THOMAS AQUINAS
AND THE CRISIS OF
CHRISTOLOGY

THOMAS AQUINAS
AND THE CRISIS OF
CHRISTOLOGY

EDITED BY MICHAEL A. DAUPHINAIS,

ANDREW HOFER, OP, AND

ROGER W. NUTT

SAPIENTIA PRESS
of Ave Maria University

Sapientia Press
of Ave Maria University
5050 Ave Maria Blvd.
Ave Maria, FL 34142
800-537-5487

Distributed by:
The Catholic University of America Press
c/o HFS
P.O. Box 50370
Baltimore, MD 21211
800-537-5487

Text and cover design: Kachergis Book Design
Cover Image: "Saint Thomas of Aquinas in front of the
crucifix where he heard Christ speaking to him" Oil on wood.
Santi di Tito, 1536–1603. Use with permission of akg-images/
Rabatti & Domingie

Printed in the United States of America.

Library of Congress Control Number: 2021940919

ISBN: 978-1-932589-85-6

CONTENTS

Many years ago, I attended a lecture presented by a prominent contributor to a volume of essays famously titled *The Myth of God Incarnate* (SCM Press, 1977). The speaker was an ordained Anglican clergyman and Regius Professor of Divinity at Oxford University. The newly published book, which had created quite a stir even beyond academic circles, developed various aspects of the general thesis that the doctrine of the Incarnation was a later mythological construction that sought to give expression to the early Christian conviction that God had acted decisively for the salvation of the world in the man Jesus. I do not remember much about the lecture itself, but one thing I will never forget is the speaker's response to a question posed during the discussion period following his lecture. When he was asked, "But what will you say about the Incarnation in your sermon on Christmas morning?" the speaker replied, "Well, of course, I will preach about the Incarnation as if it were true."

As if it were true. This hesitancy is puzzling, but also deeply significant. It involves the view that to affirm that, in Jesus of Nazareth, the only begotten Son of God, assumed a human nature is a *manner of speech*—one might call it mythological or symbolic or metaphorical—that expresses the *truth* that in him God acted uniquely to save us and that through his teaching and example God leads us to himself. A vestige of classical Christian faith remains at the level of communal devotion: on Christmas morning, one sings the traditional carols, and one preaches as if the infant in the manger were truly God and man. But the *truth* of the matter lies elsewhere. According to this and countless similar theories that have emerged since the nineteenth century and that continue to find advocates up to the present day, a full-bodied doctrinal assertion of the reality—the truth—of the Incarnation can no longer be sustained or defended at the philosophical and theological level. If there is a crisis in modern Christology, this conception of the limits of Christological affirmation is wedged at its core.

The roots of this conception lie in the powerfully influential critique of

metaphysics advanced by Immanuel Kant late in the eighteenth century. For
Kant, metaphysical inquiry discloses not the ontological structures of things
in the world that we know, but rather the cognitive structures that make our
knowledge of things in the world possible. For the many theologians who—
whether enthusiastically or begrudgingly—accepted the Kantian critique
of metaphysics, it no longer seemed possible to expound classical Christological and Trinitarian doctrines in metaphysical or ontological terms. The
ecumenical councils of the early centuries made sparing use of philosophical
concepts such as nature, substance, and person in order to articulate the in-
controvertible affirmations about the Father, Son, and Holy Spirit that were
embedded in the Sacred Scriptures and woven into the fabric of Christian
worship. These councils shunned mythical categories and adapted suitable
philosophical conceptualities not to displace but to reinforce the revealed
meaning of the Christian narrative of salvation recounted in Scripture and
celebrated in the liturgy, and to exclude heterodox interpretations of this
narrative. There was no question of a hesitant "as if it were true" when it
came to the central Trinitarian and Christological affirmations expressed
in doctrine, expounded in preaching, and celebrated in worship. For more
than a thousand years, classical theology generally followed the lead of these
councils and deployed the philosophical resources at hand to explain and
defend fundamental Christological doctrines.

What is the nature of the crisis in modern Christology? Surely a certain
hesitancy to embrace the robust theological realism of classical Christian
theology remains a key feature of this crisis. Readers of this splendid volume
of essays learn more about this. What is more, they learn that the crisis is a
complex and many-faceted one, with its disparate aspects variously amenable
to Thomistic analysis and resolution.

In the office where I work, people would say, if asked, that the crisis in
Christology is *the* crisis of contemporary Christendom—more urgent than
the other assorted crises that beset the Church in these difficult times. Striking at the very core of uniquely Christian convictions about faith, hope, and
salvation, the crisis of Christology is in the end a crisis of faith. With roots
and even parallels in the past, the crisis of Christology is, as the contributors
to this volume argue, a peculiarly modern one, shaped by typically modern
preoccupations with rationality, language, meaning, history, personal iden-

tity, pluralism, and scientific naturalism. The insights of many scholars are needed to formulate a response to the challenges posed by modern Christology, and it is a distinct blessing to have in hand a volume of essays representing such a broad range of expertise and acumen. Many essays seek the aid of the Angelic Doctor to answer the pressing question that Christ still asks, "Who do you say that I am?" and to the further question that we also raise, "What difference does it make?"

The main aspects of the crisis in modern Christology are biblical, historical, philosophical, and pastoral—*and*, as this volume's introductory essay makes clear, perhaps chiefly personal. The term *krisis*, after all, has a deeply personal meaning because it intimates the divine judgment that confronts the individual theologian as he ponders the question, "What am I going to say about Christ?" I cannot imagine that the Savior of the World would be content to hear us qualify our response with a hesitant "as if it were true."

J. Augustine Di Noia, OP
Titular Archbishop of Oregon City
Adjunct Secretary, Congregation for the
Doctrine of the Faith

THOMAS AQUINAS ON CHRIST'S JUDGMENT OF TEACHERS OF THE FAITH

Andrew Hofer, OP

In 1924, Karl Barth began his *Göttingen Dogmatics*, the first of three sets of dogmatics in his career, in this way:

> The present course is envisaged as the first and introductory part of a series on dogmatics that will stretch over three semesters. It was significant that Thomas Aquinas put at the head of his *Summa Theologica* the prayer: "Merciful God, I ask that thou wilt grant me, as thou pleasest, to seek earnestly, to investigate carefully, to know truthfully, and to present perfectly, to the glory of thy name, amen."[1]

The author is grateful to John Baptist Ku, OP, Roger Nutt, and Ephrem Reese, OP, for their comments that improved this work. The author is responsible for any remaining errors or infelicities.

1. Karl Barth, *The Göttingen Dogmatics: Instruction in the Christian Religion*, vol. 1, ed. Hannelotte Reifen, trans. Geoffrey W. Bromiley (Grand Rapids, MI: Eerdmans, 1991), §1,I, p. 3. For analysis, see Daniel L. Migliore, "Karl Barth's First Lecture in Dogmatics: Instruction in the Christian Religion," in *Göttingen Dogmatics*, preface pp. 15–62, at 16–17 and 19–21, accessed through the Digital Karl Barth Library. Barth is quoting the beginning of the *Concede mihi*, known as the *Prayer for Ordering Life Wisely*. Following the pioneering manuscript work of Claire Le Brun-Gouanvic's critical edition of William of Tocco's *Life of St. Thomas*, Paul Murray argues that this prayer, long attributed to Aquinas, is authentic. See Paul Murray, OP, *Aquinas at Prayer: The Bible, Mysticism, and Poetry* (London: Bloomsbury, 2013), 39–52, and "Beauty in the Prayer of Aquinas," *Ephemerides Theologicae Lovanienses* 95, no. 2 (2019): 235–52, at 238–41. For the prayer text preserved by Tocco, see Claire Le Brun-Gouavnic, *Ystoria sancti Thome de Aquino de Guillaume de Tocco (1323)*, Studies and Texts 127 (Toronto: Pontifical Institute of Mediaeval Studies, 1996), cap. 29, p. 156. Tocco introduces the prayer with a comment that Thomas prayed this prayer every day.

Barth continues:

If there is any mortally dangerous undertaking on earth, any undertaking in which we have reason not only at the beginning but also in the middle and at the end to take the last resort of invoking the name of the Most High, then it is that of a *Summa Theologica*, a dogmatics, and I must add that in our day and our situation such a prayer will have to be made out of materially much deeper distress and perplexity than in the time of Thomas.[2]

This most significant of the Reformed theologians of the twentieth century elaborates on the difference between Thomas's time and his own:

The manner in which Thomas pursued dogmatics leaves the impression of a holy, lofty, beautiful, and joyful work of art. Not for nothing he gives the doctor of the church a heavenly halo along with the virgin and martyr. But for us, presenting and studying dogmatics is a burden, a burden that we cannot and may not and will not avoid, but still a burden.[3]

Several paragraphs later, stressing the awesomeness of speaking about God in theology, he asks two questions: "What are YOU going to say?" and "WHAT are you going to say?"

You? What? These are the questions of dogmatics. We have to consider the fact that "in some way" we have to speak about *God*. The questions put a pistol at the breast of theologians and through them at that of the public.... This "what" means that in what is said about God there is truth and error. Is it not clear how many *fatal* possibilities await theologians when they face the dogmatic question?[4]

Karl Barth's image of a pistol to the chest of theologians, and through them to their audience, dramatizes the life-and-death consequences of speaking about the One who is. It seems to be Barth's modern variation on how Gregory the Great speaks of his own heavy burden of preaching. Gregory says that the sword of the Word passes through him to reach the heart of his neighbor.[5] For the great Christian tradition, our salvation lies within a

---

2. Barth, *Göttingen Dogmatics*, §1,I, pp. 3–4.
3. Barth, *Göttingen Dogmatics*, §1,I, p. 4.
4. Barth, *Göttingen Dogmatics*, §1,I, p. 6.
5. Gregory the Great preaches: "O how hard these things are for me to say because I hurt myself by speaking, I whose tongue does not hold the preaching as is fitting nor suffice to comprehend how far life follows the tongue. I who am often entangled in idle words and, lazy and negligent, default from the exhortation and edification of my neighbors. I who in the sight of God become mute and verbose,

right confession of faith. Those who have a solemn duty to speak about God assume a role of life-and-death importance in contemplating and articulating what the Church believes. Each theologian, no matter how learned in what others say, can hear Christ ask, "But who do you say that I am?"

This volume offers sixteen chapters by theologians who take up the theme of "Thomas Aquinas and the Crisis of Christology." That was the focus of a conference held at Ave Maria University in 2020, under the co-sponsorship of its Aquinas Center for Theological Renewal and the Thomistic Institute of the Pontifical Faculty of the Immaculate Conception at the Dominican House of Studies. The conference served this mission:

"But who do you say that I am?" At the decisive turning point in the Gospel, Jesus asks this question. Simon Peter answers correctly at first, but is soon corrected when he protests the revelation of the Cross. Christians in every age are called to confess right faith in Jesus, who suffered, died, and rose for our salvation. This conference considers a wide range of scriptural, historical, and systematic attempts at answering Jesus' question and engages in the thinking of Thomas Aquinas on it. His teaching on Christ reflects a master of the sacred page who attended adroitly to the scriptural narrative of Christ's actions and sufferings, pioneered in the West the recovery of ancient conciliar teaching, innovated in his Christological pedagogy, and elucidated Trinitarian, anthropological, sacramental, moral, and eschatological dimensions of Christology. Studying the mystery of Christ in dialogue with Aquinas can assist us in today's crisis of Christology.

The conference's presentations express various aspects of that multivalent "crisis" of Christology. "Crisis" comes from the Greek word *krisis*, which means decision, judgment, or turning point. Christ questions us about his identity, which provides the occasion also for his judgment of us. Our volume's authors answer Christ's piercing question in a variety of ways: through engagement of biblical sources, studies of the Incarnation and Christ's life, sacramental theology and Christian life, and pressing contemporary issues.

Before we come to those essays, I want us to consider the *krisis*, the judgment of the Lord himself upon the individual teacher of the faith. All of

---

mute in essentials, verbose in idle matters. But behold, God's saying about the life of the watchman compels me to speak. I cannot remain silent and yet fear to hurt myself by speaking. Let me say, let me say that the sword of God's word passes through me to pierce the heart of my neighbor." Gregory the Great, *Homilies on Ezekiel* 1.11.5; CCL 142, 171; translated in Theodosia Tomkinson, trans., *Saint Gregory the Great: Homilies on the Book of Ezekiel* (Etna, CA: Center for Traditionalist Orthodox Studies, 2008), 215–16. Cf. Heb 4:12–13 for the Word's judgment.

us theologians are under the Lord's judgment for our work. How do we recognize it? How did Thomas Aquinas? Thomas did not concern himself with what book reviews said or what tenure and promotion committees pronounced—some of the modern forms of academic judgment. He was, however, most certainly concerned about the Lord's judgment of his life of teaching. Thus he would call upon the Lord's mercy. For Aquinas, "the work of divine justice always presupposes his mercy."[6] His prayer, quoted by Barth, begins by addressing the "merciful God." Thomas relies on divine mercy to grant what he needs in his life. A tradition says that he used to recite that same prayer daily before an image of Christ.[7] It concludes in this way:

Grant me, Lord my God, intelligence in knowing you, diligence in seeking you, wisdom in finding you, conversation pleasing to you, perseverance in confidently waiting for you, and confidence in finally embracing you. Grant that as penance I may be afflicted with your hardships, as grace, make use along the way, of your favors, as glory, delight in your joys in the fatherland. Amen.[8]

Reflection on this prayer about Thomas's life can prompt us to turn to one of the most autobiographical touches in his writing. He borrows the words of a fourth-century doctor when beginning his *Summa contra Gentiles*, or the *Book on the Truth of the Catholic Faith against the Errors of the Infidels*. He submits:

Therefore, taking up confidence from divine kindness (*ex divina pietate*) I embark upon the work of a wise man, even though this may surpass my powers, and I have set myself the task of making known, as far as my limited powers will allow, the truth that the Catholic faith professes, and of setting aside the errors that are opposed to it. To use the words of Hilary: "I am aware that I owe this to God as the chief duty of my life, that my every word and sense may speak of him" (Hilary of Poitiers, *De Trinitate* 1.37).[9]

6. *ST* I, q. 21, a. 4.
7. *S. Thomae Aquinatis Opuscula Theologica*, vol. 2, ed. R. M. Spiazzi, OP (Turin: Marietti, 1954), 285.
8. Tocco, *Ystoria*, cap. 29 (Le Brun-Gouanvic, 156; trans. Murray, 43).
9. *ScG* I, c. 2, no. 2, translated in Anton C. Pegis, trans., *Saint Thomas Aquinas, On the Truth of the Catholic Faith: Summa contra Gentiles, Book One. God* (Garden City, NY: Hanover House, 1955), 62 (alt). For an enlightening study of Hilary's influence, see Joseph Wawrykow, "The *Summa contra Gentiles* Reconsidered: On the Contribution of the *De Trinitate* of Hilary of Poitiers," *The Thomist* 58, no. 4 (1994): 617–34. The founder of Aquinas's Order of Preachers, Dominic de Guzman, spoke only with God or about God, which became the model for his preachers; e.g., Testimony of William of Monferrato (August 7, 1233), the Testimony of John of Spain (August 10, 1233), the Testimony of

In each age since Thomas Aquinas, those who follow him can aspire to have that same wholehearted dedication in their teaching as men and women "consecrated in the Truth"—that is, in Christ himself (Jn 17:17)—and sanctified by the mercy they seek and dispense.[10] Aquinas's consecration to the twofold teaching office of the wise, to make known the truth and to remove errors opposing it, certainly relies upon that mercy in divine judgment. Teaching itself, a form of sharing judgments, is meant to be a spiritual work of mercy that imitates, and submits to, the Lord's own mercy in judgment.[11] We can follow the significance of that in the following three steps.

First, we sketch the morality of doing the work of theology according to Thomas. Teaching about God is a moral issue expressive of, and under, the mercy of divine judgment. Second, we explore Aquinas's appropriation of the Johannine and Augustinian emphases on Christ *as man* judging. Aquinas emphasizes not only Christ's humanity in judgment but also how the Church, the Body of Christ, shares in Christ's judgment—both now and on the Last Day. Third, we consider the aureoles, the little golden crowns, reserved for teachers of the faith in glory. Here we will also review the disaster that the sin of vainglory causes for teachers who would otherwise have received aureoles.

After those three steps, this introduction overviews the chapters of this volume's contributors. It concludes with a word of thanks and a brief meditation on Thomas's prayer before Christ crucified for its significance to our theological work under the Lord's merciful judgment.

Paul of Venice (August 16, 1233), and Primitive Constitutions of the Order of Preachers II, 31, in Simon Tugwell, trans., *Early Dominicans: Selected Writings*, Classics of Western Spirituality (New York: Paulist Press, 1982), 70, 75, 82, and 467.

10. For an overview of Aquinas and those who strive to live and teach the life that he exemplifies, see Romanus Cessario, OP, and Cajetan Cuddy, OP, *Thomas and the Thomists: The Achievement of Thomas Aquinas and His Interpreters*, Mapping the Tradition (Minneapolis: Fortress Press, 2017). I am indebted here to the authors' use of Aquinas's comments on Jn 17:17 in their summary of "The Thomists" (xiv–xvii).

11. For the spiritual almsgiving of instruction, see *ST* II-II, q. 32, aa. 1–3.

THE MORAL QUESTION OF
TEACHING THE FAITH

To begin a brief account of Thomas's understanding of the morality of teaching, we can review some fundamental truths. Made in the image of God, we human beings are rational, endowed with free will and the power to move ourselves.[12] As such, we make judgments about all sorts of matters. Since these judgments are human acts, proceeding from reason, they are either good, and thus praiseworthy, or evil, and thus blameworthy.[13] Teachers must make many kinds of judgments before communicating teachings to others. When they do teach, they lead others from the known to knowing the unknown.[14] Through the communication of their judgments, teachers assist others to make their own judgments. No one can make a judgment for another, properly speaking, although others can accept someone else's judgment by submitting their wills to it. Our judgments, including our judgments to obey God's judgment, serve as the matter for God's judgment of us. If we did not make our own judgments, on what grounds would God judge us? God does not judge irrational beasts. Given all this, teachers then bear a responsibility for their own judgments, and they may bear additional responsibility—for better or worse—for those they influence by their teaching. Teachers of the faith need divine help for their task. Without God's grace, we may perform many tasks, such as building houses and tending vineyards.[15] We need grace, however, in order to do meritorious work, including making praiseworthy judgments and teaching what we have contemplated according to God's will.[16]

In treating the virtue of justice, Aquinas explains that the word "judgment" (*iudicium*) comes originally from the right decision of the just; the term came to be applied to any right decision, whether speculative or practical.[17] Properly belonging to the virtue of justice, judgment relies on pru-

---

12. *ST* I, q. 93, and *ST* I-II, proemium.

13. *ST* I-II, q. 18, a. 9. Aquinas thinks that deliberate acts of reason must be either good or evil, and not what the Stoics call "indifferent."

14. *ST* I, q. 117, a. 1.

15. *ST* I-II, q. 109, a. 2.

16. *ST* I-II, q. 114, a. 2.

17. *ST* II-II, q. 60, a. 1, ad 1.

dence. Also, we have more than cardinal virtues to assist us. Aquinas considers how "the spiritual one judges all things" (1 Cor 2:15). That one, "by reason of the habit of charity, has an inclination to judge aright of all things according to the divine rules; and it is in conformity with these that he pronounces judgment through the gift of wisdom."[18] About this habit of charity, we can recall that the Apostle Paul says, "The love of God has been poured into our hearts through the Holy Spirit given to us" (Rom 5:5). Infused charity brings with it heavenly gifts. We teachers of the faith depend not only on the wisdom of the science of *sacra doctrina* but also on that supreme gift, the gift of wisdom, and the other gifts that would benefit our teaching.[19]

Teaching is of such importance that it can identify someone's whole life. What kind of life does a teacher have? In his evaluations of the contemplative and active lives, Aquinas categorizes the life of teaching as an active life, following the authority of Gregory the Great.[20] Aquinas distinguishes the act of teaching by a twofold object. On one hand, there is the matter or object of an interior conception. On the other hand, there is the spoken word for the sake of the hearer. If one has an interior conception for the sake of an exterior use, then that belongs to the active life. But if one has that conception for what could be called personal enjoyment, delighting in it with love, then it belongs to the contemplative life. The word spoken for a hearer is an exterior object that necessarily marks the active life. Even though Aquinas stresses the contemplative's personal enjoyment, one should not think that only the contemplative life is a life moved by love.

If we turn to a poignant comparison of the two lives recorded in Aquinas's *Commentary on John*, we discover that Thomas teaches that the active life, even though slower in understanding than the contemplative life, may be quicker to love. He gives a mystical interpretation of John's arriving at the empty tomb before Peter (Jn 20:3–10):

18. *ST* II-II, q. 60, a. 1, ad 2. For an important study featuring charity and the gift of wisdom in our deification, see Daria Spezzano, *The Glory of God's Grace: Deification According to St. Thomas Aquinas* (Ave Maria, FL: Sapientia Press, 2015).

19. For distinguishing these two kinds of wisdom, see *ST* I, q. 1, a. 6, ad 3. For the treatment of the gift of wisdom, see esp. *ST* II-II, q. 45. For an insightful treatment of showing wisdom from the vantage point of friendship, see Sr. Anne Catherine Burleigh, OP, "Wisdom as Divine Friendship According to St. Thomas Aquinas and St. Catherine of Siena" (MA thesis, Pontifical Faculty of the Immaculate Conception, Dominican House of Studies, 2019).

20. *ST* II-II, q. 181, a. 3, *sed contra*. See Gregory the Great, *Homilies on Ezekiel* 1.14.

Now it very often happens that contemplatives, because they are docile, are the first to become acquainted with a knowledge of the mysteries of Christ—but they do not enter, for sometimes there is knowledge, but little or no love follows. Those in the active life, because of their continuing fervor and earnestness, even though they are slower to understand, enter into them more quickly. In this way, those who are later to arrive are the first to penetrate the divine mysteries: "So the last will be first, and the first last" (Mt 20:16).[21]

The active life of teaching can indeed be suffused with a fervent love, a love that illuminates the lives of others.[22]

How should a teacher virtuously communicate the mysteries of the faith? Many students of Aquinas are familiar with the prologue to his *Summa Theologiae*. Read it now through the moral lens of the virtues and vices of teaching the faith:

Because the doctor of Catholic truth ought not only to teach the proficient, but also to instruct beginners (according to the Apostle: *As unto little ones in Christ, I gave you milk to drink, not meat*—1 Cor 3:1–2), the objective of our intention in this work is to treat whatever belongs to the Christian religion, in such a way as may tend to the instruction of beginners. For we have considered that students of this doctrine have frequently been hampered by the writings of various people: partly on account of the multiplication of useless questions, articles, and arguments; partly also because those things that are needful for them to know are not taught according to the order of the discipline, but according to what the explanation of the books was requiring or according to what the occasion of the argument was showing; and partly, too, because frequent repetition brought weariness and confusion to the minds of hearers. Seeking to avoid these and other like faults, we will attempt, with confidence in divine help, to set forth whatever is included in this sacred doctrine as briefly and clearly as the matter itself may allow.[23]

21. Aquinas, *Super Ioan.* 20, lect. 1, no. 2487; Fabian R. Larcher, OP, trans., *Saint Thomas Aquinas, Commentary on the Gospel of John, Chapters 9–21*, Latin/English Editions of the Works of St. Thomas Aquinas 36 (Lander, WY: Aquinas Institute for the Study of Sacred Doctrine, 2013), 461 (alt.). For an illuminating comparison of the two lives in Aquinas's thinking, see Rik Van Nieuwenhove, "'Recipientes per contemplationem, tradentes per actionem': The Relation between the Active and Contemplative Lives According to Thomas Aquinas," *The Thomist* 81, no. 1 (2017): 1–30.
22. For Aquinas's comment that it is better to illuminate than simply to shine, see *ST* II-II, q. 188, a. 6.
23. *ST* proemium (Shapcote trans. alt).

We can compare this prologue with *Quodl.* V, q. 12, a. 2 (from Aquinas's second Parisian regency, probably Advent of 1271).[24] There we read that if the teacher teaches something false, he should recant it completely, especially if it results in spiritual damage. If the teacher teaches something true, spiritual harm can still come to listeners in two ways. First, if the teacher presents deep and difficult teaching to unprepared people incapable of understanding, that teaching could put their salvation at risk. As in his *Summa* prologue, Aquinas quotes 1 Corinthians 3:1–2: "As unto little ones in Christ, I gave you milk to drink, not meat." Second, the teacher may present the material in a confused and disorganized way, not prioritizing greater things over lesser things. What if we find ourselves guilty of bad teaching? Aquinas states that teachers who cause spiritual damage are required to repair that damage if possible.[25] Bad teaching harms listeners, and it harms teachers, who may be culpable of sin. For example, giving little ones meat to eat is not merely unintelligent; it is also sinful. It could choke the immature. That guiding principle for Paul's virtuous teaching has inspired Christian teachers in every age since him.[26]

Perhaps the work of Aquinas most pertinent to the morality of teaching the faith is in his most detailed treatment of the sciences, the unfinished *Commentary on Boethius's De Trinitate*.[27] To understand Aquinas's think-

24. See Kevin White, "The *Quodlibeta* of Thomas Aquinas in the Context of His Work," in *Theological Quodlibeta in the Middle Ages*, vol. 1, *The Thirteenth Century*, ed. Christopher Schabel (Leiden: Brill, 2006), 49–133, at 85–87. White has a brilliant discussion of Aquinas's quodlibetal questions on teaching (78–87).

25. Aquinas twice quotes Gregory the Great's *Book of Pastoral Rule* (*Past.* 3, 36 and 2, 4) for these last two points about the morality of teaching.

26. For discussion of Clement of Alexandria and Origen, with attention to their appropriation of the Pauline imagery of milk and meat, see Benjamin A. Edsall, *The Reception of Paul and Early Christian Initiation: History and Hermeneutics* (Cambridge: Cambridge University Press, 2019), 93–169. Aquinas acknowledges Origen's use of this imagery in *Super Ioan.* 4, lect. 3, no. 635. For Aquinas's other uses of 1 Cor 3:1–2, see *Super Psal.* 18, no. 2; *Super 1 Thess.* 2, lect. 1, no. 34; *Super Heb.* 5, lect. 2, nos. 267–71; *Super de Trinitate*, q. 2, a. 4, co. 1.

27. I am using the Leonine Edition (LE) of Boethius's text used by Aquinas and Aquinas's text in *Sancti Thomae de Aquino Opera Omnia*, vol. 50, *Super Boetium de Trinitate, Expositio Libri Boetii de Ebdomadibus* (Rome: Commissio Leonina, 1992), 69 and 75–171, and the English translation in Armand Maurer, trans., *Thomas Aquinas: Faith, Reason and Theology. Questions I–IV of His Commentary on the De Trinitate of Boethius*, Mediaeval Sources in Translation (Toronto: Pontifical Institute of Mediaeval Studies, 1987). I am greatly indebted to Lawrence Donohoo's teaching on *sacra doctrina*. See Lawrence J. Donohoo, "The Nature and Grace of *Sacra Doctrina* in St. Thomas's *Super Boetium de Trinitate*," *The Thomist* 63, no. 3 (1999): 343–401. Among those studies Donohoo recommends are

ing there, we need to appreciate the text he is commenting on. The Roman scholastic Boethius, martyred in 525 or 526, wrote his *opusculum sacrum* on the Trinity for his mentor and father-in-law Symmachus.[28] Although Boethius credits Augustine with being his inspiration, his style—in some ways typical of the sixth-century scholasticism in both East and West—differs markedly from that of the Bishop of Hippo.[29] Aquinas himself observes that whereas Augustine sought in his *De Trinitate* to provide both authorities and reasons, Boethius gives only reasons.[30] Boethius, in fact, omits offering scriptural quotations. Now listen to how Boethius writes to Symmachus of the moral dangers in mistreating the divine matters:

For, apart from yourself, wherever I have turned my eyes, they have encountered on the one hand laziness and indolence, and on the other hand jealousy and shrewdness, so that a man who casts these matters before such monsters to be trampled under foot rather than to be appreciated, would seem to bring discredit on the study of the things of God.[31]

Commenting on this passage, Aquinas cites "Do not give what is holy to dogs" (Mt 7:6). The Gospel verse may have been in Boethius's mind; in any case, it perfectly expresses animal contempt for the sacred.[32] Aquinas quotes Matthew 7:6 not only in his commentary on Boethius's preface but also twice in q. 2, a. 4, of this work.[33]

Michel Corbin, *Le chemin de la théologie chez Thomas d'Aquin*, Bibliothèque des archives de philosophie, nouvelle série (Paris: Beauchesne, 1972), 291–474, and Leo Elders, *Faith and Science: An Introduction to St. Thomas' Expositio in Boethii de Trinitate* (Rome: Herder, 1974). Cf. Mark Jordan, "Esotericism and *Accessus* in Thomas Aquinas," *Medieval Philosophy* 20, no. 2 (1992): 35–49 (not cited by Donohoo). For a remarkable comparison between Boethius and Aquinas, see Ralph McInerny, *Boethius and Aquinas* (Washington, DC: Catholic University of America Press, 1990). For McInerny's treatment of the *De Trinitate*, see *Boethius and Aquinas*, Part Two, 97–158. McInerny writes, "When we consider the *expositio* on *De trinitate*, it seems clear that Thomas is seeking the truth of the matters under consideration in the text of Boethius rather than simply using the text of Boethius as an occasion to develop his own independent doctrine" (120).

28. For an overview of the thought of Boethius, see Henry Chadwick, *Boethius: The Consolations of Music, Logic, Theology, and Philosophy* (Oxford: Clarendon Press, 1981).

29. For Boethius's credit of Augustine, see the end of Boethius's preface. For the scholastic style of argumentation common in Greek and Latin texts of the period, see Brian E. Daley, SJ, "Boethius' Theological Tracts and Early Byzantine Scholasticism," *Mediaeval Studies* 46 (1984): 158–91.

30. LE 50, 76; trans. Maurer, 5–6. Aquinas also says here that Ambrose and Hilary provides only authorities.

31. LE 50, 69; trans. Maurer, 7.

32. LE 50, 78; trans. Maurer, 10–11; cf. Jordan, "Esotericism and *Accessus* in Thomas Aquinas," 40.

33. Aquinas cites Mt 7:6 twenty-six times in all his works, but not always in the sense of teaching the sacred.

In his study of *sacra doctrina* in Aquinas's commentary on Boethius's *De Trinitate*, Lawrence J. Donohoo observes that the second question asks the "'moral' question of whether revealed truths should be investigated."[34] Question 2 is on the manifestation of divine inquiry (*de manifestatione divinae cognitionis*), following upon question 1, on the inquiry into divine matters. Thus questions 2's investigation is precisely a manifestation or teaching. Like all of the other questions in this commentary, question 2 has four articles:

q. 2, a. 1: whether it is permissible to treat (*tractare*) divine matters by investigating[35]

q. 2, a. 2: whether there may be some science about divine matters

q. 2, a. 3: whether in the science of faith, which is about God, it is permissible to use philosophical reasons and authorities

q. 2, a. 4: whether divine matters must be veiled with obscure and new words

Thomas's treatment of this material influenced his subsequent writing of the first question of the *Summa Theologiae*. But the "moral" question of doing theology seems not to be as pronounced in the *Summa* as in this early work. Consider the following examples.

In the first article of the second question, Aquinas asks "Whether it is permissible (*liceat*) to treat divine things by investigating (*investigando*)." In the twelfth century, Bernard of Clairvaux had famously said that the mystery of the Trinity "must be worshiped, not scrutinized" (*venerandum, non scrutandum*).[36] Aquinas takes for the first objection Sirach 3:22, "Do not seek things higher than you," which he will also take as the first objection of the *Summa*'s first question.[37] There, in the *Summa*, the question pertains to the necessity of *sacra doctrina*; that is, philosophy alone does not suffice. Here in this commentary on Boethius, Aquinas stresses the moral ramifications. That first objection concludes, "Therefore, it is not permissible to

34. Donohoo, "Nature and Grace of *Sacra Doctrina*," 359.

35. A comparison to Augustine's use of *tractare* may be helpful. Augustine uses the verb *tractare* both in the sense of the way of finding what is in Scripture (*modus inveniendi*) and the way of making that known to others (*modus proferendi*). See Augustine, *On Christian Doctrine* 1.1.1. Even in the first article of the second question, it seems for Aquinas to be a matter of manifesting to others.

36. Bernard of Clairvaux, *On Consideration* 5.8.18 (PL 182, 799C). In the previous paragraph of 5.7.17 (PL 182, 798C), Bernard quotes Boethius's *De Trinitate*.

37. *ST* I, q. 1, a. 1, arg. 1.

investigate (*scrutari*) these matters."[38] The second objection continues the thought by speaking of a penalty, advocating punishment with the provocative verse, "He who is a searcher of majesty shall be overwhelmed by glory" (Prv 25:27).[39]

After several further objections and *sed contra* positions, his article's corpus communicates the moral necessity to strive toward God in our minds. It begins:

Because our perfection consists in our union with God (*coniunctione ad Deum*), we must have access to the divine to the fullest extent possible, using everything in our power, that our mind might be occupied with contemplation and our reason with the investigation of divine realities. As Psalm 72:28 says: "It is good for me to adhere to my God."[40]

The replies to the first and second objections follow from this reasoning that protects our need to strive for perfection by our mind's union with God. The first reply does emphasize that we must exceed our capacity; heretics, according to the Gloss on Romans 12:3, fall into error because they exceed their limits in thinking about either the Creator or creatures. In reply to the second objection of this first article, Aquinas writes, "To investigate thoroughly (*perscrutari*) is, as it were, to conduct an inquiry to the very end. But it is unlawful and presumptuous for anyone to inquire into the divine as though he will reach the end of comprehending it (*ut aliquis sic scrutetur divina, quasi ad finem compreensionis perventurus*)."[41]

In the third article, Aquinas asks whether it is permissible to use the rational arguments of philosophers in treating divine matters. This certainly contrasts with the approach of *ST* I, q. 1, a. 1, which asks whether any doctrine is needed in addition to the philosophical disciplines. For the fourth objection in this commentary's q. 2, a. 3, Thomas cites Jerome's self-report of experiencing a vision of judgment in his sickness. Jerome was judged by the Lord for his use of pagan writing and confessed that if ever again he should read secular books, it would be a denial of the Lord.[42] In this letter, Jerome testifies that the divine judge scourged him; after waking up from his

---

38. LE 50, 92; trans. Maurer, 35.
39. LE 50, 92; trans. Maurer, 35.
40. LE 50, 93; trans. Maurer, 37.
41. LE 50, 93; trans. Maurer, 38.
42. For Jerome's account of the vision to Eustochium, see his *Ep.* 22.

feverish dream, he found that his back was black and blue from scourging. The objection concludes about the pagan writings, "Therefore if it is wrong to study and read them [secular books] much less is it permissible to use them in treatises about God."[43] Aquinas replies to this objection by explaining Jerome's case. Jerome was so influenced by certain books of the pagans that he himself says of his reading of Scripture, "If when I came to myself I began to read the prophets, I was disgusted by their unpolished style."[44] Aquinas comments that no one would deny that such a situation is reprehensible.

In the fourth article, Aquinas asks whether divine truths should be concealed by the obscurity of words. "A teacher should so measure his words," Aquinas teaches in the article's corpus, "that they help rather hinder his hearer."[45] He distinguishes between things that on being heard would harm no one, such as truths that we are held responsible to know, from truths that could harm listeners. Truths that harm no one should not be hidden, but rather proclaimed openly to all. Truths that could harm listeners can do so in two ways. First, they could make unbelievers deride the faith, since the unbelievers would not understand them. Second, they could scandalize those who are immature, if they are too difficult for them. Aquinas quotes at length a comment from Gregory the Great in the Gloss on Exodus 21:33, regarding one leaving a pit open:

Anyone who now perceives the depths in the sacred words, should hide in silence their sublime meaning when in the presence of those who do not understand them, so that he will not hurt by interior scandal an immature believer or an unbeliever who might become a believer.[46]

Notice how Aquinas displays a great concern for the teacher's morality based upon the needs of hearers. A teacher should teach openly everything necessary for the salvation of hearers, but a teacher should hide truths too difficult for hearers that would threaten their salvation. This concealing of some truths follows upon Christ's own example of concealing secrets in parables (as given in the third *sed contra* of this article) and admonition of not giving what is holy to dogs.

43. LE 50, 97; trans. Maurer, 46.
44. LE 50, 100; trans. Mauer, 50.
45. LE 50, 101; trans. Maurer, 53.
46. LE 50, 101; trans. Maurer, 53.

When we go elsewhere to Aquinas on Christ as teacher, we can see the very pattern left by our Lord, "the most excellent teacher."[47] Christ's preeminent teaching is carried out by his disciples, sometimes in a literal imitation and sometimes in a way that shows their decidedly secondary stance in relation to Christ's own teaching. For example, of Aquinas's four articles devoted to the question of Christ's teaching in the *Tertia Pars* of the *Summa*, the first three pertain in moral considerations of: his intended audience (whether they should be only Jews or also Gentiles), his intention (whether he should avoid upsetting his listeners), and his manner of speech (whether his teaching should be veiled).[48] The fourth article pertains to whether Christ should have written anything. Even that sensitivity toward writing also appears in Boethius's *De Trinitate* and in Aquinas's commentary on it.[49] In this *Summa* question, Aquinas sees the following verse as Christ's own words: "Which I have learned without guile, and communicate without envy, and her riches I hide not" (Wis 7:13). In a sermon commenting on the child Jesus's growth in wisdom (Lk 2:52), Aquinas cites that same verse from the Book of Wisdom and explains, "Everyone can perceive that no one can advance in knowledge so well as when he shares with others what he knows

47. *ST* III, q. 42, a. 4. For the *Summa*, I am using the Laurence Shapcote translation of the Dominican Fathers of the English Province, commonly accessible and in the public domain.

48. *ST* III, q. 42, aa. 1–3. Michael Hahn has recently given an excellent study of question 42 (in conjunction with *ST* III, q. 39, a. 3). See Michael S. Hahn, "Thomas Aquinas's Presentation of Christ as Teacher," *The Thomist* 83, no. 1 (2019): 57–89. Among the scholarship that Hahn recommends is Michael Dauphinais, "Christ the Teacher: The Pedagogy of the Incarnation According to Saint Thomas Aquinas" (PhD diss., University of Notre Dame, 2000). Hahn beautifully brings out the significance of *ST* III, q. 42, a. 4, with the New Law described in the *Prima Secundae*, such as *ST* I-II, q. 106, a. 1. He may be missing how instructive Aquinas is to his readers on this subject of Christ's teaching when Hahn writes, "[Aquinas's] consideration of Christ as teacher is not aimed at providing practical guidelines for his confreres. No doubt, Christ is for Thomas an exemplary teacher, yet his manner of teaching is here examined for its own sake, as grist for contemplating the mystery of the incarnation and God's revelation in Christ" (62). In each of the four articles of q. 42, Aquinas teaches not only about Christ's teaching but also teaching in general or the teaching of Christ's disciples, e.g., *ST* III, q. 42, a. 1, ad 2, on showing greater power by working through others, such as converting the Gentiles through the disciples; q. 42, a. 2, co., on how the preacher or teacher should prefer the salvation of the multitude over the few being offended; q. 42, a. 3, co., on how anyone's teaching may be hidden in three ways; and q. 42, a. 4, co., on how writings are ordered toward the end of having the impression of teaching upon the hearts of listeners. Hahn recognizes: "In affirming this ecclesial dimension of Christ's teaching activity, Thomas underscores his commitment to the capacity of human beings to serve as fitting instruments for the mediation of divine truth, a position that is surely of a piece with the incarnational logic that has directed his Christological considerations up to this point" (78).

49. *ST* III, q. 42, a. 4.

himself. This is even an obligation (*debitum*): that someone tells others in return about the thing he got to know."[50] The morality of teaching the faith follows upon what Christ has established teachers to do in imitation of his own pattern of teaching for the salvation of hearers.[51]

CHRIST'S JUDGMENT AS MAN:
THE DIVINE SHARING OF JUDGMENT WITH THE BODY OF CHRIST

In John's Gospel, Jesus says that the Father does not judge anyone, "but he has given all judgment to the Son, so that all may honor the Son just as they honor the Father" (Jn 5:22–23). Augustine treats this by showing how all, both good and evil, will see the risen Son of Man in judgment of the nations on the Last Day. The evil cannot see the Father.[52] Aquinas follows Augustine's understanding, and in the *Summa*, he gives three reasons why judiciary power belongs to Christ according to his human nature. The first is that, because of his likeness and kinship to us, God judges the human race through the man Christ so that his judgment may be sweeter (*suavius*) to us (citing Heb 4:15).[53] Daria Spezzano expertly treats Christ as eschatological judge in this volume.[54] Here we focus on the judgment of teachers of the faith, first during this life on earth and then on the Last Day.

On earth, Christ shares his teaching authority with the Church, which

---

50. Sermon 8, *Puer Iesus*, 3.2.3, translated in Mark-Robin Hoogland, CP, trans., *Thomas Aquinas: The Academic Sermons*, Fathers of the Church, Medieval Continuation 11 (Washington, DC: Catholic University of America Press, 2010), 103.

51. For a scholar with exemplary work on Thomas on teaching, attentive to its Christological dimension, see Vivian Boland, OP, "Truth, Knowledge and Communication: Thomas Aquinas on the Mystery of Teaching," *Studies in Christian Ethics* 19, no. 3 (2006): 287–304; *St Thomas Aquinas*, Bloomsbury Library of Educational Thought (London: Bloomsbury, 2007); "St Thomas's Sermon Puer Iesus: A Neglected Source for His Understanding of Teaching and Learning," *New Blackfriars* 88, no. 4 (2007): 457–70; and "The Healing Work of Teaching: Thomas Aquinas and Education," in *Towards the Intelligent Use of Liberty: Dominican Approaches to Education*, 2nd ed., ed. Gabrielle Kelly, OP, and Kevin Saunders, OP (Hindmarsh, South Australia: ATF, 2014), 31–40.

52. Augustine, *Tractate on the Gospel of John* 21.11–17 (on Jn 5:20–23).

53. *ST* III, q. 59, a. 2.

54. See Daria Spezzano, "Is Jesus Judgmental? Aquinas on Christ as Eschatological Judge," chap. 16, in this volume.

in any age has an authority greater than even a holy doctor of the first centuries of the Church. Consider this case that Aquinas features. When arguing that the children of Jewish parents should not be baptized against their parents' will, Aquinas refers to the authority of the Church's custom. He writes, "The custom (*consuetudo*) of the Church has very great authority and ought to be jealously observed in all things, since the very doctrine of Catholic teachers derives its authority from the Church. Hence we ought to abide by the authority of the Church rather than by that of an Augustine or a Jerome or any teacher whatever."[55] Notice that Aquinas specifies that the Church's authority is preferred to that of a single teacher; he argues elsewhere that scriptural authority is preferred to that of any teacher.[56] Aquinas practices the principle of preferring not to follow a holy doctor on occasion precisely because of what the Church teaches. One famous example of this is his treatment of John Damascene and the *filioque*.[57] More pertinently for the present discussion, when Thomas treats the question of whether Christ judges as man, he mentions that John Chrysostom denies that Christ judges as man, a view that Thomas espouses within a nuanced view of God's authority to judge.[58] No single teacher, no matter how authoritative, should be

55. *ST* II-II, q. 10, a. 12. Aquinas continues that it was never the custom of the Church to baptize the children of the Jews against the will of their parents. Aquinas repeats this teaching at *ST* III, q. 68, a. 10. Cf. the Latin Church's current law in CIC can. 868 §1: "An infant of Catholic parents or even of non-Catholic parents is baptized licitly in danger of death, even against the will of the parents."

56. See also *ST* I, q. 1, a. 8, ad 2, and the lesser-known *Quodl.* XII, q. 16, a. 1. For the LE text of the quodlibetal questions, see *Sancti Thomae de Aquino Opera Omnia*, vol. 25.1, *Quaestiones de Quolibet*, Quodlibet VII, VIII, IX, X, XI (Rome: Leonine Commission, 1996), and vol. 25.2, *Quaestiones de Quolibet*, Quodlibet I, II, III, VI, IV, V, XII (Rome: Leonine Commission, 1996). I am using Turner Nevitt and Brian Davies, trans., *Thomas Aquinas's Quodlibetal Questions* (New York: Oxford University Press, 2020). In *Quodl.* XII, q. 16, a. 1, Aquinas writes, "Scriptures' commentators have expressed many of their own judgments on other matters not of faith, and hence such things can be mistaken. Even so, it is not necessary to believe what such commentators say, but only the canonical Scriptures contained in the Old and New Testament" (LE 25.2, 421; trans. Nevitt and Davies, 453 [alt.]).

57. *ST* I, q. 36, a. 2, ad 3.

58. *ST* III, q. 59, a. 2. The holy doctors in Aquinas's use provide fascinating study for how Aquinas follows them—and does not follow them. For overviews of Chrysostom's presence in Aquinas's thought (translated from the French), see Leo J. Elders, *Thomas Aquinas and His Predecessors: The Philosophers and the Church Fathers in His Works* (Washington, DC: Catholic University of America Press, 2018), 157–77, and Brian Dunkle, SJ, "Thomas Aquinas's Use of John Chrysostom in the Catena Aurea and the Tertia Pars, in *Thomas Aquinas and the Greek Fathers*, ed. Michael Dauphinais, Andrew Hofer, OP, and Roger Nutt (Ave Maria, FL: Sapientia Press, 2019), 151–64. A case of exceeding complication that merits much study is Aquinas's naming Origen well over a thousand times, sometimes ranking him among the holy doctors and other times among heretics. For an excellent overview,

confused with the Church's authority in judging matters of faith. At times, as we know all too well, the teaching of the Church and the teaching of individual teachers of the faith have been in conflict.

Aquinas uses two senses of the term "magisterium," the magisterium of the teacher and the magisterium of the pastor. After the Second Vatican Council, when some interpreted Aquinas to support a rival magisterium of theologians dissenting from the magisterium of the Church's pastors, Cardinal Joseph Ratzinger, then Prefect of the Congregation for the Doctrine of the Faith, correctly interpreted Aquinas's intent regarding magisterial judgment:

> The notion of a "parallel magisterium" of theologians in opposition to and in competition with the magisterium of the Pastors is sometimes supported by reference to some texts in which St. Thomas Aquinas makes a distinction between the "magisterium cathedrae pastoralis" and "magisterium cathedrae magisterialis" (*Contra impugnantes*, cap. 2; *Quodl.* III, q. 4, a. 1; *In IV. Sent.* d. 19, q. 2, a. 2, qc. 2, ad 4). Actually, these texts do not give any support to this position, for St. Thomas was absolutely certain that the right to judge in matters of doctrine was the sole responsibility of the "officium praelationis."[59]

Although not mentioned by Ratzinger here, other points made by Aquinas are germane to this distinction. For Aquinas, there exists a further important difference between the two magisteria regarding knowledge and power. "The superior knowledge required for a master's chair is a matter of one's own personal perfection," Thomas distinguishes, "whereas the superior power of a bishop's chair is a matter of the relationship between one person and another." Also, he insists that the office of prelate, which includes judging, is meant to be exercised with the charity that prelates must have: "It is through excelling charity (*per caritatem excellentem*) that a man is fit to hold a bishop's chair.... On the other hand, having enough knowledge is what makes

---

see Jörgen Vijgen, "Aquinas's Reception of Origen: A Preliminary Study," in *Thomas Aquinas and the Greek Fathers*, 30–88.

59. Cardinal Joseph Ratzinger, *Donum Veritatis*, Instruction on the Ecclesial Vocation of the Theologian, May 24, 1990, no. 27. I have adjusted the parenthetical references. *Contra impugnantes* cap. 2 is on whether any religious may teach. As a note of precaution, the *Corpus Thomisticum* claims to offer the *Contra impugnantes* from the Leonine Edition, but the citations do not correspond; *Contra impugnantes* cap. 2 is there listed as pars 2, cap. 1, *Contra impugnantes* cap. 3 is there listed as pars 2, cap. 2, and other variations continue. For the LE, see *Sancti Thomae de Aquino Opera Omnia*, vol. 41 (Rome: Leonine Commission, 1970); for cap. 2, see 41A, 55–63.

one fit to hold a master's chair."[60] For scriptural support for the necessity of a pastor's charity, Aquinas quotes John 21:15, "Simon, son of John, do you love me more than these?" This continues the early Church's emphasis on loving Christ as the animating pastoral virtue in caring for Christ's flock.[61]

Of all bishops, the Bishop of Rome has a particular authority to judge. Aquinas returns to this reality in different ways throughout his teaching career.[62] Because of his office in divine providence, the pope serves a role in judgment to preserve the Church from error. Aquinas explains:

Something judged possible when considered in itself can be found impossible when considered in relation to something extrinsic to it. So, I say, it is possible for those with authority in the Church to err in their judgments about anything you like, provided that we only consider the people themselves. But if we consider divine providence, it is certainly impossible for the universal Church to err in judgments about matters of faith. For the Holy Spirit guides the Church to avoid error about things necessary for salvation. As Christ promised in John 16: when the *Spirit* comes, he will teach you *all truth*. Hence, we should hold more firmly to the pope's judgment than to the opinion of any wise people about the scriptures, since it is for the pope to make determinations about the faith, which he professes with his judgments.[63]

For another example, let us consider the prologue to Aquinas's *Catena Aurea* on Matthew, which he dedicated to Pope Urban IV. There Aquinas considers the perspective of wisdom, beginning with the font of wisdom, God's own Son, and continuing with wisdom in the works of creation and even more in the Incarnation. He writes, "It was the Prince of Apostles who first of all by faith deserved to see the shining forth of this wisdom, veiled as it was by the cloud of mortality, and to confess it with firmness, with-

---

60. *Quodl.* III, q. 4, a. 1 (LE 25.2, 252; trans. Nevitt and Davies, 265 (alt.).

61. For example, for an emphasis on Jn 21:15 in Chrysostom's *Six Books on the Priesthood*, see my "The Reordering of Relationships in John Chrysostom's *De sacerdotio*," *Augustinianum* 51, no. 2 (2011): 451–71. For a beautifully Thomistic account of charity in the Church's pastoral office, see Matthew Levering, *Christ and the Catholic Priesthood: Ecclesial Hierarchy and the Pattern of the Trinity* (Chicago: Hillenbrand Books, 2010).

62. For my study that considers Aquinas on the papacy as a point of comparison to Humbert of Romans, the retired Master of his Order of Preachers, see "Humbert of Romans on the Papacy before Lyons II (1274): A Study in Comparison with Thomas Aquinas and Pope Gregory X's *Extractiones*," *The Thomist* 84 (2020): 51–102.

63. *Quodl.* IX, q. 8 (LE 25.1, 119; trans. Nevitt and Davies, 126). Cf. Donald S. Prudlo, *Certain Saints: Canonization and the Origins of Papal Infallibility in the Medieval Church* (Ithaca, NY: Cornell University Press, 2015), 182–83.

out error and fully, when he said, 'You are the Christ, the Son of the Living God' (Matthew 16:16)." Aquinas asserts that this blessed confession, which the heavenly Father revealed, laid the foundation of the Church on earth, opened the way to heaven, and merited the forgiveness of sins. Against this confession, the gates of hell, understood to be the insanity of heretics, do not prevail. Aquinas pointedly says to Pope Urban, "You are the legitimate heir of this faith and confession, Most Holy Father."[64]

For Aquinas, who developed a thirteenth-century scholastic emphasis on the articles of faith, it belongs solely to the Supreme Pontiff to determine a creed.[65] All theology needs to conform to the creed's articles, the first principles of theological work.[66] The creed most authoritatively and succinctly summarizes the faith. The pope's ability to judge the work of individual theologians to be in conformity (or not) with the creed and the Church's salvific teaching safeguards the integrity of the faith. Theologians are to recognize that authority and submit to it in the communion of faith. During Thomas's lifetime, an example of someone who was judged by Pope Alexander IV as unworthy to teach at Paris was William of Saint-Amour, the leading antagonist against the friars in the first mendicant controversy.[67] Thomas was always conscious of keeping communion with the Church's pastors, especially the pope. Shortly before he died, Thomas received Christ present in the Eucharist as viaticum, praying to him fervently and saying at the end, "I leave everything to the correction of the holy Roman Church, in whose obedience I now leave this life."[68] Aquinas's confrere Tolomeo of Lucca, who knew him well, says that he repeated many times on his deathbed this submission "to the judgment of that [Roman] Church, as the Catholic and Apostolic faith requires."[69] Mindful of his fallibility, he died obedient to the share of Christ's authority of judgment exercised by the pope. The

64. I am using the translation of *Catena Aurea: Commentary on the Four Gospels Collected Out of the Works of the Fathers by St. Thomas Aquinas*, vol. 1, *St. Matthew*, trans. John Henry Newman of the Oratory, with an introduction and translation of the Dedicatory Epistle of St. Thomas to Pope Urban IV by Aidan Nichols, OP (London: Saint Austin Press, 1999), xix–xx.

65. *ST* II-II, q. 1, a. 10.

66. *ST* I, q. 1, esp. aa. 7 and 8.

67. For William, see M.-M. Dufeil, *Guillaume de Saint-Amour et la Polémique Universitaire Parisienne 1250–1259* (Paris: A. et J. Picard, 1972).

68. Tocco, *Ystoria*, cap. 58 (Le Brun-Gouanvi, 198, my trans.).

69. Tolomeo of Lucca, *Historia Ecclesiastica Nova*, vol. 23, cap. 9, in Kenelm Foster, OP, trans., *The Life of Saint Thomas Aquinas: Biographical Documents* (London: Longmans, Green, 1959), 134.

Roman Church did indeed receive Aquinas's writings; the popes through the ages have judged Thomas, the *Doctor Communis*, to hold a singular place of brilliance for the teaching of the whole Church.[70]

Aquinas does not identify popes, however, as those who will share in a special way in Christ's judgment on the Last Day. Rather, for that he names those who led lives of voluntary poverty for the perfection of following Christ.[71] He lists three reasons for this, and here we will consider the first. By reason of congruity, voluntary poverty conforms disciples to Christ in despising the things of the world and to cleaving to Christ alone. "Consequently," he continues, "there is nothing in them to turn away their judgment from justice, so that they are rendered competent to be judges as loving the truth of justice above all things."[72] Theologians, like others, can prepare for Judgment Day by fostering voluntary poverty and extolling its ability to free us to love the truth of justice.

Yet why is there a need for a general judgment on the Last Day, and what is the significance of that for teachers? Aquinas argues that something changeable cannot be perfectly judged until it has reached its consummation. Yes, a particular judgment is rendered at death, as a life on earth has ended, but many effects of that one's life continue in time. The general judgment is needed to do justice to one's life. This includes verifying or correcting a good or evil reputation that one had during his lifetime. Our evil or good actions done in life have repercussions in the world after our life. We will not have the consummation of the good we do, or of the evil we inflict, until the end of the world. Aquinas's illustrations point to his concern about the

---

70. Here are some examples from the past century and a half: Leo XIII, *Aeterni Patris* (1879), Pius XI, *Studiorum Ducem* (1923), Paul VI, *Lumen Ecclesiae* (1974), John Paul II, *Fides et Ratio* (1998), Benedict XVI, General Audiences of June 2, 16, and 23, 2010. Also, see the Second Vatican Council's *Gravissimum Educationis*, no. 10, and *Optatam Totius*, no. 16, as well as the current *Code of Canon Law* can. 252 §3.

71. While Aquinas's interpretation has particular relevance for the mendicant controversies of the third quarter of the thirteenth century, it follows a tradition. Paschasius Radbertus writes on Mt 25:31–46: "Those who left behind all their possessions and even themselves for the sake of Christ will therefore be with the Lord at the same judgment, not that they might be judged, as I said, but that they might judge" (*Exp. in Matt. XI*, 25, 40, 1252). Translated and discussed in Owen W. Phelan, "'Beautiful Like Helen': A Study in Early Medieval Theological Method," *Catholic Historical Review* 106, no. 2 (2020): 202–26, at 218–19. Cf. Sherman W. Gray, *The Least of My Brothers: Matthew 25:31–46. A History of Interpretation*, Society of Biblical Literature Series 114 (Atlanta: Scholars Press, 1989), 163–66.

72. *In IV Sent.*, d. 47, q. 1, a. 2, qc. 2, co.; cf. *ST Suppl.* q. 89, a. 2.

judgment of teachers of faith. He writes, "From the deceit of Arius and other false leaders unbelief continues to flourish down to the close of the world." Aquinas continues, "And until then faith will continue to derive its progress from the preaching of the apostles."[73] Do you want to be like Arius or like an Apostle? If by God's grace you teach like an Apostle, you may receive both a glorious halo and, as Aquinas famously maintains, a doctor's aureole.

AUREOLES FOR TEACHERS
OF THE FAITH

As we saw above, Karl Barth recognized that Thomas Aquinas considered the Church's teachers, like virgins and martyrs, to deserve a special heavenly halo. Thomas's teaching on aureoles, the little golden crowns for certain saints in heaven, arises from the exegetical tradition sparked by the Venerable Bede's *Commentary on the Tabernacle*.[74] Reflecting on Exodus 25:25, *Et super illam alteram coronam aureolam* ("and over that [crown] another little golden crown"), Bede connects the crown with the keeping of the commandments. The additional little golden crown—that is, the aureole—is a heavenly reward that exceeds the obligation of the commandments. He writes that those who surpass the commandments receive the little golden crown "by willingly choosing the more perfect life, and can therefore expect a special reward beyond that of the rest of the faithful in return for their voluntary offering."[75] For the crown won by all the saints, Bede quotes Christ's words to the rich man of the commandments for those who wish to enter eternal life (Mt 19:17–19). For the little golden crown, he quotes Christ's words, "If

---

73. *ST* III, q. 59, a. 5.

74. For the text of the *De tabernaculo*, see D. Hurst, OSB, ed., *Bedae Vernerabilis Opera, Pars II: Opera Exegetica*, 2A: *De Tabernaculo, De Templo, In Ezram et Neemiam*, CCSL 119A (Turnhout: Brepols, 1969). For the translation, see *Bede: On the Tabernacle*, trans. Arthur G. Holder, Translated Texts for Historians 18 (Liverpool: Liverpool University Press, 1994), altered. Aquinas recognizes the Venerable Bede's prominence in interpretation, especially in *In IV Sent.*, d. 49, q. 5, a. 3, qc. 2, arg. 1, but cites the Gloss (which borrows from Bede's interpretation) in *In IV Sent.*, d. 49, q. 5, a. 1, sed contra 1. For a fascinating study in art history, see Edwin Hall and Horst Uhr, "*Aureola super Auream*: Crowns and Related Symbols of Special Distinction for Saints in Late Gothic and Renaissance Iconography," *Art Bulletin* 67, no. 4 (1985): 567–603.

75. CCSL 119A, 24; trans. Holder 24.

you would be perfect, go, sell what you have and give to the poor, and you will have treasure in heaven; and come, follow me" (Mt 19:21). Bede explains this by referring to the virgins who follow the Lamb wherever he goes (Rv 14:3–4). The English Doctor also offers a second interpretation: the little golden crown represents the glory of the body in the Resurrection that follows upon the glory of the soul.[76] This latter interpretation would apply to all the saints, but that lesser-known second interpretation is not what concerns this inquiry.

R.-A. Gauthier opines that Bonaventure perfected this allegorical teaching in his *In IV Sent.* d. 33, a. 2, q. 3, whether virginity's reward is an aureole.[77] Bonaventure makes distinctions among the three rewards for virginity: a golden crown (*aurea*) corresponds to the habitus or disposition, a fruit is given for the status, and an aureole, or little golden crown (*aureola*), signifies the beauty of wholeness (*decor integritatis*). In this question treating virgins, Bonaventure mentions other classes of saints; namely, the doctors and the martyrs. He understands the doctors to be those who lead others to the heavenly fatherland through good teaching, but he has little more to say about the doctors here. To give a precise definition from the Franciscan doctor, we can say that an aureole is a little golden crown, beyond that of a saint's golden crown or halo, owing to particular kinds of meritorious acts proper to virgins, martyrs, and doctors.

Thomas will pick up this threefold division and separate martyrs and doctors from virgins so that each has a proper treatment. This allows him to say more about the doctors than we find in Bonaventure. He has this especially in his *Scriptum on the Sentences* and in his quodlibetal questions. We will touch upon these two sources.

In his *Scriptum*, Aquinas writes that an aureole "is an exceptional reward corresponding to an exceptional victory."[78] He then matches three aureoles to the three victories needed by each of us: the victories over the flesh, the world, and the devil. A virgin receives an aureole for representing the fullest victory over the flesh, and a martyr receives an aureole for representing the fullest victory over the world. "In the conflict with the devil," Aquinas

76. Bede, *On Tabernacle* 1.6 (CCSL 119A, 24; trans. Holder, 25).
77. For Gauthier's opinion, see LE 25.2, 390, note on A.24; cf. White, "*Quodlibeta* of Thomas Aquinas," 81. For the text, see *S. Bonaventurae Opera Omnia*, vol. 4 (Quaracchi, 1889), 755–58.
78. *In IV Sent.* d. 49, q. 5, a. 5, qc. 3, co.; cf. *ST Suppl.* q. 96, a. 11.

continues, "the chief victory is to expel the enemy not only from oneself but also from the hearts of others." How? Aquinas explains, "This is done by teaching and preaching, and consequently the third aureole is due to teachers and preachers."[79]

Also concerning teachers in the *Scriptum*, Aquinas specifies that this aureole is not received solely because of prelates, who are competent to preach and teach by virtue of their office. Rather, an aureole of teaching "is due to whosoever exercises this act lawfully (*licite*)." This means that Aquinas has in mind a considerable breadth of teachers of the faith, and he unites teaching with preaching in the same reward. In Renaissance artwork, a holy woman could be shown to receive the aureole of doctors, as for example Catherine of Siena.[80] Not only is the teacher's aureole more expansive than the pastor's, but also not every prelate who goes to heaven wins it. A holy prelate needs, in fact, to have actually preached, and not simply held the office of preaching.[81] Here Thomas quotes his Vulgate translation of 1 Timothy 2:5, "He will not be crowned, unless he will have lawfully contended."

Moreover, merely teaching the faith is not a sufficient cause for someone to win a teacher's aureole. When we turn to the quodlibetal questions, we find Thomas focusing on the sin of vainglory in the life of a teacher. Would a teacher who always preached or taught out of vainglory receive an aureole after repenting before death?[82] The first objection is that teaching deserves an aureole for its fruit, which is the conversion of believers. For instance, St. Paul calls those who learn from him "my joy and my crown" (Phil 4:1). Someone who preached out of vainglory could still bear the fruit of conversions. Therefore, after repenting, he seems to deserve an aureole. Another other objection is that since a virgin who mentally corrupts her virginity,

---

79. *In IV Sent.* d. 49, q. 5, a. 5, qc. 3, co.; cf. *ST Suppl.* q. 96, a. 11 (trans. alt.). Aquinas also specifies that those who write on the faith may receive the same reward of an aureole as those who instruct orally by teaching and preaching. See *In IV Sent.* d. 49, q. 5, qc. 1, ad 5; cf. *ST Suppl.* q. 96, a. 11, ad 5.

80. Hall and Uhr, "*Aureola super Auream*," 578–83. Moreover, the liturgy commonly recognizes a saint under multiple classifications and thus could win multiple aureoles. Aquinas mentions the liturgical remembrance of Lucy as not losing her crown of virginity (if she would be murderously raped) but gaining two crowns. Artwork of the period illustrates how saints could have multiple aureoles, as, e.g., Peter of Verona—virgin, teacher, and martyr. For discussion of Peter of Verona, also known as Peter Martyr, see Hall and Uhr, "*Aureola super Auream*," 584–89. For discussion of Aquinas, who merited the double aureole of virgin and teacher, see Hall and Uhr, "*Aureola super Auream*," 589–95.

81. *In IV Sent.* d. 49, q. 5, a. 3, qc. 3, co.; cf. *ST Suppl.* q. 96, a. 7, co.

82. *Quodl.* V, q. 12, a. 1 (LE 25.2, 390–91; trans. Nevitt and Davies, 423–24).

after repenting, can still have an aureole, so too should a teacher repentant of his vainglory be able to receive an aureole.

What is Aquinas's reply? Because an aureole presupposes the crown earned by any saint, people who act out of vainglory do not win an aureole—since they do not win a crown. They have already received their reward (Mt 6:2). This means that they would go to hell. Aquinas quotes Matthew 16:26: "What does it profit a man, if he gains the whole world, but suffers the loss of his own soul?" That one, even if he should gain the whole world of souls, is himself lost and has no reward in heaven. For Thomas, there also lies a significant difference between the repentance of a vainglorious doctor and the repentance of a mentally unchaste virgin. The virgin who mentally breaks her virginity, after repenting, still has bodily integrity. She would still be able to receive the aureole of virgins earned by their lifelong virginity. Those who teach out of vainglory, by contrast, would not receive the aureole of doctors after their repentance—unless they taught anew without vainglory.

Because teachers are especially prone to vainglory, it would be good to recall Aquinas's exposition on this vice while reviewing his understanding of the doctor's aureole.[83] A disordered desire for glory may occur in three ways: (1) when we seek glory for something unworthy of glory; (2) when we seek glory from someone whose judgment is uncertain and who should not confer glory on us; (3) when we do not refer our glory to a due end, such as God's honor or our neighbor's spiritual welfare. Vainglory is opposed to the virtue of magnanimity, eschewing that virtue's placement of truth over opinion.[84] Vainglory may be a mortal sin opposed to charity in a number of ways, such as glorying in something false that is opposed to God, preferring a temporal good to God, choosing human testimony over God's testimony, or directing certain deeds—even virtuous ones—to the end of human praise. Anyone with that kind of vainglory, should he die unrepentant, would go to hell. Vainglory may also be merely a venial sin, such as being about a lesser matter. As a capital vice, vainglory has daughter vices that flow from it. Aquinas follows Gregory the Great's enumeration of these daughters: disobedience,

83. *ST* II-II, q. 132.
84. For Thomas on magnanimity, see esp. *ST* II-II, q. 129. For a fine recent study on magnanimity, see Gregory Pine, OP, "Magnanimity and Humility According to St. Thomas Aquinas," *The Thomist* 82, no. 2 (2018): 263–86.

boastfulness, hypocrisy, contention, obstinacy, discord, and love of novel-ties.[85] Do you find that these vices afflict theologians today? Some do. A study of vainglory can make an excellent examination of conscience for teachers of the faith, for it is not only what teachers communicate but also how they communicate that will be judged. In our various accounts of faith in Christ, we implore his mercy on those who listen to us that they might be led by the one Teacher who without any vainglory says, "My teaching is not my own but is from the one who sent me" (Jn 7:16).

THE VOLUME'S CHAPTERS

This volume is divided into two parts—although essays in different parts may overlap and mutually illuminate each other. Part I addresses the crisis in Christology in assessing the life of Christ. In chapter 1, the volume begins with Anthony Giambrone's "Primitive Christology as Ancient Philosophy," which offers an exploration of the relation between philosophy and theol-ogy in the Apostle Paul. Granted that in his Christology Aquinas borrows metaphysical principles from the Neoplatonic-influenced Pauline interpreter Dionysius the Areopagite, we can already discern classical metaphysics in Dionysius's professed mentor, Paul, who seizes the opportunity to speak of the "unknown God" when proclaiming Christ. Dominic Legge follows that Pauline study with "The Remedy for Confused Kenoticism: Aquinas as a Kenotic Theologian." Just like the early holy doctors who combatted heresies that propounded a confused mixture of natures in Christ when interpreting Christ's emptying himself, Aquinas provides a medicine in his careful exe-gesis of the second chapter of Paul's Letter to the Philippians to heal kenotic confusion in its later forms, including those of our own day. In chapter 3, Roger Nutt examines the claim that Aquinas asserts, upon Christ's emp-tying himself in the Incarnation, that there is a second *esse* in Christ in his disputed question *On the Union of the Word Incarnate*. Nutt shows that Aquinas argues there for a new subordinate mode of existence, not a second act of existence in Christ. This demonstrates Aquinas's consistency within that disputed question and across his other texts in applying the Church's

---

85. *ST* II-II, q. 132, a. 5.

conciliar tradition to the metaphysical question of Christ's ontological unity. Steven Long continues in the following chapter to examine Christ's *esse personale* and stresses the role of obediential potency and the metaphysics of subsistence.

The next two essays deal with Christ's human knowledge. In response to Gotthold Lessing's "ugly, broad ditch" that separates contingent truths of history from necessary truths of reason, Thomas Joseph White considers Christ's Trinitarian consciousness in chapter 5. White shows that in his humanity, Christ knew his own identity as the eternal Son of God and expressed that truth in the idioms appropriate to his time and place for the salvation of the world. In chapter 6, Simon Francis Gaine asks, "*Must* an Incarnate Divine Person Enjoy the Beatific Vision?" Reviewing what Thomas Joseph White and Dominic Legge have written about Christ's beatific vision in his humanity, Gaine adds weight to the opinion that there is a soteriological fittingness rather than an absolute metaphysical necessity to Christ's beatific vision, by appealing to the pedagogical structure of the *Summa*'s Third Part. Aquinas teaches that Christ's beatific vision is not a consequence of the union but rather one of the co-assumed perfections freely taken on for our salvation. The next two chapters consider Christ's charity. Guy Mansini writes on Christ's authority and charity in chapter 7, while John Emery expounds Aquinas's Christology of communication in chapter 8. In the former, Mansini shows that Christ's authority and charity form a unity so that Christ's authority is that of charity and his charity is that of authority. It is the same Lord Jesus who offers both God's power and mercy in a human way. In the latter chapter, Emery explains how Christ communicates salvation in his humanity through the friendship of charity. Christ gives us his charity, which transforms us to live in common with the giver.

Chapters 9 and 10 consider Christ's maleness and his priestly sacrifice, respectively, the first against a contemporary feminist interpretation that his maleness has no theological significance and the second against sixteenth-century denials of the sacrificial nature of the Mass. Christ's maleness is integral to his full humanity in Aquinas's anti-Docetic teaching. In chapter 9, Paul Gondreau offers a robust defense of Aquinas's understanding of what it means for Christ to be male and an exploration of the significance of his maleness for any sexual temptation that Christ may have faced. Reginald Lynch, in chapter 10, gives us what could be called Cardinal Cajetan's Thomistic *ressourcement* on Christ's priesthood. Following Thomas's principle of arguing with opponents with appeals only to commonly recognized authorities, Cajetan turned more explicitly and thoroughly to the Scriptures to make his case with the Reformers in his later years; among these writings we find a Thomistic exposition of the Eucharistic institution narrative and of a modal operation of Christ's priestly offering in the sacrifice of the Mass.

Part II considers the crisis of Christology in assessing our life in Christ. Here we begin with two essays on the world in the light of Christ, one on creation and the other on evolution. In chapter 11, Michael Dauphinais argues against popular spiritual teacher Richard Rohr's opinion that creation is an Incarnation of God. By returning to Aquinas's metaphysical teaching on participation in the *Commentary on John*, Dauphinais shows that the Word as Creator remains distinct from creation—neither separated from nor confused with it. That Word is made flesh in a new and most wondrous mode of God's presence within creation. Matthew Ramage follows with "Putting the Last Adam First: Evolution, Suffering, and Death in Light of Kenotic Christology." Ramage propounds a two-step argument in a *ressourcement* to Thomas Aquinas and an *aggiornamento* based on Joseph Ratzinger/Benedict XVI to appreciate Christ as the Last Adam for understanding the human condition in an evolutionary world where we experience suffering and death.

The next two essays concentrate on living out the life of faith in Christ, the first through the experiential sensing of spiritual things and the second by the sacramental minister. Gerald Boersma argues in chapter 13 that the study of the saints' spiritual tasting and touching in Christ is an extension of Aquinas's Christology. And Dominic Langevin next explores in chapter 14 "Christological Falsehood and Sacramental Truth: Intention and Faith in the Sacramental Minister." Because the sacraments give grace through the power of Christ, it makes sense that a false belief in Christ would have repercussions in sacramental theology. With Aquinas as a guide, Langevin examines how the Church considers ministerial action to contribute to sacramental signification and truthfulness, including with respect to the link between internal intention and external action.

The final two essays bring us to Christ our God's judgment of our lives of faith—or lack thereof. "Do you believe that Jesus Christ is God Almighty in the flesh?" That was a question posed to Bruce Marshall at a dinner buffet, and he uses that question to explore today's crisis of faith in chapter 15. Marshall holds that we cannot love Jesus rightly unless we tremble before him as the human being who is God our judge. Finally, in our last chapter, Daria Spezzano asks, "Is Jesus Judgmental?" Whereas many resist the idea of divine judgment, Aquinas holds that Christ is indeed our eschatological judge, and precisely for that reason we can give him praise.

CONCLUSION

Joined by this volume's other editors, Roger Nutt and Michael Dauphinais, I want to praise God for the mercy that we find in Christ's judgment of teachers of the faith. We thank the fine theologians who contributed to this volume and the many others who participated in our 2020 conference at Ave Maria. We owe thanks to Grace De Salvo, who bore the brunt of executing so many details to make our conference run smoothly. We are grateful, as well, to all the staff of both the Aquinas Center for Theological Renewal and the Thomistic Institute for various forms of assistance. We are deeply indebted to the kindness of Archbishop J. Augustine Di Noia, OP, adjunct secretary of the Congregation for the Doctrine of the Faith, for providing our book's foreword. We thank the volume's copy editor, Ashleigh McKown, for her diligence in preparing the pages of this book for publication. Lastly, we express gratitude to you, our readers, for considering with us the multifaceted theme of *Thomas Aquinas and the Crisis of Christology*.

Whereas Karl Barth chose a pistol to the breast as a symbol of judgment in his *Göttingen Dogmatics*, for Aquinas, we might say, it is Christ's Cross that best depicts the judgment of a teacher of the faith. As we saw at the beginning of this introduction, Barth contrasts Aquinas's attitude toward theology with his own and writes, "Is it not clear how many *fatal* possibilities await theologians when they face the dogmatic question?" I submit that Aquinas evinces a joyful confidence in facing the dogmatic question because he knows that God has shown us in his crucified flesh a love beyond all telling. The one on the Cross is the merciful God, God almighty in the flesh, our Teacher who wants our friendship. He is the one who died so that we might be his disciples in the divine mysteries; his breast was pierced so that God's teaching might flow down to us. Aquinas uses Augustine's likening of Christ on the Cross to a teacher on his chair four times.[86] Aquinas clearly loved thinking about Christ teaching, by word and deed, from the Cross.[87] The hagiographical depictions of Aquinas show that Christ also loved to teach Aquinas from the Cross. An early account records a dialogue between the saint and Christ crucified near the end of his life. "Thomas, you have written well about me. What reward should you receive from me for your labor?" Aquinas answered, "O Lord, nothing except you."[88] May that image of Christ teaching from the Cross help us to be confident in the divine kindness by wanting only him when pondering the thoughtful essays collected in this volume dedicated to Thomas Aquinas and the crisis of Christology.

86. Augustine, *Tractate on the Gospel of John* 119.2, on Jn 19:24–30, where Augustine calls the Cross "the chair of a master teaching." Aquinas uses that in the *Catena in Ioan*, 19, lect. 8. He also cites it in *Super Ioan*. 19, lect. 4, no. 2441; *ST* III, q. 46, a. 4, co, and in Sermon 18, *Geminet in terra*, Part 3: *Collatio in sero*, 1.1.3.

87. In addition to Sermon 18's treatment of the Cross, see esp. Aquinas's *Commentary on the Apostles' Creed* 6.2. The text and translation can be found in Nicholas Ayo, CSC, trans., *The Sermon-Conferences of St. Thomas Aquinas on the Apostles' Creed* (Notre Dame, IN: University of Notre Dame Press, 1988), 72–75. After citing Augustine, Aquinas writes, "Whoever wishes to live perfectly should do nothing other than to despise what Christ despises, and desire what Christ desires. No example of virtue is lacking at the Cross" (trans. alt.). Aquinas then explicates the virtues of love, patience, humility, obedience, and despising earthly things. The Roman Liturgy's Office of Readings for the Memorial of St. Thomas Aquinas, January 28, is taken from this passage.

88. Tocco, *Ystoria*, cap. 34 (Le Brun-Gouanvic, 162; my trans.).

PART I

THE CRISIS OF
CHRISTOLOGY IN STUDIES ON
CHRIST'S LIFE

CHAPTER I

PRIMITIVE CHRISTOLOGY AS
ANCIENT PHILOSOPHY

Anthony Giambrone, OP

In several significant recent studies, Charles Stang and his former professor Fr. Maximos Constas have been advancing the argument that modern scholarly reductions of the *Corpus Aereopagiticum* to supposed Neoplatonic antecedents have dreadfully obscured Dionysius's character as an exegete of St. Paul.[1] Their work demonstrates how categories long taken as conceptual cognates to Neoplatonic doctrine in reality have a firm anchoring in Pauline texts. "Paul animates in fact the entire corpus."[2] The implications are considerable. Martin Luther famously denounced Dionysius as *plus platonisans quam Christianisans,*[3] and while the tenor of Stang and Constas's biblical turn might seem hospitable to a long-standing aversion to Hellenistic influence on Christian theology—a triumph for purified biblical religion—I would like to take this emergent paradigm in precisely the opposite direction. The simple possibility of apprehending an author like Dionysius as an

---

1. See Charles Stang, *Apophasis and Pseudonymity in Dionysius the Areopagite: "No Longer I"* (Oxford: Oxford University, 2012); and Maximos Constas, "The Reception of St. Paul and Pauline Theology in the Byzantine Period," in *The New Testament in Byzantium*, ed. Derek Krueger and Robert Nelson, 147–76 (Washington, DC: Dumbarton Oaks, 2016); idem, "Dionysius the Areopagite and the New Testament," in *The Oxford Handbook to Dionysius the Areopagite* (Oxford: Oxford University, forthcoming). See also Alexander Golitzin, *Et introibo as altare dei: The Mystagogy of Dionysius Areopagita with Special Reference to Its Predecessors in the Eastern Christian Tradition* (Thessalonike: George Dedousis, 1994) 234–42.

2. Stang, *Apophasis and Pseudonymity*, 3.

3. WA 6.561.34–562.14; LW 36.109–10.

integrally Pauline thinker should challenge not only our image of Dionysius but also our picture of Paul.

The identical challenge might be extended to embrace any number of similar turns in present-day patristic scholarship. Like the glad recovery of Aquinas as *in sacra pagina magister*, reading Nicene thinkers, from Athanasius to Augustine, first of all as interpreters of the Scriptures is today very much in vogue. It seems to me that this seismic shift in the broad practice and character of *Dogmengeschichte*—a kind of exegetical takeover of normative Christian thought—should have real consequences for biblical exegesis at large. But let us remain with Dionysius and Platonism, invoking St. Thomas at the outset to point the way.

DIONYSIAN THEMES IN ST. THOMAS'S
BIBLICAL CHRISTOLOGY

It is well known among students of medieval theology that, following the paraphrasing work of Thomas Gallus and Robert Grosseteste's translation of the Dionysian corpus in the first half of the thirteenth century, the influence of the presumed disciple of St. Paul was enormous in the Latin schools. Albert and Aquinas (who employed instead the translation of John Sarrazin) are representative of this broad trend, and both abetted the massive influx of Platonic (and other Greek) sources into the theology of the age.[4] In this sense, all these Scholastic innovators come under the facile judgment of leading sacred science ever further astray from its authentic scriptural roots, down the Hellenized road of philosophical speculation.

It is curious in this connection that Aquinas's active instigation of William of Moerbeke's translation of Proclus's *Elements of Theology* led the saint to be the first to discern the inauthenticity of the supposedly Aristotelian *Liber de Causis*, which plainly borrows from Proclus. The same phenomenon of a Proclean debt, of course, today convinces scholars of the inauthenticity of Dionysius's Pauline connection, earning him the sobriquet "Pseudo."[5]

---

4. See Gioacchino Curiello, "'Alia translation melior est': Albert the Great and the Latin Translations of the Corpus Dionysiacum," *Documenti e studi sulla tradizione filosofica medievale* 24 (2013): 121–51.

5. While the debate over Dionysian authenticity became serious following observations of Lorenzo

Dionysius's affinities with Proclus were already noted by John of Scythopolis, interestingly, the first scholiast of the corpus and a scholar noted for skillfully detecting Apollinarian forgeries, who nevertheless defended the traditional attribution. Whatever might explain Thomas's own failure to draw the same conclusion he drew about the *Liber de Causis* in the case of the Dionysian writings[6]—a conclusion now long granted as the official consensus—it is worth observing the role played by Dionysius in Thomas's commentaries on St. Paul.

On the one hand, ironically, Dionysius's authoritative acceptance of Hebrews as a Pauline letter was used by Thomas to argue for Hebrews' own authenticity (*Super ep. ad Heb.* Proem.). On the other hand, the question of content (*materia*) was for Thomas not less interesting or important than the question of the author (*auctor*).[7] The "Pauline" character of the Dionysian corpus, dogmatically conceived, thus helps Thomas finally, not so much in the arbitration of authenticity, but in the business of recognizing what is genuinely Pauline on the theological order. For Thomas, the Christian Platonist underlines and unlocks several significant motifs in the Apostle's thought.

Perhaps the best illustration appears in the commentary on Ephesians, where Thomas engages Paul's potent Christological claim that Christ is enthroned "above every principality and power and virtue and dominion and every name that is named, not only in this world, but also in the one to come" (Eph 1:21). The text is highly suggestive, and two major Dionysian themes converge here, with resonance elsewhere in the Pauline corpus. First, the preeminent status of Christ is articulated in explicit interaction with a hierarchical angelology, eliciting from Thomas an extended discussion of Dionysius's account of the angelic choirs (*Super Eph.* §§61–64). Something similar appears in the first chapter of Hebrews, where Christ is said to be as

---

Valla in the humanistic context and the polemical atmosphere of the Reformation, simultaneous credit for demonstrating the case is usually given to two nineteenth-century scholars: Hugo Koch, "Proklos als Quelle des Pseudo-Dionysius Areopagita in der Lehre von Bösen," *Philologus* 54 (1895): 438–54; and Joseph Stiglmayr, "Der Neuplatoniker Proklos als Vorlage des sog: Dionysius Areopagita in der Lehre vom Übel," *Historisches Jahrbuch* 16 (1895): 253–73, 721–48.

6. Thomas was not unattuned to certain of Dionysius's conceptual debts. "Dionysius nearly everywhere follows Aristotle, as will be evident to anyone who diligently examines his books" (*Sent.* 2, d. 14, q. 1, a. 2).

7. See Anthony Giambrone, "The Prologues to Aquinas' Commentaries on the Letters of St. Paul," in *Towards a Biblical Thomism: Thomas Aquinas and the Renewal of Biblical Theology*, ed. Piotr Roszak and Jörgen Vijgen (Pamplona: EUNSA, 2018), 31–33.

far superior to the angels as his name is superior to theirs, and where Thomas again relies heavily on Dionysian insights (*Super Ep. ad Heb.* §§58, 86–87). The surpassing excellence of Christ's name in both of these texts represents the second, related motif associated with author of the *Divine Names*: for Thomas sees an apophatic theology of the unnamable God implicit in Paul's Christological thinking. "Lest it be thought that he [Christ] is above the name of God, he [Paul] adds 'that is named.' For the divine majesty can be neither contained nor named by a name (*nullo nomine conclude, vel nominari potest*)" (§64). The influence of Lateran IV can be discerned in Aquinas's apophatic rendition of Paul's Christology of the divine Name—Christ's name entails a greater difference from the angels' names than any difference that can be imagined, since they are infinitely apart (*Super Ep. ad Heb.* §47).[8] Dionysius's patronage of the negative theology is also evident. This is clear, for instance, from Thomas's commentary on the boldly paradoxical title of Christ in Colossians 1:13 as the "image of the invisible God" (*Super Col.* §30).

It is not my intention here to explore these motifs in their specific Thomistic context, desirable and interesting though that would be. Even less do I mean to position these ideas within Dionysian Christology, the contours of which are actually governed by different interests.[9] Instead, in what follows, both of the Christological themes actively seized upon by Thomas—the hierarchy of celestial mediators and a named-based *theologia negativa*—will be pursued, not as layered Thomistic or Dionysian motifs, alien Neoplatonic intrusions in the work of biblical exegesis, but rather as valid and even critical perspectives for a historically informed, contemporary New Testament Christology. This effort to valorize distinctively philosophical dimensions of biblical thought will be executed in direct dialogue with a common but, in my view, still too narrow postulate: monotheism as the essential matrix of primitive Christology.[10]

---

8. *Hoc nomen est valde differentius ab illo, quia quantamcumque differentiam ponis, adhuc est maiorem dare, cum distent infinitium.*

9. It is common to plot Dionysius's Christology within post-Chalcedonian sixth-century debates. In this context, he appears to promote a Diphysite viewpoint while carefully chastening his language. See István Perczel, "The Christology of Pseudo-Dionysius the Areopagite: The Fourth Letter in Its Indirect and Direct Traditions," *Le Muséon* 117 (2004): 409–46; and Ernesto Sergio Mainoldi, "Why Dionysius the Areopagite? The Invention of the First Father," in *Studia Patristica*, vol. 96, ed. Markus Vinzent (Leuven: Peeters, 2017), 430. But see also Stang, *Apophasis and Pseudonymity*, 92–116.

10. The literature endorsing this view, which focuses specifically on *Jewish* monotheism, is now vast. For a compact, early expression of the paradigm, see Paul Rainbow, "Jewish Monotheism as the

CELESTIAL HIERARCHIES AND
CHRISTOLOGICAL MONOTHEISM

One of the touchiest points in the debate over so-called Christological monotheism, at least as the discussion is presently conducted among exegetes, concerns (without ever using the title) the οὐράνιαι ἱεραρχίαι, the celestial hierarchies. Briefly, two perspectives have emerged about just how monotheistic the Jewish worldview really was in its first-century Greco-Roman setting, the worldview in which primitive Christology was born. On the one side, it is claimed that no real ambiguity troubled the bright line between the one Creator and his creatures. There was, on this view, no blurring and no mistaking when something was a "personified divine attribute," like hypostasized Wisdom, or when it was by contrast just a powerful angel.[11] On the other side of the debate, as the space between the Most High and his people on earth was so thickly forested with just such heavenly mediators and *Mittelwesen*, it is thought that overly monistic and transcendent constructions of the monotheism of the era are flatly anachronistic and misleading.[12] On this view, first-century Judaism inevitably looked much more like neighboring expressions of ancient Mediterranean religion than some would wish.

It is not difficult to detect behind the conflict of these two positions a much deeper disagreement concerning the relationship between Hellenism and Hebraism. Genuine questions about the very nature of revelation are certainly at stake in getting this relationship right; but, as often, the dichotomy as posed also forces some unnecessary and unhelpful choices. This state of affairs is exposed well by Larry Hurtado, who takes a curious middle

---

Matrix for New Testament Christology," *Novum Testamentum* 33 (1990): 78–79. Rainbow's text is a review article of Larry Hurtado's book, *One God, One Lord: Early Christian Devotion and Ancient Jewish Monotheism* (Philadelphia: Fortress, 1988), which helped greatly to begin the discussion. For a broader view of Second Temple Jewish monotheism, notably in its relation to *pagan* monotheism, see Anthony Giambrone, "*Interpretatio iudaica*: Le monothéisme juif à l'époque du second Temple," *Communio* 45 (2020): 43–60. The entire issue of the journal is consecrated to the motif *Dieu unique*.

   11. An example of this view would be Richard Bauckham, *Jesus and the God of Israel: God Crucified and Other Studies on the New Testament's Christology of Divine Identity* (Grand Rapids, MI: Eerdmans, 2008).

   12. See, e.g., Carey Newman, ed., *The Jewish Roots of Christological Monotheism*, Journal for the Study of Judaism Supplements 63 (Leiden: Brill, 1999); and Crispin Fletcher-Louis, *Jesus Monotheism* (Eugene, OR: Cascade Books, 2015).

position.[13] Situating himself between the two camps more ambiguously than some overeager apologists have understood, Hurtado acknowledges the existence in Second Temple Jewish thought of a messy metaphysical hierarchy of divine beings, yet he apprehends a decisive and distinguishing factor in the Jewish practice of exclusive worship. Only YHWH, or for Christians only YHWH and Christ, are accorded outright worship. Apart from this *latreia*, however, we would be in thick theological darkness, as Hurtado sees it.

LEX ORANDI, LEX CREDENDI?

There is significant promise in this *lex orandi lex credendi* perspective, if there are also important reasons to qualify and contextualize it. One concern is the praxis-based tendency to sideline conceptual discourse in favor of devotional behavior. Dogmatic development simply falls out. There is an ironic upside to such methodological sidelining, however. Without intending to slice this precise Gordian knot, Hurtado's simple analysis effectively siphons off philosophic from cultic paganism. He neatly (if thus with an artificial analytic clarity) decouples two deeply entangled domains, which indeed stood in a complex opposition to one another, but which have conventionally been bundled up as one polytheistic and hence dangerous non-Jewish lump. This bundling is unfortunate, for it stands to the acute disadvantage not only of philosophical thought. It also impairs our constructions of Judaism.

New clarity on the prestige of philosophy and its multiform links to ancient *latreia* is greatly needed if Christology's interface with ancient monotheism is to be properly understood. For polytheism is hardly the full Greek story, whatever certain Jewish sources would have us believe. Even the allegorizing appropriations of mythological nomenclature by Stoic theoreticians and the rationalized rereadings of pagan ritual adopted by Plutarch should be viewed as acts of theurgically inclined philosophical annexation, not evidence of rank confusion. Similarly, the oeuvre of Philo, consistently maltreated as an outlier in New Testament discussion, effects a comparable operation on the basis of a different principle of genuine harmony between

---

13. See, e.g., the recent collection of essays in Larry Hurtado, *Ancient Jewish Monotheism and Early Christian Devotion* (Waco: Baylor, 2017).

philosophy and ritual life. Indeed, Philo's project is not an idiosyncratic enterprise of intellectual syncretism, sold out to non-Jewish commitments. It is a recognizable first-century cultural form and a perennial challenge to accept Second Temple Judaism as a genuinely philosophical worldview—indeed the most philosophical of all precisely because the most majestically monotheistic.

Philo was not the first or last to think so. The Jewish Aristobulus in 200 BC was propounding the same idea. The Book of Wisdom and even Ben Sira move in the same direction. Though little is oddly made of the fact, it is no incidental curiosity of ancient ethnographical opinion that, beginning already with Aristotle and his successor Theophrastus, the Jews were openly portrayed as a race of philosophers—and that, above all, by ancient philosophers themselves.[14] The Neoplatonist Porphyry was not later innovating when he credited the Hebrews for teaching men happiness by worshipping in a pure manner the "self-produced Ruler as God" (Frag. 323).[15]

The point here is simple. If liturgical praxis is, in fact, the real criterion of division, separating the pagan from the Jewish and Christian religious worldviews, with some important if implicit consensus at the level of metaphysical doctrine, it suddenly becomes important to think more closely about the whole nonbiblical tradition of *pagan* monotheism, including its relation to Jewish worship. This has not been the approach heretofore, and the exclusively Jewish data generally discussed comprise almost entirely highly polemical material specifically targeting pagan ritual practice.[16] This distorting lens must be more consciously borne in mind; in point of actual fact, in the intellectual climate of the New Testament world, under the governing thesis of the harmony of Aristotle and Plato, there was vast sympathy for the Aristotelian argument in *Metaphysics* book *Lambda* and enormous interest in the Platonic One. If the complex dynamics of New Testament Christology are accordingly to be correctly described, it is thus essential to engage and respect what John Dillon has termed "soft monotheism," the view held by

---

14. See Menahem Stern, "Hecataeus of Abdera and Theophrastus on Jews and Egyptians," *Journal of Egyptian Archeology* 59 (1973): 159–68.

15. Andrew Smith, *Porphyrii philsophi fragmenta* (Stuttgart: Teubner, 1993). See Pieter van der Horst, "Porphyry on Judaism: Some Observations," in *Studies in Ancient Judaism and Early Christianity*, Ancient Judaism and Early Christianity 67 (Leiden: Brill, 2014), 71–83.

16. See Giambrone, "*Interpretatio iudaica*," 52–53.

basically all educated Greeks and Romans from the fifth century BC on.[17] It is a rather sobering reflection in this regard and in the strident face of both ancient Jewish and Christian accusations of the pagans' benighted polytheistic error to recall that Celsus charged the Christians precisely with transgressing proper reverence of the one God (*Contra Celsum* 8.12–14).

"SOFT MONOTHEISM" AND LITURGICAL APOPHASIS

Celsus was not alone. Against the Jewish prosecution, if "Christological monotheism" is somehow cleared of the charge of erecting "two powers in heaven," one must also be ready to pause concerning the systems of Greek *gnosis* equally indicted in this Jewish attack.[18] Such a pause before the Greek evidence is salutary—and not only for the evident affinity of Gnosticism and Christianity in rabbinic eyes. The great influence and reach of pagan monotheism are also thereby displayed.

The impressive Orphic fragment cited in pseudo-Justin (*Cohortatio ad Greacos* 15) is a fine place to start.

> One Zeus, one Hades,
> One Helios, one Dionysius,
> One god in all.[19]

This is a unique, inner-cultural form of so-called *interpretatio*, the famous process by which gods were identified with one another in antiquity (e.g., Roman Jupiter with Greek Zeus). Here the Orphic pantheon of divinities

17. John Dillon, "Monotheism in the Gnostic Tradition," in *Pagan Monotheism in Late Antiquity*, ed. Polymnia Athanassiadi and Michael Frede (Oxford: Clarendon, 2008), 69–79.

18. On this theme, see Alan Segal, *Two Powers in Heaven: Early Rabbinic Reports about Christianity and Gnosticism*, Studies in Judaism in Late Antiquity 25 (Leiden: Brill, 1977). See also, more recently, the position of Stephen Waers, "Monarchianism and Two Powers: Jewish and Christian Monotheism at the Beginning of the Third Century," *Vigiliae Christianae* 70 (2016): 401–29. The hypothesis that Gnosticism ultimately has Jewish roots must not distract from its highly Hellenized character. See Jarl Fossum, *The Name of God and the Angel of the Lord: Samaritan and Jewish Concepts of Intermediation and the Origin of Gnosticism*, Wissenschaftliche Untersuchungen zum Neuen Testament 36 (Tübingen: Mohr Siebeck, 1985).

19. For the original text, see Bernard Pouderon, *Ouvrages apologétiques: Pseudo-Justin*, Sources Chretiennes 528 (Paris: Cerf, 2009).

has collapsed and merged into one in a kind of pagan Sabellianism, culminating in a cultic exclamation—"One god in all"—that is similar to the εἷς
θεός formula found in many inscriptions. The Christian author brings forward this text in the midst of his polemic as a witness to the true doctrine of
monotheism preserved by the Greeks despite all their endless errors. If this
variety of Greek monotheism is not "Gnostic" in the technical sense, the
Orphic mysteries nevertheless had a certain mytho-philosophical color that
approximates the Gnostic milieu. The hymnic character of the Orphic cult,
moreover, made it a privileged vehicle for "soft" monotheistic sentiment and
latreia.[20] Liturgical *polyonymia* together with theogonic interest in world
generation (e.g., the Derveni Papyrus) make the *Orphica* a prime point of
reference, at least on the level of genre, for much of the material that we will
see—not least the Christological hymns.

It is possible to go further, however. Dillon is prepared to acknowledge
as "softly monotheistic" even genuinely Gnostic systems whose "reckless
multiplication of immaterial and quasi-divine entities" and radically dualistic worldview one would have thought should plainly exclude them.[21] He
cites, for instance, an extraordinary passage found in the *Apocryphon of John*
(2.33*ff.*) containing perhaps the most comprehensive expression of Gnostic
metaphysics. It is a highly apophatic, negative description of the Monad, Father of all, "existing in uncontaminated light, towards which no vision may
gaze."

We should not think of it as a god or like a god. For it is greater than a god, because it has nothing over it and no lord above it ... illimitable, since there is nothing to limit it, unfathomable, since there is nothing before to fathom it, immea-
surable, since there was nothing before it to measure it, invisible, since nothing
has seen it ...
[and so on and so on for many more lines].[22]

20. "There is only one common element to Stoics, Pythagoreans, Christians, Neoplatonists, and
composers and singers of hymns for different cults (be it the Sun, Mithra, or any other supreme God).
They all thought Orphica to be a very suitable vehicle for conveying monotheism while upholding the
legitimacy of traditional genres." Miguel Herrero de Jáuregi, "Orphic God(s): Theogonies and Hymns
as Vehicles of Monotheism," in *Monotheism between Pagans and Christians in Late Antiquity*, ed.
Stephen Mitchell and Peter van Nuffelen (Leuven: Peeters, 2010), 77–99, here 99.

21. Dillon, "Monotheism in the Gnostic Tradition," 69.

22. Marvin Meyer, trans., *The Nag Hammadi Scriptures* (New York: HarperCollins, 2008), 108.
For the Coptic text, see James Robinson, ed., *The Coptic Gnostic Library*, vol. 2 (Leiden: Brill, 2000).

If this text plainly crawls out of the "Platonic underworld," with traces of the *Parmenides'* negative predications clinging all about it, the same traces of theological negation just as plainly adhere to the lofty deity of 1 Timothy's doxologies: the "eternal, immortal, invisible, the only wise God," he "who alone has immortality and dwells in unapproachable light, whom no one has ever seen or can see" (1:17, 6:16). Romans and the Gospel of John are no less openly committed to this sovereign inaccessibility of God to the bodily senses. Pagans, Jews, and Christians were all of one mind: "No one has ever seen God." John 1:18, in fact, is in word-for-word agreement with the Jewish Aristobulus earlier cited, who notably continues the line (citing an Orphic tradition!): "No one has [ever] seen him ... he is seen only by mind" (Frag. 4).[23]

The way of pure mental apprehension naturally supported a strong apophatic fashion in Greco-Roman theology. This takes root at the latest with the Alexandrian Eudorus, who a generation before the turn of the era taught that the One transcends all attributes whatsoever.[24] Varro, at roughly the same time, imagined an aniconic golden age of Roman religion under Numa, in tune with right reason and resembling Jewish worship.[25] For Philo, the aniconism of the Jewish cult was accordingly the uncontroversial, ritual expression of a commonly accepted philosophical truth, an ascetic training of the embodied soul for its rigorous intellectual ascent to the divine realm of the incomprehensible and unseen. For "God is far away from all creation ... and the apprehension of him is removed to a very great distance from all human power of thought" (*Somn.* 1.66, LCL).

---

23. For Adela Yabro Collins's translation of the full text, see James Charlesworth, ed., *Old Testament Pseudepigrapha*, vol. 2 (Peabody, MA: Hendrickson, 2011), 840–41.

24. See John Dillon, *Middle Platonism, 80 B.C. to A.D. 220* (Ithaca, NY: Cornell University Press, 1977), 126–29.

25. See George H. van Kooten, "Pagan and Jewish Monotheism According to Varro, Plutarch, and St. Paul: The Aniconic, Monotheistic Beginnings of Rome's Pagan Cult—Romans 1:19–25 in a Roman Context," in *Flores Florentino: Dead Sea Scrolls and Other Early Jewish Studies in Honour of Florentino García Martínez*, ed. Anthony Hillhorst, Supplements to the Journal for the Study of Judaism (Leiden: Brill, 2007), 633–51.

THEOS HYPSISTOS

Even Gnostics knew that there was no lord above the invisible One. This transcendent pinnacle of the pantheon was not a theoretical abstraction, moreover. *Ho Theos* was an object of principled worship. Indeed, the most celebrated and widely attested expression of pagan monotheism takes a liturgical form: the cult of *Theos Hypsistos*, "God Most High."[26] The profound and tantalizing links of this cult to Jewish synagogue worship pose an ongoing puzzle to scholars in many respects, yet the links are nevertheless certain: archeologically attested by hundreds of inscriptions and by the apparent derivation of the cult title from the Septuagint's rendering of *El Elyon*. With good reason, this phenomenon is frequently associated with the famous "God-fearers," those sympathetic pagans so vital to the narrative progress in Acts, who entertained religious perspectives that would have resonated favorably with Philo. (In this connection, there are more than passing contacts with the solar cult of the Therapeutae that Philo so esteemed.) The riveting religious phenomenon—which filled the eastern provinces and can be dated back to the second century BC—is, in any case, a uniquely suggestive hybrid. It is not coincidental that the worship of *Theos Hypsistos* is simultaneously the most Jewish and the most philosophical of the pagan cults, nor is it accidental that it is located in such proximity to the known context of primitive Christian missionary preaching: the Hellenistic synagogue. Luke is appropriately the New Testament author most attached to the *Hypsistos* title (Lk 1:32, 1:35, 1:76, 6:35, 8:28; Acts 7:48, 16:17).

An exceptional example of the philosophical orientation of this cultic tradition appears in a celebrated inscription discovered in Oenoanda in northern Lydia in 1971. The inscription itself dates from around 150 AD and was found alongside lamps inscribed to *Theos Hypsistos*. It records a widely

---

26. Substantial research and controversy surround this famous cult. For an orientation, see Stephen Mitchell, "The Cult of Theos Hypsistos between Pagans, Jews, and Christians," in *Pagan Monotheism in Late Antiquity*, 81–148; idem, "Further Thoughts on the Cult of Theos Hypsistos," in *One God: Pagan Monotheism in the Roman Empire*, ed. Stephen Mitchell and Peter van Nuffelen, 167–208 (Cambridge: Cambridge University Press, 2010); and Jörg Lanckau, "*Hypsistos*: Cultural Translation of Jewish Monotheism in the Hellenistic Period," *Asiastische Studien/Etudes asiatiques* 65, no. 4 (2011): 861–82.

circulated oracle that resonates perfectly with the pattern of negative predications (and *polyonymia*) already observed.

> Self-born (αὐτοφυὴς), untaught, without a mother, unperturbable, not contained in any name (οὔνομα μὴ χωρῶν), known by many names (πολυώνυμος,) dwelling in fire, this is God (τοῦτο θεός) … you who ask this question about God, what his essential nature is (ὅστις ὑπάρχει), he has pronounced that Aether is god who sees all, on whom you should gaze and pray at dawn, looking towards the sunrise. (SEG XXVII, 933)

This thematization of the unnamable essential nature of God is of special interest in its contact with the title *Theos Hypsistos*, which itself clearly functions as a conceptual cult instrument. A fundamental tension between apophatic philosophical accuracy and liturgical exigency is here plainly exposed. The need to name a strictly unnamable God in order to worship him rightly is not an insignificant religious conundrum. It is, in fact, the all-important crux where the conjoined philosophical and cultic language of any true monotheism, be it Jewish or pagan, refuses to yield before Hurtado's analytical knife.

DIVINE NAMING

The theological penumbra blurring Jewish and pagan enlightenment is evident in the very biblical parentage of the name *El Elyon*, which has deep roots in Israel's long struggle with Canaanite religion. Of course, within Judaism the name does not hold the privileged cultic place of the mysterious Tetragrammaton, uniquely revealed to Moses. It is accordingly not surprising if Philo not only represents the first philosopher to apply to God significant new alpha-privative predicates including "unnamable" (ἀκατονόμαστος) and "unutterable" (ἄρρητος) (*Somn.* 1.67), notions clearly crafted under the influence of Jewish ritual *praxis*. Philo also worries about the implicit theology suggested by "Most High" language. In the end, right philosophy must chasten itself, groping inwardly to come into alignment with the revealed Jewish cult of *HaShem*. For, though biblically sanctioned, the name *Theos Hypsistos* belongs to what Tibor Grüll designates as "Megatheism" and Reinhard Feldmeier calls "Machtpredikaten": a field of agonistic superlatives, divine epithets still trapped within a comparative paradigm with God as one entity among others.[27] Like the *megistos, megistos, megistos* of Hermes Tresmegistos, the taste for superlatives and one-upmanship challenges even those gods at the very top: Juppiter Optimus Maximus, *Dios kratistos megistos* in Greek (*INikaia* 1141), boasts but one *megistos*. The titular inflation, in fact, ultimately grows so bad that, as Robert Parker says, "The world becomes strewn with best and greatest and most manifest gods" (though whether *hypsistos* itself becomes a similarly promiscuous term is disputed).[28] This is the theology of an upward straining, monolatrous, natural religion, locked in an immanent cosmological frame of univocal being. In both theory and praxis, it falls short of the necessary transcendence, philosophically grasped by the *via negativa* and ritually expressed by the Jewish paradox of the Lord's unpronounceable Name.

The *Apocalypse of Abraham* is perhaps the single most revealing and underexploited theological artifact in comprehending the character of first- and early second-century Palestinian monotheism, and notably its vital fusion with Hellenistic perspectives. Probably written in Hebrew sometime after 70 AD, the text is neatly divided into two parts. In the first Abraham, the son of Terah, an idol maker in Ur, philosophically reasons his way to a discovery of the one God and Creator of all, reconfiguring a tradition of Jewish anti-idol polemic and Hellenistic religious critique.[29] In the second part, a divine revelation in the form of a voice from YHWH—"Abraham, Abraham"—greets the newly converted former pagan and the tale joins the story of the biblical account at Genesis 12:1, culminating in an act of celestial worship. The basic organization of the work is thus quite clear. Knowledge of the one true God is partitioned between two moments: a sort of philosophical *preambula fidei* and a supernatural apocalypse, leading to true *latreia*.

27. Tibor Grüll, "'Monotheism' or 'Megatheism'? Religious Competition in Late Antiquity as Mirrored in the Inscriptions Dedicated to Theos Hypsistos," Academia.edu, https://www
.academia.edu/5382844/_Monotheism_or_megatheism_Religious_competition_in_late_antiquity_as_
mirrored_in_the_inscriptions_dedicated_to_Theos_Hypsistos; Reinhard Feldmeier, "'Der Höchste':
Das Gottesprädikat Hypsistos in der paganen Religiosität, in der Septuaginta und im lukanischen
Doppelwerk," in *Die Septuaginta—Text, Wirkung, Rezeption*, ed. Wolfgang Kraus and Siegfried Kreuzer (Tübingen: Mohr Siebeck, 2014), 544–58.

28. Robert Parker, *Greek Gods Abroad: Names, Natures, and Transformations*, Sather Classical
Lectures (Berkeley: University of California Press, 2017), 148.

29. See Giambrone, *"Interpretatio iudaica,"* 54–55.

A great deal should be said here, but suffice it to note that in the long celestial hymn sung by Abraham and his *angelus interpres*, the two fall prostrate in worship before the Lord. Their liturgy is of immense interest for its near exact echo of *Theos Hypsistos* theology.

> Eternal One, Mighty One, Holy El, God autocrat
> Self-originate, incorruptible, immaculate,
> Unbegotten, spotless, immortal
> Self-perfected, self-devised,
> without mother, without father, ungenerated
> exalted, fiery . . .
> El, El, El, El, Iaoel. (17.8-13)[30]

This incantatory fourfold repetition of El is rightly reckoned as a substitute for the Tetragrammton, as is the name Iaoel. The wanted liturgical fusion of philosophy and the divinely revealed, unpronounceable Name could not be more wonderfully evident.

DIVINE NAME THEOLOGY

The application of all this is in no way hidden, and the Dionysian patronage should by now be clear. I am pushing toward a new context and register of reception for the New Testament's Christology of the divine Name. Rather than appropriating this all-important *topos* exclusively via the Hebrew canon and through an onto-unfriendly *narrative* theology, constructing "divine identity" like a character emerging in the immanent economy of Scripture, one might instead recognize in the hymnic conferral upon Christ of that "name above every other name" an outstanding biblical effort at hyper-predication. Long before Dionysius, in fact, Plato in the *Parmenides* had already broken this ground. He speaks notably of "a feat of expression ὑπὲρ ἡμᾶς, *beyond our power*," searching some elusive way to name the ultimate principle beyond both its positive designation as "The One" (τὸ ἕν), as well beyond as its negative labelling as the "The Not Many" (τὸ μὴ πολλά)

---

30. Translation by R. Rubinkiewicz in James Charlesworth, ed., *The Old Testament Pseudepigrapha*, vol. 1 (Peabody, MA: Hendrickson, 2011), 697. The text is only preserved in an Old Slavonic version.

(*Parm.* 128b).[31] When Eudorus much later devises the language of ὁ ὑπεράνω θεός for the supreme Principle beyond Limit (Monad) and Limitlessness (Dyad), we are facing dogmatic Platonism's formulation of the surpassing feat. The Jewish tradition had its own transcendent formulation, of course. For this highest name in Philippians 2, a Name ὑπὲρ πᾶν ὄνομα, excels mere "Megatheism" precisely by coinciding with *Kyrios*, the holy Name revealed from God's extra-worldly beyond.

Obviously, the Isaianic resonance of Philippians 2 contributes hugely to its full monotheistic impact, yet such a powerful scriptural orientation must not prevent us from seeing this poem as a variation on the Hellenistic synagogue hymn. This is Christology crafted in the world of God-fearing Gentiles. For Greek ears, τὸ ὄνομα τὸ ὑπὲρ πᾶν ὄνομα is simply hard to divorce from the hymnic philosophy resonating in sites like Oenoanda, just across the Bosporus from Philippi. Here evangelical exegetes' profound aversion to Bossuet's Hellenistic "Christ cult" theory is a dangerous scholarly tic that risks radically reinscribing pre-Hengel naiveté about a pure Palestinian (read biblical) form of Judaism. When "Christological monotheism" serves as a bulwark against supposed Hellenistic infection—as it often does where the influence of Luther and Karl Barth is strong—our modeling of the first-century world has gone all catawampus. The fact is the Hellenistic synagogue was an institution even in first-century Jerusalem itself, as the Greek Theodotus inscription unambiguously proves and the *Apocalypse of Abraham* reflects. Bossuet was incorrect about the character of the Christ cult, yet the new *Religionsgeschichtliche Schule* has no less gravely mis-stepped in trying to drain primitive Christology of its profoundly Greek context.

The open paradox of Christ somehow receiving the name above every name—an evocative apophatic mystery recognized in Thomas's commentaries as we have seen—plots this Christological predication in plain view of Hellenistic theorizing on the realm of divine being, which lies beyond all names. Philo's exegesis of Exodus 3:14, for instance, takes "I am He who Is" as being "equivalent to 'my nature is to be, not to be spoken'" (ἴσον τῷ εἶναι πέφυκα, οὐ λέγεσθαι), for, as the exegete explains, "no personal name can be

31. On transcendental predication in Plato, see Rafael Ferber and Gregor Damschen, "Is the Idea of the Good Beyond Being? Plato's *epekeina tēs ousias* Revisted (Republic 6,509b8–10)," in *Second Sailing: Alternative Perspectives on Plato*, Commentationes Humanarum Litterarum 132, ed. Debra Nails and Harold Tarrant (Helsinki: Societas Scientiarum Fennica, 2015), 197–204.

assigned to the truly existent" (τῷ ὄντι πρὸς ἀλήθειαν, *Mut.* 11). Philo's own handling of the Divine Name, *Kyrios*, ultimately assigns it to God's *Logos*: a scenario to which we must shortly return (e.g., *Conf.* 146). It is already possible, however, to observe the extraordinary theological power of Philippians 2 (no less than Eph 1:21 or Heb 1:13 for that matter), which proceeds one step beyond simply naming Christ with proper transcendental precision. I use the term "proceed" with calculated intent, for Paul's text expresses the divine being of the Son by an act of naming that transpires within *ho Theos*: God names himself.

A provocative gloss on this primordial operation of immanent theo-logy (in the strongest etymological sense of a "Word of God") appears in the second-century Valentinian *Gospel of Truth.* "The Father's Name is not pronounced; it is revealed through a Son, and the Name is great ... Since the Father has no beginning, he alone conceived it for himself as a name before he created the eternal realms, that the Father's Name might be supreme over them."[32] Although the Aeons here, over whom the "invisible" Name reigns supreme, clearly insert us within the Gnostic myth, Valentinus himself, we must recall, was nearly elected Pope in Rome, and his theology cannot simply be brushed aside as a homogenous heterodox lump. Paul's own Christological "name that is named" ὑπεράνω πάσης ἀρχῆς καὶ ἐξουσίας καὶ δυνάμεως καὶ κυριότητος in Ephesians carries manifest echoes of the same idea. In any case, the many links observed between the *Gospel of Truth* and the *Odes of Solomon* attest once again to the site of this brand of theology in the hymnic setting of the synagogue and early Church.[33]

---

32. "The Name of the Father is the Son. In the beginning he gave a name to the one who came from him, while he remained the same, and he conceived him as his Son. He gave him his Name, which belonged to him. All that exists with the Father belongs to him. He has the Name; he has the Son. The Son can be seen, but the name is invisible, for it alone is the mystery of the invisible, which comes to our ears completely filled with it through his agency. Yet, the Father's Name is not pronounced; it is revealed through a Son, and the Name is great ... Since the Father has no beginning, he alone conceived it for himself as a name before he created the eternal realms, that the Father's Name might be supreme over them. This is the true Name, which is confirmed by his authority in perfect power. This Name does not derive from ordinary words or name giving, for it is invisible" (38.6–39.1). Meyer, *Nag Hammadi Scriptures,* 45–46. For the text, see James Robinson, ed., *The Coptic Gnostic Library,* vol. 1 (Leiden: Brill, 2000). Cf. Geoffrey S. Smith, *Valentinian Christianity Texts and Translations* (Berkeley: University of California Press, 2020).

33. It is also important to "normalize" certain Valentinian views by regarding wider theological currents in antiquity to which this material is related. See Guy Stroumsa, "A Nameless God: Judeo-Christian and Gnostic 'Theologies of the Name,'" in *The Image of Judeo-Christians in Ancient*

It is worth underlining, finally, in this connection, not simply the motif of the Name but also the special idiom of ὑπέρ/ὑπεράνω + πᾶς in the Philippians and Ephesians hymns, in reference to angelic powers, for it is singular usage within the New Testament and a type of superlative discourse with a suggestive affinity. The expression finds a remarkably strong parallel, for instance, in the extraordinary hymn preserved in *AposCon* 7.35.1–10.

> There is no god beside you alone,
> There is no Holy One beside you (ἅγιος οὐκ ἔστι πλὴν σοῦ),
> Lord God of knowledge (κύριος θεὸς γνώσεων), God of holy ones,
> *Holy One above all holy ones* (ἅγιος ὑπὲρ πάντας ἁγίους)
> For those who have been made holy are under your hands.
> Honored and exalted exceedingly,
> Invisible by nature (ἀόρατος τῇ φύσει)
> … unchangeable … unlimited … unapproachable … without
> Beginning … unending …
> You are the Father of Wisdom (σὺ γὰρ εἶ ὁ σοφίας πατήρ),
> the Creator, as cause, of the creative workmanship through a Mediator
> (ὁ δημιοργίας τῆς διὰ μεσίτου κτίστης ὡς αἴτιος)
> The God and Father of the Christ.[34]

This powerful monotheistic fusion of Greek philosophical concepts and biblically based liturgical praise (which in this case draws upon the very same chapter in Isaiah 45 as Philippians 2) is too vitally important to neglect in our reconstructions of primitive Christology.

CHRIST'S CREATIVE AGENCY AND "PREPOSITIONAL METAPHYSICS"

Divine Name theology in this broad philosophico-liturgical rereading is not the only key index of Christological monotheism that should be rethought and replotted in the habitat of the Hellenistic synagogue. Nor is ὑπέρ the

---

Jewish and Christian Literature, ed. Peter-Jan Tomson and Doris Lambers-Petry, Wissenschaftliche Untersuchungen zum Neuen Testament 158 (Tübingen: Mohr Siebeck, 2003), 230–43.

34. D. R. Darnell, trans., *Old Testament Pseudepigrapha*, 2 vols., edited by James H. Charlesworth, 681–82 (New York: Doubleday, 1983). For the original text, see Marcel Metzger, ed., *Les constitutions apostoliques: Tome III. Livres VII et VIII*, Sources Chrétiennes 336 (Paris: Cerf, 1987).

only preposition freighted with philosophical import. Gregory Sterling has identified a phenomenon he labels "prepositional metaphysics" that is of extremely high relevance to the whole discussion.[35] The Colossians hymn is a stellar example, but the prayer formula in Romans 11:36 is more compact and will make the point: "From him and through him and to [or for] him are all things. To him be the glory forever. Amen." The three prepositions here—ἐξ, διά, and εἰς—belong to the standard philosophical lexicon of the era, designating the material, efficient, and final causes, respectively. When Paul employs this discourse as a doxology, he is thus enunciating a simultaneous doctrine of God and of creation (theogony) with conceptual tools borrowed from metaphysical speculation, mediated as an expression of praise via Hellenistic synagogue worship. This liturgical line of transmission is confirmed through the corpus of Greek synagogue prayers preserved in the *Apostolic Constitutions* (and Christologically touched up, most frequently with a διὰ Χριστοῦ).[36]

In present New Testament discussion, one of the cornerstones of "Christological monotheism" has, of course, been Paul's reconfiguration of the *Shema* around Jesus in 1 Corinthians 8:6. Here I would merely like to highlight that prepositional metaphysics forms the essential substructure of Paul's exegesis and that the distribution of causality is more interesting than generally thought.

For us there is one God, the Father, *from whom* are all things and *for whom* we exist, and one Lord, Jesus Christ, *through whom* are all things and *through whom* we exist. (1 Cor 8:6)

Jesus Christ is here clearly inserted within a monotheistic frame. It is a reinforced monotheism, moreover, doubly expressed by both Jewish ritual and pagan philosophical language, identical to that seen in Romans 11. Jesus is designated precisely as the bearer of the Name and the instrumental, fashioning cause of all things.

Though it has thus far failed to enter the discussion, Philo, it happens,

---

35. Gregory Sterling, "Prepositional Metaphysics in Jewish Wisdom Speculation and Early Christian Liturgical Texts," *Studia Philonica Annual* 9 (1997): 219–38.

36. See, e.g., Menaham Kister, "The Prayers of the Seventh Book of the *Apostolic Constitutions* and Their Implications for the Formulation of Synagogue Prayers," *Tarbiz* 77 (2008): 205–38 (in Hebrew with English summary).

has a similar exegesis, parsing of θεός and κύριος with a somewhat doubtful two-power language: "God (θεός) is the name of the beneficent power, and lord (κύριος) is the title of the royal power" (*Somn.* 1:163; cf. *Her.* 170). The issue that arises here is how this interpretative tradition of dividing in two the divine epithet "Lord God"—an exegesis shared in common with Paul—ultimately aligns with the instrumental preposition διά, for the provenance of the preposition in Philo is clear. His middle-Platonic *Logos*, who is at once a creature and a "second god" (δεύτερος θεός, *QG* 2.62), is that image of God and archetypal firstborn of creation, the highest intermediary being, "through whom" or "by which (δι' οὖ) all the world was made (ἐδημιουργεῖτο!)" literally *demiurged* (*Spec.* 1.81; cf. *Somn.* 1.230). The *Logos* is "the shadow of God which he used like an instrument when he was making the world" (*Leg.* 3.31). The attribution of creative agency to Christ has become a solid peg in the arsenal of those touting his so-called divine identity. Whence an impertinent question: What resonance of Philo's Demiurge should be heard in this Christology, so bound to the ancient metaphysics of fashioning agency designated by διά? Wishing Philo away as a diasporic aberration is the normal response, but theologically and historically bad form.

CHRIST THE DEMIURGE?

The question of Paul's διά thus leads to our final stop on the map of primitive "Christological monotheism." We owe to Philo the neologism "polytheism," which he coined as a slur against the pagans. It is only fair, then, to give him a word in defining the Jewish monotheism around which our Christological variant wills to be built. And here nothing blurs the unmistakable, binary line that first-century Jews supposedly drew between the Creator and his creation like Philo's baffling *Logos*. The extraordinary passage in *Who Is the Heir?* 205–6 brings Philo's embrace of ambiguity to perfect expression.

To his Word (λόγῳ), his chief messenger (ἀρχαγγέλῳ), highest in age and honor, the Father of all has given a special prerogative, to stand at the border and separate the creature from the Creator (τὸ γενόμενον διακρίνῃ τοῦ πεποιηκότος). This same Word both pleads with the immortal as suppliant for afflicted mortality and acts as ambassador of the ruler to the subject. He glories in this prerogative and proudly describes it in these words, "and I stood between the Lord and you"

(Dt 5:5), that is neither uncreated as God (ἀγένητος ὡς ὁ θεὸς), nor created as you (γενητὸς ὡς ὑμεῖς), but midway between two extremes (μέσος τῶν ἄκρων), a surety to both sides. (LCL)

An exuberance of additional Philonic descriptions (*polyonymia*) complements this conceptual *metaxy* between the Father God and his world: the *Logos* is sometimes an angel, a priest, a cutter, a glue, God's image, and, importantly, both the Name of God and the "first born son of God" (cf. *Conf.* 146–47). The infinite space separating creation from its transcendent Creator poses an insuperable problem for philosophical thought, just as it does for worship: what emerges on both sides thus remains both unnamed and many named. If Philo accordingly throws a hundred metaphors at the problem and finally waffles with a *Logos* that is somehow both uncreated and created, this merely shows that even in this regime of a philosophy strengthened by the light of revelation in its firm vision of the Creator Lord, the obscure mystery of mediation was not yet fully disclosed. Like the hypostasized "Angel of the Name" in the *Apocalypse of Abraham* and other Jewish traditions, Philo's cosmic pontifex lurks in a stupefying realm of divine darkness.[37] A new doctrine of the *Logos* was needed—and it was given. Philo's Demiurge stepped out of the One God's shadow.

John's Prologue, together with the still more compact prologue of Hebrews, and the problem of the Demiurge are the great missing elements in prevailing discussions of "Christological monotheism," as far as I can see.[38] This monster *Mittelwesen* born of the *Timaeus* is quite simply the cosmic limit case where everything must be decided—and at Nicea ultimately was.[39] That Athanasius adopted a prepositional theology reminiscent of Paul (later taken up and developed by Basil) should convince us of his bona

37. On this motif, see Fossum, *Name of God.*
38. A helpful call to widen the religio-historical framework used for understanding John's *Logos* is found in Jörg Frey, "Between Torah and Stoa: How Could Readers Have Understood the Johannine Logos," in *The Prologue of the Gospel of John: Its Literary, Theological and Philosophical Contexts,* ed. Jan G. van der Watt, R. Alan Culpepper, and Udo Schnelle, Wissenschaftliche Untersuchungen zum Neuen Testament 359 (Tübingen: Mohr Siebeck, 2016), 189–234.
39. Without grasping its significant role, the Tübingen School of Platonic interpretation, with its paradigm-changing insistence on the "Unwritten Doctrines," helped prepare new insight into the important place of the Demiurge and the doctrine of cosmic Intelligence in Plato's own integral thought. See the fourth part of Giovanni Reale, *Toward a New Interpretation of Plato* (Washington, DC: Catholic University of America Press, 1997), 305–434.

fides as a biblical thinker. Origen's view of John's ἐγώ εἰμι as a Hellenistic Jewish exegesis of the divine name in Exodus 3:14 is also not eisegesis in my estimation.[40] One need read only a few pages of Philo. The awkward formulation ὁ δημιοργίας τῆς διὰ μεσίτου κτίστης ὡς αἴτιος seen above in the mongrel *Apostolic Constitutions* might leave some open questions. For the conciliarly minded exegete, the basic lines are nevertheless quite clear. No amount of creative agency or even *latreia* accorded by Christians to Christ can successfully assert his divinity without some idea of divine homo-*ousia*. And that requires some proto-Dionysian grammar of transcendent being or Thomistic notion of *ipsum esse subsistens*. Otherwise, the *Logos* will remain an Arian Artisan and worshipful super-angel: above all things, but merely atop and not entirely beyond.

The famous *Agnostos Theos* of Acts 17:23 is more than an incidental background detail in the inspiration for the grand Dionysian pseudepigraphal program.[41] It is, as Stang has shown, the founding charter for an apophatic theology of the "God beyond being." Scant notice is given, even in this new "Pauline Dionysius" paradigm, but the architectonic *exitus-reditus* dynamic rightly discerned in the programmatic opening sentence of the *Celestial Hierarchy* is articulated precisely by a citation of Romans 11:36 (minus the διά).[42] "From him and for him all things are." In other words, Paul's biblical metaphysics—or, better, Paul's classical metaphysics (which appear in the Bible)—ostensibly help animate this supposed sixth-century motif—which later becomes a thirteenth-century motif in Thomas's *Summa*—no less than

---

40. The separation of Origen the Platonist from the Christian doctor is symptomatic of the tortured views of Hellenism's relation to Christian thought. See Illaria Ramelli, "Origen, Patristic Philosophy, and Christian Platonism: Re-Thinking the Christianisation of Hellenism," *Vigiliae Christianae* 63 (2009): 217–63. Taking Origen, the student of Ammonius Saccas, to be head of the catechetical school at Alexandria and not a pagan of the same name, it is interesting to note that the only view attributed to him by pagan authors is to have considered the first principle not as the One beyond both intellect and being, but rather as itself the supreme intellect and first being. Accordingly, he would be more in line with traditional "Middle" Platonic (and Christian) conceptions than with the ideas of Plotinus. Cf. Proclus, *In Platonis Theologiam* 2.4.

41. The still classic, if somewhat dated, study on this title remains Eduard Norden, *Agnostos Theos: Untersuchung zur Formgeschichte religiöser Rede* (Helsingfors: B. G. Teubner, 1913).

42. Stang, *Apophasis and Pseudonymity*, 140, is alert to the issue, though *exitus-reditus* as such is not one of the major "Neoplatonic" categories that he concentrates upon in his analysis. As he perceptively sees, however, the process of divinization through participation in the Body of Christ represents a native Christian idiom, at once Pauline and Dionysian, for the back end of this return movement to God.

the philosophical preacher of Acts 17 also activates various other major movements in the Dionysian corpus identified by Constas and Stang. The return to the One Cause from whom all creatures came is not an unbiblical way of thinking.

If this is Neoplatonism *avant la lettre*, or rather "Middle Platonism" to employ the misleading pedagogical conceit,[43] Romans 11 remains an essential control on our designs of Christological mediation. On the one hand, the διά in 11:36 makes no mention of Christ but only the supreme God: first and final and also instrumental cause. On the other hand, it is just this perspective that clarifies Paul's innovation in 1 Corinthians 8:6. For Paul's *de Deo Uno* of the cosmic wellspring and telos is not yet the full Christian solution. The New Testament collectively communicates an experience of Israel's Lord and his *Logos* that at once explodes the doxographical frame of Greco-Roman philosophy, yet already begins reassembling the conceptual pieces in a momentous doxological act of creative destruction. In Christ, a new structure of mediation between the One God and the world is established, surpassing the gift of the Name made to Moses. And just as that true religion of Moses was radically reconfigured, yet not damaged but rather fulfilled, so the landmarks of true philosophical doctrine, coordinate with that true religious worship (even a new *Shema*), remain unmoved yet interiorly transformed in the alternative Christian vision: suffused with new clarity, content, and force, and recalibrated to a new ritual system. The final fate of Philo's ambiguous *Logos* was that it quietly disappeared, quite rightly finding no doctrinal disciples, yet the middle-Platonic double-mindedness of this Jewish contemporary of Jesus forever marks the essential theological fork in the road. On the one hand, Neoplatonic thought went enthusiastically down the path of successive emanations, first distinguishing the Demiurge from the Highest God as a buffer from the stain of matter (Numenius), before finally interring this Artisan as an obsolete cosmogonic relic (Porphyry).[44]

---

43. It should stand as a warning against undue influence of this artificial schema and periodization drawn from courses on the history of Western philosophy that no less an expert than A. H. Armstrong eventually came to see that, regarding the *Logos*, "the doctrine he had attributed to Plotinus was in fact Philo's," as Michel René Barnes observes. "Rereading Augustine's Theology of the Trinity," in *The Trinity: An Interdisciplinary Symposium on the Trinity*, ed. Stephen T. David, Daniel Kendell, and Gerard O'Collins (Oxford: Oxford University, 2002), 153. Barnes himself is engaged to limit excessive constructions of Augustine's Neoplatonic cast of mind.

44. On this history of the Demiurge concept, see the helpful study of Carl Séan O'Brien, *The*

The Christian confession, by contrast, boldly resisted this turn—with its ultimate dead end and inert transcendent Monad—as it also defied the Arian temptation, instead planting divine mediation firmly in the *manhood* of a divine *Logos* through the theurgic mechanism of a hypostatic grace: a deifying solution never even faintly dreamed of before.[45] For as the Gospels reveal and as Paul learned at Athens, there are more things in heaven and on earth than the philosophers (even Jewish ones) ever dared to imagine.

Demiurge in Ancient Thought: Secondary God and Divine Mediators (Cambridge: Cambridge University Press, 2015).

45. See the fine discussion of Pauline and Platonic theurgy in Stang, *Apophasis and Pseudonymity*, 105–16.

THE REMEDY FOR
CONFUSED KENOTICISM

Aquinas as a Kenotic Theologian

Dominic Legge, OP

Chapter 2 of the Letter to the Philippians tells us that the Son, though he was in the form of God, "emptied himself" (ἑαυτὸν ἐκένωσεν, Phil 2:7),[1] taking on the form of a slave, being found in the likeness of men. The Gospels add many rich details to this: he was born in Bethlehem; felt hunger and fatigue, sorrow and anger; and ultimately was scourged, crucified, and killed. Every Christian is therefore committed in some sense to the profession of faith that the eternal Son of God emptied himself in becoming man and suffering for us. But what, precisely, does it mean to speak of the kenosis or self-emptying of the Son?

In contemporary theology, the term "kenotic Christology" typically refers to a theological movement that initially gained momentum in the nineteenth century, with Gottfried Thomasius as an important early exponent.[2] Although there are important differences among its proponents, at least one kenotic theologian has summarized kenosis theology thus: "what is given

---

1. The verb is κενόω (*kenoō*): to make empty.

2. Thomas R. Thompson, "Nineteenth-Century Kenotic Christology: The Waxing, Waning, and Weighing of a Quest for a Coherent Orthodoxy," in *Exploring Kenotic Christology: The Self-Emptying of God*, ed. C. Stephen Evans (Oxford: Oxford University Press, 2006), 74. See also David R. Law, *Kierkegaard's Kenotic Christology* (Oxford: Oxford University Press, 2013), 38–39. For a brief but detailed and insightful history of kenotic Christology, see Bruce McCormack, "Kenoticism in Modern Christology," in *The Oxford Handbook of Christology* (Oxford: Oxford University Press, 2015), 444–57.

up in the Incarnation is not divinity but some of the divine prerogatives," so that "a kenotic understanding of Christ's Incarnation is consistent with his full divinity."[3] We could add that responsible kenoticists are typically committed to the preexistence of Christ: if the Son empties himself in time, they agree that he must have preexisted as God.[4]

Kenotic Christology sometimes comes with a Trinitarian twist. The self-emptying of the Son in the Incarnation is seen by some recent theologians not only as a feature of how the Son appears in the economy of salvation; but also, for them, it pertains to the inner life of the Trinity, such that the kenosis of the Son in time and above all his cry of dereliction on the cross enacts and reveals the eternal self-emptying of the Son, understood as the Son's "infinite distance" from,[5] or even "subordination"[6] to, the Father in the divinity.[7]

---

3. C. Stephen Evans, "Introduction: Understanding Jesus the Christ as Human and Divine," in *Exploring Kenotic Christology*, 8. According to Wolfhart Pannenberg, "Thomasius saw the solution for the difficulties of Christology in the assumption of a 'self-limitation of the divine' in the incarnation. At the incarnation, the Son gave up the *relative* attributes of divinity, that is, those which characterize the *relation* of God to the world: omnipotence, omniscience, omnipresence. He retained only the *immanent* perfections proper to God independent of his relation to the world: holiness, power, truth, and love." *Jesus—God and Man*, 2nd ed., trans. Lewis L. Wilkin and Duane A. Priebe (Philadelphia: Westminster Press, 1977), 310.

4. Law, *Kierkegaard's Kenotic Christology*, 42–43.

5. According to von Balthasar, "the Son . . . is forsaken by God on the Cross. Yet this 'infinite distance,' which recapitulates the sinner's mode of alienation from God, will remain forever the highest revelation known to the world of the diastasis (within the eternal being of God) between Father and Son in the Holy Spirit." Hans Urs von Balthasar, *Theo-Drama: Theological Dramatic Theory*, vol. 3, *The Dramatis Personae: The Person in Christ*, trans. Graham Harrison (San Francisco: Ignatius Press, 1992), 228. See also Hans Urs von Balthasar, *Mysterium Paschale: The Mystery of Easter*, trans. Aidan Nichols (San Francisco: Ignatius Press, 2000), 30–36.

6. See, e.g., Karl Barth, *Church Dogmatics*, vol. 4.1, trans. G. W. Bromiley (New York: Charles Scribner's Sons, 1956), 200–201, speaking of kenosis as rooted in the eternal relation of the Son to the Father: "We have ... to affirm and understand as essential to the being of God the offensive fact that there is in God Himself an above and a below, a *prius* and a *posterius*, a superiority and a subordination. And our present concern is with what is apparently the most offensive fact of all, that there is a below, a *posterius*, a subordination, that it belongs to the inner life of God that there should take place within it obedience."

7. Properly interpreting the complex thought of von Balthasar and Barth on these points calls for further distinctions and qualifications. This short paper cannot enter into that complexity since its goal is to explore Aquinas's views on kenosis, rather than to examine the nuances of particular contemporary authors. My point here is simply that kenosis Christology also raises intra-Trinitarian questions, and that St. Thomas provides some crucial distinctions and resources for rightly articulating a sound theology of Christ's kenosis. Thus I speak from this point forward about contemporary kenotic Christology in general, admitting that further work is needed to set forth the complexity of and distinctions between specific recent authors.

Contemporary kenotic Christology will also typically emphasize that, in Christ, God fully empathizes with us and thus becomes someone with whom we can also identify. Jesus "fully shared in the human condition in its full force," holding "no hidden divine powers in reserve"; rather, "he has chosen to endure the human situation in the same way that all of us must."[8] Kenotic theologians regard this as a special strength of their position because, in their view, it takes full account of the historical humanity of Jesus.[9] They embrace the picture that historians reconstruct of Jesus, a figure without superhuman powers, because they claim this is precisely what the Son has chosen to become: a weak and limited human being who was "ignorant, grows in knowledge, struggles with temptation," and discovers his true identity over time.[10]

For decades, students of Thomas Aquinas have been sharply critical of contemporary kenotic views like these, especially of those claims that seem to abandon the traditional Christian understanding of God as immutable and therefore impassible in his divine nature. Distinguished scholars like Bruce Marshall, Gilles Emery, Thomas Joseph White, and others have used classical Thomistic doctrines to critique contemporary kenoticism. Typically, those critiques are made on two grounds. The first concerns the divine attributes, especially divine immutability and divine impassibility, and the second concerns Trinitarian doctrine: they say that some theologians—one might think of figures like Moltmann, Jüngel, Bulgakov, Barth, and von Balthasar—hold that the Son's kenosis in time (and especially his cry of dereliction on the cross) enact and reveal the eternal self-emptying of the Son, and thus his separation and distance from the Father.[11] These Thomistic criticisms are serious, and I generally agree with them. (At the end of part I of this chapter, I will add another.)

---

8. Evans, "Introduction," 7.

9. According to Bruce McCormack, Thomasius developed his kenotic Christology with this aim in mind. Bruce McCormack, "Karl Barth's Christology as a Resource for a Reformed Version of Kenoticism," *International Journal of Systematic Theology* 8 (2006): 245.

10. Evans, "Introduction," 7.

11. For the Thomistic critiques, see, e.g., Bruce Marshall, "The Dereliction of Christ and the Impassibility of God," in *Divine Impassibility and the Mystery of Human Suffering*, ed. James F. Keating and Thomas Joseph White (Grand Rapids, MI: Eerdmans, 2009), 246–98; Bruce Marshall, "The Unity of the Triune God: Reviving an Ancient Question," *The Thomist* 74 (2010): 1–32; Gilles Emery, "Kenosis, Christ, and the Trinity in Thomas Aquinas," *Nova et Vetera*, English ed. 17 (2019): 857–60; Thomas Joseph White, "Intra-Trinitarian Obedience and Nicene-Chalcedonian Christology," *Nova et Vetera*, English ed. 6 (2008): 377–402.

In this essay, however, I will to approach the question of kenotic theology from a slightly different perspective: that of Aquinas's own exegesis of Philippians 2 and other related Scripture passages. My primary objective is to gain a positive understanding of what kenosis means in the thought of Thomas Aquinas in order to show how Aquinas's kenoticism is both more theologically sound, and better plumbs the mystery of the Incarnation, than contemporary kenotic accounts.[12]

This essay thus has two main parts. Part I focuses on Aquinas's interpretation of kenosis in view of the great ecumenical councils of the early Church. Part II then presents in positive form the features and strengths of Aquinas's balanced Christological kenoticism. In each part, I repeatedly highlight two related points: how Aquinas's scriptural exegesis is both shaped by and further advances the insights of the classical Christological dogmas, and how his analysis—and especially his reading of Philippians 2 as an anti-Monophysite text—suggests another ground for critiquing contemporary kenotic theologies.

PART I: KENOSIS AND THE CHURCH COUNCILS

Aquinas was unique among his medieval contemporaries in his study of and incorporation of the acts of the early Church councils into his theology.[13] The influence of these councils—and especially of Ephesus and Chalcedon—is often in evidence in his account of the meaning of the Son's kenosis. Gilles Emery has recently noted that Aquinas often uses the "self-emptying" reference of Philippians 2 to make an anti-Nestorian argument.[14] Specifi-

---

12. Aquinas's strengths in this domain are little known. Just last year, Gilles Emery began to remedy this with a superb article in *Nova et Vetera* on Aquinas's exegesis of Philippians 2, giving special focus to Trinitarian theology. Emery, "Kenosis." Another recent article has examined Aquinas's creative juxtaposition of kenosis (based on Phil 2:7) with his teaching that Christ is full of grace (Jn 1:14). Mateusz Przanowski, "*Formam servi accipiens* (Phil 2:7) or *Plenus gratiae et Veritatis* (Jn 1:14)? The Apparent Dilemma in Aquinas' Exegesis," in *Towards a Biblical Thomism: Thomas Aquinas and the Renewal of Biblical Theology* (Pamplona: Ediciones Universidad de Navarra, S.A., 2018), 119–33. I propose to do something similar, but focusing instead on Aquinas's strengths in Christology.

13. Martin Morard, "Thomas d'Aquin lecteur des conciles," *Archivum Franciscanum Historicum* 98 (2005): 211.

14. Emery, "Kenosis," 846–48.

cally, Aquinas denies that the Incarnation merely produces in an indwelling of the Word in the humanity of Jesus by grace, because divine indwelling in a human soul cannot rightly be termed a "self-emptying." Why? Because the one who is empty (the man Jesus) would be distinct from the one who dwells in him (the Word). Aquinas contends that a true kenosis must pertain directly to the personal subject who becomes incarnate: the Word himself.

[St. Paul] says: "He emptied himself," therefore the very same one is emptied, and is emptying. But this is the Son of God, because he himself emptied himself. Therefore the union is in the person.[15]

This is a capital starting point for a coherent kenosis theology: the emptying of the Incarnation must pertain personally to the Son. There is no question, for Aquinas, of somehow walling off or dividing the lowliness and humility of Christ from touching the Word in his very person. The same one who was in the form of God is also found in the form of a slave and in human likeness.[16] (I think that most contemporary kenoticists would agree.)

In addition to this anti-Nestorian point, we also find an anti-Arian dimension. Here we begin to see a divergence between Aquinas and contemporary kenoticism. St. Thomas emphasizes that the Incarnation does not involve any subordination of the Son to the Father with respect to his divinity. While Sacred Scripture does sometimes speak about the Son as less than the Father, Aquinas uses Philippians 2 as evidence that this "lessening" pertains only to his assumption of a human nature:

Arius ... said that the Father is greater than the Son.... But [Jesus] says "the Father is greater than me (Jn 14:28)" not as the Son of God, but as the Son of man, according to which he is not only less than the Father and the Holy Spirit, but even is less than the Angels. "We see Jesus, who was made a little lower than the angels on account of the suffering of death, crowned with glory and honor

---

15. *In Epist. ad Phil.* [Marietti ed.] c. 2, lect. 2 (no. 62): "Item dicit: *Semetipsum exinanivit*, ergo idem est qui exinanitus est, et exinaniens. Sed huiusmodi est Filius Dei, quia ipse semetipsum exinanivit, ergo est unio in persona." Aquinas makes a closely related point at *In Epist. ad Rom.* c. 1, lect. 2 (no. 35). All translations of Aquinas are my own. Unless otherwise noted, the Latin of Aquinas's texts is taken from the Leonine edition of his works.

16. As St. Thomas puts it elsewhere (relying on Eph 4:10), the one who descended from heaven, the divine Word of God, is the same as the one who ascended above the heavens, which shows that "the same one is therefore the person and hypostasis of that man, who is the person and hypostasis of the Word of God." *ScG* IV, c. 34: "Ipsa igitur est persona et hypostasis illius hominis, quae est persona et hypostasis Verbi Dei."

(Heb 2:9)." … Therefore, he is less than the Father according to his humanity, but he is equal [to the Father] according to his divinity: "he thought it not robbery to be equal with God, but he emptied himself, taking the form of a slave."[17]

Elsewhere, Aquinas makes a similar point with a more concise formula:

The Son of God "emptied himself, taking the form of a slave" [Phil 2:6]. He is called "emptied" or "brief" [Rom 9:28] not because anything was subtracted from his fullness or the greatness of his divinity, but because he took up our exile and our smallness.[18]

Or even more succinctly, from his commentary on Galatians, "'He emptied himself, etc.' He made himself small not by giving up greatness, but by assuming smallness."[19]

In my view, however, the anti-Monophysite dimension of Aquinas's exegesis is even more important for appreciating his balanced Christological kenoticism. Monophysitism principally refers to the fifth-century position (attributed to Eutyches and others) that the Incarnation produces a union in nature such that, after the Word takes flesh, there would be a single incarnate nature of Christ. At first glance, this might seem to have little to do with contemporary kenotic theology because the ancient Monophysites typically spoke of Christ's incarnate nature in high terms—indeed, as divine.

When Aquinas analyzes what is wrong with Monophysitism in the *Summa contra Gentiles*, however, he uses Philippians 2 in an argument that, it

---

17. *In Ioan.* [Marietti ed.] c. 14, lect. 7 (no. 1970): "Arius … dicens Patrem maiorem esse Filio.… Sic ergo hoc quod dicit *Maior me est*, non dicit inquantum Filius Dei, sed inquantum Filius hominis, secundum quod non solum est minor Patre et Spiritu sancto, sed etiam ipsis angelis; Hebr. II, 9: *Eum autem qui modico quam angeli minoratus est, videmus Iesum propter passionem mortis, gloria et honore coronatum.*… Sic ergo minor est Patre secundum humanitatem, aequalis secundum divinitatem; Phil. II, 6: *Non rapinam arbitratus est esse se aequalem Deo: sed semetipsum exinanivit, formam servi accipiens.*"

18. *In Epist. ad Rom.* [Marietti ed.] c. 9, lect. 5 (no. 805): "Filius Dei exinanivit semetipsum, formam servi accipiens. Dicitur autem exinanitum vel breviatum, non quia aliquid subtractum sit plenitudini vel magnitudini divinitatis ipsius, sed quia nostram exilitatem et parvitatem suscepit." See also *ScG* IV, c. 8: "Ostendit autem Apostolus eum esse minoratum secundum assumptionem formae servilis, ita tamen quod Deo Patri aequalis existat secundum formam divinam: dicit enim, *ad Philipp. II:6: Cum in forma Dei esset, non rapinam arbitrates est esse se aequalem Deo, sed semetipsum exinanivit, formam servi accipiens.*" On Aquinas's anti-Arian reading in this text, see Emery, "Kenosis," 856–88. (The whole of *ScG* IV, c. 8, is devoted to a refutation of Arian readings of Scripture.)

19. *In Epist. ad Galat.* [Marietti ed.] c. 4, lect. 2 (no. 203): "Phil. II, 7: *Exinanivit semetipsum*, etc. Parvum se fecit non dimittendo magnitudinem, sed assumendo parvitatem."

seems to me, could be rightly applied to much contemporary kenotic Christology.

Aquinas's argument is lengthy, and it has three phases. The first phase begins with a premise that the form of something designates its nature. Aquinas then writes:

It is necessary to say that in Christ there are two forms, even after the union. For the Apostle says of Christ Jesus that, "though he was in the form of God, ... he took the form of a slave (Phil 2:6–7)." But it cannot be said that the form of God and the form of a slave are the same, since nothing "takes" what it already has.[20]

Aquinas's point is that St. Paul's text logically requires a distinction between the divine nature and human nature. Otherwise, it would be nonsensical to say that Christ was in the form of God and then "took" the form of a slave. We must be saying that there are two different forms here, and thus two different natures.

Next, in phase two, Aquinas argues that it is not possible that one or the other nature would be destroyed or corrupted by the union.

Neither can it be said that the form of God in Christ was corrupted by the union, because then Christ would not be God after the union. Nor can it be said that the form of a slave is corrupted in the union, because then he would not have taken the form of a slave.[21]

This resembles an argument Thomas makes in the *Summa Theologiae* about why the union in Christ cannot take place in the nature (*ST* III, q. 2, a. 1). If there were a union in nature, this would lead to a change of the nature so that it would cease to be what it is. But this is impossible for the divine nature.[22] Aquinas does not lay all of this out in this *Summa contra Gentiles*

---

20. *ScG* IV, c. 35: "Oportet autem dicere quod in Christo sint duae formae, etiam post unionem. Dicit enim Apostolus, Philipp. II:6–7, de Christo Iesu, quod, *cum in forma Dei esset, formam servi accepit.* Non autem potest dici quod sit eadem forma Dei, et forma servi: nihil enim accipit quod iam habet."

21. *ScG* IV, c. 35: "Neque iterum potest dici quod forma Dei in Christo per unionem sit corrupta: quia sic Christus post unionem non esset Deus. Neque iterum potest dici quod forma servi sit corrupta in unione: quia sic non accepisset formam servi."

22. *ST* III, q. 2, a. 1: "Sed hoc non potest esse. Primo quidem, quia natura divina est omnino immutabilis: ut in Prima Parte dictum est. Unde nec ipsa potest converti in aliud, cum sit incorruptibilis: nec aliud in ipsam, cum ipsa sit ingenerabilis." See also *ST* III, q. 5, a. 1 ad 2, which makes a similar point with a specific reference to Phil 2:6.

text, but he does say that if you have a change in the divine nature in the Incarnation, Christ simply would not be God.

Now, phase three and Aquinas's conclusion:

> But neither can it be said that the form of a servant would be mixed together with the form of God, because when several things are mixed together, they do not retain their integrity, but each is partly corrupted. [If this were the case,] the Apostle would not have said that he "took the form of a slave," but something of the servant. And thus we must say, according to the words of the Apostle, that in Christ, even after the union, there are two forms, and therefore two natures.[23]

This argument again resembles the parallel text in the *Summa Theologiae* on a union in nature, but there is an important difference: the *Summa Theologiae* speaks more in a philosophical register about the impossibility that a nature might mix with another nature or otherwise cease to be what it is. In contrast, this text from the *Summa contra Gentiles* is more strongly scriptural, hinging on a close textual exegesis of Philippians 2. The argument's conclusion is that St. Paul's words require us to presuppose two distinct natures in Christ, even after the Incarnation.[24] This is because the divinity of Christ cannot cease to be, nor can it lose any of its divine prerogatives or attributes. The Son must really remain God in the fullest sense. At the same time, St. Paul tells us that he truly takes on a human form. Since a mixed reality would be neither God nor man, there must be two complete natures in Christ.

From Aquinas's perspective, then, contemporary kenotic Christology—at least in some of its forms—might be judged to be Monophysite, in an inverted sense: if the incarnate Son does not have a complete divine nature, integrally retaining all of its divine attributes, or if he can suffer, be tempted, die, or be separated from the Father *with respect to his divinity*, then he does not have a divine nature at all. At best, there is some new, confused reality

---

23. *ScG* IV, c. 35: "Sed nec dici potest quod forma servi sit permixta formae Dei: quia quae permiscentur, non manent integra, sed partim utrumque corrumpitur; unde non diceret quod accepisset formam servi, sed aliquid eius. Et sic oportet dicere, secundum verba Apostoli, quod in Christo, etiam post unionem, fuerunt duae formae. Ergo duae naturae."

24. Aquinas makes the same point at *De articulis fidei*, pars 1 (ll. 443–48 of the Leonine edition): "Septimus error est Euticis qui posuit in Christo unam naturam compositam ex diuinitate et humanitate; contra quod Apostolos dicit quod 'cum in forma Dei eset, formam serui assumpsit,' Phil. II:6, manifeste distinguens in eo duas naturas, diuinam et humanam."

that is neither simply divine nor simply human. To put it otherwise, it would seem that Aquinas might say that a confused kenoticism fails properly to distinguish the two natures of Christ and thus—even if it verbally pledges allegiance to a two-nature Christology—effectively presents a Christ who, during his earthly life, no longer meaningfully has two distinct natures at the same time.

PART II: THE FEATURES AND STRENGTHS OF AQUINAS'S KENOTICISM

Aquinas consistently and uniformly interprets the self-emptying of Philippians 2 (and all of the other passages in the New Testament that refer to some diminution, passibility, defect, or limitation) as referring *to* the Son, *with respect to* his human nature. The key to the solution is the classical formula of Chalcedonian orthodoxy, formulated in response to Monophysitism: there is one person who remains divine while assuming a new and lower human nature. In Chalcedon's words, one person with two natures, "without confusion or change, without division or separation. The distinction between the natures was never abolished by their union but rather the character proper to each of the two natures was preserved as they came together in one Person and one hypostasis."[25]

It is worth recalling that a principal concern at the heart of the fifth-century Christological disputes was: How can we affirm *both* that the Son of God suffered *and* that this would not imply any change or suffering in the divinity?[26] The answer given by Leo and Chalcedon—one person, two complete and unconfused natures—was carefully formulated to solve this problem. That is, Leo and Chalcedon took great pains to avoid the very difficulty revived in at least some forms of contemporary kenotic Christology: the suggestion that to confess the full truth of Christ's suffering might require one also to posit suffering in the divine nature.

25. The Chalcedonian Creed, translated in Heinrich Denzinger, *Compendium of Creeds, Definitions, and Declarations on Matters of Faith and Morals*, 43rd ed., ed. Peter Hünermann (San Francisco: Ignatius Press, 2012) [hereinafter "DH"], no. 302.

26. John J. O'Keefe, "Impassible Suffering? Divine Passion and Fifth-Century Christology," *Theological Studies* 58 (1997): 39–60.

The Chalcedonian formula also provides an important foundation for the communication of idioms, a patristic doctrine that Aquinas refines and presents in detail in the *Summa Theologiae* and elsewhere. Because the union is in the person of the Son and not in the nature, it is possible to predicate of the person of the Son everything that pertains either to his divine nature or to his human nature. This is key for Aquinas's interpretation of Philippians 2 (and many other New Testament texts as well):

> We read in Scripture both that that man [Jesus Christ] is exalted (for Acts 2:33 says: "therefore he was exalted to the right hand of God,"), and that God is emptied (Phil 2:7: "he emptied himself," etc.). Therefore, just as sublime things can be said of that man by reason of the union (such as "he is God," "he raises the dead," and so forth), so also humble things can be said of God (such as "he was born of the Virgin, suffered, died, and was buried").[27]

The communication of idioms of this passage (and of many others) works because there is a single subject in Christ, the person of the Word. Lacking such a subject, passages like Philippians 2 would leave us insoluble puzzles, a circle to be squared: how to say something of God that is incompatible with divinity.

For Aquinas, then, the authentic meaning of the kenosis of Philippians 2 can only be grasped if we keep the Chalcedonian formula in mind. Aquinas is direct: "The Apostle in Philippians 2 calls this union the emptying of the Son of God."[28] That is, for Aquinas, self-emptying simply *is* the union of the divine nature to a human nature in the person of the Son.

Thomas explains this at greater length in his commentary on Philippians:

> It says "he emptied himself, etc." But since he was filled with divinity, did he empty himself of divinity? No, because he remained what he was, and he assumed what he was not.... For as he descended from heaven (not that he ceased to be in

---

27. *ScG* IV, c. 34: "Sicut legitur in Scripturis quod homo ille est *exaltatus*, dicitur enim Act. II:33, *Dextera igitur Dei exaltatus* etc.; ita legitur quod Deus sit *exinanitus*, Philipp. II:7, *Exinanivit semetipsum* etc. Sicut igitur sublimia possunt dici de homine illo ratione unionis, ut quod sit Deus, quod resuscitet mortuos, et alia huiusmodi; ita de Deo possunt dici humilia, ut quod sit natus de Virgine, passus, mortuus et sepultus."

28. *De unione Verbi incarnati* [Latin text prepared by Walter Senner, Barbara Bartocci, and Klaus Obenauer (Stuttgart-Bad Cannstatt: Frommann-Hozboog, 2011)], a. 1: "Secundo, quia Apostolus ad Philippenses II° hanc unionem exinanitionem Filii Dei vocat."

heaven, but that he began to be in a new mode on earth), so also he emptied himself (not by laying down his divine nature, but by assuming a human nature).[29]

The force of this text depends on the distinction of natures. In fact, Aquinas "literally reprise[s] the exegesis of St. Augustine and St. Leo the Great, in particular the formula … 'he remained what he was, and he assumed what he was not,'"[30] a principle with deep roots in the patristic tradition.[31] What is more, Aquinas's reference to Christ existing "in a new mode on earth" evokes his doctrine of the divine missions. Thomas teaches elsewhere that a divine mission consists in the presence of a divine person who proceeds from another and who is made newly present on earth in a new mode, according to some new created effect.[32] Thus the Son's kenosis is the Son's visible mission; like all other divine missions, this does not change him in his divine nature but adds a new created effect—in this case, a new nature—which is grounded in his person and extends his personal procession into time.

At this point, let us pose an objection. Despite this theological jargon, at bottom, does not this produce a rather strained interpretation of Philippians 2? How can we really say that the Son "emptied himself" if he remained full of his divinity? Isn't this a hollow version of kenosis?

The answer calls for us to return again to Aquinas's texts, seeking to think through the mystery he is probing. Doing so pays rich dividends. Consider the following text from St. Thomas:

He took our own proper nature … insofar as he shared [in it] with us, assuming our nature without any change of the divine nature, and without mixing it

29. *In Epist. ad Phil.* c. 2, lect. 2 (no. 57): "Dicit ergo *sed semetipsum*, etc. Sed quia erat plenus divinitate, numquid ergo evacuavit se divinitate? Non, quia quod erat permansit et quod non erat, assumpsit.… Sicut enim descendit de caelo, non quod desineret esse in caelo, sed quia incepit esse novo modo in terris, sic etiam se exinanivit, non deponendo divinam naturam, sed assumendo naturam humanam."

30. Emery, "Kenosis," 842–43, citing Albert Verwilghen, *Christologie et sprirualité selon saint Augustin: L'hymne aux Philippiens* (Paris: Beauchesne, 1985), 209, and Laurent Pidolle, *La christologie historique du pape saint Léon le Grand* (Paris: Les Editions du Cerf, 2013), 93. For Augustine, see, e.g., s. 92.2(2), PL 38:573; s. 183.4(5), PL 38:990; s. 187.4(4), PL 38:1002. For Leo the Great, see Tr. 21.2 (CCL 138: 86–87); Epist. 28 ad Flavianum (DH no. 293); Tr. 64.2 (CCL 138A:391).

31. I am grateful to Andrew Hofer for pointing out that Augustine and Leo are themselves reprising earlier exegesis that enunciates exactly the same principle. See, e.g., Gregory of Nazianzus Or. 29.19: "What he was, he remained; what he was not, he assumed" (ὃ μὲν ἦν, διέμεινεν· ὃ δὲ οὐκ ἦν, προσέλαβεν).

32. See Dominic Legge, *The Trinitarian Christology of St. Thomas Aquinas* (Oxford: Oxford University Press, 2017), 14–23.

or confusing it with the human, such that through an ineffable emptying, about which the apostle speaks at Phil 2:7, ... there was no diminution of the fullness of his divinity, for he is not said to be emptied through a diminution of divinity, but through the assumption of the weakness of our nature.[33]

We see again the Chalcedonian elements: no change, no mixture, no confusion. But is the self-emptying fictional? Aquinas doesn't think so—rather, he thinks we are pondering a divine mystery. The person of the Word truly *does* empty himself, precisely because he truly lowers himself infinitely below what he himself is as God. He now begins to exist in and according to a weak and limited nature. It is fully true, then, to say that this limited man, capable of suffering and death, is the eternal Son in person. The divine nature has not changed nor been lowered in itself, although God in the person of the Son has indeed taken on a new way or mode of existing; namely, as man, in weakness, subject to suffering and death.

We see this very point again in another text that also opens up for us another key dimension of Aquinas's exegesis: there is an important soteriological reason why the Son must not give up any of his divine prerogatives.

How beautiful that it says he "emptied himself." For the empty is opposed to the full. But the divine nature is amply full, because every perfection of goodness is there.... But human nature, and the soul, is not full, but is in potency to fullness, because it is made like a blank slate. Human nature is therefore empty. Thus, it says he "emptied himself" because he assumed a human nature.[34]

For Aquinas, it is crucial for the sake of our salvation that the Son remain fully divine while becoming also fully human. This is because the point of the Incarnation is not simply to identify with or be in solidarity with us, or to lower himself to be like us, but rather to descend to us in order to raise

33. *In Dionysii de Divinis Nominibus* [Marietti ed.], c. 2, lect. 5 (no. 207): "acceperit propria nostrae naturae, ... communicavit nobis, assumens nostram naturam absque variatione divinae naturae et absque commixtione ipsius et confusione ad humanam naturam, ita quod per exinanitionem ineffabilem, de qua apostolus loquitur ad Philipp. 2[:7], ... nihil diminutum est de plenitudine suae Deitatis; non enim dicitur exinanitus per diminutionem Deitatis, sed per assumptionem nostrae naturae deficientis."

34. *In Epist. ad Phil.*, c. 2, lect. 2 (no. 57): "Pulchre autem dicit *exinanivit*. Inane enim opponitur pleno. Natura autem divina satis plena est, quia ibi est omnis bonitatis perfectio. Ex. XXXIII, 19: *Ostendam tibi omne bonum*. Natura autem humana, et anima non est plena, sed in potentia ad plenitudinem; quia est facta quasi tabula rasa. Est ergo natura humana inanis. Dicit ergo *exinanivit*, quia naturam humanam assumpsit."

us up to God himself. In this text, Aquinas speaks of this in the register of goodness: God is infinitely good, with every possible perfection. Human nature is created with a certain openness upward toward the divine goodness—we are *capax Dei*—but we do not have this goodness of ourselves. The opposite is true: we are more empty than full, in comparison with the infinite fullness of God. God's saving plan is precisely to give us a share in his infinite goodness through Christ's incarnation, which raises up our fallen nature and endows us sinners with a supernatural dignity and with supernatural gifts that vastly exceed even what our first parents had in their state of original grace. This is a capital point: the Son's kenosis does not aim at God becoming empty but he assumes our emptiness so as to fill us with a share in his divinity.[35]

There is something analogous in how Aquinas speaks about the beatific vision of Christ. Christ needs the beatific vision precisely so that he can be the human revealer of the Father in full, par excellence. The Father's Word becomes a man with a perfect human vision of the Father so that the revelation of the Father will be most perfectly accomplished precisely *in* and *through* his finite human mind and thus through his time-bound and limited human words, deeds, and life. The logic of kenosis in the text quoted just above is the same. A kenotic incarnation of the Son that leaves his divinity behind would not give us a Christ who is truly a savior of man, as man.

What is more, this human emptiness of the Word, remaining supremely full of the divinity, shows the marvelous love and condescension of God and is perfectly adapted to raising up our fallen minds to God himself by knowledge and by love.

---

35. When St. Thomas addresses the reasons for the Incarnation at *ST* III, q. 1, a. 2, he quotes both Leo and a text attributed to Augustine, each with a sense closely related to this point. From Leo: "Humility is assumed by majesty, weakness by strength, so that, as a remedy fitting for us, one and the same mediator of God and of men might be able both to die in one and to rise in the other. Unless he was God, he would not have brought a remedy; unless he was man, he would not have set an example." (CCL 138:87–88: "[S]uscipitur a uirtute infirmitas, a maiestate humilitas … ut quod nostris remediis congruebat, unus atque idem Dei et hominumque mediator et mori ex uno et resurgere posset ex altero. Nisi enim esset Deus uerus, non afferret remedium, nisi esset homo uerus, non praeberet exemplum.") From a sermon wrongly attributed to Augustine: "God was made man, so that man might be made God." (PL 39:1997: "Factus est Deus homo, ut homo fieret Deus.") As Bruce Marshall notes in chap. 15 in this volume, Augustine says things that are similar to this, but this text is now thought to be by another author.)

God is lovable above all other else. But due to the weakness of the human mind, just as it needs to be led by hand to knowledge of divine realities, so also it needs to be led by hand to love of them, through something known to us through the senses. The greatest among these is the humanity of Christ, as the Preface [for the Mass of Christmas] says: "as we know God made visible, we may be caught up through this in love of things invisible." And hence those things that pertain to the humanity of Christ in a certain way lead us by the hand, maximally stirring up our devotion ... [toward] what pertains to the divinity.[36]

To conclude, that the Son both empties himself as man and remains full as God is not a defect of Aquinas's Christology. Rather, it is the basis for an authentic and saving kenoticism; that is, the Son *can* accept our weakness for a saving purpose precisely because he does not relinquish his fullness as God.

36. *ST* II-II, q. 82, a. 3, ad 2: "Deus est super omnia diligendus. Sed ex debilitate mentis humanae est quod sicut indiget manuduci ad cognitionem divinorum, ita ad dilectionem, per aliqua sensibilia nobis nota. Inter quae praecipuum est humanitas Christi: secundum quod in Praefatione dicitur, *ut dum visibiliter Deum cognoscimus, per hunc in invisibilium amorem rapiamur*. Et ideo ea quae pertinent ad Christi humanitatem, per modum cuiusdam manuductionis, maxime devotionem excitant: cum tamen devotio principaliter circa ea quae sunt divinitatis consistat."

CHAPTER 3

CHRISTUS EST UNUM SIMPLICITER

On Why the *Secundarium* of the Fourth Article of Thomas Aquinas's *De Unione Verbi Incarnati* Is Not a Numerically Second *Esse*

Roger W. Nutt

PART I: INTRODUCTION AND PRELIMINARY CONSIDERATIONS

Introduction

The two natures, one person orthodoxy forged by the Council of Chalcedon seems immediately relevant to the profession and content of the original truths of the Christian faith. But the more ontologically nuanced and exacting precisions of later centuries may not present themselves to modern ears as evidently continuous with the mindset of the first followers of Christ. In the face of the questions raised about the unity of Christ and his wills and operations, the councils of Constantinople II and III, Nicaea II, and the later Greek Fathers and schoolmen offer much in the way of developing the full implications of the basic biblical truth that the "Word became flesh."[1]

An earlier version of this chapter has been accepted in *Harvard Theological Review*. Reprinted with permission.

1. Thomas Joseph White argues, "In some real sense it is true to say: ignorance of ontology is ignorance of Christ. The understanding of the Bible offered by the fathers and scholastics, then, is not something that can be justified as one possible form of reading among others (defensively, as against a post-critical anthropological turn in modern philosophy). Rather, it is the only reading that attains objectively to the deepest truth of the New Testament: a truth concerning the identity of Christ as the God-man." *The Incarnate Lord: A Thomistic Study in Christology* (Washington, DC: Catholic University of America Press, 2015), 8.

Receiving the later contributions as organic developments of biblical faith and the earlier creeds is not a task that modern theologians have found easy to accomplish, or even desirable to undertake. Pondering this challenge, then-Cardinal Joseph Ratzinger made the following observation:

> It is common enough for the theological textbooks to pay scant attention to the theological development which followed Chalcedon. In many ways one is left with the impression that dogmatic Christology comes to a stop with a certain parallelism of the two natures in Christ ... In fact, however, the affirmation of the true humanity and the true divinity in Christ can only retain its meaning if the mode of the unity of both is clarified. The Council defined this unity by speaking of the "one Person" in Christ, but it was a formula which remained to be explored in its implications. For the unity of divinity and humanity in Christ which brings "salvation" to man is not just a juxtaposition but a mutual indwelling.[2]

Ratzinger goes on to document how in the centuries following Chalcedon, individuals like Maximus the Confessor and councils like Constantinople III (680–81) developed the metaphysical "oneness" of Christ's personhood without "amputating" one of the natures or leaving them in a parallel dualism.[3] The ongoing debate over the meaning and implications of the fourth article of Thomas Aquinas's Disputed Question *De unione verbi incarnati* lies at the heart of this sustained, centuries-long post-Chalcedonian development of the mode of the union of Christ's two natures in the single subsistent Person of the Word.[4]

The *De unione* stands somewhat as a special test case in contemporary theology for how Aquinas fits in the tapestry of post-Chalcedonian Christology because some scholars argue that he offers something novel (and better) in one line of one article of this work than what is found in the rest of his corpus.[5] The intrigue around this one line in the fourth article of *De*

---

2. Joseph Cardinal Ratzinger, *Behold the Pierced One: An Approach to Spiritual Christology*, trans. Graham Harrison (San Francisco: Ignatius Press, 1986), 37–38.

3. Ratzinger, *Behold the Pierced One*, 37–38.

4. In Latin-French, Latin-German, and Latin-English, respectively, there are editions of the *De unione* that include extensive notes and theological commentary. See Marie-Hélène Deloffre, ed., *Question disputée: L'union du Verbe incarné (De unione Verbi incarnati)* (Paris: Vrin, 2000). Thomas von Aquin, *Quaestio disputata "De unione Verbi incarnati"* ("*Über die Union des fleischgewordenen Wortes*"), ed. and trans. Klaus Obenauer (Stuttgart-Bad Cannstatt: Frommann-Holzboog, 2011); the volume includes a much-needed critical Latin text prepared by Walter Senner, OP, Barbara Bartocci, and Klaus Obenauer. See also Thomas Aquinas, *De unione verbi incarnati*, trans. Roger W. Nutt (Leuven: Peeters Press, 2015), which reproduces (with permission) Obenauer's critical Latin text.

5. For a helpful historical treatment of the developments in Christology after Chalcedon that

unione verbi incarnati can be summarized as follows: in what is now held to be a rather late work,[6] many scholars have argued that St. Thomas breaks with his otherwise consistent position that Christ is one and unified in the order of being—that there is one *esse* or being in Christ—and affirms a second *esse* or being that is contributed by Christ's human nature.[7] Some of these scholars argue that this change in formulation saves St. Thomas's Christology from the error of Monophysitism.[8]

To provide just one example of his standard, single *esse* formulation, in the *Compendium of Theology*, Thomas lays out his position as follows: "If, therefore, we consider Christ as a complete suppositum having two natures, there will be only one being (*unum esse*), just as there is but one supposi-

---

touches on the teaching of many of the most important schoolmen and the speculative issues surrounding Aquinas's *De unione*, see Corey L. Barnes, *Christ's Two Wills: The Christology of Aquinas and Its Historical Contexts* (Toronto: Pontifical Institute of Mediaeval Studies, 2012).

6. For a summary of the debates over the dating of the *De unione*, see my introduction to Thomas Aquinas, *De unione verbi incarnati*, 6–9. For Obenauer's treatment of the dating of the *De unione*, see his translation of *Quaestio disputata*, 169. For Sr. Deloffre's discussion, see her *Question disputée*, 24–25. For a discussion and defense of the authenticity of the *De unione*, see Franz Pelster, SJ, "La *quaestio disputata* de saint Thomas *De unione Verbi incarnati*," *Archives de philosophie* 3 (1925–26): 198–245. Pelster's work is viewed as resolving the question of authenticity.

7. For a helpful summary of the issues surrounding the *De unione*, see David Tamisiea, "St. Thomas on the One *Esse* of Christ," *Angelicum* 88 (2011): 383–402. Tamisiea also summarizes what St. Thomas means by *esse*: "that which causes a thing to exist in reality, and is only attributed to real things contained within the categories of being identified by Aristotle" (385).

8. Thomas G. Weinandy, e.g., states, "I believe that Aquinas implicitly held two *esses* from the start (and so was never a Monophysite), but only explicitly stated this position on the one occasion in the *De Unione Verbi Incarnati*." "Aquinas: God *Is* Man. The Marvel of the Incarnation," in *Aquinas on Doctrine: A Critical Introduction*, ed. Thomas Weinandy, Daniel Keating, and John Yocum (London: T&T Clark, 2004), 67–89, at 80. See also Jean Galot, SJ, *The Person of Christ, Covenant between God and Man: A Theological Insight*, trans. M. Angeline Bouchard (Chicago: Franciscan Herald Press, 1984). Galot argues that Aquinas cannot be confidently invoked by advocates of a single *esse* understanding of Christ because in article four of the *De unione*, "St. Thomas clearly declares that 'the *esse* of the human nature is not the *esse* of the divine nature'; and that in addition to the eternal *esse* of the eternal Person there is an *esse* that belongs to the human nature, not a principal but a secondary *to be*" (17). Finally, medievalist Richard Cross has frequently critiqued Aquinas's single *esse* position. See his *The Metaphysics of the Incarnation* (Oxford: Oxford University Press, 2002); *Duns Scotus* (Oxford: Oxford University Press, 1999), esp. 114–15; and "Aquinas on Nature, Hypostasis, and the Metaphysics of the Incarnation," *The Thomist* 60 (1996): 171–202. What differentiates the *De unione* from Thomas's other accounts, Cross explains, is "his abandoning the claim that the human nature is a truth-maker precisely in virtue of its sharing in the *esse* of the *suppositum*" (*Metaphysics of the Incarnation*, 64). Cross argues that the reference to an *esse secundarium* in Christ means that Thomas holds, at least in this one case, that Christ's human nature "communicate[s] *esse* to its *suppositum*" (*Metaphysics of the Incarnation*, 63). For a response to Cross's reading of Aquinas, see James Reichman, SJ, "Aquinas, Scotus, and the Christological Mystery: Why Christ Is Not a Human Person," *The Thomist* 71 (2007): 451–74.

tum."[9] Variations of this *unum esse* formulation are standard throughout his corpus except in the one line in the fourth article of *De unione*. In this line, Thomas says that although the being of Christ's human nature "is not accidental being—because man is not accidentally predicated of the Son of God, as was said above—it is nevertheless not the principal being of its suppositum, but a subordinated (*secundarium*) being (*esse*)."[10]

As a consequence of this unique formulation, many contemporary theologians have received the *De unione* as a kind of late-career recognition by St. Thomas that the single *esse* position of the rest of his corpus was problematic, unnecessary, and in need of revision.

In the remainder of this chapter, the claim that the unique formulation found in *De unione* article four is a reversal of the single *esse* position will be challenged. The conclusion reached is that a reading of all five articles of the *De unione* as a carefully structured argument reveals a thought-out single *esse* understanding of the Incarnate Word. What is ultimately at stake in this dispute is the truth of the hypostatic nature of the union between God and man in Christ. As St. Thomas underscores, the positing of a second *esse* in Christ not only conflicts with the conciliar tradition that he appropriates but also would compromise the very truth of the hypostatic union itself.

Two Preliminary Aids

As a primer to Thomas's thinking in the five articles of the *De unione*, two items need to be reviewed so that the reader can fully appreciate the landscape of the discussion. First, from the perspective of Christological orthodoxy, considerations about the unity of Christ in the order of *esse* must be appreciated in relation to the teachings of the Councils of the first millennium. The great Fathers and councils that navigated the challenges of Arianism, Nestorianism, Monophysitism, and later heresies related to Christ's operations established more than just the grammatical parameters of orthodoxy.[11]

9. Cap. 212: "Manifestum est enim quod partes divisae singulae proprium esse habent, secundum autem quod in toto considerantur, non habent suum esse, sed omnes sunt per esse totius. Si ergo consideremus ipsum Christum ut quoddam integrum suppositum duarum naturarum, eius erit unum tantum esse, sicut et unum suppositum." The other parallel passages where Aquinas also treats Christ's *esse* are: *Quodl.* 9, q. 2, a. 2 and 3; *ST* III, q. 17, a. 2; *Scriptum super Sententias* III, d. 6, q. 2, a. 2.

10. Thomas Aquinas, *De unione verbi incarnati*, trans. Nutt, 135.

11. As early as the thirty-seventh article of the Athanasian Creed, which Aquinas quotes author-

The pivotal Council of Chalcedon in 451, for example, which developed the anti-Nestorian teaching of Ephesus (431) against the Monophysites, qualified the grammar of orthodoxy with a firm doctrine of Christ's unity. Immediately following the profession of the unconfused and unmixed union of the two natures in the one Christ, the Chalcedon declaration added:

> at no point was the difference between the natures taken away through the union, but rather the property of both natures is preserved and comes together into a single person (*prosopon/personam*) and a single subsistent being (*hypostasin/subsistentiam*); he is not parted or divided into two persons, but is one and the same only-begotten Son, God, Word, Lord Jesus Christ.[12]

Further clarification on Chalcedon's teaching that Christ was a "single subsistent being" was a priority of the teaching of Constantinople II (553) against erroneous attempts to recognize a second subsistence in Christ. This point is deeply connected to the question of Christ's *esse*, which is best understood as a development of the single subsistence doctrine. In Anathema 5, the council teaches,

> If anyone understands by the single subsistence of our lord Jesus Christ that it covers the meaning of many subsistences, and by this argument tries to introduce into the mystery of Christ two subsistences or two persons, and having brought in two persons then talks of one person only in respect of dignity ... and if he does not acknowledge that the Word of God is united with human flesh by subsistence, and that on account of this there is only one subsistence or one person, and that the holy synod of Chalcedon thus made a formal statement of belief in the single subsistence of our lord Jesus Christ: let him be anathema.[13]

Anathema 4 of the same council also develops how Christ's unity is preserved despite the presence of two real natures: "The holy Church of God ... states her belief in a union between the Word of God and human flesh which is by synthesis (*secundum compositionem*), that is by a union of subsistence (*quod est secundum subsistentiam*). In the mystery of Christ the union of synthesis (*per*

---

itatively in the *De unione*, analogical reasoning to affirm Christ's unity is used: "just as one man is a rational soul and flesh, just so the one Christ is God and man." For the text of the Athanasian Creed, see Heinrich Denzinger, *Compendium of Creeds, Definitions, and Declarations on Matters of Faith and Morals*, 43rd ed., ed. Peter Hünermann (San Francisco: Ignatius Press, 2012), §76.

12. *Decrees of the Ecumenical Councils*, vol. 1, *Nicaea I–Lateran V*, ed. Norman P. Tanner, SJ (Washington, DC: Georgetown University Press, 1990), 86–87.

13. *Decrees of the Ecumenical Councils*, 1:116.

compositionem) not only conserves without confusing the elements that come together but also allows no division."[14] This teaching on the composite mode of existence that the Word has as true God and true man according to a single subsistence is, of course, much more than a grammar of orthodoxy.

It is this quest to articulate Christ's unity in the centuries following Chalcedon that fueled the continued speculations of late Patristic and early Byzantine figures such as Leontius of Byzantium, Maximus the Confessor, and John of Damascus.[15] For example, in his famous fifth *Ambiguum to Thomas*, which is a defense of Dionysius against the charge of monoenergism, Maximus the Confessor articulates Christ's divinity and humanity as two modes of a single unified existence and not two numeric existences. "Having united His transcendent mode of existence," Maximus explains, "with the principle of His human nature, so that the ongoing existence of that nature might be confirmed by the newness of the mode of existence, not suffering any change at the level of its inner principle, and thereby make known His power that is beyond infinity, recognized through the generation of opposites."[16] This post-Chalcedonian development on Christ's unity left a deep imprint on Thomas's thinking about Christ.[17] Aquinas's knowledge of the Greek patrimony of Christian theology, read through Latin translations, in the words of Gilles Emery, "visibly makes its mark in the structure [of his] Christology."[18] Although Aquinas is often viewed as a quintessential Latin schoolman, his use of Greek patristic sources, Emery explains, "designates

14. *Decrees of the Ecumenical Councils*, 1:115.

15. For a summary of the influence of the later Greek and Fathers on Aquinas's Christology and the influence of John of Damascus on the *De unione*, see Nutt, "Introduction," in Thomas Aquinas, *De unione verbi incarnati*, 23–41. For a related treatment of the contributions of Leontius, see Brian Daley, SJ, "A Richer Union: Leontius of Byzantium and the Relationship of Human and Divine in Christ," *Studia Patristica* 24 (1993): 239–65.

16. Maximus the Confessor, *On Difficulties in the Church Fathers: The Ambigua*, vol. 1, Dumbarton Oaks Medieval Library 28 (Cambridge, MA: Harvard University Press, 2014), 45.

17. For a helpful treatment of the unique way that Dionysius influenced and informed Aquinas's Christology, see Andrew Hofer, OP, "Dionysian Elements in Thomas Aquinas's Christology: A Case for the Authority and Ambiguity of Pseudo-Dionysius," *The Thomist* 72, no. 3 (2008): 409–42.

18. Gilles Emery, "A Note on St. Thomas and the Eastern Fathers," in *Trinity, Church, and the Human Person: Thomistic Essays* (Naples, FL: Sapientia Press of Ave Maria University, 2007), 193–207, at 194. Emery also points out that in several key theological passages of Aquinas's work, citations from the Greek Fathers often double those from their Latin counterparts. Emery notes further that Aquinas's understanding of the "structure" of the hypostatic union is "fundamentally" Greek (202), and that his use of the term "instrument" (*organum*) to explain the causal merit of Christ's humanity is particularly indebted to the Greek Fathers.

Thomas as a pioneer: He was the first Latin Scholastic," for example, "tru-ly to exploit Constantinople II in Christology and exegesis. His knowledge of the Third Council of Constantinople is no less evident."[19] Disputes over Thomas's position on Christ's unity of being need to take a fuller account of his unique reception of these influences and later Greek developments.[20] Corey Barnes notes that Thomas's assimilation of these new sources and ideas about Christ's wills and operations shifts the focus of his dyothelite Christology away from accenting the perfection of Christ's human nature to "elevating as central a proper understanding of the hypostatic union."[21] This Greek-inspired development, which focused his thought on how to account for Christ's unity, seats Aquinas's various articulations within a broader framework than the Scholasticism of the thirteenth century.

Because the metaphysics of *esse* considers a thing from the perspective of its existence qua existence as the highest perfection that makes each thing to be and not from a particular aspect of its being, such as the substance under-lying a thing, it is important not to conflate *esse* with subsistence. The claim of this essay is not that the medieval metaphysics of *esse* and the doctrine of Christ's single subsistence are exactly the same consideration. The metaphys-ics of *esse* is a higher and more terminal understanding of a subsistent entity. In a question meant to parse the received definitions on the commonality and difference between theological terms like person, hypostasis and *suppos-itum*, St. Thomas clarifies the meaning of subsistence:

[Substance] is also called by three names signifying a reality—that is, "a thing of nature," "subsistence," and "hypostasis," according to a threefold consideration of the substance thus named. For, *as it exists in itself and not in another, it is called "subsistence"*; *as we say that those things subsist which exist in themselves, and not in another*. As it underlies some common nature, it is called "a thing of nature"; as, for instance, this particular man is a human natural thing. As it underlies the accidents, it is called "hypostasis," or "substance." What these three names signify

---

19. James Weisheipl points out, "Thomas d'Aquino was the first Latin Scholastic writer to utilize verbatim the acts of the first five ecumenical councils of the Church, namely in the *Catena aurea* ... and in the *Summa theologiae*." *Friar Thomas D'Aquino: His Life, Thought, and Works* (Washington, DC: Catholic University of America Press, 1983), 164. See also Martin Morard, "Thomas d'Aquin lecteur des conciles," *Archivum Franciscanum Historicum* 98 (2005): 211–365.

20. See Michael Dauphinais, Andrew Hofer, and Roger Nutt, eds., *Thomas Aquinas and the Greek Fathers* (Ave Maria, FL: Sapientia Press of Ave Maria University, 2019), esp. Khaled Anatolios, "The On-tological Grammar of Salvation and the Salvific Work of Christ in Athanasius and Aquinas," 89–109.

21. Barnes, *Christ's Two Wills*, 123.

in common to the whole genus of substances, this name "person" signifies in the genus of rational substances.[22] (emphasis added)

The question, therefore, of Christ's per se existence (subsistence) and the singularity of his *esse* must be intimately related. Without a second subsistence, what would a second *esse* be the perfection of in the order of existence? While not identical with the medieval metaphysics of *esse*, Maximus the Confessor's distinction, as noted above, between Christ's unity of existence and dual (divine and human) "modes" of that one existence presses the same point that Aquinas is attempting to spell out. Indeed, some criticisms of Thomas's single *esse* position would equally rule out the single subsistence doctrine of Chalcedon and its later developments, as would the addition of a second *esse*.[23]

As a second primer, some reference to the Christological framework established by Peter Lombard is crucial to understanding what St. Thomas and the other schoolmen were trying to pinpoint in their speculations about Christ's *esse* and unity. Lombard dutifully received the Christology of the first millennium and endeavored to give a Scholastic account of Christ's manner of existence.[24] St. Thomas makes direct reference to Lombard's famous three opinions about the hypostatic union in *De unione*, so Lombard's work is not far from his mind.[25] Lombard frames the speculative challenge posed by the Incarnation with the following: "Whether a person or nature took on a person or nature, and whether God's nature became flesh."[26] While Lombard's own position on the orthodox doctrine of the Incarnation was something disputed even by his own disciples in the twelfth century, St. Thomas is clear in the *De unione* (and the *Summa Theologiae*) that the

---

22. *ST* I, q. 29, a. 2. Taken from Thomas Aquinas, *Summa theologiae*, vol. 13, ed. John Mortensen and Enrique Alarcon, trans. Laurence Shapcote, OP (Lander, WY: Aquinas Institute for the Study of Sacred Doctrine, 2012), 310.

23. See Aaron Riches, "After Chalcedon: The Oneness of Christ and the Dyothelite Mediation of his Theandric Unity," *Modern Theology* 24 (2008): 199–224.

24. For a presentation of the theological and philosophical issues in the century prior to Aquinas that includes a thorough and original analysis of Peter Lombard's christology, see Lauge Olaf Nielsen, *Theology and Philosophy in the Twelfth Century: A Study of Gilbert Porreta's Thinking and the Theological Expositions of the Doctrine of the Incarnation during the Period, 1130–1180* (Leiden: Brill, 1982).

25. See, e.g., the corpus of *De unione*, a. 2.

26. Peter Lombard, *Sentences*, Book III, dist. 5, chap. 1, trans. Giulio Silano (Toronto: Pontifical Institute of Mediaeval Studies, 2008), 17–18. For Nielsen's original conclusion about Lombard's preference for the Third Opinion, see *Theology and Philosophy in the Twelfth Century*, 264.

Second Opinion, the "subsistence theory,"[27] is not merely an opinion but the faith of the Catholic Church.[28] A less appreciated but equally import-ant point that the Lombard leaves for subsequent generations to clarify is the status of Christ's human nature. Having laid out the "opinions" of the past generations on the hypostatic union, Lombard raises what later is re-ferred to as the problem of "Christological nihilianism." This problem serves as a catalyst for the speculations about Christ's *esse*.[29] It is called nihilian-ism because of Lombard's formulation of the problem: "Whether Christ, according to his being a man, is a person or anything. It is also usual for some to ask whether Christ, according to his being a man, is a person, or even is anything."[30] Lombard's parsing unveils the possible answers to this mercurial question: either Christ is a second person as man, which would negate the union, or he is a person as a man but not a numerically second one, which would make him, as a man, Lombard reasons, a person of the Trinity, which would then make him, as a man, God.[31] So, if he is not a person according to his being a man, then, Lombard wonders whether, as a man, he is anything at all. In short, Lombard understood that in the order of being, without positing two persons, which vacates the union, it is difficult to account for both the divinity and the humanity of Christ with just one person and being for each.[32] So the Greek patrimony of Christ's composite mode of existence as a single subsistence and Lombard's struggle to account for the human nature of Christ are two loci that spurned on medieval theo-logians like Thomas Aquinas to wrestle with the question of Christ's unity in the order of being.[33]

27. The adherents of the Subsistence Theory, Lombard explains, "profess this Christ to be only one person; however, that person was simple only before the incarnation, but in the incarnation he was made into a person composed of divinity and humanity … And so the person [of God] which before was simple and existed only in one nature, then subsists in and from two natures." Lombard, *In III Sent.*, d. 6, chap. 3, p. 26.

28. See, e.g., *ST* III, q. 2, a. 6. For a discussion of the "three opinions" in relation to developments within Aquinas's Christology over the course of his career, see Michael Raschko, "Aquinas's Theology of the Incarnation in Light of Lombard's Subsistence Theory," *The Thomist* 65 (2001): 409–39.

29. See Philipp W. Rosemann, *Peter Lombard* (New York: Oxford University Press, 2004), 131.

30. Lombard, *Sentences*, Book III, dist. 10, chap. 1, p. 41.

31. Lombard, *Sentences*, Book III, dist. 10, chap. 1, p. 41.

32. For a helpful treatment of this issue that contextualizes Thomas teaching, see Stephen F. Brown, "Thomas Aquinas and His Contemporaries on the Unique Existence in Christ," in *Christ among the Medieval Dominicans: Representations of Christ in the Texts and Images of the Order of Preachers*, ed. Kent Emery and Joseph Wawrykow (Notre Dame, IN: University of Notre Dame Press, 1998), 220–37.

33. *In Super Sent.*, lib. 3, d. 6, q. 3, a. 2, ad 1, Thomas catalogs some attempts to account for Christ's

PART II: REASONS FOR A
SINGLE *ESSE* READING OF THE *DE*
UNIONE VERBI INCARNATI

The Argumentative Progression of the
Articles Does Not Allow a "Second *Esse*"
Reading of Article Four

Many of the scholars who refer to article four to claim that Thomas abandoned a single *esse* position clutch to his use of the word *secundarium* without any reference to other articles of the Disputed Question.[34] In fact, each preceding point leading up to article four and the one article that follows it hem the consideration into narrow parameters rooted in the doctrine of the single composite subsistence of the Word as God and man. A sketch of the key hinges in this progression demonstrates why the second *esse* arguments betray Thomas's actual position.

In the first article, Thomas treats the mode of the hypostatic union in a fashion that is consistent with his other works, with his preference for the subsistence theory among the Three Opinions, and with the influence

---

human nature as an accident of the Word. Interestingly, he refers to these as accounts of "antiqui" that are inaccurate. From his early writings, Thomas considered the question of Christ's unity and the status of his human nature to be a long-standing problem and not simply one of thirteenth-century speculations. "Ad primum ergo dicendum, quod humana natura in Christo habet aliquam similitudinem cum accidente, et praecipue cum habitu, quantum ad tria. Primo, quia advenit personae divinae post esse completum, sicut habitus, et omnia alia accidentia. Secundo, quia est in se substantia, et advenit alteri, sicut vestis homini. Tertio, quia melioratur ex unione ad verbum, et non mutat verbum; sicut vestis formatur secundum formam vestientis, et non mutat vestientem. Unde antiqui dixerunt, quod vergit in accidens; et quidam propter hoc addiderunt, quod degenerat in accidens: quod tamen non ita proprie dicitur; quia natura humana in Christo non degenerat, immo magis nobilitatur." Sr. Deloffre catalogs the different ways in which the other major authors of the thirteenth century, with the issues raised by Lombard as a point of reference, framed Christ's human mode of existence in the order of being. These formulations included, among others, *esse simpliciter* and *esse personale* (used by Alexander of Hales, Albert the Great, and Bonaventure) as well as *esse hypostasis* (Albert the Great and Alexander of Hales). Conversely, many of these same authors, especially the Franciscans, employed the phrase *esse humanum* to speak of Christ's human nature. See Deloffre, *Question disputée*, 45–50. A problem arose for these authors, however, regarding Christ's unity. How can the unity of Christ be articulated in terms of *esse simpliciter* "without eliminating the reality of the human nature?" (Deloffre, *Question disputée*, 46). To address this problem, Bonaventure spoke of the categorical status of Christ's human nature in relation to the divine *esse* of the Word as "inclining toward an accident" (*vergit in accidens*) (Deloffre, *Question disputée*, 47). Bonaventure formulates this position in the commentary on Lombard's *Sentences*, Book III, dist. 6, art. 1, qu. 3.

34. See note 8 above for a list of authors and works.

of the Greek Fathers and early councils on his thought. Considering seventeen speculative objections that assert that a union between God and man in Christ must result in a conflation of the natures into something new or be only accidental, Thomas develops the distinction between person and nature to clarify precisely how the incarnate Word is truly God and man. Having established that nature is the specific difference that makes something the certain kind of being that it is, and that person is a concretely subsisting *suppositum* of a rational nature, St. Thomas draws the following conclusion: "nothing prevents some things that are not united in a nature from being united in a person, for an individual substance of a rational nature can have something that does not belong to the nature of the species: this is united to it personally, not naturally."[35]

Because it is possible for things that are not united in a nature to be united in a person, Thomas clarifies that in Christ "the non-composite divine person subsists in two natures."[36] He then makes a conclusion about Christ's being or *esse* that must be kept in mind when reading the fourth article: "the being (*esse*) of the person of the Word Incarnate is one from the perspective of the person subsisting, but not from the perspective of the nature."[37]

Having concluded in article one that the union of the two natures is according to the single subsistence of the person of the Word, Thomas then asks in the second article whether there is hypostatic (personal) unity in Christ, and, if so, how are the duality of natures maintained? The objections that Thomas considers raise two perennial concerns: first, that anything that is one by hypostasis cannot be identified as two things without duplicating the hypostases according to each nature and, second, that the infinite being of the hypostasis of the Word cannot be the hypostasis of Christ's created human nature. So the objections press the problem raised by the Lombard to their logical conclusions: Christ's human nature, as something real and not nothing, it seems, is a hypostasis. As a result, there must be two *esses* and no substantial union, which is the Nestorian heresy; or Christ's human nature takes on the status of some accidental property in relation to the Word, which would compromise the integrity of his human mode of existence.

---

35. Aquinas, *De unione verbi incarnati*, a. 1, p. 93.
36. Aquinas, *De unione verbi incarnati*, ad 6, p. 99.
37. Aquinas, *De unione verbi incarnati*, ad 10, p. 101.

Thomas dismisses any attempt to reduce Christ's human nature to an accident. Since the nature is complete, however, possessing a rational soul and body, what, if anything, would prevent it from being a suppositum and hypostasis, thereby making it a numerically second *esse*? Thomas answers this challenge in the following way:

> So, then, because the human nature in Christ does not subsist separately through itself but exists in another, that is, in the hypostasis of the Word of God—not indeed as an accident in a subject, nor properly as a part in a whole, but by means of an ineffable assumption—on that account, the human nature in Christ can indeed be called something individual or particular or singular; but nevertheless, as it is not a person, Christ's human nature cannot be called either a hypostasis or a *suppositum*. Hence it remains that in Christ there is but one hypostasis or *suppositum*, namely, that of the Divine Word.[38]

The work that Thomas does in this passage can be easily passed over without a full appreciation of its significance. Because Christ's human nature is whole and complete, it enjoys the status of individuality and singularity in the order of substance. But what enables Thomas's account to avoid the Nestorian error of vitiating the union is that in the order of being, the individual and singular nature, while being complete, is not a hypostasis or *suppositum*. This point is crucial for how one reads the formulation of article four. Thomas's explicit reference to the condemnation by Constantinople II of any attempt to add a second subsistence or person to the mystery of Christ in the body of this article shows a self-awareness of how his account of Christ's unity stands in continuity with the post-Chalcedon patrimony.

In the third article, Thomas ties the ripening implications of these principles together in preparation for the direct account of Christ's *esse*. The careful linguistic formulation of the third article can be difficult to penetrate for modern readers. The question that Thomas asks at the start of the article is "whether Christ is one in the neuter or two" (*unum neutraliter vel duo*). What Thomas is aiming for with this construction follows upon the conclusions of the previous articles. Since he is not two persons, Christ cannot be said to be *alius et alius* (one person and another), but as true God and true man, could he be said to be *aliud et aliud* (one reality and something else)? By reference to the neuter category, Thomas opens the way for a consider-

---

38. Aquinas, *De unione verbi incarnati*, a. 2, p. 113.

ation of how Christ's hypostatic unity is related to his numeric unity (after Chalcedon, some had tried to say that Christ was one person but two things, each with its own separate subsistence). All of the fourteen objections that Thomas considers press the point of Christ's duality of natures, offering variations of the following conclusion: "Therefore Christ is one reality and something else (*aliud et aliud*), and accordingly he is two."[39]

His terse response to these objections in the first *sed contra* is arresting and seemingly unorthodox: "Christ is not two persons nor two hypostases nor two *supposita* … Christ is also not two natures since human nature is not predicated of Christ. Therefore Christ is not two."[40] What could Thomas mean by asserting that Christ is not two natures? The specificity of the question is important for understanding his point. The one Christ certainly has two natures, but it is the one person of the Word who *is* both God and man. So Christ is not two natures in the sense of being two different realities in the order of being: the union of the two natures in the one subsisting person constitutes the one Christ.

Any being can be considered one thing or many things depending on whether or not the consideration is made from the perspective of its substantial unity or accidental or composite diversity. Thomas appeals to the distinction between something considered *secundum quid* (in a certain respect) or *simpliciter* (absolutely speaking) to demonstrate how this is true. Recognizing that a particular person is tall, dark, handsome, and skinny is to acknowledge many true things about them *secundum quid*. But it does not make them many things *simpliciter*. Even in the order of substance, Thomas notes, following Aristotle, that two aspects are included: the "*suppositum*, which is not [a] predicate of something else, and [the] form or nature of the species, which is [a] predicate of the *suppositum*."[41] In the case of Christ, as

---

39. Aquinas, *De unione verbi incarnati*, a. 3, arg. 6, pp. 120–21. Thomas maintains this same point in *ST* III, q. 17, a. 1, ad. 2: "Ad secundum dicendum quod, cum dicitur, Christus est aliud et aliud locutio est exponenda ut sit sensus, habens aliam et aliam naturam. Et hoc modo exponit Augustinus in libro contra Felicianum, ubi, cum dixisset, *in mediatore Dei et hominum aliud Dei filius, aliud hominis filius* subdit, *aliud, inquam, pro discretione substantiae, non alius, pro unitate personae.* Et Gregorius Nazianzenus, in epistola ad Chelidonium, *si oportet compendiose dicere, aliud quidem et aliud ea ex quibus salvator est, siquidem non idem est invisibile visibili, et quod absque tempore ei quod sub tempore. Non autem alius et alius absit. Haec enim ambo unum.*"

40. Aquinas, *De unione verbi incarnati, sed contra*, p. 123.

41. Aquinas, *De unione verbi incarnati*, a. 3, p. 125.

true particular man, the human nature is predicated of the *suppositum* of the Word, but not according to a per se (subsistence) or absolute standing as a person or *suppositum* of that particular nature but as the nature assumed by the *suppositum*. So Thomas concludes that "Christ can in some way be called one because he is one by the *suppositum*, and he can in some way be called many, or two, because he has two natures."[42] This means that "if one certain *suppositum* has many substantial natures," as is the case with Christ, "it will be one *simpliciter*, and many in a certain respect."[43] Thomas clearly forges this conclusion as a first clarification of the *esse* question in Christ. Whatever is two or multiple in Christ is recognized *secundum quid* and not in the order of being.

Thus when Thomas arrives at the famous fourth article of the Disputed Question, which asks "whether in Christ there is only one being (*esse*)," he evidently considers the question to be answered already. So much so that in the opening line of the body of the article he says, "It should be said that the argument of this question is, in a certain sense, the same as that of the previous question, because something is said to be one and a being on the same grounds."[44] Likewise, the *sed contra*, from whence the title of this paper is derived, invokes the distinction of the previous article to conclude that Christ is not two in the order of *esse*: "Everything that is one *simpliciter* is one according to being. But Christ is one *simpliciter*, as was said above. In Christ, therefore, there is one being (*esse*)."[45] What, then, does Thomas mean by his unique use of the word *secundarium* if it is not meant to indicate a second *esse*? It is clear that he means to qualify the truth of Christ's human nature according to the *secundum quid* or composite duality that follows upon the Word's possession of two existent natures.[46] In fact, he says as much in the line preceding the famous passage: "there is another being of this *suppositum*," he explains, "not insofar as this other being is eternal, but insofar as the *suppositum* was

42. Aquinas, *De unione verbi incarnati*, a. 3, p. 127.
43. Aquinas, *De unione verbi incarnati*, a. 3, p. 127.
44. Aquinas, *De unione verbi incarnati*, a. 4, p. 133.
45. Aquinas, *De unione verbi incarnati*, *sed contra*, p. 133.
46. John Emery explains Aquinas's intention as follows: "By means of this *hapax legomenon*, Aquinas does not posit a new distinct act of being in Christ; instead, he attempts to account for the creaturely character of his human nature, whose participated degree of being is different from the divine nature's limitless being." See "A Christology of Communication: Christ's Charity According to Thomas Aquinas" (PhD diss., University of Fribourg, 2017), 87.

made man temporally."[47] Why not conclude, as many have tried to claim,[48] that the *secundarium* entity, the human nature of Christ, contributes *esse* in a numerically second sense? The words of the sentence that follow his reference to the *secundarium* entity make the second *esse* conclusion impossible by clarifying that *esse* cannot be recognized without a corresponding *suppositum*: "If, however, there were two *supposita* in Christ, then each *suppositum* would have its own principal being of itself. And thus there would be in Christ a twofold being *simpliciter*."[49] Given that this is not the case, the subordinate or secondary *esse* mentioned clearly pertains to Christ's *secundum quid* duality and does not contribute *esse* in a numerically second manner because there are not two *supposita* in Christ.[50] John Froula's assessment seems to most strongly capture the sense of Thomas's intention:

Christ does have a human life and principle of his assumed created nature that is not the divine *esse*. There is a secondary, or subordinate, *esse* of the human nature of Christ that is other than the divine esse and not the divine *esse*, that is, the act by which Christ is human. It is *esse* not in the supposital sense, but in a legitimate analogical use of the word.[51]

What Christ's human nature does contribute as numerically second is specified by St. Thomas in the fifth and final article of the Disputed Question; namely, the truth of his operational duality. "It should be said," Thomas recognizes, "that Christ is one *simpliciter* on account of the *suppositum*. Never-

47. Aquinas, *De unione verbi incarnati*, a. 4, p. 135.

48. See note 8 above. In addition to the authors and positions outlined therein, for a consideration of Aquinas's ontology of the hypostatic union in relation to the work of Karl Rahner, Friedrich Schleiermacher, John Hick, Jacques Dupuis, and Jon Sobrino, see White, *Incarnate Lord*, 91–111.

49. Aquinas, *De unione verbi incarnati*, a. 4, p. 135.

50. One of the great commentators on Aquinas, Dominic Bañez (1528–1604), recognizes that an *esse* cannot be posited without a supposital reality: "The constitutive mode of a suppositis really distinct from that suppositis one thing from another ... All the more distinct then is *esse* from essence, *for esse does not come to essence except through suppositality*." *The Primacy of Existence in Thomas Aquinas*, trans. Benjamin S. Llamzon (Chicago: Henry Regnery, 1966), 49; emphasis added. For a helpful exploration of this issue, see Thomas M. Osborne Jr., "Which Essence Is Brought into Being by the Existential Act," *The Thomist* 81 (2017): 471–505.

51. John Froula, "*Esse Secundarium*: An Analogical Term Meaning That by Which Christ Is Human," *The Thomist* 78 (2014): 557–80, at 80. The article is also extremely helpful for its summary of a number of different readings of article four of the *De unione*. See also Victor Salas, "Thomas Aquinas on Christ's *Esse*: A Metaphysics of the Incarnation," *The Thomist* 70 (2006): 577–603, and Corey L. Barnes, "Albert the Great and Thomas Aquinas on Person, Hypostasis, and Hypostatic Union," *The Thomist* 72 (2008): 107–46, at 144.

theless, there are two natures in him: and therefore Christ is one agent, but there are two actions in him.”[52] The human nature truly acts in a human mode; however, the truth of the human nature and its act do not constitute a second agent of action but a second mode of being by which the one agent acts.[53] Corey Barnes recognizes Thomas's specification of Christ's unity *simpliciter* in the order of *esse*, and his *secundum quid* duality “prepares for consideration of Christ's wills and operations.”[54] If Christ had more than one *esse*, his human actions would not enjoy a theandric character.

A Brief Note on Thomas's Use of *Secundarium* in the *De Unione*

There is a final contextual thought that indicates Thomas's single *esse* mind-set in this Disputed Question. It is understandable why readers are induced to read Thomas's use of the word *secundarium* in a numerical sense because of its semantic affinity to the number two and natural cognates from the root “second.” Translating *secundarium* as “secondary,” which is not inaccurate, leads the mind to think of something numerically or quantitatively second. The fact is, however, that the comparison made in *De unione*, article four, is not between that which is *primus* and that which is *secundus*, between numerically first and second things. Rather, the contrast is between that which is “predicated” of the Word Incarnate according to the suppositum and that which is predicated according to the created nature. Comparing what is *principale* and *secundarium* in Christ is a way of affirming the modes of being that the Word has through his composite natures.[55]

---

52. Aquinas, *De unione verbi incarnati*, a. 5, ad 14, p. 145. Romanus Cessario clarifies this point in Aquinas's thought by distinguishing the person and the natures as “effective subject” and “possessive subjects.” “As a personal unity,” Cessario argues, “Christ enjoys only one effective subject, the eternal Logos. But besides the effective principle of unity which Christ receives through his uncreated personhood, he also enjoys two possessive subjects, since each nature does what remains proper to it.” *The Godly Image: Christ and Salvation in Catholic Thought from Anselm to Aquinas* (Petersham: St. Bede's, 1990), 134.

53. For a tentative but somewhat compatible reading of *De unione*, a. 4, see Michael Gorman, *Aquinas on the Metaphysics of the Hypostatic Union* (Cambridge: Cambridge University Press, 2017), esp. 161.

54. Barnes, *Christ's Two Wills*, 244.

55. This is why I have translated *secundarium* as “subordinate” in this article and my own translation of the *De unione*. *Secundarius* denotes a reality of a secondary or subordinate order and not a numeric continuum of discrete realities. Roy J. Deferrari, in *A Latin-English Lexicon of Saint Thomas*

Few scholars who have interpreted *De unione*, article four, as a break from his *unum esse* position have tested their readings on other places in his corpus where Thomas uses the distinction between *principale* and *secundarium*—a tool that he turns to not infrequently to clarify diverse aspects of a composite reality.[56]

Thomas's most concentrated use of this distinction is found in the section of the *Prima Secundae* of the *Summa Theologiae* devoted to the New Law or Gospel of Grace (qq. 106–14). It is used in this sequence as his preferred tool for clarifying the spiritual and material aspects of the New Law. In the first article (a. 106, a. 1) of this treatise, where Thomas asks whether the New Law is a "written law," he answers: "the new law is chiefly (*principaliter*) the grace itself of the Holy Spirit, which is given to those who believe in Christ."[57] The other elements of the New Law that are not the grace of the Holy Spirit, but integrally related to it, Thomas teaches are

of secondary (*secundaria*) importance, so to speak, in the New Law; and the faithful need to be instructed concerning them, both by word and writings, both as to what they should believe and what they should do. Consequently we must say that the New Law is in the first place (*principaliter*) a law that is inscribed on our hearts, but that secondarily (*secundario*) it is a written law.[58]

Likewise, in a subsequent article in the same question, Thomas makes use of the same distinction to establish the unity of the New Law while also affirming its composite nature: "There is a two-fold element in the Law of the Gospel," Thomas teaches, "there is the chief element (*principaliter*), viz., the grace of the Holy Spirit bestowed inwardly ... The other element of the

---

Aquinas (Fitzwilliam, NH: Loreto, 1948), offers the following English choices for *secundarius, a, um*: "coming in second place, subordinate, secondary, the opposite of *prinicipalis*" (1006).

56. In addition to the examples provided below, there are two other texts that demonstrate Thomas's recourse to the distinction between *principale* and *secundarium*. *ST* II-II, q. 17, a. 4, co: "In genere autem utriusque causae invenitur principale et secundarium. Principalis enim finis est finis ultimus; secundarius autem finis est bonum quod est ad finem. Similiter principalis causa agens est primum agens; secundaria vero causa efficiens est agens secundarium instrumentale." And *De veritate*, q. 23, a. 1, ad 3: "Ad tertium dicendum, quod voluntas est alicuius dupliciter: uno modo principaliter, et alio modo secundario. Principaliter quidem voluntas est finis, qui est ratio volendi omnia alia; secundario autem est eorum quae sunt ad finem, quae propter finem volumus."

57. *ST* I-II, q. 106, a. 1. Taken from Thomas Aquinas, *Summa theologiae*, vol. 16, ed. John Mortensen and Enrique Alarcon, trans. Laurence Shapcote, OP (Lander, WY: Aquinas Institute for the Study of Sacred Doctrine, 2012), 408.

58. *ST* I-II, q. 106, a. 1, trans. Shapcote.

Evangelical Law is secondary (*secundario*): namely, the things of faith, and those commandments which direct human affections and actions."[59]

Thomas returns to this distinction numerous times throughout this sequence of questions to accentuate the primacy of the grace of the Holy Spirit in relation to the material components of the New Law.[60] It is clear from this usage that Thomas in no way intends to identify those secondary (or subordinate) aspects of the New Law that are related to the grace of the Holy Spirit as a numerically "second" law. Rather, Thomas invokes this comparison to accentuate the relationship of the two aspects, spiritual and material, of the New Law as one law with an ordering to the primary reality of the grace of the Holy Spirit.

From this perspective, the position of the *De unione* is hardly as novel as it might appear when studied in Christology without reference to other instances of the distinction between that which is *principale* and *secundarium* to underscore the ultimate unity of composite realities.[61] Given the order of dependency or subordination of the *secundaria* to whatever is principal, many of the confusions surrounding article four could be avoided if *secundarium* was not presented by means of the potentially misleading cognates like "second," but with ordered comparatives like primary or principal and subordinate.[62]

59. *ST* I-II, a. 2, trans. Shapcote.

60. Thomas also uses this distinction to distinguish the primary and subordinate ends of a composite action and the primary and secondary agents of a composite motion. In both cases the secondary component depends on the primary aspect. See, e.g., *ScG* III, c. 109, no. 5: "ut scilicet secundarius finis a principali dependeat, sicut secundarium agens a principali dependet" (Leonine ed. 14:341).

61. Jason L. A. West, "Aquinas on the Metaphysics of *Esse* in Christ," *The Thomist* 66 (2002): 231–50, argues that there is no sense in which the *esse secundarium* of the *De unione* can be read without contradicting Aquinas's metaphysics and consistent arguments against the Christological heresies. West's metaphysics is correct, but his reading of the *De unione* is not. If Aquinas were distinguishing between two numerically distinct *esses* in one subsistent being, his position in the *De unione* would contradict his principles. That is not the case, however. The subordinate or *secundarium esse* is not some metaphysically incoherent attempt to affirm a half *esse* but an affirmation that the human nature of Christ is an existent particular but not a per se subsistence or person.

62. On translating the *De unione* in light of these controversies see Nutt, "Introduction," *De unione verbi incarnati*, 58–59.

CONCLUSION

What advantage is to be gained by wrestling with these complicated issues that putatively belong to a bygone age? These post-Chalcedonian attempts to articulate Christ's unity are not merely academic, Scholastic, or even Thomistic, however. They pertain to the union of God and man in Christ as affirmed in the most basic sources of the Christian faith. As Thomas Joseph White observes, key passages in the New Testament about Christ

> point us toward [a] deeper ontological mystery. How is it that God the Son and Word subsists as a human being, having a human nature, even while he retains the prerogatives of his divine identity and nature? Christ is able to cure the sick, raise the dead, and even forgive sins. Christ is also subject to human suffering, death, and resurrection from the dead. The subject who acts is one, but he acts always both as God and as man, simultaneously able to do what only God can do, and able to suffer what only a human being can suffer. To approach this mystery in its depth is to approach the heart of New Testament teaching. But this approach can only be one grounded in a distinctively metaphysical mode of Christological reflection.[63]

Like the Greek authors after Chalcedon, Aquinas sought to illumine Christ's unity and duality in terms of their metaphysical implications. By his appropriation and development of the post-Chalcedon tradition, St. Thomas understood that Jesus did not need a second *esse* to authenticate the truth of his humanity. What he assumed did not give him a new, second being; it gave him a new human mode of being, through which he loved and suffered in the single subsistent existence of the Word. Thomas's formulation of Christ's unity in the *De unione* is unique, but it is precisely the uniqueness of this formulation, so vexing to commentators, that underscores his ultimate commitment to Christ's ontological unity: the *secundarium* of this enigmatic work is not another *esse*, but the created mode of existence that Christ acted through as a human being.

---

63. White, *Incarnate Lord*, 21.

CHAPTER 4

THE SUBSISTENCE
OF CHRIST'S HUMAN NATURE WITH
THE *ESSE PERSONALE OF*
THE ETERNAL WORD

Steven A. Long

The object of this essay is to argue that the humanity of the Word subsists in the Person of the Word and does not have a separate existence, although it is a distinct nature from the divine essence. In this essay, I wish to stress two things: (1) the central and unavoidable role of obediential potency and (2) the importance of the metaphysics of subsistence that will raise its head throughout my remarks. First, I offer a few prefatory considerations; second, I state the thesis that in Christ human nature exists with the *esse personale* of the Eternal Word; third, I raise a difficulty; fourth, I explain the pertinence of obediential potency to this question; and finally, I say a few words about the *esse secondarium* or "second *esse*" of the human nature of the Word seemingly affirmed by St. Thomas in his work *De unione verbi incarnati*.[1]

PREFATORY CONSIDERATIONS

By *esse* I refer here and throughout principally to existence. There are other analogous usages of "esse," but the primary sense of *esse* is *existence*. Thus the

---

1. Thomas Aquinas, *De unione verbi incarnati*, ed. and trans. By Roger Nutt (Leuven: Peeters, 2015).

claim that there is but one *esse* in Christ is contrary to the claim that there is a second and numerically distinct existence that pertains to human nature in Christ.

Thomas notes that the term "substance" signifies in two ways and refers either to essence or quiddity, or else to a subject or "suppositum" subsisting in the genus of substance. He notes three distinct terms, all of which may be signified by the use of the term "person" in the genus of rational substances. As he writes in *Summa Theologiae* I, q. 29, a. 2, resp.:

According to the Philosopher (Metaph. v), substance is twofold. In one sense it means the quiddity of a thing, signified by its definition, and thus we say that the definition means the substance of a thing; in which sense substance is called by the Greeks ousia, what we may call "essence." In another sense substance means a subject or "suppositum," which subsists in the genus of substance. To this, taken in a general sense, can be applied a name expressive of an intention; and thus it is called "suppositum." It is also called by three names signifying a reality—that is, "a thing of nature," "subsistence," and "hypostasis," according to a threefold consideration of the substance thus named. For, as it exists in itself and not in another, it is called "subsistence"; as we say that those things subsist which exist in themselves, and not in another. As it underlies some common nature, it is called "a thing of nature"; as, for instance, this particular man is a human natural thing. As it underlies the accidents, it is called "hypostasis," or "substance." What these three names signify in common to the whole genus of substances, this name "person" signifies in the genus of rational substances.[2]

Thomas famously accepts Boethius's definition of "person" as an "individual substance of a rational nature."[3] The issue of the nature of subsistence arises with this consideration. As Thomas observed about substance in the lengthy passage quoted above, "as it exists in itself and not in another, it is called 'subsistence.'" This is substance taken as the ultimate or complete and incommunicable subject of existence. For any *created* thing to "exist in itself and not in another," it must be constituted as itself and not the other; that is, *its nature must already have been rendered incommunicable as a subject of being,* not capable of belonging to what is other than and outside itself (this is what "subsistence" *means,* to be constituted as the ultimate or *complete subject of being* that belongs to itself). Speaking of the term "individual" in

2. *ST* I, q. 29, a. 2, resp.
3. Cf. *ST* I, q. 29, a. 1, obj. 1.

the Boethian definition of person, Fr. Gilles Emery writes: "These are the two features that ground the dignity of the person, namely, (1) subsistence as denoting the substance under the aspect of its special mode of existing, and (2) intellectual nature."[4]

There is a real question as to whether the incommunicable manner of existing in itself and not in another designated by the term "subsistence" should be taken as formally constituted by a terminating mode of essence rendering it incommunicable to another subject (as Cajetan argued[5]) or as formally constituted by existence rendering the individual substance to be entitatively complete (as Billot argued[6]). But in either case, subsistence names a complete subject of being and for finite beings denotes incommunicability. Yet arguably in the case of the divine subsistence, this limitation of incommunicability does not apply because of the infinitude of the divine *esse*, perfection, and active power—I return to this consideration below. It is also of prefatory importance to note that whereas essence or nature is understood by Thomas to be a *principium quo*, a principle *whereby* something is a being, the *substance* or *supposit* is a *principium quod*; it is *that which* has being or exists.[7]

WITH WHAT *ESSE* DOES THE HUMAN NATURE OF CHRIST SUBSIST?

This raises the question, What existence pertains to the humanity of Christ? That human nature is distinct from the divine essence is evident philosophically and indeed is an object of faith, since even in the person of Christ the

---

4. Gilles Emery, OP, "The Dignity of Being a Substance—Person, Subsistence, and Nature," *Nova et Vetera*, English ed. 9, no. 4 (2011): 991–1001, 995. "Thus, the "individual substance" signifies the subsisting singular that exists through itself and in itself, according to an irreducible mode, as a complete whole, a "hypostasis" that exercises the act of existing on its own account" (995). Emery also notes: "St. Thomas specifies: 'Individual' (*individuum*) is included in the definition of the person in order to designate the individual mode of being (*individualem modum essendi*).' This means that, in Aquinas's understanding of the definition given by Boethius, the word "individual" means the incommunicable manner of existing of the real singular, the irreducibility of the singular's uniqueness" (994).

5. Cajetan, OP, on *ST* III, q. 4, a. 3.

6. L. Billot, SJ, *De Verbo Incarnato* (Rome: Typographia Polyglotta, 1895).

7. See, e.g., *ST* III, q. 17, a. 2, resp.

divine and human natures are neither commingled nor confused.[8] But *can* something be quidditatively distinct from God while yet subsisting with divine *esse*? This is difficult to understand. If the foregoing is true, however—that human nature is not divine nature and yet a human nature may exist solely with the existence of a divine Person—it would seem that this must in part be a judgment reached by negation since we have no quidditative knowledge of God Who is *Ipsum Esse Subsistens Per Se.*

Presuming that by *esse* we mean, as already stated, to refer to the act of being or actual existence and not to use the term analogically to refer to finite essence itself, the negative judgment is as follows: *human nature in Christ cannot have a separate esse from the divine esse without implying that the humanity of Christ is an accident of the divine Word rather than being substantially united to him.* As a cloak is not joined to the being of the man who wears it because the cloak is a separate subject of being with its own distinct existence, so if the human nature is a subject of being with its own separate existence, its union with the Word would render it to be merely accidentally conjoined to the Word. And thus the human nature would not be substantially united with the Person of the Word. But to the contrary, this man—Christ—is God.

It is true that in relation to the divine essence *as such* it is *ab extra* that a human nature should be assumed. Divine essence as such does not require or essentially imply the assumption of human nature, and had God never ordained the grace of union, the divine essence would not be different. It is *not* as though the human nature emanates with necessity from the divine essence, whereas the divine Persons do emanate with necessity from the divine essence. Further, the assumption of human nature occurs temporally, whereas the divine essence is simply eternal. Yet nonetheless it is not accidental *to the assumed nature as assumed* that it exists with the existence of the Person of the Word rather than possessing an existence separate from that of the person of Christ: for from its first instant of existing, it is the *humanity of the Word substantially joined to him.* Thus the human and the divine natures are affirmed as substantially belonging to the Person of the Word.[9] The hu-

---

8. Cf. *ST* III, q. 2, sed contra, quoting Chalcedon: "We confess that in these latter times the only-begotten Son of God appeared in two natures, without confusion, without change, without division, without separation—the distinction of natures not having been taken away by the union."

9. *ST* III, q. 16, a. 4, resp.

manity of Christ is the humanity of the divine second person of the Trinity since it is not a separate subject of a merely human person who is distinct from the Person of the Word. Hence it is true to say that the man, Christ, is God, although that by which he is God is not his human nature, and it is true to say that God in Christ is man, although that by which God is man in Christ is the assumed humanity. The person or *suppositum* or *subject* is the one that exists; the *nature* is a principle *of* that which exists—it is that *whereby* the person or *suppositum or subject exists*. Thus that whereby the divine Person of the Word is God, is the divine nature; and that whereby he is man, is his human nature.

It seems to be the only possible conclusion that human nature subsists with the *esse* of the Person of the Word rather than with a separate human existence. Were the human nature viewed as a mere accident of the Person of the Word, this would deny substantial union with the Person of the Word and devolve toward Christological heresy. Yet to subsist in the Person of the Word transcends the purely natural potency of any created nature whatsoever.

PROBLEMS

But how can a finite essence be "joined to" a divine person who is God, is Pure Act? Especially since it is repugnant to Pure Act that it be *limited*? Of course, the proposition is not that the divine *esse* is either *circumscriptively contained within* or *absolutely limited* by human nature, but the contrary: that the human nature exists only as belonging substantially to the Person of the Word.

A fundamental difficulty arises. In created things the nature must be incommunicable. That is, the finite individual nature must be such as to belong only to the one whose nature it is and not to anyone or anything else outside that subject. Thus as human nature is individuated in each person, it is incommunicable. The individuated human nature of Socrates is not predicated of Plato. The created subject of being, who has a nature and who has existence, can exist if and only if that subject's nature is incommunicable. For example, Socrates could not exist as an entire individual being of a rational nature if his individuated nature were also Plato's, because Socrates *is not* Plato, and Socrates *is in no way already Plato or in possession of the distinct reality of the one who is Plato.* But whereas human nature normally belongs to a human person, in Christ the human nature subsists not in a human but in a divine Person and with the *esse personale* of the Word. Since the human nature must then subsist with the *esse* of the Word, it is the humanity of Christ. How then can a nature *that is created in time* come to subsist in a divine Person Who is *eternally begotten of the Father*? It is not that to the nature *qua* nature, in and of itself, it belongs to be ordered to exist with divine *esse*. The Person of the Word is eternally begotten, and the human nature is created in time. How can a temporal being subsist with an eternal *esse*?

DIVINE SUBSISTENCE AND OBEDIENTIAL POTENCY

Respondeo. God supereminently possesses every perfection and is Pure Act, *Ipsum Esse subsistens per se* from which all things derive their limited being. Hence God can create and elevate a human nature to subsist with the *existence* of the Person of the Word, because—not being limited by potency—the Person of the Word possesses every perfection and every power of being. Hence the personal existence of the Word is, unlike finite subsistence, *communicable.*

To subsist in the Person of the Word transcends the purely natural potency of any created nature whatsoever. It is precisely for this reason that Aquinas, in speaking of the "greatest grace" of union, uses the language associated with *obediential potency,* which is the potency that every created principle or thing has *solely in relation to God and to that which God can bring forth in it.* Clearly there is no active potency for human nature to belong to a divine person: this is an effect of supernatural agency infinitely transcendent of any created principle. As St. Thomas writes in *De virtutibus in communi,* q. 1, a. 10, ad 13:

Just as from water or from earth something can be made by the power of a heavenly body which cannot be made by the power of fire; so, from the same elements something can be formed by the power of a supernatural agent which no natural agent can produce. For this reason we say that in the whole of creation there is a certain obediential potency whereby every creature obeys God by receiving into itself whatsoever God wills.[10]

The creature obeys God by receiving into itself whatever God wills, and if God wills that a nature terminate not in a created but in an uncreated *esse*, the *esse personale* of the Person of Christ, then the nature receives the grace of union with the Eternal Word. And how does St. Thomas speak of the grace of union? He speaks in language that clearly implies obediential potency. In *ST* III, q. 1, a. 3, ad 3, he writes:

A double capability may be remarked in human nature: one, in respect of the order of natural power, and this is always fulfilled by God, Who apportions to each according to its natural capability; the other in respect to the order of the Divine power, which all creatures implicitly obey; and the capability we speak of pertains to this. But God does not fulfil all such capabilities, otherwise God could do only what He has done in creatures, and this is false, as stated above.[11]

There is something similar with respect to the *lumen gloriae*. According to Aquinas, the light of glory emends the ontological imperfections of human nature prior to the beatific vision, rendering it susceptible of immediate elevation to the vision. It achieves this not in virtue of *itself* but rather as an instrumental cause.[12] In instrumental causality, the effect is more proportioned to the principal cause than to the instrumental cause, as in writing a letter the correspondence is more configured to the mind of the author than

10. *De virtutibus*, q. 1, a. 10, ad 13: "Ad decimumtertium dicendum, quod quando aliquod passivum natum est consequi diversas perfectiones a diversis agentibus ordinatis, secundum differentiam et ordinem potentiarum activarum in agentibus, est differentia et ordo potentiarum passivarum in passivo; quia potentiae passivae respondet potentia activa: sicut patet quod aqua vel terra habet aliquam potentiam secundum quam nata est moveri ab igne; et aliam secundum quam nata est moveri a corpore caelesti; et ulterius aliam secundum quam nata est moveri a Deo. Sicut enim ex aqua vel terra potest aliquid fieri virtute corporis caelestis, quod non potest fieri virtute ignis; ita ex eis potest aliquid fieri virtute supernaturalis agentis quod non potest fieri virtute alicuius naturalis agentis; et secundum hoc dicimus, quod in tota creatura est quaedam obedientialis potentia, prout tota creatura obedit Deo ad suscipiendum in se quidquid Deus voluerit."

11. *ST* III, q.1, a. 3, ad 3: "Ad tertium dicendum quod duplex capacitas attendi potest in humana natura. Una quidem secundum ordinem potentiae naturalis. Quae a Deo semper impletur, qui dat unicuique rei secundum suam capacitatem naturalem. Alia vero secundum ordinem divinae potentiae, cui omnis creatura obedit ad nutum. Et ad hoc pertinet ista capacitas. Non autem Deus omnem talem capacitatem naturae replet, alioquin, Deus non posset facere in creatura nisi quod facit; quod falsum est, ut in primo habitum est."

12. Cf. Leonine *ScG* III, c. 54.

to the nature of the pen with which it is written. It is true that—*unlike* the divine assumption of human nature—the *lumen gloriae* perfects the created person *in the intentional order*, for in the beatific vision the creature does not substantially become God but is intentionally conformed in mind and heart to the inner life and love of God. Thus the beatific vision itself is not as radical a gift as is the gift of divine union of human nature with the Person of the Word (and arguably this gift of beatific vision belongs to Christ's humanity in the gift of union, but that is another disputed question).

Nonetheless, despite this difference between the *lumen gloriae* and the gift of union, there is one formal likeness analogically shared by these different graces. The human intellect needs to be elevated and purified to be immediately capable of a vision of the divine essence which is infinitely disproportionate to, and transcendent of, the human intellect. The created intellect must be made capable of knowing without any reliance on phantasms, abstraction, or the formation of a created concept: the divine essence is both the *medium quo* and the *objectum quod* of the vision, without any natural human concept. The beatified person must be made capable of an act and object which infinitely transcend the specific proportionate powers of human nature. Similarly, in creating human nature as assumed to the Word, that nature must be caused as immediately capable of subsisting in the *esse* of the Word and without possession of or reference to any separate created *esse*. As there is no created concept for the achievement of the beatific vision, so there is no *created esse* of the human nature required or even possible for its union with the divine Word (for in that case any such *esse* would make Christ's possession of human nature an accident, and the Word would not be a man). Further, as the *lumen gloriae* makes the intellect capable of an act and object that infinitely transcend all proportion to created nature, so the grace of union makes human nature capable of existing with the *esse personale*, the personal existence, of the Word. *Esse* is the form of forms, the act of acts, the perfection of perfections, and God Who is *Ipsum Esse Subsistens Per Se* possesses infinite power. Communicating the personal existence of the Word is not impossible for God, because unlike finite persons, the Person of the Word is not restricted by the limitations of finite nature from communicating the being in which he eternally subsists.

The *esse personale* of the Word has no temporal beginning. But the human nature does have a temporal beginning. The divine *esse* does not change.

But the human nature is capable of change. Thus the personal existence of the eternal Word actuates human nature in the suppositality of the Word, *but the human nature is related to the Word differently than is the divine nature.* This, too, has its own proportionate likeness in the case of the *lumen gloriae*. Divine knowledge is related differently to the divine essence than human knowledge is related to the divine essence in the beatific vision, *yet it is the same divine essence.* As the intellect in beatific vision is actuated by God as *medium quo and objectum quod*, so the human nature in Christ is actuated not by a proportionate human *esse* but by the very *esse* of the Eternal Word.[13] This *different relation* to the *esse* of the Word seems to the present author all that an *esse secundarium*—a second *esse* pertaining to the human nature—can plausibly mean.[14]

It is worth noting that this analysis is sustained whether one follows Cajetan's famed account of subsistence or the remarkable and profound analysis of Billot. Cajetan held that subsistence pertains to the order of essence: that it is a final terminating mode of the essence that renders it fitted actually to exist as an incommunicable subject of being. Billot held that only *esse* itself could constitute such a final perfection terminating the essence as an incommunicable subject. Cajetan held that the divine assumption of the human

---

13. There is a further point that manifests this analysis. According to Thomas, higher forms possess the powers of lower forms in a higher manner, *in virtute*, which means not "virtually" but "by power." But *esse* is *most formal*, the act of acts, *the form of forms*, the perfection of perfections, and the proper name of God is He Who Is, as God is *Ipsum Esse*. Of course it is not the same as substantial form, but there is an analogical relation according to proper proportionality according as *esse* is to essence as act is to potency, and form likewise is to matter as is act to potency. The infinite divine *esse* by whose power the Word can elevate a finite nature to union with himself possesses the whole perfection of existential act. Accordingly, by the divine omnipotence, God can uphold human nature in the personal existence of the divine Word.

Somewhat similar to the way that iron in the human body belongs to the person *in virtute* and is not separated "iron" (although in this case it belongs to the human nature as such), in Christ the human nature subsists with the personal existence of the divine Word and is not a separated human substance subsisting with a numerically distinct *esse*. It does not, of course, belong to the divine nature as such, which is impossible, but it is possessed *in virtute* within the infinite formal perfection of the divine *esse*, such that the human nature may be elevated to subsist in a nobler fashion with the *esse* of the Eternal Word.

14. If one wishes to say that this is because "esse" can be used analogically of nature rather than of existence (in God, a nature identical with *esse* as existing, in the creature, identical with the *quiddity* of the creature, which is not *esse* as *actual existence*), this may be true. But it would be by virtue of the diverse relations of the human and divine natures to the one *divine esse* in the sense of *actual existence* that "esse" can signify *without* reference to time vis à vis the divine essence, and *with* reference to time in the assumed humanity of Christ.

nature of Christ prevented it subsisting as a human person rather than in the Incarnate Word. *In either case, these analyses support a unitary divine esse for Christ* (which both defended). If one thinks (as do I) that these two diverse accounts of subsistence are the most metaphysically refined alternatives, this alone inclines one to read *De unione* as not contradicting the later writing in the *Summa theologiae*. Rather, *De unione* simply acknowledges that human nature terminates in the existence of the Word in a way different than does the divine nature because the Word is eternal, whereas the human nature receives union with the Word temporally. This is a second *esse* only *secundum quid* (and in *De unione*, Thomas affirms that Christ has one being "simpliciter" and two only *secundum quid*[15]). But this is simply to say that we distinguish that whereby the Word is divine from that whereby the Word is human, even in the unitary Person of Christ: not that the humanity of Christ fails to subsist in the one *esse* of the Word.[16]

---

15. *De unione verbi incarnati*, art. 4, resp. and ad 1.

16. See also *De unione verbi incarnati*, art. 2, ad 10: "To the tenth argument, it should be said that as long as the human nature is united to the Word, it does not have its own *suppositum* or hypostasis besides that of the person of the Word because that human nature does not exist according to itself. However, if the human nature were separated from the Word, it would not only have its own hypostasis or *suppositum*, but also its own person because then it would exist through itself. So, too, a part of a continuous body, as long as it is not divided from the whole, is in potency and not in act, but this is only done by a separation."—"Ad decimum dicendum, quod humana natura, quamdiu est Verbo unita, quia non secundum se existit, non habet proprium suppositum vel hypostasim praeter personam Verbi. Sed si separaretur a Verbo, haberet non solum propriam hypostasim aut suppositum, sed etiam propriam personam, quia iam per se existeret. Sicut etiam pars corporis continui, quamdiu est indivisa a toto, est in potentia, non est actu, sed solum facta divisione." It is difficult not to think that Cajetan may have been struck by the formulation above in developing his account of subsistence as a terminative mode of the essence rendering it incommunicable (a mode constituting the essence as a proximate potency for *esse*) and so sustaining the proposition that no created substance is its own *esse*. That such a terminative mode is only intelligible in relation to *esse* is no more problematic than that essence itself is only intelligible in relation to *esse* (which does not mean that *esse* is either identical with, or an occult note of, any created essence). Further, the very language of "first" and "second" substance connotes, one might observe, what one might think of as analogical "distance" vis à vis the final *actus essendi*. The substance is a *principium quod*, and the essence is a *principium quo*, but metaphysically the first implies and requires the second as a potential principle that is rendered incommunicable and constituted in a complete subjective potency for *esse* (otherwise there is not a proper subjective potency for the actuality of a complete substance). On such an account, subsistence being a terminating mode of the essence (rendering it a complete subject that is a proximate potency for existence), the obediential potency of the essence (under the active power of God) to be elevated to terminate in the Person of the Word rather than to form a separate whole, renders intelligible what elsewise would be opaque. The analogy of this elevation with the *lumen gloriae* and the beatific vision seems to hold with analogical precision, but this is so with respect to other analyses, too (e.g., Billot's). But further consideration of Cajetan's analysis, which is remarkable, is for another day.

CHAPTER 5

THE TRINITARIAN CONSCIOUSNESS OF CHRIST

Thomas Joseph White, OP

If no historical truth can be demonstrated, then nothing can be demonstrated by means of historical truths. That is: *accidental* [i.e., contingent] *truths of history can never become the proof of necessary truths of reason.*... It is said: "The Christ of whom on historical grounds you must allow that he raised the dead, that he himself rose from the dead, said himself that God has a Son of the same essence as himself and that he is this Son." This would be excellent! if only it were not the case that it is not more than historically certain that Christ said this. If you press me still further and say: "Oh yes! this is more than historically certain. For it is asserted by inspired historians who cannot make a mistake." But, unfortunately, that also is only historically certain, that these historians were inspired and could not err. That, then, is the ugly, broad ditch which I cannot get across, however often and however earnestly I have tried to make the leap.

Epigraph. Gotthold Lessing, "On the Proof of the Spirit and of Power," in *Lessing's Theological Writings*, ed. and trans. H. Chadwick (Stanford, CA: Stanford University Press, 1957), 53–54.

CROSSING LESSING'S DITCH:
THINKING ABOUT THE HISTORICAL
JESUS AS GOD IN HISTORY

Lessing's Ditch is often said to pose a core challenge to the Church's traditional confession of faith. Yet in fact it seems to indicate two distinct and in-
terrelated challenges. The first is the famous question of continuity between
the historical Jesus of Nazareth and the New Testament portrait of Jesus as
Christ, Lord, and Son of God. Is there any real continuity between the two
ontologically, and if so, how could we even know in any certain way, epistemologically? The second challenge is philosophical in character and has
to do with the presuppositions of anti-supernaturalist rationalism. Lessing
famously asks whether any contingent truth of history can in fact provide a
proof of reason, intimating that Christianity rests upon mistaken presuppositions of inference, for reasons of its grounds of appeal. In reality, this second question is about whether we can know any universal truths other than
by means of the philosophical and scientific study of natural realities. Lessing presumably believed what he read in the newspaper about local events,
or what was reported to him of the results of scientific experiments, but only
because these truths correlated with his expectations about the world based
upon naturalistic beliefs. The quandary of Lessing's Ditch presupposes that
the supernatural claims of divine revelation in the Bible must be understood
by what David Hume and Ernst Troeltsch would later call a "principle of
analogy."[1] Any real contingent causes in the past must be just the same as
natural causes we can observe now and articulate in universal form. Consequently, natural causes alone should be referred to when we seek to explain
biblical history. There is insufficient warrant to believe in any supernatural
causality reported historically, precisely because it violates the norms of nature represented by this naturalistic presupposition.[2]

1. See David Hume's recourse to the analogy from natural causes as a unique explanatory principle
in "Of Miracles," section X of his 1748 work, *Enquiries Concerning Human Understanding and Concerning the Principles of Morals*, 3rd ed. (Oxford: Clarendon Press, 1975). Ernst Troeltsch, "Über historische und dogmatische Methode in der Theologie, Gesammelte Schriften," in *Gesammelte Schriften*,
vol. 2 (Tubingen: J. C. B. Mohr [Paul Siebeck], 1913), 728–53.

2. The idea has its early modern origins in Benedict Spinoza, *Theological Political Treatise*, ed.
J. Israel (Cambridge: Cambridge University Press, 2007). See the analysis of the naturalism of Spinoza's

From these two problems (the problem of the historical Jesus and the challenge of naturalistic causal explanation) emerge four kinds of approaches to Christology in the modern era. Each takes a position on these two questions. A first approach (which we can call naturalistic-apophatic) posits that we cannot explain the world reasonably except by recourse to natural causes, but also that we cannot reasonably get back to any historically substantial understanding of who the Jesus of history was prior to the New Testament writings. The New Testament is theology "all the way down," but insofar as it denotes supernatural mysteries, miracles, or exceptional statements of Christ regarding his preexistence, it is not rationally credible. Speaking schematically, we might say that this is the pathway of David Friedrich Strauss and Rudolf Bultmann.[3] A second kind of approach (which we can call theological and apophatic) posits that the New Testament is rightly understood as divine revelation of the Son of God in history but that we cannot reconstruct a historical account of who Jesus was prior to and in any kind of proximate independence from the New Testament. This is the way of Martin Kähler and Karl Barth. We should abandon the epistemological works' righteousness of studies of the historical Jesus and learn about the truth of Christ from the grace of the Holy Spirit that illuminates us through the medium of Scripture.[4] A third approach (which we can call naturalistic and kataphatic) posits that we cannot understand the origin of the Bible by recourse to supernatural causality, or must at least abstract from any such question when studying history, but that we can attain a fairly reliable historical portrait of the historical Jesus. Most of the mainstream *intelligentia* in the historical Jesus studies movement inhabit this niche, from Albert Schweitzer to Ernst Käsemann, and from E. P. Sanders to Geza Vermes.[5] They

---

biblical exegetical method, which had a direct influence upon Lessing, in Jonathan I. Israel, *Radical Enlightenment: Philosophy and the Making of Modernity, 1650–1750* (Oxford: Oxford University Press, 2002).

    3. David Friedrich Strauss, *The Christ of Faith and the Jesus of History: A Critique of Schleiermacher's Life of Jesus*, trans. L. Keck (Philadelphia: Fortress Press, 1977); Rudolf Bultmann, *New Testament Theology*, trans. K. Grobel (Waco, TX: Baylor University Press, 2007).

    4. Martin Kähler, *The So-Called Historical Jesus and the Historical Biblical Christ*, trans. Carl E. Braaten (Philadelphia: Fortress, 1964). Karl Barth, *Church Dogmatics*, 4 vols., ed. and trans. G. W. Bromiley and T. F. Torrance (Edinburgh: T&T Clark, 1936–75), 1:1. See, e.g., pp. 399–406.

    5. Albert Schweitzer, *The Quest of the Historical Jesus: A Critical Study of Its Progress from Reimarus to Wrede*, trans. J. Bowden (Minneapolis: Fortress Press, 2001); Ernst Käsemann, *Essays on New Testament Themes*, trans. W. J. Montague (London: SCM Press, 1964); E. P. Sanders, *Jesus and Judaism*

seek to carefully uncover a likely depiction of who Jesus was before the Gospel, so to speak, according to naturalistic criteria of explanation. The final approach (theological and moderately kataphatic) is that which posits that it is intellectually warranted to explain the unfolding of history by recourse to God's real activity in history, including in his self-revelation, incarnation, prophecy, and miracles, but that it is also feasible from New Testament sources to consider who the historical Jesus was in his own era prior to the early Christian movement and in his own historical context. Here we could arguably think of exegetes who accept methodologically the possibility of supernatural causal explanation, such as Raymond Brown, Martin Hengel, N. T. Wright, and John Meier. We can also mention theologians such as Wolfhart Pannenberg, Walter Kasper, Hans Urs von Balthasar, and Joseph Ratzinger.[6] Of course, this last category encompasses a wide variety of approaches, but all of these authors confess the divinity of Christ as a reality of history and to some extent believe that we can characterize Jesus constructively within his own historical setting before and as causally related to the unfolding of the Christian movement, with more or less confidence in the New Testament depictions of Christ as reliably historically indicative.

Catholic theologians have, it seems to me, the possibility of associating themselves with either the second or fourth of these approaches, and the key differences between them will depend upon whether and to what degree each one thinks that a historical reconstruction is either feasible epistemologically or warranted apologetically and theologically.[7]

(London: SCM Press, 1985); Geza Vermes, *Jesus in His Jewish Context* (Minneapolis: Fortress Press 2003).

6. Raymond E. Brown, *An Introduction to New Testament Christology* (New York: Paulist Press, 1994); Martin Hengel with A. M. Schwemer, *Jesus und das Judentum, Geschichte des frühen Christentums* (Tübingen: Mohr Siebeck, 2007); N. T. Wright, *Jesus and the Victory of God: Christian Origins and the Question of God* (Minneapolis: Augsburg Fortress, 1996); idem, *The Resurrection of the Son of God: Christian Origins and the Question of God* (Minneapolis: Augsburg Fortress, 2003); John P. Meier, *A Marginal Jew: Rethinking the Historical Jesus*, Anchor Bible Reference Library Series 1–5 (New York: Yale University Press, 1991–2016); Wolfhart Pannenberg, *Jesus God and Man*, 2nd ed., trans. L. L. Wilkins and D. A. Priebe (Philadelphia: Westminster Press, 1968); idem, *Systematic Theology*, vol. 2, trans. G. W. Bromiley (Grand Rapids, MI: Eerdmans, 1994); Walter Kasper, *Jesus the Christ*, trans. V. Green (London: Burns & Oates, 1976); Hans Urs von Balthasar, *Theodrama: Theological Dramatic Theory*, 5 vols., trans. G. Harrison (San Francisco: Ignatius, 1988–98); Joseph Ratzinger, *Jesus of Nazareth*, 3 vols. (New York: Image, 2007–12).

7. The Second Vatican Council dogmatic constitution on divine revelation, *Dei Verbum*, sec. 8, 12, and 19, acknowledges implicitly the warrant of New Testament historical studies, a position reiterated

For those who identify with the fourth approach, as I myself do, there remains still a fundamental question of methodological discernment. Let us presume that the principles of divine revelation do not derive from modern historical-critical study of historical Jesus as such. We know that Jesus exists now in the Resurrection and that he truly lived among us as the Son of God to redeem the human race, not because we have demonstrated it per se by historical research, but because we are enlightened by the grace of faith through the formal medium of apostolic testimony, the New Testament read within the context of the living tradition of the Church, her liturgy, her saints, and her teaching magisterium.[8] Nevertheless, it remains to be determined whether we first study Jesus in history so as to argue for the rational probability that he made high claims about himself, for example, or whether believing already in his sonship, divinity, and sinless humanity, based on the testimony of Scripture, we attempt to depict in a plausible way based on modern historical methods, how he most likely spoke of himself in his own era, and how that self-depiction, his teaching and his actions, gave rise to the early Christian movement.

The first approach is merely rational. The Christian believer attempts qua historian to enter into the secular presuppositions of his historical colleagues and to show it is merely possible or even probable that Jesus spoke of himself and the Kingdom of God in ways that did lead in turn to beliefs such as those that the early Christians held. Consequently, the study of the historical Jesus cannot be used to invalidate the faith, and perhaps at its best, it may be seen to demonstrate some truth of the faith "externally," not by yielding knowledge of the object of faith as such (known by grace alone) but by manifesting its rational intelligibility, under an aspect or part. For example, one might argue that Jesus truly took himself to be the preexistent Son of God, or that he performed miracles, or that there is no other viable way to explain

---

in its own way in the 1992 *Catechism of the Catholic Church*, §§105–33. (Unless otherwise specified, references to Church documents are taken from official translations at www.vatican.va.) But one can affirm the basic principles of the Church in this regard and remain skeptical about the epistemological warrant of any modern reconstruction of a portrait of Jesus outside of and "prior" to the depiction offered by the New Testament writings. See the recent restatement of this position, which resembles that of Kähler, by Luke Timothy Johnson, *The Real Jesus: The Misguided Quest for the Historical Jesus and the Truth of the Traditional Gospels* (San Francisco: Harper, 1996).

8. I am presuming here a Catholic ecclesiology, while recognizing that some commitment to tradition and Chalcedonian doctrine in particular is common to many Protestants who investigate these matters.

the rise of the early Christian movement historically than by reference to the Apostles' experiences of the bodily resurrection.[9] Of course, Christians may themselves differ greatly on the viability of any such arguments.

The second approach is less apologetic and more theologically constructive, and it is far more prevalent in the systematic theology guild.[10] It seeks to provide a historically informed *theological* portrait of the historical Jesus, his life, ministry, miracles, sayings, conflicts, death, and historical resurrection. It is formally speaking theological or doctrinal because it averts to the truths of the New Testament revelation as a fundamental given, but it makes subalternate use of reasonable historical arguments and associations regarding history to derive a probable or possible depiction of a Jesus of history that stands in accord with the traditional confession of Christian faith.[11]

9. At least in aspiration, this seems to be the way John Maier speaks about the method he wishes to undertake in the first volume of *A Marginal Jew*, chap. 1. Larry W. Hurtado can be seen as documenting post-resurrection early Christian intellectual history in this way in *Lord Jesus Christ: Devotion to Jesus in* Earliest Christianity (Grand Rapids, MI: Eerdmanns, 2005), where he argues that the worship of Christ (as God) is primitive and organically developmental in early Christianity.

10. This practice is found diversely in Pannenberg and Kasper, Balthasar and Ratzinger. N. T. Wright does not necessarily present himself in this way, but I take it that in reality he fits in this category methodologically. As I take it, this kind of theological stance trascends the distinction between "Christology from below," which uses historical illustrations and arguments to manifest revealed principles and argue for their historical cogency, and "Christology from above," which begins from the confessional givens of the New Testament and the dogmatic and theological tradition of the Church and may then subsequently express the principles in a historical way by use of illustrations and arguments derived from a historical-critical methodology.

11. I am appealing here to two ideas found in Aquinas. The first is that the supernatural mystery of the Trinity revealed in Christ is discernable and intelligible in virtue of the grace of faith, which permits the intellect to make a new judgment in the reality of the mystery. As such, faith as a gift allows us access to the "formal object" of faith. Second, Aquinas distinguishes the material object of a given science from the formal medium by which it is known. For example, one may know something about God (the subject matter in question) either through the formal medium of natural reason (philosophical metaphysics) or through the formal medium of revelation (and the assent of supernatural faith). The theologian may make use of both formal mediums but subordinate one to the other, making use of philosophical metaphysics in the service of faith. Sometimes, however, a given "science" does not have a pure autonomy of object and method but is "sub-alternated" to another, as musical denotation depends on principles of mathematics, and theology depends upon the possibility of a perfect knowledge of God by grace (one that is possessed ultimately by the saints in heaven). Exegesis inevitably considers the mysteries of the faith revealed in the New Testament, whether it acknowledges these or not, since they are overtly presented in historical fashion in the Old and New Testaments. Consequently, to the extent that exegesis is something that one can do without overtly referring to theologically revealed mysteries, it is merely a "sub-alternated" science or method, not a subordinate one. In short, exegetical consideration of the "formal truth" contained in Scripture does not have pure scientific autonomy. The exegete ultimately either has to try to make sense of divinely revealed truth (as expressed in its historical context) or reject that there is such a revelation (based on nonhistorical philosophical, naturalistic

After all, what we do typically when we try to present people in history is to construct a likely narrative and contextual depiction that explains a series of causes and effects under a given set of conditions. Here that kind of historical methodology is simply sub-alternated to the study of God made human, his life, teaching, death, and resurrection.[12] I take it that the latter approach is the most warranted for Catholic theology. This being stated, we can return to the problems posed by Lessing's Ditch and think of how modern Catholic theology might respond to them.

Based on what I have argued above, Catholic theologians can and should adopt a twofold approach. First, they approach the matter by averting intellectually to the formal object of faith, the knowledge of the Son of God in history that is made known by divine revelation and the grace of faith. The apostolic doctrine of the New Testament and the Church's dogmatic teaching, then, are not proven to natural reason but first believed and assent is given to the intelligibility of the mystery as a gift of grace, not a conquest of natural reason. To argue for the latter approach exclusively would be in this context epistemological Pelagianism. In reality, as the apostolic teaching suggests, authentic knowledge and apprehension of Jesus as the eternal Son of God made man are made possible only by the grace of faith, which allows one to believe in the apostolic testimony and perceive its truth inwardly. "Simon Peter replied, 'You are the Christ, the Son of the living God.' And Jesus answered him, 'Blessed are you, Simon Bar-Jona! For flesh and blood has not revealed this to you, but my Father who is in heaven'" (Mt 16:16–17). "No one can say 'Jesus is Lord' except by the Holy Spirit" (1 Cor 12:3).

Second, one may also approach the question of who the historical Jesus was from the point of view of natural reason, assembling and judging the historical evidence of the various depictions of Jesus in the New Testament (or other sources) as providing likely evidence of the historical figure himself, or as merely possibly doing so, or as probably not doing so, with various degrees

---

principles). I have treated this question in greater detail in *The Incarnate Lord: A Thomistic Study in Christology* (Washington, DC: Catholic University of America Press, 2015), 53–61. See Aquinas, *ST* I, q. 1, aa. 2, 3, 5, 7, 8; II–II, qq. 1–2.

12. As noted previously, I take it that this epistemological stance obtains whether one begins with the Church's confession of Chalcedonian faith (Jesus Christ is true God and true man) and then proceeds to articulate its inner historical content (so-called Christology from above) or begins from a historical description of Jesus in view of an argued discernment of the principles of faith manifest in the historical portrait as rendered (so-called Christology from below).

of likelihood in each category. Most scholars, for example, think it is highly probable that Jesus of Nazareth was baptized by John or that he spoke about the Kingdom of God. Few scholars ascribe historical reliability to stories or sayings attributed to Jesus in the Gospel of Thomas (though there are exceptions). Between the two extremes of highly probable and highly improbable, there is a vast range of reasonable conjectures concerning a multitude of singular features of the historical life and teaching of Jesus. Historical Jesus scholars, then, each assemble a vast collection of historical conjectures that they argue to be reasonable and probable, placing them individually into a system of mutual reinforcement so as to create by a mixture of art, historical reasoning, and factual basis a collective portrait of Jesus. The Catholic theologian may make use of some set of arguments collated from within this vast field, subordinate to and in the service of the theological approach indicative of the first approach (theological consideration of the revelation of Jesus given by the New Testament). In other words, in the dual-approach method I am describing, the formal object of faith comes first and is primary: the confession that Jesus is God; has become incarnate; has lived a revelatory human life among us; been crucified, died, and raised bodily from the dead; and is the source of grace. The presentation of the unfolding of his human life in its historical context is not obligatory for faith, but the theologian can make use of such modern methods to depict his life, teaching, and ministerial aims within that context in ways that are consonant with both divine revelation and responsible modern historiography.[13]

13. Of course, what I am saying here also presupposes from a philosophical point of view that one opposes Lessing's natural presuppositions, which are influential and utterly contestable from the standpoint of natural reason. The human being does learn about necessary truths of human reason through historically contingent circumstances and makes use of such learning all the time. Human beings as embodied rational agents learn principally through traditions of their communities by trusting in the reports of others, and they infer truths about nature and the created order over time through repeated experiences of the very ontological structure of things that they encounter in singular repeated fashion, not through a priori laws of reason. Finally, God—if God exists as the author of all else that is—can of course become incarnate in principle since God precisely as the cause of all that exists is omnipotent. Consequently, just because he is the author of being, he is able to manifest himself in creation and history in ways that exceed the realm of nature and our understanding of nature. It is not odd to think he should wish to do so either, from a philosophical point of view, if God wishes us to know him interpersonally, since all human beings as embodied rational agents typically come to know others through an encounter with them in sensible form. Consequently, it cannot be shown to be irrational for God to encounter us personally by becoming human. In fact, exegetical positions that take Lessing's Ditch as an epistemologically warranted starting point are based primarily on naturalistic philosophical

"GOD WAS IN CHRIST
RECONCILING THE WORLD
TO HIMSELF" (2 COR 5:19):
WAS JESUS HIMSELF AWARE OF
THIS, AND IF SO, HOW?

I have noted two challenges that Lessing poses to any modern form of Chalcedonian Christology: that concerning the possibility of a historical depiction of Jesus and that concerning the reality of supernatural revelation in history. The vexing topic of the human self-consciousness of Christ touches upon both of these questions in key ways. After all, the Gospels themselves depict Jesus as being humanly aware of the significance of his own identity as the Son of God, and as seeking to draw out a confession of faith from the Apostles: "Who do men say that I am?" (Mk 8:27; see also Mt 16:13–20 and Jn 14:9). How, then, might theologians rightly understand the self-consciousness and aims of Jesus in his own original historical context, based upon the New Testament portrait of him that we have from the Apostles? How might this depiction be defended historically as probable in respect to the historical Jesus, as the historical origin or "founder" of the early Christian movement? Does the self-consciousness of Jesus manifest in some way his ontological status—that he is the preexistent Son of God and therefore is one in being and nature with the Father and the Spirit? Relatedly, as he is depicted in the New Testament, does he manifest awareness of this filial identity, and does his deity have any effect upon the natural operation of his human intellect?

Clearly, it is reasonable to argue that if God became human and manifested his identity to us in a human way through his words and gestures,

---

presuppositions, not historical discoveries that they procure from study of the New Testament. Just to the extent that they do so, they are not based on sound principles of natural reason. The advantage of Lessing's challenge, however, is that it invites both Christians and non-Christians to treat the Bible as a human text (even if it is also divinely inspired) and so to think out in deeper ways how and why it was humanly written, in what circumstances, and for what ends, all of which ultimately is helpful to the cause of historical realism, since the mystery of God is truly revealed in and through real communities of living people, beginning in ancient Israel and culminating in the early Church. The study of this process is not threatening to a reasonable form of Christian faith but is beneficial when conducted responsibly.

life and death, then he, God the Son, was humanly aware of his own transcendent identity in some way. At the same time, it is the also the case that Jesus's historical consciousness needs to be understood against the backdrop of his historical context, in the culture of Second Temple Judaism. If both these claims are true, then Jesus must have expressed his filial consciousness, his human awareness of his divine identity, in ways that were typical of his time.[14]

Yet again here we face options. We might accord ourselves to the fourth of my approaches mentioned previously and think that the Son of God in his human life among us assumed a state of such lowliness that he was even somehow unaware of his divine status or only able to perceive it faintly and imperfectly. Or perhaps the question can simply be left to the side. Wolfhart Pannenberg, for example, claims that Jesus understands himself as a reformer of the law and a designated minister of God bringing about a supreme initiative in view of an eschatological Kingdom of divine rule.[15] As is well known, Pannenberg believes in the divinity of Christ and argues theologically and historically for the reality of the bodily resurrection of the Lord.[16] He allies this modest view of Jesus's historical self-awareness with these other high claims by arguing for its fittingness, for ontological and soteriological reasons. Ontologically, it signals the free kenotic self-emptying of the eternal Son who lives out his eternal obedience to the Father precisely

---

14. In the words of the *Catechism of the Catholic Church*, §§472–74: "This human soul that the Son of God assumed is endowed with a true human knowledge. As such, this knowledge could not in itself be unlimited: it was exercised in the historical conditions of his existence in space and time. This is why the Son of God could, when he became man, 'increase in wisdom and in stature, and in favor with God and man' (Lk 2:52), and would even have to inquire for himself about what one in the human condition can learn only from experience. This corresponded to the reality of his voluntary emptying of himself, taking 'the form of a slave' (Phil 2:7). But at the same time, this truly human knowledge of God's Son expressed the divine life of his person. 'The human nature of God's Son, not by itself but by its union with the Word, knew and showed forth in itself everything that pertains to God.' [St. Maximus the Confessor, *Qu. et dub*. 66 PG 90, 840A] Such is first of all the case with the intimate and immediate knowledge that the Son of God made man has of his Father. The Son in his human knowledge also showed the divine penetration he had into the secret thoughts of human hearts. By its union to the divine wisdom in the person of the Word incarnate, Christ enjoyed in his human knowledge the fullness of understanding of the eternal plans he had come to reveal. What he admitted to not knowing in this area, he elsewhere declared himself not sent to reveal (cf. Mk 13:32 and Acts 1:7)." I have attempted to reflect on this issue in greater depth in "The Infused Science of Christ," *Nova et Vetera*, English ed. 16, no. 2 (2018): 617–41.

15. Pannenberg, *Systematic Theology*, 2:328–34.

16. Pannenberg, *Systematic Theology*, 2:343–72.

in and through this human self-expression of intellectual searching and un-knowing.[17] It is fitting soteriologically because it shows that Christ not only suffered innocently in the crucifixion but also nesciently, not understanding perfectly what transpired. In this respect he descended innocently into our alienation from God as one who is without sin, so as to exchange places with us, by a kind of penal substitution, one only now envisaged in light of mod-ern historical studies.[18] Karl Rahner takes a slightly different approach: the historical Jesus saw himself as the ultimate eschatological emissary of God, the one who would bring Israel's history of prophetic witness to the reign of God to its perfection for all the nations. He referred to God as his Father. His resurrection not only confirms this mystery of Jesus's self-designation as eschatological prophet but also manifests plainly that his designation of God as his Father was implicitly indicative of his ontological Sonship and his preexistent Deity.[19] For both Pannenberg and Rahner, Jesus is recognized as God most especially in light of his resurrection, and not owing to his his-torical human consciousness or aims. The Gospels are written in the wake of the Easter mystery and could be seen to project back onto the historical Jesus certain features of post-paschal illumination present in the Christian community. Their approach thus removes from us any theological burden of having to demonstrate that prior to his bodily resurrection, Jesus Christ in history possessed an elevated self-awareness or consciousness of his own transcendent identity as the preexistent Son of God.

---

17. Pannenberg, *Systematic Theology*, 2:377: "In his form of life as Jesus, on the path of his obedi-ence to God, the eternal Son appeared as a human being. The relation of the Son to the Father is char-acterized in eternity by the subordination to the Father, by the self-distinction from the majesty of the Father, which took historical form in the human relation of Jesus to God. This self-distinction of the eternal Son from the Father may be understood as the basis of all creaturely existence in its distinction from God, and therefore as the basis of the human existence of Jesus, which gave adequate embodiment in it is course to the self-emptying of the Son in service to the rule of the Father. As the Incarnation of the Logos was the result of the self-emptying of the eternal Son in his self-distinction from the Father, so the self-humbling of Jesus in obedience to his sending by the Father is the medium of the manifesta-tion of the Son on the part of his earthly life." Pannenberg sees the intra-Trinitarian, eternal kenosis of the Son as the foundation of his human obedience and notes in his exposition that he is following Karl Barth in this motif, based on the arguments found in *Church Dogmatics* IV, 1, section 59.

18. Pannenberg, *Systematic Theology*, 2:416–29.

19. Karl Rahner, *Foundations of Christian Faith: An Introduction to the Idea of Christianity*, trans. W. V. Dych (New York: Seabury, 1978), 228–64.

AN ALTERNATIVE PROPOSAL:
THE THEANDRIC HUMAN CONSCIOUSNESS
OF CHRIST

At this point we can note that the way we treat the question of the consciousness of Christ in Catholic theology relates profoundly to the way we understand the two natures of Christ and their relations. How is the human nature of Jesus—which includes of course his human mind and heart—affected or influenced by his identity as the Son of God and by his divine nature? And likewise, what is the soteriological importance of Christ's historical consciousness? Does he save us primarily through kenosis and by the solidarity of identification with us in our human condition? Is the Resurrection the core way in which we discover the divinity of the Lord? As Bruce Marshall has noted, a prominent trend in modern Christology can be characterized by the twofold phrase "before the resurrection, all hail the historical critical method, after the resurrection, all hail the Nicene creed."[20] It is true that Pannenberg and Rahner, and with them biblical scholars like N. T. Wright, make room for a broad array of visions of the historical Jesus as a subject in history whose ordinary human consciousness could be marked by his cultural context and whose self-designation and perhaps even self-assessment could evolve in a human way, all while preserving a confession of Chalcedonian faith. Nor can they be accused of a classical Monophysitism that downplays the reality of the Lord's authentic humanity. Precisely in their effort to underscore the historicity of the human Christ, however, they do seem to minimalize the reality of his divine nature, at least insofar as it has any impact upon his human nature in his concrete historical context. Consequently, core elements of the Gospel's depiction of Jesus Christ seem to be missing and soteriological dimensions of the Incarnation obscured. Here I will identify briefly only a few significant ways in which this is the case.

Most centrally, what is missing in the influential modern theological accounts mentioned above is the acknowledgment that Jesus's knowledge of his own identity is a key dimension of the mystery of the Incarnation and likewise has important soteriological consequences. Jesus, precisely because

20. I'm indebted for this helpful phrase to personal conversation with Professor Marshall.

he knows who the Father is, knows who he himself is as the Son of the Father. "No one knows the Father but the Son and no one knows the Son but the Father and those to whom the Father reveals him" (Mt 11:27). The so-called Johannine thunderbolt of Matthew's Gospel is of only secondary importance as a probable historical record of Jesus's very words. It is of primary importance as evidence of a *theological claim* about the historical Jesus made by the early Church: Christ as man knew himself to be the exclusive Son of the Father and sought to transmit this saving knowledge to us. Analogously, the Gospel of John underscores that the Son made man knows who the Holy Spirit is: "When I go to the Father, I will send you the Paraclete the spirit of Truth" (Jn 14:6). When we receive the Spirit of Christ, we receive the Spirit he came into the world to give us, which he intended to effect through his voluntary acceptance of death.

Obviously, the depictions of Jesus's self-knowledge in Matthew and John are elevated in nature and have overt soteriological reverberations. The two main ones are these. First, an integral dimension of Jesus's visible mission (the Son's coming into the world) is to reveal to us in a human way, within our history, who the Father is, who he is, and who the Spirit is. To speak in a later idiom: the visible mission of the Son-made-man both reveals and effectuates knowledge of the Trinitarian life of God, the eternal processions of the persons of the Trinity. Second, and relatedly, Jesus is only the Savior of the human race because he can and does reveal to us this truth. Salvation is not only about his atoning death (as Pannenberg risks to make it), or even about union with the divine (as Rahner risks to make it), but also about initial and eventually perfected human knowledge of the Trinity. Salvation is effectuated ultimately, in other words, by our union with God through knowledge and love of God by faith in this life and by vision in the next. Jesus of Nazareth can only illuminate us—as distinct from being illuminated himself by the Father in his resurrection—if he is able during his earthly life to manifest the truth about God in his teaching, actions, miracles, and suffering unto death.[21] He manifests to us in his historical earthly life that he is one with the Father, and is truly God with us, giving us to know God in himself.

21. Aquinas makes an argument to this effect in *ST* III, q. 9, a. 2. See also *ST* III, q. 7, a. 1, where Aquinas notes that Christ as man must have a plenitude of habitual grace in order to complete his saving mission and to communicate truth and grace to others as the mediator of salvation.

We may join these reflections with two further claims, one regarding the theandric acts of Christ and one regarding the soteriological offering of the Cross. Theandric acts are acts Jesus can perform in virtue of his divinity and his humanity operating simultaneously.[22] For example, he is depicted in all four canonical Gospels as someone who is aware of his capacity to act in union with God to accomplish miracles, as signs of the Kingdom and presumably as anticipations of the mystery of the Resurrection. "When he entered the house, the blind men came to him; and Jesus said to them, 'Do you believe that I am able to do this?' They said to him, 'Yes, Lord.' Then he touched their eyes, saying, 'According to your faith be it done to you'" (Mt 9:28–29). The mysterious power of God resides in him, and he can deploy this power actively when he should so wish.[23] Actions of this kind implicitly

22. Aquinas, *ST* III, q. 19, a. 1, ad 3: "To operate belongs to a subsisting hypostasis; in accordance, however, with the form and nature from which the operation receives its species. Hence from the diversity of forms or natures spring the divers species of operations, but from the unity of hypostasis springs the numerical unity as regards the operation of the species: thus fire has two operations specifically different, namely, to illuminate and to heat, from the difference of light and heat, and yet the illumination of the fire that illuminates at one and the same time is numerically one. So, likewise, in Christ there are necessarily two specifically different operations by reason of His two natures; nevertheless, each of the operations at one and the same time is numerically one, as one walking and one healing." *ST* III, q. 19, a. 1, ad 1: "Dionysius places in Christ a theandric, i.e., a God-manlike or divine-human, operation not by any confusion of the operations or powers of both natures, but inasmuch as His Divine operation employs the human, and His human operation shares in the power of the Divine. Hence, as he says in a certain epistle (*Ad Caium* iv), 'what is of man He works beyond man; and this is shown by the Virgin conceiving supernaturally and by the unstable waters bearing up the weight of bodily feet.' Now it is clear that to be begotten belongs to human nature, and likewise to walk; yet both were in Christ supernaturally. So, too, He wrought Divine things humanly, as when He healed the leper with a touch. Hence in the same epistle he adds: 'He performed Divine works not as God does, and human works not as man does, but, God having been made man, by a new operation of God and man.'" All citations from the *ST* are taken from *Summa Theologica*, 1920 English Dominican Translation (New York: Bengizer Brothers, 1947). On the theandric action of Jesus as pertaining to modern theological options, see also White, *Incarnate Lord*, chaps. 1 and 5.

23. John Damascene, *The Orthodox Faith*, III, c. 15: "The power of miracles is the energy [i.e., natural operation] of His divinity, while the work of His hands and the willing and the saying, *I will, be thou clean* (Mt 8:3), are the energy [i.e., natural operation] of His humanity. And as to the effect, the breaking of the loaves (Jn 6:11), and the fact that the leper heard the 'I will,' belong to His humanity, while the multiplication of the loaves and the purification of the leper belong to His divinity. For through both, that is through the energy of the body and the energy of the soul, He displayed one and the same, cognate and equal divine energy. For just as we saw that His natures were united and permeate one another, and yet do not deny that they are different but even enumerate them, although we know they are inseparable, so also in connection with the wills and the energies we know their union, and we recognize their difference and enumerate them without introducing separation. For just as the flesh was deified without undergoing change in its own nature, in the same way also will and energy are deified without transgressing their own proper limits. For whether He is the one or the

manifest the numinous unity of Jesus with the God of Israel, and Jesus is of course depicted as being humanly aware of his capacity to act thus as the Son of the Father. Based on this understanding of the mission of Jesus, his Trinitarian consciousness is present manifestly or implicitly in all that he says and does as Son: within his miracles, parables of the Kingdom, authority claims, prophecies regarding the Crucifixion and Resurrection, and eschatological foretellings. The theandric activity of Jesus as both God and man implies the presence in him of a distinctive human awareness and judgment, as Jesus connotes his interpersonal relation to the Father and the Spirit through a range of actions and teachings.

This Trinitarian consciousness of Jesus is also present in his act of self-offering in the passion and the crucifixion. The three Synoptic authors depict Christ as predicting his death and intimating that it has a universal saving meaning.[24] One may also argue that Jesus's denotations of himself as the "Son of Man" are eschatological in meaning, and that his several associations of himself with the Suffering Servant of Isaiah 53 are meant to have redemptive connotations.[25] In John 10:18, he is depicted as stating explicitly that he intends to lay down his life in death and to take it up again, in resurrection, in view of the salvation of the world.

The upshot of such statements is significant for classical soteriology. Anselm of Canterbury argues in the *Cur Deus Homo* that the redemption is accomplished in part because the Son of Man willingly gave his life to the Father out of love for the Father and the human race, meritoriously, even in the midst of trials and sufferings. This self-offering was meritorious for man because it was the offering of a sinless human being, but it was of infinite value because it was the offering of one who is God.[26] This vision of

---

other, He is one and the same [person], and whether He wills and energizes in one way or the other, that is as God or as man, He is one and the same [subject or hypostasis]." P. Schaff and H. Wace, ed.; E. W. Watson and L. Pullan, trans., *Nicene and Post-Nicene Fathers, Second Series*, vol. 9 (Buffalo, NY: Christian Literature Publishing, 1899).

24. Mk 8:31: "the Son of Man must suffer many things ... and be killed, and after three days rise again." See also Mk 9:22, 10:33–34; Mt 16:21, 17:22, 20:17–18; and Lk 9:22, 17:25, 18:31–33.

25. E.g., most famously, Mk 10:45: "For the Son of man also came not to be served but to serve, and to give his life as a ransom for many."

26. See Anselm, *Why God Became Man*, I, cc. 11–25; II, cc. 6–7, especially as interpreted by Aquinas, *ST* III, q. 48, aa. 1–4, and *ScG* IV, c. 55. B. Davies and G. R. Evans, eds., *Anselm of Canterbury: The Major Works* (Oxford: Oxford University Press, 2008); *Summa contra Gentiles IV*, trans. C. J. O'Neil (Garden City, NY: Doubleday, 1956).

substitutionary atonement, in which Christ has offered himself in our stead, in true love and obedience where we have failed to love and obey, is at the center of the Catholic liturgy, in which the Church humbly and obediently claims to offer the merits of Christ to the Father in the sacrifice of the Mass and to commune in the grace of self-offering he extends to the Church so that she may herself in turn offer herself with Christ.[27] All this presumes in some real sense that the Jesus of history truly intended to offer his life for the sins of the world and was conscious of doing so. If we accept the prevalent modern model of Christology that minimizes Jesus's historical self-consciousness of his own identity, these features of New Testament revelation and sacred Tradition are rendered obscure in significant ways.

PROPORTIONATE HISTORICAL CAUSALITY AND THE HIGH CLAIMS OF CHRIST

If we are to pursue the line of argument I am making, we must confront a theological objection. Are we not obliged to understand all the aspects of Jesus's self-awareness as presented in the New Testament that I am mentioning here merely as post-paschal theologoumena? That is to say, are they not all retrospective projections of the early Christian community back onto the historical life of Christ, meant to articulate in explicit fashion what was only implicitly contained in his historical life, and understood after his resurrection? After all, it is precisely the appeal of theologians like Pannenberg and Rahner that they can accede to the theological substance of the New Testament teaching about the meaning of Jesus and the real, ontological significance of his life, even while maintaining a more modest view of his initial historical self-awareness. The advantage of this viewpoint, seemingly, is that we are allowed to maintain our dogmatic commitments while maintaining simultaneously only a minimal and therefore apologetically defensible set of claims about the historical Jesus, his aims, sayings, and deeds. Likewise, by drawing attention to the epistemological importance of the Resurrection,

---

27. *Catechism of the Catholic Church*, §§1362–72.

which alone allows us to realize the deeper truth about Christ, we under-score accurately where the real difference lies between believers and nonbe-lievers with regard to the confession of Jesus as Christ, Lord, and Son. This objection assuredly represents a coherent alternative viewpoint. However, there are four intellectually problematic ideas that it presupposes.

First, the idea that a later historical figure has a more perfective or en-riched view than an earlier figure is not always realistic. For example, is it true that the writings of later Platonists typically improve upon the earlier thinking of Plato? Do their writings convey more energy and depth than his, as they bring his initial intuitions to perfection or debate their possible interpretations and consequences? The same might be said of Aristotle, or Augustine, or Aquinas. Often the original source is the most powerful. Like-wise, as Romano Guardini pointed out in his seminal work *The Humanity of Christ*, the grand statements of Matthew or John that we see placed on the lips of Jesus are indeed presentations after the fact by the early Christian community, but they might also be diminutions marked by a lesser plenitude of perfection in their expression than the grandeur of the original statements themselves.[28] Historical development is not always perfective or evolutive in the world of ideas. In fact, it is almost always the case that the spiritual source is greater than the recipient who reports or transmits.

Second, one can see the apologetic value of the stance I am criticizing. It seems to allow for the full human realism of a Jesus having only a mod-est special knowledge coupled with a divine realism concerning the Incar-nation and Resurrection. But the apologetic value of this idea should not be overstretched. If God truly can become human, and learn in a human way through a culture in a time and place, and also can raise the dead bodily to re-deem the real world, then he surely also can convey divine truth to the human intellect of Christ within the course of his ordinary human history, within the context of Second Temple Judaism. There is no difficulty for God in his causality to both respect all that is integrally human and to be present and to manifest himself effectively in and through all that is integrally human.

Third, there is an argument from fittingness for a more elevated human self-understanding in Christ. This argument begins from the premise that

28. Romano Guardini, *The Humanity of Christ: Contributions to a Psychology of Jesus*, trans. R. Walls (New York: Random House, 1964).

he should have the historical plenitude of knowledge in himself and convey it to his Church. This is the case because he is the savior of the Church, not a member awaiting salvation only after resurrection. That is to say, if Christ is the savior of other human beings and their unique fontal source of grace, then it is fitting that he should be the source of epistemological knowledge also in the order of grace and have it in the most perfective sense. The ambiguity that results, otherwise, is that Christ should receive eventual knowledge of his own identity from another (e.g., from the Father, not during the Son's human life among us but only after the Resurrection), and the Apostles should know more or the same truths as Christ does, at the same time, by a means other than his instruction (e.g., also by being illumined by the Father after the Resurrection). The Christological communication of salvation is obscured in this way. This criticism is even strengthened if we consider that, according to the theory under discussion, the early Christians can be said to have had an explicit knowledge of Christ's identity during the course of their historical lives that Jesus himself did not have during the course of his historical life. But it is unfitting to claim that the Apostles after the Resurrection and the Pentecost should as first-century Jews within their context have a more perfect explicit knowledge of the Lord than he had during the course of his life, especially since they are members of his same epoch and culture.

Finally, there is a historical principle of causal explanation that follows from the last point. It is most reasonable to think that many of the teachings of the Apostles concerning Christ, his identity and redemptive death, his intentions and the sacraments, came from Jesus himself, not merely from a set of realizations and experiences that transpired after the Resurrection. An obvious example concerns the words of the narrative of the institution of the Eucharist: "and when he had given thanks, he broke it, and said, 'This is my body which is for you. Do this in remembrance of me.' In the same way also the cup, after supper, saying, 'This cup is the new covenant in my blood. Do this, as often as you drink it, in remembrance of me'" (1 Cor 11:24–25). As Martin Hengel has argued, it is difficult to see how we could locate the origin of the various institution narratives of Mark and Matthew, Luke and Paul in anyone other than the historical founder of Christianity.[29] And yet

29. See Martin Hengel, *The Atonement: The Origins of the Doctrine in the New Testament*, trans. J. Bowden (Philadelphia: Fortress, 1981).

to institute a ritual of sacrifice making allusion to Exodus 24:8 taking place outside the temple, with twelve appointed followers present as the seeming symbol of a new Israel, all suggests an elevated consciousness on the part of the one instituting the rite. Here the theory of causal explanation for the genesis of the Church overlaps closely with the previous argument from fittingness, that Jesus should especially and above all understand what he was doing, and that the Apostles should understand it only afterward in the Spirit, and even then less perfectly than the Lord.[30]

JESUS'S HEBRAIC TRINITARIAN CONSCIOUSNESS

In the final part of this essay, I would like to suggest briefly how one might hold that the historical Jesus possessed an elevated human consciousness of his own identity and unity with the God of Israel while expressing himself in the idioms and cultural modes of expression of his time. I will consider briefly four topics. First, from the point of view of Aquinas's Christology, how might we understand the real integrity of the acquired knowledge of Christ in relation to his beatific vision and infused knowledge? Second, how might the historical consciousness of Christ be affected by his cultural linguistic context in his acquired learning and teaching? Third, what do we mean by the Trinitarian consciousness in a Thomistic light? Fourth, how

---

30. See in this respect the 1985 document of the International Theological Commission, *The Consciousness of Christ Concerning Himself and His Mission*, which maintains four propositions concerning Christ's human consciousness as normative for Catholic theology: (1) "The life of Jesus testifies to his consciousness of a filial relationship with the Father." (2) "Jesus was aware of the purpose of his mission: to announce the Kingdom of God and make it present in his own Person, in his actions, and in his words, so that the world would become reconciled with God and renewed. He freely accepted the Father's will: to give his own life for the salvation of all mankind. He knew the Father had sent him to serve and to give his life 'for many' (Mk 14:24)." (3) "To realize his salvific mission, Jesus wanted to unite men with the coming Kingdom and to gather them around himself. With this end before him, he did certain definite acts that, if taken altogether, can only be explained as a preparation for the Church, which will be definitively constituted at the time of the Easter and Pentecost events. It is therefore to be affirmed of necessity that Jesus willed the foundation of the Church." (4) "The consciousness that Christ had of being the Father's emissary to save the world and to bring all mankind together in God's people involves, in a mysterious way, a love for all mankind so much so that we may all say: 'The Son of God loved me and gave himself up for me' (Gal 2:20)." This fourth proposition seemingly underscores the universality of Christ's soteriological intention.

might we think about the Hebraic Trinitarianism of the historical Jesus, by which he expressed his identity in the language and modes of his time? Here I mean only to indicate pathways of interpretation, to intimate a larger view that is possible.

Aquinas on Acquired Knowledge

As is well known, Aquinas denies that the Christ of the Gospels has faith or that he believes in his own divinity. Rather, he knows as man by an intuitive and immediate knowledge who he is subjectively, as the Son of God, and in this same light has an immediate knowledge of the Father and the Holy Spirit.[31] What is more, he also has a habitual infused or prophetic knowledge by which he is given to know not always but only habitually what is needed for the sake of his mission, regarding the future, the state of the souls of those around him, the capacity he has to heal this or that person, and so forth.[32] These two forms of knowledge overlap in part regarding their objects but differ according to mode. Christ's immediate knowledge of the Father is constant, nonconceptual, and intuitive and stems in a sense from his hypostatic union, since it permits him to know himself in his person, the Father and the Holy Spirit.[33] It has an economic and soteriological function for Aquinas. Christ as man possesses the plenitude of the knowledge of God in view of his mission. It is a dimension of the way in which he is fully human, and head of the Church, able to communicate this grace to others instrumentally.[34] Meanwhile, the infused science of Christ is actualized habitually, determined by infused species, and is given in view of Christ's particular needs in his mission.[35] Both of these forms of graced knowledge, however, are embedded within and respect the integrity of Christ's natural acquired

31. On Aquinas's teaching regarding the beatific vision in the earthly life of Christ, see *ST* III, qq. 9–10; White, *Incarnate Lord*, chap. 5; and Simon Gaine, *Did the Saviour See the Father? Christ, Salvation, and the Vision of God* (London: Bloomsbury T&T Clark, 2015).

32. *ST* III, q. 11.

33. See on this Thomas Joseph White, "*Dyotheletism* and the *Instrumental* Human *Consciousness* of Jesus," *Pro Ecclesia* 17 (2008): 396–422.

34. I take it there is an intimate connection between the arguments of *ST* III, q. 7, a. 1, q. 8, aa. 1–2, and q. 9.

35. *ST* III, q. 11, a. 5.

knowledge.[36] As Jean-Pierre Torrell has noted, Aquinas is the first medieval to make prominent use of the notion of a natural human acquired knowledge in Christ, so as to underscore the reality of his humanity, his natural abstract manner of knowing, and the phantasmal and linguistic conditions of his knowledge as man.[37]

Historical Conditions of the Consciousness of Christ

None of these Thomistic themes just indicated pertain directly, of course, to the question of what consciousness is. Aquinas himself rarely uses this word in Latin, *conscius*, though he does interestingly ascribe it to the Father in the mystery of the Transfiguration, saying that the Father is conscious of the Son.[38] If we are to think about Jesus's natural self-awareness as man in a modern light and thus to think about his consciousness, we should note the following. First, although "consciousness" can be understood in many ways, it is reasonable for our purposes to provide a generic definition. Generally speaking, consciousness is any form of self-awareness in an agent of knowledge that results from and accompanies the activity of knowledge, be it sensate or intellectual in kind. In short, one is conscious when one is aware of one's self knowing something. The mode in which one is self-conscious depends upon the medium of knowledge. One can be aware in a sensate way of one's sensate act of knowing other realities. One can be intellectually aware of one's self in the intellectual act of knowing other realities. The generic definition, then, is based on the self-awareness that accompanies knowledge, and the specific definition is based on the mode or medium of knowledge by and through which one is aware of one's self knowing.[39] This

36. This is the general argument of my "Infused Science of Christ."

37. See Jean-Pierre Torrell, "Le savoir acquis du Christ selon les théologiens médiévaux," *Revue Thomiste* 101 (2001): 355–408.

38. *ST* III, q. 45, a. 4: "Since, therefore, it is in baptism that we acquire grace, while the clarity of the glory to come was foreshadowed in the transfiguration, therefore both in His baptism and in His transfiguration the natural sonship of Christ was fittingly made known by the testimony of the Father: because He alone with the Son and Holy Ghost is perfectly conscious (*conscius*) of that perfect generation."

39. For my reflections on consciousness, from a philosophical point of view, I am indebted in a general way to reflections in Bernard Lonergan, *The Ontological and Psychological Constitution of Christ*, *Collected Works*, vol. 7 (Toronto: University of Toronto Press, 2002). "Consciousness is an interior

definition is helpfully broad because it can be applied to both nonhuman animals and to human beings. In turn, it also permits a generic definition of human consciousness that includes both our specifically sensate animal features of knowledge and our distinctively rational, conceptual, and voluntary forms of self-awareness. It is therefore applicable to the experiences we have of ourselves, in and through our external and internal senses, as well as our intellectual and volitional states.

Second, consciousness implies presence to self. As noted, self-awareness is distinct from knowledge of another reality outside ourselves. It takes place in virtue of that knowledge and through a formal medium, and it depends upon it. When we contemplate the beauty of a natural reality (like a tree or a mountain), or speak to another person in conversation, we also are aware of ourselves as agents of knowledge and in a sense are present to ourselves, sensibly and intelligibly, in virtue of our knowing activity.

Third, consciousness can only formalize itself in and through concepts wed to cultural linguistic contexts with their various symbols and conventional norms of thought. If, for example, Jesus was aware of himself as the Son of God in virtue of his graced immediate knowledge and his infused science (stemming from his created grace), he must nevertheless also have been humanly aware of who he is in an ordinary conscious way, through the medium of his ordinary human self-awareness (stemming from his human nature). This would require that he reflect upon himself in the linguistic tropes and symbols of Second Temple Judaism, not only in order to make himself understood but also more fundamentally because he is human. To think discursively as man, he must make use of acquired knowledge, by which he reflects conceptually and expresses himself in the language and signs of his culture.

---

experience of oneself and one's acts, where 'experience' is taken in the strict sense of the word. 'Experience' may be taken in a broad or in a strict sense. Broadly speaking it is roughly the same as ordinary knowledge; strictly speaking it is a preliminary unstructured sort of awareness that is presupposed by intellectual inquiry and completed by it" (157). Consciousness here is understood not as the "perception of an object" (mere knowledge) but rather as an awareness of one's self as a subject. Consciousness, therefore, is more fundamental than thinking and is preconceptual, but it also is present as a dimension of "objective" thinking: the dimension of self-reflexivity, or self-awareness in thinking. Christ's linguistic and conceptual thinking as a first-century Jew pertains to his consciousness, therefore, just as much as his preconceptual (affective, intuitive, and sensible) human experience of himself in the world. Yet the former is part of his consciousness only insofar as he is also aware of himself as a subject in and through his objective thinking about the world, himself, and the like.

Trinitarian Consciousness

If Jesus of Nazareth expressed himself in a typically human way, as one who is conscious of himself within the given culture and linguistic tropes of his age, he did so nonetheless as one who was also humanly aware that he is the transcendent Son of God and who was aware, however numinously, that he can and does act in unity with the Father and with the Holy Spirit.[40] His human consciousness therefore is Trinitarian in form insofar as he is aware (in however clear or vague a way) that he is a subject who is eternally from the Father, who has come into the world to redeem the world, and because he knows he is the recipient of the Spirit of the Father upon whom the Spirit reposes, and who will send the Spirit upon others.[41] This interpersonal Trinitarian set of intuitions, we might say, stands as the backdrop of all of Jesus of Nazareth's human activity and intentions.

This interpersonal form of knowledge has a distinctive soteriological importance as well. As depicted in the Gospels, the historical Jesus is aware, however clearly or vaguely, of his divine origin and capacity to work with the Father and the Spirit. Consequently, his actions of miraculous healing, like his words and parables, as well as his suffering and death, *reveal a set of personal relationships* that he is aware of as man. They reveal his personal intimacy with the Father and the Spirit, and therefore implicitly manifest to us the true inner identity of God as Trinity.[42] This knowledge is salvific because

40. Jn 5:36: "the works which the Father has granted me to accomplish, these very works which I am doing, bear me witness that the Father has sent me." Jn 10:25: "The works that I do in my Father's name, they bear witness to me." Jn 10:37–38: "If I am not doing the works of my Father, then do not believe me; but if I do them, even though you do not believe me, believe the works, that you may know and understand that the Father is in me and I am in the Father." Jn 15:26: "But when the Counselor comes, whom I shall send to you from the Father, even the Spirit of truth, who proceeds from the Father, he will bear witness to me."

41. See on this topic Dominic Legge, *The Trinitarian Christology of St. Thomas Aquinas* (Oxford: Oxford University Press, 2018), 172–86.

42. Commenting on Jn 14:10, "I am in the Father and the Father is in me," Aquinas writes: "The belief that Christ was God could be known from two things: from his teaching and from his miracles. Our Lord mentions these. 'If I had not done among them the works which no one else did, they would not have sin' (15:24). Referring to his teaching he says, 'If I had not come and spoken to them, they would not have sin' (15:22). We also read: 'No man ever spoke like this man!' (7:46). The blind man, referring to his works, said: 'Never since the world began has it been heard that any one opened the eyes of a man born blind' (9:32). Our Lord shows his divinity by these two things. Referring to his teaching, he says, The words that I say to you, by the instrument of my human nature, I do not speak of myself,

it communicates to us an awareness of who God truly is in himself and inaugurates the possibility of our genuine union with God by faith, hope, and charity, culminating in the configuration to Christ our head in the grace of the Resurrection. Because Jesus knows the Father, he can reveal the Father to us in his human speech and gestures (denoting his relation of origin). Because Jesus knows who he is as Son, he can reveal his own identity (denoting himself as Lord and Son). Because he is aware of the Spirit, he can promise to send the Spirit upon us and tell us about his activity (denoting the procession and mission of the Spirit). In each of these modes he is communicating saving knowledge of the Holy Trinity.

Hebraic Trinitarianism

If this set of claims is true, then we can also think about Christ's human self-expression of his Trinitarian identity within the context of first-century Israelite culture. How or in what *culturally locative* way is he humanly aware that he is God, the Son of God, one with the Father, and so forth? Here we are asking how the historical Jesus himself, prior to the records given to the Gospels, might have spoken about himself in his own historical context within the setting of late Second Temple Judaism, so as to convey to another an impression of his own identity and give rise to the early Christian movement, including the forms of designation that are attributed to him in the Gospel and epistles. Let us consider a few potential examples.

First, we see in the New Testament that Jesus makes use of both functional and ontological Sonship language. Does this form of speech have a historical intelligibility if we consider it within the context of Jesus's own historical lifetime, in the context of Israelite Judaism? Consider the parable of the usurping tenant farmers from Matthew 21:33–46. Jesus is depicted as telling a story of the prophets of ancient Israel who are represented as emissaries of a landowning king, systematically rejected by the Israelites who

---

but from him who is in me, that is, the Father: 'I declare to the world what I have heard from him,' the Father (8:26). The Father, therefore, who speaks in me, is in me. Now whatever a human being says must come from the first Word. And this first Word, the Word of God, is from the Father. Therefore, all the words we speak must be from God. So, when anyone speaks words he has from the Father, the Father is in him. Referring to his works, he says, the Father who dwells in me does the works, because no one could do the works that I do: 'The Son can do nothing of himself' [5:19]." *Commentary on the Gospel of St. John*, Marietti ed., trans. F. Larcher (Albany, NY: Magi Books, 1998), para. 1893.

took the land to be their own, until such time as the King decides to send his Son who the tenants kill, thinking that they will inherit the land once and for all. This simple story is not Hellenistic in origin but seemingly marked by Israelite sensibilities and in that context is clearly deeply provocative in character.[43] It presents a bird's-eye view of the divine economy of prophecy that culminates in the mission of the Son. But the Son is himself not merely distinct in function but also in personal identity since he is the Son of the King and not a mere servant. Jesus's self-awareness of his functional and ontological distinctiveness is reflected here in parabolic form and is communicated in a way that is accessible to the widest possible audience. This kind of popular preaching can be seen reasonably as a way that Jesus of Nazareth initially indicated implicitly his unique sonship. To this simple example we could add the many and varied ways that Jesus in the Gospels seemingly refers to himself not only as a son of God but as the exclusive Son of God, denoting his awareness of a unique ontological status.

A second example: we find clear indications in Jesus's self-designating speech in the Gospels of a divine name theology. John's Gospel famously depicts Christ applying the divine name to himself, for example, in 8:48–59, where he claims that "before Abraham was I am." Jesus also seems to use the phrase in Mark, both in 6:50 while walking on the sea of Galilee and in 14:62 at his trial before the high priest, where he says "I am" to denote his own identity or presence.[44] The phrase is ambiguous in both instances and may suggest an intimation of the divine identity subtly manifest in Jesus's historical speech acts. In Matthew's resurrection scene (28:19), no doubt highly schematized, the Apostles encounter Christ on a mountain in Galilee that echoes Sinai and receive anew the name of God, "Go and baptize in the name of the Father, the Son and the Holy Spirit."[45] These various literary portraits of Jesus are clearly highly affected by post-paschal context and Christian confessional awareness. Nevertheless, someone had to have been the first person to designate Jesus as Lord by making use of the divine name, and in fact the Gospels are in accord in depicting Jesus of Nazareth himself

---

43. See the argument to this effect by James H. Charlesworth, *Jesus within Judaism* (New York: Doubleday, 1988), 131–64: "Jesus' Concept of God and His Self-Understanding," esp. 139–43.

44. See the reflections of Hurtado, *Lord Jesus Christ*, 285–86, and Joel Marcus, *Mark 1–8: A New Translation with Introduction and Commentary*, Anchor Bible (New York: Doubleday, 2000), 432.

45. Hurtado, *Lord Jesus Christ*, 331–32, 338–39.

as this person. Subsequent Christians would speak of Christ as Lord, presumably with the implication of the Hebraic euphemism, by which the divine name was denoted in Greek as *Kyrios*. So we see Paul express the divine name of Christ clearly in many passages such as Philippians 2:6–11, where he is given the "name above any other name."[46] Consequently, there is a real possibility of historical continuity between Jesus's own self-designation as I Am, and the early Christian movement's designation of him as the "Lord Jesus Christ."[47]

Finally, there are the many possibly implicit or overt allusions Jesus makes to his own preexistence.[48] "I came to cast fire on the earth, and would that it were already kindled" (Lk 12:49). "Do not think that I have come to bring peace on earth; I have not come to bring peace but a sword" (Mt 10:34). "For this I was born and for this I have come into the world, to bear witness to the truth" (Jn 18:37). The statements of origin may only refer to a temporal mission, but they also could be meant to signify an origin in God and a preexistent mission. Again, we find the New Testament offering us a historically plausible depiction of Jesus articulating a seed idea that later appears in other New Testament writings articulated in thematic fashion: that God so loved the world that he sent his only begotten Son (Jn 3:16) and that when the time had fully come, God sent forth his Son, born of a woman, born under the law (Gal 4:4).[49]

---

46. Regarding the Pauline divine name theology of Phil 2:6–11, see Richard Bauckham, *God Crucified: Monotheism and Christology in the New Testament* (Grand Rapids, MI: Eerdmans, 1998), 66–77.

47. The case is strengthened when we see Christ's self-depiction as "one with the Father" or as having the authority that pertains normally to God to forgive sins, (re)interpret the law, or denominate the significance of the temple and the "sacraments" of ancient Israel.

48. See on this point Simon Gathercole, *The Pre-Existent Son: Recovering the Christologies of Matthew, Mark and Luke* (Grand Rapids, MI: Eerdmans, 2006).

49. The case is strengthened when we observe the eschatological self-designations of Jesus as the ultimate emissary of God, the Son of Man, the principle of judgment (e.g., Mk 8:38; Mt 16:27). The idea of him being the "omega" of salvation history is mirrored by his being the "alpha" who comes into the world and has his authority from the Father. We find this protology and eschatology correlated in the New Testament in Col 1:15–20, in the Rv 4–5 theology of the eschatological Lamb correlated with Rv 21–22, in Paul's theology of the Son's resurrection in Rom 13–3, and in 1 Cor 15:45 as simultaneously a manifestation of the preexistent Sonship and as a cosmic principle of re-creation denoting the final state of things. Is it really so difficult to envisage this later Christological teaching of the Apostles as coming from the Jesus of history, at least in seed, under slightly different idioms?

CONCLUSION

My conclusion from these reflections is threefold. First, it is fitting that Christ should possess a human self-consciousness of his own divine identity and that he should give expression to it in and through the cultural idioms of his day, for ontological reasons, precisely because of his divine identity and owing to the reality of his human nature and his historically situated, acquired human knowledge. Second, there are soteriological implications to this view. Christ must know who the Trinity is to reveal to us who God is and to offer his life meaningfully to the Father on behalf of the human race. Therefore we should be inclined to see the New Testament prescriptions to Jesus of an elevated awareness of his identity as historically realistic, again for theological reasons. Third and finally, it is possible if not necessary to depict the historical Jesus as one who denoted himself as having a divine identity and a Trinitarian consciousness within the historical conditions of his age, communicated through the medium of Hebraic idioms, of Sonship, divine naming and preexistent mission. Lessing depicts in summary fashion the crisis of Christology: it concerns belief in the modern world in the reality of God's presence among us in history, and in the capacity we might have in the modern era to tell a concrete historical story of the way God's human life among us unfolded. Catholic theologians and scriptural exegetes have every reason to make use of modern historiographical methods in the service of the explication of the New Testament and the articulation of the mystery of faith. They can do so, however, precisely so as to illustrate what the first letter of St. John announces both to the Church and to whole human community, that through the medium of faith we have come into living contact with the very mystery of God dwelling among us in the flesh:

That which was from the beginning, which we have heard, which we have seen with our eyes, which we have looked upon and touched with our hands, concerning the word of life—the life was made manifest, and we saw it, and testify to it, and proclaim to you the eternal life which was with the Father and was made manifest to us—that which we have seen and heard we proclaim also to you, so that you may have fellowship with us; and our fellowship is with the Father and with his Son Jesus Christ. And we are writing this that our joy may be complete. (1 Jn 1:4)

CHAPTER 6

MUST AN INCARNATE DIVINE PERSON ENJOY THE BEATIFIC VISION?

Simon Francis Gaine, OP

One part of the current crisis in Christology, a crisis that involves the kind of Savior we need, has been the state of Christ's human knowledge while on earth. Was he clueless, or was he clued in? Catholic theologians have traditionally held the latter. Like many such theologians, St. Thomas Aquinas taught that part of the way Christ was clued in was his earthly possession of the beatific vision in his human mind, a view that fell out of favor among Catholic theologians in the middle of the twentieth century. Objections included its meagre attestation in Scripture and the Fathers, and its alleged incompatibility with the earthly Christ's authentic humanity, especially in regard to his intellect, freedom, suffering, and even the presence in him of faith.[1] More recently, in responding to these objections, disciples of St. Thomas have led a return to his teaching that Christ always enjoyed this knowledge and that there were reasons why he *had* to have it.[2] But in what sense of "must," *must* Christ have enjoyed the beatific vision?

The arguments Thomists have employed in favor of his vision's necessity have generally fallen into two kinds, soteriological and metaphysical. The

The author expresses his thanks to Fr. Dominic Ryan, OP, and Fr. Oliver Keenan, OP, for the helpful comments they made on an earlier draft of this chapter.

1. See Simon Francis Gaine, OP, *Did the Saviour See the Father? Christ, Salvation and the Vision of God* (London: Bloomsbury T&T Clark, 2015).

2. For the recent fortunes of the thesis, see Gaine, *Did the Saviour See the Father?*, 3–14.

first—soteriological—contends that, given the content of God's saving plan, in which human beings are called to the beatific vision, Christ needed that vision to be our Savior. Aquinas used such an argument when he said in the *Summa Theologiae* that Christ possessed that vision in order to bring us to the same vision too:

> Human beings are brought to this end of beatitude through the humanity of Christ, as is said in Hebrews [2.10]: "It befitted him, for whom all things are and through whom all things are, in bringing many sons to glory, to perfect the author of their salvation through suffering." And so the beatific knowledge which consists in the vision of God had to belong to Christ the human being pre-eminently, since the cause ought always to be more powerful than what it causes.[3]

While Aquinas's argument hardly excludes metaphysical elements, it is at bottom soteriological: through the Fall, humanity lost the original grace that ordered it to the beatific vision, but now the blessed Christ has come as the fitting Savior to lead us through grace to share his vision of glory. As such, this argument does not entail any absolute necessity of the beatific vision for Christ; rather, this knowledge is necessary to equip him in a most fitting way for God's freely chosen plan of salvation. This necessity is more one of fittingness than an absolute necessity, and as far as this kind of argument goes, the beatific vision is not required for an incarnation in all possible worlds.

The second kind of argument—metaphysical—typically contends, in contrast, that the vision follows by strict necessity from the very fact of the hypostatic union, implying that this would hold even if the Son, or any other divine person, had become incarnate without any salvific purpose. The nineteenth-century Neo-Thomist Matthias Joseph Scheeben made just such an argument in his *Mysteries of Christianity*.[4] His view is that, in contrast to us, who live initially without the beatific vision and only afterward are admitted to it, Christ cannot inhabit any state prior to that vision. Since Christ is the divine Son of God by nature, even in his humanity he must

---

3. St. Thomas Aquinas, *ST* III, q. 9, a. 2.

4. Matthias Joseph Scheeben, *The Mysteries of Christianity* (St. Louis, MO: Herder, 1947), 325–26. On Scheeben, see Aidan Nichols, OP, *Romance and System: The Theological Synthesis of Matthias Joseph Scheeben* (Denver, CO: Augustine Institute, 2010), esp. 330–31. On his doctrine of Christ's beatific vision, see R. M. Schmitz, "Christus Comprehensor: Die 'Visio Beatifica Christi Viatoris' bei M. J. Scheeben," *Doctor Communis* 36 (1983): 347–59.

enjoy the fullness of divine Sonship. What this entails is that he can never be separated from God in the way that would be involved in any state less than the beatific vision. In other words, Christ had "fully achieved glory and beatitude from the very first instant."[5] Scheeben evidently supposed that this fact must hold, whatever the circumstances of the Incarnation:

Not only could this be so, it had to be so, unconditionally. It is unthinkable that the Son of God would not from the beginning have stood in closest and highest union with His Father even in His human nature, and that He would have strengthened and perfected this union only by degrees. But such would be the case if He had not from the first instant looked upon His Father face to face, if He had had to stand afar off like a stranger, and if, as a result, He had not been able to embrace His Father with that love in which the blessed in heaven are consumed. As there is no closer union with God than hypostatic, personal union, there can be no kind of union with God by knowledge and love that did not exist from the beginning in consequence of the hypostatic union of Christ's humanity with the Son of God. Owing to the hypostatic union, that humanity from the moment of its conception was present in God's bosom, to which creatures are raised only gradually and imperfectly; and in God's bosom it had also to gaze upon God's countenance, and to embrace God not with a love of longing and striving, but with a love of possession and fruition.[6]

In short, the hypostatic union necessarily entails a perfection of Christ's soul that cannot but include beatific knowledge. It seems to me that, if this did indeed hold for the Son, it must hold equally, *mutatis mutandis*, for the Father and the Holy Spirit too: *any* incarnate divine person must possess this supernatural perfection as a necessary consequence of his incarnation. Whatever an incarnation's purpose, then, the beatific vision will just follow automatically from the perfect human mind necessarily assumed by any divine person in any possible world.

While a soteriological argument is always one of fittingness and never of absolute necessity, however, a metaphysical argument may be presented in terms of fittingness as well as of strict entailment. The appeal of theologians to the hypostatic union and the perfection of Christ's soul has not led in every case to a conclusion presented as of absolute necessity. As well as those who have followed Scheeben, there are also those who formulate such

5. Scheeben, *Mysteries of Christianity*, 325.
6. Scheeben, *Mysteries of Christianity*, 325–26.

arguments in terms of a necessity of fittingness only, making it "most fitting" rather than altogether necessary for an incarnate divine person to enjoy the perfection of this vision.[7] Aquinas himself seems to have done something similar in the case of one of his arguments for Christ's habitual grace, where he concludes from the hypostatic union to his most fitting possession of this grace:

> We must say that habitual grace must be supposed in Christ ... on account of the union of his soul with the Word of God. For the nearer something receptive is to an inflowing cause, the more it participates in its influence. But the influx of grace is from God, as it says in Psalm [83.12], "The Lord will give grace and glory." Therefore it was most fitting that his soul received the influx of divine grace.[8]

Thus while Scheeben held habitual grace to follow the hypostatic union by absolute necessity,[9] as with the beatific vision, Aquinas treated habitual grace here as "most fitting" to it.[10] Whether Aquinas held that the beatific vision itself was "most fitting" or instead followed by absolute necessity from the fact of the Incarnation has been disputed.[11] I shall return to this question toward the end of this essay, after an examination of the character of some contemporary arguments in favor of the earthly Christ's beatific knowledge.

In my own defense of Christ's beatific vision in *Did the Saviour See the Father? Christ, Salvation and the Vision of God*, I preferred a soteriological argument to one of absolute metaphysical necessity. Those who have argued that Christ's beatific vision was a necessary part of his "very metaphysical structure"[12] I treated as conflating the orders of being and knowledge, such that the presence of the Word in the hypostatic union was confused with the presence of the Word as object of knowledge. I maintained that Aquinas, in contrast, carefully distinguished the orders of being and knowledge and the divine presence in each. In this way, while I did not reject the metaphysical

7. E.g., Guy Mansini, OSB, "Understanding St. Thomas on Christ's Immediate Knowledge of God," *The Thomist* 59 (1995): 91–124.

8. *ST* III, q. 7, a. 1.

9. Scheeben, *Mysteries of Christianity*, 322–24.

10. Whether or not Aquinas held overall that habitual grace follows the Incarnation by absolute necessity is in fact disputed. See Dominic Legge, OP, *The Trinitarian Christology of St Thomas Aquinas* (Oxford: Oxford University Press, 2017), 135–45.

11. Luigi Iammarrone, OFM, "La visione beatifica di Cristo Viatore nel pensiero di San Tommaso," *Doctor Communis* 36 (1983): 287–30; Mansini, "Understanding St. Thomas."

12. William G. Most, *The Consciousness of Christ* (Front Royal, VA: Christendom, 1980), 168.

argument that the beatific vision was, like habitual grace, "most fitting" to an incarnate divine person, I did not endorse the argument that it followed by absolute necessity. Instead, I agreed with Marie-Joseph Nicolas that a "more rigorous theology of the incarnation" allows for God's power to cause an incarnation in the order of being without a (beatific) union in the order of knowledge.[1]

In this light, I attempted to explore the divine wisdom of choosing an incarnation that in fact had beatific knowledge follow from the hypostatic union and concluded that the reason for this choice was fundamentally soteriological: God's salvation of us as revealed in Scripture. I noted that when Karl Rahner in his own theology supplanted Christ's beatific vision with the "direct vision" he held to be entailed by the Incarnation, he took this metaphysical necessity to be an advantage over the Thomist account, which he correctly interpreted as requiring some kind of witness for Christ's beatific knowledge in Scripture.[2] My response was to treat the Thomist reliance on Scripture as an advantage that sought a closer relationship between systematic theology and biblical exegesis, where the biblical text raises questions for the theologian.[3] Rather than pursue a theory of the kind proposed by Rahner in relative isolation from Scripture, I formulated a basically soteriological argument for Christ's possession of the beatific vision designed to make sense of the saving Teacher we find in the Gospels.[4] In this way, I continued an earlier trend in Thomism to treat Christ's knowledge in terms of his teaching needs.[5] The picture of Christ found in Gospels as one teaching us divine truth in a human way raised for me the theological question of how Christ is equipped to perform this saving work.[6] In seeking theological understanding of what we find here in Scripture, I drew on the scriptur-

---

1. Gaine, *Did the Saviour See the Father?*, 17. The quotation is from Marie-Joseph Nicolas, OP, "Voir Dieu dans la 'condition charnelle,'" *Doctor Communis* 36 (1983): 384–94 (385).

2. Gaine, *Did the Saviour See the Father?*, 15–16. See also Karl Rahner, SJ, "Dogmatic Reflections on the Knowledge and Self-Consciousness of Christ," in *Theological Investigations*, vol. 5, *Later Writings* (London: Darton, Longman and Todd, 1966), 193–215.

3. Gaine, *Did the Saviour See the Father?*, 18.

4. See Gaine, *Did the Saviour See the Father?*, esp. 39–41, 71–102.

5. Cf. Simon Francis Gaine, "Is There Still a Place for Christ's Infused Knowledge in Catholic Theology and Exegesis?," *Nova et Vetera*, English ed. 16 (2018): 601–15 (605–6).

6. See also Simon Francis Gaine, "How Could the Earthly Jesus Have Taught Divine Truth?," In *Christ Unabridged: Knowing and Loving the Son of Man*, ed. George Westhaver and Rebekah Vince (London: SCM, 2020), 82–93.

al doctrine of the beatific vision and its theological explication by Aquinas, seeking understanding of the earthly Christ's knowledge in the light of the beatific knowledge enjoyed by the saints.[7] In other words, the conclusion that beatific knowledge in fact followed the hypostatic union brings us deeper understanding of how the earthly Christ taught us saving truth. My argument, while including metaphysical elements, was at bottom soteriological.

It is hardly unimportant whether an argument for Christ's beatific knowledge is basically metaphysical or soteriological, and I present two reasons for this. First, arguments for Christ's beatific vision are, I find, typically assumed even by teachers of theology to be always ones of absolute metaphysical necessity based on Christ's perfection, and such arguments are often assumed to be weak and so are dismissed in the classroom without serious consideration.[8] This means that a soteriological argument can be easily overlooked if it is assumed to be simply metaphysical. Second, soteriological arguments have the inherent advantage of presupposing that God could have done otherwise and that an incarnate divine person as such need not possess beatific knowledge, which at the same time throws into relief the wisdom of God's choice in actually blessing Christ in this way.[9] For these reasons it is crucial that a soteriological argument be perceived for what it is. So, having found that contemporary defenders of Christ's beatific vision are sometimes perceived as presenting arguments that are more metaphysical than soteriological, when this is by no means the case, I offer here the following response. I suggest that two of these contemporary defenders, Fr. Thomas Joseph White and Fr. Dominic Legge, while in no sense neglecting metaphysics in their Christologies, in fact present arguments for Christ's beatific vision that are significantly soteriological. In conclusion, I make an argument from Aquinas's structuring of the *Summa* that he himself in fact ruled out metaphysical arguments for the absolute necessity of Christ's vision.

In chapter 5 of his collection of Christological essays, *The Incarnate Lord,*

---

7. Gaine, *Did the Saviour See the Father?*, 71–102.

8. Cf. Jean Galot, "Le Christ Terrestre et la vision," *Gregorianum* 67 (1986): 429–50; J. P. Galvin in F. Schüssler Fiorenza and J. P. Galvin, eds., *Systematic Theology: Roman Catholic Perspectives* (Dublin: Gill & Macmillan, 1992), 293n89; Thomas Joseph White, OP, *The Incarnate Lord: A Thomistic Study in Christology* (Washington, DC: Catholic University of America Press, 2015), 240–46.

9. See my account of contemporary appropriation of Aquinas's Christology in Matthew Levering and Marcus Plested, eds., *The Oxford Handbook of the Reception of Aquinas* (Oxford: Oxford University Press, 2021), 673–88.

White proposes an argument for Christ's beatific vision, which he says Aquinas did not explicitly make but follows from his Christological principles.[10] He adds that the arguments Aquinas did explicitly make are soteriological,[11] and this might lead us to suppose that White's argument will not be a soteriological one, but instead more metaphysical. And that is perhaps how it sounds when he says that affirmation of Christ's beatific vision "was and is essential for maintaining the unity of his person in and through the duality of his natures, and most particularly in safeguarding the unity of his personal agency in and through the duality of his two wills (human and divine)."[12] It sounds as though he is going to say that there is no possible world in which there could be any hypostatic union of two natures in one person, *any* unity of personal agency in two wills, without a beatific vision to maintain those unities. That is not, however, how the argument unfolds.

White is concerned to distance himself from the standard metaphysical argument for Christ's beatific vision from his perfection, at least as it is presented by its critics.[13] But he is also concerned that Christ's human acts manifest—presumably to us—his divine filial personhood.[14] But that manifestation to us cannot take place, he says, without a perfect cooperation between Christ's human and divine wills in all his human actions, and not just in some of them. Such cooperation cannot take place, he adds, without Christ having knowledge of the divine will in his human mind: the divine will has to be humanly known for deliberate human cooperation with it to take place. White maintains that the requisite knowledge can only be provided by the beatific vision.[15] This is because the beatific vision gives the human mind continuous evidential certainty of the content of the divine will, and for White no other certainty will do, not even the certainty that pertains to the indirect knowledge of faith.[16] But at no point does he argue it would be altogether impossible for a divine person to become incarnate without such evidential certainty. At most he says that it would be "entirely

10. White, *Incarnate Lord*, 238–39.
11. White, *Incarnate Lord*, 238–39n2.
12. White, *Incarnate Lord*, 238.
13. White, *Incarnate Lord*, 245–46.
14. White, *Incarnate Lord*, 239.
15. White, *Incarnate Lord*, 247, 251, 254–56.
16. White, *Incarnate Lord*, 257–60.

unfitting"[17] for Christ to have had faith because, while still the Word incarnate, he would have lacked direct evidential certainty of the divine will and so instead ended up with the capacity to act *as if* he were a human subject distinct from the Word.[18] Presumably, then, had he acted according to that capacity, we might have concluded to a Nestorian heresy because Christ's human actions would not have properly manifested his divine personhood. But White does not deny that God *could* have given Christ faith instead, absolutely speaking: it is rather that that would have impaired his imparting saving knowledge to us, something unfitting for our salvation. So in the end the argument is at base soteriological: it was so that he can give us saving knowledge of his divinity that Christ had to have the beatific vision so that his human acts would manifest to us his divine filial personhood through the perfect cooperation of his divine and human wills. The argument is at bottom more soteriological than metaphysical.

So now to Fr. Dominic Legge. We must bear in mind that his monograph *The Trinitarian Christology of St Thomas Aquinas* does not set out to argue for the necessity of Christ's beatific vision, but rather to demonstrate the Trinitarian character of Aquinas's Christology. Legge does not concern himself so much with the Incarnation of any divine person in all possible worlds,[19] but with the Trinitarian implications for the actual incarnation of the Son, where what is at stake is chiefly Trinitarian doctrine rather than any metaphysical account of perfection. But a metaphysical argument of a Trinitarian kind may be suggested by such passages as this: "The visible mission of the Son in the incarnation brings with it, by way of an intrinsic relationship grounded in the eternal processions, the invisible mission of the Holy Spirit to Christ's humanity in the fullest possible measure, and consequently every grace, gift, and charism that a human nature can receive."[20] Among these Legge includes the beatific vision, as is clear from the quotation's context in his chapter on "The Holy Spirit and Christ's Human Knowledge." If one could then demonstrate that the Spirit's grace, and indeed the fullness of such grace, were absolutely necessary for Christ's humanity, and that the be-

---

17. White, *Incarnate Lord*, 256.
18. White, *Incarnate Lord*, 255, 260–61.
19. But see Legge, *Trinitarian Christology*, 123–27.
20. Legge, *Trinitarian Christology*, 178.

atific vision were similarly necessary to that fullness, one could conclude that the beatific vision itself followed on his incarnation by absolute necessity.

When we dig into Legge's argument, however, it is not as clear as it first appears that the argument is a purely metaphysical one. Legge certainly sees the eternal inseparability of the persons of Son and Spirit as undergirding a certain inseparability of the temporal missions of the Son and Spirit, meaning that the Son's incarnation must involve in him the presence of the Spirit through habitual grace.[21] But the necessity of this Legge places on the uncreated side of the divine persons and not on the created side of Christ's humanity and habitual grace: his human nature cannot in any way require grace.[22] But can the inseparability of the divine persons guarantee that the Spirit is sent in the mission of the Son rather than just be present in it? It seems to me that the absolute necessity of linking the Incarnation and the Spirit's grace must require necessity on the created as well as on the uncreated side, since a temporal mission always includes a created effect in addition to the divine person sent.[23] In other words, not only must the eternal divine persons of Son and Spirit be inseparable, but also so must the temporal effects of their missions be absolutely inseparable, in this case the humanity of Christ and the Spirit's grace. In the case of the two invisible missions of Son and Spirit, Aquinas himself had located an intrinsic relationship between them not only in the inseparability of the divine persons but also in the common root of the temporal effects of wisdom and love in habitual grace.[24] It seems to me more challenging, however, to establish a comparable inseparability of the *visible* mission of the Son and the invisible mission of the Spirit, because a comparable common root of the created effects of the missions is more difficult to find. Habitual grace can hardly be such a common root so long as we maintain, with Aquinas and Legge, that habitual grace follows rather than precedes the union.[25]

Another possibility for establishing an absolute inseparability of Christ's humanity and the Spirit's grace might be a return to the standard meta-

---

21. Legge, *Trinitarian Christology*, 149–50.
22. Legge, *Trinitarian Christology*, 152–53.
23. *ST* I, q. 43, a. 5; Legge, *Trinitarian Christology*, 24–58.
24. *ST* I, q. 43, a. 5, ad 3. Legge omits this point when he quotes this reply. See Legge, *Trinitarian Christology*, 150.
25. *ST* III, q. 7, a. 13; Legge, *Trinitarian Christology*, 146–57.

physical argument found in Scheeben that the perfection of Christ's mind necessarily entailed habitual grace. But Legge nowhere makes that appeal. I suggest that at most he should suppose, as Aquinas did, that habitual grace is most fitting for any incarnate divine person and is necessary for God's plan of salvation. And when it comes to why the *fullness* of the Spirit and of his grace is required, rather than *just* the Spirit and grace, though he links Christ's fullness of grace to the excellence of the hypostatic union, Legge speaks in soteriological terms at this point in his book: Christ, as Head of his Body, has the fullness of the Spirit and of grace, so as to impart them to us.[26] Moreover, Legge adds to Aquinas no explicit metaphysical argument that the fullness of grace necessarily entails the immediate glory of the beatific vision.[27] It seems then that we can extract no seamless argument of absolute metaphysical necessity from Legge's book, but rather one that both appeals to soteriology and also holds back from absolute necessity.

In both cases, then, the appeal of these contemporary advocates of Christ's beatific vision is to soteriological arguments and arguments of fittingness rather than to any of strict metaphysical necessity. In conclusion, I suggest that this tendency should draw encouragement from the fact that Aquinas himself ruled out such metaphysical arguments by the way he structured the *Summa*'s Third Part. That Aquinas did not argue for Christ's beatific knowledge in terms of absolute necessity has been supported with reference to his use of the language of fittingness and his ordering of the *Summa*'s questions.[28] Here I appeal to the way he divided the text of the *Summa*'s Third Part into groups of questions. After treating the nature assumed in the union (qq. 3–6), he treated what was "co-assumed" in the union (qq. 7–15), and then "consequences" of the union (qq. 16–26). The divisions of co-assumed and of consequences Aquinas seems to have drawn together from different sources.[29] The division of co-assumed had already appeared in the Franciscan *Summa* attributed to Alexander of Hales, and the division of consequences in the works of Aquinas's Dominican teacher St. Albert the Great. Under co-assumed, the *Summa Halensis* had treated

---

26. Legge, *Trinitarian Christology*, 172–231.
27. Cf. Legge, *Trinitarian Christology*, 175–78.
28. Mansini, "Understanding St. Thomas."
29. See Ghislain Lafont, OSB, *Structures et Méthode dans la Somme Théologique de Saint Thomas d'Aquin* (Bruges: Desclée de Brouwer, 1961), 348.

penalties taken on by Christ apart from his basic nature for our salvation. These co-assumed defects were taken on voluntarily: some defects Christ co-assumed and others he did not.[30] Aquinas expanded the division of co-assumed by adding to defects *perfections* that Christ likewise took on over and above that nature, including the beatific vision. Such defects and perfections Albert had treated under "consequences" or effects of the union. Albert had already used "consequences" in making sense of the structure of Peter Lombard's *Sentences*, and Aquinas had done the same.[31] In his *De Incarnatione*, Albert had divided consequences overall into "effects" and "ends" of the union, the ends being Christ's passion and resurrection.[32] In the *Summa*, Aquinas removed the passion and the Resurrection from consequences of the union to a later division, thus treating consequences more or less as the union's effects. But while Albert treated Christ's knowledge among consequences or effects of the union,[33] Aquinas treated it not under consequences but under the co-assumed.

How can we make sense of Aquinas reassigning to the co-assumed what his Dominican teacher had treated under consequences? Aquinas did not give an explicit explanation of how he understood the division he had made. Clearly, all the co-assumed perfections are *in terms of order* "consequent" to the divine person and his assumed nature and thus are consequences in a wider sense of the term. So, for example, Aquinas maintained that Christ's co-assumed habitual grace is consequent to the uncreated grace of union.[34] In that wider rather than proper sense, everything "co-assumed" can be considered a consequence of the union. Moreover, many things considered by Aquinas under consequences of the union depend on something co-assumed and could therefore be considered "co-assumed" in a wider derivative sense. While the proper sense of the term would be restricted to what is basically co-assumed, the wider sense would include what is further co-assumed on that basis. To that extent some consequences can be counted "co-assumed" in this wider sense.[35]

---

30. Alexander of Hales et al., *Summa Theologica* III tr1 q4, tit1 d3.

31. St. Albert the Great, *Commentarii in III Sententiarum* d6; Aquinas, *Scriptum super libros sententiarum*, III d8.

32. Albert, *De Incarnatione*, tr4, proem; tr6 q1.

33. *De Inc.* tr4 q1.

34. *ST* III, q. 7, a. 13.

35. It can only be in this wider sense that I referred in Gaine, *Did the Saviour See the Father?*, 162,

Something, however, must set apart the union's consequences in the proper sense from what was co-assumed in the proper sense.[36] Since it is not possible to address here the whole question of this distinction, I restrict myself to a few remarks. It seems to me that the "co-assumed" encompass basic perfections and defects, voluntarily taken on for our salvation that neither followed by absolute necessity from the nature assumed nor are effects of some prior co-assumed perfection.[37] Though Aquinas may have removed many matters from Albert's "consequences," the consequences of the union nevertheless remained for him a broad category. They seem to me to include some saving effects that followed on what was directly co-assumed in the union. Christ's priesthood, for example, is a fitting consequence of what had already been treated in the *Summa*, including his co-assumed fullness of grace. But under consequences are also included what followed by absolute necessity from the assumption of human nature in the union without consideration of the co-assumed. For Aquinas, Christ's unity of personal being seems to be a metaphysically necessary consequence for any truly hypostatic union.[38]

In conclusion, it seems to me that, had Aquinas considered the beatific vision to follow by absolute necessity from the hypostatic union without reference to anything co-assumed, he would surely have included it among consequences of the union. Matters concerning Christ's knowledge would have easily nestled well in a coherent order between Aquinas's treatment of Christ's being (q. 17) and his treatment of Christ's will (q. 18).[39] But in fact he diverged from Albert—surely deliberately—by removing consideration

---

to Christ's co-assuming of perfect freedom. From the point of view of Aquinas's proper terminology, Christ's freedom would be a consequence of the union that presupposed his co-assumption of beatific knowledge.

36. For some discussion, see Lafont, *Structures et Méthode*, 390–92.

37. Aquinas does not argue, e.g., that the beatific vision is an effect of Christ's fullness of grace (cf. *ST* III, q. 9, a. 2). Unlike some more recent Thomists—Jacques Maritain, *On the Grace and Humanity of Jesus* (New York: Herder, 1969), 101; White, *Incarnate Lord*, 260n45—he does not argue that infused knowledge is an effect of beatific knowledge (cf. *ST* III, q. 9, a. 3). Although he argues from the act of beatific knowledge to the presence of habitual grace, he does not treat grace as an effect of the vision (cf. *ST* III, q. 7, a. 1). Moreover, he does not treat Christ's instrumental power to work miracles as an effect of his grace (*ST* III, q. 13, a. 2).

38. *ST*, III, q. 17.

39. The only aspect of Christ's knowledge that might more plausibly fit under consequences would be the soul's natural knowledge of first principles. See *ST* III, q. 9, a. 1. Given that everything else under Christ's knowledge fits better under the co-assumed, however, Aquinas treated it where he did.

of the beatific vision into the expanded division of co-assumed. This suggests to me that Christ's beatific vision was not, for Aquinas, an absolutely necessary effect of the union of the assumed nature with the divine person, nor even a fitting consequence of something co-assumed, but instead was freely co-assumed in itself as a basic supernatural perfection of Christ's human nature. If that is the case, then contemporary advocates of Christ's beatific vision, who support it on soteriological rather than strict metaphysical grounds, can take encouragement from their theological master.

CHAPTER 7

THE AUTHORITY AND
CHARITY OF CHRIST

Guy Mansini, OSB

If the authority and charity of Christ are the topics of this essay, part of its burden is to show why we should consider them together—why in the end they make a sort of unity.

They make a sort of unity in three ways. First, together they manifest to human intelligence enlightened by faith the complete reality of Christ as to his person and natures. Second, they belong together at the phenomenal level because the authority of Christ is the authority of charity, and the charity of Christ is the charity of his authority. Third, they unite in this further fashion; namely, that Christ's authority is a filial authority, and his charity is a filial charity.

We will see these things accordingly as we pay attention to how the authority and charity of Christ show themselves to us, which is to say, how Christ shows them to us. Further, we are interested in seeing how the authority and charity of Christ must show themselves to us. In this regard, this essay is or wants to be one in what Robert Sokolowski calls "the theology of disclosure."[1] The point of such a theology is to uncover not simply what God reveals to us, but how he does it; it means to uncover the necessities embedded in how God uncovers (reveals) himself to us. In the theology of

1. See Robert Sokolowski, *The God of Faith and Reason* (Washington, DC: Catholic University of America Press, 1982), chap. 8, and *Eucharistic Presence: A Study in the Theology of Disclosure* (Washington, DC: Catholic University of America Press, 1994), chap. 1. Proximate to the topic of this essay there is also "The Revelation of the Holy Trinity," in his *Christian Faith and Human Understanding* (Washington, DC: Catholic University of America Press, 2006), 131–48.

disclosure, we want to see the light and not just what the light shows us. If we pay no attention to what is to be seen, however, we cannot see how the light works, what necessities it obeys or presupposes. If there is nothing to be seen, then we cannot notice the light, and we may as well be in darkness. Furthermore, if we never pay attention to the light, we will miss some of the intelligibility of what is to be seen, too.

These abstractions will prove themselves in the performance or not. But there is still one more introductory word before the performance. In illustrating how Christ's authority and charity appear to us, and their unity, we will presuppose what St. Thomas Aquinas took them to be, that is, what he took to be the nature of authority and charity. We will also be attentive to what he can teach us about how they are disclosed to us.

THE AUTHORITY OF CHRIST

The authority of Christ manifests the person of Christ to us accordingly as his authority is displayed principally in his teaching.[2] His miracles also display it, but only with the aid of speech. If he just healed, we would not know on whose authority he healed. But when he says to the paralytic, "My son, your sins are forgiven," and then orders him, "I say to you, take up your pallet and go home" (Mk 2:5, 2:9), we know he works by his personal authority as also that he authoritatively reveals that he is the Son of man and that he personally has power on earth to forgive sin (Mk 2:5, 2:10). So his authority is displayed principally in his teaching.[3]

Preliminary Remarks

As to the teaching, there are four things to note here in a preliminary and schematic way: first, about persons and their finality; second, about the goal of the universe; third, about authority; and fourth, about the manifestation of persons.

2. Richard Bauckham finely suggests the link between authority and identity in his *Jesus: A Very Short Introduction* (Oxford: Oxford University Press, 2011), chap. 6.

3. The authority of Jesus is also manifested in a similarly subsidiary way in his commands to demons and to the wind and waves.

The Nature of Persons

First, persons are individuals of an intellectual or rational nature. Their defining finality is therefore unto the knowledge of the truth, and to be sure, the truth about the highest and most truthful thing, which is God.[4] This means also that their first and preeminent way of interacting with one another simply according to what they are and what they are naturally inclined to is at the level of knowledge. Their principal and friendliest way of influencing one another will be by teaching, by imparting knowledge, and indeed knowledge in its highest form, *scientia*, and about the highest things. So in the treatise on the divine government, when St. Thomas deals with that government as mediated by men one to another and precisely in what makes them personal, which is the rationality they owe to their soul or substantial form, he treats first of *teaching*.[5] The original headship of Adam had to do not only in his being the first father of men, but also in his authority as teacher of men,[6] where an "authority" is one who knows, who is expert, whose opinion therefore is weighty, authoritative.[7]

The End of the Universe

The importance of teaching is borne out also if we think of the goal of the universe, which is truth. Since the universe comes from an intellect, its last end will be the good of an intellect, which is the truth.[8] Of course, the last end of the created universe will be to make the truth known to *created* intellects, who do not differ from the uncreated God in that their defining good, the good to which they are ordered by nature, is to know the truth.[9] And just as soon as he has established that the end of the universe is truth in the *Sum-*

---

4. Thomas Aquinas, *ST* I, q. 95, a. 2, c. I cite the *Summa* according to the edition of P. Caramello (Rome: Marietti, 1952, 1956).

5. *ST* I, q. 117, a. 1. See Yves Congar, OP, "Tradition et *Sacra Doctrina* chez Saint Thomas d'Aquin," in *Église et Tradition*, ed. Johannes Betz and Heinrich Fries (Le Puy and Lyon: Éditions Xavier Mappus, 1963), 157–89, at 161; Andrew Meszaros, *The Prophetic Church: History and Doctrinal Development in John Henry Newman and Yves Congar* (Oxford: Oxford University Press, 2016), 202–3.

6. *ST* I, q. 96, a. 4. Adam as a teacher is treated before he is treated as a progenitor in q. 98.

7. Congar, "Tradition et *Sacra Doctrina*," 172–73.

8. St. Thomas Aquinas, *Summa contra Gentiles, Book One: God*, trans. Anton Pegis (Notre Dame, IN: University of Notre Dame Press, 1975), chap. 1, no. 2.

9. *ST* I-II, q. 3, aa. 5 and 8.

ma contra Gentiles, St. Thomas notes that the first cause of the universe, the subsistent Wisdom of God, tells us that he has taken flesh and come into the world in order to make the truth known.[10] "For this I was born, and for this I have come into the world, to bear witness to the truth" (Jn 18:37). Doubtless, he bears witness to the truth by teaching. The Second Adam takes up the work of the failed First Adam.

Authorities

Just as in a hierarchical universe there is a hierarchy of beings, of truths, and of goods, as well as a hierarchy of knowers and legislators, so we may expect there to be also a hierarchy of authoritative teachers, and this is verified in the supernatural order in the Church. Christ, however, will be an authority in an absolute sense. For St. Thomas, an *auctor* is not simply a trustworthy teacher, but a teacher as the first author or originator of the teaching.[11] "For 'author' adds to the *ratio* of a principle that it is not from another."[12] So in the Trinity, the Father alone is *auctor* relative to the other persons. But relative to the created order and the Church, Christ is the *auctor* of Christian doctrine just as much as, insofar as he is divine, he is the *institutor* of the sacraments with *potestas auctoritatis* such that they give grace.[13] Relative to us, then, no greater authority can be conceived. For as the consubstantial and eternal Word of his Father, he knows the truth of God and of all things the divine power has made in wisdom. And he possesses this knowledge also as he is a man, beholding the essence of God in vision, even on his pilgrim way.[14]

If we know who Christ is and what he says, his authority as the First Truth will be a sure warrant for assenting to what he says. St. Thomas: "man, to achieve perfect certitude about the truth of faith, had to be instructed

10. *ScG*, I, c. 1, no. 2.

11. See Roy J. Deferarri, *A Lexicon of Saint Thomas Aquinas* (Washington, DC: Catholic University of America Press, 1948), at *auctor, auctoritas*.

12. "Sed nomen 'auctoris' addit super rationem principii hoc quod est non a aliquo." St. Thomas, *In I Sent.*, ed. Pierre Mandonnet (Paris: Lethielleux, 1929), d. 29, q. 1, a. 1, c.

13. For Christ as *auctor* and teacher of Christian doctrine, see *ST* III, q. 11, a. 6, ad 2, and q. 12, a. 3, c. For God as *institutor* of the sacraments, see *ST* III, q. 64, a. 2, and for Christ's *potestas auctoritatis* relative to the sacraments, see q. 64, aa. 3 and 4.

14. *ST* III, q. 9, a. 2; q. 10, a. 2. For the translation of the knowledge of vision into knowledge communicable to us in our words, see Simon Francis Gaine, *Did the Saviour See the Father? Christ, Salvation and the Vision of God* (London: Bloomsbury T&T Clark, 2015), 96–102.

by God Himself made man, that man might in the human fashion grasp the divine instruction."[15] We come to know that it is God who instructs us, however, just insofar as the authority of Christ is displayed to us *within* or *through* the very teaching itself. Moreover, if the authority of Christ is displayed and made manifest in his teaching, that is the only way it can be made manifest.[16] This is not true of purely human teachers. For human teachers, there are external accreditors, university authorities who grant degrees, accrediting agencies who grant certificates.[17] To be sure, there may be some display of authority in their teaching itself: if the hearers are brought to insight, the authority of the teacher is demonstrated—manifested in the magisterial performance. But this is absolutely true of the authority of Christ. If we are initially invited to credit Jesus of Nazareth by reference to an authority seemingly distinct from his because of the Voice and the Dove at his baptism, the way we initially credit some professor by his university degree, or the fact that some institution has hired him, in the end we must find his authority to be verified in himself, such that the verification or self-authentication of his teaching itself leads us to recognize who he is.[18] This is in the nature of the case: it would be monstrous to measure the divine authority of Christ by any standard or warrant outside of it. Scripture forbids us to do this (Heb 6:13–20; cf. Isa 45:23).[19] It is in the nature of the case that Jesus's teaching must be, as a human teaching, altogether unique because it is altogether self-supporting and credible in itself.[20]

---

15. *Summa contra Gentiles, Book Four*, trans. Charles J. O'Neil (Notre Dame, IN: University of Notre Dame Press, 1975), chap. 54, no. 4.

16. There are subsidiary ways, as noted above, but they don't really work without words.

17. See Matthias Joseph Scheeben, *Handbook of Catholic Dogmatics. Book One: Theological Epistemology. Part One: The Objective Principles of Theological Knowledge*, trans. Michael J. Miller (Steubenville, OH: Emmaus Academic, 2019), no. 71: "We call authority ... any kind of credibility of another person whereby that person becomes for us the occasion or cause of accepting a truth."

18. St. Thomas takes it for granted that the Father and Spirit warrant the authority of Jesus at his baptism. See St. Thomas Aquinas, *Commentary on the Gospel of John Chapters 1–8*, trans. Fabian R. Larcher, OP (Lander, WY: Aquinas Institute for the Study of Sacred Doctrine, 2013), c. 5, lect. 6, at 5:37, no. 819.

19. See on this Michel Henry, *Words of Christ*, trans. Christina M. Geschwandtner (Grand Rapids, MI: Eerdmans, 2012), chap. 8, esp. p. 87.

20. Juan Alfaro, SJ, *Fides, Spes, Caritas: Adnotationes in Tractatum de Virtutibus Theologicis* (Rome: Gregorian University Press, 1968), chap. 9, art. II.

The Manifestation of Persons

Jesus of Nazareth is a human teacher, but his teaching must just in itself be the act of and ordered to the manifestation of a divine *person*. That it is the act of a divine person follows from the teaching of Chalcedon and Constantinople II. It follows from the communication of idioms that was affirmed at Ephesus. It is expounded by St. Thomas in the Third Part of the *Summa* at qq. 16 and 19, on the communication of idioms and Christ's theandric acts. But also his teaching is ordered to the *manifestation* of his person. For together with their moral acts, that is how persons show themselves, how they communicate the self they are. For persons, selves, are minds (angels) or principally minds (human beings). "The function of man is an activity of soul which follows or implies a rational principle," Aristotle says.[21] Or, as Sokolowski has it in a perhaps fresher idiom, a person is an "agent of truth"—a person aims at installing truth in his action and expressing it in his word.[22] The rational principle Aristotle speaks of colonizes the passions in the moral virtues, and it cultivates itself in contemplation of what is most real.[23] As to the last, we say what we are, who we are, by saying what things are, what the important things are, and especially by saying what we take the whole of things to be. For us, coming to say what the whole is constitutes part of our construction of ourselves.[24]

Moreover, that the manifestation of the whole and of ourselves in speech is a good thing just in itself we know not only from our experience of ourselves as persons and from the unique good and pleasure of friendship, but also from revelation, since the first procession within the Godhead is the procession of what manifests the divine understanding; namely, the procession of the Word. It is part of the nature of all persons that they are bound

---

21. *Nicomachean Ethics*, Book I, chapter 7, 1098a7–8, trans. W. D. Ross, in *The Basic Works of Aristotle*, ed. Richard McKeon (New York: Random House, 1941).

22. Robert Sokolowski, *Phenomenology of the Human Person* (Cambridge: Cambridge University Press, 2008), 1, prefers this phrase over "rational animal" because it indicates that truth is our accomplishment and not just passively received. See also 12–18 for some introductory exploration.

23. *Nicomachean Ethics*, Book I, chapter 13, 1103a3–10.

24. Of course, if our speech is a constant reiteration of trivialities and gossip, a repetition of what consumers and the crowd say, never arising above the chatter of Heidegger's *Gerede*, and if we never stop to construe the whole of things, then that, too, declares a sort of a person, a person who refuses to be a person.

up with speaking as one who manifests or as a manifestation or as dependent on a manifestation. It is part of the nature of all persons that they are spoken of (for the intelligibility of created persons as well as that of Father and Spirit also come to expression in the Word). Moreover, the Father loves to speak the Word, and the Son loves to be spoken. Just as the manifestation of the Father is by his Word, so the manifestation of a divine Person to us must similarly be achieved by speech and action that is informed by speech. Such manifestation, however, will have a certain absolute and self-authenticating character to it, as noted previously. As for Christ, then, we cannot have saving faith in his word unless we know it is a human word of a divine person. But we cannot know it is the word of a divine person except from within this word itself.

Jesus's Authoritative Teaching

In fact, the teaching of Jesus does manifest his authority, the authority of a divine person, in both its content and its manner.

Preaching the Kingdom

As to its content, his very first message, that the Kingdom of God is at hand, is something that God alone can know.[25] At the same time, this news is not presented even as some prophet would present his message with an introductory "thus saith the Lord" (Mk 1:14; Mt 4:17).[26] That is to say, its manner of presentation as much as what is presented bespeaks a greater than human authority and betrays the presence, indirectly but truly, of divine authority.[27] The content and the manner work together in showing Jesus's authority, for he commands repentance and belief on the strength of his word alone (Mk 1:15; Mt 4:17).[28] Who must he be if he does this rightly?

---

25. St. Thomas remarks that Jesus communicates his divinity by revealing things hidden to ordinary human knowledge. *Commentary on John 1–8*, c. 1, lect. 15, at 1:42, nos. 303–5.

26. It is true that John the Baptist is not reported as announcing the Kingdom with a "thus saith the Lord" (Mt 3:2), and yet he is obviously subordinate to Jesus: "he who is coming after me is mightier than I, whose sandals I am not worthy to carry" (Mt 3:11).

27. I mean "indirectly" in the sense of Bauckham, *Jesus*, 57–61.

28. See again Scheeben, *Handbook*, no. 71: "the strict and *specific* concept of authority is present only when the acceptance of a truth by faith can be ... *imperatively demanded*."

The Sermon on the Mount

The same unity of content and manner works in the Sermon on the Mount. He emends the law and fulfills it (Mt 5:17, 5:21–22, 5:28, 5:31–32, 5:33–34, 5:38–39). The law in question is a divine law. As St. Thomas says, he presents himself as Lord or as legislator.[29] He presents himself as having the authority so to act, such that the crowd is astonished that he teaches "with authority" (Mt 7:29). It is an authority, moreover, with "the power of penetrating the heart."[30] It does not coerce belief, however. "Where does this man get this wisdom?" the people of Nazareth ask, and take offense at him (Mt 13:54, 13:57). The author of freedom leaves our freedom intact even when he commands us to believe.

The Fourth Gospel

It is in John's Gospel, however, that the unity of content and manner of teaching come most forcefully together, where the content is his own identity as the Son of God. As Juan Alfaro observes, we know that Jesus is the Son because we believe him as Son. He can communicate his identity to us as Son only if he asks us—commands us—to believe that he is who he is on the sole warrant of his word to that effect. The grammar of the Gospel indicates this: we are to believe "in him" (*pisteuein* + *eis* with the accusative), which is to say, we are to believe who he is because we believe him telling us so (*pisteuein* with the dative).[31] Jesus can be believed on the basis of his works, his miracles (Jn 2:23, 7:31). This faith, however, is fragile and infirm, contrary to the very nature of faith (Jn 8:30–59).[32] Thus St. Thomas says that it is more perfect simply to believe his teaching itself.[33]

---

29. St. Thomas Aquinas, *Super Evangelium S. Matthaei Lectura*, ed. R. Cai, OP (Rome: Marietti, 1951), c. 7, lect. 2, at 7:29, no. 678.

30. *Super Evangelium S. Matthaei Lectura*, c. 7, lect. 2, at 7:29, no. 678, my translation. In the *Summa*, St. Thomas will say that it is because of the dignity of Christ's teaching that he does not write it on parchment but, as befits the "the most excellent teacher," "impresses his teaching on the hearts of his hearers." *ST* III, q. 42, a. 4, c.

31. Juan Alfaro, SJ, *Esistenza Cristiana* (Rome: Gregorian University Press, 1975), 61–64. See, e.g., Jn 8:30 and 8:31, although here the RSV misleads us, translating 8:31 as if it were *pisteuein eis*.

32. Contrary to the nature of faith: *ST* II-II, q. 4, aa. 1 and 8.

33. St. Thomas Aquinas, *Commentary on the Gospel of John 1–8*, c. 2, lect. 3, at 2:23, no. 418, and c. 7, lect. 3, at 7:31, no. 1070. In the *Summa*, St. Thomas lists four elements accounting for the "power (*potestas*) of Christ in teaching: its confirmation by miracles; its "effectiveness in persuading"; "the authority

So at John 9:35, Jesus asks the man born blind if he believes "in the Son of God,"[34] and he identifies himself, the speaker, as such. The man answers "I believe" and worships. He believes the words of Jesus accordingly as he is Son of God and believes that he is the Son of God. St. Thomas comments:

Christ reveals himself to the man born blind, who desired him [the Son of God], when he says "you have seen him, and it is he who talks with you." Here, Christ is giving him a teaching of faith ... the teaching itself is given when he says, "it is he who talks with you" ... These words refute the error of Nestorius, who said that in Christ the suppositum of the Son of God is different from the suppositum of the Son of man. They refute it because the one who spoke these words was born from Mary and was the Son of man, and the very same one is the Son of God, as our Lord says.[35]

The Son of Mary teaches that he is the Son of God and asks to be taken at his word. And the very fact that he can so ask implies that he is the Son.

In John 11:26–27, Jesus asks Martha if she believes he is the Resurrection and the life. She believes Jesus's word but answers that she believes that he is "the Christ, the Son of God." St. Thomas:

Augustine ... says that Martha answers this way because it gives the reason for all that our Lord had said. It is as though she were saying: "whatever you say about your power and the effect of salvation, I believe it all; because I believe something more, which is the root of all these things," that is, "that you are the Christ, the Son of the living God."[36]

And he explains:

Martha's profession is complete, for she professes Christ's dignity, his nature and his mission, that is, to be made flesh.

She professes his dignity when she says, "You are the Christ." ... Then she professes that Christ's nature is divine and equal to the Father; she says "the Son of the living God." In calling him uniquely the Son of the living God, she affirms the truth of his sonship.[37]

(auctoritas) of the speaker"; and the rectitude of his life (ST III, q. 42, a. 1, ad 2). I am saying that the second and third elements work together and are, so to speak, interior to one another.

34. Manuscripts also read "Son of man," and so the RSV. But I take "Son of God," following the Vulgate.

35. St. Thomas Aquinas, Commentary on the Gospel of John 9–21, trans. Fabian Larcher, OP (Lander, WY: Aquinas Institute for the Study of Sacred Doctrine, 2013), c. 9, lect. 4, at 9:35, no. 1357.

36. Commentary on John 9–21, c. 11, lect. 4, at 11:27, no. 1519.

37. Commentary on John 9–21, c. 11, lect. 4, at 11:27, no. 1520.

The answer of Martha attains to the personal reality of Christ, following his own teaching.[38]

It is just because of his personal reality, therefore, that his teaching has the effect it does. At John 7:46, the officers sent to arrest Jesus explain why they failed: "No man ever spoke like this man!" and the chief priests suppose they now believe Jesus. St. Thomas explains:

let us realize how good these officers were … They deserve our praise for three reasons. First, because of their admiration: for they admired Christ because of his teachings, not his miracles. And this brought them nearer to the truth … Second, we should praise them because of the ease with which they were won over: because with just a few words, Christ had captivated them and had drawn their love. Third, because of their confidence …

And these things are to be expected, for Jesus was not just a man, but the Word of God; and so his words had power to affect people. "Are not my words like fire, says the Lord, and like a hammer breaking a rock?" (Jer 23:29). And so Matthew says: "he was teaching them as one who had authority" (Mt 7:29).[39]

The power of the words of the incarnate Word enables the hearers to see that they are self-authenticating words. In this way, his teaching manifests an authority, an authority that can be measured by no created reality, the authority of a divine person.

THE CHARITY OF CHRIST

The charity of Christ manifests the humanity of Christ according to the humanity of Christ that is displayed in an undeniable way in his passion and death. Just because the person of Christ cannot die in its divinity, and just because only a man can suffer and die, and just because Jesus dies out of charity and without charity would not die for us, his charity shows his humanity.

---

38. See also *Commentary on John 9–21*, c. 15, lect. 5, at 15:22, no. 2049: "Christ showed himself to them in person and taught them."

39. *Commentary on John 1–8*, c. 7, lect. 5, at 7:46, no. 1108.

Charity

Charity is the friendship between God and men[40] and is the created term of the mission of the Holy Spirit to the souls of the just.[41] Since the Word became incarnate as he really is, he became incarnate as breathing the Holy Spirit, and thus he necessarily sends this Spirit into the soul of the nature he assumes from Mary.[42] In this way, the Holy Spirit is in Christ's humanity as the Spirit is in us and as founding the way he is in God, which is to say, as the beloved in the lover.[43] In this way, the Holy Spirit and charity are the uncreated and created principles of all Christ's loving acts and preeminently those he demonstrates on the cross, loving God and loving us.[44] As St. Thomas says, "there is no act of charity more perfect than the one by which a *man* bears even death for another" (emphasis added), and he finds warrant for this in John 15:13, "greater love has no man than this, that a man lay down his life for his friends."[45] All the more is this true since Jesus lays down his life for us in order to pay the penalty of our sin, and "the death of Christ had its satisfying power from His charity in which He bore death voluntarily."[46]

The Incarnation itself, the union of the divine and human natures, stems from the divine charity.[47] But this charity is enacted in the works accomplished through the humanity of Christ.[48] "No one can know how much Christ has loved us," St. Thomas says.[49] If we do not know Christ's love, moreover, we know nothing of the redemption, and so nothing of the Incarnation, which was for the redemption.

40. *ST* II-II, q. 23, a. 1. In a. 2, charity is a *habitus*, so a form superadded to the will, inclining it to acts of charity.

41. *ST* I, q. 43, a. 5, ad 2.

42. See Dominic Legge, OP, *The Trinitarian Christology of St. Thomas Aquinas* (Oxford: Oxford University Press, 2017), 147–53.

43. In God, *ST* I, q. 27, a. 3, and as the beloved is in the lover, *ST* I-II, q. 28, a. 2.

44. St. Thomas Aquinas, *Commentary on the Letter of Saint Paul to the Hebrews*, ed. J. Mortensen and E. Alarcón, trans. Fabian Larcher, OP (Lander, WY: Aquinas Institute for the Study of Sacred Doctrine, 2012), c. 9, lect. 3, at 9:14, no. 444.

45. *ScG* IV, c. 55, no. 17.

46. *ScG* IV, c. 55, no. 25, replying to the 22nd argument of c. 53.

47. *ScG* IV, c. 55, no. 5.

48. *ScG* IV, c. 54, nos. 8–9.

49. St. Thomas Aquinas, *Commentary on Ephesians*, in St. Thomas Aquinas, *Commentary on the Letters of Saint Paul to the Galatians and Ephesians*, ed. J. Mortensen and E. Alarcón, trans. Fabian R. Larcher, OP [Galatians], and Matthew L. Lamb [Ephesians] (Lander, WY: Aquinas Institute for the Study of Sacred Doctrine, 2012), c. 3, lect. 5, at 3:19, no. 180.

For whatever occurred in the mystery of human redemption and Christ's Incarnation was the work of love. He became incarnate out of charity: "for his exceeding charity with which he loved us even when we were dead in our sins, has quickened us together in Christ" (Eph 2:4–5). That he died also sprang from charity: "greater love than this no man has, that a man lay down his life for his friends" (Jn 15:13). And "Christ hath also loved us and hath delivered himself up for us, an oblation and sacrifice to God" (Eph 5:2). On this account St. Gregory exclaimed: "O the incalculable love of your charity! To redeem slaves you delivered up your Son." It follows that to know Christ's love is to know all the mysteries of Christ's Incarnation and our redemption. These have poured out from the immense charity of God, a charity exceeding every created intelligence and the knowledge of all of them.[50]

In this magnificent passage, we begin first with the charity of Christ as God, for when St. Thomas says that "he became incarnate out of charity," the subject is a "pre-incarnate" subject, the Son in his divinity. The charity out of which he becomes incarnate is therefore a charity common to the Three Divine Persons, the charity that God can be said to be.[51] But the charity by which Christ dies is the created charity infused into his soul with habitual grace at his conception.[52] Whence it may be observed that, although Christ's death manifests his humanity bodily, his charity, created though it be, does not so clearly *manifest* his humanity in its highest part, in his soul. It is this very failure of created charity to manifest itself as created that enabled Peter Lombard to identify the charity of Romans 5:5, poured into our hearts by the Holy Spirit, with the Holy Spirit himself.[53] For St. Thomas, the charity poured into our hearts through the Holy Spirit (Rom 5:5) must be created, else our acts of loving God and neighbor in fulfillment of the new law are not our own.[54] But just as such, because of its excellence and divinity, just because it is a supernatural likeness of the love of God and the

---

50. *Commentary on Ephesians*, c. 3, lect. 5, at 3:19, no. 178. The reference to Gregory the Great refers to the Exultet, widely attributed to him in the Middle Ages.

51. *ST* II-II, q. 23, a. 2, ad 1; see Jean-Hervé Nicolas, OP, *Synthèse Dogmatique: De la Trinité à la Trinité* (Paris: Beauchesne, 1985), no. 149, pp. 176–77.

52. *ST* I, q. 43, a. 7, ad 3; III, q. 7, aa. 1, 2, and 13; q. 34, a. 1.

53. Cf. St. Thomas, *In I Sent.*, d. 17 (Paris version), q. 1, a. 1, notes on the text of Lombard, 29–30, and *In I Sent.*, d. 17 (*Lectura romana*), d. 17, q. 1, a. 2, all in St. Thomas Aquinas, *On Love and Charity: Readings from the "Commentary on the Sentences of Peter Lombard,"* trans. Peter A. Kwasniewski, Thomas Bolin, OSB, and Joseph Bolin (Washington, DC: Catholic University of America Press, 2008).

54. *ST* II-II, q. 23, a. 2, c.

Holy Spirit, it does not show itself as something *human*.[55] Christ's created and human charity manifests itself as created not in itself but through the obedience to the command of the Father it elicits.

Human Charity Displayed in Obedience

Part of the mystery of our redemption is the freedom with which Christ delivered himself up for us. Of this freedom St. Thomas is assured because of Ephesians 5:2, already quoted above, and also because of Galatians 2:20, which speaks of Christ "who loved me and gave himself up for me." St. Thomas explains that the Father delivers Christ up out of love (cf. Rom 8:32), and the Son delivers himself up out of obedience and love, while Judas acts out of avarice and treachery.[56] He comes to closer quarters with this "delivering up" by the Father in the later commentary on Romans. God's not sparing his Son but delivering him up to death at 8:32 is identified as his inspiring Christ's will with love, with the *affectus caritatis*.[57] This charity is evidently created. Moreover, it is the source of Christ's obedience. And his obedience, which is necessarily the act of a subordinate to a superior, manifests his humanity in its higher part, his soul.

This sense of obedience is sometimes resisted today for those who, following Karl Barth and Hans Urs von Balthasar, wish to postulate an obedience of the Son to the Father within the Trinity and prior to the Incarnation. It is true that the Son is "sent" into the world by the Father (e.g., Gal 4:4). But St. Thomas understands the missions of Word and Spirit into the economy of salvation to designate their processions, the Word from the Father and the Spirit from Father and Son, with a fitting term *ad extra*, within the economy, which accomplishes some work or declares their presence. So grace and charity are the terms of the invisible mission of the Spirit into the

---

55. For Jean-Luc Marion, Christ's gaze is the phenomenalization of charity; see Stephen E. Lewis, trans., *Givenness and Revelation* (Oxford: Oxford University Press, 2016), 71.

56. *Commentary on Galatians*, in St. Thomas Aquinas, *Commentary on the Letters of Saint Paul to the Galatians and Ephesians*, c. 2, lect. 6, at 2:20, no. 110.

57. St. Thomas Aquinas, *Commentary on the Letter of Saint Paul to the Romans*, ed. J. Mortensen and E. Alarcón, trans. Fabian Larcher, OP (Lander, WY: Aquinas Institute for the Study of Sacred Doctrine, 2012), c. 8, lect. 6, at 8:32, no. 713; see also and earlier, *ScG* IV, c. 55, no. 19, reply to 16th argument of c. 53.

souls of the just, making them holy,[58] and the humanity of Christ is the term of the visible mission of the Son.[59] But since the sending is principally simply the procession of the person who is then made present in the economy by a created, temporal term, it connotes no subordination in nature of the one sent to the one sending.[60] The persons sent, Word and Spirit, are not "obeying" in an act of their own will some act of another will, the Father's, distinct from their own will. The persons just are the single mind and will of God, the one essential act of understanding and willing that God is.[61]

For obedience, however, there must be two wills. And the Son cannot be obedient to his Father except in his human will, the will that is part of his humanity.[62] Obedience may be the obedience of a slave, or a servant, or a son.[63] The obedience of Christ is the obedience of a Son, and the obedience with which he fulfills his Father's will and his command to lay down his life therefore springs from charity, his created charity. And indeed, just because his charity was most perfect, his obedience was maximal, too. So the *Contra Gentiles.*

> There is no act of charity more perfect than the one by which a man bears even death for another [and he cites Jn 15:13] … Therefore one finds that Christ bearing death for the salvation of men and for the glory of God the Father was extremely obedient to God and carried out a perfect act of charity.[64]

This same line of thought is continued in the great *Summa*. Question 47 of the *Tertia Pars* asks after the efficient cause of Christ's passion, and the second article asserts that he died out of obedience. This obedience, however, makes one thing with his love, or we should say, makes his charity more visible: he fulfills the moral precepts of the law out of his love for his Father and for us (ad 2); and again, "even the precepts of charity he fulfilled out of

58. *ST* I, q. 43, a. 3.

59. *ST* I, q. 43, a. 2

60. *ST* I, q. 43, a. 1.

61. *ST* I, q. 14, a. 4; q. 19, a. 1.

62. Sokolowski, *Eucharistic Presence*, 75; G. Mansini, "Obedience Religious, Christological and Trinitarian," *Nova et Vetera*, English ed. 12 (2014): 395–413.

63. Dorotheos of Gaza, *Dorotheos of Gaza: Discourses and Sayings*, trans. Eric P. Wheeler (Kalamazoo, MI: Cistercian Publications, 1977), "On the Fear of God," 109–21, at 110–11; cf. *ST* II-II, q. 104, a. 3, for the three kinds of goods for the sake of which one may obey a superior.

64. *ScG* IV, c. 55, no. 17, reply to the 14th argument of c. 53.

obedience, and he was obedient to Father's command out of love" (ad 3).[65] And as in the Romans commentary, so in the third article of q. 47, this charity is God's work in him: God "inspired his will to suffer for us by infusing him with charity."[66]

It is especially noteworthy that for St. Thomas, the obedience of Christ is learned experientially, for that is how he understands the saying in Hebrews that Christ "learned obedience through what he suffered" (5:8):

one who learns something comes voluntarily to learn it. But Christ accepted our weakness voluntarily; consequently, he says that "he learned obedience," i.e. how difficult it is to obey, because he obeyed in the most difficult matters, "even to the death of the cross" (Phil 2:8).

This shows how difficult the good of obedience is, because those who have not experienced obedience and have not learned it in difficult matters, believe obedience is very easy. But in order to know what obedience is, one must learn to obey in difficult matters ... Therefore, although Christ knew by simple recognition [from eternity] what obedience is, he nevertheless "learned obedience by the things which he suffered."[67]

This emphasis on the experiential character of Christ's knowledge of obedience will be matched by an emphasis on his experiential knowledge of our misery, as we will shortly see.

Joy: An Interior Effect of Charity

That the Lord dies from charity is shown also by the fact that in accepting his passion and death, he manifests the interior effects of charity, joy, and mercy.[68] Love causes joy, St. Thomas says, either because of the presence of the beloved or because the good proper to the beloved belongs to him.[69] Love just of itself makes the beloved present to the lover as a sort of proportion to or disposition unto the beloved, and in this way the charity of Christ makes

65. My translation.
66. My translation.
67. *Commentary on Hebrews*, c. 5, lect. 2, at 5:8, no. 259.
68. For the interior effects of charity, see *ST* II-II, qq. 28–30. Something will be said about peace below.
69. *ST* II-II, q. 28, a. 1, c; also *Commentary on Galatians*, c. 5, lect. 6, at 5:22, no. 330.

his Father present to him.[70] And just as man, the Lord rejoices in his Father's immutable possession of what is proper to divinity, the perfect possession of the infinite Good in an infinite act of understanding it that flowers in perfect beatitude.[71] We should think that Christ's vision of the divine essence and his possession of his Father in this way also makes more excellent the quality of his love of his Father.[72]

As for his love of us, prior to his passion and our redemption and its application for the justification of sinners, he cannot rejoice because we already return his charity. Still, St. Thomas recognizes from the outset of his theological career that there is a certain joy in suffering for the beloved:

> the lover … is inclined through love to act according to the demands and needs of the beloved, and such activity is most of all delightful to him, as being suitable to his form. For this reason, whatsoever the lover does or suffers for the beloved, the whole of it is delightful to him, and he is ever more stirred up, insofar as he experiences greater delight in the beloved in all he does or suffers for his sake.[73]

The joy caused by love, so also by charity, can therefore be mixed with suffering and with sadness that the beloved does not yet possess the good proper to him.[74] St. Thomas finds this verified in the Letter to the Colossians, where Paul prays for them "that their hearts may be encouraged [consoled] as they are knit together in love [charity]" (2:2). He observes that "it is consoling to a friend of God to endure evils for his sake," and says there is joy in such consolation.[75]

St. Thomas also finds this state of affairs verified in Christ, when he deals with the Agony in the Garden in his commentary on Matthew:

---

70. For the presence of the beloved in the lover, see *ST* I-II, q. 28, a. 2. For this presence as an *inclinatio* unto the beloved, see *ST* I, q. 27, a. 4, c. See also T. C. O'Brien's new Blackfriar's translation of the *Summa, Father, Son and Holy Ghost* (Ia. *33–43*, vol. 7 (New York: McGraw Hill, 1964), Appendix 2, "The Holy Spirit: Love."

71. For divine beatitude, see *ST* I, q. 26, a. 1. That charity rejoices in God's blessedness: *ST* II-II, q. 23, a. 3, ad 2, with q. 23, a. 4, c, and q. 28, a. 1, c and ad 3.

72. See *ST* I-II, q. 3, a. 4; q. 4, aa. 1–4.

73. *In III Sent.*, d. 27, q. a. 1, c, in St. Thomas Aquinas, *On Love and Charity*, 121.

74. *ST* II-II, q. 28, a. 2.

75. *Commentary on Colossians*, in St. Thomas Aquinas, *Commentary on the Letters of Saint Paul to the Philippians, Colossians, Thessalonians, Timothy, Titus, and Philemon*, ed. J. Mortensen and E. Alarcón, trans. Fabian Larcher, OP (Lander, WY: Aquinas Institute for the Study of Sacred Doctrine, 2012), c. 2, lect. 2, at 2:2, no. 79; and that consolation brings joy, no. 78.

the death of Christ was a cause (*materia*) of sadness accordingly as it was considered in itself [by Christ]; but accordingly as it was referred to reason, by referring it to its end [our salvation], he thus rejoiced.[76]

Mercy: An Interior Effect of Charity

We pass to another interior effect of charity. Mercy arises from charity "insofar as someone counts the misery of another as his own on account of being united to him in love," St. Thomas says in the *Summa*.[77] And in his commentary on Hebrews, at 2:17, he asks whether Christ the merciful high priest was not merciful to us from all eternity, since, again, "mercy consists in having a heart grieved at another's misfortune," and the Son of God has loved us eternally with divine charity. The answer to this question is important for understanding St. Thomas's appreciation of the mercy of Christ as a man. The "grief" of a loving heart is constituted first "by merely recognizing the misfortune, which is the way God recognized our wretchedness without suffering." But there is another way for Christ as man, as

mercy consists in having a heart grieved at another's misfortune ... in another way by experiencing (*per experientiam*) our misfortune, which is how Christ experienced our misery, especially during the passion.

And thus it is said that he who was merciful through apprehension of our misery was merciful by experience: "I shall cry out and say, here I am, because I the Lord your God am merciful" (Isa 58:9).[78]

So to speak, we know his charity for us as a man because of his experiencing our misery out of the charity that moved his humanity, and then, too, we know his charity as God because he chose eternally so to experience it as a man. In this way, we are led from the misery we can ourselves sense and imagine and feel to the experience of Christ of the same misery, thence to the infinite mercy of God, which is impossible to comprehend but easy to

---

76. *Super Evangelium S. Matthaei Lectura*, c. 26, lect. 5, at 26:38, no. 2225. Christ also gave thanks for his passion at the Last Supper, c. 26, lect. 4, at 26:27, no. 2195.

77. *ST* II-II, q. 30, a. 2, c (my translation).

78. *Commentary on Hebrews*, c. 2, lect. 4, at 2:17, no. 153. See here Joel Matthew Wallace, "*Inspiravit ei voluntatem patiendi pro nobis, infundendo ei caritatem*": *Charity, the Source of Christ's Action According to Thomas Aquinas* (Siena: Cantagalli, 2013), 243–47.

imagine in its created similitude in Christ.[79] Christ demonstrates his mercy in forgiving the woman caught in adultery (Jn 8:1–11); moreover, he *taught* mercy (Mt 5:7) and *commanded* mercy (Mt 12:7).[80] We may well say that the mercy of Christ has a singular place in the declaration of his charity.

The line of thought on the experience of Christ the man is continued in the commentary on Hebrews 2:18. Paul speaks of Christ as man, "in that nature which he assumed in order to experience (*experietur*) in himself that our cause is his own." This redounds to our good, to our confidence in his love and mercy. And again: "He became merciful and faithful because in suffering and being tempted he has a kinship (*convenientiam*) to mercy."[81]

Christ knows our misery for mercy's sake, therefore, as he knows the difficulty of obedience, experientially. This is a most convincing proof of his human charity because it is a most condescending act whose term is ultimately his passion and death. The experiential knowledge of Christ will come forward again, below. But already we can see that his experiential knowledge of us and our condition plays a key role in explaining the approachableness, even the attractiveness, of Christ.

To sum up, the authority of Christ in his human teaching shows us the person of Christ, which is not distinct from his divine nature, and the charity of Christ, obedient and merciful and experiencing our condition as it does, shows us a humanity like ours in all things but sin.

AN AUTHORITATIVE CHARITY
AND A CARITATIVE AUTHORITY

If we knew only Christ's authority, he would frighten us. If we knew only his charity, we might wonder how it could help us. Christ's authority and charity belong to one man, however, and should not be considered separately from one another. They qualify one another. Working together, they attract us to him.[82]

---

79. *ScG* IV, c. 55, no. 7, 3rd argument: "The condition of man required that God instruct man sensibly about Himself as Man."

80. *Commentary on Hebrews*, c. 2, lect. 4, at 2:17, no. 153.

81. *Commentary on Hebrews*, c. 2, lect. 4, at 2:18, no. 154.

82. See Hans Urs von Balthasar, *Love Alone Is Credible*, trans. D. C. Schindler (San Francisco:

An Authoritative Charity: The Authority of Christ's Charity

The authority of Christ's charity is both obvious and evident, so we can be brief.

Freely Exercised

Christ is in charge of the exercise of his charity and its deployment. That is, it is discharged "authoritatively." He lays down his life for his sheep because he loves them, and so the Father loves him (Jn 10:15, 10:17). But he says also: "No one takes it [my life] from me, but I lay it down of my own accord. I have power to lay it down, and I have power to take it again" (Jn 10:18). "Power" here is *exousian*, and we can just as well translate "authority." The discharge of charity thus also displays his authority.

A New Law

In addition, the Lord has the authority to impose charity as a new law. "A new commandment I give to you, that you love one another; even as I have loved you, that you also love one another" (Jn 10:34). The authority of Christ thus makes charity authoritative for us. St. Thomas says that the law of Christ is called the law of charity not only because this distinguishes it from the old law, and not only because he perfectly fulfills it, but also because he expressly "promulgates this law [the new law] in terms of charity," and by this all men will know Christians are his disciples (Jn 13:35).[83]

Ignatius Press, 2004), 56: "The sole [and original and ultimate] authority [of revelation] is the Son, who interprets the Father in the Holy Spirit as divine Love. For it is only here, at the source of revelation, that authority (or majesty) and [divine] love can—and necessarily so—coincide." But it is Christ's human love that is the manifestation of divine love (99).

83. *Commentary on Galatians*, c. 6, lect. 1, at 6:2, no. 348.

A Caritative Authority: The Charity
of Christ's Authority

Teaching from Love

In the first place, the teaching of Christ, manifesting his authority as it does, is also a function of his charity. Christ rejoices in the Spirit as he teaches the Trinity to mere children at Luke 10:21. But again, joy is an interior effect of charity. Just as Aristotle supposed that the most excellent friendship centered on a sharing of knowledge about the best things,[84] so the friendship of charity will be devoted to sharing the revealed knowledge of God. We will see this again below.

Auctor sanctificationis

In the second place and more comprehensively, while the Holy Spirit is the gift (*donum*) of our sanctification, Christ is the *auctor* of our salvation, which he accomplishes through his humanity by his work and his teaching,[85] a teaching that itself gives grace.[86] This last point is important for understanding how it is that human beings can come to recognize his authority and assent to his teaching. Recognizing Christ's person and assenting to his word occurs in faith, and faith is not within the compass of our unaided powers.

Christ's words have the power to penetrate to the heart, as noted above. This power of penetration of Christ's exterior word has to be matched by an interior word of the Spirit, both working unto the heart's assent.[87] So the Lord teaches us, saying that "no one can come to me [in faith] unless the Father who sent me draws him" (Jn 6:44). This drawing is through the inspiration of the Holy Spirit, according to which we realize the goodness

---

84. *Nicomachean Ethics*, Book 9, chapter 12: 1172a12–13, and Book 10, Chapter 7:1177a34–1177b1. For Joseph Owens, friendship is contained focally, but not specifically, in the happiness of contemplation; see his *Human Destiny: Some Problems for Catholic Philosophy* (Washington, DC: Catholic University of America Press, 1985), 22–23. This does not take into account the peculiar pleasure Aristotle recognizes in the shared consciousness of friendship; see Book 9, chapter 9: 1070a13–1070b19.

85. *Auctor* of salvation, *ST* I, q. 43, a. 7, c; *per instructionem et operationem*, *In I Sent.*, d. 16, q. 1, a. 3. See Gilles Emery, OP, "*Theologia and Dispensatio*: The Centrality of the Divine Missions in St. Thomas's Trinitarian Theology," *The Thomist* 74 (2010): 515–61, at 530–33.

86. *Commentary on John 9–21*, c. 20, at 20:22–23, no. 2539.

87. Legge, *Trinitarian Christology*, 55, 224–25.

and attractiveness of faith, and without this interior teaching of the Spirit we cannot assent to the exterior teaching of Christ's word. "No matter what a person may teach by his exterior actions, he will have no effect unless the Holy Spirit gives an understanding from within."[88] But just as the Spirit proceeds eternally from the Father and the Son within the Trinity, so within the economy of salvation he is sent into our hearts by the incarnate Christ (Jn 7:39).

Charity and the Religious Life

In the third place, the relation between teaching and charity is borne out by St. Thomas's theology of the religious life. Charity is the essence of the spiritual life in which we love both God and man,[89] and it is enabled by following the evangelical counsels[90] in the vowed life.[91] But the best exercise of charity just in itself is a matter of teaching, of communicating the revelation of God.[92]

The third [and last] degree of charity consists in enriching our neighbor with such spiritual benefits as are supernatural and exceed human reason. Such benefits are, instruction in divine truth, direction to God, and the spiritual communication of the Sacraments.[93]

Wherefore the best Order of religious life is that devoted to sharing with others the fruits of one's study of Scripture and one's understanding of revealed truth out of charity.[94] Jean-Pierre Torrell adverts to this when he speaks of St. Thomas's own Dominican vocation.

---

88. *Commentary on John*, c. 14, lect. 6, at 14:26, no. 1958. See also c. 16, lect. 3, at 16:13, no. 2103, and c. 17, lect. 6, at 17:26, no. 2269.

89. St. Thomas, *De perfectione spiritualis vitae*, chaps. 2 and 3 in the Leonine edition (LE) of *Sancti Thomae de Aquino Opera Omnia*, vol. 41 (Rome: Santa Sabina, 1970), at LE 41B, 69–70. This corresponds to chaps. 1 and 2 of the English translation in F. J. Procter, ed., *The Religious State* (Westminster, MD: Newman Press, 1950), 5–9. The Corpus Thomisticum website (http://www.corpusthomisticum .org/) claims to offer the Leonine edition of this text, but its numbering (like Procter's old translation of a different edited text) does not correspond to the Leonine edition.

90. St. Thomas, *De perfectione*, chap. 7 (LE 41B, 71–72); trans. Procter, *Religious State*, chap. 6.

91. St. Thomas, *De perfectione*, chap. 12 (LE 41B, 80–81); trans. Procter, *Religious State*, chap. 11.

92. St. Thomas, *De perfectione*, chaps. 15–17 (LE 41B, 86–89); trans. Procter, *Religious State*, chap. 14.

93. St. Thomas, *De perfectione*, chap. 17 (LE 41B 89, ll. 20–14; trans. Procter, *Religious State*, chap. 14, pp. 81–82.

94. *ST* II-II, q. 188, aa. 4–6.

To announce what one has understood of the Gospel truth to someone deprived of it is to come to the aid of the worst poverty and to participate in the highest act of divine mercy.[95]

But mercy is an interior effect of charity.

The Religious Life and the Sacrifice of Teaching

The religious life is indeed the perfect realization of the priesthood of the faithful for St. Thomas.[96] The spiritual sacrifice of this priesthood insofar as it is an offering of the goods of the soul consists in prayer and devotion, but also in praise and teaching.[97] Preaching and teaching are acts of mercy, spiritual alms, but also sacrifices.[98] Teaching is an exercise of both the love of neighbor and the love of God. G. Emery comments as follows.

The office of teaching and of preaching seems to him [Thomas] as a genuine spiritual sacrifice, insofar as it consists in the application of the soul of another to contemplation, and so comprises the offering of the soul of the other.... The commentary on the Psalms explains equally that there is a double spiritual sacrifice, not only that of the praise of God, but also that of doctrine by which one instructs the neighbor; Thomas makes good the example of Christ who, living justly, taught: "The fruit of this doctrine is not only the understanding of the truth in view of beatific contemplation [for oneself], but the end pursued is also the conversion of sinners" [In Ps. 50, 15]. An Order instituted for preaching and study thus includes two forms of spiritual sacrifice according to St. Thomas: that of every religious life that accomplishes by way of a "holocaust" the sacrifice of goods to God in prolonging the sacrifice of the baptized; and that of the teaching that aims at the contemplative union with God and within which the offering of self extends to the offering of another.[99]

95. Jean-Pierre Torrell, OP, *Thomas Aquinas*, vol. 2, *Spiritual Master*, trans. Robert Royal (Washington, DC: Catholic University of America Press, 2003), 380–81.

96. Gilles Emery, OP, "Le sacerdoce spirituel des fidèles chez saint Thomas d'Aquin," *Revue Thomiste* 99 (1999): 211–43, at 238.

97. Emery, "Sacerdoce spirituel," 231, 238–39.

98. Alms, according to *In IV Sent.*, d. 49, q. 5, a. 3, qla 3, ad 1; and sacrifices, according to *De perfectione*, chap. 27, ad 12 (LE 41B, 106, ll. 289–304); trans. Procter, *Religious State*, chap. 23, ad 12, pp. 144–45. Cf. *ST* II-II, q. 182, a. 2, ad 3.

99. Emery, "Sacerdoce spirituel," 239. See also M. Morard, "Sacerdoce du Christ et sacerdoce des chrétiens dans le *Commentaire des Psaulms* de saint Thomas d'Aquin," *Revue Thomist* 99 (1999): 119–42, esp. at 138–40.

FILIAL AUTHORITY AND CHARITY

The unity of Christ's authority and charity is also manifested by the fact that his authority is a filial authority and his charity a filial charity. His entire humanity is, according to Aquinas, "filial" in its entirety and in every exercise of its powers, since it exists only by the *esse personale*—the personal being—of the Son.[100] This is the one being of God, but it is the one being as proceeding from the Father. So whatever Christ as a man does and says manifests the Father in manifesting himself as Son.[101] This manifestation is in its fullness addressed to faith and recognized in its fullness only by faith. D. Legge puts it this way:

Of course, while one who sees Christ's humanity truly sees the incarnate Son, it does not necessarily follow that he would recognize Christ as the Son and thus know the Father.... it is only when they [the disciples] recognized that he was truly the Word of God in the flesh that they not only "saw" but also "knew" him and the Father.[102]

We are interested in those invitations to faith in the self-authenticating teaching of Christ, those places where the authority of Christ comes to light, offers itself for recognition. There is, in other words, a sort of gradation of intensity in how the Son manifests himself in his teaching. There is a scale from "the Kingdom of heaven is like a grain of mustard seed" (Mt 13:31) to "you have heard that it was said ... but I say to you" (Mt 5:21–22), to "something greater than Solomon is here" (Mt 12:42) and "before Abraham was, I am" (Jn 8:58).

Filial Authority

Christ fairly obviously and directly claims the authority of a Son with the parable of the vineyard and tenants (Mt 21:33–43). Once again, however, the communication of the filial character of his authority is bound up not only

---

100. *ST* III, q. 17, a. 2, c. See Legge, *Trinitarian Christology*, 106–14.

101. Legge, *Trinitarian Christology*, 116.

102. Legge, *Trinitarian Christology*, 121–22. The appeal is to the *Commentary on John 9–21*, c. 14, lect. 3, at 14:9, no. 1886.

with the content but also with the manner of his teaching. This is what the Fourth Gospel insists upon, and in a twofold way, first with regard to the origin of his teaching and second with regard to its manner, the nature of the witness he gives to himself.

Content

As to the content of his teaching, Christ says he speaks only what he hears from his Father. So, at John 7:16, "My teaching is not mine, but his who sent me." St. Thomas comments:

> since the doctrine of anyone is nothing else than his word, and the Son of God is the Word of God, it follows that the doctrine of the Father is the Son himself. But this same Word belongs to himself (*est sui ipsius*) through identity of substance. What belongs to you if not you yourself? "However, he does not belong to himself through his origin," as Augustine says.

But then this also follows:

> "my doctrine" … is the Father's; that is, my doctrine is not mine as from myself, but it is from the Father: Because the Son has even his knowledge from the Father through an eternal generation.[103]

John 8:26 is clear also: "I declare to the world what I have heard from him [who sent me]," of which St. Thomas says this "hearing" is the Son's eternal generation.[104]

The Structure of His Testimony

Then there is what we might call the structure of Christ's testimony. The issue is introduced in the fifth chapter of John, and at John 5:31, Jesus says: "If I bear witness to myself, my testimony is not true; there is another who bears witness to me." Following John Chrysostom, St. Thomas takes this other to be John the Baptist.[105] But Christ receives testimony from no man (5:34), that is, in order to come to know who he is.[106] He knows who he is from the interior "testimony" of the Father in the Father's generation of

---

103. *Commentary on John 1–8*, c. 7, lect. 2, at 7:16, no. 1037, translation slightly altered.

104. *Commentary on John 1–8*, c. 8, lect. 3, at 8:26, no. 1187. See also c. 12, lect. 8, at 12:50, no. 1726; c. 14, lect. 3, at 14:10, no. 1893; c. 15, lect. 3, at 15:15, no. 2017; and c. 17, lect. 2, at 17:8, no. 2201.

105. *Commentary on John 1–8*, c. 5, lect. 6, at 5:32, nos. 802 and 805.

106. *Commentary on John 1–8*, c. 5, lect. 6, at 5:32, no. 808.

him.[107] Commenting on 5:37, "the Father himself who has sent me has given testimony about me," Thomas understands this to be the testimony of the Father's voice at Christ's baptism and transfiguration.[108] But again, if the Father testifies to him, it is only for the sake of others, that they may know who he is.

The question of Christ's testimony is rejoined and resolved in chapter 8, where the Lord seems to contradict what he said at 5:31, as to whether he bears witness to himself: "Even if I do bear witness to myself, my testimony is true, for I know whence I have come and whither I am going." Why does this make his testimony true? St. Thomas: "It is like saying, according to Chrysostom, my testimony is true because I am from God, and because I am God, and because I am the Son of God."[109] The person of Christ, his self, is a received self. He can fittingly give testimony to a received self only if it is a received testimony. That is, the word he speaks about himself must match his reality: he speaks a received word about a received self, and only in this way does his truth and identity come properly to light. Just so, his identity as Son, as the proceeding Word, comes to light in this way.[110]

Manifesting Manifestation

The names of the Second Person of the Trinity as Son and Word and Image all designate him as a "principled" reality: he is Son *of* his Father, Image *of* an Exemplar, Word *of* a Speaker. As Son, it is fitting that he be born of Mary; as Image, it is fitting he undertake the work of reparation. And just because he is Word, he is suitably a teacher, for a teacher's words manifest him as a speaker, and he manifests the Father.

But insofar as he is the Word, he fittingly undertakes the office of preaching and teaching, because a word manifests the speaker, and he himself manifested the Father. "Father, I have manifested your name to men" (Jn 17:6).[111]

---

107. *Commentary on John 1–8*, c. 5, lect. 6, at 5:32, no. 809.

108. *Commentary on John 1–8*, c. 5, lect. 6, at 5:32, no. 819.

109. *Commentary on John 1–8*, c. 8, lect. 2, at 8:14, no. 1149.

110. Just so, Jean-Luc Marion speaks of the "perfect inauthenticity" of Christ, *Givenness and Revelation*, 85.

111. *In III Sent.*, ed. Maria Fabianus Moos (Paris: Lethielleux, 1933), d. 1, q. 2, a. 2.

His teaching manifests him as the one who manifests the Father. This is brought to sharper focus in the *Commentary on John*, as Legge notes.[112]

> Note that the Apostle says: "For what person knows a man's thoughts except the spirit of the man which is in him?" (1 Cor 2:11), which we should understand as saying "except insofar as he wants to manifest himself." A person manifests what is hidden within (*suum secretum*) by his words, and it is only by the words of a person that we can know what is hidden within (*secretum hominis*). Now "no one comprehends the thoughts of God except the Spirit of God" (1 Cor 2:11), therefore no one can acquire a knowledge of the Father except by his Word, which is his Son: "no one knows the Father except the Son" (Mt 11:27).[113]

It is not just any of his thoughts that Christ speaks; he reveals his "secret," who he is, the eternal Word, and so his Father. "This is the characteristic work (*proprium opus*) of the Son of God, who is the Word, and the characteristic of a word (*cuius est proprium*) is to manifest the one speaking."[114] Christ does not accomplish his mission unless he manifests himself as purely and completely the manifestation of the Father.

It was noted above in remarks preliminary to considering the teaching of Christ that we light up ourselves by lighting up not just things in the world, but what we take the world itself to be. Christ lights up himself by lighting up his Father, who is in the beginning, before there is any world.

Charity

The charity of Christ also plays a role in the manifestation of his person as Son. There are three paths to consider here: first, from the obedience to the Father that springs from Christ's charity and to which obedience corresponds the gift of piety, filial piety; second, from the effect of Christ's charity, which is peace among men, which is also a work of wisdom, and to which corresponds the reward of the seventh beatitude, according to which peacemakers shall be called sons of God; third, more directly from that very gift of wisdom, the gift of the Holy Spirit that St. Thomas immediately associates with charity, the wisdom whose exemplar is the Second Persons of the

---

112. Legge, *Trinitarian Christology*, 79.
113. *Commentary on John 9–21*, c. 14, lect. 2, at 14:6, no. 1874. I have altered Larcher's translation.
114. *Commentary on John 9–21*, c. 16, lect. 2, at 17s:6, no. 2194.

Trinity, to Christ's human experience of and conformity to the Word in his action and teaching.

In each case, charity works unto the display of the filial character of Christ through some gift of the Holy Spirit that accompanies it.[115] This is to say that his filial character is displayed through the acts that the gifts dispose one to make at the instigation of the *instinctus* of the Holy Spirit.[116] While all the just must be moved not only by reason but also by the illumination and motion of the Spirit to their final end, an end beyond the scope of reason even to discern and the ways to which are similarly beyond the power of reason to grasp,[117] it most of all befits Christ so to be illumined and led by the Spirit, since he occupies not just any place in the pattern of the economy of salvation but is the keystone of the arch.[118]

The Gift of Piety

The gift of the Holy Spirit corresponding to the virtue of justice and so to obedience, one of its potential parts, is piety. By the *virtue* of piety, one is prompt to pay one's debts, as much as one can, to one's parents and homeland, debts of submission and honor and reverence.[119] But by the *gift* of piety, a gift of the Spirit, one is moved to pay these debts to God. It is a gift of filiality, uniting us to God as children to a father:

the Holy Spirit moves us to this that we have a kind of filial affection to God: according to the teaching of Romans 8:15: "Receive the Spirit of the adoption of sons, in which we cry out, Abba, Father."[120]

But from charity, as we have seen, there arises obedience, such that Christ loves his Father and so loves to obey the command of his Father.[121] The gift of piety will move him as a child, in a filial way, to obey his Father's command. That is what we see in the Gospels, in prayer (Mk 1:35), in his thanks-

---

115. A good introduction to St. Thomas on the Gifts can be found in Edward O'Connor, CSC, Appendix 4, "The Evolution of St. Thomas's Thought on the Gifts," in *St. Thomas Aquinas, Summa Theologiae, vol. 24 (1a2ae 68–70): The Gifts of the Spirit* (New York: McGraw-Hill, 1964).

116. *ST* I-II, q. 68, a. 2.

117. *ST* I-II, q. 68, a. 1, and a. 2, c and ad 3. See Legge, *Trinitarian Christology*, 202–6.

118. *ST* III, q. 7, aa. 1 and 5.

119. *ST* II-II, q. 101, aa. 1 and 2.

120. *ST* II-II, q. 121, a. 1, c. See Wallace, *Inspiravit ei voluntatem*, 393, 397.

121. E.g., *ST* III, q. 47, a. 2, ad 2.

giving (Mt 11:25), in his obedience in the garden, and on the cross, when he commends himself reverently to the Father, returning gifts to God (Lk 23:46; Jn 19:30). The affective unity of Christ, considered in his charity and obedience and piety, is a filial unity.

Peacemaking

The third interior effect of charity of which we have said little up to now is peace, since it has the effect of uniting the wills of many agents in one willing.[122] But peace is not the work only of charity. The seventh beatitude, concerning peacemakers, is especially to be associated with the gift of wisdom, which is itself a conformation to the subsisting Wisdom of God, the term of his invisible mission to the souls of the just.[123]

For peacemakers are said as it were to make peace either in themselves or also in others. And this happens for both through this, that those things in which peace is constituted are brought back to due order: for peace is "the tranquility of order," as Augustine says in Book XIX of *The City of God* [c. 13, no. 1]. But to order something belongs to wisdom, as is evident through the Philosopher at the beginning of the *Metaphysics* [Book I, c. 2].[124]

Now by his passion, Christ reconciles us to God and one another, and so makes peace. So at Colossians 1:20, where Christ is said to make peace by the blood of his cross, Thomas says:

wills that were before in conflict are made to harmonize in Christ. For example, the wills of men, of God, and of the angels. The will of men, because Christ is a man; and the will of God, because Christ is God. There was also conflict between the Jews, who wanted the law, and the gentiles, who did not want the law. But Christ created harmony between the two, because he was from the Jews, and he freed us from the legal observances.

This harmony was accomplished "through the blood of his cross."[125]

So he makes peace in the order of his action or operation, especially by his obedience and piety, and as conformed to the wisdom of God by the working of the gift of wisdom in him, all of which things are filial. He displays who he is in a sort of operative filiality, if you will.

---

122. *ST* II-II, q. 29; see also *Commentary on Hebrews*, c. 13, lect. 3, at 13:20, no. 766.
123. *ST* I, q. 43, a. 5, ad 2.
124. *ST* II-II, q. 45, a. 6. See Wallace, *Inspiravit ei voluntatem*, 397–98.
125. *Commentary on Colossians*, c. 1, lect. 5, at 1:20, no. 53.

Furthermore, if by his passion and death Christ makes peace, then he does the work of wisdom, establishing the tranquility of order, and if he could *merit* it, would merit to be called a son of God according to the seventh beatitude. His charity and obedience, piety and wisdom rather manifest his personal identity as Son and do not constitute it. But we merit such status according as by own charity and obedience, piety and wisdom, we share in his sufferings.

The Gift of Wisdom

Just as charity bespeaks a likeness to the Holy Spirit, so the gift of wisdom bespeaks a likeness to the Word, as we just said. Here is the key text of which we have yet to take full account.

Because the Holy Spirit is Love, the soul is assimilated to the Holy Spirit through the gift of charity ... But the Son is the Word, and not just any word, but the Word breathing Love ... Therefore it is not according to just any perfection of the intellect that the Son is sent, but it is according to that intellectual instruction by which it breaks forth into the affection of love ... And therefore Augustine says significantly that the Son is sent "when he is known and perceived by someone": for perception means a kind of experimental perception. And this is properly called wisdom—as it were a kind of savoring knowledge according to Sirach 6:23.[126]

The gift of wisdom thus assimilates the soul to the Word and enables a connatural knowledge, an experimental knowledge, of what befits the wisdom of the Word, of the Son, both speculatively and practically.[127] And this gift so directs the soul according to the divine rules that it finds sweetness and rest in what otherwise would be bitter and onerous.[128] To the point, the gift of wisdom in Christ's intellect enables him to know by experience the goodness and sweetness of his passion and of obediently submitting to it. And just because its exemplary cause is the Word himself, the gift of wisdom gives this experiential knowledge a filial character.[129]

---

126. *ST* I, q. 43, a. 5, ad 2.

127. *ST* II-II, q. 43, a. 3, c. For the experiential knowledge of the persons imparted by the gifts, see Gilles Emery, OP, *The Trinitarian Theology of St. Thomas Aquinas*, trans. Francesca Aran Murphy (Oxford: Oxford University Press, 2007), 392–95.

128. *ST* II-II, q. 45, a. 3, ad 3.

129. See Joel Matthew Wallace, *Inspiravit ei voluntatem*, 386–94.

Charity and the gift of wisdom work together in Christ unto a knowledge and a love displayed in his work of redemption because each gives rise to knowledge and each gives rise to love. For St. Thomas, charity is not only affective but cognoscitive, as Thomas explains in his commentary on Philippians 1:9. It gives a connatural knowledge of the good, an experiential recognition and discernment of the good as conformed to the Holy Spirit.

when a person has a habit, if that habit is right, then right judgment of things pertaining to that habit follows from it.... therefore a person with charity has a correct judgment both in regard to things knowable ... and in regard to things to be done.[130]

This knowledge extends to discerning the difference between good and evil and between the good and the better. The exercise of the gift of wisdom, however, is the exercise of a word that breaks forth in into love. It gives a practical knowledge, proximate to love, of the good and discerns it to be good according to the wisdom of God to which the gift is conformed in the person of the Word, as already noted. Both charity and wisdom therefore conspire, as gifts of the Holy Spirit, to lead Christ to the work of his passion and death. This is a knowledge, an affective knowledge leading to action (operation) that is available to no one except Christ and those who are in him, else the princes and principalities of this world would never have crucified the Lord of glory and in that way contributed to their own demise and dethronement (1 Cor 2:7–8).

It would be a mistake to think that the gifts of the Holy Spirit that charity brings to Christ extended only to the Spirit's guidance of Christ's own life. The gifts of wisdom and understanding, bearing on divine things, and the gift of knowledge, bearing on human things, bear also on things to be done (as was just said of the gift of wisdom).[131] Together with the gift of counsel, they bear also on Christ's guidance of the lives of others. That is, they bear on his teaching. This is easier to see if we think of him carrying it out in the contingent circumstances of his life. His knowledge of God *per es-*

---

130. *Commentary on Philippians*, in St. Thomas Aquinas, *Commentary on the Letters of Saint Paul to the Philippians, Colossians, Thessalonians, Timothy, Titus, and Philemon*, c. 1, lect. 2., at 1:9, no. 17. See Wallace, *Inspiravit ei voluntatem*, 235–38.

131. For understanding (*intellectus*), *ST* II-II, q. 8, aa. 1 and 2; for knowledge (*scientia*), II-II, q. 9, aa. 1 and 2.

sentiam, in vision, is perfect from the first moment of his conception.[132] His infused knowledge was similarly always perfectly available to him. He does not deliver all that he knows to his disciples in one instant block of teaching, however, for such would not fit the capacities of his hearers. In revealing himself and his authority, in teaching the new law, he has to teach now one thing and now another. Just here, then, the gifts of the Holy Spirit play their proper role, catching the inspiration of his own Spirit, beyond what he could know by his human reason, and in addition to what he knows as God does in vision and as the angels do by infused species, and in a way not deducible from this abiding twofold knowledge, so that his charity inclines him to teach now this, and now that.[133] In this way, the very teaching that reveals his authority and person is always under the guidance of a charity led by the Spirit, always under the guidance of an experiential knowledge of divinity that leads him to teach the right things at the right time to the right people, such that it would be truer to say of him than of any other teacher: "Do not be anxious how or what you are to answer or what you are to say; for the Holy Spirit will teach you in that very hour what you ought to say" (Lk 12:11–12).

Just according as they are intellectual gifts, wisdom and understanding and knowledge find their exemplar in the Second Person of the Trinity. And in that way, their exercise declares his person and authority. But also, insofar as the gifts are ways in which charity is channeled and vectored now in this, now in another way, this display of authority is always also a demonstration of charity.

CONCLUSION

Christ's authority in and of itself makes him distant from us. Or, rather, it makes us distant from him. "Depart from me, for I am a sinful man, O Lord" (Lk 5:8). But the charity of Christ brings him close to us, and in St.

---

132. *ST* III, q. 12, a. 2, ad 1.

133. *What* Christ knows as to the content of revelation via the gifts he knows via infused knowledge; see Legge, *Trinitarian Christology*, 185. But I am saying that his infused knowledge does not include the knowledge of the times and seasons of its dispensation—how, concretely, it is to be shared.

Thomas's account, experientially close to us. He knows by experiencing our misery how much we stand in need of mercy. He knows by experience how hard it is to rise to God in an obedience to difficult commands. This is super important, first, for our love of him, and next and second, for our confidence in our ability to follow him. If he teaches the law of love authoritatively, commanding us to follow him on this way, he is not commanding us to do anything he did not do first, more fully, more perfectly, with a more perfect taste of the difficulty of our starting point and the difficulty of rising up from it by humility and obedience. Furthermore, third, as he came through the gift of wisdom to know the goodness of his passion and death, we can in the same way come to know the goodness of our sharing in his sufferings, tasting the things ordained by the wisdom of God that surpass human understanding. In the fourth place, if as a man he has by seeing the essence of God a humanly perfect knowledge of his Father, he knows the divine persons also connaturally, experientially, via charity and in the gifts of the Holy Spirit. We cannot now share in the knowledge of vision. But we can share in this life in the experiential knowledge of divine things St. Thomas imputed to Christ. Fifth, knowing what is good for us via the Spirit, he teaches us also only as guided by the Spirit of charity. In this way, the very authority of Christ shares in the charity by which he comes close to us.

We know from the New Testament that Jesus of Nazareth was an attractive, popular man. Great crowds went out to listen to him (Mk 1:45, 3:7), and they followed him from place to place (Mt 14:13–14, 15:39). It is an understatement to say that people liked to be around him; they came near to crushing him (Mk 3:9). The crowds so pestered him and the disciples that they could not even eat (Mk 3:20). He asked the people what they went out to see when they went out to see John the Baptist (Mt 11:7). What did they go out to see when they went out to see Jesus? They went out to see authority joined to charity. They went out to see the great dumbfounding constellation of power and mercy, one who experienced them more profoundly than they did themselves, one who also experienced their God, whom he called Father. They went out to see the authority of a Teacher, led by the Spirit, obedient in charity to the One who sent him, who could give life.

CHAPTER 8

AQUINAS'S CHRISTOLOGY OF
COMMUNICATION

John Emery, OP

INTRODUCTION:
THE QUEST FOR A CHRISTOLOGY
OF COMMUNICATION

Contemporary portrayals of Christ's saving agency adeptly present it in a manifold way that avoids reducing the ensemble to just one manner of salvation.[1] In fact, following an established practice based on Sacred Scripture,[2] studies on soteriology rightfully and lucidly list a number of ways in which Christ's saving agency can be conceived without the intention of choosing one to the exclusion of all others.[3] This positive staple of Catholic theology can, of course, be found in Aquinas's own works; notably, in questions 48 and 49 of the *Tertia Pars* of his *Summa Theologiae*.[4]

1. See, e.g., Bernard Sesboüé, *Jésus-Christ l'unique médiateur: Essai sur la rédemption et le salut*, vol. 1, *Problématique et relecture doctrinale*, Jésus et Jésus-Christ 33 (Paris: Desclée, 1988).

2. See, e.g., *ST* III, qq. 48–49, where Thomas develops different aspects of Christ's saving agency during his passion.

3. See, e.g., Sesboüé, *Jésus-Christ*, 1:123–390; International Theological Commission, *Select Questions on Christology*, 1979, Part 4, nos. 4–8, website of the Holy See, January 28, 2020, http://www.vatican.va/roman_curia/congregations/cfaith/cti_documents/rc_cti_1979_cristologia_en.html; International Theological Commission, *Select Questions on the Theology of God the Redeemer*, 1995 [1994], Part 3, website of the Holy See, January 28, 2020, http://www.vatican.va/roman_curia/congregations/cfaith/cti_documents/rc_cti_1995_teologia-redenzione_en.html; Olegario González de Cardedal, *Cristología*, Sapientia Fidei: Serie de Manuales de Teología (Madrid: Biblioteca de Autores Cristianos, 2001), 516, 519, 523–46.

4. See notably *ST* III, q. 48, a. 6, ad 3.

Contemporary Christology, however, rarely accounts for this multiplicity or for its cohesion. This situation could be portrayed as a "soteriological disconnect." Walter Kasper opines: "the traditional soteriology makes a very fragmentary and disorganized impression; the extremely various biblical and traditional metaphors . . . and theories of redemption . . . are simply juxtaposed, not developed systematically from a single point of view."[5] Gerald O'Collins gives a similar assessment.[6] The question arises as to why there are many ways in which Christ saves us and how they are united. Although Aquinas does not explicitly pose this question, the response is provided in his work. I wish to argue that Christ's charity as man—that is, the charity that animated each of his saving causalities—offers us a path forward. Our claim that Christ's charity lends cohesiveness to the ensemble of his saving agency is based on St. Thomas's definition of charity as a friendship founded on the communication of beatitude.

Communication has the potential to provide a unified account of Christ's saving agency because it looks to what is common to God and man, and avoids setting divine and human agency in opposition.[7] By analyzing each manner in which salvation is effected through the lens of communication, one comes to realize that an ascending account of Christology—where human agency plays a prominent role—is in fact but a continuation and a greater expression of a descending one—in which divine agency comes to the fore—since the former is rooted in the latter. From this vantage point, one can come to consider all other soteriological categories as being at the service of God's communication to and with spiritual creatures. Some theologians, who do not especially purport to develop or follow Aquinas, have alluded to the appeal held by a Christology of communication; Karl Rahner,[8] Wal-

---

5. See Walter Kasper, *Jesus the Christ*, trans. V. Green, 4th repr. (London: Burns & Oates, 1985; 1st ed., 1976), 253.

6. See Gerald O'Collins, SJ, *Christology: A Biblical, Historical, and Systematic Study of Jesus*, repr. (Oxford: Oxford University Press, 2013; 2nd ed., 2009; 1st ed., 1995), 297: "no period of Christianity can claim to have produced a truly unified systematic soteriology."

7. See González de Cardedal, *Cristología*, 305–10, who praises Thomas's Christology in the *Tertia Pars* for its "admirable equilibrium" between the descending and ascending perspectives (309).

8. See International Theological Commission, *Select Questions on the Theology of God the Redeemer*, part III, n. 30, which summarizes Rahner's basic understanding of Christ's redeeming work thus: "He depicts Jesus as the unsurpassable symbol that manifests God's irreversible universal salvific will. As a symbolic reality, Christ effectively represents both God's irrevocable self-communication in grace and the acceptance of that self-communication by humanity."

ter Kasper,[9] and Jean Galot come to mind.[10] These and other voices bear witness to the need for a new outlook on the study of Christ; however, they are not accompanied by a thorough analysis of what this entails.[11] Only an unfolded and worked-out theological notion of communication is capable of integrating the different ways in which Christ works our salvation, so as to incorporate them into a coherent whole. St. Thomas's theology is conducive to this because it offers us a nuanced usage of *communicatio*. Notably, this is found in his explanation of charity as friendship. This very fact is not devoid of importance for our purpose here. For Aquinas, a saving causality based on communication amounts to a saving causality based on friendship: Christ causes salvation not by coercing others, but by acts of friendship that give rise to other acts of friendship. In what follows, we will study Aquinas's theological concept of communication, its affinity with Christ's charity, his own communication, and how his saving causalities are based on communication in order to cause it in us.

9. Kasper, *Jesus the Christ*, 250: "[Christ is] in person, God's self-communication in love" (modified). The scholar also speaks of Christ as "God's self-communicating love in person" (252) and "[Christ is the] mold and receptacle for God's self-communication" (267).

10. See Jean Galot, SJ, *Le problème christologique actuel* (Paris: Éditions C.L.D., 1979), 86–93, who explains that the sacrifice of Christ, as well as our own, is the fruit of a divine communication: "La nature humaine, d'une manière absolue dans le Christ et d'une manière participée dans les autres hommes, devient parfaite en raison du sacrifice, et cette perfection résulte d'une communication de la perfection divine" (92–93).

11. Cf., e.g., Kasper, *Jesus the Christ*, 259–66, where the scholar refers to Christ's "three offices" ("prophet and teacher," "priest," "pastor and king") but only presents them side by side in what amounts to a piecemeal rendering of Christ's saving agency, and one that is only loosely connected with the Holy Spirit; Galot, *Le problème*, 51–55, who speaks of the work of salvation as a "liberation of love" that is found in both the liberator and the liberated; O'Collins, *Christology*, 306–14, whose presentation of Christ's saving work consists mainly in a list of "eight themes" that pertain to "*love*," "the richest key" for its interpretation, but does not articulate how these aspects of love concur in one agency and how this agency affects that of the redeemed (the scholar notably commences his soteriological account with man's need for salvation and not with God's love or gift; 280–82); and Roch A. Kereszty, *Jesus Christ: Fundamentals of Christology*, 3rd ed. (Staten Island, NY: St Pauls, 2015; 1st ed., 2002), 411–42, who indicates that God's goal when redeeming man is perfect communion with him, and sees sin and the cross of Christ as rejection and acceptance of the divine gift, respectively (428–49).

AQUINAS'S IDEA OF
COMMUNICATION

The fact that St. Thomas's idea of communication can be best grasped by studying his treatment of charity is extremely fitting: through charity, the invisible divine missions are made present in us, we are united operatively with God himself, the image of God in us is fulfilled, human beings are made perfect as the Father is perfect, the whole of the supernatural moral order is set in motion, and, of course, "charity never ends" (1 Cor 13:8).[12] Charity is "breathed forth" within us through the living knowledge the Word infuses in us: together, these two gratuitous effects—supernatural knowledge and love—constitute the apex of the life of God in us.[13]

Aquinas boldly and originally defines charity as friendship by drawing on Aristotle's understanding of friendship and completing it. Based on the Stagirite's usage of κοινωνία and κοινωνέω,[14] a usage that agrees with that of Scripture and the Church Fathers,[15] the Dominican centers his explanation of charity as friendship on communication: "Given that there is some communication of man toward God inasmuch as He communicates his beatitude to us, it is fitting (*oportet*) that some manner of friendship be founded upon this communication."[16] An attentive reading of the first article of his last full account of charity in the *Secunda Secundae* reveals that this term is given three different yet analogous meanings.[17] This analogy has deep metaphysical roots: these three forms of communication participate in the actuality given by God and work together in the same process. The communication

12. See, e.g., *ST* I, q. 8, a. 3, c; I, q. 43, a. 3, c and ad 2; I, q. 93, a. 7, c; I, q. 93, a. 8, c; I-II, q. 67, a. 6, c; II-II, q. 23, aa. 7–8; II-II, q. 24, a. 8; II-II, q. 184, aa. 1–2.

13. *ST* I, q. 43, a. 5, ad 2.

14. See, e.g., Aristotle, *Nicomachean Ethics*, Book 8, chapter 11 (z9), 1159b24–32; Book 8, chapter 14 (z12), 1161b11; Book 9, chapter 9, 1170b10–12; Book 9, chapter 12, 1171b32–34.

15. See Ceslas Spicq, OP, *Agapè dans le Nouveau Testament: Analyse des textes*, Études Bibliques 2 (Paris: J. Gabalda et Cie, Éditeurs, 1959), 165; Benoît-Dominique de La Soujeole, OP, *Introduction to the Mystery of the Church*, trans. M. J. Miller (Washington, DC: Catholic University of America Press, 2014), 452–60.

16. *ST* II-II, q. 23, a. 1, c. See also *In III Sent.* d. 27, q.. 2, aa. 1–2; *In Eth.* 8, II, ll. 89–116 (9–11, m1559–1561); *ST* I-II, q. 65, a. 5, c; II-II, q. 24, a. 2, c.

17. The passage quoted above (*ST* II-II, q. 23, a. 1, c) refers to the first two forms of the communication upon which charity is founded; a third form can be found in *ST* II-II, q. 23, a. 1, ad 1, where friendship with God is said to include "communication or living-together" (*communicatio vel conversatio*).

on which charity is founded is (1) a giving that makes the recipient come to possess something in common with the giver, (2) a having in common, and (3) an acting or living in common.[18] Considered from the vantage point of their action, this threefold communication involves (1) divine initiative and action, (2) the reception of a gift by the recipient, and (3) the development of that gift through the recipient's cooperation. The synergy between the act of God and the act of his created friend enables the latter to be borne, so to say, by God's very act of giving himself because God's communication of sanctifying grace or beatitude is present at every stage. Understanding communication in this way leads to viewing salvation as a sole movement that comprises both a descending and an ascending stage, such that the latter stems from the former and the former is present in the latter.

Three points should be further clarified. First, every creature receives a first communication of being and actuality corresponding to that creature's nature. Although the Trinity is present in it, according to this first mode a creature is not itself united to God as a friend, nor does it share in the very life of God.[19] Some creatures have an aptitude to receive a second mode of communication from God that surpasses their nature because they are created according to and *toward* the image (*ad imaginem*) of God. This new communication is a participation in the very life of God, according to which God loves us as his friends.[20] It should be noted that, although both the natural and supernatural communications somehow develop according to the three forms or stages of communication discussed above, this applies most fully and properly to the latter. Aquinas's preferred definition of charity in the *Secunda Secundae* does not refer to its communication as "grace" but as

18. The secondary literature on the meanings of *communicatio* is extremely abundant. The first contributions in the early part of the twentieth century by Cocconier and Keller vied for the prevalence of either the third or second sense, respectively: Marie-Thomas Cocconier, "La charité d'après saint Thomas d'Aquin: à propos d'une boutade de Bossuet," *Revue thomiste* 12 (1904): 641–60; Marie-Thomas Cocconier, "Ce qu'est la charité d'après saint Thomas d'Aquin (2° article)," *Revue thomiste* 14 (1906): 5–30; Josephus M. Keller, OP, "De virtute caritatis ut amicitia quaedam divina. S Thomas, 3. dist. 27, q. 2, a. 1 et 2. 2, q. 23, a. 1," in *Xenia Thomistica*, vol. 2, ed. S. Szabó, OP (Rome: Typis Polyglottis Vaticanis, 1925), 233–76; Marie-Joseph Keller, OP, and Marie-Benoît Lavaud, OP, "La charité comme amitié d'après S. Thomas," *Revue thomiste* 12 (1929): 445–75. Gradually the senses were integrated into an analogous whole comprising the first sense; see, e.g., Joseph Bobik, "Aquinas on *Communicatio*, the Foundation of Friendship and *Caritas*," *Modern Schoolman* 64 (1986): 1–18.

19. See *In I Sent.* d. 37, q. 1, a. 2, c and ad 2; *Comp. theol.* I, 214, ll. 46–50; *Sup. Col.* 2, II (*v.*9; m96).

20. See *In II Sent.* d. 26, q. u, a. 1, ad 2; *In III Sent.* d.19, q. u, a. 5, qla. 1, c and ad 1; d. 32, q. u, a. 2, c; *ST* I, q. 20, a. 2, ad 3; I-II, q. 110, a. 1, c; *Sup. Io.* 15, V (*v.*21; m1936).

"beatitude"; in doing so, he shows us that true beatitude is communicated to God's friends already in this life, albeit in an inchoate form.[21] The vision of the divine essence brings about the consummate form of what we receive in this life. To be clear, the second mode of divine presence equates to the presence of the invisible missions, sanctifying grace and beatitude; the state of grace in this life is inchoate beatitude.[22] The communication of being according to nature equates to God's first mode of presence; beatitude is the second mode of divine presence, wherein the invisible divine missions inform our operative union with God. Beatitude, inchoate or consummate, is nothing other than operative union with God: performing acts of knowledge and love of God in a most intimate union with him.

Second, Aquinas explains that the love involved in friendship—love of friendship or of benevolence—arises from the impulse to communicate one's actuality or perfection.[23] In other words, our love of friendship flows from something that perfects us or actualizes us, thus enabling us to give to others. In the case of charity, to be a friend of God implies communicating something to him, not only receiving it from him.[24] This involves the full acceptance of God's gift, that is, to be made like it and to be made one with it. In this regard, as the three forms or stages of the communication pertaining to the second mode of divine presence imply, whoever loves according to that friendship that is charity will strive to give to God, in himself or in his loved ones (our neighbors), the very fruit of the communication received from him.[25]

---

21. In addition to *ST* II-II, q. 23, a. 1, c, see II-II, q. 23, a. 5, c; II-II, q. 24, a. 2, c; II-II, q. 25, a. 2, ob. 2; II-II, q. 25, a. 3, c; II-II, q. 25, a. 6, c; II-II, q. 25, a. 10, c; II-II, q. 25, a. 12, c; II-II, q. 26, a. 1, c; II-II, q. 26, a. 2, c; II-II, q. 26, a. 7, ob. 3.

22. Save for the hypostatic union, all supernatural effects belong to one communication: "grace and glory, appertain to the same genus, because grace is nothing but an inception ('inchoatio') of glory in us" (*ST* II-II, q. 24, a. 3, ad 2), a fact upon which St. Thomas bases the unity of the virtue of charity (*ST* II-II, q. 23, a. 5, c). To receive sanctifying grace in this life is to receive beatitude "in its cause" (*In III Sent.* d. 19, q. u, a. 5, qla. 1, c), or as its "seminal form (*ratio seminalis*)" (*ST* I, q. 62, a. 3, c). See also *Sup. Heb.* 12, V (*v.*28; m723); *Sup. Io.* 16, VI (*v.*23a; m2140).

23. See *ST* I-II, q. 27, a. 3, c. See also *In II Sent.* d. 3, q. 4, a. u, c.

24. Cf. *De Caritate* a. 2, c: "loving the good in which the blessed participate so as to have or possess it does not render man well disposed toward beatitude, since those who are evil ('mali') also desire that good; however, loving that good in itself ('secundum se') so that it endures and is diffused ('diffundatur'), and so that nothing is done against this good, renders a man well disposed toward that association [or society] of the blessed." Cf. also *In III Sent.* D. 29, q. u, a. 3, ad 4; *ST* II-II, q. 28, a. 1, c.

25. The twenty-five articles Aquinas devotes to the treatment of the object and order of charity in

Third, acts of charity in this life are tied or linked to the acts of charity in heaven: the former fulfill an order preordained by God to the latter.[26] There is not only a formal continuity, according to what is essential in these acts, but also a causal continuity, one effected by God with our cooperation. This is called merit. When someone performs an act of charity founded on inchoate beatitude (or grace), he or she fulfills its ordering to consummate beatitude (or glory) at the same time. Merit is our collaboration in the fulfillment of this ordering.[27] Thus meriting eternal life does not amount to forcing God's hand to reward something that he had not decided to give already; neither does it involve doing something that he himself does not do in us and with us. Merit is a development of God's gift: it is a new stage in the development of his grace. As a development of the communication of beatitude, it presupposes God's "preordination" or an ordering of someone and his or her act to attain a higher and fuller communication of beatitude.[28] The Holy Spirit works in and with the recipient of this communication by infusing charity into him and moving him to love God and his communication. The ensuing act is one of intimate friendship and brings about the full unfolding of the communication that God gives to us. Insofar as this act merits, it is an act performed by two agents: each one authors it in its entirety.[29] In this meriting act, both the agency of the recipient and its fruit are gratuitous because they are both freely given by God: he gives to us that we collaborate with a gift designed to incorporate us into its gratuitousness at every step of the way.

---

the *Secunda Secundae* (*ST* II-II, qq. 25–26) can be seen as the deployment of charity's love of friendship that aims to give to God the very communication it receives and upon which it is founded (see also *In III Sent.* Dd. 28–30; *De Caritate* aa. 7–9).

26. For the "virtual" equality between grace and glory, see *ST* I-II, q. 114, a. 3, ad 3.

27. The main element in Aquinas's mature study on merit in the *Prima Secundae* is the "divine ordering" ('ordinatio') or "preordering" ('praeordinatio'): *ST* I-II, q. 114, aa. 1–4. See, e.g., William D. Lynn, SJ, *Christ's Redemptive Merit: The Nature of Its Causality According to St. Thomas*, Analecta Gregoriana 115 (Rome: Gregorian University Press, 1962), 34–44; Bernard Catão, *Salut et rédemption chez S. Thomas d'Aquin: L'acte sauveur du Christ* (Paris: Aubier, 1965), 135–41; Joseph P. Wawrykow, *God's Grace and Human Action: Merit in the Theology of Thomas Aquinas* (Notre Dame, IN: University of Notre Dame Press, 1995), 9–12, 80–83, 147–64, 180–90, 241.

28. In *ST* I-II, q. 114, a. 6, c, the divine preordering or "motion" defines what can be merited and for whom. Merit presupposes divine mercy and grace; see *ST* I-II, q. 114, a. 3, ad 2; I, q. 21.

29. In addition to the preordering to eternal life, in order to fulfill this preordering that surpasses a creature's capacity, we need to be moved by the Holy Spirit (*ST* I-II, q. 114, a. 3, c and ad 3) and to receive charity so as to cooperate with this Spirit (*ST* I-II, q. 114, a. 4, c).

CHRIST'S CHARITY AT THE CORE OF
THE DIVINE DISPENSATION

The central place held by charity within God's economy naturally leads to inquiring about the place of Christ's charity within this saving dispensation. To do so, it is expedient to continue to have recourse to the modes of divine presence as the framework that best represents Aquinas's thought and, most of all, enables us to grasp the connections he establishes within his treatment of the divine economy.[30] Having referred to the first two modes already, let us now consider the relation between the mode of divine presence pertaining to charity and the unique mode of divine presence in the incarnate Son's humanity. This third mode coincides with the visible mission of the eternal Word, just as the second does with the invisible missions of the eternal Word and the Holy Spirit. Both these modes of divine presence exceed the natural order: they involve grace, union with God, supernatural sonship, and a more perfect Trinitarian likeness.

First, the grace that corresponds to the third mode of divine presence is the grace of union, which is the union inasmuch as it is gratuitous.[31] This is

---

30. See Yves M.-J. Congar, OP, *The Mystery of the Temple: Or The Manner of God's Presence to His Creatures from Genesis to the Apocalypse*, trans. R. F. Trevett (London: Burns & Oates, 1962; 1st French ed., 1958), 238–39, esp. no. 3; Erik Persson, "Le plan de la Somme théologique et le rapport 'Ratio–Revelatio,'" *Revue Philosophique de Louvain* 56 (1958): 545–72; Marie-Vincent Leroy, OP, "La convenance de l'Incarnation," *Revue thomiste* 109 (2009): 419–65, here 422–25; Romanus Cessario, OP, "Is Aquinas's *Summa* Only about Grace?," in *Ordo sapientiae et amoris. Image et message de saint Thomas d'Aquin à travers les récentes études historiques, herméneutiques et doctrinales: Hommage au professeur Jean-Pierre Torrell, OP à l'occasion de son 65e anniversaire*, ed. C.-J. Pinto de Oliveira, OP (Fribourg, Switzerland: Éditions Universitaires, 1993), 197–209; Guillermo A. Juárez, *Dios Trinidad en todas las creaturas y en los santos: Estudio histórico-sistemático de la doctrina del Comentario a las Sentencias de Santo Tomás de Aquino sobre la omnipresencia y la inhabitación* (Córdoba, Argentina: Edición del Copista, 2008), 596–97; Benedict XVI, "General Audience: Saint Thomas Aquinas (3), 23 June 2010," website of the Holy See, January 28, 2020, http://www.vatican.va/content/benedict-xvi/en/audiences/2010/documents/hf_ben-xvi_aud_20100623.html; Gilles Emery, "L'inhabitation de Dieu Trinité dans les justes," *Nova et Vetera* 88 (2013): 155–84, here 148. The *exitus-reditus* schema as applied to the economy—to human beings in particular—has a number of shortcomings and is not very helpful; moreover, it is not truly representative of Aquinas's theology, as he only draws on it in his *Commentary on the Sentences* in connection with the divine processions but foregoes it in the *Summa Theologiae*. The schema was popularized by Marie-Dominique Chenu, *Toward Understanding Saint Thomas*, ed. and trans. A.-M. Landry, OP, and D. Hughes, OP (Chicago: Henry Regnery, 1964; 1st French ed., 1950). The schema is more apt when applied to the divine missions and to Christ (Jn 13:3) in particular.

31. See *ST* III, q. 6, a. 6, c; III, q. 2, a. 10; III, q. 8, a. 13.

the highest and maximal grace because it fulfills the "end," or purpose, of grace most perfectly,[32] that is, the "union" between God and man.[33] Nothing is as gratuitous as the grace of union; all other graces, including habitual sanctifying grace, participate in its gratuitousness as in their exemplar.[34] Second, since the hypostatic union is the "maximal union" between God and man,[35] it encourages us to believe that the next greatest union between God and man is attainable; namely, the union between the divine essence and our intellect in the beatific vision.[36] The latter is the highest operative union possible or the highest degree of union within the second mode of divine presence. Third, another way of regarding these modes is through the lens of sonship. Christ's natural divine filiation as man is the exemplar of the divine filiation attached to the second mode of divine presence in us: our adoptive sonship is a likeness of and a participation in Christ's natural one.[37] Finally, as with the eternal Son's generation, the creation of spiritual creatures involves a special likeness to their principle. They have been created in the image of the Trinity, and this image is fulfilled when they become like each of the eternal processions (the generation of the Son and spiration of the Holy Spirit). This occurs through the acts of the spiritual powers of the soul—that is, by knowing and loving God supernaturally—something that is brought about by the invisible divine missions.[38] This most perfect like-

32. *ScG* IV, c. 46 (5, m3828); *Sup. Io.* 1, VIII (*v.*14d; m188); *ST* III, q. 2, a. 10, ad 1.

33. *In III Sent.* d. 13, q. 1, a. 2, qla. 1, c; *Sup. Io.* 17, V (*v.*22; m2246); *Comp. theol.* I, 214, ll. 50–56 and 78–81; *ST* III, q. 7, a. 12, c.

34. See *ST* III, q. 24, a. 3, sc and c.

35. *ST* III, q. 2, a. 9.

36. See *ScG* IV, c. 54 (2, m3923); c. 55 (6, m3937); *Comp. theol.* I, 201, ll. 17–22.

37. See *Sup. Rom.* 1, III (*v.*4; m48); *Sup. Io.* 1, VIII (*v.*14c; m187); *ST* II-II, q. 45, a. 6, c; III, q. 3, a. 8, c; III, q. 23, a. 3, c; III, q. 23, a. 4, c; III, q. 24, a. 3, c.

38. See *ST* I, q. 93, esp. aa. 7 and 8. See also I, q. 60, a. 5, ad 4; I-II, q. 109, a. 3, ad 1; Jean-Pierre Torrell, OP, *Christ and Spirituality in St. Thomas Aquinas*, trans. B. Blankenhorn, OP (Washington, DC: Catholic University of America Press, 2011; 1st French ed., 1996), chap. 3; Gilles Emery, *The Trinitarian Theology of Saint Thomas Aquinas*, trans. F. A. Murphy (Oxford: Oxford University Press, 2007; 1st French ed., 2004), 395–96; G. Emery, "L'inhabitation," 178–83; Daria Spezzano, *The Glory of God's Grace: Deification According to St. Thomas Aquinas*, Faith and Reason: Studies in Catholic Theology and Philosophy (Ave Maria, FL: Sapientia Press, 2015), 98–103. For Aquinas's evolution from a "static" notion of the divine image in man to a "dynamic" one that is realized through supernatural spiritual operations, see D. Juvenal Merriell, *To the Image of the Trinity: A Study in the Development of Aquinas' Teaching*, Studies and Texts 96 (Toronto: Pontifical Institute of Mediaeval Studies, 1990); Klaus Krämer, *Imago Trinitatis: Die Gottebenbildlichkeit des Menschen in der Theologie des Thomas von Aquin*, Freiburger theologische Studien (Freiburg im Breisgau: Herder, 2000), 235–62 and 286–334;

ness among creatures imitates the infinitely perfect Image who is the second divine Person.

The relationship between the two supernatural modes of divine presence in the incarnate Word finds its fulcrum in Christ's charity: this is the point at which both modes converge (in fact, all three modes do). The maximal divine communication pertaining to the third mode consists in the hypostatic union. In and of itself, it does not include the created operative union with God, nor a communion with the divine Persons that is fully human. Though not necessary, among all the communications pertaining to the second mode, Christ's is certainly the most fitting. To speak of the fittingness of the charity infused into Christ's human soul is to take into account the specific gratuitousness of beatitude and sanctifying grace, one that is not confused with any other.[39] Likewise, the maximal union and grace corresponding to the hypostatic union make it most fitting and a quasi "consequence" for Christ's humanity to receive the fullest measure of this second mode of divine presence owing to its maximal affinity with the third mode, thus enjoying the greatest operative union and sanctifying grace among created beings.[40] This combined fittingness, however, does not lessen the gratuitousness of their association in Christ. In other words, though most fitting, Christ's maximal charity is the most gratuitous divine effect outside of the hypostatic union. Again, the most gratuitous communication in no way undermines the next most gratuitous one, even though it might seem absurd to us that the latter does not follow almost of necessity from the former, since it is Christ himself as the eternal Word who sends the vivifying Holy Spirit

---

John P. O'Callaghan, "Imago Dei: A Test Case for St. Thomas's Augustinianism," in *Aquinas the Augustinian*, ed. M. Dauphinais, B. David, and M. Levering, (Washington, DC: Catholic University of America Press, 2007), 100–144; Bernhard Blankenhorn, OP, *The Mystery of Union with God: Dionysian Mysticism in Albert the Great and Thomas Aquinas* (Washington, DC: Catholic University of America Press, 2015), 239–47.

39. For Christ as being in need of receiving sanctifying grace, see *ST* III, q. 7, a. 1, ad 1–3.

40. See *ST* III, q. 7, a. 13, c and ad 2. See also *De Ver.* q. 29, a. 5, c; *Sup. Matt.* 28, u (*v.*18; m2460); *Comp. theol.* I, 214, ll. 112–116; *ST* III, q. 26, a. 2, ad 1. See Dominic Legge, OP, *The Trinitarian Christology of St Thomas Aquinas* (Oxford: Oxford University Press, 2017), 144–53, who analyzes *ST* III, q. 7, a. 13; cf. Simon F. Gaine, OP, "Review of *The Trinitarian Theology* [sic] *of St Thomas Aquinas*, by Dominic Legge, OP," *New Blackfriars* 99 (2018): 108–10, who rightfully points out a gap in Legge's argument concerning the necessity of the invisible missions in Christ's humanity because he overlooks the distinction between the visible and invisible missions.

to his own individual human nature[41] and imprints the fullest likeness of himself in his own humanity, created in the image of the Trinity.[42]

CHRIST AND COMMUNICATION

If communication is such a key element in Aquinas's theology dealing with man's fulfillment, surely one should expect this concept to be no less significant in Aquinas's account of Christ, "who as man is the way by which we tend toward God."[43] Indeed, the first article of the *Tertia Pars* portrays the Incarnation as a communication: "it pertains to the concept (*ratio*) of the highest good that it *communicates* itself to a creature in the highest manner."[44] One can contend that this description should not be circumscribed to the hypostatic union itself, since, as we have seen in the previous section, the communication consisting in the third mode of divine presence—the visible mission of the Word—is intimately bound to the communication consisting in the second mode of divine presence. Thus when the Savior is sent visibly as a communication, it is little wonder that he is sent to communicate beatitude in the flesh he assumed. Furthermore, Christ is sent not just to mediate or cause this communication extrinsically, but in a way that befits communication: Christ's own communication of beatitude as man is involved in God's saving communication of beatitude to all.

No matter how fitting it is for Christ to receive as man the most perfect communication corresponding to the second mode of divine presence, he is ultimately endowed with it because he is called to be the principle of this communication. Put another way, what he receives is tied to what he gives, since true communication must include receiving and giving. The roots of these affirmations are found in the Trinity Itself, where the Son is—together

---

41. See, e.g., *Contra err. graec.* II, 1, ll. 45–82; Gilles Emery, "Missions invisibles et missions visibles: Le Christ et son Esprit," *Revue thomiste* 106 (2006): 51–99, here 79–81; idem, *The Trinity: An Introduction to Catholic Doctrine on the Triune God*, trans. M. Levering (Washington, DC: Catholic University of America Press, 2011; 1st French ed., 2009), 188–94; Legge, *Trinitarian Christology*, 160–71, 219–23. Note that Christ does not receive adoptive sonship because sonship concerns a person: where there is but one person, there is but one filiation (*ST* III, q. 23, a. 4).

42. See *ST* III, q. 5, a. 4, ad 1. Cf. *Sup. Io.* 6, III (v.27b; m898).

43. *ST* I, q. 2, prol.

44. *ST* III, q. 1, a. 1.

with the Father—the Principle of the Spirit. The Son receives all that he is from the Father and gives, with the Father, all that he is to the Holy Spirit. Even the Son's ability to breathe forth (or "spirate") the Holy Spirit is received from the Father.[45] Aquinas brings this out when describing the Son's visible mission as the sending of the "Author of sanctification."[46] In this title based on Scripture (Heb 2:10), we can discover in a condensed form the whole mystery of Christ: (1) the intra-Trinitarian relations upon which the Son's visible mission and its conditions depend—the Son is the sole proceeding Person that is the principle of another within the Trinity; (2) the place of the mystery of Christ within God's plan of communication in accordance with the concept for his visible mission—he is sent visibly in a nature that reveals that he is a principle that is capable of acting, sanctifying, and communicating; and (3) the fact that Christ is sent as man (i) to make us like his natural divine filiation so as to lead us to the Father as his sons and daughters, (ii) to obtain for us the realization of the image of God in us by making us like his divine image inasmuch as he is the Word and the perfect Image of the Father, and (iii) to be the principle of the Holy Spirit as man insofar as he is the Word that breathes forth Love, thus kindling the love of charity within us. Thus the sending of the Son as author of sanctification reveals the implications of this visible mission: the proceeding principle (i.e., One who proceeds from the Father and is one principle with him of the Holy Spirit) becomes man so as to communicate what he is as a divine Person and what he possesses in full as man.[47]

Explaining the role Christ's communication of beatitude as man has in God's dispensation benefits from two traditional teachings that Aquinas draws upon to explain Christ's saving relationship with us. The first of the two is the Aristotelian (metaphysical) doctrine of the Principle of the Max-

---

45. See Council of Florence, "Laetentur caeli," in Heinrich Denzinger, *Enchiridion symbolorum, definitionum et declarationum de rebus fidei et morum*, 37th ed., ed. P. Hünermann (Freiburg im Breisgau: Herder, 1991), no. 1301; Emery, *The Trinity*, 145.

46. See *ST* I, q. 43, a. 7, c and ad 4; cf. *ST* I-II, q. 101, a. 4, ad 2; *ST* III, q. 34, a. 3, c.

47. "Author of sanctification" is clearly a title pertaining to the dispensation or economy, since Aquinas only refers to the Father as "author" within the Trinity, while the Son is also the "principle" of the Holy Spirit with the Father (*In I Sent.* d. 29, q. u, a. 1, c; d. 31, q. 2, a. 1, c; *Sup. Matt.* 11, III (*v.25*; m955); *Sup. Io.* 1, I (*v.1*; m48); *ST* III, q. 21, a. 3, c and ad 2; *ST* III, q. 48, a. 5, ad 2); with regard to their operations outside the Trinity, however, all three Persons are called "author," including the Son in his humanity: see John Baptist Ku, *God the Father in the Theology of St. Thomas Aquinas* (New York: Peter Lang, 2013), 149–69, 187–93.

imum: the first and maximum in a genus is the cause of all those contained in that genus;[48] the second is the Pauline portrayal of Christ as Head.[49] Aquinas sees the former as a way of understanding more thoroughly the latter: Christ as Head is a first and maximum cause of all those contained in the genus of creatures receiving the communication of beatitude. In spite of the prevalence of the term "maximum" when referring to this metaphysical teaching, for Aquinas it is the priority of the principle, or the fact that it is "first," which determines how it is applied.[50] The headship of Christ implies that because he is established as the first, according to a metaphysical order, within the genus containing all those who benefit of the second mode of divine presence, he possesses the maximal communication of beatitude and is able to cause this communication in others. To be clear, it is not enough for Christ as man to possess this maximal communication in order to cause it in others; instead, it is his priority as established by God that accounts for this causality.[51] In fact, the communication of beatitude is so gratuitous that any association with God in causing it also needs to be established expressly and gratuitously. Needless to say, this priority of Christ as man is most fitting because he is the sent Principle of the Holy Spirit: the order between the Son and the Holy Spirit, as well as between the effects of grace that are their likenesses—wisdom and charity—harmonizes with the priority of Christ as a human principle of sanctification.

48. See Aristotle, *Metaphysics*, 2 (α), 1, 993b24–25. See, e.g., Vincent de Couesnongle, OP, "La causalité du maximum: L'utilisation par saint Thomas d'un passage d'Aristote," *Revue des Sciences philosophiques et théologiques* 38 (1954): 433–44; Vincent de Couesnongle, OP, "La causalité du maximum: Pourquoi saint Thomas a-t-il mal cité Aristote?," *Revue des Sciences philosophiques et théologiques* 38 (1954): 658–80. In combination with other principles taken from Aristotle, the *Liber de Causis*, Dionysius, and Boethius, St. Thomas applies this teaching to a variety of subjects on at least ninety-three occasions, most notably in *ST* I, q. 2, a. 3, c (§ 4). In particular, with regard to Christ, see *In III Sent*. d. 1, q. 2, a. 2, sc2; d. 10, q. 2, a. 1, qla. 3, ob. 2; *In IV Sent*. d. 43, q. u, a. 2, qla. 1, sc1 [*Suppl*. 76, 1, sc1]; *ScG* IV, c. 27 (1, m3635); *Sup. Rom.* 1, III (v.4; m48); *ST* III, q. 22, a. 4, c; III, q. 56, a. 1, c; III, q. 56, a. 1, ad 3. In *ST* III, q. 4, a. 4, ob. 2, the principle is used to contend that the Word should have assumed a per se human nature after the manner of the Platonists.

49. Thomas treats Christ's headship in *In III Sent*. d. 13, q. 2, a. 1; *De Ver*. q. 29, a. 4; *Sup. 1 Cor.* 11, I (v.3; m587); *Sup. Eph.* 1, VIII (v.22; m69); *Sup. Col.* 1, V (v.18–20; m47–52); *Comp. theol.* I, 214, ll. 105–51; *ST* III, q. 8, a. 1, c; III, q. 8, a. 4, c.

50. St. Thomas evolves on this matter: his later works set priority as the first among the traits of Christ's headship: see *Sup. Col.* 1, V (v.18; m47–49); *ST* III, q. 8, a. 1, c; III, q. 8, a. 4, c.

51. For examples of Aquinas arguing from Christ's priority to his causality, see *Sent., prol.*; *In I Sent*. d. 32, q. 1, a. 3, c; *In III Sent*. d. 1, q. 2, a. 2, sc2; d. 10, q. 2, a. 1, qla. 3, ob. 2; *In IV Sent*. d. 43, q. u, a. 2, qla. 1, sc1 [*Suppl*. 76, 1, sc1]; *ST* I, q. 45, a. 6, ob. 1 and ad 1; III, q. 22, a. 4, c; III, q. 56, a. 1, c.

Christ as head is a homogeneous cause of all other spiritual creatures' supernatural communication as well as of the friendship based on it. Thus his headship is not limited to a matter of dignity or government; rather, Christ as head causes a continuous influx of communication in his members.[52] The question as to how he does this receives an answer that is varied and yet cohesive because all of Christ's soteriological causalities are based on the deployment of his friendship and intend the establishment and development of friendship in those who benefit from his saving agency in an act of friendship. Our response to this question in what follows will show how each of Christ's salvific causalities is itself based on some aspect of his own communication of beatitude, and how each contributes in some way to our own reception and development of this saving communication of beatitude upon which friendship with God is founded.

CHRIST'S SAVING CAUSALITIES AS "COMMUNICATION"

Christ's "Ontological" Exemplary Causality

It is apposite to begin a presentation of Christ's saving causalities with exemplarity because it is the foundation of all causality inasmuch as every cause produces something that bears some likeness of itself.[53] This means that the perfection or actuality communicated to something is always modeled after its exemplar. When the giver is the exemplar—as is the case with Christ, whose exemplarity is simultaneously efficacious—communication actually refers directly to this result: both the giver and the recipient come to possess the same perfection or actuality. We are not dealing here with exemplary causality simply as the example set for someone to follow, but with the re-

---

52. While in his earlier explanations of Christ's headship, Aquinas refers to his influx as a *gubernatio* (*De Ver.* q. 29, a. 4, c), in his later works he clearly teaches that Christ as head causes grace in his members; see, e.g., *ST* III, q. 8, a. 1, c; III, q. 8, a. 4, c.

53. For instances of St. Thomas's recourse to the principle "omne agens agit sibi simile," see, e.g., *In I Sent.* d. 36, q. 2, a. 3, c; *In IV Sent.* d. 1, q. 1, a. 4, qla. 4, c; *ScG* II, c. 6 (5–6, m882–883); c. 21 (9, m977); c. 41 (7, m1173); *III*, c. 21 (6, m2022); *In de div. nom.* 1, 3 (m86); *De Pot.* q. 3, a. 1, c; q. 3, a. 6, c; q. 7, a.1, ad 8; q. 7, a. 5, c; *Comp. theol.* I, 101, ll. 12–32; *ST* I, q. 4, a. 3, c; I, q. 19, a. 2, c; I, q. 19, a. 6, c; I, q. 50, a. 1, c; I, q. 115, a. 1, c. See also *ST* I, q. 6, a. 4, c; I, q. 45, a. 6, c; I, q. 45, a. 7, c.

lation of likeness between the cause and the effect, or between the actuality of the former and the latter. This foundational exemplarity can be called an "ontological" exemplarity because the being of the recipient, or effect, is like that of the cause.[54] This priority of the exemplary causality of Christ is suggested by Aquinas himself when discussing the fittingness of the second divine Person's incarnation (instead of that of the other two divine Persons) in the *Tertia Pars*: the first reason given for this fittingness is the Word's exemplary causality.[55]

Though every cause produces an effect that is somehow similar to itself, the nobler the cause, and the more successful its causation is, the greater this likeness will be, not necessarily because the distance between the cause and the effect is lessened or done away with, but because all that is found in the effect has some likeness to the cause. The dignity of Christ's saving causality can be verified in that its effect is so much like himself. Indeed, the fact that Christ has been sent to save and even to "serve" (Mt 20:28) does not diminish him in any way; on the contrary, because saving or serving is tantamount to communicating or causing, Christ's humanity is so ennobled by God that the fullness of his own communication as man enables him to communicate an actuality that is so much like himself, thus coming to imitate God the most.[56]

The first and maximal exemplar of the communication of beatitude is the Trinity. Whereas this exemplarity is analogous with its created effect, by becoming incarnate and receiving as man the fullness of this communication, the Word becomes our "quasi-univocal" exemplar.[57] This means that,

---

54. This is Torrell's expression. In addition to *Christ and Spirituality in St. Thomas Aquinas*, see his "Imiter Dieu comme des enfants bien-aimés: La conformité à Dieu et au Christ dans l'œuvre de saint Thomas," in *Novitas et veritas vitae: Aux sources du renouveau de la morale chrétienne, Mélanges offerts au Professeur Servais Pinckaers*, ed. C.-J. Pinto de Oliveira (Paris: Cerf, 1991), 53–65, here 59–62; "La causalité salvifique de la résurrection du Christ selon saint Thomas," *Revue Thomiste* 96 (1996): 179–208, esp. 193–96; "Le Christ dans la 'spiritualité' de saint Thomas," in *Christ among the Medieval Dominicans: Representations of Christ in the Texts and Images of the Order of Preachers*, ed. K. Emery Jr. and J. Wawrykow (Notre Dame, IN: University of Notre Dame Press, 1998), 197–219, here 202–8, 215–18; *Le Christ en ses mystères: La vie et l'œuvre de Jésus selon saint Thomas d'Aquin*, vol. 2 (Paris: Desclée, 1999), 629–34.

55. See *ST* III, q. 3, a. 8, c: "the Word of God ... is the exemplary likeness of all creatures: ... the artificer ('artifex') restores his work ('artificiatum'), if it is ruined, by the conceived artistic form whereby he made it." See also *ST* III, q. 5, a. 4, ad 1.

56. See *ST* I, q. 20, a. 4, ad 1; *In III Sent.* d. 32, q. u, a. 5, qla. 4, c and ad 1–2.

57. *In III Sent.* d. 13, q. 2, a. 1, c; *In IV Sent.* d. 43, q. u, a. 2, qla. 1, c. It is "univocal" because there

although the perfection of his communication or participation is different from ours, the mode or type of communication is the same; namely, the second mode of divine presence.[58] The Incarnation effectively renders God our proximate exemplar: he saves us in accordance with it, and at the same time it plays a role in our own cooperation in this salvation.

As a proximate exemplary cause, Christ's communication models our own. This occurs on a number of levels. First of all, he is the exemplar according to which the divine Persons transform us. This is certainly evident in the case of our future glorious resurrection from the dead. As Paul teaches (1 Cor 15), we will be raised as Christ was raised.[59] Other cases in which this ontological exemplarity of Christ is manifest is his predestination, which "is the exemplar of our predestination,"[60] as well as his filiation, to which we "appropriate" the "exemplar" of our "adoptive filiation."[61] As with the Resurrection and predestination, charity is infused in our will in the same way as it is infused in Christ's human will: the Father loves us according to his love for the Son in his humanity (Jn 17:26b);[62] Christ loves us according to the love the Father has for him (Jn 15:9a);[63] and the Holy Spirit, who infuses charity (Rm 5:5), conforms and "assimilates" us to, or makes us like, Christ.[64] As already suggested, Christ's exemplarity is present in every other soteriological causality: each one of them aims at making human beings receive or develop a communication like Christ's, and a love like his.

---

is one genus: the communication of beatitude; it is "quasi"- univocal because not every member of this genus participates in it to the same degree.

58. See *Sup 1 Cor.* 11, I (*v.1*; m583); *Sup. Gal.* 4, VI (*v.19*; m244); *Sup. Io.* 1, XIII (*v.27a*; m248); 12, I (*v.6*; m1604); 12, III (*v.12*; m1626); *In salutationem angelicam* 3 (m1126).

59. In addition to the two passages just cited above in note 57, see *ST* III, q. 56, a. 1. Cf. *ST* III, q. 45, a. 1, c.

60. *ST* III, q. 24, a. 3, c.

61. *ST* III, q. 23, a. 2, ad 3. See also *Sup. Rom.* 8, VI (*v.29*; m706).

62. See *Sup. Io.* 17, V (*v.23*; m2251); 17, VI (*v.26*; m2270).

63. See *Sup. Io.* 15, II (*v.9a*; m1999).

64. See *De Pot.* q. 10, a. 4, c; *Sup. Rom.* 8, II (*v.10*; m629); *Sup. Io.* 3, I (*v.5*; m442); *In Symb. Apost.* 8 (m969). Aquinas employs the term *assimilare* profusely when referring to the process whereby something is made like something else.

Christ's Revealing or "Moral"
Exemplary Causality

What is found in Christ is, first and foremost, what God works in us. If we can imitate Christ, it is not only because we can get to know him, but because God is transforming us according to the exemplar who is Christ. In the case of Christ's and our own glorious (bodily) resurrection, this exemplarity is purely ontological; with other mysteries, revealing or moral exemplarity enables us to collaborate in the process whereby we become like Christ. Put another way, Christ's revealing or moral exemplary causality builds upon Christ's "ontological" exemplarity. As eternal Word, Christ is the exemplar of all creatures according to the first mode of divine presence.[65] The second mode of divine presence, however, requires knowledge on the part of its recipients. Obviously, his mission to reveal divine communication is well served by assuming a proximate and "quasi-univocal" exemplarity. He is thus able to reveal to us God's saving plan by means of both his "deeds and words," which complement one another.[66] All that Christ preaches is also revealed by his exemplary actions, while the revealing or moral exemplarity of these actions is guaranteed by his words.

In his *Commentary on John*, Aquinas affords greater attention to a two-fold illumination by Christ: he enlightens us exteriorly and interiorly.[67] If his exterior illumination in words and deeds is efficacious and leads us to believe, it is because of the interior illumination. This is obviously no ordinary human knowledge. Here, the invisible missions work through the visible mission of the Son: what he is, says, does, and experiences transforms us owing to the action of the invisibly sent Persons. Thus the supernatural infused knowledge we obtain from Christ's revealing and moral exemplary causalities enables us to play our own part in our transformation according

---

65. See *ST* I, q. 34, a. 3; III, q. 3, a. 8, c. See also *In I Sent.* d. 10, q. u, a. 1, c; *ST* I, q. 33, a. 3, ad 1; I, q. 45, a. 6, c.

66. Second Vatican Council, *Dogmatic Constitution on Divine Revelation "Dei Verbum"* (1965), no. 2, website of the Holy See, January 28, 2020, https://www.vatican.va/archive/hist_councils/ii_vatican_council/documents/vat-ii_const_19651118_dei-verbum_en.html.

67. See *Sup. Io.* 1, XVI (*vv.*43–44; m313); 3, I (*v.*2; m428); 5, IV (*v.*25; m780); 15, V (*v.*24b; m2055); Paweł Klimczak, OP, *Christus Magister: Le Christ Maître dans les commentaires évangéliques de saint Thomas d'Aquin*, Studia Friburgensia 117 (Fribourg, Switzerland: Academic Press Fribourg, 2013), 174–203.

to Christ's ontological exemplarity. This is a powerful motive in Aquinas's soteriological discourse: we are transformed into what we know with living faith or what the invisible missions of the Word and the Holy Spirit lead us to truly know and love.[68]

This twofold illumination (exterior and interior) worked by Christ is clearly at the service of God's communication of beatitude, a process that, because it involves the spiritual reception of a gift, requires our cooperation through the spiritual acts of knowledge and love. Here, the invisible missions of the Word and the Holy Spirit perfect our intellect and will by rendering them like themselves through their infused gifts of knowledge and love. Their two missions, however, work in an orderly fashion that follows the order of the processions in the Trinity. This order concurs with the order found among our spiritual powers: the Word's mission logically precedes that of the Holy Spirit, just as knowledge is a precondition for love.[69] Both the missions and the acts they cause in us (with our cooperation) are inseparable because, like the eternal Word himself, the knowledge he infuses in us breathes forth love.[70] It can therefore be said that Christ's full illumination is present in human beings when they perform an act of charity.

Christ's Instrumental Causality

Aquinas is the first theologian to explain how Christ's humanity is an instrumental efficient cause of grace: God infuses grace in and through Christ's humanity.[71] Just as the invisible missions cooperate with the exemplary

---

68. See *Sup. 2 Cor.* 3, III (*v.*18; m114): "given that all knowledge occurs through the likening ('per assimilationem') of the knower to the known, it is necessary that those who see [God], be in some way transformed into God." *Sup. Rom.* 8, VI (*v.*29; m704): "due to the fact that [the Son] illuminates the saints with the light ('de lumine') of wisdom and grace, He makes them become conformed to himself." See also *Sup. Io.* 1, XI (*v.*18; m216).

69. See *ST* I, q. 27, a. 3, ad 3.

70. For the simultaneousness of the missions, see *Sup. Col.* 2, II (*v.*9; m97); I, 43, 5, 2–3; Emery, *Trinitarian Theology*, 390–95. On the Son as "Word that breathes forth Love," see *In I Sent.* d. 15, q. 4, a. 1, ad 3; *ST* I, q. 43, a. 5, ad 2; *Sup. Io.* 6, V (*v.*45; m946). See also *In I Sent.* d. 27, q. 2, a. 1, c.

71. See, e.g., *ST* I-II, q. 112, a. 1, ad 1; III, q. 8, a. 1, ad 1. For studies on Aquinas's understanding of the instrumental causality of Christ's humanity (including his evolution), see Theophil Tschipke, OP, *Die Menschheit Christi als Heilsorgan der Gottheit* (Freiburg im Breisgau: Herder, 1940); Torrell, "La causalité salvifique," 186–89; Eduardo M. Taussig, "La humanidad de Cristo como instrumento según Santo Tomás de Aquino: Evolución de Sto. Tomás en el recurso a la noción de instrumento para iluminar diversos problemas cristológicos" (PhD diss., Pontificia Studiorum Universitas a S. Thoma

causality of the Son's visible mission, so too the instrumental causality of this visible mission cooperates with the invisible missions. Christ's humanity participates in the invisible missions of the Son and the Holy Spirit, while these missions move his humanity in order to communicate beatitude, or sanctifying grace.

Strictly speaking, God does not require an instrument; if he chooses to employ one, it is for our benefit, since his supernatural communication is transmitted in a way that is more fully human. The instrument God assumes is itself full of the communication that it is moved to convey to others, since it is an "animate" and spiritual instrument, capable of receiving the communication of grace by cooperating with it.[72] This communication enables Christ's human nature to work "in communion" with his divine nature, to quote Leo the Great.[73] Within that communication, the instrument and the principal cause act as one. Here, the instrument's action qua instrument includes the instrument's own action. Thus each of Christ's mysteries involves a slightly different cooperation with the invisible missions, resulting in a communication of grace that is bound to a specific human act of Christ. By means of each of the things he did and suffered, Christ communicates grace as man for the common goal of our salvation, as well as for a specific aspect of this salvation, which finds its exemplary cause in that particular mystery. Hence being used as an instrument brings with it a privilege; that is, that the acts of Christ determine, as it were, the saving action of God according to their exemplarity, a determination already eternally disposed by God.[74] Christ's mysteries show us what the divine communication works in

Aq. in Urbe, Rome, 1990); Bernhard Blankenhorn, OP, "The Instrumental Causality of the Sacraments: Thomas Aquinas and Louis-Marie Chauvet," *Nova et Vetera*, English ed. 4 (2006): 255–94; Marie-Hélène Deloffre, "Introduction," in Thomas d'Aquin, *Questions Disputées sur la vérité: Question XXIX, La grâce du Christ (De gratia Christi)*, trans. M.-H. Deloffre (Paris: Vrin, 2015), 9–148, here 53–69.

72. *ST* III, q. 7, a. 1, ad 3.

73. *ST* III, q. 19, a. 1, c and ad 2 (here, St. Thomas quotes Leo's Tome to Flavian: Denzinger, *Enchiridion symbolorum*, no. 294). See also *ST* III, q. 62, a. 1, ad 2.

74. In the *Tertia Pars*, Aquinas sets Christ's exemplary and efficient causalities side by side while explaining many of his mysteries, e.g., Christ's baptism (*ST* III, q. 39, a. 2); temptations (III, q. 41, a. 1); passion (III, q. 48, a. 6; III, q. 49, a. 1); death (III, q. 50, a. 6); resurrection (III, q. 56, aa. 1–2); ascension (III, q. 57, a. 6). The sacrament of baptism is also presented in this way: *ST* III, q. 62, a. 1, ad 2. For the relation between interior illumination and instrumental causality, see Klimczak, *Christus Magister*, 203–9.

us, so that we can collaborate with the grace instrumentally communicated to us by this very mystery. This synergy between Christ's exemplary causality and the instrumental causality of his humanity hinges on his being sent as a proximate quasi-univocal cause of grace.

It is worth mentioning one more aspect of Christ's causality of communication that works through his instrumental causality: Christ's humanity is a "conjoined instrument," not a separate one.[75] This implies that it is the closest to the principal cause and therefore the *first* among all instruments— the "Head instrument": all other instruments need to be moved by it and require the influx of grace that issues from its fullness of grace. The perfect communication found in Christ's humanity moves the whole instrumental organism of grace; insofar as this organism also signifies what it transmits, it can be called a "sacramental" order. Ultimately, the humanity of Christ is a conjoined and first instrument because it receives and possesses the same supernatural communication as we do, and enjoying the priority and fullness of this communication, his humanity is also able to cause it in others.[76]

Christ's Saving Causalities
Depending on Merit

The remaining soteriological causalities treated by Aquinas form a whole based on Christ's merit: in satisfaction, sacrificial reconciliation, and redemption, it is his charity's merit that works our salvation.[77] Through Christ's satisfaction the merits of his passion free us from the punishment due to our sins; his sacrifice reconciles us with the Father and makes us his friends on account of the value of these same merits; the grace merited by

---

75. See *De Ver.* q. 29, a. 5, c; *ScG* IV, c. 41 (12–13, m3798–3799); *De unione Verbi incarnati* q. 5, a. 1; *ST* III, q. 56, a. 1, c; III, q. 64, a. 5, ad 2. See also *ST* III, q. 2, a. 6, ad 4. Instead, the sacraments of the New Law are considered "separate instruments" of grace; see, e.g., *ST* III, q. 62, a. 5, c; III, q. 64, a. 5, ad 2.

76. In addition to the already cited passages, see *De Ver.* q. 27, a. 4, c; *Quodl.* 12, q. 9, a. u [15], c (m12, q. 10, a. u [14]); *ST* III, q. 63, a. 5, ad 1; III, q. 64, a. 3, c; III, q. 64, a. 4, c.

77. This is already suggested by *ST* III, q. 48, a. 6, ad 3: "inasmuch as [the passion] is referred to the will of Christ's soul, it acts by mode of merit; in turn, when it is considered in the very flesh of Christ, [a] it acts by mode of satisfaction … [b] by mode of redemption … [c] by mode of sacrifice." The latter three saving causalities (a–c) presuppose Christ's human will and charity, which are directly associated with his merit. In questions 48 and 49 of the *Tertia Pars*, satisfaction, sacrifice, and redemption are consistently described as depending on charity and merit for the exertion of their causality.

Christ's passion redeems us by liberating us from sin and the evil of fault (*malum culpae*).

As discussed above, the main element of merit is its preordination: without it, no matter how great Christ's charity or communication of beatitude was, he would not have been able to merit. Not even Christ could have merited without this preordination.[78] Christ's preordination destined him to merit as the head of all those who merit:[79] when meriting, Christ did so as an individual and as "a mystical person."[80] Thus, through Christ's meritorious causality, we are in some way incorporated into his own communication.

This unique preordering corresponds to Christ's priority as head: all of his members will benefit from this priority. For Aquinas, the conditions of Christ's earthly existence were adapted to this preordination. (A) He was a pilgrim or wayfarer; that is, he was in that state in which someone is able to merit because there was something he did not yet possess that he needed to merit for himself: the overflow of beatitude from the deepest part of his soul to the rest of his humanity. (B) His charity was suited to what he was preordered to merit because it was founded on the communication of consummate beatitude.[81] Thus, by developing the communication of the beatitude that he received as man, through his cooperation with it, he obtained two fruits: (1) the overflow of his own beatitude into his physical body as well as into the functions of his soul that are associated in some way with this body and (2) the communication of beatitude for his mystical body, which

---

78. Though this main element of merit is not discussed explicitly in the *Tertia Pars*, this teaching is implied in its explanations of Christ's predestination (*ST* III, q. 24, a. 1, ad 3; III, q. 24, a. 3, c and ad 3) and headship (III, q. 19, a. 4, c). See Lynn, *Christ's Redemptive Merit*, 145–57, and Catão, *Salut et rédemption*, 135–41 (who has a better grasp of the significance of these notions for Christ's saving agency than Lynn). See also Philippe-Marie Margelidon, OP, *Études de Christologie Thomiste: De la grâce à la résurrection du Christ* (Perpignan: Artège, 2010), 109–37, whose overview of the French-speaking Thomists' studies on merit during the twentieth century (Hugon, Michel, Héris, Bouëssé, J.-H. Nicolas, and M.-J. Nicolas) shows that they overlook Christ's preordination as the main explanatory element of his merit.

79. See *ST* I-II, q. 114, a. 6, c; III, q. 48, a. 1, c; III, q. 49, a. 1, c. Cf. *ST* III, q. 8, a. 5, c.

80. *In III Sent.* d. 18, q. u, a. 6, qla. 1, ad 2; *In IV Sent.* d. 49, q. 4, a. 3, ad 3; *De Ver.* q. 29, a. 7, sc3 and ad 11; *Sup. Col.* 1, VI (*v.*24; m61); *ST* III, q. 15, a. 1, ad 1; III, q. 19, a. 4, c; III, q. 48, a. 2, ad 1; III, q. 49, a. 1, c; *Sup. Psalm.* 21, 1 (two-thirds of the way through the *lectio*); 30, 1 (one-third of the way through the *lectio*).

81. See *In III Sent.* d. 15, q. 2, a. 1, qla. 3, ad 3; d. 18, q. u, a. 2, c; *De Ver.* q. 10, a. 11, ad 3; q. 26, a. 10, ad 14–15; q. 29, a. 6, c; *Comp. theol.* I, 231, ll. 15–55; *Sup. Io.* 4, VI (*v.*43; m667); *ST* I, q. 62, a. 9, ad 3; III, q. 15, a. 10; III, q. 19, a. 3, c and ad 1.

encompasses all those who have received, now receive, and will receive this communication. In other words, the same meritorious act of charity was ordered to attain the highest fulfillment of grace ever merited: (1) the overflow of beatitude from his human spirit (*mens*) to the rest of his (individual) humanity, and, at the same time, (2) all the grace participated by his members. The amount, so to speak, of the former was more than enough to account for the latter. Because his maximal charity was proportioned to what he was called to merit for himself—the overflowing of his own beatitude from the higher part of his soul to the rest of his humanity—his maximal merits were "overabundant" with regard to the "whole world," and even for "many," "a hundred thousand," or, still, "infinite worlds," "if they exist," as Aquinas teaches.[82]

Christ's meritorious priority as head benefits his members because every grace, other than those received by Christ's humanity at his incarnation (the grace of union and his maximal communication of beatitude), is merited by Christ, and every meritorious development of grace has already been merited by Christ. Thus, for us, to merit is to receive a participation in Christ's merit or to be incorporated into his merit. Put another way, the sole beatitude among human beings that is absolutely unmerited by Christ is his own fullness of grace and beatitude as a wayfarer; everyone else receives an inchoate beatitude that is merited by Christ and a consummate beatitude that is merited by Christ and themselves. Hence our acts of charity are deeply marked by the meritorious causality of Christ's charity and are performed within our relationship with him: every act of charity configures us to his act of charity and joins us to it. Given that Christ merits the beginnings of our friendship with God as well as its utter fulfillment, it can be said that he is the milieu in which we live and develop this friendship. There can be no friendship with God outside of Christ's humanity and his communication of beatitude.

---

82. *Sup. Io.* 1, VIII (*v.*14d; m190): merits a "superabundant grace for infinite worlds, if they exist"; *Comp. theol.* I, 215, ll. 91–99, and *Sup. Io.* 3, VI (*v.*34b; m544): a satisfaction or propitiation that is sufficient for "many worlds, if they exist"; *In Symb. Apost.* 4 (m917): an atonement that is sufficient "even for a hundred thousand worlds, if they exist"; *Sup. Col.* 1, VI (*v.*24; m61): a redemption that is sufficient for "many worlds." Most of these expressions comment on 1 Jn 2:2.

CONCLUSION

Studies of Christ and his saving work have generally failed to present a cohesive account of the multiple ways in which Christ saves us. Instead, Aquinas offers a much more integrated soteriological presentation. This is ultimately owing to Christ's charity and, especially, to the Dominican theologian's idea of communication. Following Aristotle, St. Thomas sees communication as the decisive element of friendship. A close analysis of his understanding of friendship reveals three forms of communication that are at play there: (1) a "giving" so that something may be had in common by the giver and the recipient; (2) the resulting "having" in common in the recipient; and (3) the recipient's "acting" or "living in common" with the giver. As expounded upon above, the larger context of charity's threefold communication is Aquinas's theological framework based on the modes of divine presence, which are also three in number: charity is a friendship founded upon the communication of beatitude, which is the second mode of divine presence. Within this framework, one can more readily appreciate the affinity between the second mode—the invisible divine missions—and third mode—the visible mission of the Son.

Christ's charity is at the core of the entire divine dispensation and is connected to every form of supernatural communication. This is especially evinced by studying such notions as "grace," "union with God," "divine filiation," and "Trinitarian likeness." Furthermore, St. Thomas considers the Incarnation itself to be the maximal communication; it is fittingly called upon to dispense to others the next highest mode of communication. These affirmations can be traced back to their Trinitarian roots: the Son, who receives all that he is from the Father and gives (with the Father) all that he is to the Holy Spirit, is sent in a way that reveals his personal property—that is, that he is the "Author of sanctification," or the visible principle of the Holy Spirit in his humanity. Aquinas provides us with two related principles, one metaphysical, the other scriptural, so as to grasp more fully what this authorship of sanctification entails: because Christ is the first and therefore the maximum among those who receive grace or beatitude, he is the cause of this communication within this genus.

Finally, the question as to how Christ does this receives a manifold and yet unified response, since each saving causality revolves around communication. Through the lens of communication, Christ's charity *reveals* to us his communication of beatitude as the quasi-univocal *ontological exemplar* of our own communication, thus drawing us to his humanity and "compelling" us (2 Cor 5:14) to cooperate with the communication we receive through this *instrument* (his humanity) by means of our own act of charity, which in turn configures us to the communication *merited* by Christ and incorporates us into it through our own merit.

By shedding light on how Christ's saving causalities are connected—and how the knowledge of Christ's charity is one that surpasses all other knowledge (Eph 3:19)—Aquinas's idea of communication proves to be important for theology today. There are at least four reasons for this. First, it manifests that God's design is ordered and unified. That is, the central place held by Christ's communication and charity highlights the significance of considering the modes of divine presence and the divine missions in the systematic study of theology. Second, the unified account of soteriology elucidates the importance of our collaboration in the transformation worked by the invisible missions of the Son and the Holy Spirit. These missions have the principal aim of conforming our intellect and will to the divine Persons, and yet, thanks to Christ's humanity and his human charity, the entire human being is affected by this work of likening (*assimilatio*). Third, charity is shown to be connected not just to moral theology, but primarily to Trinitarian theology and to Christology since it is fundamentally developed within Christ's own charity, as well as in the divine missions to the soul. This systematic basis of charity should permeate moral theology wherever the influence of charity extends. Thus the good moral life preached by the Gospel is shown to be the life in Christ and according to his Holy Spirit. Finally, the preeminent role of communication and charity in soteriology, largely neglected until recently, offers a spacious and fertile terrain for the theologian, and for any Christian, one that should yield fruits of renewal for our time and for future generations.

CHAPTER 9

AQUINAS ON CHRIST'S
MALE SEXUALITY AS INTEGRAL
TO HIS FULL HUMANITY

Anti-Docetism in the Common Doctor

Paul Gondreau

Few today know that at the time of the Renaissance, artists commonly spot-lighted Christ's male sexuality as a way of emphasizing his full humanity. One characteristic device was to remove the infant Christ's clothes in order to reveal his genitals, as in representations of the Nativity or the Visit of the Magi.[1] A few centuries earlier, the Byzantine author St. Theodore the Stu-dite (†826) made a similar move, as he rested his defense of icons on Christ's full humanity, in particular on his maleness. Icons depict Christ not in some kind of androgynous or asexual manner, Theodore observed, but as a male individual (just as, we might add, icons of the Blessed Virgin depict her as a female or icons of St. Joseph as a male, etc.).[2]

Thomas Aquinas, medieval schoolman, also pronounced on Christ's

---

1. See Leo Steinberg, *The Sexuality of Christ in Renaissance Art and in Modern Oblivion*, 2nd ed. (Chicago: University of Chicago Press, 1996). Steinberg shows that many Renaissance paintings of the infant Christ and of the dead Christ, motivated by an incarnational theology, depict a veritable *ostenta-tio genitalium*, a deliberate viewing of Christ's genitals. Supplying ample images for support, Steinberg writes: "In many hundreds of pious, religious works, from before 1400 to past the mid-16th century, the ostensive unveiling of the Child's sex, or the touching, protecting or presentation of it, is the main action.... And the emphasis recurs in images of the dead Christ, or of the mystical Man of Sorrows" (3).

2. See Theodore the Studite, *Writings on Iconoclasm*, trans. Thomas Cattoi, Ancient Christian Writers 69 (Mahwah, NJ: Paulist Press, 2015).

male sexuality, the present reader might be surprised to learn, as part of a larger effort at promoting Christ's full humanity. In a little-known passage from his *Commentary on the Sentences* that proves a theological treasure trove, Aquinas stakes a position on Christ's sexuality that, to my knowledge, knows no historical precedent. It concerns a query on whether Christ had to assume any particular sex at all.[3] In the backdrop looms the ever-present tendency in Christian thought (including in our own day) of Docetism, the tendency to deny or downplay Christ's full manhood.[4] That God became man, that God substantially and not merely accidentally or temporarily took on a "true human body" and a "rational soul," Aquinas more than once calls the greatest of all wonders.[5] It is not hyperbole to consider St. Thomas one of Christian tradition's foremost champions of Christ's full humanity, with a pronounced anti-Docetic strain running throughout his writings.[6] This anti-Docetic determination is nowhere more evident than when Aquinas ventures into such a far-reaching implication of the "wonder" of the Incarnation as that of Christ's male sex.

In what follows, I examine this passage from the *Sentences* commen-

---

3. This query is appended to an Augustinian-sparked consideration of whether Christ assumed the "more honorable sex" (*sexus honorabilior*), which Augustine answers affirmatively; see *De div. Quaest. 83*, q. 11 (CCSL 44a.18). Peter Lombard takes this issue up for discussion in *Sent.* 3, d. 12, ch. 4 (ed. Brady, 83), from which it passed to the thirteenthcentury *Sentences* commentaries. In addition to his own *Sentences* commentary, Aquinas addresses this particular issue also in *ST* III, q. 31, a. 4, ad 1.

4. From the Greek *dokeo*, "to seem," and traceable to apostolic times (see 2 Jn 7: "Many deceivers … will not acknowledge the coming of Jesus Christ in the flesh"), Docetism alleges that Christ only *appeared* to have come in the flesh. For more on Docetism, see Fernando Ocáriz, Lucas F. Mateo-Seco, and José Antonio Riestra, *The Mystery of Jesus Christ: A Christology and Soteriology Textbook*, trans. Michael Adams and James Gavignon (Portland, OR: Four Courts Press, 2011), 55–58. As the authors note: "Docetism was not a clearly defined sect. It was rather a tendency to be found in many sects, particularly Gnostic ones.... These [Docetic] errors … derive partly from Manichaean and Gnostic doctrines which regarded matter and more specifically the human body as something evil and therefore totally inappropriate for God to assume" (55–56).

5. "Nothing more wondrous could be accomplished than that God should become man." *In Ioan.*, ch. 2, lect. 3 (no. 398). He offers the same wording in *Summa contra Gentiles* IV, c. 27. For Aquinas's affirmation that Christ assumed a true human body (*verum corpus humanum*) and a rational soul (*animam rationale*), which he considers to be established both by the principle of hylemorphism (matter-form composition) and by the witness of the NT; see *ST* III, q. 5, aa. 1–4.

6. Jean-Pierre Torrell observes that Aquinas seeks to affirm "wherever possible that Christ is a man fully subject to the laws of humanity." *Le Christ en ses mystères: La vie et l'oeuvre de Jésus selon saint Thomas d'Aquin*, 2 vols. (Paris: Desclée, 1999), 1:118 (translation mine). See also my "Anti-Docetism in Aquinas' *Super Ioannem*: St. Thomas as Defender of the Full Humanity of Christ," in *Reading John with St. Thomas Aquinas: Theological Exegesis and Speculative Theology*, ed. M. Dauphinais and M. Levering (Washington, DC: Catholic University of America Press, 2005), 254–76.

tary, highlighting its biblical, patristic, and conciliar resonances relative to Christ's full humanity, as well as its Aristotelian-inspired metaphysical commitments. Then, in a second move, I address the fact that Aquinas was largely charting new ground on the more general issue of human sexuality (also traceable to the *Sentences* commentary), in that he sought to tether sexual difference closely to human biology and thus to God's creative handiwork. This new "positive teaching on sexuality," to quote the moral theologian Servais Pinckaers, was foundational to the position Thomas takes on Christ's male sex.[7] In a third and final move, I consider how Aquinas's view that sexuality, inclusive of biological design, marks a source of moral excellence invites particular consideration of the virtue of chastity or virginity in Christ. Here, with the support of the emerging field of neurobiology, where structural differences between the male and female brains have come to light, I argue that Christ, owning a male-structured nature, mastered his sexuality in a male-conditioned way, in a "manly" way. I close with a consideration of the possibility of sexual temptation in Christ's life.

CHRIST'S FULL HUMAN CONSUBSTANTIALITY AND HIS MALE SEX

First, the passage from the *Sentences* commentary. It reads:

Christ had to be like his brethren in all things natural, as Heb 2:17 says. *Yet sex is natural to man (sexus est de naturalibus hominis).* Therefore, he had to assume a sex.... [Further] Christ came to restore [or redeem] human nature by his very assumption; and for this reason it was necessary that he assume everything following upon human nature, namely, all the properties and parts of human nature, among which is sex; and therefore it was proper for him to assume a particular sex.... He assumed a sex not in order to use it but for the perfection of nature.[8]

---

7. Servais Pinckaers, *The Sources of Christian Ethics*, trans. Mary Thomas Noble (Washington, DC: Catholic University of America Press, 1995), 440.

8. *In III Sent.*, d. 12, q. 3, a. 1, qa. 1, sol. 1, co. and ad 2; emphasis added. The title of the query is *Utrum Christus debuerit sexum aliquem*, Whether Christ had to assume any particular sex.

A Biblical Witness That Invites a
Philosophical Exegesis

That Aquinas opens with a citation of Hebrews 2:17 is instructive. Ever the biblical theologian, Aquinas could easily have chosen other New Testament texts that bear on Christ's assumption of a sexed nature, in particular, those that provide simple acknowledgment that he was male: "Behold [Mary], you shall conceive in your womb and bear a son," says the angel Gabriel in Luke 1:31, where son means biological male, which the circumcision of this same son, recounted in Luke 2:21, manifestly confirms. What undoubtedly draws Aquinas to the Hebrews passage, however, is its appeal to human nature ("like his brethren in all things natural"), an appeal that readily lends itself to a robust philosophical exegesis and coherence. Aquinas promptly offers such an exegesis.

"Sex Is Natural to Man":
Metaphysical Christology

"Sex is natural to man," Thomas writes, a phrase charged with metaphysical thrust and one that stands practically without precedent in the history of Christian thought, in terms both of strict anthropology and of its Christological relevance. While he fails to mention it explicitly here, Aquinas will elsewhere expressly link sex to the animal-like (and thus biological) structure of human nature: "[Sexuality] is natural to man by reason of his animal life … as our bodily organs clearly attest," he writes in the *Summa*.[9]

For a deeper metaphysical account of the same, we can turn to another early work, the *De ente et essentia*. There Aquinas assigns human sexuality to the category of an essential property of our animal nature. Eyeing the hylemorphic structure of the human being, he holds that there are certain essential features of human nature (he calls them proper accidents) that, while not entering into the definition of the human being as a rational animal per se, nonetheless proceed immediately, and thus essentially, upon this definition. Certain essential attributes, or essential compositional accidents,

---

9. *ST* I, q. 98, a. 2. In ad 1, Thomas affirms that the human being owns "an animal life in his body."

thus follow immediately upon our animality (expressive of the body or of our matter) and upon our rationality (expressive of the soul or of our form). If risibility provides an example of an attribute following upon human rationality, sexuality, or binary sexual dimorphism (maleness and femaleness), stands out as a compositional attribute that proceeds upon our animality, or upon our animal bodiliness: "the diversity of male and female among animals derives from matter" is how Aquinas puts it.[10] As risibility is to the rational soul, so is binary sexual difference to the animal body. Not a pure or contingent accident (like hair color), sex is a proper or essential accident of the body.

So when Thomas holds that Christ's sexed nature owes to his having assumed "all the properties and parts of human nature," the "property" of human nature that pertains to sex is that of a compositional attribute (or proper accident) of the body, while the "part" concerns the animal side of human nature. Later in the *Summa*, he makes Christ's assumption of the animal part of human nature explicit: "Nothing implanted in our nature by God was lacking in the human nature assumed by the Word of God.... Hence the Son of God necessarily assumed together with his human nature whatever belongs to animal nature."[11] Though this passage from the *Summa*, where the specific concern centers on Christ's possession of a sensitive appetite (the human animal-like ordering to bodily goods), fails to name Christ's male sex as an example of that which belongs to his "animal nature," the earlier passage from the *Sentences* commentary leaves little doubt.

We shall return to the relationship between sexuality and human animality in the second part of this study. For the moment, however, note that for Aquinas, "animal nature" in reference to man does not carry the pejorative sense that it often does in modern thought. Bearing the influence of Cartesian rationalism, modern thought tends to equate animal nature, along with all things biological, with the subhuman. Further, the effort to ground sexuality in our animal-like structuring is not to *reduce* sexual difference wholly to our bodily animality, as if laying aside the social and psychological aspects of human sexuality.

---

10. Aquinas, *De ente et essentia*, ch. 5.
11. *ST* III, q. 9, a. 4; q. 18, a. 2.

The Patristic and Conciliar Resonance

There is more to Aquinas's statement that Christ assumed "all the properties and parts of human nature." Charged not simply with deep philosophical thrust, this phrase sounds a clear patristic and conciliar resonance as well. Thomas, in fact, seems to offer this phrase as a condensed précis of the conciliar proclamation of Christ's full humanity. (Scholars have long documented Aquinas's unparalleled thirteenth-century familiarity with the conciliar decrees of the early Church.)[12]

Certainly, the overt patristic allusion comes earlier in the passage, specifically when Thomas writes, "Christ came to restore [or redeem] human nature by his very assumption." The celebrated soteriological principle, so seminal in patristic thought, unmistakably reverberates here, as it does throughout all of Aquinas's writings. In its classic formulation, the principle states, "What was not assumed was not healed or saved" (Thomas prefers to cite John Damascene's use of the principle).[13] Possibly tracing back to Irenaeus's theory of recapitulation, the principle originates more than likely with Origen: "man would not have been saved entirely if Christ hadn't clothed himself in man entirely," writes the Alexandrian.[14] For the whole of man to be saved, Christ had to take on the whole of man—he had to take on everything essential pertaining to human nature, including sexuality.

The soteriological principle played a crucial role in the patristic response to Apollinarianism, the heresy that denied Christ's rational soul (named after Apollinaris of Laodicea, Apollinarianism maintained that the Word, *Logos*, took the place of Christ's human mind, or *nous*). Officially condemning Apollinarianism in 381, the First Council of Constantinople employed the key term *enanthrōpeō*, "to become man," the Church's clearest attestation to date of Christ's full humanity.[15] When Thomas affirms that Christ as-

---

12. See, e.g., C. G. Geenen, "The Council of Chalcedon in the Theology of St. Thomas," in *From an Abundant Spring: The Walter Farrell Memorial Volume of The Thomist*, ed. Staff of *The Thomist* (New York: P. J. Kennedy, 1952), 172–217; and Martin Morard, "Thomas d'Aquin, lecteur des conciles," *Archivum franciscanum Historicum* 98 (2005), 211–365.

13. See Damascene, *De fide orth.*, III.6 (ed. Buytaert, 188).

14. Origen, *Discussion with Heraclitus*, 7.

15. *Decrees of the Ecumenical Councils*, 2 vols., ed. Norman P. Tanner (Washington, DC: Georgetown University Press, 1990), 1:24.

sumed "all the properties and parts of human nature," he seeks among other things, then, intentionally to echo the profession of Constantinople I. If, as per this council and contra Apollinaris, to be human is to have a rational soul with a mind (*nous*), it is also, Aquinas shies not from saying it, to have a sexuality, to be a biologically structured man or woman.

Over and above an allusion to Constantinople I, this phrase, "all the properties and parts of human nature," echoes especially the Council of Chalcedon in 451, the high point of the ancient Church's efforts to proclaim the full truth of Christ's humanity (and divinity). Chalcedon responded to the heresy of Monophysitism (or Eutychianism), which compromised Christ's full human nature by positing in Christ not two natures, a human nature and a divine nature, but one blended or mixed nature, making Christ a kind of theandric mutant. To counter this, Chalcedon appropriated the celebrated term of Nicaea, *homoousios* (consubstantial), used to affirm Christ's divinity, and applied it to Christ's humanity: "Christ is consubstantial (*homoousios*) with the Father as regards his divinity," the council professes, "and consubstantial (*homoousios*) with us as regards his humanity."[16] Christ shares in our human nature fully, not partially.

Chalcedon did not stop there. Continuing to hold Monophysitism (as well as Nestorianism) squarely in its scope, the council's profession of faith employed another, even more crucial turn of phrase (its celebrated phrase): "One and the same Christ, Son, Lord, only-begotten, acknowledged in two natures which undergo no confusion (*asugchytōs*), no change (*atreptōs*), no division (*adiairetōs*), no separation (*achōristōs*)."[17] Christ's human nature was not compromised or diluted by its being joined to the divine nature, since, still quoting the council, "the property of both natures is preserved, [while] com[ing] together into a single person and a single hypostasis."[18] The integrity and distinct identity of Christ's human nature were preserved.

All this Aquinas holds in mind when he maintains that Christ assumed "all the properties and parts of human nature, among which is sex." Genuine human consubstantiality as the early Church defined it *must*, on Aquinas's reading, mean the Word's assumption of a sexed nature.

16. *Decrees*, 1:86.
17. *Decrees*, 1:86.
18. *Decrees*, 1:86.

For the Sake of the Integrity of the Human Body

We come to the last line of the *Sentences* commentary passage, "(Christ) assumed a sex not in order to use it but for the perfection of nature." Besides the obvious reference to Christ's virginity or celibate state ("not in order to use it [his sex]"), the metaphysically charged phrase "for the perfection of nature" recapitulates what has been noted above and thus points to what the next section of this study will cover. For the moment, we can simply note that Aquinas is so firm on the basic goodness of human sexuality and on the integral role it plays in our hylemorphic design that he insists it shall remain in our resurrected bodies. He writes:

The diversity [of sex] befits the perfection of [our] species.... And therefore just as humans will rise again in diverse statures, so too, in diverse sexes. And although there be a difference between the sexes, nevertheless there will be no shame (*confusio*) in the mutual sight, for there will be no sexual desire inciting them to base acts, which is the cause of this shame.... The difference between the sexes and [genital] members will be for restoring the perfection of human nature (*ad naturae humanae perfectionem reintegrandam*) both in the species and in the individual.[19]

"Restoring the perfection of human nature" (or "restoring the integrity of the human body," as he puts it elsewhere)[20]—strong, robust words on human sexuality that practically stand without precedent in the history of Christian thought. Though Augustine proves an exception to this, as he asserts that sexual difference shall remain in the resurrected state, since it owes to human nature ("He who created both sexes will restore both").[21] The eastern Cappadocian Fathers, for their part, favor the express opposite view, holding that unity in Christ, in whom "there is neither male nor female" (Gal 3:28), means

19. *In IV Sent.*, d. 44, q. 1, a. 3, qa. 3, and qa 4, ad 2. Beth Mortensen, Peter Kwasniewski, and Dylan Schrader, trans. (Green Bay, WI: Aquinas Institute, 2018), 74–75, with adaptations.

20. *ScG* IV, c. 88. Laurence Shapcote, trans. (Green Bay, WI: Aquinas Institute, 2018), 541: "None of those members [i.e., sexual members] will be lacking [in the bodies of those who rise again], although they will not have their use; yet not without purpose, since they will serve to restore the integrity of the human body (*ad integritatem naturalis corporis restituendam*)."

21. Augustine, *City of God*, Bk. 22.17; here the Bishop of Hippo also writes: "They seem to be wiser who make no doubt that both sexes will rise.... From those bodies [of man and woman], then, vice shall be withdrawn, while nature shall be preserved. And the sex of woman [or of man] is not a vice, but nature." Marcus Dods, ed. (Edinburgh: T&T Clark, 1871), 2:509–10.

the dissolution of sexual difference in the resurrection.[22] As we shall see in the next section, Aquinas offers sharp words on what certain Greek Fathers opine regarding the role of sexuality in our natural design.

Importantly, Thomas's position on sex belonging to the resurrected body holds for Christ's resurrected body as well: his risen body retains its sexed design, its male structuring, for the sake of "the integrity of [his] human body"—just as the Virgin Mary, assumed "body and soul" into heaven, retains the female structuring of her body. The risen Jesus who showed his hands and his side to his Apostles was not an androgynous or epicene, undifferentiated individual; he was, and remains, a man, a male individual with all the biological structuring, all the bodily integrity, that this entails, albeit in a glorified mode. From his conception to his everlasting glorification, Christ's male-structured body remains a constitutive part of his human identity.

"Toxic Masculinity" and Gender Ideology: Objections to Christ's Maleness

At this point, we should note that, apart from the objections of simple, outright Docetism, placing the theological spotlight on such a sensitive topic as Christ's male sexuality invites obvious suspicion (to put it mildly) from today's wider culture beholden to what, following Pope Benedict XVI, we could term a "new philosophy of sexuality."[23] This is especially the case when

22. For the position of the Cappadocian Fathers, see the important essay by Verna Harrison, "Male and Female in Cappadocian Theology," *Journal of Theological Studies* 41, no. 2 (1990), 441–71. For instance, Basil of Caesarea asserts: "For there is no male or female in the resurrection, but there is one certain life and it is of one kind, since those dwelling in the land of the living are well pleasing to their Master" (*Homily on Psalm 114* [PG 29.492C]; cited on p. 451). Gregory of Nazianzus writes: "This is the great mystery planned for us by God, who for us was made human and became poor, to resurrect the flesh and recover his image and refashion the human, that we might all become one in Christ ... that we might no longer be male and female" (*Or.* 7.23 [PG 35.785C]; cited on p. 459). Gregory of Nyssa affirms the same even more stridently; see his *On Those Who Have Fallen Asleep* (GNO 9.63); cited on p. 469.

23. By this, Benedict meant a view where "sex is no longer [seen as] a given element of nature," but instead as "a social role that we choose for ourselves." See "Address of His Holiness Benedict XVI on the Occasion of Christmas Greetings to the Roman Curia," website of the Holy See, December 21, 2012, http://w2.vatican.va/content/benedict-xvi/en/speeches/2012/december/documents/hf_ben-xvi_spe_20121221_auguri-curia.html. His predecessor, Pope Pius XI, offered a similar locution. Writing his encyclical letter on Christian marriage, *Casti Connubii*, in 1939, partly in response to the Anglican Church's decision to allow the use of contraception in marriage, Pius denounced what he called his own day's "new and utterly perverse morality" (§3).

we consider how the notion of "toxic masculinity" has emerged as the latest iteration of this new philosophy of sexuality. That we find influential voices expressing a maligning attitude toward the male sex should give pause to the endeavor of treating theologically Christ's maleness or manliness. A prime example of this maligning attitude comes from no less an authority than the American Psychological Association (APA). In a recent report titled *Harmful Masculinity and Violence*, the APA labels as "harmful" Western culture's tendency to relate maleness to "masculine ideals" and to "heterosexism." There is little doubt that "masculine ideals" is "code" for "toxic masculinity" and all forms of male aggression (even of the ordered sort), including male headship, and that "heterosexism" equates with heteronormativity in all of its forms, including, we can assume, such traditional views as men as providers and protectors of women.[24]

Another objection arises from the fact that gender ideologues, determined to champion the irrelevance of human biology, as least as regards sex, deny any intrinsic link between sexuality and biological structuring (for Aquinas, this link is essential). The same APA report gives voice to this view as well, insisting: "The concept of gender roles is not cast as a biological phenomenon, but rather a psychological and socially constructed set of ideas that are malleable to change." Gender or sexual difference—in this case, masculinity or maleness—is completely severed from the realm of biology and, in a Cartesian-styled move, is instead relegated to a "malleable idea" conjured up by the human psyche or human society.[25] Little wonder Pope Francis has decried modern gender theory as an "error of the human mind" that "seeks to cancel out sexual difference" and that denies the "valuing [of] one's own body in its femininity or masculinity."[26]

24. "Harmful Masculinity and Violence: Understanding the Connection and Approaches to Prevention," American Psychological Association, September 2018, https://www.apa.org/pi/about/newsletter/2018/09/harmful-masculinity.

25. We should note, of course, that an ambiguous cloud hangs over the notion of gender and what it means in its current cultural usage. Sometimes it signifies sexual self-identity as distinct from one's biological sex, sometimes it refers to one's sex as it pertains to social role and function, sometimes other things—though in the very least it signifies differentiated sex.

26. This is an amalgam of citations from Francis: *Laudato Si'*, no. 155; "Pastoral Visit of His Holiness Pope Francis to Pompeii and Naples," website of the Holy See, March 21, 2015, http://www.vatican.va/content/francesco/en/speeches/2015/march/documents/papa-francesco_20150321_napoli-pompei-giovani.html; "General Audience, Saint Peter's Square," website of the Holy See, April 15, 2015, http://w2.vatican.va/content/francesco/en/audiences/2015/documents/papa-francesco_20150415_udienza-generale.html.

For a second piece of evidence of this culture-wide dismissive attitude toward biology—examples could be produced ad nauseam—one could point to the recent landmark decision by the US Supreme Court in *Bostock v. Clayton County*. Redefining sex (and the legal rights attending it) to include homosexual and transgender self-identification, this decision renders nonsensical any meaningful biological difference between male and female. If an individual with the male XY genetic karyotype has the legal right to be regarded as a woman, then nominalism has eclipsed biology. "Our legal regime has repudiated the Book of Genesis and the scriptural account of God as creator," retorts R. R. Reno.[27]

The upshot is clear: when applied to the topic of Christ's male sexuality, such repudiation of "male and female He created them" (Gn 1:27) or such labeling of "masculine ideals" as "harmful" (i.e., toxic masculinity) can spell nothing less than silence on this aspect of Christ's humanity. The risk of emasculating Christ looms before us, just as Docetism (or semi-Docetism) ever does.

"The Maleness of Jesus Has No Theological Significance"

To be sure, certain feminist theologians have long favored the semi-Docetic emasculation of Christ's manhood. Scandalized by the "naïve physicalism" (or "naïve biology," we might say) of giving weight to the particularity of Jesus's maleness, these theologians are fearful that such focus "collapses the totality of Christ into the human man Jesus," to quote the feminist Elizabeth Johnson.[28] Another, Rosemary Radford Ruether, asking whether a male savior "can save women," holds that, in the final analysis, "the maleness of Jesus has no theological significance."[29] Preferring to stress the undiffer-

---

27. R. R. Reno, "A Striking Display of Sophistry," *First Things*, June 16, 2020, https://www.first things.com/web-exclusives/2020/06/a-striking-display-of-sophistry?fbclid=IwAR1t11PxQ4oPCogxC HFYV6nBRlq9kPTOMNwAQECEk-Yz1BDHtTswOZfrIic.

28. Elizabeth A. Johnson, "The Maleness of Christ," in *The Special Nature of Women?*, ed. Anne Carr and Elisabeth Schüssler Fiorenza, Concilium 6 (London: SCM Press, 1991), 108–16, at 113 and 115; see also idem, "Redeeming the Names of Christ," in *Freeing Theology: The Essentials of Theology in Feminist Perspective*, ed. Catherine Mowry LaCugna (Harper: San Francisco, 1993), 115–37; and Anne Carr, "Feminist Views of Christology," *Chicago Studies* 35, no. 2 (1996): 128–40.

29. Rosemary Radford Ruether, "Christology: Can a Male Savior Save Women?," in *Sexism and*

entiated, ahistorical humanity of Christ, these feminists warn us that if we accentuate Christ's maleness, we risk obscuring the way Christ's redemptive accomplishments extend to all without distinction: male and female, Jew and Gentile, slave and free man, "for you are all one in Christ Jesus" (Gal 3:28).[30] Not without weight, these feminist concerns merit a response.

Reply to the Feminist Objections

Predicated on a view of human nature as undifferentiated by sex, this feminist position, it needs to be unequivocally asserted, is a deficient anthropology. For human nature *is* differentiated by sex. We possess bodies of differentiated biological design, a design encoded in the nucleus of each and every cell in the human body. It is impossible to dissociate sexual difference from the embodied, animal-like (and thus biological) structure of human nature. And our bodies, along with our souls, are a constitutive part of our human identity, including Jesus's.

Admittedly, this feminist objection would prove difficult to overcome if men and women, male and female, constituted distinct species. But they do not. Like odd and even, where each shares fully in the essence of number, while at the same time carrying numerical signification that the other does not, so men and women belong to the same human species, while marking two distinct "modes" of being human.[31] As Aquinas again observes, binary sexual difference constitutes an accidental difference. Granted, maleness and femaleness are accidents of the highest sort: not pure or contingent accidents (like skin color), they are "proper" accidents, as Aquinas calls them, that is, essential compositional attributes that follow upon our animal bodiliness. But they remain accidents all the same. An individual is human, then, in

---

God-Talk: Toward a Feminist Theology (Boston: Beacon Press, 1983), 116–38, at 137. For a general overview of feminist Christology, see Michele Schumacher, "Feminist Christologies," in *The Oxford Handbook of Christology*, ed. Francesca Murphy (Oxford: Oxford University Press, 2015), 408–24.

30. "Christ is not necessarily male, nor is the redeemed community only women, but a new humanity, female and male." Radford Ruether expressly favors a Christ abstracted from his historical existence: "Christ, as redemptive person and Word of God, is not to be encapsulated 'once-for-all' in the historical Jesus" ("Christology," 138).

31. The comparison of male and female to odd and even comes from Thomas himself, drawing upon Aristotle (see his *Commentary on the Metaphysics*, Bk. X, lect. 11 [no. 2128]), as noted by John Finley, "The Metaphysics of Gender: A Thomistic Approach," *The Thomist* 79 (2015): 585–614, at 607.

the very measure that one is either a man or a woman. Christ was human in the very measure that he was a man, a male individual. His salvific accomplishments, even if accomplished in the male sex, thus extend to the entire human species.

Further, Christ's male flesh, as Aquinas puts it, is "of infinite worth"—for men and women alike—since his flesh belongs to a divine Person.[32] The doctrine of the hypostatic union means that the particulars of the Incarnation (Jesus's maleness, but also his Jewishness, etc.) subsist in a divine Person who, as God, transcends all particulars and all limits of time and place. The whole of God and the whole of his infinite power are at work in every existential particularity of the life of Jesus.

Certainly, to many, not just feminists, it seems scandalous that the God of all peoples should unite himself substantially to one particular human individual, to a man, to the male Jesus, thereby granting him "the name which is above every name" (Phil 2:9). Yet that is the Christian confession. Jesus is himself God "particularized," embodied, who gained universal salvation through the historical life, death, and resurrection that he accomplished through his male body. Accomplished not in the abstract, human salvation was accomplished in all that Christ did and suffered in the flesh, as Aquinas is wont to say.[33] And Christ's flesh was male flesh. The feminist objections should serve as a reminder that we must ever be on our guard against the Gnostic tendency to choose universal (spiritual) salvation with no necessary, immediate link to historical particularity. "The Christian faith can never be separated from the soil of sacred events," writes Joseph Ratzinger (the future Pope Benedict XVI), "from the choice made by God, who wanted to speak to us, to become man, to die and rise again, in a particular place at a particular time."[34]

---

32. "The dignity of Christ's flesh is not to be estimated solely from the nature of flesh, but also from the Person assuming it—namely, inasmuch as it was God's flesh, the result of which was that it was of infinite worth." *ST* III, q. 48, a. 2, ad 3.

33. "Christ gives life to the world through the mysteries that he accomplished in his flesh." Aquinas, *In Ioh.* VI, l.4 (no. 914); see also V, l.5 (no. 791). More generally, Aquinas likes to say it is the humanity of Christ that leads us to God, as in the prologue to the entire *Summa* itself, "Christ, who, as man, is our way to God"; or again in *In Ioh.* VII, l.4 (no. 1074), "the humanity of Christ is the way that leads us to God." See as well *ST* III, q. 48, a. 6; and Torrell, *Le Christ en ses mystères*, 1:15n6.

34. Joseph Ratzinger, *Theology of the Liturgy: The Sacramental Foundation of Christian Existence*, in *Collected Works*, ed. Michael J. Miller, trans. John Saward et al. (San Francisco: Ignatius Press, 2014), 11:101. The Protestant theologian Karl Barth appreciated the same. For Barth, the universality of the

So just as stressing the Jewishness of Jesus, a favorite topic of current biblical scholarship, hardly calls into question the fact there is "neither Jew nor Gentile" in Christ (Gal 3:28), so neither does underscoring Jesus's maleness subvert the fact that there is "neither male nor female" in Christ. Jesus is no generality, he is not "humanity," as is no human being. To be human, one must be a man or a woman, and the historical fact is that Christ was a man (just as it is a historical fact that the Virgin Mary was a woman). This is not to assert the superiority of maleness over femaleness or vice versa; it is simply to recognize that a true human individual must be either male or female. To underscore Jesus's maleness is to affirm his real humanity.

AQUINAS AND THE "METAPHYSICAL BIOLOGY" OF HUMAN SEXUALITY

At this point, we shift our attention to consider what accounts for Aquinas's unprecedented decision to affirm the necessity of Christ's assumption of a sexed nature. Servais Pinckaers helps identify the reason. In a little-regarded section near the end of his much-acclaimed *Sources of Christian Ethics*, Pinckaers notes that Aquinas was largely charting new ground on the more general issue of human sexuality. By tethering human sexuality to the biologically structured animal-like side of human nature, and thus to God's creative handiwork, Aquinas advanced a decided "positive teaching on sexuality" relative to the Augustinian tradition (inclusive of Peter Lombard) and the Franciscan school that preceded him.[35] If Thomas anchored his approach to human sexuality in human biology—that is, in our animal-like, biologically structured bodies—the Augustinian tradition and the Franciscan school instead placed the focus on the way marriage corrects concupiscence and the disordering effects of original sin on human sexuality.[36]

Son of God is revealed in the particularity of the Son's assumption of Jewish flesh, and he bemoans the "all too generalised views of the man Jesus" that lose sight of "the simple truth that Jesus Christ was a born Jew." G. W. Bromiley and T. F. Torrance, eds. *Church Dogmatics*, IV.1 (Edinburgh: T&T Clark, 1961), §59, 166–67.

35. Pinckaers, *Sources*, 438–40. Pinckaers observes that Aquinas introduces this new perspective on sexuality at the outset of his career, in *In IV Sent.*, distinctions 26–42.

36. Pinckaers does not hesitate to point out, however, that this does not mean that a deprecating

Aquinas was also contending with the problematic patristic view, somewhat widespread among the Greek Fathers (Thomas cites Gregory of Nyssa, but Athanasius, John Chrysostom, and the other Cappadocian Fathers could be included) and not unknown in the Latin West (e.g., Ambrose), that God endowed us with a sexed nature, inclusive of genitals, only because God "foreknew the mode of generation [sexual union and the pleasure accompanying it] that would take place after sin."[37] "But this view is unreasonable (*hoc non dicitur rationabiliter*)," replies Thomas rather acerbically to the Bishop of Nyssa. Favoring a Platonic-inspired regard for the body as alien to our human makeup, these Greek Fathers, and the Cappadocians in particular, ground human sexuality in sin—"[which] is probably why," the patristic scholar Verna Harrison points out apropos the subject matter of this essay, "his [Christ's] maleness never became an issue in Greek patristic Christology."[38] Aquinas, however, sees sexual dimorphism (binary sexual difference) as natural to us on account our God-given animal-like embodied nature: "[Sexuality] is natural to man by reason of his animal life ... as bodily organs clearly attest," he writes immediately after his rejoinder to Gregory.

Nor should we think that Thomas's quarrel was merely with the patristic past. Proving that an even more extreme position remained a live option in the thirteenth century, Aquinas's contemporary Mechthild of Magdeburg (†1280) wrote that God created our first parents with "no shameful members" (genitals), but that "when they ate the forbidden food, they were [afterward] ignominiously altered in body."[39] The anthropological differences relating to our sexual design between Aquinas on the one side and certain Greek Fathers (in this case, Gregory of Nyssa) or various of his Latin contemporaries on the other could not be any starker.

---

view of marriage was espoused, as Bonaventure offers "very beautiful texts ... on the mutual support, love, and friendship of husbands and wives" (*Sources*, 439).

37. Citation here of Aquinas, *ST* I, q. 98, a. 2. See Gregory of Nyssa, *De hominis opificio*, 17 (PG 44.189); and John Chrysostom, *In Genesim*, hom. 16 (PG 53.126).

38. Harrison, "Male and Female in Cappadocian Theology," 456–59, at 458.

39. "Their bodies were to be pure, / For God created for them no shameful members, ... / But when they ate the forbidden food, they were ignominiously altered in body." Mechthild of Magdeburg, *Das fliessende Licht der Gottheit*, III.9, "Von dem Anfang aller Dinge, die Gott aus Minne erschaffen hat," ed. Margot Schmidt (Einsiedeln: Benziger Verlag, 1956), 141–42; cited in Leo Steinberg, *The Sexuality of Christ in Renaissance Art*, 249.

Metaphysical Biology and the
Basic Goodness of Sexuality

Alasdair MacIntyre holds that what we see on display here in Aquinas is his commitment to what he terms a "metaphysical biology."[40] That is, a commitment to human biology as ensuing upon an Aristotelian-inspired hylemorphic (matter-form) conception of human nature. As a matter-form composite, the human being has the "matter" of an organic, biologically structured body, specifically of an animal-like sort, and the form of a rational, immaterial soul.

If Aquinas's metaphysical biology draws heavily upon Aristotle, as MacIntyre observes, it is no less biblically inspired. For evidence, we need only consider how Thomas calls out the view that "bodily things (res corporalis) were caused by an evil God" (the referent here is Albigensianism, even if not named) as the "worst of all heresies (pessima haeresis)"—and heresy is a denial of some revealed truth. Such a view is tantamount to heresy, since it counters the biblical witness that, as Thomas puts it, "bodily nature was instituted by the good God (natura corporalis sit a Deo bono instituta)."[41] Important for this present study, Aquinas embeds these words amidst his affirmation of the goodness of human sexuality, specifically, of the sexual inclination and its ensuing marital act "by which children are procreated."

For Aquinas, then, when considering sexual difference, we must begin with our "bodily nature instituted by the good God," that is, with our animal-like, biologically structured bodies. (Sexual difference pertains neither to God nor the angels because neither possess bodies.) Not coincidentally, modern genomic science has shown that sexual difference rests ultimately upon the complementary genetic karyotypes of XX (for females) and XY (for males). Sexual difference, maleness or femaleness, is written into our very biological design, in that it is encoded in the nucleus of each and every cell of our bodies.[42]

---

40. See Alasdair MacIntyre, *After Virtue: A Study in Moral Theory*, 2nd ed. (Notre Dame, IN: University of Notre Dame Press, 1984), 148; see also the preface to his *Dependent Rational Animals: Why Human Beings Need the Virtues* (Chicago: Open Court, 1999).

41. *In IV Sent.*, d. 26, q. 1, a. 3 (trans. Mortensen, 8–9).

42. "The X and Y chromosomes are known as the sex chromosomes for the obvious reason that they determine, with almost perfect predestination, the sex of the body." Matt Ridley, *Genome: The Autobiography of a Species in 23 Chapters* (New York: HarperCollins, 2000), 108.

While Augustine deserves honorable mention, Aquinas seems to be among the first in the history of Christian thought to affirm vigorously, simple and obvious though it may seem, that before the Fall and its deleterious consequences on human nature, there stands our God-given animal-like nature with its sexed design.[43] By the time he writes the *Summa*, Aquinas would not hold back: primordially expressive of God's creative will, sex constitutes a *tantum bonum*, "a great good indeed."[44] Hence Pinckaers's remark that "sexuality was recognized [by Aquinas] as something basically good and a source of moral excellence."[45]

Foundational to the position he takes on Christ's male sex, then, is this new "positive teaching on sexuality." Recognizing sexuality as basically good and a source of moral excellence, Aquinas has little difficulty, no matter the lack of precedence, in appreciating the full bodily implications of Christ's humanity, inclusive of his male sexuality.

Sexual Difference in
Modern Neurobiology

Emerging research in the field of neurobiology has uncovered crucial structural differences between the male brain and the female brain, thereby lending key support to Aquinas's biologically based view of sexual difference.[46] With the proviso that these encephalic differences lend no support to the view that one (say, the male brain) proves superior over the other, as both admit of respective and complementary advantages, here I shall offer a few brief highlights of these findings, since they bear on the question of Christ's male structuring.[47]

43. Augustine's affirmation of this is implicit when he writes in *City of God*, Bk. 22.17: "Before they sinned, the man and the woman were naked, and were not ashamed. From those bodies, then, vice shall be withdrawn [at the time of the Resurrection], while nature shall be preserved. And the sex of woman [or of man] is not a vice, but nature" (ed. Dods, 2:509).

44. *ST* I, q. 98, a. 1.

45. Pinckaers, *Sources*, 439. See Aquinas, *ScG* III, c. 126; *De ente*, chap. 5; and *In II Sent.*, d. 20, q. 1, a. 2.

46. Writing in 2017, the neurobiologist Larry Cahill observes: "The past 15 to 20 years in particular witnessed an explosion of research (despite the prevailing biases against the topic) documenting sex influences at all levels of brain function. So overpowering is the wave of research that the standard ways of dismissing sex influences ... have all been swept away, at least for those cognizant of the research." "An Issue Whose Time Has Come," *Journal of Neuroscience Research* 95 (2017): 12–23, at 12.

47. For these findings, I lean heavily on the physician and psychologist Leonard Sax, *Why Gender*

In terms of size, the male brain is on average ten percent larger than the female brain and has a higher rate of blood flow, though the male brain loses some of its density while undergoing quicker post-pubertal aging. As regards smell, women have more cells in the olfactory bulb, the part of the brain that controls smell, by a factor of nearly two to one, with the result that women smell differently than men. With respect to sound, girls on average experience a greater sensitivity to sound than boys by about eight decibels. Concerning sight, the male brain enjoys more resources in the system that specializes in speed and direction, while the female brain owns more resources in the system that specializes in color, detail, and texture.

Additionally, researchers have found that connections in the male brain run between the front and the back of the same side of the brain, which optimizes communication within the same hemispheres of the brain; connections in the female brain, on the other hand, run from side to side between the left and right hemispheres, thereby optimizing communication between the hemispheres. This allows men generally to function better at spatial tasks and motor control, whereas women generally perform better at verbal tasks that involve memory and intuition.

As regards sexual desire and activity, the male brain owns more extensive testosterone circuits, the hormone that mediates male aggression and the male sex drive, whereas the female brain engages more the cerebral cortex and has more extensive oxytocin circuits, the so-called bonding hormone, hardwiring women neurobiologically in a particular way for relationships. As a result, women experience optimal sexual pleasure within the context of a committed relationship, more so than for men, whose sexual drive is oriented more to "objectification" (or to physical attraction, it might be better to say) and pleasure.[48] The physician and psychologist Leonard Sax puts it

---

Matters: What Parents and Teachers Need to Know about the Emerging Science of Sex Differences, 2nd ed. (New York: Harmony, 2017). See also Charles Murray, *Human Diversity: The Biology of Gender, Race, and Class* (New York: Twelve, 2020); in particular, chap. 3, "Sex Differences in Neurocognitive Functioning," and chap. 5, "Sex Differences in the Brain," where one will find references to all the relevant studies. One could also look at the linguistics professor Deborah Tannen's *You Just Don't Understand: Women and Men in Conversation* (New York: HarperCollins, 1990).

48. "Women's sexual experience is 'happening' more in the cerebral cortex and is therefore more connected with the rest of what's going on in their mind. The sexual experience in men is less connected with the cortex, less connected with the outside world.... 'For women, an important goal of sex is intimacy; the best context for pleasurable sex is a committed relationship. This is less true for men.'" Sax, *Why Gender Matters,* 122–23. The citation is from the psychologist Leitita Anne Peplau, "Human

this way: "Most girls, and most women, are looking first and foremost for a *relationship*. Most boys, and more than a few men, are interested first and foremost in *sex*."[49]

Psychological research bears out the behavioral outcomes relative to sexual desire and activity that one would expect to see in light of the neurobiological structuring. Studies show that men, possessing a more objectification- and pleasure-oriented sex drive, display a stronger sexual appetite than women and are more motivated to pursue sexual opportunities.[50] Other studies indicate that men exhibit a decidedly greater willingness to engage in casual sex than women,[51] and that a much greater occurrence of sexual pathologies and sexually deviant behavior exist among men (as testified by the current epidemic of pornography, largely a male problem, to name just one example).[52] Behind these findings the moral theologian will spy

---

Sexuality: How Do Men and Women Differ?," *Current Directions in Psychological Science*, 12 (2003): 37–44.

49. Sax, *Why Gender Matters*, 229; emphasis his. Sax further notes that this holds regardless of whether the sexual desires are of a heterosexual or homoerotic bent; the sex drive of women who identify as lesbian remains relationship oriented, while that of men who identify as homosexual remains objectification and pleasure oriented (see 118 and 122; see also 228–29). This finding would not have surprised Aquinas, who observes that the disorder of "insensibility," a dislike for sexual pleasure, "is not found in many, since men are more incline to pleasure." *ST* II-II, q. 153, a. 3, ad 3.

50. For a summary of these studies, see R. F. Baumeister, K. R. Catanese, and K. D. Vohs, "Is There a Gender Difference in Sex Drive? Theoretical Views, Conceptual Distinctions, and a Review of Relevant Evidence," *Personality and Social Psychology Review* 5 (2001): 242–73.

51. The classic study on this is Russell D. Clark and Elaine Hatfield, "Gender Differences in Receptivity to Sexual Offers," *Journal of Psychology and Human Sexuality* 2, no. 1 (1989): 39–55. What the opening abstract reports is worth citing: "In [our] experiments ... male and female confederates of average attractiveness approached potential partners with one of three requests: 'Would you go out tonight?' 'Will you come over to my apartment?' or 'Would you go to bed with me?' The great majority of men were willing to have a sexual liaison with the women who approached them. Women were not. Not one woman agreed to a sexual liaison." This study, with some modifications, was repeated several years later, with similar results; see Mercedes Tappé, Lisamarie Bensman, Kentaro Hayashi, and Elaine Hatfield, "Gender Differences in Receptivity to Sexual Offers: A New Research Prototype," *Interpersona: An International Journal on Personal Relationships* 7, no. 2 (2013): https://interpersona.psychopen. eu/article/view/121/html. The opening abstract from this latter study summarizes: "In all three [of our] experiments men were more likely than women to accept sexual offers."

52. This according to the psychologist Paul Vitz, from his paper , "Men and Women: The Psychology of Their Differences and Their Complementarity," delivered at the annual symposium of the Catholic Women's Forum of the Ethics and Public Policy Center, Washington, DC, June 26, 2019. See also the study by Samantha J. Dawson, Brittany A. Bannerman, and Martin Lalumière, "Paraphilic Interests: An Examination of Sex Differences in a Nonclinical Sample," *Sexual Abuse: A Journal of Research and Treatment* 28, no. 1 (2016): 20–45, https://journals.sagepub.com/doi/ pdf/10.1177/1079063214525645; see in particular its conclusion: "Our results suggest a reliable and sub-

concupiscence and the *fomes peccati* (the affective "spark" to sin), to advert to Scholastic vocabulary, a disordering traceable to original sin that has undoubtedly adversely affected the male neurobiological wiring.

The upshot from this is that what men, generally speaking, must master and control in a particular way, certainly more so than women, are sexual appetites and aggressive impulses. Men are particularly prone to a disordered use of their sexual desires and thus face a distinct challenge in being chaste, that is, in mastering and rightly ordering their sex drive. Lust emerges as an especially male problem. Indeed, I think it sound to affirm, beyond the more general *fomes peccati*, a more specific type of *fomes* in men, a *fomes luxuriae*: an affective spark to lust characteristic of the male fallen condition. The male neurobiological predisposition to physical attraction (i.e., to objectification) and to seeking sexual pleasure becomes, as a consequence of original sin, a condition of "lying in wait"; thus a "spark (*fomes*)" to lust—that is, a spark that can stoke or rouse and thereby exacerbate this male neurobiological predisposition.

The male *fomes luxuriae* aside, the foregoing cursory, and somewhat hurried, overview of the neurobiology helps to appreciate the wondrous extent of God's fashioning of sexual difference—with complementarity as its clear intended purpose. "Male and female he created them" (Gn 1:27) only hints at the much grander reality. God has embedded sexual complementarity so deeply into our design that it reaches unto the very structure of the brain.

Sexual Difference in the Soul

If sexual difference and complementarity reach unto the structure of the brain, it remains to consider whether it extends to the soul, given the hylemorphic design of the human being. Not a centaur, with a clean line of separation between the animal and the rational, the human being remains first and last a unified, integrated being. As Pinckaers observes, "in the hu-

---

stantial sex difference in paraphilic [i.e., sexually deviant] interests, such that men report less repulsion to a variety of paraphilic acts than do women, and more men than women report being actually aroused by particular paraphilic activities" (37). The study also observes: "Sex drive appears to provide the best explanation for the sex difference in paraphilic interests.... Sex drive, comprised of measures assessing sexual compulsivity and hypersexuality, was found to significantly and fully mediate the sex difference in overall paraphilic scores" (34–35).

man person the biological dimension [inclusive of our sexuality] is vitally integrated in a spiritual nature."[53]

As a spiritual substance, however, the soul in itself can be neither male nor female. Sexual difference owes not to the soul, but to the biological design of our animal-like bodies, to "animal nature," as Aquinas again puts it, ultimately to the XX and XY karyotypes. Insofar, then, as the soul qua immaterial form is concerned, there is no male or female soul.

At the same time, the soul bears an essential relation to the body since it remains the form of the body—the form of *this* or *that* body, "the form individualized by signate matter," to quote Thomas.[54] Insofar as we are considering the soul qua joined or related essentially to a particular body—to a male body or a female body—we are dealing with a soul that, as Aquinas expresses it in another key passage, is "commensurate with" or "adapted to" that individual's male or female body:

This distinction [of form causing a difference within a species] results from … the various coaptation [or commensuration] of souls to bodies (*secundum diversam commensurationem animarum ad corpora*), because this soul is adapted (*commensurata*) to this and not to that body, and that soul to another body, and so on…. Now it is as forms that souls need to be adapted (*commensuratas*) to their bodies.[55]

While Aquinas here fails to mention sexual identity, his point nonetheless holds for a particular body's essential properties, such as maleness or femaleness. Insofar, then, as we are speaking of a soul qua commensurate with or adapted to/individualized by the male or female body to which it is joined and essentially related, we can speak of female souls and male souls.[56]

---

53. Pinckaers, *Sources*, 440–41.

54. *ST* I, q. 119, a. 1. Here Thomas distinguishes between human nature "in general" and "in the individual," with the latter signifying "individualized signate matter, and *the form individualized* by that matter…. Thus to the true human nature of Peter and Martin belongs *this* soul and *this* body." Emphasis added.

55. *ScG* II, c. 81 (trans. Shapcote, 322–23); see also *De spiritualibus creaturis*, a. 9, ad 4.

56. John Finley holds the same: "While the soul on its own is not gendered … presumably the soul of a human male can be derivatively considered a male soul, and the same in the case of a female, since the soul's identity is marked by its being the soul of the male or female body" ("Metaphysics of Gender," 594). W. Norris Clarke argues this as well in *The One and the Many* (Notre Dame, IN: University of Notre Dame Press, 2001), 103–4. Thus, as Finley notes, Edith Stein goes too far in holding that sex difference stems from the soul, "resulting in a male and female 'species'" (606n50); see Stein, *Essays on Women* (Washington, DC: ICS Publications, 1996), 187.

Christ's Male Soul and
Male-Structured Body

We return to Christ and consider how the foregoing bears on his humanity. Regarding his body, we have a clearer idea of what it means to affirm Christ's maleness in the full biological sense. To say he possessed a male-structured body is to say he owned the XY genetic karyotype and all that this gives rise to, including male genitals, the bone and muscle structure proper to men, and a male-structured brain designed to send male-specific neurotransmitters and to release male-specific biochemicals and hormones that largely determine male-specific behavior. That the anti-Docetic Aquinas, committed completely and full on to a biologically grounded approach to human sexuality, would affirm as much there can be little doubt.

As for Christ's soul, we know that, related essentially to his male body as its proper form, his soul would, as with all male individuals, have been commensurate with or adapted to this same (male) body. In this way we can affirm a masculine or male soul in Christ.

Further, because the latest findings of neurobiology have uncovered newer and deeper ways of appreciating the extent to which our bodies—in particular, our brains—enjoy a female-specific or male-specific design, we gain deeper insight into what it means to say Christ's soul is commensurate with or adapted to his male-structured body. Since the soul remains the principle and source of all the body's vital movements, the human brain cannot perform the functions for which it is designed apart from the soul that is adapted to it: "integral to 'this soul's' essence is that it is the act of 'this body,'" writes John Finley, "[with the upshot that] the body's organization and development [and action] flow from the soul."[57] Hylemorphism extends to all human action, including that of every organ. In Christ's case, this means that, materially speaking, his male-specific behavior is accounted for by his male-structured brain (designed to send male-specific neurotransmitters and to release male-specific biochemicals and hormones), while formally speaking it is accounted for by his male-adapted soul.

Placing in relief Christ's male-specific design and the male-specific

---

57. Finley, "Metaphysics of Gender," 598.

behavior that ensues invites consideration of the moral quality of this behavior. The issue carries special interest when we bear in mind that the male-structured brain accounts for a sex drive that, because oriented to physical attraction (objectification) and pleasure, typically proves a challenge in mastering and controlling, resulting in problems with lust. To this topic, then, we turn.

SEXUALITY AS A SOURCE OF MORAL EXCELLENCE IN CHRIST'S LIFE

To repeat what was noted above, Aquinas's regard for the basic goodness of sexuality runs so deep that he sees sex, biological structuring and all, as a "source of moral excellence" (Pinckaers). Let us trace out a bit this position.

The Sensitive Appetite and Moral Virtue

Human sexuality, on Thomas's account, provides the basis of a natural inclination, one that we share in common with the animal kingdom. Aquinas terms this the inclination to sexual intercourse (procreative by its nature, as he names it, literally, the "union of male and female," *coniunctio maris et feminae*) and the rearing of offspring.[58] Ontologically speaking, this inclination is expressive of a natural appetite for sex, of a natural sex drive, similar to our natural appetite for food (recognizable when we grow hungry, whether or not there are objects of food before us).

Distinct from and foundational to any elicited desire for a particular object of sex or of food, this natural ontological appetite provides the source for the two ensuing "psychological" appetites. The first Thomas terms the *appetitus sensitivus*, the "sentient" or "sensitive appetite," which denotes our lower ordering to particular bodily goods (such as to sexual pleasure) as ow-

---

58. "There is in man an inclination to things that pertain to him more specially according to that nature which he has in common with other animals. In virtue of this inclination, those things are said to belong to the natural law which nature has taught to all animals, such as sexual intercourse (*coniunctio maris et feminae*), education of offspring and so forth." Aquinas, *ST* I-II, q. 94, a. 2.

ing to the animal-like dimension of human nature.[59] The second concerns the higher intellectual or rational appetite (*appetitus intellectivus*), known more commonly as the will, by which the human person enjoys an ordering to rational (spiritual) goods (such as to unitive love in the case of sex) and ultimately to God, the *summum bonum*. Together these two appetites, the sensitive subordinate to the intellectual and both perfective of the natural appetite (inclusive of human biology), order the human being to his proper fulfillment, concomitant with his corporeal-spiritual hylemorphic design.[60]

The lower sensitive appetite gives rise to animal-like movements (internal movements) toward bodily goods apprehended as such by the senses. Aquinas names these *passiones animae*, passions or emotions (inclusive of sexual desire and sexual pleasure). These movements, the passions or emotions, are taken up into the rational dimension of human life, inasmuch as reason and will finalize them and integrate them into the proper human good. It belongs to moral virtue to accomplish this task. Drawing upon Aristotle, Thomas writes: "moral virtue perfects the appetitive part of the soul by directing [the passions or emotions] to the good defined by reason," as, indeed, passion or emotion constitutes the "proper matter" of the moral virtues.[61]

There are various passions or emotions, each one bearing on a particular moral virtue. When it concerns passions or emotions of a sexual sort (desire and pleasure), rooted in and perfective of the natural sexual inclination, the proper matter of the virtue of chastity emerges. What begins at the ontological, biological level of human nature—sexual inclination—and then extends to the sentient animal level—elicited sexual passions—becomes "humanized" and integrated through the virtue of chastity. As Pinckaers expresses it, sexuality becomes "integrated in the totality of human nature, particularly through its coordination with spiritual inclinations," and so "is realized in man in a different and far richer way than in animals."[62] Sexual inclination

59. *ST* I-II, q. 94, a. 2 ad 2.

60. I am indebted to Michael D. O'Connor for these remarks on natural appetite and the ensuing psychological appetites. "The Orientation of Human Sexuality: A Thomistic Study of the Inclination to Conjugal Union (STD diss., Pontifical University of Saint Thomas Aquinas, 2020), chap. 4. See also Sean B. Cunningham, "Natural Inclination in Aquinas" (PhD diss., Catholic University of America, 2013). For Aquinas's overview of the natural appetite and the psychological appetites, see *ST* I, q. 80, aa. 1–2.

61. *ST* I-II, q. 59, aa. 4–5. See Aristotle, *Nicomachean Ethics*, Book II, chapter 6 (1106b15–16). For much more on this, see my own "The Passions and the Moral Life: Appreciating the Originality of Aquinas," *Thomist* 71 (2007): 419–50.

62. Pinckaers, *Sources*, 438.

and biological design, encompassing sentient appetitive movements, burgeon into moral excellence, specifically in the form of chastity.

The Mean of Virtue Is in Our
Sexual Structuring

For Thomas, the key question centers on how one conceives the regulation or direction of sensibility exercised by our rational powers, reason and will. On this point, he famously stakes a position that differs sharply from what one finds, for instance, in Bonaventure.[63] For Bonaventure, moral virtue simply "tames" our lower animal-like urges and passions by what he terms a forced "submission to reason (*optemperat rationi*)," somewhat akin to calling a dog to heel on a leash.[64]

Aquinas, by contrast, holds that moral excellence, hardly dragging along our animal-like bodily impulses as on a leash, instead elevates our passions to the level of reason, as co-partners in the work of virtue. Moral virtue reforms our bodily desires and passions to the extent that they become "rational by participation (*rationale per participationem*)," to cite Aquinas's key phrase (itself indebted to Aristotle).[65] We could liken Thomas's position somewhat to the dog that is so perfectly trained that it acts quasi-rationally, in that it never need discipline or a leash, even when crossing the path of another dog. In this way our sentient movements of affectivity become "disposed to obey reason promptly (*prompte*)," as Aquinas puts it, whereby they speak the same voice as reason, walking hand in hand with reason and will as active assistants and collaborators in the life of virtue.[66]

---

63. For a deeper examination of how Aquinas's position figures in the history of Western thought, see again my "Passions and the Moral Life," 419–50. For Aristotle's position, which Aquinas draws upon, see *Nicomachean Ethics*, Book I, chapter 13 (1102b13–1103a3).

64. Bonaventure, *In III Sent.*, d. 33, a. 1, q. 3, ad 1 (ed. Quar., 717). One finds a similar position in John Duns Scotus (*Op. Ox.*, Bk. III, d. 33, q. 1) and later in modern philosophers like Descartes (*The Passions of the Soul*, Pt. 1, art. 47; Pt. 2, art. 137 and 148) and Immanuel Kant (*Groundwork of the Metaphysics of Morals*, section 1, ed. and trans. Mary Gregor [Cambridge: Cambridge University Press, 1998], 12–14 and 17).

65. Aquinas, *In Ethic.*, Bk. I, ch. 13, lect. 20; C. I. Litzinger, trans. (Notre Dame, IN: Dumb Ox Books, 1993), 80; see Aristotle, *Nicomachean Ethics*, Book I, chapter 13 (1102b26–35). For the classic study of this issue, see M.-D. Chenu, "Les passions vertueuses: L'anthropologie de saint Thomas," *Revue philosophique de Louvain* 72 (1974): 11–18.

66. *ST* I-II, q. 68, a. 3.

Thomas, at the very inception of his career, does not hold back in expressly affirming the same of human sexuality. Commenting on the sexual inclination and its ensuing "act by which children are procreated," Thomas stares down the tradition and asserts rather astoundingly: "It is impossible to say ... that the mean of virtue (*medium virtutis*) cannot be found in it."[67] Human sexuality provides a source for moral virtue, specifically of chastity. "Sexuality, including with it the sensibility [sensitive appetite], could be the foundation for the virtue of temperance in the form of chastity," writes Pinckaers.[68]

For Aquinas, then, virtuous character, moral excellence, arises from our natural appetite (such as for food and sex) and from our subsequent lower animal-like inclination to bodily goods, inclusive of the desire for and enjoyment of sexual pleasure, as from a font.[69]

Christ's Perfect Interior Mastery of His Sexuality: Christ as *Exemplum Castitatis*

As for how the foregoing pertains to Christ, Aquinas cuts straight to the point: if we can affirm in general that "the moral virtues are in the irrational part of the soul ... and so much the more as the virtue is more perfect," then this holds preeminently for Christ, "since the virtues were in their highest degree in him."[70] Christ was sinless, with the result that he was "not troubled by the passions of the soul nor the desires of the flesh," to quote the Second Council of Constantinople (553).[71] This conciliar teaching owes to the fact that, because he was sinless, Jesus was not subject to concupiscence nor the

---

67. *In IV Sent.*, d. 26, q. 1, a. 3 (trans. Mortensen, 9). No matter the "intensity of pleasure (*delectationis intensio*)" of the marital act absorbing the mind while it occurs, Thomas goes on in ad 6 of this article to defend the reasonableness of this act (virtue, after all, signifies behavior in accord with reason); in this instance, the pleasure does "not take away the ordering of reason (*non tollit rationis ordinem*)," since "even if one is not so ordered at that moment, nevertheless such a person is pre-ordered by reason (*a ratione praeordinatus*)."

68. Pinckaers, *Sources*, 439.

69. See *ST* I-II, q. 24, a. 3, ad 1; and q. 56, a. 4.

70. *ST* III, q. 15, a. 2.

71. Constantinople II, twelfth anathema (*Decrees of the Ecumenical Councils*, ed. Tanner, 1:119). For the teaching of this council as a source for Aquinas, see Martin Morard, "Une source de saint Thomas d'Aquin: le Deuxième Concile de Constantinople (553)," *Revue des sciences philosophiques et théologiques* 81 (1977): 21–56.

fomes peccati (the affective "spark" to sin); both terms, concupiscence and *fomes peccati*, express the interior affective disorder introduced in the human condition by original sin, inasmuch as the postlapsarian sensitive appetite inclines to its proper object (a bodily good) irrespective of the good of reason. Spared this disorder, and thus spared from having the governance of his reason compromised in any way, Christ enjoyed consummate interior rectitude, similar to Adam before the Fall.[72] So, when affirming a sensitive appetite (or a "will of sensuality") in Christ, Aquinas at once qualifies this appetite as "rational by participation" (equivalent to saying "the moral virtues are in the irrational part of the soul").[73] This establishes Christ as the supreme model of virtue, the *exemplum virtutis*, as Thomas calls him.[74] So when in the Sermon on the Mount Jesus enjoins his disciples to strive for moral perfection (Mt 5:48), he knows that by his own example he leads the way.

What follows as regards the moral quality of Christ's sexuality is paramount. Since sexuality can be the foundation for the virtue of temperance in the form of chastity in those beset by concupiscence and the *fomes peccati* (or what I have called above the *fomes luxuriae* in the case of men, the male spark to lust), we can assert the same, yet to an exceedingly higher degree, in one such as Christ who enjoyed perfect interior rectitude. In no way can we attribute lust in any form to him.

We should not take this to mean, however, that Jesus was spared the typical male neurobiological structuring orienting men to physical attraction and to pleasure. Natural biological design suggests otherwise, and "what is natural to man was neither acquired nor forfeited by sin," as Aquinas insists.[75] Like any man, Jesus owned a male-structured brain that largely determined male-specific behavior. All the same, since his male structuring did not suffer the rousing or stoking influence of concupiscence and the *fomes peccati* (or, more specifically, the *fomes luxuriae*, the male spark to lust), his self-mastery over his sexual appetites remained unmitigated; reason's interior mastery of sexuality reigned supreme in him. This signals Christ as the

---

72. For more on concupiscence and the *fomes peccati* as effects of original sin, on what distinguishes them, and on how they pertain to Christ, see my *The Passions of Christ's Soul in the Theology of St. Thomas Aquinas* (Münster: Aschendorff, 2002; repr., Providence, RI: Cluny Media, 2018), 340–49.

73. *ST* III, q. 18, a. 2.

74. *ST* III, q. 15, a. 1.

75. *ST* I, q. 98, a. 2.

exemplum castitatis, the supreme model of the virtue of chastity, with his sexuality—male biological structuring and all—as the source of it.

Moreover, on the subject of Christ's perfect interior rectitude, it must be stressed: as he was spared the *fomes peccati*, defined by Thomas as "an inclination of the sensual appetite to what is contrary to reason,"[76] so Jesus would have been spared any sort of disordered sexual inclination or "orientation." This would include homoeroticism, as this inclines to inherently disordered acts, that is, acts "contrary to reason."[77] In this connection and not coincidentally, Jesus himself espoused a "heteronormative" view of sex in his teaching, in that he affirmed the male-female anthropology of the Genesis creation account and the view that sex is ordered to the joining of male and female in marriage (see Mk 10:4–12).[78] Little matter that he was silent on the issue of homosexuality. His silence finds explanation in the simple fact that it was not an issue for his Jewish audience ("no social visibility" is how one biblical scholar characterizes the issue of homosexuality in Jesus's Jewish milieu) and in his undoubted tacit agreement with the moral censure of homosexual practice in the Book of Leviticus and the rest of the Torah (see Lv 18:22 and 20:13, as well as Gn 19:1–29 and Jgs 19:11–25).[79]

Jesus as the Model of Manly Chastity

With the foregoing in mind, we can approach Christ's moral exemplarity from two distinct angles. On the one hand, as a human being and as savior

76. *ST* III, q. 15, a. 2.

77. In its 1986 *Homosexualitatis Problema*, §3, the Congregation for the Doctrine of the Faith asserts: "Although the particular inclination of the homosexual person is not a sin, it is a more or less strong tendency toward an intrinsic moral evil; and thus the inclination itself must be seen as an objective disorder." "Letter to the Bishops of the Catholic Church on the Pastoral Care of Homosexual Persons," website of the Holy See, October 1, 1986, www.vatican.va/roman_curia/congregations/cfaith/documents/rc_con_cfaith_doc_19861001_homosexual-persons_en.html. The *Catechism of the Catholic Church*, §§2357-58, more or less repeats this by holding that the homosexual inclination is "objectively disordered," as it orders one to "acts [that] are intrinsically disordered." For much more on this, see O'Connor, "Orientation of Human Sexuality," 29–34, 105–9, and 214–49.

78. For much more on this and on Jesus's esteem for marriage, see my "Jesus and Paul on the Meaning and Purpose of Human Sexuality," *Nova et Vetera*, English ed. 18, no. 2 (2020): 461–503, at 464–69.

79. For more on this, see Gondreau, "Jesus and Paul on the Meaning and Purpose of Human Sexuality," 491–93. The citation is from Jean-Baptiste Edart, Innocent Himbaza and Adrien Schenker, *The Bible on the Question of Homosexuality*, trans. Benedict Guevin (Washington, DC: Catholic University of America Press, 2012), 114.

of the human race, Christ serves as *exemplum virtutis* for all people, men and women alike. On the other hand, and no matter if feminist theologians should rue the point, as a male individual, Christ serves as a particular model of virtue for men, for those who share a male structuring with him—just as the Virgin Mary serves as a particular model of virtue for women. Concerning his male sexuality, then, it bears insisting: Christ serves as a particular model of chastity for men. No small matter, given that men face a particular challenge in being chaste, endowed as they are with a neurobiological predisposition to objectifying women and to seeking sexual pleasure for its own sake. Too often, concupiscence and the *fomes luxuriae*, the disordered affective condition characteristic of men, stirs this condition to actual moral disorder.

As a model of manly chastity, Jesus exemplifies an integrated sexuality in a male-specific or male-appropriate manner. Though men in their fallen condition might commonly struggle to varying degrees with a disordered sex drive, Christ's male sex drive at all points served his proper moral good and indeed was a source burgeoning into his moral good. Not insignificantly, then, does Jesus direct his injunction against lustful desires primarily at men, as his express mentioning of women (*gynaika*) suggests: "Anyone who looks at a woman lustfully has already committed adultery with her in his heart" (Mt 5:28).[80] He enjoins on men the same manly chastity that he possessed, the same male-conditioned integrated sexuality, integrated, that is, to serve the disinterested gift of self in an other-oriented manner.

The Gospel witness makes clear: Jesus formed deep, intimate relationships with both sexes. These relationships remained completely non-genital or non-erotic and were wholly virtuous. Jesus opted for a life of virginity (in accordance with the will of the Father, we can assume), that virtue defined by the perpetual renunciation of all sexual pleasure. And lest we think he chose virginity out of a harbored disdain for marriage, as if by default, his teaching on the impermissibility of remarriage after divorce proves otherwise: Jesus favored a highly elevated understanding of marriage as an in-

---

80. As an aside, we know that if the current epidemic of pornography—an especially male problem—is expressive of lust besetting men more than women, evidence shows that women, given their neurobiological propensity for relationship, sometimes struggle with what we might term "narrative pornography" (such as romance literature). If men have a tendency to "look" at women lustfully, women sometimes favor "reading" about men lustfully, i.e., within the context of a relationship.

dissoluble and sacred union, and not merely a natural one (see again Mk 10:4–12). He further holds to husband and wife possessing equal status, a consequence of his revoking the Mosaic right to divorce, as only men enjoyed this right (the Talmud, the body of rabbinical commentary on the Torah, is unequivocal on this point).[81] Pushing social boundaries—to the point of risking offense or even scandal—as they impinge upon women, Jesus models what it means to look upon women not as objects, but as persons with equal dignity to whom men owe respect.

Ample evidence stands behind this latter claim (beyond his rescinding the male right to divorce): his holding women up as models of discipleship (Lk 10:42) and accepting them as disciples (an unheard-of practice for his day, given that rabbis were prohibited from teaching women, as in accordance with the Talmud's claim that "women are of light mind" and its concomitant injunction to "teach Torah … to your sons, but not your daughters");[82] his allowing women to travel with him (Lk 8:1–3); his speaking with women in private (Jn 4:7–26) and allowing his feet to be kissed by a sinful woman (Lk 7:38), both of which were scandalous in his Jewish culture, which tended to view women as a sexual temptation (for which reason the Talmud instructs women to avoid speaking with men they encounter, to stay indoors as a general rule, and to cover themselves as much as possible, in particular their heads);[83] his exhibiting special affection for women in

81. The Talmud states that only the husband can initiate a divorce (see Dt 24:1–2) and that this can be for any reason—an ancient form of "no-fault" divorce. In the Mishnah (the first part of the Talmud), the School of Hillel states that a man may divorce his wife "even due to a minor issue, e.g., because she burned or over-salted his dish, as it is stated: 'Because he has found some unseemly matter in her' [Dt 24:1]," while Rabbi Akiva adds, "He may divorce her even if he found another woman who is better looking than her and wishes to marry her, as it is stated in that verse: 'And if it comes to pass, if she finds no favor in his eyes' [Dt 24:1]" (b. Git. 90a; available online at Sefaria, accessed October 18, 2020, www.sefaria.org/Gittin.90a?lang=bi). Jewish law thus relegated women to secondary status, to the property of their husbands.

82. The two Talmudic citations are from b. Kiddushin 30a:6 and 80b:5, accessed October 9, 2020, www.sefaria.org/Kiddushin.30a?lang=bi; and www.sefaria.org/Kiddushin.80b?lang=bi. The Mishnah makes this a disputed point, however; see, e.g., b. Sotah 3:4; accessed October 9, 2020, www.sefaria. org/Mishnah_Sotah.3.4?lang=bi&with=all&lang2=en. Also, the Talmud does praise the intellectual talents of a certain Beruriah, the wife of a rabbi who, as the Talmud puts it, "was so sharp and had such a good memory that she learned three hundred *halakhot* [laws] in one day from three hundred Sages." B. Pesachim 62b:9; accessed November 25, 2020, www.sefaria.org/Pesachim.62b?lang=bi. Yet Beruriah seems to have very much marked the exception than the rule.

83. Thus, for instance: "And who is considered a woman who violates the precepts of Jewish women? One who, for example, goes out of her house, and her head, i.e., her hair, is uncovered; or she

need of healing (Lk 13:10–17); his showcasing women in many of his parables (Lk 15:8–10)—and the list goes on.[84]

Admittedly, the image of a chaste celibate Christ curries little favor or understanding in a culture otherwise beholden to a "new philosophy of sexuality." In such a climate as this, it is not surprising that revisionist portrayals of Christ's sexuality often find a favorable reception. Consider, for instance, Dan Brown's popular novel *The Da Vinci Code*, or Nikos Kazantzakis's novel *The Last Temptation of Christ* (made into a critically acclaimed film by Martin Scorsese), both of which imagine a romantic relationship between Jesus and Mary Magdalene. The 2019 Netflix film *The First Temptation of Christ*, which stages a gay Jesus bringing a "boyfriend" home to Nazareth, provides another example. Regardless of these inventive takes, the textual evidence (to say nothing of the doctrinal truth that stands upon it) supports a quite different view. In this regard, it is Chaucer who hits the mark when he writes in his prologue to the Wife of Bath's tale, "Christ lived always in perfect chastity." Jesus models consummate authentic human love.

Sexual Temptation

Notwithstanding the foregoing, excluding all forms of lust from Jesus's life does not necessarily preclude the experience of sexual temptation. Luke 4:13 mentions that Jesus endured "every temptation (*panta peirasmon*)," while Hebrews 4:15 affirms that Jesus was tempted as we are "in all things (*kata panta*)." It is plausible to argue, which I shall do now, that in principle this may have included sexual temptation and that this would have been of two possible types. The first concerns his sensitive appetite, with a bodily sexual good as its object, and the second his rational appetite, his will, with the

---

spins wool in the public marketplace; or she speaks with every man she encounters.... The prohibition against a woman going out with her head uncovered is not merely a custom of Jewish women. Rather, it is by Torah law, as it is written [in Numbers 5:18]." B. Ketubot 72a:10 and 19, accessed October 17, 2020, www.sefaria.org/Ketubot.72a?lang=bi. For other textual evidence from the Talmud, see b. Shabbat 13a:4–10 and 13b:1, accessed October 10, 2020, www.sefaria.org/Shabbat.13a?lang=bi; and b. Kiddushin 80b:4–7, accessed October 10, 2020, www.sefaria.org/Kiddushin.80b?lang=bi. For more on this in the Talmud, see Rabbi Nisan Dovid Dubov, *The Laws of Yichud: Permissibility and Prohibition Regarding the Seclusion of a Man and Woman* (Brooklyn, NY: Sichos In English, 2006).

84. The feminist Rosemary Radford Ruether accedes that Jesus liberated women from the "web" of secondary social status ("Christology," 137).

rational good of marriage as its object. Navigating this highly sensitive topic will require the use of crucial distinctions that seek to render proper account of both Christ's full humanity and his sinlessness.

Tempted by the Bodily Good of Sex

Regarding the first, the temptation presented by a bodily object of sex, since this concerns the sensitive appetite (the lower animal-like ordering to particular bodily goods), such a temptation would have been directly analogous to his being tempted in the desert by the bodily good of bread (see Lk 4:3). Not an inherent evil, of course, food marks a most necessary good (necessary for the preservation of life). But it is not the highest good. And since Jesus was fasting at the time of the temptations in the desert, whereby he was observing the principle that man, because ordered to higher goods, "does not live by bread alone" (Lk 4:4), he would have sinned had he commanded the stone to turn into bread. That is, the sin would not have been on account of his wanting to eat the stone-turned-into-bread per se, since otherwise he often desired to eat and did eat, but of the circumstances—he was fasting—of his so wanting.

Sex likewise marks a necessary bodily good (necessary for the preservation of the species). But since Jesus, following the will of the Father, was vowed to perpetual virginity, whereby he renounced this good completely (not all must propagate in order to ensure the continuation of the species), he would have sinned had he desired some object of sex. Thus, just as he refused to desire the stone-turned-into-bread, so he would have refused—throughout his entire life—the desire for any bodily object of sex (which would have concerned the female sex, since he would not have experienced homoerotic inclinations).

The parallels extend further. As with the temptations in the desert, a sexual temptation of this sort would have come from without, not from within (even if internally "he was hungry," as per Luke 4:2). This means that the temptation would not have arisen from an interior disordered movement of affectivity, with concupiscence and the male *fomes luxuriae* as its root cause: "Although Christ suffered no internal assault on the part of the *fomes peccati*," writes Aquinas, "he sustained an external assault on the part of the world and the devil, and won the crown of victory by overcoming them."[85]

---

85. *ST* III, q. 15, a. 2, ad 3; see also q. 39, a. 5: "The *fomes peccati* assails us from within, while the world and the devil assail us from without." Thomas culls this distinction from John Damascene, *De*

At the crux of the issue is whether Christ *desired* a bodily object of sex—
that is, a woman in the sense of physical attraction. Morally speaking, it is
one thing to have a natural appetitive drawing toward a bodily good as desirable (or toward an *appetibile*, to use Thomas's term for a desirable object),
in itself not sinful, quite another actually to desire that good, sinful if the
good (*appetibile*) is illicit.[86] As regards an object of sex, then, the sinless and
perpetually virgin Christ could experience the former—he could experience
a given woman as desirable (i.e., as physically attractive) or as appetible, particularly since he possessed a male-structured brain "wired" for sexual physical attraction.[87] But Jesus would never have desired a woman in the fully
elicited sense nor taken an interior delight (*delectatio*) in the same, which
Thomas maintains is when the sin generally speaking begins in temptation,
"and then reaches perfection with the consent."[88]

The sensitive appetite, as a power, remains distinct from its movements,
the passions. Even prior to its movements (the passions), the sensitive appetite signifies an inbuilt ontological inclination toward a suitable object on
account of sentient or bodily need; it signifies a drawing toward or connatural affinity with a bodily good apprehended as such by the senses (just as the

---

fide orth., III.20 (ed. Buytaert, 260). Gregory the Great insists that Jesus was tempted "only by suggestion" and not by an interior movement of disordered affectivity (*Hom. in Evang.*, I, hom. 16, n. 1 [PL
76: 1135]). Hence *ST* III, q. 41, a. 1, ad 3: "Temptation that comes from the enemy can be without sin,
since it occurs merely by suggestion from without." For more on this in Aquinas, see Torrell, *Le Christ
en ses mystères*, 1:224–42.

86. *ST* I-II, q. 80, a. 1; and III, q. 41, a. 4, ad 4. On this J.-H. Nicolas writes: "we must offer the
subtle yet well founded following distinction: *to experience a good as desirable and to desire this good.* We
can acknowledge the first in Jesus." *Synthèse dogmatique*, De la Trinité à la Trinité (Fribourg: Éditions
universitaires, 1985), 407–8; emphasis his, translation mine.

87. Psychologists speak of an "arousal template," which refers to the way the brain subconsciously
determines one's sexual palette, or the type of individual that one is sexually drawn to. Having "had to
be made like his brethren in every respect" (Heb 2:17), Jesus presumably had such an arousal template.
See Patrick Carnes et al., who define the arousal template as a pattern that corresponds to "the total
constellation of thoughts, images, behaviors, sounds, smells, fantasies, and objects that arouse us sexually." *In the Shadows of the Net: Breaking Free of Compulsive Online Sexual Behavior*, 2nd ed. (Center
City, MN: Hazeldon, 2007), 58. See also Michael Bader, *Arousal: The Secret Logic of Sexual Fantasies*
(New York: Thomas Dunne Books, 2002). I owe this insight on the arousal template to Michael D.
O'Connor, who argues that the cogitative sense, the internal sense power that "does a sort of thinking
with the senses," as well as the memory and imagination, together participate in the functioning of the
arousal template ("Orientation of Human Sexuality," chap. 4).

88. "[With temptation] the sin begins with the interior delight … and then reaches perfection
with the consent." Aquinas, *In Matt.*, ch. 4, lect. 1; see Gregory the Great, *Hom. in Evang.*, I, hom. 16,
n. 1 [PL 76: 1135]).

rational appetite, the will, signifies a drawing toward or connatural affinity with a rational good apprehended as such by the intellect).[89]

To say Jesus was tempted by a woman he found physically attractive is to say nothing other than that, given his possession of a sensitive appetite and a male-structured brain, he felt a connatural, inbuilt drawing toward or affinity for certain women that were physically attractive to him. Like his natural appetite for food, Jesus owned a natural appetite for sex, a natural sex drive. Yet this appetite remained indeterminate, drawing him to food and drink and to sex merely indeterminately or in a general sense. His sensitive appetite then sought to make his natural appetency determinate by drawing him to specific bodily objects (like a cup of quality wine or an attractive woman, not simply to food and drink or to sex in general). If his natural appetite for sex provided the ontological "ground" for the possibility of his being sexually tempted, he could only be tempted by a specific sexual object (i.e., by a woman that was attractive to him)—tempted, in other words, at the psychological level (at the level of the sentient powers of his soul)—through his sensitive appetite.

Since appetite signifies a basic tendency to be attracted by its proper object, it is not difficult to imagine Jesus's sentient or animal-like appetency predisposing him for temptation in his life relative to some woman/women he found physically attractive (analogous to how he was predisposed to be tempted by food that he found desirable—tempted, that is, when circumstances warranted that it was not proper for him to eat, such as with the proffered stone-turned-into-bread in the desert). In other words, even in temptation that originates from without (whether from the devil or from the world), there is an internal dimension that the temptation "plays on" and seeks to trigger, including in the sinless Christ: the inbuilt appetitive drawing, that is, the appetite as a power (distinct from the appetite's elicited movements).

Indeed, if Jesus experienced no bona fide drawing toward the *appetibile* in question, whether that be an object of food or of sex, his temptations would be reduced to a masquerade and to pure playacting. For Jesus, temptation to sin implies the external suggestion (sometimes from the devil, some-

---

89. "Appetite is nothing other than a certain inclination toward something on the part of what has the appetite." *ST* I-II, q. 8, a. 1. See also I, q. 78, a. 1, ad 3.

times from the world, or perhaps both) that "plays on" his internal appetitive drawing toward a certain good—yet a good deemed illicit for circumstantial reasons (fasting in the case of the stone-turned-into bread, perpetual virginity or celibacy in the case of a woman that was physically attractive to him). It would thus be sinful if he should take delight in and desire it. It is one thing to affirm that Jesus underwent the inbuilt drawing toward a woman he found physically attractive by virtue of his sensitive appetite and the particular "wiring" of his male-structured brain, quite another to assert that he experienced inordinate *movements* of his sensitive appetite toward the same. We can attribute the former to him, not the latter, not the "reaching out" by way of elicited desire: he promptly, easily, and with delight desired to live his sexuality in full accord with right reason, which in his case means in accord with the virtue of virginity.

Tempted by the Rational Good of Marriage

Not merely expressive of man's bodily or animal nature, human sexuality participates hylemorphically in the rational dimension of human nature as well. Unlike animals, human beings seek to integrate sexual intimacy within an entire shared life of profound loving friendship (or of unitive love, as it is commonly referred to today). Human beings thus find themselves drawn appetitively both to sex as a bodily good and to what the 1983 Code of Canon Law terms (though with foundation in the language of Aquinas) a *consortium totius vitae*, a partnership between man and woman that encompasses the whole of life; in other words, to marriage, which attains to the highest degree of human interpersonal knowing and loving. For this reason, Aquinas holds that marriage enjoys the rank of *maxima amicitia*, "highest friendship."[90] This latter good, marriage, marks the sexual object of the rational appetite, the will.

We should bear in mind that both appetites, sensitive and rational, exist in an integrated whole (the human individual) and function together in a synergetic fashion. The human being finds that he is endowed with a natural sex drive, a natural appetite for sex (tier one), with both sentient and

90. See Canon 1055 §1; and Aquinas, *ScG* III, c. 123 (here, in addition *to maxima amicitia*, Thomas uses the language of *totius domesticae conversationis consortium*).

rational dimensions (tiers two and three, respectively).[91] Jesus would prove no exception. He could thus be tempted on both sentient and rational levels synergistically. That his rational appetite could have been drawn to—tempted by, because vowed to perpetual virginity—the *consortium totius vitae* of marriage is not difficult to imagine, given his view of marriage as a great and noble good, as was noted earlier.

Significantly, the Gospels do present an episode in which we see Jesus tempted in another area of his life at both the sensitive and rational levels in synergetic fashion. In the garden of Gethsemane, Jesus faced his impending physical and spiritual torment, horrendous in the extreme and which would culminate in his death. Undergoing an aversion to this in both his sensitive appetite ("He began to be greatly distressed and troubled. And he said to them, 'My soul is very sorrowful'"; Mk 14:33–34) and in his rational appetite ("'Father, all things are possible to thee; remove this cup from me'"; Mk 14:36), he experienced the temptation not to follow through.

Of import as regards Jesus's rational appetite, the original Koine Greek of Luke's Gospel embeds a distinction in willing—though it does not translate into English—in its treatment of Jesus's prayer in Gethsemane: "'Father, if you will (*boulei*) it, remove this cup from me; nevertheless not my will (*thelēma*), but yours be done'" (Lk 22:42). Here Luke suggests that Jesus underwent both a spontaneous and naturally instinctive type of willing (*thelēsis*) and a more reflective or deliberated type of willing (*bouleisis*).[92] Learning of this distinction through John Damascene, Aquinas enshrines the distinction in Scholastic language, penning the following at the outset of his career: "In Christ there was both a *voluntas ut natura*, which equates with *thelēsis*, and a *voluntas ut ratio*, which corresponds to *bouleisis*."[93]

In short, *voluntas ut natura* (*thelēsis*) signifies an instinctive type of willing or desire. Jean-Pierre Torrell terms this "the pure and simple willing of

---

91. I am adapting the language here of Sean Cunningham, "Natural Inclination," 325.

92. For the classic exegetical study of this distinction, see Paul Joüon, "Les verbes ΒΟΥΛΟΜΑΙ et ΘΕΛΩ dans le Nouveau Testament," *Revue des Sciences religieuses* 30 (1940): 227–38.

93. *In III Sent.*, d. 17, a. 1, sol. 3, ad 1. See Damascene, *De fide orth.*, III.23 (ed. Buyt., 265–66). For Aquinas's treatment of this distinction as it concerns Christ's agony in the garden, see *ST* III, q. 18, a. 5; see also *In III Sent.*, d. 15, q. 2, a. 3, sol. 2; and *Comp. theol.*, I, chap. 233. For an in-depth study of this, see my own "St. Thomas Aquinas, the Communication of Idioms, and the Suffering of Christ in the Garden of Gethsemane," in *Divine Impassibility and the Mystery of Human Suffering*, ed. James F. Keating and Thomas Joseph White (Grand Rapids, MI: Eerdmans, 2009), 214–45.

the good before any kind of qualification," as when a person instinctively recoils from the thought of chemotherapy when diagnosed with cancer, given the severe ill side effects of the treatment.[94] *Voluntas ut natura* signifies nothing other than the experience of the pull of the rational appetite toward its proper connatural object (a rational good).[95] In this sense, it is directly analogous to what we saw above regarding the sensitive appetite. Just as the sensitive appetite can undergo a natural drawing toward a bodily good as desirable, so the will can do the same, which *voluntas ut natura* denotes: it can undergo a natural tendency toward its proper good as rationally desirable. Distinct from this, *voluntas ut ratio* (*bouleisis*) concerns an elicited type of willing or desire that "reaches out" toward the object in question as following upon the deliberation of reason (i.e., upon full reflected knowledge of the good in question), as when the same person willingly undergoes chemotherapy, no matter an initial *ut natura* aversion, in hopes of returning to good health.

If, then, Jesus was tempted in his rational part by the good of marriage (tempted because he freely renounced this good for the sake of his mission), tempted by the general prospect of a lifelong partnership with a woman, he would have experienced an *ut natura* type of willful desire, an inbuilt connatural drawing of his will toward marriage as rationally desirable. He would not have experienced an *ut ratio* type of willful desire; he would not have willfully desired marriage in the elicited sense, nor taken an interior willful delight (*delectatio*) in marriage. Recall that the appetite can only but choose its proper object (a bodily good for the sensitive appetite, a rational good for the will). Accordingly, just as sin consists always in choosing wrongly a certain type of good, an illicit good (like sexual pleasure in the case of adultery), so temptation to sin always implies temptation to choose some type of good, but an illicit good (like sexual pleasure with a person one is not married to, or marriage for one who has renounced this partnership of life for the sake of the kingdom of heaven). Vowed to perpetual virginity in accordance with the will of the Father, Jesus would never have desired

94. Torrell, *Le Christ en ses mystères*, 2:360 (translation mine).
95. I use the phrase "willfully desirable" to distinguish this movement of the will from that of the sensitive appetite, given that the same terms are often used to name the movements of both appetites (love, desire, etc.), as Thomas notes (*ST* I, q. 82, a. 5, ad 1). Still, if Aquinas calls the movements of the sensitive appetite passions, those of the will he terms intellectual affections (*ScG* I, c. 89).

marriage in the fully elicited sense with his will, similar to the regard of his sensitive appetite for an attractive woman. Though a noble good, marriage remained "off limits" for Christ.

Granted, one can speak of how Christ's rational appetitive drawing to marriage was realized at a higher, spiritual level through his nuptial union with the Church. But that does not mean that he did not find a partnership of life with a woman—marriage as a carnal union—attractive, perhaps deeply attractive. Nothing more than an attraction it remained, however; an elicited willful desire for it was absent from Christ's life.

CONCLUSION

If we wish to take the ever-present threat of Docetism seriously, which Aquinas certainly does, we must not fear to tread on the subject of Christ's male sexuality, on his being a male individual. Not to suggest the superiority of the male sex, this is merely to affirm that God became human, and to be human one must be either a man or a woman. It is a historical fact: Christ was a man. Possessing therefore a male-structured body (inclusive of a male-structured brain) and even a male-adapted soul, he accordingly acted in male-specific manner. Because he was sinless, his male-conditioned behavior always attained to perfect, manly virtue. He experienced no form of lust, no disordered sexual desire (whether of a heterosexual or homoerotic sort), even if it was possible for him to experience sexual temptation (which would have been of a heterosexual nature). He enjoyed unmitigated mastery of his sexual appetites, living in harmonious accord with the virtue of virginity, with his sexual design as its very source.

CHAPTER 10

CAJETAN ON CHRIST'S PRIESTLY SACRIFICE

Ressourcement Thomism in the Sixteenth Century

Reginald M. Lynch, OP

During the sixteenth century, the questions raised by the Protestant Reformation posed new challenges for many aspects of Catholic teaching. Although not always framed as direct challenges to the settled dogma of Chalcedonian Christology, many of the proposals made by the Reformers touched on the broader theological implications of the Church's accepted Christological orthodoxies such as the life of grace in relation to Christ, the sacraments as instruments of the Incarnation, and the sacramental and sacrificial nature of the Mass in relation to Christ's self-oblation on the cross. Even in those cases in which these new doctrines did not challenge Catholic dogma directly, the Reformation often had a fragmenting effect on the theological tradition as a whole. Many Catholic theologians working in this period took up the challenge of rearticulating the intrinsic connections between topics such as the Incarnation and the Eucharist on both speculative and biblical grounds. After his first encounter with Martin Luther as papal nuncio in 1518, Thomas de vio Cajetan (d. 1534) would spend over a decade engaging Protestants with principles drawn from Thomas Aquinas and arguing for the biblical foundations of the Catholic theological synthesis.

Many of the most controversial topics raised by the Reformers involved the Eucharist, the liturgical practices that surrounded it, and the relationship between these practices and Christ's cross. Scripturally, the theological connection between Christ's priestly sacrifice on the cross and the liturgical praxis of the Church is made clear: in the Letter to the Hebrews, for example, we find strong affirmations of the singularly efficacious character of Christ's priesthood and its relationship to the Church; complementary to this, Paul underscores the soteriological significance of the sacrifice of Christ's blood on the cross (Col 1:20) and the importance of the Church's liturgy as a participation in the body and blood of Christ (1 Cor 10:16). Following some theological cues found in these and other New Testament texts, both Luther and Zwingli were quick to confirm a sacramental and symbolic connection between the cruciform sacrifice of Christ as priest and the Eucharistic memorial that takes place in the Church's liturgy, while at the same time denying the sacrificial character of this same Eucharistic liturgy.

This chapter begins by exploring Cajetan's teaching on Christ's priestly sacrifice in his commentary on the *Summa*, where Cajetan presents Christ's priesthood as the perfection of a Christological anthropology and argues that in the New Law, a true sacrifice is offered by the Church's ministers in the context of the Eucharistic liturgy that cannot be reduced to the private interior offerings of individual Christians. Next, I examine Cajetan's opusculum *De cena* and his interpretation of the institution narrative in his commentaries on the New Testament, where he argues that Christ's words at the Last Supper not only institute a liturgical memorial, but also form the basis for a kind of modal operation of Christ's priestly offering in the context of the Mass itself.

CAJETAN ON THE *SUMMA*

Cajetan began commenting on the *Summa* early in the sixteenth century, finishing his commentary on the *Prima Pars* in 1507. His commentaries on the *Prima Secundae* and *Secunda Secundae* appeared in 1511 and 1517, respectively. Although Cajetan would become interested in biblical commentary after his encounter with Martin Luther, he continued to work on his *Summa* commentary, completing his treatment of the *Tertia Pars* in 1520–22.[1] In

1. James A. Weisheipl, "Cajetan (Tommaso de Vio)," in *New Catholic Encyclopedia*, 1st ed. (NCE[1]), vol. 2 (Washington, DC: Catholic University of America, 1967), 1053–55.

this text, Cajetan offers important cometary on questions 22, 48 and 78, all questions that are central to Aquinas's own teaching on Christ's priesthood and the Eucharist in the *Tertia Pars*. Without relativizing the centrality of Christ's sacrifice on the cross in any way, Aquinas introduces in question 22 a broader anthropological conception of priestly sacrifice in which the whole of Christ's life and ministry comes to be understood as a kind of offering or oblation on behalf of the human family.[2] To establish this, Cajetan builds on Augustine's distinction between visible and invisible sacrifices, quoting a text from the *City of God* that Aquinas invokes in the text of question 22 itself. Following Augustine, Aquinas distinguishes between the inward offering of a person's spirit to God and those outward offerings that become the visible sacraments of this interior offering.[3] For Aquinas, sacrifice is required of humanity for three reasons: the remission of sin, preservation in the state of grace, and the perfection of the union between the human soul and God. Aquinas argues that, through the humanity of Christ, these benefits are conferred on the whole of humanity. In his self-oblation, Christ is not only the priest who offers but also the perfect offering.[4] Augustine's distinction between interior and exterior sacrifice allows Aquinas to emphasize the anthropological importance of the interior offering, of which the visible exterior sacrifice is a sign. Although fully man, because of the perfect charity of Christ's soul, the three anthropological reasons for sacrifice that Aquinas names cannot in fact refer to defects in Christ's humanity that are to be remedied. Rather, his perfection in charity makes him a perfect victim.[5] For Aquinas, sacrifices are made so that the human soul may be raised to God.[6] In his commentary on this text, Cajetan builds on this, emphasizing that if all that is given to God is called a sacrifice, in the case of Christ's self-offering, it is the whole of his humanity itself that is offered, which has the universalizing effect of raising the souls of all to God.[7]

---

2. Cajetan, in *ST* III,[a] q. 22, a. 2. Leonine ed. 11:258. On Cajetan's interpretation of the *Tertia Pars*, see William Baum, *The Teaching of Cardinal Cajetan on the Sacrifice of the Mass: A Study in Pre-Tridentine Theology* (Rome: Angelicum, 1958). For a detailed treatment of Cajetan on the relationship between the priesthood of Christ and the ministry of the ordained priesthood in the Church, see Charles Morerod, "Le prêtre chez Cajetan," *Revue Thomiste* 99, no. 4 (1999): 245–80.

3. *ST* III,[a] q. 2, a. 2, co. See *De civ.* 10.5. CCL 47: 277.15–16.

4. *ST* III,[a] q. 22, a. 2, co.

5. *ST* III,[a] q. 22, a. 2, co., ad 3.

6. *ST* III,[a] q. 22, a. 2, co.

7. Cajetan, in *ST* III,[a] q. 22, a. 2. Leonine ed. 11:258.

Implied in Aquinas's treatment of Christ's priesthood in question 22 of the *Tertia Pars* is his earlier discussion of sacrifice as a moral act in the *Secunda Secundae*. Here Aquinas uses this same text from the *City of God* to emphasize the primacy of interior, spiritual sacrifice in relation to outward sacrificial acts.[8] In a proper and immediate sense, Aquinas names sacrifice as a specific, external act of the virtue of religion that is elicited by the virtue of religion directly;[9] in a broader sense, however, because religion is a general virtue, all acts—even those proper to other virtues—can be considered as acts of sacrifice when done for the purpose of reverencing God.[10] Given that the proper sense of sacrifice denotes a specific external act of the virtue of religion, however, because of the primacy that Aquinas attributes to interior sacrifice, an external action of this kind can only be properly named a sacrifice because it functions as a sign or sacrament of an interior reality. For Aquinas, therefore, an intrinsic relationship exists between the interior acts of the virtue of religion—which are devotion and prayer—and the exterior acts of this same virtue. Commenting on Aquinas, Cajetan affirms a distinction between these proper interior acts, characterizing devotion and prayer as interior oblations, and the broader sense in which all virtuous acts can be said to be sacrifices when operated by the virtue of religion.[11] In the life of the Church, however, Cajetan recognizes a third category, which is distinguished from the personal interiority of devotion and prayer and the more general sense in which all human acts, whether interior or exterior, can be offered to God out of reverence: for Cajetan, the liturgical offering performed by the Church—which is both public and external—is properly sacrificial in character. For Cajetan, this third species of sacrifice builds on principles that are at work in Aquinas's general treatment of sacrifice as an anthropological phenomenon, where Aquinas himself has suggested that, although all external acts may be spoken of as sacrifices in a general sense, there is a form of external act that can be elicited directly as a sacrifice in the proper sense by the virtue of religion. What makes Cajetan's third, liturgical species of sacrifice plausible is Aquinas's treatment of the interplay between human moral acts and legal specification. In the case of sacrifice, Aquinas

---

8. *ST* IIa-II,ae q. 81, a. 7, ad 2.
9. *ST* IIa-II,ae q. 81, a. 1, ad 1; *ST* IIa-II,ae q. 85.
10. *ST* IIa-II,ae q. 81, a. 4, ad 1.
11. Cajetan, in *ST* IIa-II,ae q. 85, a. 4. Leonine ed. 9:219.

argues that although the external act of sacrifice does belong to natural law in a general sense, the specific determination of this act is bound up in the exercise of positive law.[12] This means that, for Aquinas, legal determination has the ability to shape and specify the form of external sacrificial acts. While many pre-Christian cultures attempted this in various ways, the Law of Moses contained clear ceremonial precepts that delineated the shape and form of those external and public human acts that were intended to serve as sacramental signs of the interior sacrifice of devotion and prayer; under the New Law of grace, Christ's instructions at the Last Supper have the function of positive law in this context. Rather than the multitude of sacrifices offered under the Law of Moses or even those other exterior offerings that are made by Christians out of devotion, Cajetan emphasizes that it is the Eucharist alone that fulfills the sacrificial precept of the New Law.[13]

Returning to the *Tertia Pars*, in question 48, Aquinas portrays the sacrifice of Christ on the cross as the perfection and archetype of all sacrifices. As the proper exterior act that sacramentally expresses his perfect interior offering of his whole humanity, Aquinas uses Christ's offering to establish the concept of sacrifice within the Christian context of charity, using Augustinian texts drawn from *The City of God* and *De Trinitate*.[14] In the sixth chapter of Book 10 of the *City of God*, Augustine argues that, when understood in its proper sense, sacrifice functions within the bond of charity that unites the rational creature to God.[15] For Augustine, the Incarnation of Christ forms the context for the exercise of Christ's sacrifice because the hypostatic union of Christ's human and divine natures unites both in one offering, that which is offered and the one to whom it is offered. For Augustine, this supreme union of love functions as a sacrificial archetype in which the Church's daily sacrificial offering is contextualized.[16] Aquinas argues that it is the charity of Christ's passion that displays this union between priest, victim, and recipient in a most acceptable way.[17] In his commentary on this text, Cajetan

---

12. *ST* IIa-II,[ae] q. 85, a. 1, ad 1.

13. Cajetan, in *ST* IIa-II,[ae] q. 85, a. 4. Leonine ed. 9:219.

14. *ST* III,[a] q. 48, a. 3, co. *De civ.* 10.6. CCL 47:278.1–3; *De civ.* 10.20. CCL 47:294.1–14; *De Trin.* 4.19. CCL 50:186.15–17.–187.18–20.

15. *De civ.* 10.6. CCL 47:278.1–3.

16. *De civ.* 10.20. CCL 47:294.1–14. Aquinas also cites *De Trin.* 4.19. CCL 50:186.15–17.–187.18–20.

17. *ST* III,[a] q. 48, a. 3, co.

paraphrases the Augustinian texts that Aquinas uses, emphasizing that any action that accomplishes our deeper union with God through charity should be named a sacrifice itself in the full sense.[18]

For Cajetan, the Christian effectively participates in the charity of Christ's sacrifice by means of their own analogically proportioned acts of charitable sacrifice—although this certainly extends to all human activity in the perfection of the virtue of charity, as he continues to engage Reformed perspectives during the 1520s, Cajetan will remain convinced that the external and public ritual of the Catholic Mass constitutes a special liturgical participation in Christ's passion that stands distinct from these more general offerings, and in which a true and proper sacrifice is offered according to Christ's instruction. Concerning the relationship between Christ's priesthood and the exercise of his priesthood within the Church, in his commentary on question 78 of the *Tertia Pars*, Cajetan argues that an instrumental relationship exists between Christ's priesthood and the ordained ministerial priesthood that functions as both a sign and a cause. When an ordained priest speaks the words of Christ to consecrate the Eucharist in the context of the Mass, this liturgical use of the words of institution functions as not only a sign of Christ's speech at the Last Supper, but also as an instrumental efficient cause. Although not able to achieve such supernatural effects by their own natural potency, Cajetan argues that by their nature as creatures, the priest himself and the natural elements of bread and wine stand ready to respond to this new initiative of divine causality, allowing themselves to become instruments of God's intent—as a result, Cajetan argues that by means of the act of consecration working through the instrumental efficiency of the ordained priest, the Eucharist is a sign of both Christ's priestly sacrifice and its effect.[19] Although the biblical commentaries that Cajetan would author during the 1520s would be methodologically distinct from his earlier system-

---

18. Cajetan, in *ST* III,ᵃ q. 48, a. 3. Leonine ed. 11:466.

19. Cajetan, in *ST* III,ᵃ q. 78, a. 4. Leonine ed. 12:212. Cajetan's use of obediential potency in this context is framed against Scotus, who Cajetan argues conflates the questions of creation ex nihilo and the re-creation of an existing substrate in a univocal manner. Although Cajetan comments extensively on the second article of this question, in this context he discusses the connection between the liturgical use of the institution narrative and the sacramental validity of the Eucharist, addressing the legitimacy of various other liturgical practices that differ from that of the Roman rite. Cajetan, in *ST* III,ᵃ q. 78, a. 2. Leonine ed. 12:207. On the relationship between human nature and priesthood under the natural law and under the law of grace, see Serge-Thomas Bonino, "Le sacerdoce comme institution naturelle selon Saint Thomas d'Aquin," *Revue Thomiste* 99, no. 4 (1999): 33–58.

atic work in many ways, in this new context, Cajetan would continue to develop his own theological articulation of many of the principles that he identified in his commentaries on Aquinas. In part because of questions raised by the Reformers, in these later commentaries, Cajetan would pay particular attention to the way in which the cross and the Mass could both be grounded in the one priestly sacrifice of Jesus Christ, extending and developing many of the insights expressed in germ in his commentary on the *Summa*.

CAJETAN AND ZWINGLI

Between his initial contact with Luther until his death, Cajetan would produce numerous works on topics that were directly related to the Reformation.[20] Although Cajetan completed his first biblical commentary in 1524,[21] his response to Zwingli's 1525 *De vera et falsa religione* represents one of the first mature applications of his newfound interest in biblical methodology to the questions that were raised by many Reformers.[22] In his biblical commentaries Cajetan sought to respond to the arguments of the Reformers by using authorities that they themselves acknowledged, believing that the apologetic efficacy of his own arguments would depend on his ability to defend the Church's doctrine using authorities that were acknowledged by his opponents.[23] In his 1531 response to the Augsburg Confession, Cajetan justifies this approach by appealing to the example of Christ himself, who, when responding to the criticisms of the Sadducees, made appeals to biblical sources in the Pentateuch so that his arguments would be grounded in a source that his opponents acknowledged.[24] Aquinas recommends a similar apologetic

20. For a bibliography of these works, see Jared Wicks, *Cajetan Responds: A Reader in Reformation Controversy* (Washington, DC: Catholic University of America Press, 1978), 245–46. See also A. Vacant and E. Mangenot, eds., *Dictionnaire de Théologie Catholique* (DTC), vol. 2 (Paris: Letouzey et Ane, 1905), 1313–29. (See specifically DTC 2:1320–25). See also NCE[1] s.v. "Cajetan (Tommaso de vio)."

21. Cajetan, *Jentacula Reverendiss: Dn. Thomas de vio Caietani, cardinalis s. Xysti, praeclarissima LXIIII, notabilium sententiarum Noui testamenti literalis exposito, in duodecim capita distincta* (Lyon: Lugduni, 1551).

22. Cajetan, *Instructio Nuntii circa Errores Libelli de Cena Domini, sive De Erroribus Contingentibus in Eucharistiae Sacramento*, ed. Franciscus A. von Gunten (Rome: Angelicum, 1962).

23. Wicks, *Cajetan Responds*, 41.

24. Cajetan, *De sacrificio Missae*, c. 1. As in *Reverendissimi domini domini Thomae de Vio Caietani*

approach in the *Summa contra Gentiles*. When arguing against opponents, he advocates the use of the New Testament against heretics, the Old Testament against the Jews, and reason against the Muslims and pagans.[25] In his response to Zwingli's *De vera et falsa religione*, Cajetan adopts a similar rhetorical approach, arguing for Catholic doctrine from scriptural texts that were central to Zwingli's arguments.

In *De vera et falsa religione*, Zwingli adopts a symbolic understanding of the relationship between Christ's oblation on the cross and the Eucharist, arguing that New Testament language that seems to indicate the real presence of Christ should be understood symbolically. For Zwingli, when Christ tells his disciples that the cup at the Last Supper is his blood, it should be understood that he means to indicate that the cup is a symbol of his blood.[26] Although Zwingli believes that the Catholic affirmation of the Mass as a sacrifice must necessarily lead to a series of new sacrifices after Christ's singular offering on the cross, in his response, Cajetan insists that the offerings of the cross and the altar are not formally distinct but are in fact the same sacrifice, distinguished from each other only by the *mode* in which the offering is made. Turning to Christ's sacrifice on the cross, Cajetan argues that Christ's offering can be related to the reality of his death in two separate modes— corporally, Christ's mode of offering was made in his actual death (*in re mortis*); in another sense, according to a spiritual modality Christ's offering is now made in the Church in the mystery of death (*in mysterio mortis*).[27] In this context, the concept of *mysterium* indicates a sacramental reality.[28] For Cajetan, however, this sacramental reality is not confined to the concept of sign—as an offering made *in mysterio mortis*, Christ's self-oblation is contained in this offering as well.[29] Recalling the distinction between interior and exterior sacrifices employed by Augustine and Aquinas, Cajetan argues

---

Cardinalis.S.Xisti: De sacrificio Missae, De Communione, De Confessione, De satisfactione, De sanctorum inuocatione, Adversus lutherano iuxta scripturam Tractatus (Paris: Petri Regnault, 1531), 4.

25. *ScG* I, c. 2.

26. Zwingli, *De vera et falsa religione* (Zurich, 1525), 266–67.

27. Cajetan, *Errores de cena Domini*, c. 9. As in Franciscus A. von Gunten, ed., *Instructio Nuntii circa Errores Libelli de Cena Domini, sive De Erroribus Contingentibus in Eucharistiae Sacramento* (Rome: Angelicum, 1962), 58–59 (44). See also Wicks, *Cajetan Responds*, 168.

28. See Reginald Garrigou-Lagrange, "Le sens du mystère chez Cajétan," *Angelicum* 12 (1935): 3–18.

29. Cajetan, *Errores de cena Domini*, c. 9 (Rome: 1962), 58–59 (44).

that although made according to a spiritual modality, this offering is manifested visibly by the sacramental species of the Eucharist.[30]

A significant portion of Cajetan's criticism of Zwingli's position concerns the interpretation of Christ's priestly offering in the Letter to the Hebrews. Interpreting the ninth chapter of Hebrews, for Zwingli, the concept of offering sacrifice is necessary and univocally bound to suffering, the shedding of blood and to death.[31] As a result, the prohibition against repeated offerings found in Hebrews 9:25–26 prevents any Eucharistic form of offering, even within the context of the Church's liturgy. Zwingli builds on the soteriological role attributed to Christ's blood in this text, arguing that only *this* blood can forgive sins, and its offering cannot be repeated.[32] For Zwingli, all sacrifice involves the shedding of blood, and such offerings are ended definitively with Christ's cross. The law of grace does not establish offerings or sacrifices as such, but rather offers a symbolic participation in Christ's single self-offering, as it is memorialized in the Church's liturgy.[33]

For Cajetan, Zwingli's interpretation of Hebrews is contingent on a univocal definition of sacrifice, in which the concept of sacrifice is intrinsically connected to the realities of physical suffering and death. Although Cajetan readily acknowledges that the Letter to the Hebrews teaches that Christ's singular offering was sufficient for all time and cannot be repeated, for Cajetan the teaching of the literal sense of Hebrews applies in this case to Christ's corporal sacrifice on the cross. In this, Cajetan and Zwingli are in agreement—for Cajetan, however, the analogical language of modal distinction allows him to distinguish between this corporal modality of sacrifice and a spiritual modality in which the same sacrifice is offered.[34] Because this second, spiritual modality has the capacity to not only signify but also contain the reality it offers, Cajetan's approach is also able to accommodate a Catholic understanding of the substantial presence of Christ in the Eucharist. Here, the flexibility of Cajetan's analogical language resolves a tension created by Zwingli's insistence on a univocal association between the con-

---

30. Cajetan, *Errores de cena Domini*, c. 9 (Rome: 1962), 58–59 (44).
31. Zwingli, *De vera et falsa religione* (Zurich, 1525), 272.
32. Zwingli, *De vera et falsa religione* (Zurich, 1525), 271–72.
33. Zwingli, *De vera et falsa religione* (Zurich, 1525), 270.
34. Cajetan, *Errores de cena Domini*, c. 9 (Rome: 1962), 59–60 (45).

cept of sacrifice and the bloody reality of corporal offering. While the body and blood of Christ are truly contained by the sacramental elements of the Eucharist, as a spiritual modality of Christ's sacrifice, his corporal death on the cross and his body and blood in death are signified rather than present in fact.[35] Because of this modal distinction, Cajetan argues that although it is Christ who is contained and offered in the Eucharist, one need not conclude that referring to the presence of Christ's sacrifice in the Eucharistic liturgy must also necessarily imply that the corporal crucifixion and death of Christ are repeated at every Mass.[36]

Although much of the disagreement between Cajetan and Zwingli on this point involves the interpretation of Hebrews, Cajetan is careful to tether the spiritual modality of Christ's sacrifice to the positive instruction found in the institution narratives, where Christ himself instructs the Church to "do this in memory of me."[37] Here, another disagreement emerges between Cajetan and Zwingli that concerns the relationship between Christ's sacrifice and the Eucharist. Although the words of institution seem to indicate the presence of Christ's body and blood in the Eucharistic elements, for Zwingli, these symbols are not exhausted by the elements of bread and wine themselves but reference the Church assembled as Christ's body and constituted as such by the consumption of the Eucharist.[38] Because Zwingli has excluded any notion of sacrifice or offering that does not involve the shedding of blood and death, in this case he therefore restricts himself to symbolism alone. For Cajetan, however, the words of institution are central to the signate relationship that exists between the Christ's priestly activity in the sacrifice of the Mass and the corporal modality of Christ's sacrifice on the cross. Although not contained in reality under the Eucharistic elements of bread and wine, the death of Christ and the physical shedding of his blood are signified in important ways by the actions commanded by Christ in the institution narrative and performed by the Church in his commemoration. These same words, which are used by the priest in confecting the Eucharist, refer to Christ's blood, indicating that it "will be shed for you and for many." For Cajetan, however, the most important sign of Christ's corporal and cru-

---

35. Cajetan, *Errores de cena Domini*, c. 9 (Rome: 1962), 60 (45).
36. Cajetan, *Errores de cena Domini*, c. 9 (Rome, 1962), 60 (46).
37. Cajetan, *Errores de cena Domini*, c. 9 (Rome: 1962), 58–59 (44).
38. Zwingli, *De vera et falsa religione* (Zurich, 1525), 268.

ciform sacrifice that is found within its spiritual modality is the independent consecration of Christ's body, and then his blood, in each Eucharistic liturgy. Although physically separated in the corporal modality of Christ's sacrifice, in the course of the Eucharistic liturgy, a "sacramental separation" of Christ's body and blood occurs, which signifies the corporal separation of these elements on the cross and the physical suffering and death this implied, even as the substantive reality of the same body and blood is made present for the life of the Church.[39]

THE INSTITUTION NARRATIVES

In the years following the publication of *De cena*, Cajetan produced a commentary on the four Gospels between 1527 and 1528 and a commentary on the Pauline epistles in 1529.[40] In these works, Cajetan comments on each of the biblical accounts of the institution narrative as it appears in the Gospels of Matthew and Luke, and in Paul's first Letter to the Corinthians. In his commentary on the institution narrative in the Gospel of Matthew (26:20–29), Cajetan focuses on the words from this narrative that are used by the priest to consecrate the Eucharist: this is my body (*hoc est corpus meum*). For Cajetan, the Reformers do not pay sufficient attention to the grammatical significance of the words that Scripture records. Cajetan argues that while *hic* might imply setting or situation, the demonstrative pronoun *hoc* must be understood in a substantive manner. Concerning the substance indicated by *hoc*, Cajetan emphasizes that it is Christ's own body that is substantially present, and that this reference is directed to what Christ is holding in his own hands while speaking these words. Implicitly, therefore, Christ's words do not refer only to the assembly of the Church who are gathered to celebrate the Eucharist—in this case, those Reformers who would prefer an exclusively ecclesial interpretation of Christ's words are in fact refusing the proper sense of the scriptural text itself, relying instead on a metaphorical interpretation.[41] Further, Cajetan argues that the choice of the term *est*,

---

39. Cajetan, *Errores de cena Domini*, c. 9 (Rome, 1962), 60 (46).

40. Michael O'Connor, *Cajetan's Biblical Commentaries: Motive and Method* (Leiden: Brill, 2017), XIII, 57, et al.

41. "Hoc. Non dicit *hic*, id est, in hoc loco, sed dici *hoc:* quod est pronomen demonstratiuú

instead of a more symbolic term, underscores the substantive presence of Christ's body in the Eucharist when coupled with the term *hoc*. Concerning the substance referenced by the phrase *hoc est*, Cajetan argues that Christ's words rule out the possibility that these words indicate bread and wine in any substantive way; rather, Christ himself makes it clear that the substance in question is his body. Although Cajetan's arguments are grounded in the literal sense of Scripture, it is clear that his knowledge of the Aristotelian categories has aided his interpretation in this case. Although Cajetan is careful to distinguish the phrase *hoc est* from other references that might be understood in a purely qualitative or special sense, he insists further that the substance referenced by *hoc est* need not be understood as qualitatively situated in any way. Instead, the substance of Christ's body is referenced directly and in a general sense, without implying that it is situated in any particular qualitative or spatial way.[42] This distinction allows Cajetan to turn his attention to what Christ's speech effects. Rather than an observation about an existing substance, Christ's speech is a sign of this truth coming to be as well.[43] Although human cognition has the ability to speak truly about existing substances as situated categorically and existing in reality, the speech of Truth himself has an efficacious relationship with substance itself. As a result, Cajetan's interpretation of the literal sense of the institution narrative allows for a substantive understanding of Christ's presence in the Eucharist that is effected by the priestly speech of Christ. Rather than a doctrinal aberration, therefore, for Cajetan, the concept of transubstantiation reflects something essential about the literal sense of Matthew 26:26 because it speaks truly about the substance that Christ holds in his hands both before and after Christ says, *this is my body*. If a substantive change does not occur as Christ utters these words, the claim made by Christ would be false. In this case, a simple replacement of one substance with another natural substantial change would also render the speech of Christ false—if the substance of bread and wine were simply annihilated and replaced with the substance of Christ's body, the initial object referenced by the term *hoc* at the beginning of Christ's speech would simply cease to be, and his statement

---

substantiae. Et est propriissimus non metaphoricus sermo, ut haeretici interpretantur." Cajetan, *In Matt.*, c. 26:26 (Iacobi & Petri Prost, 1639), 118.

    42. Cajetan, *In Matt.*, c. 26:26 (Iacobi & Petri Prost, 1639), 118.

    43. Cajetan, *In Matt.*, c. 26:26 (Iacobi & Petri Prost, 1639), 118–19.

as a whole would necessarily be untrue. By contrast, the concept of transubstantiation allows for a different kind of change that, although substantial, does not fundamentally replace the subject referenced by *hoc* at the outset with something else completely. Christ is truly and substantially present in the Eucharist under the appearance of bread and wine, and the truth of this presence is effected by the words of institution.[44]

In addition to the true and substantive presence of Christ's body, in the following text of the institution narrative, Cajetan also sees a reference to Christ's self-oblation of this same body on the cross. Although in the text of Matthew, Christ concludes with the phrase "this is my body" before turning to the consecration of the chalice, in Luke and First Corinthians, Christ adds that this same body will be handed over.[45] Commenting on the Gospel of Luke, Cajetan argues that this reference to the giving of his body cannot be interpreted metaphorically, but instead must be understood as a reference to Christ's natural and true body that was crucified on the cross. Here, Cajetan focuses on Luke's use of *dare* (to give), noting that it is not the future tense but rather the present tense of the verb that is used in this case, indicating that at the time Christ uttered these words, his betrayal and passion had already begun.[46] In the rendition of this phrase in First Corinthians, however, Cajetan notes that, at least in some versions of the Latin text, Paul chooses the verb *frangere* (to break) in place of *dare* or *tradere*. Cajetan argues that the use of *frangere* by Paul in this context forms a specific reference to the physical modality of Christ's self-offering that occurred on the cross and ended in his death.[47] Although the Lukan account of the institution narrative is similar to Paul's, for Cajetan, Luke's use of *dare* (to give over) in this case functions as a more generic sign of Christ's passion, whereas Paul's reference to "breaking" adds specificity and clarity.[48] As a sign of the physi-

---

44. Cajetan, *In Matt.*, c. 26:26 (Iacobi & Petri Prost, 1639), 119.

45. See Lk 22:19 and 1 Cor 11:24.

46. "Quod pro vobis datur. Ne intelligerent mysticum aut metaphoricum corpus, verum ac naturale explicat, dicendo, *quod pro vobis datur*, ipsummet corpus est quod datur morti crucis. Et non dicit *dabitur*, sed *datur*: quia iam inceptum erat dari, iam venditus erat." Cajetan, *In Lucam*, c. 22:19. As in *Evangeliacum commen* (Venice, 1530), 130a.

47. Cajetan, *In 1 Cor.*, c. 11:24–25. As in *Epistolae Pauli et aliorum Apostolorum* (Venice, 1531), 59b. Cajetan completed his commentary on First Corinthians in October 1528. Cajetan, *Epistolae Pauli et aliorum Apostolorum* (Venice, 1531), 72a.

48. Cajetan, *In 1 Cor.*, c. 11:24b. As in *Epistolae Pauli et aliorum Apostolorum* (Venice, 1531), 59b.

cal dimension of Christ's crucifixion, Cajetan believes that Paul's emphasis in this particular case makes the signate connection between the repetition of the words of institution during the Eucharistic liturgy and the corporal sacrifice of Christ even more clear. In Cajetan's view, Paul's terminology indicates that the spiritual modality of Christ's sacrifice does not replace its corporal one, but rather functions as a sign of the corporal sacrifice, even as the body and blood of Christ crucified are made substantively present by the use of these same words.

Continuing to follow the text of the institution narrative in First Corinthians, Cajetan emphasizes that, after identifying the Eucharist as his own body that was broken for our sake (*hoc est corpus meum, quod pro vobis frangitur*), Christ himself commands that *this* be done (*hoc facite*) in commemoration of him (*in meam commemorationem*). For Cajetan, Christ's command to *do this* emphasizes the sacrificial nature of the Eucharist—as both a sacrament and a sacrifice, the Eucharist is distinct from the other sacraments of the Church because it involves doing or offering something according to Christ's instructions. As a true sacrifice made in a spiritual and unbloody modality, it is not formally distinct from Christ's sacrifice on the cross but rather is done in memorial of this singular corporal offering.[49] Returning to his commentary on Luke, we find Cajetan emphasizing that the fulfillment of Christ's command in the life of the Church involves not only repeating his words, but also *doing* what Christ did. The sacrificial oblation that Christ references in the institution narrative, already begun with Judas's betrayal and consummated on the cross, is *done* in the context of the Church's liturgy through the actions that Christ describes in the institution narrative: bread is taken and thanks is given; the same is consecrated, taken up then given to be eaten.[50] As something done *in memory*, therefore, the Mass is offered as a memorial not only of what Christ said, but also of what he did. Although the corporal modality of Christ's sacrifice is offered once, Cajetan argues that when the spiritual modality of this same sacrifice is offered as a memorial, the Mass has the capacity to transcend the historical singularity of cross and offering inestimable benefits in the present.[51]

---

49. Cajetan, *In 1 Cor.*, c. 11:24b. As in *Epistolae Pauli et aliorum Apostolorum* (Venice, 1531), 59b–60.

50. "Hoc facite. Non dicit *hoc dicite*, sed *facite*: quia mádat fieri quod ipse fecit scilicet accipete panem, gratias agere, frangere, consecrare, sumere ac dare." Cajetan, *In Lucam*, c. 22:19. As in *Opera omnia*, vol. 4 (1639), 263. See also *Evangeliacum commen* (Venice, 1530), 130a.

51. Cajetan, *In Lucam*, c. 22:19. As in *Opera omnia*, vol. 4 (1639), 263.

CONCLUSION

Although Cajetan would die in 1534, his work on the subject of Christ's priestly sacrifice and its relationship to the Eucharist would prove influential in many ways. After his commentary on Aquinas's *Summa* was formally endorsed by Pope Pius V in 1570 and included in subsequent printings of Aquinas's text, his reading of Aquinas would come to exercise a great deal of authority among later Thomists.[52] Although his biblical commentaries were not circulated as widely as his commentary on the *Summa*, many of the arguments that first appeared in Cajetan's earlier biblical commentaries during the 1520s were integrated into his later *De Missae sacrificio*, which Cajetan wrote in response to the Augsburg Confession in 1531 and was more widely circulated than some of his earlier commentaries.[53] Although Cajetan died before the convocation of the Council of Trent in 1545, he was a respected authority for many bishops and theologians who attended the council.[54] Although not cited explicitly, a number of conceptual parallels between the council's 1562 decree on the Mass and Cajetan's earlier work can be identified. Echoing Cajetan's response to Zwingli, the council draws a modal distinction between the cross and the altar as a means of defending a Catholic understanding of the singular and unrepeatable nature of Christ's self-offering that is taught by the Letter to the Hebrews. Like Cajetan, Trent also turns to the institution narratives, rather than the literal sense of Hebrews alone, to find biblical warrant for the sacrificial character of the liturgical rite of the Mass itself, arguing that the teaching of both of these scriptural sources can be preserved in their full sense if the commemorative sacrifice indicated by the institution narratives is understood as a modality of the singular sacrifice described in Hebrews, rather than a separate sacrifice that is differentiated from that of the cross in a quantitative or formal way.[55]

The incorporation of these principles—likely inspired by Cajetan—into

---

52. DTC 2:1320.

53. See Cajetan's *De Missae sacrificio* in *Reverendissimi domini domini Thomae de Vio Caietani Cardinalis.S.Xisti: De sacrificio Missae, De Communione, De Confessione, De satisfactione, De sanctorum inuocatione, Adversus lutherano iuxta scripturam Tractatus* (Paris: Petri Regnault, 1531). O'Connor, *Cajetan's Biblical Commentaries*, XVI.

54. Jared Wicks, "Thomism between Renaissance and Reformation: The Case of Cajetan," *Archiv für Reformationsgeschichte* 68 (1977): 11n7.

55. Conc. Trident. Sess. 22, cap. 1. Tanner, 733.

the Tridentine decree on the nature of the Mass underscores their utility and doctrinal clarity. On one level, Trent implicitly endorses the value of Cajetan's later biblical work, where he develops a theological grammar that is both consonant with the literal sense of the Letter to the Hebrews and able to account for the full textual implications of the institution narratives. Although methodologically distinct from his earlier work on the *Summa* in many ways, when Cajetan's later texts are read against the backdrop of his earlier speculative work, it becomes clear that the arguments and principles that Cajetan articulated in his biblical period were not simply apologetical reformulations of speculative truths that had already been articulated with greater precision in Cajetan's earlier work. Rather, Cajetan's later biblical work on the sacrificial dimension of the Eucharist represents an authentic development of his own thought on this subject; by offering a more robust account of the liturgical modality of Christ's priestly sacrifice, Cajetan applies the principles of Aquinas's thought in a new context, responding directly to the challenges of his own day.

PART II

THE CRISIS OF CHRISTOLOGY IN ASSESSING OUR LIFE IN CHRIST

CHAPTER 11

CREATION IS
NOT AN INCARNATION

Responding to a
Contemporary Crisis in
Catholic Christology in Light of
Aquinas's Teaching
on Participation

Michael A. Dauphinais

A contemporary crisis in Catholic Christology concerns the relationship between the Incarnation and creation. A current trend views the Incarnation as an expression of evolutionary creation. Rather than telling us something specific about Jesus Christ, this view proposes that the Incarnation reveals the truth about creation; namely, that creation itself is an Incarnation. According to this view, all of creation is filled with God's presence. All of creation is evolving to higher unity with God. Rather than focusing on Jesus Christ and his Church, this way of interpreting the Incarnation shifts the focus to the whole of creation. For instance, in his *Incarnation: A New Evolutionary Threshold*, Diarmuid O'Murchu presents the Incarnation as the lens through which to see creation and vice versa: "This is a book about Incarnation, which, for the moment, I understanding to mean *God's*

A version of this chapter appears as "Pantheistic versus Participatory Christologies: A Critical Analysis of Richard Rohr's Universal Christ in Light of Thomas Aquinas's *Commentary on John*," *European Journal for the Study of Thomas Aquinas* 39 (2021).

embodiment in creation as experienced and named by human beings."[1] O'Murchu writes, "Without body, however, the Spirit goes nowhere; *it is in and through bodies that spirit becomes grounded and generic at every level of creation's evolution.*"[2] In every level of creation, there is the incarnation of the spiritual in the material. In her *The Emergent Christ: Exploring the Meaning of Catholic in an Evolutionary Universe*, Ilia Delio likewise presents creation as the incarnation with an evolutionary thrust: "Every act of evolving nature is the self-expression of God, since the very act of nature's transcendence is the energy of divine love. God unfolds in the details of nature; thus, evolution is not only *of* God but *is God incarnate.*"[3] Delio writes, "These emerging Christ fields are new basins of attraction, transcending institutional religion, signaling a new religious consciousness, a new God-centeredness that inspires and empowers co-creativity for a new humanity and a new earth."[4] According to Delio, evolutionary creation is the Incarnation, ever moving forward and more fully incarnating divine love.

This chapter focuses on a recent book that articulates this creation-centered approach to Christology in a popular and winsome manner: Richard Rohr's *The Universal Christ: How a Forgotten Reality Can Change Everything We See, Hope For, and Believe.*[5] Rohr is a Franciscan spiritual teacher who has reportedly helped a number of people discover greater integration and peace in their earthly lives. He is sometimes known among circles of people who are—and those who work with those who are—recovering from addictions.[6] He has authored numerous books on spirituality and Christian mysticism and communicates in an accessible and engaging manner. *The Universal Christ* has become a *New York Times* bestseller and includes blurbs from celebrity figures such as Melinda Gates and Bono. Rohr may appear an odd selection for the present analysis because he is a popular

---

1. Diarmuid O'Murchu, *Incarnation: A New Evolutionary Threshold* (Maryknoll, NY: Orbis Books, 2017), 44; italics original.

2. O'Murchu, *Incarnation*, 62; italics original.

3. Ilia Delio, OSF, *The Emergent Christ: Exploring the Meaning of Catholic in an Evolutionary Universe* (Maryknoll, NY: Orbis Books, 2011), 51; italics original.

4. Delio, *Emergent Christ*, 145.

5. Richard Rohr, *The Universal Christ: How a Forgotten Reality Can Change Everything We See, Hope For, and Believe* (New York: Convergent Press, 2019).

6. Richard Rohr, *Breathing under Water: Spirituality and the Twelve Steps* (Cincinnati, OH: Franciscan Media, 2011).

author who writes and speaks outside the typical context of university or seminary education. I suggest that his book offers a helpful insight into—and is reflective of—a serious contemporary crisis in Christology. This essay presents Fr. Rohr's central claims about Jesus Christ and the presence of God in creation and then offers a critique of them in light of Aquinas's teachings with particular attention to his *Commentary on John*.[7] This essay attempts to show that Rohr's claims are ultimately inadequate and erroneous and that Aquinas's participatory account of creation and the Incarnation allows him to cultivate an awareness of God's presence in all of creation while also maintaining the salvific uniqueness of the Incarnation.

ROHR'S REINTERPRETATION OF CHRISTIANITY: CREATION AS INCARNATION

Rohr seeks to unveil a new key to our experience of the world and of one another. The subtitle of his book reads, *How a Forgotten Reality Can Change Everything We See, Hope For, and Believe*. The unveiling of the whole of reality is the central aim of his reinterpretation of Jesus Christ. I present Rohr's teaching following the division of his book into two main parts: first, the rediscovery of the universal Christ and the first incarnation of creation; and second, the way in which the historical Jesus reveals the universal patterns of this first incarnation.

Rohr claims that Christianity has focused too heavily on the particular instance of the historical Jesus and so has missed the real point of Christianity: the revelation of the universal Christ as always already present everywhere and in everything. This may be seen in two questions he articulates

---

7. For a critical review of Fr. Rohr's book, see Michael McClymond, "'Everything Is Christ'—and Other Muddled Messages from Richard Rohr," *Gospel Coalition*, September 16, 2019, https://www.thegospelcoalition.org/reviews/universal-christ-richard-rohr. For an adulatory review, see Cathleen Falsani, "In New Book, Richard Rohr Says the 'Universal Christ' Changes Everything," *National Catholic Reporter*, April 1, 2019, https://www.ncronline.org/news/spirituality/new-book-richard-rohr-says-christ-changes-everything. For another sympathetic portrayal, see Eliza Griswold, "Richard Rohr Reorders the Universe," *New Yorker*, February 2, 2020, https://www.newyorker.com/news/on-religion/richard-rohr-reorders-the-universe.

in his introduction: "What if Christ is a name for *the transcendent within every 'thing' in the universe?*" and "What if Christ is *another name for everything*—in its fullness?"[8] Rohr shifts the attention of the reader to the creation of the cosmos as the *"first Incarnation."* He writes, "The incarnation, then, is not only 'God becoming Jesus.'" Instead, all of creation is the Incarnation or the "enfleshment of spirit": *Everything visible, without exception, is the outpouring of God.*"[9] Gesturing at the preexistent and cosmic visions of Christ as articulated in John 1:1–18, Colossians 1:15–20, and Ephesians 1:3–14, Rohr claims that this cosmic Christ has been overlooked by a focus on the historical Jesus in his particularity.[10] He summarizes the supposed error, "in Christianity, we have made the mistake of limiting the Creator's presence to just one human manifestation, Jesus."[11] Rohr wishes, instead, for the reader to see God's presence in all creation. He writes, *"God loves things by becoming them."*[12]

The shift to seeing creation itself as the Incarnation of God, for Rohr, opens up a new way of seeing God's presence in the world. He wishes the reader to find a pan-human spirituality: *"If all of this is true, we have a theological basis for a very natural religion that includes everybody."*[13] Rohr moves from the particular Jesus to the universal Christ to help everyone to discover the presence of God already in the world, in their neighbors, and in themselves.

Rohr invites his readers to adopt this new way of seeing the world opened up by Jesus, one of inclusivity rather than exclusivity. He writes, *"In Jesus Christ, God's own broad, deep, and all-inclusive worldview is made available to us."*[14] Rohr says that Christianity has missed this change of perspective

8. Rohr, *Universal Christ*, 5.

9. Rohr, *Universal Christ*, 12–13.

10. Rohr, *Universal Christ*, 17. "Numerous Scriptures make it very clear that Christ has existed 'from the beginning' (John 1:1–18, Colossians 1:15–20, and Ephesians 1:3–14 being primary sources), so the Christ cannot be coterminous with Jesus. But by attaching the word 'Christ' to Jesus as if it were his last name, instead of means by which God's presence has enchanted all matter throughout all of history, Christians got pretty sloppy in their thinking. *Our faith became a competitive theology with various parochial theories of salvation, instead of a universal cosmology inside of which all can live with an inherent dignity.*"

11. Rohr, *Universal Christ*, 16. There's a deep irony here that this contrast presumes a dualistic view of God-as-present-in-Jesus vs. God-as-present-in-all-creation.

12. Rohr, *Universal Christ*, 16, 20. All italicized texts are from the original.

13. Rohr, *Universal Christ*, 21.

14. Rohr, *Universal Christ*, 32.

offered to us by Jesus Christ and so fell into exclusivity, and worst of all used Jesus as the principle of exclusion. He writes, "too often, we have substituted the messenger for the message." Rohr says that Christians have been too concerned with worshipping Jesus rather than "actually *following* what he taught—and he did ask us several times to follow him, and never once to worship him."[15] Per Rohr, the goal of the Christian is not to see the historical Jesus but to see the universal Christ: "A mature Christian sees Christ in everything and everyone else."[16] Rohr asserts that this divine omnipresence necessitates radical inclusivity: "*The only thing [Jesus] excluded was exclusion itself.*"[17] Rohr asserts that "we need both a Jesus and a Christ" in his effort to keep them divided from each other. Jesus remains a moment on the journey to Christ. He writes, "When your isolated 'I' turns into a connected 'we,' you have moved from Jesus to Christ."[18] Moving from Jesus to Christ allows Rohr's readers to see creation as the primary incarnation of the universal Christ and so to an all-inclusive vision of creation.

In order to move from the historical Jesus to the universal Christ, Rohr wants to move away from the Christ of the creeds. Rohr explains, the creeds "reaffirm a static and unchanging universe, and a God who is quite remote from almost everything we care about each day.... The Christ of these creeds is not tethered to earth—to a real, historical, flesh-and-blood Jesus of Nazareth."[19] Per Rohr, the historical Jesus is witness to the universal Christ, to the universal presence of God in creation, to the idea that all creation is incarnation. Rohr describes the turn from the creedal Christ to the universal Christ as a paradigm shift. Just as Christianity has been a

---

15. Rohr, *Universal Christ*, 32. This approach seems squarely within the expression often attributed to Unitarian theology that Christianity should be "the religion of Jesus, not the religion about Jesus." While Rohr wants to move from Jesus to Christ, the influential Adolf von Harnack moved from Christ to Jesus in his influential lectures and book originally published in German in 1902, *What Is Christianity?*, trans. Thomas Bailey Saunders (Minneapolis, MN: Fortress Press, 1986). Von Harnack moved away from Christ to Jesus in order to move "away from dogma, onward to love," something distinctly observable in Rohr. Joseph Ratzinger summarizes von Harnack's approach: "the watchword is obvious: back past the *preached Christ*, the object of divisive belief, to the *preaching Jesus*, back to the summons to the unifying power of love under the one Father with all our brothers" (199; italics added). *Introduction to Christianity*, trans. J. R. Foster and Michael J. Miller (San Francisco, CA: Ignatius Press, 2004)

16. Rohr, *Universal Christ*, 33.

17. Rohr, *Universal Christ*, 34.

18. Rohr, *Universal Christ*, 37.

19. Rohr, *Universal Christ*, 104–5.

"two-thousand-year-old paradigm shift from Judaism," Rohr now proposes another paradigm shift from Christianity as a particular religion to Christianity as an awareness of the universal Christ. He asserts the fruit that he hopes this shift will bear: *Jesus can hold together one group or religion. Christ can hold together everything.*"[20] No longer is the Incarnation something that only happened in Jesus or is the incarnate Word only worshipped by Christians—now everything is incarnation.[21]

In presenting creation as incarnation, Rohr deploys a foundational dichotomy between dualism and nondualism. He affirms that dualism sees God as separate from his creation, whereas nondualism sees God within all creation. Rohr is not clear about when exactly dualism entered into and corrupted the original nondualistic Christian message. He asserts variously that dualism came in with the rise of the Christian emperors and the early councils and creeds, with the Reformation and the Enlightenment, or even that it has bound the first two thousand years of Christianity.[22] Likewise, he identifies nondualistic or holistic Christianity at times with Paul's conception of the cosmic Christ, the Eastern Church, mystics, or the third millennium we have just entered.[23] At other points, he contrasts dualistic and nondualistic ways of thinking as rational thinking or the "binary mind" versus a "contemplative way of knowing."[24] Moving from dualism to nondualism thus moves from a particular and exclusive emphasis on Jesus as the object of creedal faith to a universal and inclusive emphasis on the universal Christ

20. Rohr, *Universal Christ*, 47.

21. Rohr attempts to defend his claim against those who might allege that this view is pantheistic: "Paul merely took incarnationalism to its universal and logical conclusions. We see that in his bold exclamation 'There is only Christ. He is everything and he is in everything' (Col 3:11). If I were to write that today, people would call me a pantheist (the universe is God), whereas I am really a pan*en*theist (God lies within all things, but also transcends them), exactly like both Jesus and Paul" (*Universal Christ*, 43).

22. Rohr writes, "To legitimate our new religion in the Roman Empire, Christians felt that we have to prove that Jesus was independently divine," then refers to the Councils of Nicaea (325) and Chalcedon (451) and concludes, "we were more interested in the superiority of our own tribe, group, or nation than we were in the wholeness of creation. Our view of reality was largely imperial, patriarchal, and dualistic" (*Universal Christ*, 45).

23. Rohr writes, "We must point out that these hidden but fully corporate understandings in Paul, since most Western dualistic minds have been preconditioned to read his letters in a purely anthropocentric and individualistic way" (*Universal Christ*, 168). "In the fourteenth century, the book's author would've enjoyed the last remnants of mystical holism before it was taken away by the dualistic—but also necessary—ravages of the Reformation and the Enlightenment" (*Universal Christ*, 163).

24. Rohr, *Universal Christ*, 204–5.

without creeds. By way of example, Rohr exhorts his reader, "We kept ourselves so busy trying to process the idea of Jesus as the personal incarnation of God, and a God that an empire (East or West!) could make use of, that we had little time or readiness to universalize that message to all 'flesh' (John 1:14), much less of all creation (Romans 8:18–23)."[25] Rohr here reinterprets the Incarnation, "the Word became flesh" (Jn 1:14), from a dualistic claim about Jesus to a nondualistic truth about all creation.

After presenting creation as the Incarnation of the universal Christ, Rohr uses this theme to reinterpret the mysteries of Jesus's life, death, and resurrection. Rather than seeing Jesus as unique (dualistic), Rohr presents Jesus as unveiling patterns present in all creation (nondualistic). In the second part of his book, Rohr goes through Jesus's story to show how it is witness to the universal Christ of creation. For instance, the Eucharist, the Crucifixion, and the Resurrection show the reader the deeper reality of all creation.

As presented by Rohr, the Eucharist reveals God's presence in all creation. He writes, *"Seeing [the Eucharist] as a miracle is not really the message at all"*; instead, the Eucharist is *"the pattern of everything—and not just this thing."*[26] To focus on the unique presence of God in the Eucharist, to see him in the Eucharist and not elsewhere, is to remain in dualistic thinking. The point of the Eucharist, instead, is that it is not unique, "not just this thing," but common, "the pattern of everything." Rohr concludes, *"The universe is the Body of God, both in its essence and in its suffering."*[27] The Eucharist, according to Rohr, not only allows us to see the universe as the essence of God, but also allows God to see in a new way: *"We are not just humans having a God experience. The Eucharist tells us that, in some mysterious way, we are God having a human experience!"*[28] As he puts it, "It is all one continuum of Incarnation."[29] Rohr's language here of "one continuum" expresses his commitment to embrace a nondualism. By discovering the universal Christ, we discover that creation itself and everything in creation is always and already the Incarnation of God. Just as everything is Incarnation, so everything is Eucharist.

25. Rohr, *Universal Christ*, 204.
26. Rohr, *Universal Christ*, 134.
27. Rohr, *Universal Christ*, 134.
28. Rohr, *Universal Christ*, 137.
29. Rohr, *Universal Christ*, 138.

Rohr likewise approaches the crucifixion as illuminating a universal pattern of creation. To accomplish this holistic and universal view, he rejects what he terms the "penal substitutionary atonement theory" and the dualistic quid pro quo it presupposes and engenders. Owing to the dualistic understanding of the cross, "Salvation became a *one-time transactional* affair between Jesus and his Father, instead of an ongoing *transformational lesson* for the human soul and for all of history."[30] The nondualistic approach opens up the relevance of the cross. He writes, "The cross is not just a singular event. It's a statement from God that *reality has a cruciform pattern.*"[31] Just as everything is Incarnation, so everything is Crucifixion.

According to Rohr, Jesus's resurrection exemplifies the evolutionary movement of all creation. The Resurrection announces the universal Christ to be the alpha and the omega of the evolving cosmos. Rejecting what he describes as an individualistic or *"privatized salvation,"* Rohr says that God is "saving and redeeming the Whole ... in [the] Cosmic Sweep of Divine love."[32] From this view of God's universal salvation, Rohr asks us to shift our view of the Resurrection, again from a dualistic to a nondualistic viewpoint: "from a one-time miracle in the life of Jesus that asks for assent and belief, to a pattern of creation that has always been true."[33] Rohr writes, *"Resurrection and renewal are, in fact, the universal pattern of everything.... Every time you take in a breath, you are repeating the pattern of spirit taking on matter, and thus repeating the first creation of Adam....* You are an incarnation, like Christ, of matter and spirit operating as one."[34] Just as everything is Incarnation, so everything is Resurrection.

Here we turn to a brief response to Rohr's central claims. Rohr constantly reminds his reader to learn to see the universal Christ—the presence of God—everywhere and in everything. Employing memorable turns of phrase, he connects Christian teachings to the everyday, ordinary, and unavoidable experiences of human existence. To be human, to be created, is al-

30. Rohr, *Universal Christ*, 141.

31. Rohr, *Universal Christ*, 147.

32. Rohr, *Universal Christ*, 167. Rohr avers, "The true Gospel democratizes the world. *We are all saved in spite of our mistakes and in spite of ourselves. We are all caught up in the cosmic sweep of Divine grace and mercy"* (*Universal Christ*, 166).

33. Rohr, *Universal Christ*, 169.

34. Rohr, *Universal Christ*, 99.

ways and already to be in the presence of God. And yet Rohr's reformulation of the Christian life and faith overlooks the unique and efficacious reality of the Incarnation.

When Rohr reinterprets creation as incarnation, he flattens out reality in a way that distorts the Christian message. No longer distinct, the Creator and creation dissolve into one another. No longer distinct, Jesus and the rest of humanity dissolve into one another. In Rohr's reenvisioning, everything is Incarnation; everything is Eucharist; everything is Crucifixion; everything is Resurrection. Although it is true that everything is filled with the divine presence, God is not present in everything in the same manner. By undermining distinctions among modes of divine presence, something that he views as dualistic, Rohr affirms a nondualistic, flattened sense of the presence of God, in the rocks, in the animals, in human beings, in Jesus Christ, and thus inevitably in God himself. All such divine presences are "all one continuum of incarnation." Such a view constitutes and exemplifies a contemporary crisis in Christology.

AQUINAS ON THE
PROLOGUE OF JOHN

The prologue to the Gospel of John offers an excellent place to consider how the Incarnation is related to the creation. John 1:1 echoes Genesis 1:1, "In the beginning," and so retells the story of creation now in light of the Incarnation. In the first eighteen verses, we witness affirmations of distinct modes of the divine presence: in the Word of God himself (Jn 1:1–2); in all creation made through the Word (Jn 1:3); in all rational creatures who share in the light of the Word (Jn 1:4); in those who become children of God (Jn 1:12–13); and in Jesus Christ, the Word became flesh (Jn 1:14). How are we to receive such a powerful revelation of God's presence in creation and in the Incarnation?

Aquinas offers rich accounts of creation and Incarnation through the metaphysics of participation. Participation moves beyond Rohr's limited opposition of dualistic and nondualistic ways of thinking about God. Dualism and nondualism both occur within one plane of reality: either-or versus both-and; particular versus universal; transactional versus transformational; the personal incarnation of Jesus or the universal incarnation of the Christ. Participation offers a more adequate response to reality and so to the biblical revelation. It rejects both dualism and nondualism while recognizing the partial truth of each approach. Dualism rightly affirms that the Word is uniquely present in Jesus of Nazareth; nondualism rightly affirms the Word is also present in each human being. Dualism incorrectly presupposes a God separate from the world; nondualism incorrectly presupposes a God at one with the world. A participatory view of reality allows for a primacy and uniqueness to God's existence while at the same time affirming how God is present in all of creation in various ways.

Aquinas offers a helpful summary of participation when he introduces God's action of creation in his *Summa Theologiae* I, q. 44, a. 1. To begin, he cites Paul's doxology in Romans about the presence of God, "of Him, and by Him, and in Him are all things" (Rom 11:36). Aquinas then continues,

every being in any way existing is from God. For whatever is found in anything by participation (*per participationem*), must be caused in it by that to which it belongs essentially.... Therefore all beings apart from God are not their own being, but are beings by participation. Therefore it must be that all things which are diversified by the diverse participation of being, so as to be more or less perfect, are caused by one First Being, Who possesses being most perfectly.

Aquinas employs the idea of participation to articulate the doctrine of creation. Aquinas elsewhere describes participation as follows: "when something receives in particular fashion that which belongs to another in universal (or total) fashion, the former is said to participate in the latter."[35] Thus Aquinas sees that all of creation participates in the Creator. The Creator is neither separate from nor confused with his creation. Participation instead distinguishes the Creator from creation and describes creation's relationship with—and dependence upon—the Creator.[36] God alone possesses existence in its fullness. Created realities only participate in that perfect existence. As such, Aquinas says that creatures may therefore share in God's perfection of

---

35.. Commentary on the *De Hebdomadibus*, lect. 2, Leon. 50.271:71–73, as cited and translated by John F. Wippel, *The Metaphysical Thought of Thomas Aquinas: From Finite Being to Uncreated Being* (Washington, DC: Catholic University of America Press, 2000), 96.

36. For a recent study that focuses on Aquinas, see Andrew Davison, *Participation in God: A Study in Christian Doctrine and Metaphysics* (Cambridge: Cambridge University Press, 2019).

being "so as to be more or less perfect." By speaking of creation as a participation in God, Aquinas avoids the dualist-nondualist dichotomy and accomplishes three necessary insights: first, he maintains radical uniqueness
of God's existence; second, he shows that all creatures participate in that
existence; and third, he allows for creatures to participate in God's existence
to various degrees.

Let us examine Aquinas's treatment of the prologue of in his *Commentary on John* and discover how he utilizes his understanding of participation
to present the Incarnation in relationship to creation.[37] Following Aquinas's
own division of the prologue of John, I first examine Aquinas's presentation
of how creation itself and the rational creature in particular participate in
the divine creative Word.[38] Second, I examine his presentation of the saving
participation of the children of God in the Incarnation of the Word. Aquinas helpfully differentiates the reality of creation *through* the Word of God
from the truth that Jesus Christ is the unique Incarnation *of* the Word.[39]

The Gospel of John begins, "In the beginning was the Word." In commenting upon the meaning of "Word," Aquinas employs the idea of participation. He emphasizes the differences between human words, interior
and exterior, and the divine Word. Yet the difference is not so great to lead
to incoherence. Human words, especially in their interior dimension as understandings of reality, share—or participate—in the unique divine Word.
Aquinas writes, "although there are many *participated* truths, there is just
one absolute truth, which is truth by its very essence, that is, the divine act of
being (*ipsum esse divinum*); and by this truth all words are words."[40] Because

---

37. Joseph W. Koterski, SJ, shows how Aquinas's *Commentary on John* consistently employs a Platonic notion of participation while rejecting the Platonic idea of an independent existence of forms or
ideas as well as the Neoplatonic theme of a necessary emanation. This adapted Platonic participation
rests on the understanding of the Word of God as co-eternal with the Father and thus equally sharing
in God's free creation of the universe. See "The Doctrine of Participation in Aquinas's *Commentary on
John*," in *Being and Thought in Aquinas*, ed. Jeremiah M. Hackett, William E. Murnion, and Carl N.
Still (Albany: State University of New York Press, 2004), 109–21.

38. See *Commentary on John*, ch. 1, lect. 1, no. 23, in which Aquinas divides John 1 in two parts,
with the first five verses manifesting the divinity of Christ and then with the remainder manifesting
the Incarnation of the Word.

39. See the prologue of the *Commentary on John*, in which Aquinas observes that the Gospel of
John was written after the other Gospels in order to affirm the divinity of Christ which became increas-
ing in doubt over time.

40. *Commentary on John*, ch. 1, lect. 1, no. 33; emphasis added.

the Word of God is nothing other than the divine *esse* itself, the Word is the one truth and thus unlike all of our partial words and incomplete truths as well as that one truth by which all our "words are words."

Here we notice two distinct, yet related, modes of the divine presence. Aquinas describes the first mode of presence as belonging to the Word of God, who is "truth by its very essence, that is, the divine act of being." The divine act of being is appropriate to the divine nature, being completely unlimited by any particular modes of being, unlimited by space and time, *ipsum esse subsistens*, sheer actuality, sheer and original truth itself. The second mode of divine presence is the way in which the rational creature exists by coming to know and speak a conglomeration of truths, of judgments, and words.[41] Such a mode of divine presence in the rational creature depends upon the utterly unique and perfect mode of divine presence that is the Word as Creator.[42]

Aquinas continues to comment on the first verse of John to show that the Word fully exists as God. Against the error of Arius, who claimed that the Son was less than the Father, Aquinas argues that the verse "the Word was God" means that the Word is co-eternal and consubstantial with the Father. Against the error of Sabellius, who claimed that the Word was merely another mode of the Father, Aquinas argues that the preposition in "the Word was *with* God" manifests a distinction of persons so that the Son is equal to the Father and yet not identical to the Father.[43] Aquinas also rejects the possibility that the affirmation that the "Word was God" might be

41. Aquinas distinguishes between the speech of human beings and the noise of animals by saying that the latter only communicate passions and feelings. In his *Commentary on Aristotle's Politics*, he writes, "speech is proper to men, because it is proper to them, as compared to the other animals, to have a knowledge of the good and the bad, the just and the unjust, and other such things that can be signified by speech" (I, I, 37).

42. Gilles Emery, OP, writes, "St. Thomas often explains that all natural human knowledge is a participation in the Word" (citing Aquinas, "He shines in everyone's understanding; because whatever light and whatever wisdom exists in men has come to them from participating in the Word" [*Commentary on John*, ch. 1, lect. 13, no. 246]) in his "Biblical Exegesis and the Speculative Doctrine of the Trinity in St. Thomas Aquinas's *Commentary on John*," in *Reading John with St. Thomas Aquinas: Theological Exegesis and Speculative Theology*, ed. Michael Dauphinais and Matthew Levering (Washington, DC: Catholic University of America Press, 2005), 23–61, 37.

43. *Commentary on John*, ch. 1, lect. 1, no. 45. See also, "And so, and the Word was with God, indicates: the union of the Word with the Father in nature, according to Basil; their distinction in person, according to Alcuin and Bede; the subsistence of the Word in the divine nature, according to Chrysostom; and the authorship of the Father in relation to the Word, according to Hilary" (no. 51).

meant in a metaphorical manner. Contra Arius's claims, the Word possesses the attributes of eternity, "he was in the beginning with God," and omnipotence since "all things were created through him."[44] The Word shares fully in the divinity of the Father because the Word fully possesses the existence and wisdom by which God is God the Creator. Aquinas affirms this truth by distinguishing the Word from his creatures: "the Word is called God absolutely because he is God by his own essence, and *not by participation*, as men and angels are."[45] Participation becomes the key way in which Aquinas distinguishes the Word as fully divine from all creatures that receive their being through the Word. Aquinas writes, "our Lord is saying that he is the source or beginning with regard to all creatures: for whatever is such by essence is the source and the cause of those things which are by participation."[46] As the Creator, the Word is *distinct from*—neither *separate from* nor *confused with*—his creation because he is creation's source or present cause.[47]

Aquinas employs participation to show how rational creatures arrive at wisdom. Participation thus shapes not only the existence of creatures but also their activities. He writes, "there is one absolute wisdom elevated above all things, that is, the divine wisdom, by *participating* in which all wise persons are wise. Further, there is one absolute Word, by *participating* in which all persons having a word are called speakers. Now this is the divine Word which of itself is the Word elevated above all words."[48] The divine truth, the divine wisdom, the divine Word is the fullness of actuality and as such shares itself uniquely with intelligent creatures in their activity of learning truths, gaining wisdom, and speaking words. Moreover, Aquinas describes rational creatures as not only coming to know this or that truth, "but truth itself, which can be manifested and is manifestive to all."[49] Truth is to be

---

44. *Commentary on John*, ch. 1, lect. 1, no. 62.

45. *Commentary on John*, ch. 1, lect. 1, no. 57; emphasis added.

46. *Commentary on John*, ch. 8, lect. 3, no. 1183, originally cited by Gilles Emery, OP, who writes, "The creative causality of the Son is manifested by the rule of the causality of the *primum*: that which sovereignly possesses a perfection is the cause of that which has this perfection in a second way (by participation)." "Biblical Exegesis and the Speculative Doctrine," 40.

47. *Commentary on John*, ch. 1, lect. 10, no. 207, "by [Christ's] essence he is the uncreated truth, which is eternal and not made, but is begotten of the Father; but all created truths were made through him, and these are certain *participations* and reflections of the first truth, which shines out in those souls who are holy" (emphasis added).

48. *Commentary on John*, ch. 1, lect. 1, no. 33; emphasis added.

49. *Commentary on John*, ch. 1, lect. 2, no. 97, "*ipsa veritas quae manifestabilis est et manifestativa*

shared, not only in its discrete modes of distinct truths, but also truth in itself, as one.[50]

Aquinas further draws upon the idea of participation to discuss the Word as "the light of men" (Jn 1:4). The intellectual vision of rational creatures differs from that of nonrational animals. Rational creatures "alone [are] capable of the vision of God ...; for although other animals may know certain things that are true, nevertheless, man alone knows the nature itself of truth."[51] This ability to know truth itself, ultimately to come to know God, is not something that human beings possess on their own but something they share in from truth itself. Aquinas says that the expression "the light of men" might also refer to God's own light, in this case, "a light in which we participate." He continues, "we would never be able to look upon the Word and light itself except through a participation in it; and this participation is in man and is the superior part of our soul."[52] The intelligence of the human being is nothing other than a sharing in the very intelligence of God.[53] To summarize this creative presence of God, each creature's being shares in the divine being, and each rational creature's wisdom shares in the divine wisdom. [54] To be a rational creature is to be able to acknowledge our

---

omnium." The capacity to know truth itself is present in all human beings and angels. As Aquinas will show in the rest of his commentary on John 1, the incarnate Word, Jesus Christ, is the one who fulfills this capacity and even makes the Father known to us (Jn 1:18) in a way otherwise unknown to us and beyond our natural capacities.

50. Aquinas holds that this participation in the Word as wisdom takes place through the Spirit when he comments on the verse "the Holy Spirit will teach you all things" (Jn 14:26): "Just as the effect of the mission of the Son was to lead us to the Father, so the effect of the mission of the Holy Spirit is to lead the faithful to the Son. Now the Son, once he is begotten Wisdom, is truth itself: 'I am the way, and the truth, and the life' (John 14:6). And so the effect of this kind of mission [i.e., of the Spirit] is to make us sharers (*participes*) in the divine wisdom and knowers of the truth. The Son, since he is the Word, gives teaching to us; but the Holy Spirit enables us to grasp it" (*Commentary on John*, ch. 14, lect. 6, no. 1958).

51. *Commentary on John*, ch. 1, lect. 3, no. 101.

52. *Commentary on John*, ch. 1, lect. 3, no. 101.

53. See also, "For all men coming into this visible world are enlightened by the light of natural knowledge through participating in this true light, which is the source of all the light of natural knowledge participated in by men" (*Commentary on John*, ch. 1, lect. 5, no. 129).

54. Aquinas frequently repeats the theme of human wisdom as a participation in divine wisdom, "the minds of the wise are lucid by reason of a participation in that divine light and wisdom" (*Commentary on John*, ch. 1, lect. 3, no. 103). Even those who are foolish and in darkness are not fully excluded from this participation in the divine wisdom, "whatever truth is known by anyone is due to a participation in that light which shines in the darkness; for every truth, no matter by whom it is spoken, comes from the Holy Spirit" (no. 103).

own incompleteness: I am not my own being or my own wisdom, but I receive all of this from my Creator.

Alongside the uniqueness of the Word as God and of the participation in the Word appropriate to the rational creature, Aquinas also develops another level by which *all creatures* participate in the Word of God. Developing the affirmation that all things are created through the Word, Aquinas quotes Augustine's *De Trinitate*, "the Word is the art (*ars*) full of the living patterns (*rationes*) of all things."[55] This is a startling claim in many ways: all of creation, even inanimate creation, nonetheless has its origin in an intelligent and living pattern or *ratio* in the Word of God. Aquinas here goes so far as to employ the language of patterns or *rationes* of reality, the same language employed by Rohr. Moreover, Aquinas repeats the expression of the Word as the *ars* full of the living patters of creatures at least two more times.[56] Aquinas explains his usage as follows:

> the patterns (*rationes*) which exist spiritually in the wisdom of God, and through which things were made by the Word, are life, just as a chest made by an artisan is in itself neither alive nor life, yet the exemplar of the chest in the artisan's mind prior to the existence of the chest is in some sense living, insofar as it has an intellectual existence in the mind of the artisan…. [Now] the creature in God is the creating essence (*creatura in Deo est creatrix essentia*). Thus, if things are considered as they are in the Word, they are life.[57]

Nonliving creatures may be said to possess life in God who is continually sharing his being with them as the Creator and knowing their forms to be through his Word. Participation allows Aquinas to speak of the living presence of the Word in inanimate creatures without falling into pantheism. The

---

55. *Commentary on John*, ch. 1, lect. 2, no. 77, "*Verbum est ars plena omnium rationum viventium.*" Aquinas's quote shortens Augustine's *De Trinitate*, 6.11: "One perfect Word to which nothing is lacking, which is like the art of the almighty and wise God, full of all the living and unchanging ideas (*ars quaedam omnipotentis atque sapientis dei plena omnium rationum uiuentium incommutabilium*) which are one in it, as it is one from the one with whom it is one." Gerald Boersma has a helpful essay on Augustine's understanding of the way in which the Word of God is present in the patterns of creation: "The *Rationes Seminales* in Augustine's Theology of Creation," *Nova et Vetera*, English ed. 18, no. 2 (2020): 413–41.

56. See also *Commentary on John*, ch. 1, lect. 2, no. 87, when Aquinas affirms, "the Word, who is the art of the Father, full of living patterns (*rationes*)." See also, "since the cause of all effects produced by God is a certain life and an art full of living patterns (*rationes*)" (no. 90).

57. *Commentary on John*, ch. 1, lect. 2, no. 91. The translation at aquinas.cc translates *rationes* as "archetypes," for which I have substituted "patterns" (https://aquinas.cc/la/en/~Ioan.C1.L2.n91).

patterns or *rationes* of all creation have an existence in God in his one act of understanding; and they have another existence in created things as those created things participate in the pattern or *ratio*.

When Aquinas speaks of the divine ideas in the *Summa Theologiae*, he explains that these patterns are that by which creatures not only exist but that by which they share in varying likeness to the Creator. Participation illustrates a likeness of all creatures to God. Aquinas writes, "every creature has its own proper species, according to which it participates in some degree in likeness to the divine essence. So far, therefore, as God knows His essence as capable of such imitation by any creature, He knows it as the particular pattern (*rationem*) and idea of that creature."[58] Participation thus makes possible imitation.

Aquinas articulates orders of existence that are not properly characterized as either dualistic or nondualistic. Instead, they are participatory levels of sharing in the fullness of being; namely, the divine essence. Aquinas discerns a "fitting order (*congruus ordo*)" in the first verses of John and how it re-presents the story of creation: "in the natural order of things, existence is first; and the Evangelist implies this in his first statement, 'in the beginning was the Word' (John 1:1). Second, comes life; and this is mentioned next, 'in him was life.' Third comes understanding; and that is mentioned next; 'and the life was the light of men.'"[59]

In addition to the three levels in which creation participates in the Word,

58. *Summa Theologiae* I, q. 15, a. 2. The translation at aquinas.cc translates *rationem* as "type," for which I have substituted "pattern" (https://aquinas.cc/la/en/~ST.I.Q15.A2.C.3). See Josef Pieper's commentary on and citation of this passage in "The Negative Element in the Philosophy of St. Thomas Aquinas," in *The Silence of Saint Aquinas* (South Bend, IN: St. Augustine's Press; repr., 1999), 66. Pieper argues that Aquinas's understanding of truth depends upon his teaching of creation. Since things not only exist, but exist having been created, the truth of things depends on their fundamental correspondence to the divine mind whose knowledge itself creates things. Unlike the creative divine mind, the human mind thus receives the truth of things in a way that is noncreative. In other words, God's knowledge is the cause of created realities; created realities are the cause of human knowledge. Thus Pieper writes, "The 'truth of things' [will be missed] unless we make it explicit that these things are *creatura*, that they have been brought into being by the creative knowledge of God." The result of this dependence of all things on God's creative knowledge has implications for how we interact with the world. Pieper continues, "it is the creative fashioning of things by God which *makes it possible* for them to be known by men" (55).

59. *Commentary on John*, ch. 1, lect. 3, no. 100. Aquinas says that "the light of men" (Jn 1:4) may also be interpreted as the order of grace: "the Evangelist considers here the restoration of the rational creature through Christ.... [T]he Son of God assumed flesh and came into the world to illumine all men with grace and truth" (no. 104).

there is a redemptive participation of the rational creature in the incarnate Word.[60] Aquinas comments on "without me you can do nothing" (Jn 15:5):

For our works are either from the power of nature or from divine grace. If they are from the power of nature, then, since every action of nature is from the Word of God, no nature can act to do anything without him. If our works are from the power of grace, then, since he is the author of grace, because grace and truth came by Jesus Christ (John 1:17), then it is obvious that no meritorious work can be done without him.[61]

In all of our being and acting, we are dependent upon the perfect being and acting of the Word. And, yes, not in the same way. Aquinas distinguishes between created participation in the Word and graced participation in the same Word incarnate. After treating primarily the role of Christ as the divine Word in the first five verses of John, Aquinas turns in the remainder of the first chapter to consider the "the incarnation of the Word" and how Christ restores and illumines us in grace and truth.[62]

Aquinas employs the notion of participation to comment on the Gospel of John's presentation of John the Baptist and Jesus Christ. Aquinas observes that while both John and Jesus bear witness, they do so in different modes. Aquinas describes Christ as bearing witness "as the existing light itself," whereas John "bears witness only as participating in that light."[63] The dif-

60. Michael Waldstein distinguishes without separating the natural and graced levels of participation: "creatures are made after the exemplar of the eternal Son in his eternal procession. This exemplarity, which is fundamental in the natural order of creation, continues in the supernatural order of grace and divinization: created persons gain life by union with the Son, by participation in his sonship." "The Analogy of Mission and Obedience: A Central Point in the Relation between *Theologia* and *Oikonomia* in St. Thomas Aquinas's *Commentary on John*," in *Reading John with St. Thomas Aquinas*, 92–112, 110.

61. *Commentary on John*, c. 15, lect. 1, no. 1993. Originally cited by David Burrell, CSC, "Creation in St. Thomas's *Super Evangelium S. Joannis Lectura*," in *Reading John with St. Thomas Aquinas*, 115–26, 125. Burrell describes the uniqueness of Aquinas's presentation of creation as "non-duality" because "creatures can never be separated from their creator" since they rely on the first cause for their very existence or *esse* (125). While I agree with Burrell that Aquinas's understanding of creation necessarily rejects any dualist accounts of God's relationship to the world, I find it more helpful to follow Aquinas's own language of participation rather than "non-duality." Participation maintains the hierarchical ordering of the Creation as the ever-present cause of creation as well as of the incarnate Word as the ever-present cause of redemption. On Aquinas's interpretation of this passage as referring to the order of created nature as well as that of grace, see Guy Mansini, OSB, "'Without Me You Can Do Nothing': St. Thomas with and without St. Augustine on John 15:5," in *Aquinas the Augustinian*, ed. Michael Dauphinais, Barry David, and Matthew Levering (Washington, DC: Catholic University of America Press, 2007), 159–80.

62. *Commentary on John*, ch. 1, lect. 4, no. 108.

63. *Commentary on John*, ch. 1, lect. 5, no. 117.

ference between John and Jesus is neither dualistic nor nondualistic. They are neither fully separate nor fully the same. Instead, John's participatory witness comes from—and depends upon—the fully realized witness of Jesus Christ.

In interpreting the role of John the Baptist's witness, Aquinas presents faith as a mode of participation in Jesus Christ. The Gospel narrates that the purpose of John's witness was "so that through him all men might believe" (Jn 1:7). For Aquinas, belief unites the believer to the object of faith. He presents belief as the graced participation in God's own light: "the salvation of man lies in participating in the light."[64] Aquinas presents two stages to this participation: "first they would believe through faith, and later enjoy him through vision in heaven."[65] Participation thus moves from imperfect to perfect.[66]

Faith is the beginning of a new manner of sharing in this divine life. Faith is when we cease prideful trust in the completeness of our vision of ourselves, of the world, and of God and begin to see reality as God sees, to know as God knows. Such language is not metaphorical since faith is nothing other than our higher—or more perfect—sharing in "the existing light itself" who is Jesus Christ. Aquinas describes this reality in the *Summa Theologiae* when he explains the way in which faith may truly be called a kind of knowledge: "faith ... does not proceed from the vision of the believer, but from the vision of Him who is believed."[67] Faith is a secondhand—or participatory—knowledge by which we believe what Christ sees.[68] In his *Commentary on John*, Aquinas puts it simply, "the Son of God is light by his very essence; but John and all the saints are light by participation."[69] By grace and by faith, the rational creature participates in the Word incarnate. Aquinas comments on "He was the true light" (Jn 1:9) and writes, "the Word

---

64. *Commentary on John*, ch. 1, lect. 5, no. 122.

65. *Commentary on John*, ch. 1, lect. 5, no. 120.

66. *Commentary on John*, ch. 1, lect. 5, no. 120.

67. *ST* I, q. 12, a. 13, ad 3.

68. Aquinas teaches that we come to know the saving truth about God through the Word as incarnate: "As to nature (*secundam naturam*), in Christian doctrine the beginning and principle of our wisdom is Christ, inasmuch as he is the wisdom and Word of God, i.e., in his divinity. But as to ourselves (*quoad nos*), the beginning is Christ himself inasmuch as the Word has become flesh (John 1:14), i.e., by his incarnation" (*Commentary on John*, ch. 1, lect. 1, no. 34).

69. *Commentary on John*, ch. 1, lect. 4, no. 123.

of God was not a false light, nor a symbolic light, nor a participated light, but the true light, i.e., light by his essence."[70] Aquinas thus rejects Arius, who held that "Christ was not true God, but God by participation."[71] Aquinas affirms that Jesus Christ has a fully created human nature but should not be called a creature since that would imply the Arian position.[72] Jesus Christ is the eternal Word now incarnate.

Jesus's uniqueness as the Word incarnate allows other human beings to share in his divine light, his divine truth, his divine love. When seen through the lens of participation, Jesus's uniqueness creates communion. Because Christ enjoys the divine presence in a manner unlike us, we become able to enjoy the divine presence in a manner like his. Earlier we observed that the living patterns or *rationes* of created things exist in the divine Word as well as in created realities. The difference in the Word's unique perfection of existence does not separate creatures from the Word but allows creatures to participate in the Word's existence and even his understanding or *ars* as Augustine and Aquinas describe. In fact, these participatory patterns are what allows creatures to imitate the Creator. Beyond these modes of imitation, there are more perfect modes of imitation made possible through the Incarnation. The uniqueness of Christ as the perfect light itself is what allows the faithful in this life and the saints in heaven to share in this divinizing light.[73]

Nonetheless, Aquinas is attentive to the difference between God's creative and incarnate presence. Aquinas finds this distinction between creation and incarnation when the Gospel affirms that "he was in the world" (Jn 1:10) and then that "he came in to the world" (Jn 1:11). To affirm that God was "in the world" requires us to distinguish God's being from creaturely being: God is "neither localized nor a part of the universe."[74] Turning this imagery upside down, Aquinas says that "the entire universe is in a certain sense a part, since it participates in a partial way in his goodness." The

---

70. *Commentary on John*, ch. 1, lect. 5, no. 125.

71. *Commentary on John*, ch. 1, lect. 5, no. 126.

72. *ST* III, q. 16, a. 8.

73. Aquinas describes being elevated by the light of glory as a kind of deiformity in *ST* I, q. 12, a. 5: "By this light the blessed are made *deiform*—i.e., like to God, according to the saying: 'When He shall appear we shall be like to Him, and we shall see Him as He is' (1 John 3:2)."

74. *Commentary on John*, ch. 1, lect. 5, no. 133.

relationship between God and creation is an asymmetrical relation. God's presence in things ought not to be imagined as another creaturely mode of presence that would be in competition with the creature's own existence. Instead, Aquinas says that God "acts by creating . . . [and] by acting gives existence."[75] Aquinas summarizes this by affirming that "God is in all things by his essence, presence, and power."[76] That "he came into the world" announces that the one who assumed a full human nature was also the one who is continually creating the world. Aquinas eloquently juxtaposes these two modes of presence, the presence of the Creator Word and the presence of the incarnate Word: "the Son of God came into the world and yet was in the world. For he was there, indeed, by his essence, power, and presence, but he came by assuming flesh. He was there invisibly, and he came in order to be visible."[77] Aquinas here emphasizes the dissimilarity of God's presence in Jesus Christ from his presence in creation. Creation is not a larger category of incarnation of which Jesus Christ is a particular instance, perhaps even the highest instance. Yet neither would it be true to see creation and incarnation as opposed to one another. Aquinas portrays a harmony between these two modes of divine presence since the Word who is already present in creation is now present in creation through the Incarnation in a singular manner.

The newness of the Incarnation reshapes rational creatures in its image. The unique sonship of Christ is not kept to himself but is shared with others. Following the narrative on John, Aquinas turns to the verse "he gave them power to become children of God" (Jn 1:12). He emphasizes the way in which the Incarnation is the ever-present cause of our newness. Aquinas writes, "the coming of the Son of God is great, because by it we are made sons of God" quoting Galatians 4:4–5 in support. He praises the fittingness that "we, who are sons of God by the fact that we are made like the

---

75. *Commentary on John*, ch. 1, lect. 5, no. 133.

76. *Commentary on John*, ch. 1, lect. 5, no. 134. This expression is familiar to readers of the *Summa Theologiae*: "God is in all things by His power, inasmuch as all things are subject to His power; He is by His presence in all things, as all things are bare and open to His eyes; He is in all things by His essence, inasmuch as He is present to all as the cause of their being (*causa essendi*)" (I, q. 8, a. 3).

77. *Commentary on John*, ch. 1, lect. 5, no. 144. See *ST* I, q. 43, a. 1, in which Aquinas presents the visible mission of the Son—i.e., the Incarnation—"as meaning a new way of existing in another; thus the Son is said to be sent by the Father into the world, inasmuch as He began to exist visibly in the world by taking our nature."

Son (*assimilamur Filio*), should be reformed through the Son (*reformemur per Filium*)."[78] As we saw earlier, participation is the ground of likeness and imitation. So our reformation is accomplished through the Son as we are assimilated to the Son, made like unto him. Here we are deeply united with the unique sonship of Jesus Christ. Aquinas articulates three ways in which human beings become sons of God, "through sanctifying grace, through the perfection of their actions, and through the attainment of glory."[79] To be children of God sets the human creature on a path that begins now but ends in a communion beyond that which is capable in this present mode of earthly existence.

As observed previously in Aquinas's exposition of John, this new participation in Christ is made possible because of the difference between Christ and the rest of humanity. He alone is the natural Son of God; the rest of us are adoptive sons. He enjoys a divine presence that is both like and unlike ours. Aquinas traces carefully the grammar of "children of God ... who are born, not of blood, nor of the will of the flesh, nor of the will of man, but of God (*ex Deo*)" (Jn 1:13) to emphasize the distinction:

since only the Son of God, who is the Word, is of the substance of the Father and indeed is one substance with the Father, while the saints, who are adopted sons, are not of his substance, the Evangelist uses the preposition "out of (*ex*)" saying of others that they are born of God (*ex Deo*), but of the natural Son, he says that he is born of the Father (*de Patre*).[80]

Adoptive sons and daughters are *ex Deo*; the natural son is *de Patre*. Aquinas notes the way that Scripture speaks of Christ both as the "only-begotten" (Jn 1:18) and as the "first-born" (Rom 8:29) and explains the possible contradiction in this same way. Christ alone is a natural son, so "only-begotten," and yet this natural sonship is the source of others to receive sonship, so "first-born."[81] Our adoptive sonship participates in his natural sonship. Aquinas thus avoids a dualistic separation between Jesus Christ and us as well as a nondualistic identification between Jesus Christ and us.

78. *Commentary on John*, ch. 1, lect. 6, no. 149.
79. *Commentary on John*, ch. 1, lect. 6, no. 156.
80. *Commentary on John*, ch. 1, lect. 6, no. 162.
81. Aquinas writes, "Christ is called the only-begotten of God by nature; but he is called the first-born insofar as from his natural sonship, by means of a certain likeness and participation, a sonship is granted to many" (*Commentary on John*, ch. 1, lect. 7, no. 187).

Aquinas further addresses the uniqueness of the presence of God in Jesus Christ when he comments on "the Word was made flesh, and dwelt among us" (Jn 1:14). That "flesh" here indicates a fully human nature, body and soul, requires an understanding of the fruit and purpose of the Incarnation. Aquinas writes, "the Word assumed human nature in order to repair it. Therefore, he repaired what he assumed."[82] The Word's unique personal union with our common human nature is the path of salvation. Aquinas highlights the distinctive language of "the Word was made flesh" to argue that Christ is not merely a prophet. Because Christ possesses the unity of person rather than a prophetic indwelling of the divine person alongside the human person (or supposit), this allows us to affirm that God became man and that man became God, even so far as to say that God is man.[83]

When Aquinas comments on the second half of John 1:14, "and dwelt among us," he identifies diverse levels of how God dwells in his creation through the idea of participation. Aquinas identifies the confusion of modes of indwelling as the heresy of Nestorius, who held that there were two natures and two persons in Jesus Christ. Aquinas explains,

Nestorius misunderstood this phrase ["and dwelt among us"] and said that the Son of God was united to man in such a way that there was not one person of God and of man. For he held that the Word was united to human nature only by an indwelling through grace. From this, however, it follows that the Son of God is not man.[84]

Instead of the graced indwelling proper to the saints, in Christ there is the personal union by which the Word assumes a human nature that now subsists in the Person of the Word. Aquinas goes on to interpret the meaning

---

82. *Commentary on John*, ch. 1, lect. 7, no. 168. The word *reparo*, here translated as repair, may also mean restore, renew, make good, refresh, revive. Roy J. Deferrari, *A Latin-English Dictionary of St. Thomas Aquinas* (Boston, MA: St. Paul Editions, 1986).

83. "And so the Evangelist expressly said 'was made,' and not assumed, to show that the union of the Word to flesh is not such as was the lifting up of the prophets, who were not taken up into a unity of person, but for the prophetic act. This union is such as would truly make God man and man God, i.e., that God would be man" (*Commentary on John*, ch. 1, lect. 7, no. 170). Aquinas rejects the one-person two-supposit Christology allowed for in Peter Lombard's *Sentences* on the basis that "According to this opinion the proposition, that God was made man and man was made God, is not true" (*Commentary on John*, ch. 1, lect. 7, no. 171). Aquinas treats the importance of maintaining certain grammatical and propositional formulations about Christology in *ST* III, q. 16, aa. 1–2, e.g., that "God is man (*Deus est homo*)" and "man is God" in the case of Jesus Christ.

84. *Commentary on John*, ch. 1, lect. 7, no. 174.

of the verse by affirming the unity of the Person while maintaining the distinction of the divine and human natures: "the Word dwelt in our nature; therefore, he is distinct in nature from it. And so, inasmuch as human nature was distinct from the nature of the Word in Christ, the former is called the dwelling place and temple of the divinity."[85] The assumption of the human nature to the divine Person of the Word means that the Word dwells in the human nature of Christ in the very unity of the Person. This allows Aquinas to affirm the reality of the Incarnation against Nestorius and to confess that the "Son of God is man." In the case of the saints, however, the Word dwells in them "through grace" so that their personal identity remains albeit now enlivened by the Word.[86] The personal indwelling of the Word in Christ's human nature causes the graced indwelling of the Word in the saints.[87]

When Aquinas turns to the earthly life of Jesus, he presents Jesus Christ as the unique and efficacious revelation of God. Contra Rohr, Jesus does not merely give witness to the patterns already present in creation, patterns of the universal Christ. Were this the case, Jesus would merely exemplify what we was already available to human reason. Instead, Aquinas presents Christ as the definitive cause and teacher of our salvation. When Aquinas comments on John 1:16, "of his fullness we have all received," he distinguishes between the fullness of the divine presence in Mary and the saints and that of Jesus Christ. Christ's fullness not only perfects his human nature but also is the cause of the perfection of the saints.[88] Aquinas describes "a fullness of efficiency and overflow, which belongs only to the man Christ as the author of grace."[89] As the author of grace, Christ possesses fully what he shares with others. This is essential to the understanding of participation: the fullness of reality causes others to share in that fullness. Aquinas

85. *Commentary on John*, ch. 1, lect. 7, no. 173.

86. See Daniel Keating, who uses participation to show what divine indwelling does and does not entail: "Christian life as an existence in the Trinity does not remove us from the sphere of being and remaining creatures.... Ours is a 'participation' in the divine nature, but this participation is dependent on the utter difference between Creator and creature remaining intact." "Trinity and Salvation: Christian Life as an Existence in the Trinity," in *The Oxford Handbook of the Trinity*, ed. Gilles Emery, OP, and Matthew Levering (New York: Oxford University Press, 2011), 442–53, 452.

87. See *ST* III, q. 59, a. 2, ad 2: "It belongs to God alone to bestow beatitude upon souls by a participation with Himself; but it is Christ's prerogative to bring them to such beatitude."

88. *Commentary on John*, ch. 1, lect. 10, no. 202: "the fullness of grace in Christ is the cause of all graces that are in intellectual creatures."

89. *Commentary on John*, ch. 1, lect. 10, no. 201.

explains further, "For Christ received all the gifts of the Holy Spirit without measure, according to a perfect fullness; but we *participate*, through him, of some portion of his fullness; and this is according to the measure which God grants to each."[90] The Holy Spirit is given fully to the human nature of Jesus Christ.[91] Thus when we participate in Christ, we receive from Christ the same Holy Spirit that his human nature received as united to the person of the Son. Jesus's uniqueness does not separate him from the rest of us but rather makes possible our communion in him.

When Aquinas comments on John 1:18, "No man has ever seen God: the only begotten Son, who is in the bosom of the Father, has made him known," he titles his lecture simply "the revelation of the Son" and presents the Son's revelation as a form of teaching (*doctrina*).[92] Aquinas draws three conclusions from this verse: first, we need this teaching; second, the Son is uniquely able to offer it; and third, the teaching itself makes God the Father known.[93] We do not currently see God properly because of ignorance and errors arising from our broken human experience as well as the inability to see God as he is in this earthly life. Christ, however, sees God properly since the Son is fully like the Father as a natural son, the only natural son, consubstantial with the Father. Aquinas describes Christ as "the competent (*sufficiens*) teacher" of this necessary wisdom of the truth about God.[94] The perfect vision of the divine Son allows the created soul of Jesus Christ to know God truly without knowing him as the divine nature knows itself him.[95]

Aquinas shows a continuity and discontinuity between the prophets and Christ by means of participation. The eternal Word spoke through the prophets and now speaks as Jesus Christ. Whereas the prophets made God known "to the extent that they shared (*particeps*) in the eternal Word," the teaching of Christ "surpasses all other teachings in dignity, authority and

90. *Commentary on John*, ch. 1, lect. 10, no. 202; emphasis added.

91. Dominic Legge, OP, writes, "Christ is greater than every other prophet; possessing the fullness of the Holy Spirit, Christ's prophetic knowledge surpasses that of all others," in *The Trinitarian Christology of Thomas Aquinas* (New York: Oxford University Press, 2017), 184. Legge presents the perfection of Christ's human knowledge as dependent upon the invisible mission of the Holy Spirit (172–86).

92. For a consideration of Aquinas's treatment of the teaching of Christ and revelation, see my "The Role of Christ and the History of Salvation in Aquinas's Theology of Revelation," *Angelicum* 96, no. 3 (2019): 293–328.

93. *Commentary on John*, ch. 1, lect. 11, no. 208.

94. *Commentary on John*, ch. 1, lect. 11, no. 215.

95. *Commentary on John*, ch. 1, lect. 11, no. 219.

usefulness, because it was handed on *immediately* by the only begotten Son, who is the first wisdom."[96] The Son teaches *through* the prophets; in Jesus Christ, the Son himself teaches *immediately*. The Son is the first wisdom as the creative divine Word who now also subsists in a human nature. As such, the Son's identity as the Son of the Father is what he teaches and thus makes the Father known. In each of these ways, Christ's teaching is always to be shared. The reality of the Incarnation allows first wisdom itself to hand on himself "immediately" to the human race.[97] His unique existence as the Word of God incarnate allows him to communicate to others a new and distinctive mode of participation in God.

CONCLUSION

Rohr criticizes the tradition's emphasis on the unique mode of divine presence in the incarnation and instead presents the message of the universal Christ as a recovery of the ubiquity of the divine presence.[98] This trend in contemporary Christology rightly affirms the divine presence in all creation and sees this as the ground of the Incarnation. This same trend, however, incorrectly reduces the presence of God in the Incarnation—as well as in the sacraments or in charity—to that presence already in creation. To accomplish this project, Rohr separates the universal Christ from the historical Jesus. The historical Jesus now unveils universal patterns of creation, patterns of the universal Christ's presence in all created things. According to Rohr, we need to turn from a dualistic focus on God present in Jesus and the Church to a nondualistic vision of the universal Christ present in all cre-

96. *Commentary on John*, ch. 1, lect. 11, no. 221.

97. Aquinas holds that Christ teaches through the teaching of his Apostles and disciples: "most of all he wanted to teach his disciples, who were destined to be the teachers of the entire world" (*Commentary on John*, ch. 6, lect. 1, no. 864). Michael Sherwin, OP, helps us to see how Christ immediately teaches through the mediation of his disciples: in his divinity, Christ "is the first cause of all learning ... and able to employ his creatures as instruments and secondary causes of his teaching. They thus become teachers by participation and truly merit the title *magistri*." "Christ the Teacher in St. Thomas's *Commentary on the Gospel of John*," in *Reading John with St. Thomas*, 173–93, 184.

98. Rohr includes the following epigraph at the beginning of his book: "The only really absolute mysteries in Christianity are the self-communication of God in the depths of existence—which we call grace, and in history—which we call Christ. —Fr. Karl Rahner, Jesuit priest and theologian, 1904–1984."

ation. In short, we need to turn from—or perhaps with—the historical Jesus to the universal Christ. According to Rohr, to focus on Jesus as the unique and personal Incarnation—as affirmed in the Catholic creeds—separates God from creation and Jesus from us.

Rohr's reinterpretation of creation as incarnation comes with a cost and collapses reality into a monistic or pantheistic view. In Rohr's presentation, the Incarnation is no longer a presence by union distinct from a presence by grace in those joined to God. The graced reality of charity and faith likewise are no longer a presence by grace distinct from the manner in which God is present in all creation.[99] Rather than seeing how the Incarnation of the Word changes everything, Rohr empties the Incarnation of the Word in Jesus Christ of any specific meaning or efficacy. Rohr rejects a dualistic view that separates the Creator from the creation and adopts a nondualistic view that makes creation divine. Rohr likewise rejects a dualistic view that separates incarnation from creation and adopts a nondualistic view that makes creation to be an incarnation. Even God appears as merely another mode of the created order, albeit the highest and most spiritual aspect of creation. By trying to see everything as incarnation, Rohr ends up simply presenting everything as creation or, to press the point more forcefully, creation as everything.

Aquinas allows us to respond to this contemporary crisis in Christology by articulating God's various presences via participation rather than a flattened view arising from the contrast of dualism versus nondualism. The doctrine of participation distinguishes pointedly between God's perfect existence and the existence of all created realities, which receive their existence from God. The created realities we encounter thus are discovered to be neither separate from nor identified with God but distinct from God. Participation articulates the way in which all creation receives its being and operation from the perfection of the Word and all rational creation receives its active understanding from the perfection of the Word. Moreover, participation expresses the way in which the children of God receive their higher participation in the divine nature from the personal union of the human nature of Jesus to the divine Word.[100]

Aquinas distinguishes among various levels of God's presence as he inter-

99. Rohr dedicates his book to his beloved dog, Venus, and writes, "Without any apology, lightweight theology, or fear of heresy, I can appropriately say that Venus was also Christ for me."
100. See 2 Pt 1:4, "sharers of the divine nature."

prets the prologue of John.[101] God himself is being itself, the sheer fullness of actuality, who creates the cosmos. The divine nature exists as the Father eternally expressing his Word (or begetting eternally his Son) in his Spirit. All of creation and of the re-creation that comes through redemption come to be through the Word. Whatever exists at all receives its partial existence from the fullness of divine existence and so imitates the divine Word's creative patterns or *rationes*, the living art (*ars*) of the Father. Whatever exists in the manner of a rational creature receives its partial rationality from the fullness of rationality in the divine existence and in the divine Word and so may come to discern the Creator, who is truth itself. In the Incarnation, the humanity of Jesus Christ is the perfected humanity conjoined fully to the natural sonship of the divine Word. Whatever exists as a rational creature in the communion of sonship through grace thus receives its partial sonship from the fullness of sonship present in the incarnate Word. Further, whatever exists in the perfected communion of sonship in glory exists in and from this same incarnate Word.

The reality of the Incarnation is necessarily a story about distinctions among God's modes of presence. God is present in himself as the Creator in a way distinct from his presence in creation. This allows human beings to be freed from idolatrous attempts at trying to find God incorrectly in created things and so turn to the living God as the Creator. God is present in Jesus Christ as the Word made flesh in a way that is unique from his presence in other rational creatures. This is what allows human beings to be healed from

101. In his *Commentary on the Sentences*, Aquinas offers a concise summary of three distinct modes by which God is present in creation: "Now a creature may be united to God in three ways. First, by way of likeness (*similitudinem*) only, insofar as in a creature is found some likeness to the divine goodness, but not that it reaches to God according to its substance; and this union is found in all creatures as a likenesses to the divine goodness. As such, this is a common mode by which God is in all creatures by essence, presence, and power (*per essentiam, praesentiam et potentiam*). Second, a creature may reach to God himself with respect to its substance, and not only by likeness; and this is by way of activity (*operationem*). This occurs when anyone adheres to first truth itself by faith and to the highest good itself by charity. As such, this is another mode by which God is particularly in the saints by grace (*per gratiam*). Third, a creature attains to God himself not only according to activity but also according to being (*esse*): not, indeed, as its being is the act of essence, because a creature is not able to cross over into the divine nature; but inasmuch as it is the act of the hypostasis or the person, to whose union the creature has been assumed: and thus we have the final way by which God is in Christ by way of union (*per unionem*)" (*In I Sent.*, dist. 37, q. 1, a. 2). I am indebted to Fr. Gilles Emery, OP, for this reference. The translation is mine. As we have seen in the *Commentary on John* and the *Summa Theologiae*, Aquinas continually refers to an additional mode of God's presence in creation in the rational nature. See, e.g., *ST* I, q. 93, a. 4, where Aquinas distinguishes between the image of God in the rational creature by creation and that by re-creation.

isolation and wounds and elevated to a sharing in God's eternal communion. These very distinctions are undermined by the attempt to reinterpret the creation as incarnation. We can avoid the deformities caused by dualistic thinking better by following Aquinas's teaching on participation. The Creator is not separate from the creature but is the creature's constant source and cause. The Incarnation is not separate from the reborn creature but is the reborn creature's constant source and cause. The distinctions between Creator and creature and between incarnation and creation are what allow salvation to take place.

The uniqueness of the divine Word incarnate allows the rational creature to be reformed and healed so that we may live as children of God by grace and faith in this life and by glory and vision in the next. This definitive reality of the Incarnation includes all of the earthly mysteries from the first moment of the Incarnation up to and including the ascension to the right hand of the Father and his eventual return to render justice to the living and the dead. The Incarnation is not the same as the presence of the Word in all rational creatures even in those united to God by faith and love. Instead, Jesus's human nature exists in the personal union of the Word. This personal union of human nature with the divine Son of God allows Aquinas to confess the truth of the Incarnation; namely, that "the Son of God is man." The historical Jesus thus does not merely witness the universal Christ, as does John the Baptist. No, the human nature of Jesus witnesses his own divine identity as the Son of God who came from the Father. Because the Son of God is man according to the personal union, the rest of humanity may let ourselves be taught by Christ the teacher and thus participate not merely in the Word's patterns or *rationes* displayed in all creation but in the Word's eternal filial relationship to the Father. Aquinas thus helps us to see that the Incarnation is much more than creation. The Incarnation not only renews creation but also elevates creation to participate in God's eternal life. Rather than presenting creation as the Incarnation, Aquinas presents "Christ, who as man, is our way to God."[102] Aquinas's participatory Christology lets the divine Word be encountered in creation while safeguarding the unique saving and healing efficacy of encountering that same Word incarnate in Jesus Christ.

---

102. *ST* I, q. 2, prologue: *"Christo, qui, secundum quod homo, via est nobis tendendi in Deum."*

CHAPTER 12

PUTTING THE
LAST ADAM FIRST

Evolution, Suffering, and Death in Light
of Kenotic Christology

Matthew J. Ramage

INTRODUCTION

This essay addresses a Christological crisis in which I find myself engrossed week in and week out, in person and online, among my students and peers alike. It consists in the urgent need to articulate rightly the relationship between the First Adam and the Last Adam in our modern context. Advances in evolutionary biology strongly suggest that human life has been subject to suffering and death from its very outset. But the classical theological synthesis assumed by most Catholic theologians until the mid-twentieth century is that prelapsarian man suffered neither pain nor death.[1] Some scholars conclude that the right approach is to reject the doctrine of original sin, while

---

1. For an extensive survey of this classical synthesis in the context of a comprehensive overview of the Tradition vis-à-vis this topic, see Nicholas Lombardo, OP, "Evil, Suffering, and Original Sin," in *The Oxford Handbook of Catholic Theology*, ed. Lewis Ayres and Medi Ann Volpe (Oxford: Oxford University Press, 2019), 139–50. For conciliar teachings germane to this point, see Carthage (419), canon 109; Second Council of Orange (529), canons 1–2; Trent, Decree on Original Sin (1546), canons 1–2, 4; *Gaudium et Spes*, Vatican II (1965), 18. This latest conciliar treatment of the matter speaks of "that bodily death from which man would have been immune had he not sinned." The biblical foundations of this theology can be found in Wis 1:13, 2:23–24; Rom 5:21, 6:23; and Jas 1:15. As we will see below, Ratzinger argues for a development of this tradition in which the doctrine of original sin remains intact while the question of whether all physical suffering and death followed upon sin remains open.

many ordinary Catholics I talk to respond to the same challenge by rejecting evolution.[2] The main contention of my essay will be that recovering the primacy of Jesus Christ in our theological anthropology may shine light on the origin and meaning of human suffering and death—that kenotic Christology allows us to bridge the gap between these two seemingly incompatible claims.

In view of this end, I chart a path forward through a *ressourcement* of the wisdom bequeathed to the Church by Thomas Aquinas while at the same time undertaking a needed *aggiornamento* of the Tradition with the help of Joseph Ratzinger's keen work at the intersection of Christology and human origins. Putting these thinkers' respective Christologies into dialogue with one another, I explore what it means for Christ to be the true Adam and how his *kenosis* illumines the relationship of sin, suffering, and death.

PART I: THOMAS AQUINAS

Christ the True Adam in Aquinas's Biblical Theology

The Last Adam (1 Cor 15)

Several biblical passages are important for Aquinas in connection with Christ being the definitive man, but it is appropriate to begin with the text where Paul explicitly identifies Christ as the last Adam: "The first man Adam became a living being'; the last Adam (ὁ ἔσχατος Ἀδάμ) became a life-giving spirit" (1 Cor 15:45).

Given that billions of humans have existed after Christ ascended to heaven, it is obvious that Scripture is not claiming Christ to be the last man in a chronological sense. In his commentary on 1 Corinthians 15, Aquinas thus ponders why it is fitting that Christ should be called "last." This terminology reveals an order of principles, he explains. As in nature, the imperfect is prior to the perfect (itself an idea consistent with modern evolutionary theory that was unknown to Thomas), so in human nature the spiritual (perfect)

---

2. For Catholic theologians who respond to the data of evolutionary biology by rejecting the doctrine of original sin, see Jack Mahoney, *Christianity in Evolution: An Exploration* (Washington, DC: Georgetown University Press, 2011), and John Haught, *God after Darwin: A Theology of Evolution* (Boulder, CO: Westview Press, 2008).

is not prior. If order is to be preserved, "the imperfect must be first, namely, what is animal, then the perfect, namely, what is spiritual" (cf. 1 Cor 13:10).[3] For Thomas, accordingly, Genesis's narration of Adam being formed from the dust of the earth indicates his mortality, whereas Christ the second man coming "from Heaven" refers to the reality of his being "spiritual and immortal," a state we one day hope to share; for, "if we have been united with him in a death like his, we shall certainly be united with him in a resurrection like his" (Rom 6:5).[4]

Christ's True Human Nature
and Its Defects (Phil 2:6–8)

If 1 Corinthians 15 serves as the most explicit biblical basis for the identification of Christ as the Last Adam, then one of the prime texts for understanding what precisely that entails is Philippians 2:6–8:

[Though Christ Jesus] was in the form of God, [he] did not count equality with God a thing to be grasped, but emptied himself, taking the form of a servant, being born in the likeness of men. And being found in human form he humbled himself and became obedient unto death, even death on a cross.

In commenting on this text throughout his corpus, the Angelic Doctor underscores the truth of Christ's real human body and real human soul as well as the ordinary way he lived as a man among men—in short, what it means for him to be found *in forma servi* and to live in an ordinary way as a man among other men, being obedient not only to his heavenly Father but also to his parents, to the governing authorities, and to the Torah.[5]

In his commentary on Philippians 2:7, Aquinas takes the expression *se-*

---

3. Aquinas, *Super I Cor 15*, lect. 7, no. 994, in *Commentary on the Letters of Saint Paul to the Corinthians*, trans. Fabian R. Larcher (Lander, WY: Aquinas Institute for the Study of Sacred Doctrine, 2012).

4. Aquinas, *Super I Cor 15*, lect. 7, no. 997.

5. See Aquinas, *Super Phil.* 2, lect. 2, no. 60, in *Commentary on the Letter of St. Paul to the Philippians, Colossians, Thessalonians, Timothy, Titus, and Philemon*, trans. Fabian R. Larcher (Lander, WY: Aquinas Institute for the Study of Sacred Doctrine, 2018); Aquinas, *Super Gal.* 4, lect. 1, no. 195, in *Commentary on the Letter of St. Paul to the Galatians and Ephesians*, trans. Fabian R. Larcher (Lander, WY: Aquinas Institute for the Study of Sacred Doctrine, 2012); Aquinas, *ST* III, q. 5, a. 2, trans. Fathers of the English Dominican Province (Westminster, MD: Christian Classics, 1981). All quotations from *ST* will be from this translation.

metipsum exinanivit to mean "he emptied himself." Gilles Emery observes that such an exegesis was not common among Thomas's contemporaries, and the uniqueness of his approach can be seen in two ways. First, Aquinas picks up on how the Pauline corpus itself contrasts the "emptiness" of Christ's humanity with the "fullness" of his divinity (cf. Col 2:9). Second, Thomas interprets this emptiness as "signifying the potentiality of the soul or the human nature with respect to the acquisition or reception of a perfection or plenitude."[6]

Emery describes the Angelic Doctor's exegesis of Philippians 2:7 as resolutely anti-Nestorian, indicating that the principal doctrinal error he was seeking to avoid was the notion that the Incarnation boils down to an "inhabitation by grace."[7] Aquinas is adamant that the Son did not assume a human hypostasis but rather a human nature, and it is for this is reason, he argues, that Paul did not say "taking a servant" (*servum accipiens*) but rather "taking the form of a servant" (*formam servi accipiens*).[8] In a nutshell, Christ's *kenosis* means: "He took the nature to his own person, so that the Son of God and the Son of man would be the same in person."[9] And "He is not said to have 'emptied himself' by diminishing his divine nature, but by assuming our deficient nature."[10]

---

6. Gilles Emery, OP, "Kenosis, Christ, and the Trinity in Thomas Aquinas," *Nova et Vetera* 17, no. 3 (2019): 839–69, at 844. Emery also observes that Thomas's understanding of *exinanitio* is especially noteworthy given that he was aware of another verb form (*vacuatum*) that was equivalent in meaning. See Aquinas, *Catena Aurea: Commentary on the Four Gospels* (Oxford: J. H. Parker, 1842), cap. 1, lect. 1.

7. Emery, "Kenosis, Christ, and the Trinity in Thomas Aquinas," 846–47, 852.

8. Aquinas, *Super Phil.* 2, lect. 2, no. 58.

9. Aquinas, *Super Phil.* 2, lect. 2, no. 58.

10. Aquinas, *In de div. nom.* 2, lect. 5, no. 207, in *In librum beati Dionysii de divinis nominibus,* ed. Ceslas Pera (Turin: Marietti, 1950). The translation of the above text is taken from Emery, "Kenosis, Christ, and the Trinity in Thomas Aquinas," 853n70. Thomas further demonstrates the balance and wisdom of his approach in a fascinating "mystical" (*mystice*) exegesis of Phil 2:7 found within his treatment of Jn 13:4 ("He [Jesus] rose from supper, laid aside his garments, and girded himself with a towel"). Citing Phil 2:7, the Angelic Doctor states that Christ's actions at the Last Supper indicate his *kenosis* (*exinanitio eius*). It is certainly not the case that the Lord abandoned his majestic dignity, but rather he hid it by assuming our smallness (*non quidem quod suae dignitatis maiestatem deponeret, sed eam occultaret, parvitatem assumendo*). To this, Thomas adds a reference to Isaiah: "Truly, thou art a God who hidest thyself" (Isa 45:15). Finally, Christ's donning a towel is understood here as signifying that he took on our mortality (*assumptio nostrae mortalitatis*)—in other words, having the form of a servant, being born in the likeness of men (Phil 2:7). Of course, by this interpretation being deemed *mystice*, Aquinas recognizes that it was not necessarily the intention of John himself to make this precise connection but that it is nevertheless a truth that emerges from the text's literal sense. Aquinas, *Super Ioan.* 13, lect. 2, no. 1746, in *Commentary on the Gospel of John 9–21*, trans. Fabian R. Larcher

Integral to Thomas's understanding of this passage is his acknowledgment that Christ's humanity had all the defects and properties that assuming a nature tainted by original sin entails—death, hunger, thirst, tiredness, and the like—except sin.[11] Moreover, this applies not only to the body (*defectus corporis*) but also to his soul (*defectus animae*). Thus not only was Christ's body passible but he also had innocent passions like pain, fear, sorrow, anger, and wonder in his soul.[12] And it was fitting for Christ to bear these human infirmities and defects, for in doing so he assumed the penalties of original sin, enhanced our faith in the Incarnation, and gave us all an example of patience "by valiantly bearing up against human passibility and defects."[13]

Like Us in All Things but Sin (Heb 2:14–18)

Aquinas's treatment of Hebrews emphasizes the reality that Jesus suffered real temptations, only without sin. The texts that are of particular interest are as follows:

Since therefore the children share in flesh and blood, he himself likewise partook of the same nature, that through death he might destroy him who has the power of death, that is, the devil, and deliver all those who through fear of death were subject to lifelong bondage ... [H]e had to be made like his brethren in every respect, so that he might become a merciful and faithful high priest in the service of God, to make expiation for the sins of the people. For because he himself has suffered and been tempted, he is able to help those who are tempted (Heb 2:14–18).

For we have not a high priest who is unable to sympathize with our weaknesses, but one who in every respect has been tempted as we are, yet without sin. Let us then with confidence draw near to the throne of grace, that we may receive mercy and find grace to help in time of need (Heb 4:15–16).

Thomas begins his discussion of Hebrews 2:14–15 with a clear distinction regarding the meaning of the "flesh and blood" nature that Christ assumed. In

---

(Lander, WY: Aquinas Institute for the Study of Sacred Doctrine, 2013). Thomas's emphasis on the truth that "Christ made himself little by taking on our littleness" (*Christus se paruum fecit nostram paruitatem accipiendo*) also appears in the sermon *Puer Iesus*, Leonine ed., 44/1:104, in Thomas Aquinas, *The Academic Sermons*, ed. Mark-Robin Hoogland, CP (Washington, DC: Catholic University of America Press, 2010), 87–107.

11. Aquinas, *ST* III, q, 14, a. 1; Aquinas, *Super Phil.* 2, lect. 2, no. 60.

12. Aquinas, *ST* III, q, 15, a. 1

13. Aquinas, *ST* III, q, 14, a. 1.

Scripture, this expression sometimes denotes the body itself (cf. Gn 2:23; Job 10:11). Elsewhere, it refers to the vices of flesh and blood—"Flesh and blood have not revealed this to you" (Mt 16:17). Still other times, it signifies the corruptibility of flesh and blood: "flesh and blood cannot inherit the kingdom of God, nor does the perishable inherit the imperishable" (1 Cor 15:50). With this in mind, Thomas clarifies that the expression as used in Hebrews embraces two of the above meanings but "does not refer to vices, for Christ assumed a nature without sin, but with the possibility of suffering, because he assumed a flesh similar to the sinner 'in the likeness of sinful flesh'" (Rom 8:3).[14] In other words, it is to be understood as referring to "the very substance of animated flesh," which includes the possibility of suffering.[15] And so is it fitting, for Christ is not our brother in guilt, but he is so in bearing its punishment: "Therefore," Thomas says, "it behooved Him to have a nature that could suffer."[16]

Another relevant feature of Hebrews 2:15 that fascinates Thomas is the idea that Christ freed us from the fear of death.[17] But he asks, Why did Christ free us immediately from the cause of death and its fear but not also from death itself? One reason is that freeing us from bodily death would have led men to serve Christ only for their bodily good, which in turn would destroy the merit of faith and hope. Another is that bodily evils enable us to merit eternal life when we endure them virtuously, as demonstrated in

---

14. Aquinas, *Super Heb.* 2, lect. 4, no. 138, in *Commentary on the Letter of St. Paul to the Hebrews*, trans. Fabian R. Larcher (Lander, WY: Aquinas Institute for the Study of Sacred Doctrine, 2012).

15. Aquinas, *Super Heb.* 2, lect. 4, no. 139. For an important Patristic source that speaks to Christ taking on human nature in its entirety, see Athanasius, *On the Incarnation of the Word* (Crestwood, NY: St. Vladimir's Seminary Press, 2000). Of the many texts that could be marshalled to support Aquinas's treatment, we might recall Athanasius's teaching that "the Lord touched all parts of creation, and freed and undeceived them all from every deceit" (Athanasius, *On the Incarnation of the Word* §45, at 82). And then there is this marvelous passage: "The Word perceived that corruption could not be got rid of otherwise than through death; yet He Himself, as the Word, being immortal and the Father's Son, was such as could not die. For this reason, therefore, He assumed a body capable of death, in order that it, through belonging to the Word Who is above all, might become in dying a sufficient exchange for all, and, itself remaining incorruptible through His indwelling, might thereafter put an end to corruption for all others as well, by the grace of the resurrection" (Athanasius, *On the Incarnation of the Word* §9, at 35). And of course we would be remiss not to recall St. Gregory of Nazianzus's immortal line "The unassumed is unhealed." Letter 101, *The First Letter to Cledonius the Presbyter*, in *On God and Christ: The Five Theological Orations and Two Letters to Cledonius*, trans. Lionel Wickham (Crestwood, NY: St. Vladimir's Seminary Press, 2002), §5, at 158.

16. Aquinas, *Super Heb.* 2, lect. 4, no. 150.

17. Aquinas, *Super Heb.* 2, lect. 4, no. 144.

the life of the early Church: "through many tribulations we must enter the kingdom of God" (cf. Acts 14:21).[18]

Returning to Christ's human nature, Aquinas's exegesis of Hebrews 4:15 highlights what it means for him to have been "tempted as we are, yet without sin." Here, Thomas describes Christ's sufferings and temptations as establishing a kinship of mercy between him and us.[19] As we are tempted, so too Christ was tempted in the desert by the devil (cf. Mt 4). In this way, he truly knows our wretchedness by experience (*scit, per experientiam, miseriam nostram*), which, as God, he knew from all eternity by simple knowledge (*scivit per simplicem notitiam*).[20] According to Thomas, Christ was tempted in order to give us an example of how to handle temptation. He cites St. Peter to this effect: "Christ suffered for us, leaving you an example that you should follow in his footsteps" (1 Pt 2:21), and "Christ, therefore, having suffered in the flesh, be you also armed with the same thought" (1 Pt. 4:1). Additionally, he continues, if Christ had not experienced temptations, he could not have had true compassion ("to suffer with"). And, of course, if he had sinned, Jesus would not have been able to save us, but rather he himself would have needed saving.[21]

How, precisely, was Christ tempted? The Angelic Doctor immediately rules out one kind of temptation—that "from the flesh" (*a carne*), as this "always involves sin." In this lies an important difference between our experience of temptation and that of Christ, who had not the slightest movement of sin: "who did not sin, neither was guile found in his mouth" (1 Pt 2:22).[22] In other words, "in Christ there was no rebellion of the lower powers against the higher, but He suffered for us in the flesh."[23] Nevertheless, Christ was tempted by being enticed with prosperity (Mt 4:3) and terrified with adversity (Mt 27:40).

18. Aquinas, *Super Heb.* 2, lect. 4, no. 146.
19. Aquinas, *Super Heb.* 2, lect. 4, no. 146.
20. Aquinas, *Super Heb.* 2, lect. 4, no. 146.
21. Aquinas, *Super Heb.* 2, lect. 4, no. 237.
22. Aquinas, *Super Heb.* 2, lect. 4, no. 237.
23. Aquinas, *Super Heb.* 2, lect. 3, no. 236.

Human Sin, Suffering, and Death in
Aquinas's Biblical Theology

Having laid out the Angelic Doctor's understanding of the Last Adam, we now turn our attention to created human nature as it exists in those of us who have yet to be fully conformed to the likeness of Jesus Christ.

Death Is Natural to Man,
but God Did Not Create Us in a State of
Pure Nature (Rom 5)

A good place to begin is with Thomas's commentary on Romans 5:12–14, in which the Apostle tells us: "As sin came into the world through one man and death through sin, and so death spread to all men because all men sinned" and that "death reigned from Adam to Moses, even over those whose sins were not like the transgression of Adam, who was a type of the one who was to come." To explicate the Pauline notion that death entered the world through sin, Thomas cites Wisdom 1:12: "Ungodliness purchases death" (Wis 1:12; RSV: "Do not invite death by the error of your life"). To this he adds that Romans 5:12 must refer to original and not actual sin, for otherwise Paul would have said that sin entered the world through the devil, as actual sin did (Wis 2:24: "through the devil's envy death entered the world").[24]

Despite this biblical evidence connecting death with sin, Thomas notes that death seems to arise not from sin but from the nature of our bodies, seeing as they are material and thus corruptible by their very nature.[25] In light of this, he explains that human nature can be considered in two ways. According to our body's structural principles, death is indeed natural. But Thomas does not believe that man was created with purely natural endowments. In other words, he never experienced the state of *natura pura*. Aquinas finds confirmation of this teaching in Ecclesiastes 7:30: "God made man upright (*rectum*)." Through this grace of original justice that man possessed, divine providence initially prevented man from experiencing suffering and death.[26]

---

24. Aquinas, *Super Rom.* 5, lect. 3, no. 407, in *Commentary on the Letter of St. Paul to the Romans*, trans. Fabian R. Larcher (Lander, WY: Aquinas Institute for the Study of Sacred Doctrine, 2018).

25. Aquinas, *Super Rom. 5*, lect. 3, no. 416; Aquinas, *De malo*, q. 5, a. 5, s.c. 2, in *St. Thomas Aquinas on Evil*, trans. Richard Regan (Notre Dame, IN: University of Notre Dame Press, 1995).

26. Aquinas, *In II Sent.* d. 30, a. 1, q. 1. For a lengthy treatment of this point, see Jean-Pierre

Building on this foundation, Thomas explains in detail the harmonious relationships experienced by our first parents:

This justice was a state in which man's mind was under God, the lower powers of the soul under the mind, the body under the soul, and all external things under man, with the result that as long as man's mind remained under God, the lower powers would remain subject to reason, and the body to the soul by receiving life from it without interruption, and external things to man in the sense that all things would serve man, who would never experience any harm from them.

Divine providence planned this for man on account of the worth of the rational soul, which, being incorruptible, deserved an incorruptible body (*debebatur sibi incorruptibile corpus*). But because the body, which is composed of contrary elements, served as an instrument for the senses, and such a body could not in virtue of its nature be incorruptible, the divine power furnished which was lacking to human nature by giving the soul the power to maintain the body incorruptible.[27]

Thomas compares God's would-be act of perpetually preserving the health of our first parents to a metalworker maintaining his sword in such a way that it never rusts. As a sword remains intact as long as it is maintained, so man would not have died had he only allowed God to preserve his life.

No Suffering before the Fall

The Angelic Doctor teaches that prelapsarian man's flesh, subjected to his intellect, did not endure suffering or illness of any kind.[28] Sinless man would have used things in conformity with their design, with the result that thistles and thorns (which in Thomas's view already existed prior to man's entry into the world) originally served as food for animals and not to punish man.[29] Likewise, harmful plants and animals did not injure us thanks to

---

Torrell, OP, "Nature and Grace in Thomas Aquinas," in *Surnaturel: A Controversy at the Heart of Twentieth-Century Thomistic Thought*, ed. Serge-Thomas Bonino, OP (Ave Maria, FL: Sapientia Press, 2007), 155–87.

27. Aquinas, *Super Rom.* 5, lect. 3, no. 416; Aquinas, *De malo*, q. 5, a. 5, ad 16.

28. Aquinas, *Super Rom.* 8, lect. 1, no. 608. See also Aquinas, *ST* I, q. 72, a. 2, ad 3; Aquinas, *De Malo*, q. 5, a. 4, ad 7; Aquinas, *De veritate*, q. 25, a. 7, trans. James McGlynn (Chicago: Henry Regnery, 1953). For an insightful exploration of how Aquinas might have emended his precise position on this topic had he been privy to modern biology's understanding of infectious diseases and immunology, see Jordan Haddad, "Modern Biology's Contribution to Our Understanding of Christ's Sufferings," *Church Life Journal*, August 8, 2018.

29. Aquinas, *ST* II-II, q. 164, a. 2, ad 1.

God's providential protection.[30] Interestingly, Thomas nevertheless insists that the nature of animals was unchanged by man's sin. Although they posed no threat to us, a natural antipathy between certain animals has always existed, and there was (nonhuman) death before the Fall. Lions, then, were never herbivores.[31] The Angelic Doctor's great respect for the nature of things evinced here, combined with his openness to respectfully emending the Tradition when necessary, makes one suspect that—had he known of their existence—Thomas may well have contended that our hominin ancestors too had died.[32]

While Aquinas did not believe that our first parents suffered, it is significant that he did acknowledge the presence of passions in them, thereby affirming their true humanity. He contends that Adam and Eve experienced all of those passions "that casteth not down" (*non affligens*)—those involving the present good (e.g., joy and love) and those that regard future good to be had at the proper time (desire and hope).[33] Indeed, he says, "Perfection of moral virtue does not wholly take away the passions, but regulates them."[34] At the same time, he holds that "sorrow, guilt, and unhappiness are incompatible with the perfection of the primitive state" (*perfectioni enim primi status repugnat tam dolor, quam culpa et miseria*).[35]

---

30. Aquinas, *In II Sent.* d. 14, a. 5, q. 1, ad 7. I am indebted to Piotr Roszak for knowledge of this text.

31. Aquinas, *ST* I, q. 96, a. 1, ad 2. Indeed, in *ST* I, q. 48, a. 2, ad 3, Thomas offers the lion's predatory nature as an illustration that "God and nature and any other agent make what is best in the whole, but not what is best in every single part, except in order to the whole, as was said above." The reason for this, he explains, is that "many good things would be taken away if God permitted no evil to exist." Accordingly, Thomas observes that "fire would not be generated if air was not corrupted, nor would the life of a lion be preserved unless the ass were killed." Although Aquinas does not deploy the image of the dying and rising grain of wheat that Ratzinger does to make this point, one can see important common ground between these two thinkers who are convinced that God has always allowed evils—perhaps even death from the very beginning of creation—in order to bring about greater good. I find that *ST* I, q. 22, a. 2, likewise illumines this point well: "Corruption and defects in natural things are said to be contrary to some particular nature; yet they are in keeping with the plan of universal nature; inasmuch as the defect in one thing yields to the good of another, or even to the universal good ... Since God, then, provides universally for all being, it belongs to His providence to permit certain defects in particular effects, that the perfect good of the universe may not be hindered, for if all evil were prevented, much good would be absent from the universe."

32. Aquinas, *ST* I, q. 96, a. 1, ad 2.

33. Aquinas, *ST* I, q. 95, a. 2.

34. Aquinas, *ST* I, q. 95, a. 2, ad 3.

35. Aquinas, *ST* I, q. 95, a. 2.

The Fallout of the Fall

As we know well, man's state of innocence did not endure for long. Given the unity of the human race, the sin of Adam led to a series of cascading disorders that affected not just him but in turn all who ever since have partaken in the same nature.[36] Like an iron sword left to its own, man after turning his mind from God became corruptible, that is, subject to death from intrinsic sources and to violence from external ones.[37] Sin thus understood by Thomas is the accidental or indirect cause of human death. In other words, sin created a circumstance that permitted the direct cause of death (i.e., our bodily nature) to follow its natural course. Or, as Thomas explains in his commentary on the *Sentences*, death and suffering are not in themselves penalties (*poenae*) due to original sin but rather mere natural deficiencies (*naturales defectus*) that are common to every creature (*omnem creaturam*). If, however, we consider human nature as it was actually created (*instituta*) in a state of grace and original justice, suffering and death are indeed rightly understood as penalties.[38]

Aquinas offers a further analogy to clarify his point. As a man removing a stone from the pillar it had been holding up causes the entire edifice to come crashing down, so the loss of grace entailed by the rupture of our relationship with God resulted in damage to all of our other relationships—within our own soul, with other humans, with creation, and between our body and soul—and resulted in death, illness, and the other defects of our human nature.[39] Nothing was added to or subtracted from our nature after the fall; it was rather the loss of "the proper *relationship* of the body under control of the soul" that resulted in human suffering and death.[40]

It is also noteworthy that the relationship fallout from Adam's sin did not merely return humans to a state of *natura pura*. Aquinas makes this very point as he comments on the man from the parable of the Good Samaritan

---

36. Aquinas, *Super Rom.* 5, lect. 3, no. 410.

37. Aquinas, *Super Rom.* 5, lect. 3, no. 416.

38. Aquinas, *In II Sent.* d. 30, a. 1, q. 1. See also Torrell, "Nature and Grace in Thomas Aquinas," 162–63, 167, and the various texts he references, including Aquinas, *De Malo*, q. 4, a. 2, ad 1; q. 5, a. 1, ad 13.

39. Aquinas, *ST* I-II, q. 85, a. 5.

40. Aquinas, *De malo*, q. 5, a. 4, ad 7 (emphasis mine).

who fell among robbers on his way down to Jericho (Lk 10:30). Luke tells us that this individual was "wounded" and "stripped," which Thomas takes to mean that he was stripped of his gratuitous gifts and wounded in his natural ones. Again, nothing belonging to the substance of man was lost after sin: "Man's nature is the same before and after sin, but the state of his nature is not the same" (*eadem est natura hominis ante peccatum et post peccatum, non tamen est idem naturae status*).[41] Jean-Pierre Torrell summarizes this point well in saying that sin "made [man] not only unable to attain the supernatural end to which God had called him, but even unable to do the good that would have been within reach of his natural powers in the state of integral nature."[42] As we will see momentarily, Ratzinger also connects man's incapacity to live a life of virtue and attain salvation to the doctrine of original sin.

PART II: JOSEPH RATZINGER

On the subject of human suffering, foremost among the differences between Aquinas and Ratzinger is undoubtedly that the latter is privy to discoveries within the field of evolutionary biology. Evolution by natural selection reveals that death played an essential role in getting us from bacteria to humans. More to the point, it strongly suggests that the first humans were subject to death by virtue of their having descended from hominin ancestors who had been dying for millions of years before our species arrived on the scene of history. Can the evolutionary story about suffering and death coexist with Catholic doctrine of human origins? I believe that the key to a possible reconciliation may lie in examining how Ratzinger's kenotic Christology informs his anthropology.

---

41. Aquinas, *ST* III, q. 61, a. 2, ad 2.
42. Torrell, "Nature and Grace in Thomas Aquinas," 176; Aquinas, *ST* I-II, q. 85, a. 1, s.c. On our difficulty in receiving grace after sin, see Aquinas, *De malo*, q. 2, a. 11.

Christ the True Adam in
Ratzinger's Biblical Theology

Throughout his corpus, Ratzinger variously refers to Jesus as the "last man" (*letzte Mensch*), "exemplary man" (*exemplarischen Menschen*), "second Adam" (*zweite Adam*), "definitive Adam" (*endgültige Adam*), and even "Counter-Adam" (*Gegenadam*).[43] According to Ratzinger, man becomes man only when God becomes man: "in him is manifested for the first time the truth about what is meant by the riddle named 'man.'"[44] Winsomely summarizing this view, he relates: "From the standpoint of Christian faith one may say that for *history* (*Geschichte*) God [Christ] stands at the end, while for *being* (*Sein*) he [Christ] stands at the beginning."[45] Cast in Thomistic language, Christ the end is last in the order of execution, yet he is first in the order of the God's intention for creation.[46]

But what, precisely, does it mean for Christ to be the archetypal human being? As the definitive man, Jesus is pure relation, the one who empties himself in a complete gift to the other, who is entirely "transition" (*Pasch*) and for that reason "binds humanity and divinity into a unity."[47]

43. Ratzinger deployed this last formulation in his 1957 Mariology course at the Freising Seminary, the notes for which are housed in the Benedikt XVI Institut in Regensburg and have been expertly summarized in Emery de Gaál, "Mariology as Christology and Ecclesiology: Professor Joseph Ratzinger's Only Mariology Course," in *Joseph Ratzinger and the Healing of Reformation-Era Divisions*, ed. Emery de Gaál and Matthew Levering (Steubenville, OH: Emmaus Academic, 2019), 93–120. Following de Gaál, I refer to the manuscript of Ratzinger's Mariology lecture notes as *Scriptum*. For the term *Gegenadam* or "Counter-Adam," see de Gaál, "Mariology as Christology and Ecclesiology," 98, and *Scriptum*, 6.

44. Joseph Ratzinger, "On the Understanding of 'Person' in Theology," in *Dogma and Preaching* (San Francisco: Ignatius Press, 2011), 181–96, at 192.

45. Joseph Ratzinger, *Introduction to Christianity* (San Francisco: Ignatius Press, 2004), 242 [*Einführung in das Christentum*, 228].

46. For this language, see Aquinas, *ST* I-II, q. 1, a. 1, ad 1.

47. Ratzinger, *Introduction to Christianity*, 234, 236, 240. Commenting on Jn 12:32 ("And I, when I am lifted up from the earth, will draw all men to myself"), Ratzinger prolongs this meditation, "This sentence is intended to explain the meaning of Jesus' death on the Cross ... The event of the crucifixion appears there as a process of opening, in which the scattered man-monads are drawn into the embrace of Jesus Christ, into the wide span of his outstretched arms, in order to arrive, in this union, at their goal, the goal of humanity" (239–40). Ratzinger's understanding of Christ as "pure relation" in the above text is in keeping with his understanding that the defining feature of the human race is our ability to be "directly" or "immediately" in relation to God. See his "Belief in Creation and the Theory of Evolution," in *Dogma and Preaching* (San Francisco: Ignatius Press, 2011), 141–42. See also *God and the World* (San Francisco: Ignatius Press, 2002), 75.

Ratzinger by no means rejects the reality of man's immortal soul, though he does prefer to articulate

The Relationship of Sin, Suffering, and Death

An Existential Analysis of Death and
the Purpose of the Fall Narrative

The ineluctable nature of our call to find holiness through suffering is evident to us every day as creatures living in a fallen world. But the field of evolutionary biology challenges a long-standing feature of the Church's thought regarding man's relationship with suffering and death: the ancient tenet that both are present in our lives only as the result of original sin. Instead of jettisoning the doctrine of original sin on the one hand or discounting evolutionary science on the other, Ratzinger says that evolutionary biology has much to contribute to our grasp of creation and sin by helping us get down

---

the nature of soul according to his preferred personalist framework: "The distinguishing mark of man (*Das Unterscheidende des Menschen*), seen from above, is his being addressed by God, the fact that he is God's partner in a dialogue ... [H]aving a 'spiritual soul' means precisely being willed, known, and loved by God in a special way; it means being a creature called by God to an eternal dialogue and therefore capable for its own part of knowing God and of replying to him. What we call in substantialist language 'having a soul' (*haben Seele*) we will describe in a more historical, actual language as 'being God's partner in dialogue' (*Dialogpartner Gottes sein*) ... This does not mean that talk of the soul is false (as is sometimes asserted today by a one-sided and uncritical biblical approach); in one respect it is, indeed, even necessary in order to describe the whole of what is involved here. But, on the other hand, it also needs to be complemented if we are not to fall back into a dualistic conception that cannot do justice to the dialogic and personalistic view of the Bible" (*Introduction to Christianity*, 354–55).

Also, while he certainly accepts the broad strokes of evolutionary theory, Ratzinger roundly rejects a materialist account of man and the cosmos. For instance, in a rare writing published after this retirement, the emeritus pontiff wrote, "Only if things have a spiritual reason, are intended and conceived—only if there is a Creator God who is good and wants the good—can the life of man also have meaning" ("The Church and the Scandal of Sexual Abuse," Catholic News Agency, April 10, 2019, https://www.catholicnewsagency.com/news/full-text-of-benedict-xvi-the-church-and-the-scandal-of-sexual-abuse-59639). In an earlier essay specifically dedicated to the relationship of faith and evolution, he wrote similarly, "[Belief in creation] expresses the conviction that the world as a whole, as the Bible says, comes from the Logos, that is, from creative mind (*schöpferischen Sinn*) and represents the temporal form of its self-actuation (*die zeitliche Form seines Selbstvollzugs*) ... To believe in creation means to understand, in faith, the world of becoming revealed by science as a meaningful world that comes from a creative mind" ("Belief in Creation and the Theory of Evolution," 139–40). In the same essay, he writes, "Spirit is created and not the mere product of development, even though it comes to light by way of development" (*auch wenn er in der Weise der Entwicklung in Erscheinung tritt*)" (141). For an application of this to the afterlife, see Ramage, *The Experiment of Faith* (Washington, DC: Catholic University of America Press, 2020), 122–29. Even as he prefers to speak of the resurrection of the human person as a whole rather than the immortality of souls, these pages make it clear that Ratzinger resolutely rejects a materialist account of the soul and affirms the Christian hope for eternal life.

to the essentials of Pauline Christology and rendering it comprehensible again to modern man.[48]

Professor Ratzinger confronted the problem that evolution poses for traditional teaching in his 1964 Münster course on creation. Already at this early date, he was well aware that maintaining a strict causal and temporal connection between human sin and the onset of our mortality is difficult to square with the scientific data. This knowledge, in conjunction with his understanding that the Adam narrative was written in a mythopoetic key, leads Ratzinger to insist that "the purpose of the doctrine of the original state is not to recount a piece of empirical history and thus to expand our knowledge of history into the prehistoric, but to express the difference between the God-willed meaning of the creature man and the historically existing being man."[49] Further, Ratzinger suggests that when Paul speaks of death in Romans, "This does not mean physical dying, but that dying must have another meaning. It is about the state of separation from God."[50] Nevertheless, Ratzinger notes, there can be "no doubt" (*kein Zweifel*) that the Bible points to "a very close relationship between sin and death" (*zwischen Sünde und Tod eine sehr enge Verbindung*) and that this connection is based upon a "massive scriptural foundation" (*auf ein massives Schriftfundament stützen*).[51]

A similar position comes into view later in Ratzinger's commentary on *Gaudium et Spes* 18, wherein the council Fathers toed the traditional line

---

48. Ratzinger, *Introduction to Christianity*, 239. This particular comment comes after a sustained reflection on the contributions of Teilhard de Chardin's evolutionary Christology: "One can safely say that here the tendency of Pauline Christology is in its essentials correctly grasped from the modern angle and rendered comprehensible again, even if the vocabulary employed is certainly rather too biological." As he does with any thinker, Ratzinger here appropriates whatever truth he can from a given author, ancient or modern, while remaining critical where necessary.

49. Here and in what follows, citations from this course are identified according to the name of the course itself: *Schöpfungslehre* (1964). I have translated these unpublished lecture notes (*Vorlesungsmitschriften*) of Professor Ratzinger's courses on creation housed at the Institut Papst Benedikt XVI in Regensburg from the original German texts. Some I have taken directly from the notes manuscript, while other times I have taken them from the selections provided in Santiago Sanz, "Joseph Ratzinger y la doctrina de la creación: Los apuntes de Münster de 1964 (y III). Algunos temas debatidos," *Revista Española de Teología* 74 (2014): 453–96. When drawing from Sanz's selections, I also provide the location in his text where the citation occurs. The particular text cited here is located in Ratzinger, *Schöpfungslehre* (1964), 253; Sanz, "Joseph Ratzinger y la doctrina de la creación," 493n126.

50. Ratzinger, *Schöpfungslehre* (1964), 208.

51. Ratzinger, *Schöpfungslehre* (1964), 207.

that man would have been immune from death had he not sinned. On this text, council *peritus* Fr. Ratzinger remarks that the document's authors were well aware of the various problems germane to its teaching, and it is for this reason that they rejected a number of proposals to mention the preternatural gifts or to discuss the specifics of original sin and man's original condition.[52] Agreeing with the Fathers' decision, Ratzinger nevertheless expresses regret that the council had punted on a major difficulty; namely, "The thesis [that man would have been immune from death had he not sinned] in its classical dogmatic form is scarcely intelligible to present-day thought."[53] He then proposes an alternative. This teaching "could be made [intelligible] by means of an existential analysis of the constitutive features of human life which established a distinction between death as a natural phenomenon and death as seen in the personal categories proper to human life."[54]

What is death, then, if we approach it from this point of view? When we familiarize ourselves with the entirety of his corpus vis-à-vis this question, it becomes clear that Ratzinger wants to avoid pigeonholing the doctrine of original sin into so close a connection with death that it contradicts what we know through modern science. His personalist, existentialist approach therefore endeavors to get down to the essence of what it is about death that troubles man: the experience of dread, absurdity, and rebellion (or, in Thomistic terms, sorrow, guilt, unhappiness, and affliction).[55] From there, he sets out to explore how we might recast traditional teaching on the relationship between sin and death as an existential rather than historical proposition.

Suffering and Death Stem from
the Evolutionary Dynamic and from the
Cruciform Shape of This World

Ratzinger's emphasis on the crucified Christ as the exemplary man goes hand in hand with his view that the root *ratio* for human suffering and death is not sin but rather our finite creaturely condition inhabiting a world that is and was always intended to be cruciform. If we take the Paschal Mystery as

52. Joseph Ratzinger, "The Dignity of the Human Person," in *Commentary on the Documents of Vatican II*, vol. 5, ed. Herbert Vorgrimler (New York: Herder and Herder, 1969), 115–64, at 141.
53. Ratzinger, "Dignity of the Human Person," 141.
54. Ratzinger, "Dignity of the Human Person," 141. I am grateful to Nicholas Lombardo, OP, for calling my attention to this passage.
55. Ratzinger, "Dignity of the Human Person," 141.

the key to interpreting reality as such, it stands to reason that the experience of redemptive suffering that so characterized the Final Adam's entire earthly existence is constitutive of the human vocation as such.

In his 1985 Carinthian lectures, Ratzinger deployed images of creation that suggest that the entire cosmos has a kenotic structure: "If we read the Bible as a whole, the paschal mystery, the mystery of the dying grain of wheat appears before us already among the ideas of creation."[56] This cosmic vision traces all the way back to Ratzinger's time in the academy. Specifically, the following statements from Ratzinger's 1964 course on creation illustrate his conviction that the world itself has a cruciform shape:

The fate of death is not a special destiny of sinful man, but the mystery of death is the stamp of the whole creation (*die Prägeform der ganzen Schöpfung*).[57]

Suffering and death are the foundational principles (*Grundprinzipien*) upon which the whole interplay of the world is built."[58]

Suffering and death are not peripheral, but belong to the structuring principles (*Bauprinzipien*) of the world; they are embedded in the grain itself, and whoever wanted to take that away would dissolve the world as such (*würde die Welt als so auflösen*).[59]

Taken together, Ratzinger concludes that all the evidence we have at our disposal today "makes it impossible to uphold the said teaching (i.e., original sin) *in the usual way*" (*in der üblichen Weise*).[60]

As we now know that suffering and death have always been integral ingredients in the evolutionary process, Ratzinger thus cautions against insisting that human beings were initially exempt from this experience. In sections of his course dedicated to the preternatural gifts, we read that the Church's teaching "does not include the thesis that there was no earthly death without sin."[61] He then elucidates this position in great detail, as can be glimpsed in his saying:

---

56. Joseph Ratzinger, *Gottes Projekt: Nachdenken über Schöpfung und Kirche* (Regensburg: Pustet, 2009), 63 (my translation).

57. Ratzinger, *Schöpfungslehre* (1964), 211.

58. Ratzinger, *Schöpfungslehre* (1964), 215.

59. Ratzinger, *Schöpfungslehre* (1964), 215.

60. Ratzinger, *Schöpfungslehre* (1964), 215. The emphasis here is mine, attempting to show that Ratzinger of course is not denying the doctrine of original sin, but rather questioning common interpretations of it.

61. Ratzinger, *Schöpfungslehre* (1964), 208.

According to the usual teaching, the main consequences of the Fall are concu-piscence and rule of death ... But the phenomenology of man shows that pre-cisely these two realities of man [desires/suffering and death] are as indispensable (*wegzudenken*) to him as the suffering from the world ... What applies to desire (*Trieb*) also applies to pain, (*Schmerz*), to the presence of death in our lives. As man is built (*So wie der Mensch gebaut ist*), pain and suffering are a necessary con-stituent (*notwendiges Konstitutiv*) of his physical existence.[62]

This text reveals that, at least as of 1964, Ratzinger explicitly taught that physical suffering, death, and the presence of our concupiscible desires were not the result of the Fall but rather constitutive of the graced condition of human nature in which we were created. Moreover, a number of later writ-ings indicate that Benedict XVI continued to think along these lines even through his tenure as Supreme Pontiff. In his encyclical *Spe Salvi*, we thus read that man does not want to die, and yet "neither do we want to continue living indefinitely, nor was the earth created with that in view."[63] What is more, later in this text Benedict distinguishes two reasons that suffering is present as part of human existence. On the one hand, it stems "partly from the mass of sin which has accumulated over the course of history, and con-tinues to grow unabated today." On the other hand, "Suffering stems partly from our finitude."[64] From statements like these, it appears that Benedict thinks suffering is constitutive of the human experience itself on this side of eternity regardless of the mass of sin that exacerbates it. That said, the emer-itus pontiff refrains from deeming it part of human nature as such. Indeed, if this were the case, it would raise significant problems, such as: What, then, do we make of life in heaven? Do Christ, Mary, and the saints suffer forever? Or do they cease to be human? Ratzinger never addresses these questions, but it is unlikely that he would countenance affirmative answers to them.[65]

---

62. Ratzinger, *Schöpfungslehre* (1964), 216.

63. Benedict XVI, *Spe Salvi*, §11.

64. Benedict XVI, *Spe Salvi*, §36.

65. Moreover, even if Ratzinger holds that suffering and death are constitutive of human nature in this world, it is highly unlikely that Ratzinger would countenance the view that suffering exists within God, who is love. It seems clear to me that when Ratzinger speaks of the deep connection that exists between love and suffering, he has us creatures in mind and leaves it at that. As an indication of this, Benedict explains that, while there are no passions in God, he does have compassion: "God cannot suffer, but he can 'suffer *with*.'" Benedict XVI, *Jesus of Nazareth: From the Baptism in the Jordan to the Transfiguration* (New York: Doubleday, 2007), 87.

There Can Be No Love without Suffering

Not only does Benedict consider suffering and death integral to our created universe, but he also insists that they are necessary for human flourishing in this present world. So strongly does he hold this conviction that Professor Ratzinger said that "a person without suffering (*leidloser*) in the world in which we live would be a monster and unrealizable … Suffering and death are essential to the structure of things" (*wesentlich zur Struktur der Dinge*).[66] Ratzinger would later add in *Eschatology*: "Of course, suffering can and should be reduced … But the will to do away with it completely would mean a ban on love (Ächtung der Liebe) and therewith the abolition of man."[67]

In his interview *God and the World*, Cardinal Ratzinger spoke similarly:

Pain is part of being human. Anyone who really wanted to get rid of suffering would have to get rid of love before anything else, because there can be no love without suffering (*Und wer das Leiden wirklich abschaffen wollte, müßte vor allen Dingen auch die Liebe abschaffen, die es ohne Leiden gar nicht gibt*), because it always demands an element of self-sacrifice, because, given temperamental differences and the drama of situations, it will always bring with it renunciation and pain.

When we know that the way of love—this exodus, this going out of one-self—is the true way by which man becomes human, then we also understand that suffering is the process through which we mature. Anyone who has inwardly accepted suffering becomes more mature and understanding of others, becomes more human (*menschlicher*). Anyone who has consistently avoided suffering does not understand other people; he becomes hard and selfish.[68]

It turns out, then, that for Ratzinger, "suffering is the inner side of love" (*Leiden eine Innenseite von Liebe ist*), which gives each of us the opportunity to be "reshaped" (*umgestalten*) by learning how to suffer well.[69]

Perhaps this sheds some insight into God's will to create life by means of evolutionary processes. For, if we are to truly be conformed to the image of Christ and rise with him, we must give ourselves away in a sincere gift of self through suffering and death. Pope Benedict himself said as much:

66. Ratzinger, *Schöpfungslehre* (1964), 215; Sanz, "Joseph Ratzinger y la doctrina de la creación," 493nn125.

67. Joseph Ratzinger, *Eschatology: Death and Eternal Life* (Washington, DC: Catholic University of America Press, 1988), 103. [*Eschatologie*, 91.]

68. Ratzinger, *God and the World*, 322.

69. Ratzinger, *God and the World*, 323.

In suffering there is also a profound meaning, and only if we can give meaning to pain and suffering can our life mature. I would say, above all, that there can be no love without suffering (*non è possibile l'amore senza il dolore*), because love always implies renouncement of myself, letting myself go and accepting the other in his otherness ... The inseparability of love and suffering, of love and God, are elements that must enter into the modern conscience to help us live.[70]

As I understand him here, the reason that Benedict considers suffering and death so essential to our experience is that our lives only find their fulfillment in the taking up of our master's cross, that *theosis* comes only through *kenosis*.

Benedict's thought in this regard is especially clear on other occasions where he explicitly casts our experience of suffering in a Christological context. Thus at a General Audience we hear him saying, "The Cross reminds us that there is no true love without suffering, there is no gift of life without pain" (*non esiste vero amore senza sofferenza, non c'è dono della vita senza dolore*).[71] Yet the then pontiff immediately added, Jesus's closeness to us in his *kenosis* means that our suffering "without ceasing to be suffering becomes, despite everything, a hymn of praise."[72]

In closing out this point, we must of course remember that the emeritus pontiff is speaking and writing in a postlapsarian world—"the world in which we live," as he said on one occasion referenced above.[73] It is therefore ultimately not clear whether or not Ratzinger thinks unfallen man would have been immune from death and suffering. One thing seems clear, though: Ratzinger views suffering as essential for human fulfillment in this vale of tears and has been around from the beginning. And in this we find an important point of contact with Aquinas, who also held that suffering and death predated the existence of man.

70. Benedict XVI, Meeting with the Clergy of the Dioceses of Belluno-Feltre and Treviso, July 24, 2007.

71. Benedict XVI, General Audience, September 17, 2008.

72. Benedict XVI, *Spe Salvi*, §37.

73. Ratzinger, *Schöpfungslehre* (1964), 215; Sanz, "Joseph Ratzinger y la doctrina de la creación," 493nn125.

CONCLUSION

In the end, I consider Aquinas's and Ratzinger's kenotic Christologies as two necessary ingredients in any anthropology that would seek to illumine the presence of suffering and death in our evolving universe. I believe that putting these two into dialogue with one another is necessary for telling a coherent story about who man is, why he suffers and dies, and in what lies his ultimate vocation.

Thomas's thought remains crucial and timely. Moreover, a number of erudite Thomists currently working on this problem have demonstrated that the traditional teaching on the original state may be understood in ways that are compatible with the evidence of universal common ancestry that has been unearthed through evolutionary science. For example, it has always struck me as evident that, given our ancestry and barring a special grace from God, humans would have inherited suffering and death from our hominin ancestors, along with inclinations that are rightly considered disordered in humans. As a response to this problem, I find particularly helpful Nicanor Austriaco's recasting of the preternatural gifts as "preteradaptive gifts." Austriaco writes, "Human beings by their very nature are prone to interior disarray because what we are inclined to know, what we are inclined to choose, and what we are inclined to desire often do not coincide. The gift of integrity was given to our first parents to overcome this interior disorder."[74]

For his part, Ratzinger emphasizes that the world itself has a paschal structure and steers clear of speculating about a causal or temporal connection between original sin and the onset of suffering and death that Thomas makes explicit. But it seems likely that Ratzinger sees the deep connection between suffering and love as something that belongs to our condition in this present world and not constitutive of human nature itself. Yet even if on Ratzinger's view suffering and death are natural to man in this world, sin is not—just the capacity for it that comes with being free yet not confirmed in grace. If we are to believe St. Paul, even that evil which is to be pinned

---

74. Nicanor Austriaco, OP, "How Did God Create Homo Sapiens through Evolution?," in *Thomistic Evolution: A Catholic Approach to Understanding Evolution in the Light of Faith*, 2nd ed., ed. Nicanor Austriaco et al. (Tacoma, WA: Cluny Media, 2019), 156.

squarely on the shoulders of us humans ultimately proves to be an occasion for joy (cf. Rom 5:20). *Felix culpa.* Or, in the words of Aquinas, "God allows evils to happen in order to bring a greater good therefrom."[75]

What would the original human experience of suffering and death have looked like on Ratzinger's view? From his various works, we may infer that it would have looked much like the life and dormition of the Blessed Virgin, whom Aquinas and Ratzinger both regard as sinless and yet having experienced suffering, sorrow, and death before being assumed. Or, to pivot from Mariology back to Christology, suffering before the Fall likely would have looked like Christ's suffering in Gethsemane and on the cross—not a desirable experience itself but the occasion for a synergy of wills in which man handed himself over to God, saying, "Not my will, but thine be done!" (Lk 22:42).[76] Another way Ratzinger captures this is by saying that if Jesus is the exemplary man, then his existence concerns all mankind.[77] This point is so important for the emeritus pontiff that, in his view, Christology is anthropology,[78] and man's Christification is the *telos* of evolution.[79]

In light of the above, I would suggest that the above approach might be further explicated by applying Aquinas's language to our contemporary context that the Angelic Doctor himself had no way of envisioning. As we have seen, Thomas responds affirmatively to the question of whether or not mankind's progenitors experienced passions. We also know, however, that Aquinas considers the first humans to have been free from the passions of sorrow, guilt, unhappiness (*dolor, culpa, miseria*), and affliction (*affligio*) that attended any difficulties they experienced. Given our knowledge of evolution and Ratzinger's approach detailed above, I would propose using these categories to consider the possibility that unfallen man would have experienced suffering of many kinds, but that—as we see in the life of Christ— it would not have caused in him any of the misery and affliction that we

---

75. Aquinas, *ST* III, q. 1, a. 3, ad 3. See also *ST* I, q. 2, a. 3, ad 1, with Thomas's reference to Augustine, *Enchiridion*, xi.

76. For a brief and clear exposition of Maximus's teaching on the two wills of Christ, see Benedict XVI, General Audience: St. Maximus the Confessor, June 25, 2008.

77. Ratzinger, *Introduction to Christianity*, 236.

78. For a discussion of this point in Ratzinger's commentary on *Gaudium et Spes*, see Ratzinger, "Dignity of the Human Person," 118–19, and remarks on the text in Emery de Gaál, *The Theology of Pope Benedict XVI: The Christocentric Shift* (New York: Palgrave Macmillan, 2010), 107–8.

79. Ratzinger, *Introduction to Christianity*, 236–37. [*Einführung in das Christentum*, 223.]

experience because of our inept, rebellious response to trials. To put it in Ratzinger's personalist language, I would say that the problem is not pain per se but rather our *relationship* with the pain—whether we receive it as a gift, accepting it as part of God's plan for us, or if we instead rebel against it. I am therefore attracted to the possibility that the grace lost by our forebears not being something that would have prevented us from dying but rather that which *would allow us to die well*—with Christ and in Christ in a cruciform gift of self-abandonment to the Father's will.

Even so, I do not see how we will ever have certainty on the question of whether or not original justice would have entailed human immortality and impassibility. Indeed, in one of his lectures, Ratzinger interprets the cherubim and flaming sword placed outside Eden (Gn 3:24) as a symbol of the reality that "the empirical history of the paradise state is no longer within reach."[80] Lacking direct experience of what a sinless world might look like, all we can do is to propose ways by which kenotic Christology might help to illumine the realities of suffering and death that are so integral to life in our evolving world as we know it. This essay has contended that Aquinas and Ratzinger offer ways to do this that are congruous at a deep level.

There may be other ways to harmonize the role of death so integral to evolution by natural selection with the doctrine of original sin. For instance, St. Maximus the Confessor offers a way to affirm that suffering and death have been around from the beginning *and* at the same time remain somehow causally connected to sin. Maximus proposes the possibility that "God created matter in this way from the beginning, according to His foreknowledge, in view of the transgression He had already seen in advance."[81] Seen from

80. Ratzinger, *Schöpfungslehre* (1964), 214; Sanz, "Joseph Ratzinger y la doctrina de la creación," 492n123. On our lack of experience of a sinless world and consequent inability to know what it would be like, see also Luis Ladaria, *Teología del pecado original y de la gracia*, 2nd ed. (Madrid: Biblioteca de Autores Cristianos, 2001), 47.

81. Maximus the Confessor, *Ambigua*, 8, trans. Nicholas Constas, in *On Difficulties in the Church Fathers: The Ambigua*, vol. 1 (Cambridge, MA: Harvard University Press, 2014), 145. I am grateful to Nicholas Lombardo, OP, for sharing this reference with me. For a survey of this and other patristic views on this topic, see his "Evil, Suffering, and Original Sin," in *The Oxford Handbook of Catholic Theology*, ed. Lewis Ayres and Medi Ann Volpe (Oxford: Oxford University Press, 2019), 141. See also Maximus, *Ambigua*, 42, and Maximus, *On Difficulties in Sacred Scripture: The Responses to Thalassios* (Washington, DC: Catholic University of America Press, 2018), 59, 61. For an illuminating discussion of these patristic texts, see also Hans Urs von Balthasar, *Cosmic Liturgy: The Universe According to Maximus the Confessor*, trans. Brian Daley, SJ (San Francisco: Ignatius Press, 1988), 187.

this perspective, suffering and hardships have always been part of God's plan to help man "come to an awareness of himself and his proper dignity" and thereby detach himself from the material things of this world that keep him from God. This perspective has the benefit of maintaining the connection between original sin and the experience of physical suffering and death while cohering with the likelihood that the suffering and death that have always been part of earthly reality, allowed by God in order to make room for love. To recast Maximus's insight along Ratzingerian lines, one might say that God created a world with suffering not primarily in view of *sin* but rather in view of *love*.

In the end, our knowledge of the events that transpired at the origin of human history is limited. Yet, thankfully, the most important thing about our human nature is something we do in fact know with certainty: that the crucified and risen Jesus is the true and definitive Adam who reveals man to himself, and that we will therefore find ourselves only through a sincere gift of self in union with our Lord's *kenosis*. Seen in this light, the very imperfection of our evolving world with all the suffering it entails affords us creatures the opportunity to become ever more like Christ—and thereby more like God. No matter where each of us comes down on the issue of whether human suffering and death would have been part of a sinless world, my hope is that this essay has cast fresh light on this profound relationship between suffering and love and on what the New Adam has to do with it all.

CHAPTER 13

"NO ONE KNOWS WHO DOES NOT FIRST TASTE"

The Spiritual Senses in Aquinas's Christology

Gerald P. Boersma

Knowledge of divine realities by way of experience or connaturality is an important feature of St. Thomas's religious epistemology. This theme is particularly prominent in two contexts: first, in the discussion of the invisible missions of Son and Spirit to the soul of the believer, and second, in the discussion of wisdom and understanding that are the gifts of the Holy Spirit. In these contexts, Thomas draws especially on the language of *taste* and *touch* to articulate how the spiritual senses operate with respect to apprehending the things of God. After briefly surveying the category of experiential knowledge generated by the invisible missions and the gifts of wisdom and understanding, I argue that the spiritual senses are an extension of St. Thomas's Christology. The spiritual senses express the experiential movements—especially of taste and touch—that belong to the saint as a member of Christ's mystical body.

EXPERIENTIAL KNOWLEDGE AND THE INVISIBLE MISSIONS

In the *Commentary on the Sentences*, Aquinas contrasts speculative knowledge of God with the experiential knowledge of God generated in the soul that is the terminus of the invisible missions: "Each of them (Son or Spirit) is sent when he is known. This is to be understood as not only a speculative knowledge (*cognitione speculativa*), but also a knowing that has a certain experiential character (*quodammodo experimentalis*). This is shown by what follows: '[known] and perceived,' ([*cognoscitur*] *atque percipitur*) which suggests an experience properly speaking (*proprie experientiam*) in the gift possessed."[1] The origin of the phrase "known and perceived" (*cognoscitur atque percipitur*) is the fourth book of Augustine's *De Trinitate* and is the wellspring of considerable medieval commentary.[2] Peter Lombard suggests that the African doctor hereby distinguishes two ways the Son is "sent": he is "known" (*cognoscitur*) when he is sent in the flesh in the Incarnation (i.e., a visible mission), and he is "perceived" (*percipitur*) in the souls of the just when he is experienced in love (i.e., an invisible mission). Subsequent commentary on Lombard's *Sentences* gave considerable attention to the Augustinian phrase "known and perceived" (*cognoscitur atque percipitur*) as articulating the distinction between the visible and invisible divine missions.[3] In the subsequent distinction in the *Scriptum*, Thomas maintains, "In the invisible mission of the Holy Spirit, grace overflows into the soul on account of the fullness of the divine love. And through that effect of grace, the experiential knowledge of this divine person is received by one to whom this mission is made (*cognitio illius personae diuinae experimentalis ab ipso cui fit missio*)."[4]

To what degree is this experiential knowing *intellectual*? This is a much-debated question. Some commentators hold that Thomas intends a wholly emotional, nondiscursive, noncognitive type of knowing. Others give a thoroughly intellectualist vector to *experimentalis cognitio*. I will return

---

1. *In I Sent*. d. 15, a. 3, q. 5, *expos. expositio secundae partis textus* (translation mine).

2. Augustine, *Trin* 4.28 (trans. Edmund Hill): "[The Word] is precisely sent to anyone when he is known and perceived (*cognoscitur atque percipitur*) by him, as far as he can be perceived and known to the capacity of a rational soul either making progress toward God or already made perfect in God. So the Son of God is not said to be sent in the very fact that he is born of the Father, but either in the fact that the Word made flesh showed himself to this world; about this fact he says, *I went forth from the Father and came into this world* (Jn 16:28). Or else he is sent in the fact that he is perceived in time by someone's mind, as it says, *Send her to be with me and labor with me* (Wis 9:10). That he is born means that he is from eternity to eternity—he is *the brightness of eternal light* (Wis 7:26). But that he is sent means that he is known by somebody in time."

3. Cf. John F. Dedek, "Quasi experimentalis cognitio: A Historical Approach to the Meaning of St. Thomas," *Theological Studies* 22 (1961): 357–90.

4. *In I Sent*. d. 16, a. 2, q. 1, co. (translation mine).

to this question later. Regardless, it is clear that for Thomas, the indwelling of the divine persons in the soul of the just effects a new type of unitive or connatural knowledge of God that is experiential. In the Dominican's discussion of the divine missions in the *Summa* (*ST* I, q. 43), he argues that the Son is sent "not in accordance with every and any kind of intellectual perfection, but according to the intellectual illumination, which breaks forth into the affection of love."[5] Drawing once again on the much-discussed quotation from Augustine, Thomas remarks, "Thus Augustine plainly says: *The Son is sent, whenever He is known and perceived* (cognoscitur atque percipitur) *by anyone.* Now perception implies a certain experimental knowledge (*experimentalem ... notitiam*); and this is properly called wisdom (*sapientia*), as it were a sweet knowledge (*sapida scientia*)."[6] Tasting, savoring, and relishing are the verbs Thomas uses to expresses the connatural or experiential knowledge of God given to the saint in the invisible missions.

EXPERIENTIAL KNOWLEDGE
AND THE GIFTS OF WISDOM
AND UNDERSTANDING

The second context in which Thomas addresses experiential or connatural knowledge of God is his discussion of the gifts of wisdom and understanding. In Christian maturity, the distinct and radical union of God and the soul effected in baptism manifests itself through the gifts and virtues. The Thomist tradition identifies these as habits; that is, the gifts and virtues articulate the divine life insinuated in the intellectual and moral fiber of the baptized.[7] The life of God becomes "connatural" to the saint. The intel-

---

5. *ST* I, q. 43, a. 5, ad 2. All quotations from the *Summa Theologiae* are from the translation by the Fathers of the English Dominican Province (New York: Benziger, 1948).

6. *ST* I, q. 43, q. 5, ad 2: *Et ideo signanter dicit Augustinus quod filius mittitur, cum a quoquam cognoscitur atque percipitur, perceptio enim experimentalem quandam notitiam significat. Et haec proprie dicitur sapientia, quasi sapida scientia.* Bernard McGinn notes, "Thomas, like most medieval thinkers, derived *sapientia* from *sapida scientia*, that is, knowledge that 'tastes' its object, rather than merely considering it from afar or abstractly." "'Contemplatio Sapientialis': Thomas Aquinas's Contribution to Mystical Theology," *Ephemerides Theologicae Lovanienses* 95 (2019): 327.

7. The Spanish Dominican Francisco *Marín-Sola, in The Homogeneous Evolution of Catholic Dog-*

lectual gifts of wisdom and understanding allow for a new sense (a taste or touch) for divine truth that is principally not speculative but affective.[8]

Three texts from the *Summa* demonstrate the connection between the intellectual gifts and connatural knowledge of divine truth.[9] First, in addressing the nature of *sacra doctrina* (*ST* I, q. 1, a. 6), Thomas distinguishes two ways according to which wisdom renders judgment: by inclination (*per modum inclinationis*) and by cognition (*per modum cognitionis*). Thomas quotes Dionysius, whose mentor Hierotheus was "taught not by mere learning, but by experience of divine things (*patiens divina*)."[10] Second, in the question on wisdom (*ST* II-II, q. 45), Thomas contends, "It belongs to the wisdom that is an intellectual virtue to pronounce right judgment about Divine things after reason has made its inquiry (*ex rationis inquisitione*), but it belongs to wisdom as a gift of the Holy Ghost to judge aright about them on account of connaturality (*quandam connaturalitatem*) with them."[11] Here Thomas advances the same quotation from Dionysius: "Hierotheus is perfect in Divine things, for he not only learns, but also experiences Divine things (*patiens divina*)."[12] Divine caritas obtains this unique, connatural wisdom: "Now this sympathy or connaturality for Divine things is the result of charity, which unites us to God, according to 1 Corinthians 6:17: 'He who is

---

ma, trans. Antonio T. Piñon (Manilla: Santo Tomas University Press, 1988), describes how connatural knowledge becomes a habit, i.e., a new *sensing* nature:

> That faith, that grace, that charity, those virtues, those gifts—especially the gifts of wisdom, understanding, and knowledge—are objective supernatural realities, *second natures*, grafted onto what in modern parlance would be called the *subconscious* of our being. By means of them we are able to perceive, judge, and develop connaturally, intuitively, through contact, quasi experimentally, many supernatural truths which the speculative theologian comes to know only through science, as a conclusion, through study, through laborious reasoning. (403)

8. *ST* II-II, q. 162, a. 3, ad 1: "Knowledge of truth is twofold. One is purely speculative … the other knowledge of truth is affective." Although the discussion of connatural knowledge is most explicit in Thomas's theology of the gifts of the Holy Spirit, the broader category of "affective knowing" equally undergirds his theology of the virtues and emotions. See Thomas Ryan, "Revisiting Affective Knowledge and Connaturality in Aquinas," *Theological Studies* 66 (2005): 49–68.

9. An important locus for Thomas's treatment of connatural knowledge through the gift of wisdom is the early sentence commentary (*In III Sent.* d. 34–36). Here Thomas also identifies the union with God through charity as the cause of a supernatural wisdom that involves a "taste of experience" (*In III Sent.* d. 34, q. 1, a. 2, 2c).

10. *ST* I, q. 1, a. 6, ad 3.

11. *ST* II-II, q. 45, a. 2.

12. *ST* II-II, q. 45, a. 2; translation altered.

joined to the Lord, is one spirit.'"[13] Finally, in *ST* II-II, q. 97, a. 2, ad 2, we read,

> There is a twofold knowledge of God's goodness or will. One is speculative (*speculativa*) … the other knowledge of God's will or goodness is affective or experimental (*affectiva seu experimentalis*) and thereby a man experiences in himself the taste of God's sweetness, and complacency in God's will (*experitur in seipso gustum divinae dulcedinis et complacentiam divinae voluntatis*), as Dionysius says of Hierotheos (*Div. Nom.* ii) that "he learnt divine things through experience (*ex compassione*) of them." It is in this way that we are told to prove God's will, and to taste His sweetness (*gustemus eius suavitatem*).[14]

The identical quotation from Dionysius in all three texts from the *Summa* underscores both the *immediacy* of experiential or connatural knowledge and the soul's *passivity* to such knowledge.[15] Connatural knowledge is affective knowledge of God, which belongs to the saint who "experiences in himself the taste of God's sweetness."[16] The saint has become morally and intellectually acclimatized to divine things through experience and has developed new spiritual senses to savor the things of God.[17]

13. *ST* II-II, q. 45, a. 2.

14. *ST* II-II, q. 97, a. 2, ad 2.

15. Thomas's most extensive discussion of Dionysius's description of his master Hierotheus "suffering divine things" is (unsurprisingly) in the *Commentary on the Divine Names*, which I treat below (*DDN*, c. 2, lect. 4, nos. 189–92). Bernhard Blankenhorn's masterful study *The Mystery of Union with God* (Washington, DC: Catholic University of America Press, 2015) considers the Dionysian features of Thomas's account of union with God. Blankenhorn points out that Eriugena's Latin translation of Dionysius is the source of not only Gallus's "affective" interpretation, but also of the interpretation given by Albert and Aquinas. Eriugena translates Hierotheus's experience of "not only learning but suffering divine things" as "not only learning but also an affection for divine things (*affectus divina*)" (42).

16. The seventeenth-century Dominican John of St. Thomas, in *The Gifts of the Holy Spirit*, trans. Dominic Hughes (New York: Sheed and Ward, 1951), 4.4, offers what is perhaps the most trenchant treatment of connatural knowledge of divine truth realized through the gifts of wisdom and understanding. He accents the saint's distinct union with God as the wellspring of this wisdom:

> Its [the gift of wisdom] judgment is unique, proceeding from a special impulse, by which the mind is elevated to judge with promptitude, and by which the soul is united and subjected to God from a connaturality and experience of divine things.… The gift of wisdom does not judge from any knowledge derived from study and reasoning about causes or even by a light which manifests them in themselves. It judges from a connaturality and union with the supreme cause which is possessed as it were through experience. (124–25)

John of St. Thomas underscores the immediacy and intimacy of connatural knowledge given through gifts of wisdom and understanding. This immediacy is also the emphasis in St. Thomas's treatment, for which reason the spiritual senses—especially touch and taste—play such a decisive role in his account of the intellectual gifts.

17. Cf. *ST* II-II, q. 24, a. 11: "For just as the sense of taste judges flavors according to its own dis-

THE *CORPUS MYSTICUM*
AND THE SPIRITUAL SENSES

Experiential or connatural knowledge is not simply a heightened spiritual sensitivity, some type of unique spiritual superpower. The recurring emphasis in Thomas's treatment of the invisible missions and the gifts of the Holy Spirit falls on the participatory character of this connatural knowledge. The formal cause of the spiritual senses is the saint's union with God, whereby he experientially discerns divine things in participation with Christ the Head as a member of his mystical body.[18] Although Thomas's entire corpus contains only approximately fifteen explicit references to the "spiritual senses," the bulk of those are found in discussion of Christ's mystical body.[19]

The efficient cause of the spiritual senses is baptism, which communicates a new spiritual life along with the attendant spiritual senses of that life. The baptized are united to God and incorporated into Christ's mystical body. The gift of divine filiation given in baptism allows the soul to become the terminus of the invisible missions and bestows the gifts of the Spirit according to which the soul is moved with docility to the promptings of the

---

position, so too a man's mind judges something to be done according to his own habitual disposition. Hence, in *Ethics* 3 the Philosopher says, 'As each one is, so will such-and-such an end seem to him.'" John of St. Thomas comments, "The formal nature by which wisdom knows the highest causes is an internal experience of God and divine things. It is a taste, love, delight, or internal contact, of the will with spiritual things. By reason of its union with spiritual truth the soul is, as it were, made connatural to things divine.... The divine reasons through which wisdom proceeds to give its account are not known in their essence by this gift of wisdom, but lovingly, mystically, and for a connaturality and union, or interior experience of divine things" (*Gifts of the Holy Ghost*, 4.6, 4.8, 125–26).

18. *ST* III, q. 69, a. 5. A key text is *In Philipp.* lect. 2.52, in which Aquinas details how the five spiritual senses realize by "experience" the Apostle's injunction: "Let this mind be in you, which was also in Christ Jesus."

19. Richard Cross maintains that Thomas makes only fifteen explicit references to the spiritual senses in his oeuvre. "Thomas Aquinas," in *The Spiritual Senses: Perceiving God in Western Christianity*, ed. Paul Gavrilyuk and Sarah Coakley (Cambridge: Cambridge University Press, 2012), 185. A lemma search in the "Library of Latin Texts" (Brepols) for various forms of *sensus spiritualis* indicates the paucity of Thomas's treatment of the topic. Of the approximately twenty-five references to forms of *sensus spiritualis* (and eighteen to various forms of *sensus interior*), the majority concern the spiritual interpretation of Scripture. Texts that I do not treat here but that have bearing on the doctrine of the spiritual senses of the soul include *ST* III, q. 8, a. 2, c; *In III Sent.* d. 13, a. 2, q. 3, obj. 2; *In IV Sent.* d. 5, a. 1, q. 3, 2 c; *De Ver.* 27, 3 obj. 5; *De Ver.* 27, 4 c; *Super I Cor.* 11, lect. 1; *Super I Cor.* 12, no. 17; *Super II Cor.* 11, lect. 1; *Super epistolam ad Ephesios lectura*, 1.8.71.

Spirit. It is important to note that the spiritual senses are not reserved to a spiritual elite—say, mystics—but are part and parcel of the new life bestowed in baptism.[20]

It is axiomatic for Thomas that the soul receives knowledge of sensible realities through the physical senses in an experiential mode.[21] A parallel epistemology operates with respect to divine truth. The spiritual senses perceive the things of God in an experiential manner. Just as our natural life is equipped with physical senses to apprehend the material quiddity of sensible realities, so, in an analogous fashion, the supernatural life given in baptism is equipped with spiritual senses to apprehend divine realities.

20. Admittedly, the spiritual senses of some are more "attuned" to the things of God than others. Thomas's treatment of folly (*stultitia*) (*ST* II-II, q. 46) is an important locus for discussion of the spiritual senses. Folly dulls the spiritual senses and, in its extreme, metastasizes into fatuity, which denotes the "entire privation of the spiritual sense" (*ST* II-II, q. 46, a. 1). Thomas describes folly as the loss of taste or *sapor* for divine things and develops the etymology provided by Isadore of Seville (*Etymologiarum libri X*, 10 [PL 82.393C]):

> For "*sapiens*" [wise] as Isidore says (*Etym.* x) "is so named from *sapor* [savor], because just as the taste is quick to distinguish between savors of meats, so is a wise man in discerning things and causes." Wherefore it is manifest that "folly" is opposed to "wisdom" as its contrary, while "fatuity" is opposed to it as a pure negation: since the fatuous man lacks the sense of judgment, while the fool has the sense, though dulled, whereas the wise man has the sense acute and penetrating. (*ST* II-II, q. 46, a. 1, c)

In keeping with Thomas's general epistemology, wisdom is ordered to judgment; wisdom is the "savor of discretion and sense" (*ST* II-II, q. 46, a. 1, ad 2). Folly, its contrary, "denotes dullness of sense in judging, and chiefly as regards the highest cause, which is the last end and the sovereign good" (*ST* II-II, q. 46, a. 2, c). Folly may either be a natural deficiency or can be the result of sin. The spiritual senses of the person who has plunged himself into earthly things have become so dull that they are rendered incapable of perceiving divine things. They are condemned by the verdict of the Apostle Paul: "'The sensual man perceiveth not the things that are of the Spirit of God,' [1 Cor 2:14] even as sweet things have no savor for a man whose taste is infected with an evil humor: and such like folly is a sin" (*ST* II-II, q. 46, a. 2). Acute spiritual senses render perceptive judgments with respect to good and evil; "taste" and "savor" describe the operation of this intuitive sense of wisdom.

The *Commentary on Job* offers a similar example. Commenting on Job 12:11 ("Does not the ear judge words when it hears them, and when the palate relishes the taste of food, does it not discriminate? There is wisdom in the ancients and prudence comes with advanced age"), Thomas remarks that wisdom and prudence are required to judge what the senses deliver. This involves experience, however, and experience is obtained only with time ("advanced age"). Hearing and tasting designate two types of experiential knowledge. Hearing, which is the "most teachable of all the senses," is correlated with wisdom and regulates the contemplative life. Taste, which has to do with food and the necessities of life, is correlated to prudence and regulates the active life. Thomas concludes, "From the judgment of the two senses, he shows the value of experience in both speculative things and practical things." *Commentary on the Book of Job*, vol. 28 (Lander, WY: Aquinas Institute 2016), 12.2, p. 154. *In Iob XII*, 11–14, Leonine, 26:81, ll. 163–226.

21. Cf. *ST* I, q. 54, a. 5, c: "We have experience when we know single objects through the senses."

The ecclesiology of the *corpus mysticum* serves as the foundation of Thomas's doctrine of the spiritual senses. According to this ecclesiology, the members participate in the spiritual realities predicated of the Head. In his treatment of the effects of baptism, Thomas writes, "Just as the members derive sense and movement from the material head, so from their spiritual Head, i.e. Christ, do His members derive spiritual sense (*sensus spiritualis*).... It follows from this that the baptized are enlightened by Christ as to the knowledge of truth (*cognitionem veritatis*), and made fruitful by Him with the fruitfulness of good works (*bonorum operum*) by the infusion of grace."[22] Here we see the participatory character of the spiritual senses that gives a more literal connotation to the traditional locution *sentire cum ecclesiae*. The senses exist perfectly in Christ the Head and overflow to those who comprise his mystical body. The members do not possess the spiritual senses autonomously, but on account of their incorporation in the Head. The final cause of the spiritual senses is the intellectual illumination of the truth and fecundity in good works, which is a share in Christ's own light and grace.

Thomas's insistence on the real union of Head and members leads him to correct Peter Lombard, who in his *Sentences* maintains that while all the spiritual senses are in Christ, only the sense of touch obtains for the members. Lombard holds that just as in the physical body all five senses are found in the head and only touch in the members, so too only touch and not the other spiritual senses obtains for the members of the mystical body.[23] Further, Lombard admits only a "likeness" of the spiritual senses in the members, as they do not participate in "the same grace as to the essence" that belongs to the Head. In his *Scriptum*, Thomas disagrees with the Master, insisting that a real union of Head and members constitutes the mystical body:

22. *ST* III, q. 69, a. 5.
23. Peter Lombard, *Sent.* 3, d. 13, n. 2. Lombard holds that Christ alone is filled with every grace because in him dwells the fullness of divinity. He quotes Augustine (*Ep.* 187): "Just as 'in our body there is a sense in each of the members, but not so much as in the head: for in the head there is sight and hearing and smell and taste and touch, but in the others there is only touch,' so also in Christ *dwells the fullness of divinity*, because he is the head in which are all the senses; but in the saints there is, as it were, touch alone, for to them the spirit was given according to measure, when they took *from his fullness* [Lk 2:40]. How 'we took from his fullness,' is to be understood. But they took from his fullness not according to essence, but according to likeness, because they did not receive the same grace as to essence, but a like one."

"In the Saints there is only touch." This seems to be false, because Origen, *On Leviticus*, distinguishes five spiritual senses, saying that spiritual sight occurs when we see God; hearing when we hear who speaks; smell, by which we smell the good odour of Christ; taste, when we taste his sweetness; touch, when we touch, with John, the Word of life. All of these things are in all the saints. So they do not have merely touch. I reply by saying that the spiritual senses can be distinguished [1] by likeness to the acts of corporeal senses (*per similitudinem ad actus sensuum corporalium*), and thus they are in all the saints, as Origen says, and [2] by likeness to certain properties of the senses (*per similitudinem ad quasdam proprietates sensuum*), according to which touch is necessary, and the others not, and in this way, because there are in the saints all things necessary to salvation, whereas in Christ there are all things which simply pertain to the perfection of grace, it follows that all the senses are said to be in Christ, whereas in others there is only the sense of touch.[24]

The striking claim is not just that the spiritual senses refer to the distinct ways the saint perceives Christ, but also that the believer sees, hears, smells, tastes, and touches with Christ's senses. Contrary to Lombard, who admits only a "likeness" of the spiritual senses in the members, Aquinas holds that if all the senses exist perfectly in Christ the Head, they must also obtain for his members. In Christ, who was a *comprehensor* in this life, they obtain perfectly, whereas for the members of his mystical body, they operate sufficiently for salvation.[25]

The distinction at work in this paragraph serves to balance competing authorities. Origin of Alexandria first develops a doctrine of five spiritual senses corresponding to the five physical senses. Origin held that the members of Christ's mystical body share in *all* the senses of the Head. This significant feature of Greek mystical theology was widely known in the Middle Ages because of its transmission in the *Glossa*.[26] Peter Lombard instigates a

---

24. *Super Sent.*, lib. 3 d. 13 q. 3 a. 2 qc. 3 expos. Trans. Cross, "Thomas Aquinas," 187.

25. I see nothing in this paragraph that warrants Richard Cross's supposition that the *sancti* refer to the *comprehensores* possessing the beatific vision. Rather, the spiritual senses discussed seem the possession of the saints *in via*. See Cross, "Thomas Aquinas," 187.

26. See Karl Rahner, "The Doctrine of the 'Spiritual Senses' in the Middle Ages," in *Theological Investigations*, vol. 16, *Experience of the Spirit: Source of Theology* (New York: Crossroad, 1983), 106; Boyd Taylor Coolman, *Knowing God by Experience: The Spiritual Senses in the Theology of William of Auxerre* (Washington, DC: Catholic University of America Press, 2004), 113n10. Elsewhere, Boyd Coolman underscores how the doctrine of the mystical body underwrites the theology of the spiritual senses throughout the twelfth century, including William of St. Thierry, Hugh of St. Victor, Hildebret, Herveus, Peter Lombard, and especially Alexander of Hales. He also notes the uniqueness of

new and vexed discussion when he maintains that Origen (and the *Glossa*) contradicts Augustine. In *Epistle* 187, Augustine develops the metaphor of bodily sense perception to explain the distinction of Christ the Head, in whom alone the "the fullness of divinity dwells" (Col 2:9), from his members. Just as a physical head possess all five senses but only touch operates in the rest of the body, so too the Headship of Christ's assumed humanity is of a singular grace far exceeding any of his members. Lombard appeals to Augustine in maintaining that the members of Christ's mystical body only possess the spiritual sense of touch. The distinction Aquinas proposes is that the members of the mystical body *act* with Christ's spiritual senses, but that the proper nature of the spiritual senses belong exclusively to Christ the Head. This permits Aquinas to affirm with Origen (and the *Glossa*) that Christ's members fully participate in all the spiritual senses of the Head and affirm with Lombard (and Augustine) the uniqueness of Christ's assumed humanity.

Richard Cross maintains that Thomas does not have an account of "spiritual senses" as a distinct faculty for apprehending spiritual realities. He holds that "sensory language is not evidently anything other than metaphorical."[27] This seems to run contrary to Thomas's theology on two counts. First, the spiritual senses are metaphorical only on the supposition that the new "life" of baptism is also metaphorical (i.e., not ontological). But the relation between natural and supernatural life is analogous rather than metaphorical. Baptism gives a real and new supernatural life that is analogous to and continuous with natural life. As natural life is equipped with sense perception, so too supernatural life is equipped with spiritual senses. Thomas argues that although the spiritual senses are "first and principally" senses of the soul, the unity of body and soul entails that spiritual sense operate "secondarily" in the body in an "instrumental" mode.[28] Second, the spiritual senses of the members of Christ's mystical body are a participation in the sense and movement of the spiritual Head. As such, the spiritual senses can be metaphorical only on the supposition that the doctrine of the *corpus*

Lombard's controversial opinion proposed in *Sent.* 3, d. 13. See "Alexander of Hales," in *The Spiritual Senses: Perceiving God in Western Christianity*, ed. Paul Gavrilyuk and Sarah Coakley (Cambridge: Cambridge University Press, 2011), 121–39.

27. Cross, "Thomas Aquinas," 186.

28. *ST* III, q. 8, a. 2.

mysticum as a whole is metaphorical.[29] Thomas is clear, however, that the relation between head and members is a real (rather than linguistic) relation. He writes, "The head influences the other members in two ways. First, by a certain intrinsic influence, inasmuch as motive and sensitive force flow from the head to the other members; secondly, by a certain exterior guidance, inasmuch as by sight and the senses, which are rooted in the head, man is guided in his exterior acts."[30] The "intrinsic influence" of Christ the Head is his justifying power given in an unmediated manner to his members. The "exterior guidance" of Christ the Head is given to his members in a mediated mode, as bishops direct the members of the body, for example.

"NO ONE KNOWS WHO DOES NOT FIRST TASTE"

Commenting on Psalm 34 [33]:8 ("O taste, and see that the Lord is sweet"), Thomas offers greater detail on how the spiritual senses operate distinctly as *experiences* of God, which coalesce in a type of spiritual sensorium:[31]

29. Admittedly, Thomas does describe the mystical body as "metaphorically called one body" (*corpus similitudinarie dictum*). But he does so in contrast to a "natural body." The mystical body, like a domestic or civil multitude, borrows the term "body" to express an "ordered multitude" (*ST* III, q. 8, a. 1). But this does not entail that the term "mystical body" is a linguistic contrivance. The mystical body is still a "real" body. Helpful here is the medieval theological articulation of the *triforme corpus Christi* that distinguished between (1) "physical body" of the incarnate Christ, (2) the "mystical body" of the Eucharist, (3) and the "real body" of the Church. (The designations "mystical" and "real" were reversed on account of the Berengar controversy, so that the Eucharist was subsequently held to be the "real body" in distinction to the "mystical body" of the Church.) Cf. Henri de Lubac, *Corpus mysticum: The Eucharist and the Church in the Middle Ages*, trans. Gemma Simmonds (Notre Dame, IN: University of Notre Dame Press, 2006).

30. *ST* III, q. 8, a. 6.

31. This sensorium is perhaps best understood as a spiritual analogue to the inner sense or *sensus communis*. A number of times, Thomas refers to the *sensus interior* in a way that corresponds to his account of the *sensus communis* (or common sense). The *sensus communis* mediates between the lower power of the exterior senses and the higher power of intellect. It can be considered in relation to both. First, with respect to the external senses, it is passive and receptive. The *sensus communis* is responsible for sensory unification, simultaneously integrating the various external sense experiences into a coherent whole. Second, the *sensus communis* is proximate to the higher power of the intellect and on account of this affinity participates in the power of understanding, which it exercises when it judges the deliverances of the senses. As such, a hierarchal chain structures Thomas's process of cognition, which proceeds from the material external senses to the immaterial internal sense (*sensus communis*) and, finally, to the spiritual power of the intellect. The relevant texts are spread throughout Thomas's

When the Psalmist says *taste and see how sweet*, he urges an experience.... [Regarding taste] he does two things: first he urges the experience; second he describes the effect of the experience, when he says *and see how*. And so he says *taste and see*, etc. Now the experience of anything comes through the senses but in different ways, depending on whether the object is close or at some distance. If it is removed at a distance (*de absente*), then the experience of it comes through sight, smell or hearing. If it is close (*de praesente*), then touch and taste come into play, but each in its own way. For touch senses the outside (*de extrinseca*) of the object, whereas taste senses the inside (*de intrinseca*). Now God is not far from us nor outside us, but rather He is in us, as Jeremiah 14 says: *You are in us, O Lord*. Thus the experience of divine goodness is called tasting (*experientia divinae bonitatis dicitur gustatio*).... Next he shows that the effect of this experience is twofold: the certitude of understanding (*certitudo intellectus*) and the security of love (*securitas affectus*). With respect to the first effect he says *see*. For in corporeal things, something is first seen and then tasted, but in spiritual things something is first tasted and then seen, because no one knows who does not first taste: and for this reason he first says "taste," and then "see."[32]

The spiritual senses allow for experiential knowledge of God but according to a differentiated mode of experience, depending on the kind of sense that is involved. Spiritual sight, smell, and hearing apprehend divine reality at a distance—they grasp reality remote from us (*de absente*). Touch and taste, by contrast, imply an immediacy and contact with divine realities proximate to us (*de praesente*).[33] The intimacy of the soul indwelt by the divine persons

corpus: *Summa contra Gentiles* I, c. 61; *De Ver.* 15, l; *ST* I, q. 78, a. 4, ad 2; I, q. 77, a. 3, obj. 4 and ad 4; I, q. 57, a. 2; *Questiones disputate de anima*, 13 obj. 15 and ad 15; 20 obj. 17 and ad 17. Traditional Thomistic interpretation of the *sensus communis* includes Mark Gaffney, *The Psychology of the Internal Senses* (St. Louis: Herder, 1942); George Klubertanz, *Notes on the Philosophy of Human Nature* (St. Louis: St. Louis University Press, 1949); H. D. Gardeil, *Introduction to the Philosophy of St. Thomas Aquinas*, vol. 3, *Psychology* (St. Louis: Herder, 1956). A helpful overview is Stephen Laumakis, "The Sensus Communis Reconsidered," *American Catholic Philosophical Quarterly* 82 (2008): 429–43.

32. *In psalmos* 33, n. 9, ed. S. Fretté, *Doctoris angelici divi Thomae Aquiatis opera omnia*, 34 vols. (Paris: Vivès, 1871–80), 18:419. Translation mine, drawing on Gregory Froelich, "The Aquinas Translation Project," accessed October 28, 2020, http://hosted.desales.edu/w4/philtheo/loughlin/ATP/index.html, and Cross, "Thomas Aquinas," 188.

33. The paring of touch and taste goes back to Aristotle, for whom each sense correlates to one of the four elements: we see with water, hear with air, smell with fire, and touch with earth. Taste is considered a species of touch. Here Aristotle makes a fascinating remark germane to the topic of experiential knowledge: "This explains why the sensory organ of both touch and taste is closely related to the heart. For the heart, as being the hottest of all the bodily parts, is the counterpoise of the brain" (*De Sensu* 438b30–439a3). In treating of the spiritual senses, Thomas not only follows Aristotle in holding taste and touch together, but also seems to transpose Aristotle's physiognomic insight regarding the heart as the seat of taste and touch to a spiritual register. Connatural knowledge is a knowledge of the heart that operates through spiritual touch and taste.

and animated by the gifts of the Spirit suggests that touch and taste better express the soul's experiential knowledge of divine realties. Thomas advances a further distinction between these last two spiritual senses. Touch apprehends divine realities outside of us (*de extrinseca*), whereas taste apprehends divine realties within (*de intrinseca*). The interiority of the experience of God in the soul is the reason the psalmist enjoins the believer to *taste* God. The divine goodness—which is God himself—is savored within: "Thus the experience of divine goodness is called tasting (*experientia divinae bonitatis dicitur gustatio*)."

It is telling that here Thomas prioritizes the senses of taste and touch to express the immediacy of the soul's experience of God. In this respect, he does not adopt the traditional philosophic hierarchy of the senses that proceeds from the "lowly" bodily senses of taste and touch to the "higher" spiritual senses of hearing and vision. Aquinas departs (at least in this instance) from an established pattern of articulating the hierarchy of the spiritual sense that emerged with Origen and was adopted by Augustine, Gregory the Great, and Bonaventure. This broadly Platonic pattern held the "intellectual" senses of sight and hearing to be more appropriate to express how we know the immaterial God than the "corporeal" senses of touch or taste that are eminently somatic and often associated with the dangers of bodily pleasure.[34]

---

34. The distinction between the higher intellectual senses and the lower corporeal senses goes back to classical philosophy (Cf. *Timaeus* 47). Aristotle identifies touch and taste with "animal" senses as opposed to the "human" senses of seeing and hearing (*On the Soul*, 413–29). Christian discourse of spiritual sensation evinces significant exceptions to this hierarchy. Mystical writers such as Bernard of Clairvaux, Hadewijch of Brabant, Jan Ruusbroec, and others seem to prefer taste and touch to express their experiential knowledge of God. And even among figures such as Augustine, Gregory the Great, Bonaventure, and Aquinas, who in the main favor seeing and hearing as expression of the soul's union with God, one can discover significant exceptions. Cf. Gordon Rudy, *The Mystical Language of Sensation in the Later Middle Ages* (London: Routledge, 2002); Gavrilyuk and Coakley, *Spiritual Senses*; Hans Urs von Balthasar, *The Glory of the Lord: A Theological Aesthetics*, vol. 1, ed. Joseph Fessio, SJ, and John Riches (San Francisco: Ignatius, 1982–89), 365–80; Mariette Canévet, "Sens spirituel," in *Dictionaire de spiritualité*, 14:598–617. Boyd Coolman has demonstrated the priority of the spiritual sense of touch for Alexander of Hales: "He arranges them on a continuum of proximity to their object: vision and audition are most remote; smell, taste, and touch are respectively closer to their objects. Tellingly, he does not construct a vertical hierarchy here of 'lower' to 'higher' senses. He observes, rather, a progression from faith's vision and audition of divine *veritas*, through hope's olfaction of divine things, to charity's taste and especially touch of divine *bonitas*, a movement from the most distant to the most intimate and certain knowledge of God." Coolman, "Alexander of Hales," 128.

Thomas typically follows the traditional hierarchy of the senses, prioritizing seeing and hearing on account of their exalted place in the discovery of knowledge. Thomas offers three reasons why

After considering the psalmist's exhortation to experience the divine goodness by taste, Thomas considers the effect of this experience as having bearing on the "certainty of the intellect" (*certitudo intellectus*) and the "security of the affect" (*securitas affectus*). Here we touch on the difficult question raised earlier: Does experiential or connatural knowledge of God belong more properly to the intellect or the will? In the question on wisdom (*ST* II-II, q. 45), Thomas gives a succinct answer: "The wisdom that is a gift has a cause in the will, viz., charity, but it has its essence in the intellect."[35] Experiential knowledge of God is certainly a type of *knowledge*, but it is a "loving knowledge"—a knowledge *of* divine love and knowledge *by means* of divine love. It involves both the will and the intellect. While it belongs to the intellect to illumine, it belongs to the will to move the intellect. Love pulls the object of affection to itself; it focuses the intellect, giving it greater attention and interest in the object of its delight. We might say that the "loving taste" of the will carries the intellect toward its object as something experienced.[36]

In the *Commentary on the Divine Names*, Thomas considers the power of divine inspiration given to Dionysius's master, Hierotheus, which was more acute and penetrating

---

Aristotle's claim for the superiority of sight at the outset of the *Metaphysics* is true. First, sight knows in a more perfect way because the operation of vision is the most spiritual and immaterial of the senses. Only sight involves a "spiritual modification" in that the eye receives the immaterial form of color. Sight alone is exempt from the "material modification" of both the sense organ and the medium in the process of sensation. As such, sight operates in a more spiritual manner, enabling it to judge sensible objects in a more certain and perfect mode than the other senses (*Metaphysics* I.1.6). Second, sight has the capability to obtain and deliver more information than the other senses (*Metaphysics* I.1.7). Finally, sight (along with touch) apprehends the sense object itself rather than a secondary effect. Hearing and smell only apprehend the accidental qualities that flow away from the sense object. (Thus it is the odor of the food, not the food itself, that I smell. Likewise, the sound of footsteps indicate to me a passing person, but the person is not the sound of the footsteps that I hear.) While the proper objects of sound and smell diminish with time, the proper objects of touch and sight remain: "The judgment of sight and touch is extended to things themselves, whereas the judgment of hearing and smell is extended to those accidents which flow from things and not to things themselves" (*Metaphysics* 1.1.8).

35. *ST* II-II, q. 45, a. 2.

36. Marín-Sola remarks, "Love excites and concentrates our attention, it makes one dwell on the loved object more constantly and with greater fixedness. This concentration of attention is tantamount to an increase in cognitive power.... The lover fixes his gaze intensely, and even exclusively on the beloved; he thus receives impressions with great force and greater purity, and discerns more quickly certain properties or features that others fail to notice, or come to notice much later. It is the Beloved Disciple who before all others recognizes the risen Christ on the shore, and exclaims: 'It is the Lord'" (*Homogeneous Evolution of Catholic Dogma*, 400–401).

than is commonly made to many, "not only learning, but also suffering divine things"—that is, not only receiving the knowledge (*scientia*) of divine things in the intellect, but also by loving, [he] was united to them through affect (*per affectum*). For passion appears to pertain more to appetite than to cognition, for realties known are in the knower according to the knower's mode and not according to the mode of the realities known, but the appetite moves to the realities according to the mode by which they are in themselves, and so in a way he is moved (*afficitur*) to the very realities.[37]

A gap between knower and known defines the nature of *scientia*; I grasp the cognitive object not in itself but in a new manner, "according to the mode of the knower." The intellect desires its object under a new ratio of "knowable," entailing a residual duality that is ever present between knower and known. This cogitative gap does not apply to the will, which does not seek a distinct intellectual account of its object of affection, but seeks rather to penetrate and unite itself to the very object of its affection. It does not want to engage the object as "knowable" but to "experience" it.

Love holds the object desired under the light of the intellect, disposing the intellect to its illuminating task. But even on the supposition that love moves the intellect to greater attention, specifying its illuminating task, surely we cannot say that love *knows*. Can affection add anything to intellectual illumination? While it is true that only the intellect knows, the will enters into the formal causality of knowing. John of St. Thomas helps to unpack Aquinas's theology on this point:

The will does not formally illumine the intellect. However, it can causally furnish the intellect with greater light, in so far as love makes the object more united to the soul, more immediately attached to it and tasted by it. Thus the object is presented anew to the intellect with a different suitability and proportion to the will. The object is felt as if by an immediate experience.... Thus the intellect proceeds to judge of things and divine truths according as it knows them in this loving experience of God.[38]

While the intellect apprehends the object of knowledge at a remove, as distinct from itself, love apprehends the object of its affection by uniting with

---

37. *DDN*, c. 2, lect. 4, no. 191, as quoted by Blankenhorn, *Mystery of Union with God*, 417.
38. John of St. Thomas, *Gifts of the Holy Spirit*, 4.15 (p. 180).

it.[39] And so connatural or experiential knowledge has its seat in the will; that is, it is driven by the impetus of love for union, even as its essence remains in the intellect inasmuch as it is a genuine knowledge.

Sight and hearing are standard conceptual metaphors for intellectual experience. By contrast, touch and taste are standard conceptual metaphors for affective experience. Perhaps this is because the former involve mediation. We see and hear things at a distance, mediated through air, light, water, or something else. Because knowledge engages its object at a distance—the intellect grasps reality extrinsic to itself—knowledge involves mediation. Touch and taste, by contrast, involve a direct, unmediated, and intimate union. The intellectual virtue of faith is typically allied with sight and hearing: its divine object is mediated ("through a glass dimly"). Faith comes through what is heard and is realized in seeing. Love, which has its seat in the will, is unmediated; it does not seek to know its object at a distance but desires union with it. Love desires to possess, to enjoy that which it loves. And so the unique type of divine knowledge that is experiential or connatural is not content to know God through the intellect, at a remove, by way of faith (through hearing and seeing), but aims also at a knowledge generated by the experience of love (through touch and taste). In Thomas's words, it "has its cause in the will, viz., charity, but it has its essence in the intellect." It is for this reason, contends Thomas, that the order "taste and see" proposed by the psalm is fitting. Unlike material reality, which I first see and then taste (e.g., I first see the apple and then reach out to taste it), the love of spiritual things is prior to my knowledge of them: "In spiritual things something is first tasted and then seen, because no one knows who does not first taste: and for this reason he first says 'taste,' and then 'see.'"[40]

Aquinas's theology of the spiritual senses is the outworking of his conception of the *corpus mysticum*—of the intimacy between the Head and the

---

39. In the question on charity (*ST* II-II, q. 24, a. 1, ad 2), Thomas remarks that while charity's proper seat is the will rather than the intellect, it "is not alien to reason" but has an "affinity to reason."

40. *In psalmos* 33, n. 9. A similar motif is found in Bernard of Clairvaux: "Doubtless the Lord is sweetness (*suavitas*), but unless you have tasted, you will not see (*nisi gustaveris, non videbis*). For it is said: 'Taste and see that the Lord is sweet.' This is hidden manna, it is the new name which no one knows except him who receives it. Not learning, but anointing teaches it; not knowledge (*scientia*), but conscience (*conscientia*) grasps it." Bernard, *Ad clericos de conversione*, sermon 13, par. 25 (Leclercq, Talbot, and Rochais, *Sancti Bernardi opera*, 4:99–100; trans. Rudy, *Mystical Language of Sensation*, 63, slightly altered).

members. The soul that because of baptismal incorporation into Christ is made the terminus of the invisible missions and the recipient of the gifts of the Spirit apprehends divine things with new spiritual senses. These senses obtain perfectly for Christ the Head and are participated in by his members. The immediacy and intimacy of such experiential knowledge of God in this life are the reason Thomas prioritizes the spiritual sense of taste above the others. And indeed he contends that, at least for spiritual reality, "no one knows who does not first taste."

CHAPTER 14

CHRISTOLOGICAL FALSEHOOD
AND SACRAMENTAL TRUTH

Intention and Faith in the
Sacramental Minister

Dominic M. Langevin, OP

INTRODUCTION

A crisis of Christology has effects for sacramental theology and practice. Whereas the sacraments were instituted by Christ and extend his salvation, it stands to reason that shaking the Christological tree trunk shakes, or at least affects, the sacramental branches up above. To what extent are the sacraments affected? Can defective Christology vitiate the sacraments? More broadly, can any bad theology vitiate the sacraments?

The subjective faith of the sacramental minister is an area where such questions could find particular focus. This chapter examines whether and how a true sacrament can be done by a theologically false minister. This seems like a strange juxtaposition, and it is. But the Church's magisterium and the sacramental theology of St. Thomas Aquinas provide some guidance through the issues while also leaving unanswered questions that deserve our exploration.

Christian faith can be described as an internal act and an external act. With respect to the latter, the believer confesses faith through scriptural statements, credal articles, and theological propositions, using external signs that manifest the internal assent to the object of belief, the triune God who reveals himself to us as First Truth. Aquinas distinctly defines the virtue of faith by reference to "truth" (*veritas*) and "falsity" (*falsitas*). In his first article on the virtue in the *Summa Theologiae*, Thomas says that "in faith, if we were to consider the formal aspect of the object, it is nothing other than First Truth (*veritas prima*)."[1] The third article of that question investigates the possibility of falsity intermingled with faith. Thomas responds, "Nothing can fall under faith except insofar as it stands under First Truth. Under this, nothing false (*falsum*) can stand, just as non-being cannot stand under being, and evil under goodness. Whence, [the conclusion] is set down that something false cannot fall under faith."[2] The interior act of faith has a correspondence to Truth, and the exterior act of faith can be judged by correspondence to truth and falsity.

The sacraments present a similar dynamic, particularly with respect to the external act of faith. St. Thomas Aquinas defines that "a 'sacrament' … is a sign of a sacred thing insofar as it is sanctifying men."[3] The focus on signification leads to a particular way to evaluate sacramental activity. If the various elements of a sacrament are present, Thomas says that the sacramental rite is "true."[4] The signification is correct. There is "truth" in the sign, and as a result, the sacrament is efficacious in grace. Parallel to this language of a "true" sacramental rite, the canonical tradition and some theologians would say that this rite is "valid."[5] In contrast, a failed attempt at a sacrament is a Thomistically "false" or canonically "invalid" sacrament.[6]

A true sacrament entails various elements.[7] A short, compact definition

1. *ST* II-II, q. 1, a. 1. Texts from the *Summa* will be cited according to the corrected Leonine edition of *Summa theologiae*, 3rd ed. (Turin: San Paolo, 1999). All translations of Aquinas are my own.

2. *ST* II-II, q. 1, a. 3.

3. *ST* III, q. 60, a. 2.

4. E.g., *ST* III, q. 60, a. 8: the phrases *veritas sacramenti* and *veritas eius* (where *eius* means *sacramenti*) are used six times in the corpus and responses; q. 64, a. 10: *veritas sacramenti* is used twice in the corpus.

5. E.g., in the 1983 *Code of Canon Law* promulgated by Pope John Paul II, canon 841 depends upon the distinction between the validity and the liceity of sacramental rites, recognizing the possibility for invalidity and illiceity. On this distinction, see John M. Huels, *Liturgy and Law: Liturgical Law in the System of Roman Catholic Canon Law* (Montreal: Wilson & Lafleur, 2006), 73.

6. For examples of Thomas's description of sacramental errors as *falsitas*, see, e.g., *ST* III, q. 60, a. 8, ad 1; and q. 68, a. 4. In the latter, Thomas writes, "in the sacramental signs, there ought not to be any falsity. Now, a sign is false when the signified thing does not correspond to it."

7. Taken together, these elements have been called the "substance," "essence," "necessities," or "definition" of a sacrament. For some examples of this nomenclature (including magisterial ones) and

that includes all essential elements may be elusive to obtain. The Council of Florence says, "All [the] sacraments are accomplished by three elements: namely, by things as the matter, by words as the form, and by the person of the minister who confers the sacrament with the intention of doing what the Church does. If any of these is absent, the sacrament is not accomplished."[8] A more recent theological attempt at a definition holds, "For the essence of any sacrament are required an external and sensible sign, interior grace, an institution done by God, and an appropriate minister."[9]

A sacramental minister plays an integral role in the signification of a sacrament. He perfects the sacramental matter (a thing or gesture, of which he himself may also be the actor) by doing the sacramental form (the verbal pronunciation of a formula). In this, the minister does a specific human act that has been instituted by Christ and that is gracefully moved by Christ, precisely for the communication of divine grace to a sacramental recipient.

As a human act, the sacramental act of a minister bears the traits of personal intellect and will that distinguish such acts from those of a mere animal or of a human being who is acting without reason. A sacramental act is an intended act. "Intention is not ... an extrinsic condition, even [an] indispensable [one]; much more than this, it is a constitutive element of the sacrament."[10] The merely physical production of the gestures and words in-

---

for discussion of it, see Emmanuel Doronzo, OMI, *De Sacramentis in Genere* (Milwaukee: Bruce, 1946), 408–11.

8. Heinrich Denzinger, Peter Hünermann, Robert L. Fastiggi, and Anne Englund Nash, eds., *Compendium of Creeds, Definitions, and Declarations on Matters of Father and Morals* (San Francisco: Ignatius, 2012), para. 1312. This *Compendium* will hereafter be abbreviated as *DH*. The Florentine text seems to have been based upon the following statement by Aquinas: "It is, indeed, common to all the sacraments that they confer grace ...; and it is common to all of them that each sacrament consists in words and corporeal realities (*res*), as in Christ, who is the author of the sacraments, there is the Word become flesh.... Whence, the words by which the sacraments are sanctified are called the forms of the sacraments; whereas the realities sanctified by such words are called the matters of the sacraments.... Also, in whichever sacrament, there is required the person of the minister, who confers the sacrament with the intention of doing what the Church does (*cum intentione faciendi quod facit Ecclesia*). Of these three, if anything is absent—that is, if there is not the due form of words, if there is not the due matter, or if the minister of the sacrament does not intend to confer the sacrament—the sacrament is not performed." *De articulis fidei et Ecclesiae sacramentis*, in *Opera Omnia*, Leonine ed., vol. 42 (Rome: Editori di San Tommaso, 1979), 253.

9. Dominic M. Prümmer, OP, *Manuale Theologiae Moralis secundum Principia S. Thomae Aquinatis*, 8th ed., 3 vols., ed. Engelbert M. Münch, OP (Freiburg im Breisgau: Herder, 1935–36), 3:7 (para. 5).

10. Jean-Hervé Nicolas, OP, *Synthèse dogmatique: De la Trinité à la Trinité* (Fribourg: Éditions Universitaires Fribourg Suisse, 1985), 742.

volved with the sacramental form and matter is not enough. The minister must intend those gestures and words as a united sacramental act. In the *sacramentum tantum* of a sacrament, the ministerial intention informs the sacramental form, which informs the sacramental matter.

The importance of ministerial intention, as well as the recipient's intention, was recognized in colorful narrative form in early theological presentations, which nonetheless likely reflected pastoral cases. For instance, patristic and medieval pastors and theologians wondered about a scenario of children at play wherein one child "enacts" the baptism of another, unbaptized child.[11] And they considered the scenario of a theatrical actor's "baptism" of another, unbaptized actor.[12] Beyond such extraordinary cases, the necessity and dynamics of sacramental ministerial intention became normal objects of theological investigation and were insisted upon by the magisterium.[13] The possibility of a lack of ministerial intention is recognized today in more typical pastoral and ministerial settings. For instance, a rehearsal for a Catholic wedding will often involve the engaged couple's practice of the formula for the exchange of consent, with the officiant's guiding preface, "This is just practice. This is not the real thing. The wedding is tomorrow, not today."

Under normal settings, the minister's intention is moved by and informed by faith. True faith and true sacramental intention go together. Right Christian faith, and only the right Christian faith, leads to and supports the full Christian sacramental life. In contrast, a defective faith, such as forms of Protestantism, leads to a sacramental deficiency.[14] And yet we

---

11. Marcia L. Colish, *Faith, Fiction, and Force in Medieval Baptismal Debates* (Washington, DC: Catholic University of America Press, 2014), 4, 97–103.

12. Colish, *Faith, Fiction, and Force*, 4, 93–97.

13. Concerning theological investigation, from a variety of different schools and styles, see, e.g., Christian Pesch, SJ, *De Sacramentis*, 4th ed., 2 vols., Praelectiones Dogmaticae 6–7 (Freiburg im Breisgau: Herder, 1914–20), 1:121–31 (paras. 262–88); Prümmer, *Manuale Theologiae Moralis*, 49–57 (paras. 61–69); Doronzo, *De Sacramentis in Genere*, 438–70; Felix M. Cappello, SJ, *De Sacramentis in Genere, de Baptismo, Confirmatione et Eucharistia*, 7th ed., Tractatus Canonico-Moralis de Sacramentis 1 (Turin: Marietti, 1962), 32–39 (paras. 38–44); Nicholas Halligan, OP, *The Sacraments and Their Celebration* (New York: Alba House, 1986), 4–7; and Jean-Philippe Revel, *Traité des sacrements: Baptême et sacramentalité*, 2 vols. (Paris: Cerf, 2004–5), 2:276–84. Below, I describe briefly the magisterium's insistence on needed ministerial intention when I examine the phrase "to do what the Church does" and the rebuttal against François Farvacques. At this point, though, we can note that perhaps the first magisterial statement that explicitly mentions ministerial "intention" as a distinct sacramental requirement is in the year 1208 by Pope Innocent III (*DH* 794).

14. Anscar Vonier, *A Key to the Doctrine of the Eucharist* (Bethesda, MD: Zaccheus, 2003), 6–10.

Catholics affirm that Protestant Christians can truly do the sacrament of baptism, for instance. This could seem strange insofar as both faith and the sacraments are defined by St. Thomas with reference to truth or falsity. It could seem internally contradictory for a man to be somehow false in his faith and yet the minister of a true sacrament.

In this chapter, I examine whether the quality of a minister's faith makes a difference to the performance and efficacy of a sacrament.[15] This investigation presumes the presence of all other elements of a truthful sacrament: for instance, proper sacramental matter and form, a subject's capacity to receive the sacrament, and any needed ministerial reception of the sacrament of holy orders. But for an emergency baptism, for example, would it make a difference if the minister were the Blessed Virgin Mary, who undoubtedly possessed the most perfect faith; a Catholic parish priest who is theologically orthodox on all dogmatic matters but also holds a crazy theory or two on smaller theological matters; or a Southern Baptist preacher who beforehand tells the baptismal recipient and assembled congregation that "baptism does not regenerate"?[16] How does faith, sacramental intention, and sacramental truthfulness intersect in these ministers? Among possible sacramental ministers, are we limited to those who have perfect theological acumen?

In the following pages, I describe the sacramental framework that leads to the Church's presupposition that the minister's right or wrong personal faith does not affect sacramental truthfulness. We begin with the patristic discussions and arrive at Aquinas's account. Then, I present two modern magisterial decisions that illustrate a tension within or challenge to that

---

15. Using Thomistic Scholastic language concerning the tripartite structure of a sacrament, this essay focuses on the *sacramentum tantum* and whether a heretical minister can perform the *sacramentum tantum*. If that is done, by the perfective causality of the sacraments, *ex opere operato*, the *res et sacramentum* and *res tantum* result (presuming that the recipient poses no obstacles).

16. On the latter point, see Anthony R. Cross, "Baptismal Regeneration: Rehabilitating a Lost Dimension of New Testament Baptism," in *Baptist Sacramentalism 2*, ed. Anthony R. Cross and Philip E. Thompson, Studies in Baptist History and Thought 25 (Milton Keynes, UK: Paternoster, 2008), 150, which makes special reference to guidelines given to missionaries by the International Mission Board of the Southern Baptist Convention. While not all Baptists are unified on this point, the rejection of any regenerative role to baptism has been a consistent feature of many Baptists over the course of history. "In the English Baptist tradition, both General and Particular, ... although believers' baptism was insisted upon, the rite was not regarded as conveying any spiritual gifts. At most it was a faithful response to the gift of faith and the Spirit." Bryan D. Spinks, *Reformation and Modern Rituals and Theologies of Baptism: From Luther to Contemporary Practices* (Aldershot, Hants, UK: Ashgate, 2006), 100.

framework. The cases involve Anglican ordinations and Mormon baptisms. I try to extend the Thomistic framework in order to account for such cases. We will see that a minister's faith has the potential to influence his likelihood to have a false ministerial intention. Faulty faith can block a right intention such that an intrinsically false rite is performed or such that, even if a physically correct rite is performed, the rite is shorn of the necessary Christian signification and is thus ineffective. I conclude the chapter by asking some questions about contemporary theological and pastoral implications.

PATRISTIC BACKGROUND

Over the centuries, Catholic theology and the Church's magisterium have elaborated an understanding of sacramental ministers that generally mitigates the importance of personal defects with respect to correct faith. This theological position was articulated initially in the third through fifth centuries with respect to the sacraments of baptism and holy orders, specifically whether to accept the sacramental ministrations of heretics and how to reconcile fallen-away Catholics. These sacraments were of particular importance because their reception entailed an important, lifelong, ecclesially visible change (what would be recognized as sacramental character). Ritual alternatives to sacramental reconciliation involved rebaptism or reordination. An initial historical locus of theological development was the rebaptism controversy in the 250s between St. Cyprian of Carthage (d. 258), who did not accept the baptism given by heretics, and Pope St. Stephen I (d. 257), who did accept their baptism. A second locus was the fight between the Donatists (who were strongest in the fourth and fifth centuries) and St. Augustine (354–430). That dispute concentrated upon whether to accept the permanent baptismal status of sinful Catholics and the sacramental ministrations of sinful Catholic ministers, but it also included the question of heretical Christians and heretical ministers.

Two scriptural and traditional truths were in tension.[17] First, the sacraments are divine vessels of God's grace wherein the human ministers are

17. The following analysis comes from Bernard Leeming, SJ, *Principles of Sacramental Theology* (London: Longmans, Green, 1957), 497–98.

"stewards of the mysteries of God" but not their owners (1 Cor 4:1). As St. Paul critiqued the Corinthians, "Each one of you says, 'I belong to Paul,' or 'I belong to Apollos,' or 'I belong to Cephas,' or 'I belong to Christ.' Is Christ divided? Was Paul crucified for you? Or were you baptized in the name of Paul?" (1 Cor 1:12–13). The Corinthians were not "baptized in the name of Paul" but baptized with the sacrament of Christ. The sacramental minister—for instance, Paul—is the agent of a superior sacramental agent, Christ. Second, the Church is Christ's assembly of the holy ones.[18] Sin and the means of righteousness are opposed to each other. The Church is the community of "one Lord, one faith, one baptism" (Eph 4:5). It was a historical struggle for members of the Church to recognize that she possesses the true faith and the sacramental means of holiness while elements of her gifts can exist outside of her visible communion.

Catholic views about baptisms done by those who deny Christ's divinity, such as Arians, provide an interesting historical test case. Unfortunately, Catholic perspectives on this matter were muddled, and our historical record is even more muddled. For instance, there is the example of the followers of Paul of Samosata, a third-century Christological Adoptionist or Trinitarian Dynamic Monarchian. He certainly did not hold for the eternal divinity of Christ. Concerning his followers, called Paulianists or Paulinists, the Council of Nicaea (325) required the rebaptism of any who converted.[19] St. Athanasius, around the years 356 to 362, affirmed that Arians used a Trinitarian formula for their baptisms but that these acts were invalid because of a defective Trinitarian faith.[20] But St. Epiphanius of Salamis indicated in 378

---

18. See, e.g., 1 Cor 1:2.

19. Leeming, *Principles of Sacramental Theology*, 508–9. Council of Nicaea, canon 19: "With regard to the Paulianists who subsequently seek refuge in the Catholic Church, it is decided that they must, by all means, be rebaptized" (*DH* 128).

20. *Orations against the Arians*, 2.42: "I am speaking now of baptism. If the initiation is given into the name of the Father and the Son, and yet they [i.e., the Arians] are not speaking of a true Father since they deny what is from him and like his being and they deny also the true Son and invent for themselves another who is created from non-being, how is the baptism which they administer not completely empty and useless, a mere pretense which in fact is of no aid to piety? For the Arians do not give it 'into the Father and the Son' (Mt 28:19) but into Creator and creature and into Maker and made. As a creature is other than the Son, so also what they purport to give is other than the truth, even if they make a pretense of naming the name of the Father and the Son, because this is what is written in the Scripture. But the one who gives the baptism is not simply the one who says, 'Lord' (Mt 7:21), but the one who joins calling on the name to holding the right faith. For this reason, therefore, the Lord did not merely command to baptize, but first he says to 'teach' and then to 'baptize into the name of the

that converts from Arianism were generally not rebaptized though at least one group of Catholics was rebaptizing them.[21] Pope St. Siricius in 385 said in the strongest terms that converted Arians were not to be rebaptized.[22] Similarly, St. Gregory the Great, writing in 601, confirmed that converted Arians should not be rebaptized, in contrast to other heretics who should be so treated because of their more grievously deficient Trinitarian or Christological beliefs. Gregory's words reveal a wide range of pastoral practice relative to non-Catholics' faith and sacramental rites:

From the ancient instruction of the Fathers, We have learned that those in heresy who are baptized in the name of the Trinity, when they return to the holy Church, should be recalled to the bosom of Mother Church either by the anointing of chrism or by the imposition of hands or by the mere profession of faith. Wherefore, the West renews the Arians for entering the Catholic Church by the imposition of hands, while the East does so by the unction of holy chrism. Monophysites and others, however, are taken back only on the basis of the true profession of faith because the holy baptism that they received while among the heretics receives then the power of cleansing when either the former have received the Holy Spirit by the imposition of hands or the latter have been united to the heart of the holy and universal Church by means of the profession of the true faith.

Heretics, however, who are not baptized in the name of the Trinity, such as the Bonosians and the Cataphrygians—since the former do not believe in Christ, the Lord,[23] and the latter in a perverse manner believe the Holy Spirit to be a

---

Father and the Son and the Holy Spirit (Mt 28:19), so that right faith may come about through teaching, and the initiation of baptism may be accompanied by faith." Translation from Khaled Anatolios, *Athanasius* (New York: Routledge, 2004), 136–37.

21. Marta Szada, "The Debate over the Repetition of Baptism between Homoians and Nicenes at the End of the Fourth Century," *Journal of Early Christian Studies* 27 (2019): 646; Leeming, *Principles of Sacramental Theology*, 511. From Epiphanius's remarks, it seems that these Catholic rebaptizers were on the fringes of Catholic life. See Epiphanius, *De Fide*, 13.6–7, as found in *The Panarion of Epiphanius of Salamis, Books II and III: "De Fide,"* 2nd ed., trans. Frank Williams (Leiden: Brill, 2013), 671.

22. "[You have indicated] that many of those baptized by the impious Arians are hastening to the Catholic faith and that some among our brothers wish to baptize them again: this is not allowed, for the apostle forbids it to be done [cf. Eph 4:5; Heb 6:4f.] and the canons oppose it, and the general decrees sent to the provinces by my predecessor Liberius, of venerable memory, after the annulment of the synod of Rimini, likewise forbid it. We receive these [Arians] into the community of the Catholics, along with the Novatianists and the other heretics, in the manner decided in the synod: through the sole invocation of the sevenfold Spirit by the imposition of a bishop's hand, as is likewise observed throughout all of the East and the West. If you do not wish to be separated from our communion by means of a synodal decision, you also, from now on, must not deviate in the least from this practice." Letter "Directa ad decessorem" to Bishop Himerius of Tarragona, February 10, 385, chapter 1, §2, found as *DH* 183. See the discussion in Szada, "Debate over the Repetition of Baptism," 646–47.

23. It seems that the Bonosians denied the divinity of Christ, although the view of their founder

328 The Crisis of Christology in Assessing Our Life in Christ

certain depraved man, Montanus— ... are baptized when they come back to the Catholic Church, because when they were in error they did not receive baptism in any way since it was not done in the name of the Holy Trinity. And this cannot be called a repeated baptism, since the first, as we have said, was not given in the name of the Trinity.[24]

The Church's response to non-Catholic groups, according to Gregory, varies according to two factors: a group's (1) beliefs about the Trinity and Christ and (2) sacramental ritual, especially its Trinitarian character. The more important aspect is the second: whether the baptism is done "in the name of the Holy Trinity." So, as for the Arians, while there were important voices both for and against the rebaptism of Arian converts, the Church generally settled by the late fourth century upon the theology and practice of not rebaptizing them.[25] In contrast, Catholics held that those who did not baptize in the name of the Trinity did not baptize at all.[26]

The Catholic allowance for a sacramental minister's theological error resulted from the gradual appreciation of the sacraments' instrumental nature.[27] In the 370s, St. Optatus of Milevis in modern-day Algeria distinguished the baptismal minister's action from God's action, highlighting that baptism's spiritual cleansing surpasses human power and instead depends upon divine causality.[28] St. Augustine extended this to say that Christ is the primary minister of any sacrament. Furthermore, on the ecclesiological question, Augustine affirmed that any true sacrament, even one done by a non-Catholic, is a sacrament of the Catholic Church. Lastly, Augustine began analogies between Christ and the sacramental minister whereby

---

on this matter is uncertain. They may have had a variety of baptismal practices, even including baptism with a Trinitarian formula, though this latter possibility was evidently not known or accepted by Gregory. See X. Le Bachelet, "Bonose," in *Dictionnaire de théologie catholique* (Paris: Letouzey et Ané, 1903–72), 2:1027–31.

24. Letter "Quid caritati nihil" to the bishops of Iberia (Georgia), ca. June 22, 601, found as *DH* 478.

25. Szada, "Debate over the Repetition of Baptism," 662.

26. See Everett Ferguson, *Baptism in the Early Church: History, Theology, and Liturgy in the First Five Centuries* (Grand Rapids, MI: Eerdmans, 2009), 398–99.

27. For the points in this paragraph, see Leeming, *Principles of Sacramental Theology*, 149–57, 512–18.

28. For the dating of Optatus's work *On the Schism of the Donatists against Parmenian*, see M. J. Edwards, "Optatus of Milevis, c. 4th cent. CE," *Oxford Classical Dictionary*, accessed November 3, 2020, http://doi.org/10.1093/acrefore/9780199381135.013.8015.

the minister could be understood as an instrument. For instance, Augustine compared the minister to a canal for water, a farmer who is evil in one way but who can still sow seed, air that allows light to get through, and a self-interested speaker who nonetheless authentically communicates reality to his hearers. Augustine's distinction between the *sacramentum* and the *res*—that is, the liturgical rite and the effect of sacramental grace—helped to show how an erroneous minister could truly perform the sacramental rite while the recipient, himself also erroneous in faith, may receive the *sacramentum* but not the *res*. Lastly, Augustine argued that if the sacraments were dependent upon the invisible theological qualities of their ministers, it would be impossible to have a stable sacramental system, and the salvific gift of Christ would be ill designed and all for naught.

Patristic and early medieval concerns about ministers plagued by sin and theological error could have led to those time periods' theories of occasional and dispositive sacramental causality, which minimized the minister's causation of grace.[29] Herein, the minister's role was necessary for the performance of the sacramental rite, and both the minister and the rite were necessary for the divine gift of sacramental grace. But it was understood that grace was given by God directly to the recipient's soul, for grace—a completely spiritual reality—could not be communicated by any physical cause, including the physical mediation of the sacramental rite and its minister.[30]

Furthermore, the early and high medieval periods provide ample evidence of pastors and theologians who thought that a theologically erroneous minister could not even supply the sacramental rite.[31] For instance, there is the messy history of occasional reordinations in the eighth through twelfth

29. For background about the different theories of sacramental causality, one may profitably consult Revel, *Traité des sacrements: Baptême et sacramentalité*, 2:62–121; Roger W. Nutt, *General Principles of Sacramental Theology* (Washington, DC: Catholic University of America Press, 2017), 99–137; and Reginald Lynch, OP, *The Cleansing of the Heart: The Sacraments as Instrumental Causes in the Thomistic Tradition* (Washington, DC: Catholic University of America Press, 2017), 10–66.

30. For the history of medieval efforts to understand sacramental causality, see John F. Gallagher, CM, *Significando Causant: A Study of Sacramental Efficiency*, Studia Friburgensia, New Series 40 (Fribourg: University of Fribourg Press, 1965), 55–81. For a helpful explanation of occasional causality's understanding of the communication of grace, see Revel, *Traité des sacrements: Baptême et sacramentalité*, 2:64–68.

31. For further background about patristic and medieval views on baptism and faith, see Colish, *Faith, Fiction, and Force*, esp. 91–226, though this study focuses more on the baptismal recipient than the baptismal minister.

centuries.[32] In another example, important theologians such Hugh of St. Victor and Peter Lombard denied that a heretic could celebrate a valid Eucharist.[33]

ST. THOMAS AQUINAS

Greater theological illumination came in the thirteenth century. St. Thomas was extremely helpful in this matter. He described how, normally, faith and the sacraments can be and should be held together.[34] Each one is a form of "spiritual contact" with Christ and his saving mysteries.[35] St. Thomas wrote, "the power of Christ's Passion is joined to us through faith and the sacraments though in different ways. For the connection that exists through faith occurs through an act of the soul, whereas the connection that exists through the sacraments occurs through the use of exterior things."[36] Faith is "spiritual contact" through purely spiritual means; the sacraments are "spiritual contact" through means that include the physical. There is a hierarchy among these forms of contact. Faith comes first, and the sacraments build upon them. "The sacraments are certain signs protesting the faith by which man is justified."[37] Thus Thomas would sometimes use the phrase "faith and the sacraments of faith."[38] As Abbot Vonier would write, "The sacramental

32. Leeming, *Principles of Sacramental Theology*, 530–35.

33. Leeming, *Principles of Sacramental Theology*, 537, 539–40.

34. Concerning the following discussion about faith and the sacraments as instrumental means for spiritual contact with Christ, see Vonier, *Key to the Doctrine of the Eucharist*, 2–9.

35. *Spiritualem contactum. ST* III, q. 48, a. 6, ad 2. See also *ST* III, q. 49, a. 1, ad 4; q. 62, a. 5, ad 2; and q. 62, a. 6.

36. *ST* III, q. 62, a. 6.

37. *ST* III, q. 61, a. 4.

38. Some version of *fides et fidei sacramenta*: e.g., *Summa contra Gentiles* IV, c. 55 (1961 Marietti ed., para. 3940); *ST* III, q. 48, a. 6, ad 2; q. 49, a. 3, ad 1; q. 49, a. 5; q. 64, a. 2, ad 3; *Quodlibet* XII, q. 12, corpus (Leonine ed., vol. 25/2 [Paris: Cerf, 1996], p. 413); *Contra doctrinam retrahentium a religione*, c. 10 (Leonine ed., vol. 41C [Rome: St. Thomas Aquinas Foundation, 1969], p. 59); *In II Epist. ad Corinthios*, c. 12, lect. 1 (1953 Marietti ed., para. 445); and *In Epist. ad Romanos*, c. 8, lect. 1 (1953 Marietti ed., para. 596). An interesting example is Thomas's exposition of Heb 3:14, "For we are made participants in Christ if, however, we hold fast to the beginning of his substance to its safe end." Thomas wrote: "We are made participants in grace, first, through the reception of faith, as stated in Eph 3:17, 'That Christ may dwell by faith in your hearts.' Second, through the sacraments of faith, as stated in Gal 3:27, 'Whoever is baptized in Christ puts on Christ.' Third, through participation in the Body of Christ, as stated in 1 Cor 10:16, 'The bread that we break, is it not a participation in the Body of the Lord?'"

system is grafted on faith; … it is, shall we say, the reward of faith. Because of her faith the Church is granted those further powers of reaching Christ which make Christ not only the object of devout contemplation, but of physical possession."[39] So in the Thomistic understanding, the sacraments are practiced from a foundation of faith, which should order the actions of the minister and the recipient.

Another important factor for Thomas's analysis of a sacramental minister and his faith is his thought on sacramental causality. Compared to his predecessors and contemporaries, Thomas integrated into sacramental theology a more robust Aristotelian understanding of primary and instrumental causalities, leading to his understanding of perfective sacramental causality. With this theory, it is true to say that God, the sacramental minister, and the sacramental rite all cause grace, though in different ways.[40] Compared to theories of occasional and dispositive causality, Thomas's perfective causality gave increased scope for concerns about ministerial intentionality. But Thomas also gave tools to deal with those concerns.

Thomas's understanding of sacramental instrumentality is on display when he evaluates the question of theologically erroneous ministers. Key texts are *Summa Theologiae* III, q. 64, a. 8, on a minister's intention, and a. 9, on a minister's faith. Thomas says that a theologically erroneous minister can still do a true, efficacious sacrament "because a minister in the sacraments works instrumentally" and "acts not by his proper power but by Christ's power."[41] Thomas adds a condition: "provided that there are present the other things that are of the necessity of the sacrament." What are those "other [necessary] things"? Thomas specifies two: first, the "intention" "to do what the Church does"[42] and second, "the form of the Church in the bestowal of the sacraments."[43] By the first condition, the minister is not a mindless robot. Distinct from "an inanimate instrument," Thomas says, "an animate instrument, as is a minister, not only is moved but even, in a certain manner,

---

(*In Epist. ad Hebraeos*, c. 3, lect. 3 [1953 Marietti ed., para. 188]). Concerning a particular sacrament identified as a "sacrament of faith," see, e.g., the following references to baptism: *ST* III, q. 66, a. 1, ad 1; a. 3; and a. 10, ad 2.

39. Vonier, *Key to the Doctrine of the Eucharist*, 8.

40. *ST* III, q. 62, a. 1.

41. *ST* III, q. 64, a. 9.

42. *ST* III, q. 64, a. 9, ad 1.

43. *ST* III, q. 64, a. 9, ad 2.

moves himself, insofar as he moves by his own will his [bodily] members for work. And thus his intention is required, by which he should subject himself to the principal agent, such that it is evident that he should intend to do what Christ and the Church do."[44] Thomas will specify that a "habitual" interior intention is at least required.[45] A minister's theological error about a particular sacrament can be serious: for instance, denying even the sacrament's causation of grace.[46] But so long as he does the Church's *sacramentum tantum* (i.e., minimal liturgical rite, "the form of the Church") and has the intention to do what the Church does, the sacrament is true and efficacious. Normally, one can presume that the doing of the *sacramentum tantum* entails a right intention, though Thomas does allow that even the *sacramentum tantum* can be vitiated if "the contrary should be expressed exteriorly on the part of the minister."[47]

THE LATE MEDIEVAL
AND EARLY MODERN
MAGISTERIUM

Moving from the opinions of theologians to the pronouncements of the magisterium, the latter has been much more circumspect with respect to flawed ministerial faith than ministerial sinfulness. For instance, the Council of Trent confirmed, for every sacrament, the sacramental efficacy of a "a minister in the state of mortal sin."[48] But when it comes to ministers of

---

44. *ST* III, q. 64, a. 8, ad 1.

45. As opposed to an "actual intention." *ST* III, q. 64, a. 8, ad 3. The nomenclature concerning types of intention varies. On this point, see Nicholas Halligan, OP, *The Administration of the Sacraments* (New York: Alba House, 1962), 12. As an example of a Thomist with a different or more refined nomenclature, Emmanuel Doronzo, OMI, using a division of "actual" vs. "habitual" vs. "virtual" vs. "interpretative" intentions, specifies that a "virtual" intention is required on the part of the minister, in the sense that some preconceived interior intention by the minister moves (by a power: the Latin *virtus*) his exterior acts at a particular time (as opposed to, e.g., a drunk priest who is merely going through the so-called "habitual" exterior motions because he has done the exterior motions a thousand times before). Doronzo, *De Sacramentis in Genere*, 466–70.

46. *ST* III, q. 64, a. 9, ad 1.

47. *ST* III, q. 64, a. 8, ad 2.

48. "If anyone says that a minister in the state of mortal sin, though he observes all the essentials that belong to the effecting and conferring of the sacrament, does not effect or confer the sacrament,

flawed faith, the magisterium's explicit dogmatic formulations have guaranteed only the ministrations of baptizers. Concerning this sacrament, the Council of Florence in 1439 taught, "The minister of this sacrament is the priest, to whom by reason of his office it belongs to baptize. But in case of necessity not only priests or deacons, but also laymen or laywomen or even pagans and heretics may baptize, provided they observe the Church's form and intend to do what the Church does."[49] And in 1547, the Council of Trent declared, "If anyone says that baptism, even that given by heretics in the name of the Father and of the Son and of the Holy Spirit, with the intention of doing what the Church does, is not true baptism, let him be anathema."[50] So the magisterial understanding is that if the sacramental form and matter are correctly performed, the faith of a baptizer is not pertinent to whether the sacramental rite is effective for salvation.[51] This fits within the theologians' general consensus that a minister's defective faith need not vitiate the integrity of a sacramental rite.

ANGLICAN ORDERS

There are two modern cases where the magisterium has judged that defective ministerial faith has led to defective ministerial intention and thereby to fundamentally defective sacramental rites. Both involve non-Catholic

---

let him be anathema." Session 7, "Decree on the Sacraments," *DH* 1612. See also the *Catechism of the Catholic Church* (Washington, DC: Libreria Editrice Vaticana/United States Catholic Conference, 2000), para. 1128: "From the moment that a sacrament is celebrated in accordance with the intention of the Church, the power of Christ and his Spirit acts in and through it, independently of the personal holiness of the minister. Nevertheless, the fruits of the sacraments also depend on the disposition of the one who receives them." Note that the phrase "the personal holiness of the minister," according to the traditional terminology of sacramental theology, signifies the minister's subjective state of grace and moral actions besides the act of faith.

49. "Bull of Union with the Armenians *Exsultate Deo*," *DH* 1315.

50. Session 7, "Decree on the Sacraments," *DH* 1617.

51. Going beyond the magisterium, one avenue by which Tridentine and post-Tridentine commentators approached our topic was by discussing the differences between external and internal intentions on the part of the sacramental minister and recipient. Given its complexity and indirect connection to our subject, however, I abstain from presenting that matter as a whole but only present aspects as needed for our discussion of ministerial faith. For further background, see Raphael De Salvo, OSB, "The Dogmatic Theology on the Intention of the Minister in the Confection of the Sacraments" (STD diss., Catholic University of America, 1949).

communities, even a non-Christian community. Whereas the principles of Christian sacramental signification and efficacy remain the same whether a sacrament is performed by a Catholic or non-Catholic, we can gain insights about the sacraments by seeing how the magisterium has judged the sacramental activity of non-Catholics.[52]

Pope Leo XIII in his 1896 Apostolic Letter *Apostolicae Curae* declared that Anglican ordinations have been and are invalid.[53] The liturgical rite in question was from the Ordinal of King Edward VI, drafted by Thomas Cranmer and promulgated by the king in 1550 as a replacement for the Roman Pontifical. Leo XIII identified two sacramental deficiencies: a defect of form and a defect of intention. With respect to form, the Edwardine Ordinal changed what could be considered the minimal sacramental form. That alone could invalidate the attempt at a sacrament. Furthermore, the defect of form was matched by—indeed, motivated by—a defect of intention. Pope Leo noted how right intention could be presumed if a Church-approved liturgical rite is used with the intention to do what the Church intends. Then the pope added:

If the rite be changed, with the manifest intention of introducing another rite not approved by the Church and of rejecting what the Church does and what by the institution of Christ belongs to the nature of the sacrament, then it is clear that not only is the necessary intention wanting to the sacrament, but that the intention is adverse to and destructive of the sacrament.[54]

---

52. It is not as if there are seven Catholic sacraments and, in contrast, some number of separate Protestant sacraments. There are only seven sacraments. Catholics live them fully. Non-Catholic Christians may live them to a greater or lesser degree.

53. Historical and theological accounts of the subject have often been polemical, including after the Second Vatican Council by Catholic commentators who wish to question Leo XIII's judgment. For historically sensitive accounts that defend Leo XIII's decision, see Francis Clark, SJ, *Anglican Orders and Defect of Intention* (London: Longmans, Green, 1956); *The Catholic Church and Anglican Orders* (London: Catholic Truth Society, 1962); "Les ordinations anglicanes, problème oecuménique," *Gregorianum* 45 (1964): 60–93; and Paul R. Rust, OMI, "Leo XIII's Decision on Anglican Orders," *Homiletic and Pastoral Review* 61 (1961): 949–51 and 1041–53. For accounts that desire a reevaluation of the matter, see John Jay Hughes, *Absolutely Null and Utterly Void: The Papal Condemnation of Anglican Orders, 1896* (Washington, DC: Corpus, 1968); *Stewards of the Lord: A Reappraisal of Anglican Orders* (London: Sheed and Ward, 1970); George H. Tavard, *A Review of Anglican Orders: The Problem and the Solution* (Collegeville, MN: Liturgical Press, 1990); and R. William Franklin, ed., *Anglican Orders: Essays on the Centenary of Apostolicae Curae, 1896–1996* (London: Mowbray, 1996).

54. DH 3318.

What was the intention of the drafters of the Anglican ordinal? Leo specified:

Being fully cognisant of the necessary connection between faith and worship, between the law of believing and the law of praying, under a pretext of returning to the primitive form, they [the drafters] corrupted the liturgical order in many ways to suit the errors of the innovators. For this reason, in the whole *Ordinale* not only is there no clear mention of the sacrifice, the consecration, the priesthood, or the power of consecrating and offering the sacrifice, but, as We have just stated, every trace of these things, which had been in such prayers of the Catholic rite as they had not entirely rejected, was deliberately removed and struck out.[55]

So the crafting of the Anglican liturgical rite and its subsequent use occurred through an erroneous faith that rejected what the Church intends to do in the sacrament. And the continued use of the Edwardine Ordinal by erroneous ministers meant that apostolic succession was lost and that Anglican ordinations are "absolutely null and utterly void," in Leo's famous phrase.[56] Christ's sacramental dispensation were not able to sustain such false faith, intention, and form.

MORMON BAPTISM

The second modern case pertinent to our subject concerns baptism. In 2001, the Congregation for the Doctrine of the Faith (CDF), with the approval of Pope St. John Paul II, responded to a *dubium* by declaring that Mormon baptism is invalid.[57] This could seem surprising. At the external level, Mormon baptism is essentially identical to a Catholic baptismal rite. The Mormon book of *Doctrine and Covenants*, which constitutes part of the community's scriptural canon, specifies:

---

55. *DH* 3317a.
56. *DH* 3319. Commentators have argued over what Pope Leo meant in saying that there was a defect of intention. Francis Clark analyzed those arguments exhaustively and determined that the defect was not just in the rite but properly "in the mind of the minister of the sacrament." Clark, *Anglican Orders and Defect of Intention*, 71–97. Clark also specified how Leo's objections were two in number, about two separable factors—namely, the sacramental form and the minister's intention (85–86, 168–69).
57. *DH* 5090.

Baptism is to be administered in the following manner unto all those who re-pent—The person who is called of God and has authority from Jesus Christ to baptize, shall go down into the water with the person who has presented himself or herself for baptism, and shall say, calling him or her by name: ["]Having been commissioned of Jesus Christ, I baptize you in the name of the Father, and of the Son, and of the Holy Ghost. Amen.["] Then shall he immerse him or her in the water, and come forth again out of the water.[58]

Given these ritual elements and given that the Councils of Florence and Trent said that a baptizer's faith is not pertinent, it would seem that a Mormon baptism should be true and efficacious. Indeed, previous to the 2001 CDF decision, CDF officials in 1976 and 1991 had given private replies indicating that Mormon baptism was to be treated as valid.[59] In 2001, however, the response was negative.

With this decision, an explanation was offered on the congregation's behalf by a CDF consultor, then Father Luis Ladaria, SJ, now in 2020 the congregation's cardinal-prefect. Ladaria's explanation does not have the same weight as the *dubium* response, but it does give a sense of the mind of the congregation.[60]

Ladaria said that the presumption in favor of recognizing baptism existed "even in the case of a false understanding of Trinitarian faith, as for example in the case of the Arians." Ladaria recognized that Mormon baptism had been considered valid by Catholic authorities. But Ladaria explained that, upon further study, Mormon baptism is invalid because Mormons do not have a traditional belief in the Trinity, let alone a traditional belief in Christ, for they do not hold for the divinity of Christ. Mormons present themselves as Christians but are not.

58. *The Doctrine and Covenants of the Church of Jesus Christ of Latter-Day Saints* (Salt Lake City: Church of Jesus Christ of Latter-Day Saints, 2013), section 20, verses 72–74. If we were to apply Scholastic language to this ceremony, while the ritual matter occurs after the verbal form and while there is not an exact physical union between form and matter, the two are close enough such that we could say that there is a moral union. Thus, on a ritual level, the physical elements of a Christian baptism are present in Mormon baptism.

59. For a partial description of the complex history of Vatican congregational responses to the question of Mormon baptism (the Congregation for Divine Worship and the Discipline of the Sacraments was also involved), see Owen F. Cummings, "Is Mormon Baptism Valid?," *Worship* 71 (1997): 150–51. Note that the data of this article are now incomplete because the article was written before the 2001 CDF response.

60. Luis Ladaria, SJ, "The Question of the Validity of Baptism Conferred in the Church of Jesus Christ of Latter-Day Saints," *L'Osservatore Romano*, weekly English ed., August 1, 2001, 4.

Ladaria identified four essential elements of a Christian baptismal rite: "the matter, the form, the intention of the minister, and the right disposition of the recipient." Only the first is correctly found in a Mormon baptism; the last three are gravely defective. But do not Mormons use a Trinitarian verbal formula? Ladaria wrote that non-Trinitarian belief renders hollow the Mormon use of Trinitarian language in the baptismal form:

The similarities with the formula used by the Catholic Church are at first sight obvious, but in reality they are only apparent. There is not in fact a fundamental doctrinal agreement. There is not a true invocation of the Trinity because the Father, the Son and the Holy Spirit, according to the *Church of Jesus Christ of Latter-day Saints*, are not the three persons in which subsists the one Godhead, but three gods who form one divinity.

So, in the case of Mormons and their baptismal rite, higher questions of Trinitarian belief—and departure from Trinitarian truth—have implications for sacramental signification and efficacy. Ladaria rendered clear those implications:

The differences are so great that one cannot even consider that this doctrine is a heresy which emerged out of a false understanding of the Christian doctrine. The teaching of the Mormons has a completely different matrix. We do not find ourselves, therefore, before the case of the validity of Baptism administered by heretics, affirmed already from the first Christian centuries, nor of Baptism conferred in non-Catholic ecclesial communities.

In other words, a sacramental rite must have a historically Christian origin and theological character.

This historical and theological background impinges upon the actions of a Mormon believer. This is true for both the minister and the recipient. Concerning the first, Ladaria wrote:

Such doctrinal diversity ... prevents the [Mormon] minister ... from having the intention of doing what the Catholic Church does when she confers Baptism, that is, doing what Christ willed her to do when he instituted and mandated the sacrament of Baptism. This becomes even more evident when we consider that in their understanding Baptism was not instituted by Christ but by God and began with Adam.

For Mormons, the sacrament of baptism is not fundamentally connected with Christ. Thus the Mormon minister cannot intend the baptism intended by the Church of Christ. Ladaria added that the Mormon baptismal recipient, who is never a child under the age of reason[61] and who is thus guided by Mormon belief in a way parallel to the minister, also cannot have the intention to receive a Christian sacrament. Both the Mormon minister and recipient have a radically false belief about God, Christ, and Christian baptism such that they cannot intend to do what the Christian Church does in baptism.

Ladaria gave some other, lesser arguments. But the ones that are most important in his exposition are (1) defect of form and (2) defect of ministerial intention because of a fundamentally different faith.

TO DO WHAT THE CHURCH DOES

These two modern cases deny sacramental validity because of defective form and intention rooted in erroneous faith. There has been much theological commentary on the Anglican orders decision.[62] With respect to the Mormon baptism issue and the CDF declaration, Catholic commentary has tended to be on the canonical side rather than the properly theological.[63]

Much depends upon the notion that a sacramental minister must intend "to do what the Church does."[64] The phrase dates to the turn from the

---

61. Mormons are baptized beginning at the age of eight years old. See *Doctrine and Covenants of the Church of Jesus Christ of Latter-Day Saints*, 18:42 ("all men must repent and be baptized, and not only men, but women, and children who have arrived at the years of accountability") and 20:71 ("no one can be received into the church of Christ unless he has arrived unto the years of accountability before God, and is capable of repentance"). The age of "accountability" in Mormon families is clarified by 68:25 as "eight years old," and the youngest age for baptism in such families is set at 68:27: "children shall be baptized for the remission of their sins when eight years old."

62. The primary work with respect to our question is Clark, *Anglican Orders and Defect of Intention*. While it focuses on ministerial intention, it also has a chapter on defect of form.

63. Urbano Navarrete, SJ, "Response of the Congregation for the Doctrine of the Faith about the Validity of Baptism Conferred in the Church of Jesus Christ of Latter-Day Saints," *L'Osservatore Romano*, weekly English ed., August 1, 2001, 5; Gordon Read, "Mormon Baptism Revisited," *Canon Law Society Newsletter* (*London*) 126 (2001): 91–95; William B. Smith, "Is Mormon Baptism Valid?," *Homiletic and Pastoral Review* 102, no. 8 (2002): 70–72; and Patrick R. Lagges, "Mormon Baptism Revisited," *Catechumenate* 25, no. 1 (2003): 25–35.

64. On the use and meaning of this phrase, see Doronzo, *De Sacramentis in Genere*, 438–49; De

twelfth century to the thirteenth.[65] It explicitly entered into magisterial use in 1418 at the Council of Constance against the followers of Wycliffe and Hus[66] and in 1439 at the Council of Florence, which stated that a necessary component of each sacrament is "the person of the minister who confers the sacrament with the intention of doing what the Church does."[67] The Council of Trent was more explicit, stating, "If anyone says that the intention at least of doing what the Church does is not required in the ministers when they are effecting and conferring the sacraments, let him be anathema."[68]

A minister's intention to do what the Church intends seems normal. "Common sense ... presumes that in the case of sacraments the minister intends to do a religious act, to do it in accord with the meaning of the rite which he uses, and in accord with the mind of the religious body of which he is a minister."[69] But just doing the external rite is not enough.[70] A positive internal intention is needed. This was made clear by the Holy Office under Pope Alexander VIII in 1690, when it condemned the following proposition purportedly held by the Jansenists and certainly held by the Augustinian François Farvacques (1622–89): "Baptism is valid when conferred by a minister who observes all the external rite and form of baptizing but within his heart resolves, 'I do not intend what the Church does.'"[71] A sacrament is an ecclesial act, and its minister must be open to that ecclesial dimension.[72]

Salvo, "Dogmatic Theology on the Intention of the Minister," 24–26; and Leeming, *Principles of Sacramental Theology*, 450–55. When St. Thomas uses this idea, he adds the Christological dimension, showing how Christ and the Church work together: the minister "should intend to do what Christ and the Church do." *ST* III, q. 64, a. 8, ad 1.

65. The phrase (some version of *intentio faciendi quod facit Ecclesia*) was first used by Praepositinus of Cremona (1130/35–1210; chancellor of Paris), though the idea is found earlier in Peter the Chanter. Doronzo, *De Sacramentis in Genere*, 438.

66. *DH* 1262.

67. "Decree for the Armenians," *DH* 1312.

68. Session 7, "Decree on the Sacraments," *DH* 1611.

69. Leeming, *Principles of Sacramental Theology*, 483.

70. Thus insufficient is any focus on the external intention alone, which purportedly was the understanding of Ambrosius Catharinus, OP (1484–1553), and Alphonso Salmerón, SJ (1515–85).

71. *DH* 2328. "The Augustinian theologian François Farvacques held that even if the minister secretly resolves not to do what the Church does, nevertheless the sacrament is valid." Leeming, *Principles of Sacramental Theology*, 467.

72. Revel, *Traité des sacrements: Baptême et sacramentalité*, 2:242–47.

REFINING OUR UNDERSTANDING
OF MINISTERIAL FAITH
AND INTENTION

The above data need to be synthesized into a more refined understanding concerning the faith and intention of the sacramental minister. Per se, a person's faith is not essential to his potential to serve as a sacramental instrumental minister. Per accidens, however, his faith may lead him to an intention substantially inconsistent with that of the Church such that any attempted ritual actions cannot be true Christian sacraments. Using St. Thomas's principles and more recent magisterial pronouncements, we can articulate some aspects toward a theological definition about the juxtaposition between the minister's faith and intention.

The conditions separating a truthful participation from a false participation in Christ's sacramental dispensation are more easily identified by disqualifications, things that prevent a sacramental act. I see four possible disqualifications of varying levels of certainty.

For all of the following conditions, I have two opening presuppositions, and I will later add a third presupposition. First, I am trying to delineate points that will serve for all of the sacraments. Baptism offers a test case at one extreme, for even a pagan can baptize. Another sacrament may have higher standards.[73] Second, as I specified at the beginning of this essay, I pre-

---

73. E.g., some have questioned whether or argued that active faith is needed on the part of the man and woman who are entering into the sacrament of marriage. The International Theological Commission has twice offered reflections on the issue: first, in 1977, in "Propositions on the Doctrine of Christian Marriage," esp. sections 2.3, 3.3, and 3.5–6, and in "Christological Theses on the Sacrament of Marriage," esp. sections 7–9; and second, in 2020, in "The Reciprocity between Faith and Sacraments in the Sacramental Economy," esp. part 4. The first documents are available in International Theological Commission, *Texts and Documents: 1969–1985*, ed. Michael Sharkey (San Francisco: Ignatius, 1989), 163–83; the latter document is available at the website of the Holy See, accessed September 11, 2020, http://www.vatican.va/roman_curia/congregations/cfaith/cti_index.htm. For the position in favor of a requirement of active faith, see Ladislas Örsy, SJ, "Faith, Sacrament, Contract, and Christian Marriage: Disputed Questions," *Theological Studies* 43 (1982): 379–98; Susan K. Wood, "The Marriage of Baptized Nonbelievers: Faith, Contract, and Sacrament," *Theological Studies* 48 (1987): 279–301; and Michael G. Lawler, "Faith, Contract, and Sacrament in Christian Marriage: A Theological Approach," *Theological Studies* 52 (1991): 712–31. Against their position, see Peter J. Elliott, *What God Has Joined: The Sacramentality of Marriage* (New York: Alba House, 1990), 192–99; and David L. Schindler et al., "Faith and the Sacrament of Marriage: A Response to the Proposal of a New 'Minimum Fidei'

sume that the potential minister is using a correct sacramental matter and form and fulfills all other ministerial requirements (e.g., an ordained priest as the minister of the Eucharist). We only want to focus on what difference a faith-based ministerial intention makes. Otherwise, with those other ministerial conditions in place (as well as the recipient's conditions), the normal Catholic perspective is that the doing of the sacramental rite confers the sacrament.

A first disqualification that separates a true intention from a false one is when the minister has no knowledge of the Church of Christ or denies that there is a Church of Christ. This condition fits the problem of Mormon baptism. Its elaboration by the magisterium responds to increased ecclesial sensibilities, with the rise of ecumenism and the science of ecclesiology over the past two centuries. This heightened awareness has included the study of the sacraments as ecclesial acts. If a minister has no knowledge of a sacrament as an ecclesial act or if he denies this truth, then he cannot have the intention to do what the Church does.

A second disqualification is when the minister denies that Christ instituted in some fashion the sacrament in question. Ladaria described this in the case of Mormon baptism. The disqualification concerns the denial of the sacrament as a whole. It does not pertain to the denial of some part of a sacrament, for instance, its efficacy. So this condition is not speaking about Protestant baptisms wherein the minister does not believe that the sacramental rite confers grace. Even mainline Protestants have recognized that Christ instituted certain sacraments as ordinances, as rituals commanded by Christ, even if those Protestants deny sacramental causality. Rather than that, this second disqualification concerns the denial that Christ instituted or ordained a sacrament. Such a faith against the Christian root of the sacrament cannot intend to do what the Church intends.

One could speculate whether two further disqualifications are in order. A third condition would hold that a rite is invalid if the minister denies the Trinity or the divinity of any Trinitarian Person. We saw how patristic Catholics denied the baptism of some non-Trinitarians, such as Adoptionists.

Requirement," *Communio* 42 (2015): 309–30. We need not resolve this marriage question in this article. I would point out, however, the crucial difference between (1) what is required for the *sacramentum tantum* to occur truthfully and (2) what is required for the *res et sacramentum* to result in a fruitful *res tantum*.

But we also saw how this was a disputed question in the Arian controversy. Ladaria himself says that Arian baptisms were recognized as valid. And yet Ladaria's primary explanation of the defectiveness of Mormon baptism hinges on the non-Trinitarian though Trinitarian-looking belief of Mormons. It is hard to see how this does not apply equally to Arian baptism or indeed to any baptism that does not recognize the equal divinity of the Father and the Son and the Holy Spirit. A denial of the Trinity denies the source of the sacrament. In the case of baptism, an intention against the Trinity would seem to render a charade the sacramental form with its Trinitarian invocation. Looking to the patristic witness, Ladaria's explanation matches St. Athanasius's condemnation of Arian baptism, not Pope St. Siricius's or Pope St. Gregory's allowance of Arian baptism. If the Arian problem were more pronounced today, would the magisterium make the prudential, pastoral judgment that an Arian minister intends what the Church does, and that that Arian minister does a valid sacrament?

For a fourth possible condition, we return to the example of a Protestant minister's denial of the intrinsic efficacy of baptism while yet doing true baptisms. Aquinas dealt with such a case in *ST* III, q. 64, a. 9, ad 1. The Holy Office said that such Protestant baptisms are truly sacramental.[74] But Leo XIII's argument about defect of intention in Anglican ordinations specified that part of the defect was the denial of an essential aspect of the sacrament—namely, to create a minister of sacrifice. Leo specified that such a denial cannot coexist with the intention to do what the Church does. Therefore a fourth disqualification for any sacramental rite could be the denial of an essential effect of the sacrament in question. Frankly, on this point, it is difficult to see how the various magisterial statements fit together. It is a question that needs a fuller answer.

Having elaborated these conditions, allow me to add another presupposition. I presume the typical operating procedure whereby a person's faith informs his intention. In contrast, if a person wishes to not have an anti-Catholic or anti-sacramental intention, then a typically erroneous minister could make a specific intention to do what the Church does. In that

---

74. Leeming, *Principles of Sacramental Theology*, 472–73. The Holy Office decisions are from 1833, 1872, 1877, and 1949 (the last of which affirmed the baptisms of Disciples of Christ, Presbyterians, Congregationalists, Baptists, and Methodists). The latter two decisions respond to dubia sent from the United States.

case, a person typically disqualified by his faith could form a sufficient intention and be a truthful minister. For instance, even a Mormon priest could, on a specific occasion, intend to do what the Church intends and thereby do a true baptism.

CONCLUDING IMPLICATIONS

Much of the theology of sacramental ministrations has had to be worked out in moments of crisis. Our time may surpass earlier ones in how far ostensibly Christian ministers are willing to depart from rather basic biblical and dogmatic principles of Christianity. Additionally, even more than the fragmentation during the patristic Christological controversies or during the Reformation, today's climate allows or encourages creedal diversity even within ecclesial communions. This fragmentation and anti-ecclesiality place new pressures on the possibility of sacraments outside the visible Church.

For instance, when some Catholic priests nowadays receive a young convert from the Episcopalian communion, they ask if the Episcopalian baptism used the traditional Trinitarian formula or some false alternative like "the name of the Creator, and of the Redeemer, and of the Sanctifier." That latter alternative was declared an invalid form by the CDF and Pope Benedict XVI in 2008.[75] Today, the choice to use such a form suggests defective ministerial intent, an intention against doing what the Church does.

If such false Trinitarian faith among certain Episcopalians has actively taken the step of inventing a replacement for a biblically based baptismal formula, how should we evaluate a minister with a similarly erroneous faith but without the creative energy or interest to invent a new formula? Extending our pastoral example from above, what if a Catholic priest were to receive a convert ostensibly baptized by John Shelby Spong, now retired from being the Episcopalian bishop of Newark? The latter is well known for having denied the physical truth of the Resurrection. That is just the start. He has

---

75. "Responsa ad proposita dubia de validitate baptismatis," February 1, 2008, in *Acta Apostolicae Sedis* 100 (2008): 200; also available at the website of the Holy See, accessed September 11, 2020, http://www.vatican.va/roman_curia/congregations/cfaith/documents/rc_con_cfaith_doc_20080201_validity-baptism_en.html.

also written that he does not "define God as a supernatural being"; that "the Holy Trinity is not now and never has been a description of the being of God [but that] it is rather the attempt to define our human experience of God"; that "since [he does] not see God as a being, [he] cannot interpret Jesus as the earthly incarnation of this supernatural deity"; and that he "[does] not believe that this Jesus founded a church" or "that he created sacraments."[76] Spong has been controversial but has not been censured by his Episcopal Church. He is still within the Episcopalian communion. Should we automatically accept as true or valid a baptism done by Spong even if done with a Trinitarian formula? We can desire that he intend to do in baptism what the Church does. But it is well possible that his defective faith could entail defective intention, leading to a false sacramental rite.

Unfortunately, our postmodern, increasingly post-Christian religious climate in America is going to involve more examples like Spong. This is not to say that the average Catholic believer has to worry about radically dissenting sacramental ministers within the Church. We can prudently be confident that the overwhelming majority of Catholic sacramental ministers intend to do what the Church does. But our ecumenical and interreligious context—and fragmentation—means that the Catholic pastor, layman, and theologian will increasingly be confronted with questions about ministerial intention.

The sacramental theology of St. Thomas Aquinas teaches us how ministerial action contributes to sacramental signification, sacramental truthfulness, including the link between internal intention and external action. The broader dogmatic and moral theology of St. Thomas will be needed in order to understand how true faith supports true sacramental signification, how God's sacramental system can work despite some ministerial error, and how extremely false ministerial faith can corrupt sacramental signification.

76. John Shelby Spong, *A New Christianity for a New World: Why Traditional Faith Is Dying and How a New Faith Is Being Born* (New York: HarperCollins, 2002), 3, 4, 5, and 61.

CHAPTER 15

GOD ALMIGHTY IN THE FLESH

Christology and the Crisis of Faith

Bruce D. Marshall

I. WISDOM IN DISNEYLAND

Many years ago, sometime in the late 1980s or early 90s, I was having dinner with a group of like-minded theologians at the annual meeting of the American Academy of Religion. This was in Anaheim, California, more or less across the street from the original Disneyland, and the restaurant was host to a decidedly mixed clientele. When I went up to the buffet for seconds (or quite possibly for thirds), I found myself standing next to a man in jeans and cowboy boots. I can't remember why, but he struck up a conversation with me, and asked me what I was doing in town. "I'm here," I said, "for a big meeting of professors from all over the country." "Oh?" he replied. "What sort of professors?" "Religion professors," I told him. "Is that right? Well you know, what you religion professors need to do is face the question of Jesus Christ." "Oh?" I said. "How's that?" Looking keenly at me, he asked, "Do you believe that Jesus Christ is God almighty in the flesh?" I hesitated briefly, and said, "Yes, I do." Pleased, if a bit startled, he said, "Well OK. Good for you," and went back to his table.

That the human being Jesus, the son of Mary who was handed over to death for our transgressions, is in reality nothing less than God almighty in our flesh—this is the glowing center of our faith in him, the core of Christian belief. The Apostle John puts this with incomparable clarity, at the beginning of his First Letter. "The one whom we have heard, whom we have seen with our own eyes, upon whom we have looked," whose flesh, indeed, "we have touched with our own hands"—this is none other than "the one who was from the beginning," "the Word of life," "the eternal life that was in the beginning with the Father and has appeared to us" (1 Jn 1:1–2). When we hear the human speech of Jesus, we hear the Word of life speaking to us. When we see the human flesh of Mary's Son, we see the one who was in the beginning with the Father, and when those of us who have not seen his flesh have that flesh announced to us, the one who was in the beginning with the Father is announced to us (cf. 1 Jn 1:5). When we touch that flesh, we touch the Word of life himself, and when his flesh touches ours in the holy Eucharist, the eternal life that was in the beginning with the Father is on our tongue.

The human being born of Mary who hung on the cross for us is, as the Definition of Chalcedon repeatedly insists, "the very same" as the Word who was in the beginning with the Father.[1] Jesus of Nazareth and the Father's eternal Only-Begotten are one and the same. They are not one and another; they are one, not two. They are one and the same subject, one and the same irreducible individual, or, in the language of Chalcedon, one and the same "person" and "hypostasis." The flesh of Jesus is therefore the flesh of God, the flesh of the Only-Begotten. The human heart of Jesus is, as Catholics are accustomed to pray, "the heart of the eternal Father's Son" (*Cor Iesu, Filii Patris aeterni, miserere nobis*). The flesh of Jesus is not God, since human nature is not divine nature. But his flesh is the flesh *of* God; it belongs to God the Son, as much as yours and mine belong to us. The flesh of Christ is, as St. Thomas says, the *caro Dei*, the flesh of God. The value of this flesh is infinite, Thomas insists—*habebat dignitatem infinitam*—not on account of the nature of flesh as such, but because of the person, the Only-Begotten of the Father, who has assumed it, and whose flesh it therefore is—because, in other words, this is the very flesh of God.[2] This flesh, never to be loosed from the Word of the Father who has assumed it, is eternally life-giving for us because of the one whose flesh it is, as 1 John emphasizes. Just this flesh touches ours

1. Six times in the first paragraph of the Definition alone (*DH* 301), and twice more in the second (*DH* 302).

2. *Summa Theologiae* III, q. 48, a. 2, ad 3: "dignitas carnis Christi non est aestimanda solum secundum carnis naturam, sed secundum personam assumentem, inquantum scilicet erat caro Dei, ex quo habebat dignitatem infinitam."

in the Eucharist and gives us life, as St. Cyril of Alexandria insists, "because it is the very-own flesh of the Word of God the Father."[3]

Just as my Disneyland interlocutor said, Jesus Christ is God almighty in the flesh. To know who he is, to grasp his very identity and not simply some truths about him, is to know just this. Or, in the more comprehensive designation of the Nicene Creed, Jesus Christ is "true God," as much as the Father who eternally begets him is true God. Just this true God, "God from God," is enfleshed by the Holy Spirit, incarnate of the Virgin Mary for us men and for our salvation.

At just this point, Western Christianity, both Catholic and Protestant, is now beset by a crisis of faith, and has been for close to two centuries. At its most basic—or, we might say, its most blatant—this crisis consists in the unambiguous denial, precisely by Christians, that Jesus is true God, God almighty in our flesh. In the early nineteenth century, Protestant theologians in Germany began to look for alternatives to the traditional doctrine of an incarnate divine person, a person fully the subject of both divine and human natures. With often remarkable intellectual ingenuity, they aimed for something like a functional equivalent of the traditional doctrine. The aim was an understanding of Christ's person that would enable Christians to maintain the utter religious centrality of Jesus, yet without incurring the hopeless burdens, as these theologians saw it, of the traditional doctrine of God become flesh—a teaching that had come to seem not only indefensible, both metaphysically and epistemically, but also religiously irrelevant.

First in Germany and then more widely, Protestant theologians repeatedly sought a Christology that clearly maintained, in Friedrich Schleiermacher's phrase, that Jesus is "redeemer alone and for all," without having to maintain that Jesus is God almighty in the flesh.[4] The solution was to see in Jesus the perfect *homo religiosus*, the human being who confronts us not with God in the flesh, but with a perfect human relationship with God, a relationship for which we sense in ourselves the need, but not the ability to bring it about. By way of the Christian community, we can have contact with this archetypal *homo religiosus* and thereby come into the relationship

---

3. From Cyril's 11th anathema against Nestorius, text in *DH* 262.

4. Friedrich Schleiermacher, *The Christian Faith*, 3rd English ed. (London: Bloomsbury, 1999), §11.4, 58.

with God for which we secretly long, a relationship like his, though not fully equal to it. For Schleiermacher the redemptive power of Jesus, the religious impact of this unsurpassable embodiment of the religious perfection we all seek, lay in his wholly unimpeded "God-consciousness." But Protestant theologians proposed many other (and, they thought, better) ways of thinking about Jesus as the perfect *homo religiosus* well into the twentieth century. There were also, to be sure, many other Protestant theologians who continued to argue for the traditional doctrine of the Incarnation, including some within the intellectual orbit of the distinctively modern movement to deny it which I have just been sketching. The Lutheran Isaac August Dorner comes to mind, among others.[5]

II. FAITH WITHOUT FEAR

This post-Enlightenment theological project of Christocentrism without incarnation, redemption in Christ without an enfleshed divine person for the redeemer, never took deep root in Catholicism, not least because of salutary anti-modernist discipline imposed by the Holy See in the early twentieth century. Its day seems largely past in Protestant theology as well. There are plenty of people, of course, who deny that Jesus is true God, but fewer of them are likely to be Christians than was the case a generation or more ago.

Among Catholics, however, a less blatant, a more indirect and implicit, way of *treating* Jesus as though he were not true God has surely become widespread. This almost never takes the form of an outright denial of the traditional doctrine that the human being Jesus is the eternal Son of the Father, incarnate for our salvation. Instead we fail to act and speak as though

---

5. Dorner (1809–84) devoted considerable historical and systematic labor to arguing that the categories of modern thought (particularly, in his case, those of post-Kantian German philosophy) could be adapted to the requirements of traditional faith in the Incarnation. See *Entwicklungsgeschichte der Lehre von der Person Christi von den ältesten Zeiten bis auf die neueste dargestellt*, 2nd ed. (Berlin: Gustav Schlawitz, 1851–56), English translation: *History of the Development of the Doctrine of the Person of Christ* (Edinburgh: T & T Clark, 1863–78). See also *System der Christlichen Glaubenslehre*, 2nd ed. (Berlin: Wilhelm Hertz, 1886–87), English translation: *System of Christian Doctrine*, 2nd ed. (Edinburgh: T & T Clark, 1888–91). For a helpful approach to Dorner in English, see Claude Welch, *God and Incarnation in Mid-Nineteenth Century German Theology: Thomasius, Dorner, Biedermann* (New York: Oxford University Press, 1965).

when we have to do with Jesus, we have to do with nothing less than God almighty in the flesh. I use the word "treat" deliberately: we do not deny that Jesus is God, but we treat him as though his utterances were merely human words, and not the human speech of almighty God. We treat him as though his human actions and sufferings were not those of almighty God in the flesh, the actions and sufferings of the Word of power who upholds all things (cf. Col 1:17), of the one who will with divine authority forever separate the sheep from the goats (Mt 25:31–46), the one who in fulfillment of the prophet's word opens and no one can close, who closes and no one can open (Rv 3:7).

We can be a little more precise about this way of acting and thinking. What is the nature of the God who becomes flesh in Jesus Christ? A God of infinite mercy but not, it often seems, a God who is at the same time infinitely just. Or more subtly, what is it of God that becomes incarnate in Christ? His mercy, without question, but not, it seems, his justice, at least not equally with his mercy and inextricable from it. Of course no Catholic theologian, at least to my knowledge, maintains the remarkably unlikely metaphysical proposition that only part of God becomes incarnate, some attributes but not others. Nor is there recourse to the more sophisticated route of nineteenth-century Protestant kenoticism, for which a divine person whole and entire becomes human, but in order to do so must suspend certain characteristics of his divine nature, let them go dormant, especially those seemingly incompatible with the limitations of human consciousness. On the contrary, in contemporary Catholicism the tendency to treat the human being Jesus as though he were not God almighty in the flesh often stands side by side with a flamboyant assertion of the Incarnation of the Son, of God's complete descent into our flesh and our suffering condition.

When we have to do with Jesus, this outlook insists, we most certainly have to do with true God, in that we here find the human face of divine mercy. There, however, the matter can safely be allowed to rest. That in having to do with Jesus we also, and unavoidably, come face-to-face with divine justice we are far less ready to recognize, and tend to pass over in silence. In so doing, we treat Jesus as though he were not true God. We speak of him and act toward him with complete confidence that he will seek out the lost sheep yet as though he will not separate sheep from goats; we embrace our profession that he is God incarnate of the Virgin Mary for our salvation and try not to think of our profession that this same God made flesh will come in glory to judge the living and the dead with divine justice. His mercy may be almighty, virtually unstoppable, but his justice is allowed to disappear, more or less completely, from view. Or, as Paul teaches, that in Christ it is precisely the justice of God that has appeared for our salvation (Rom 3:25–26) seems to be a teaching of the Gospel for which we no longer have any feel or sense.

We can get a better idea of this outlook, and of the way it tends to undermine the Church's faith that Jesus is true God, by looking at some of its effects, what we could call its symptoms. Perhaps chief among these is the remarkable disappearance, in Western Catholic religious life, of the fear of God. We treat our faith in Jesus as though it relieved us of the need, or the obligation, to fear God. The Western pastoral and theological tradition, we need to recall, usefully distinguished between two different ways of fearing God, what were called servile fear and filial fear, the fear appropriate to slaves and the fear appropriate to children.[6] The one consists in the dread of punishment, and is naturally the sense of the term more readily suggested by the current use of the English term "fear." It is rooted in self-love, the self's desire to avoid what is disagreeable to it. This is not to say that it is valueless. It can be the starting point for something better, a fear based on love for the one who is feared, and a dread of losing the love, the favor, the good opinion of the beloved. This would be more naturally rendered for us by terms like "reverence" and "respect." When Jesus tells his Apostles that he no longer calls them slaves but friends (Jn 15:15), he is not inviting them to abandon all fear but to have a properly filial fear toward him, and toward the Father who sent him. To have this fear is to love with trembling and awe the Father who is boundlessly merciful to us in Jesus his Son, recognizing that his mercy and all in which it consists—the Incarnation, the cross, the glorification of the Son—is not owed to us. This mercy is a free gift which, as such, does not have to be given to us and which moreover can be forsaken and lost by us. This especially, the fear rooted in gratitude and love, is what seems to have disappeared, and not simply what the tradition called servile fear.

6. For a classic explanation of this distinction, see *ST* II-II, q. 19. Fear so understood, it should be noted, is a gift of the Holy Spirit annexed to the theological virtue of hope. As its ultimate aim hope desires the vision of God, and to reach this aim relies on God's help, his love and power, and not on our own strength.

The eclipse of a salutary fear of God comes to the surface in many ways. I'll mention three, the first two practical and specifically Catholic, the third more theological and shared with Protestants.

1. The practice of sacramental confession has decreased dramatically among Catholics in Western Europe and North America over the past generation or two. This is not simply a reflection of declining Mass attendance. Even Catholics who attend Mass regularly go to confession less frequently than they used to. Among the reasons for this seems to be a sense that the mercy of God comes to us without any need for repentance on our part, that is, without any need for us to recognize in word and deed the just claim of God against us on account of our sins. "Take heed, lest you fall," the Apostle warns the Corinthians (1 Cor 10:12), but we seem not to worry that we might fall, perhaps because we take for granted the mercy of God if we do.

Our loss of a sense that the mercy of God is meant to lead us to repentance, and thereby to the sacrament of reconciliation, encourages Catholics to approach the Eucharist without having any recent memory of a good confession. The problem here is not simply canonical, the failure to follow a rule, but religious and spiritual. We have largely ceased to sense the intimate, inextricable connection of God's mercy and forgiveness with our fear and repentance. "There is forgiveness with you, that you may be feared," the psalmist cries from the depths (Ps 130:4). "The Lord pities those who fear him," and his steadfast love "is from everlasting to everlasting upon those who fear him" (Ps 103:13, 103:17). So too Mary, full of grace and schooled in the songs of Israel, sings of the Lord, "He has mercy on those who fear him, in every generation" (Lk 1:50), and every generation of Christians, even our own, has sung with her of the fear that precisely the mercy of the Lord is meant to call forth from each of us.

Having severed mercy from repentance, we approach the Eucharist without filial fear, without a sense that our maker and redeemer is here fully present for our salvation in his flesh and blood, hidden under these sensible things so that we might, with awe, be able to approach him—*quae sub his figuris vere latitas*, as St. Thomas says. Before each communion, we say we are not worthy to receive him in this way, not worthy for him to enter under our roof. If we take this to heart, we will surely recognize that we might in fact receive him unworthily, and should diligently prepare to receive him well, especially through repentance. This is part of what having filial fear involves. Approaching the Eucharist with healthy fear means recognizing that the fathomless mercy held out to us here makes an equally fathomless claim upon us, a claim we can begin to meet by contrition and confession before communion.

2. That the crisis of clerical sex abuse in the Catholic Church exhibits a profound loss of the fear of God is perhaps too obvious to require any explanation. It seems plain that the perpetrators of these crimes lack the fear of God, especially when they profess to believe that they have done nothing wrong, and that the Church's belated penalties against them are unfair. Sometimes there can, no doubt, also be a pathological element involved in such cases, which does not come down only to virtue forsaken. What is more surprising—shocking, in fact—is the readiness of some bishops and others responsible for the Church's discipline of clergy to act as though there were simply no divine justice to which they or anyone else would have to answer in this matter. The only pastoral and doctrinal issue in play, so it has often seemed, is God's undoubted mercy toward even the gravest sinners, untethered to any sense of God's justice toward these same sinners, and still more toward their victims. Thus one well-known archbishop, now dead, was asked under deposition in the criminal trial of one of his clergy why he repeatedly moved the man from one parish to another despite continual accusations of abuse wherever he went. "Because," he replied, "I believe in redemption." Or, he might equally have said, "because I believe in mercy." That there is no true mercy, least of all divine mercy, without justice seems to have escaped him. One is hard pressed to see here a trace of even servile fear, which does what justice requires at least for dread of punishment, to say nothing of the salutary fear that dreads to offend God.

3. A third index of the vanishing fear of God, this one more theological than directly practical. Not a few theologians, Catholic as well as Protestant, now insist on what could be called a dogmatic universalism with regard to salvation. The salvation of every human being, or indeed of every rational creature, fallen angels (i.e., demons) included, is for the dogmatic universalist not simply a possibility for which we can reasonably hope.[7] For the dogmat-

---

7. Whether the salvation of all rational creatures is a possibility that must be left open or one that has, on the contrary, been foreclosed by scriptural and traditional teaching that some (especially some fallen angels) are certainly lost, is itself a debated matter that I won't pursue here.

ic universalist, the salvation of all is an established fact of which Christian faith ought to make us certain, an actuality, not simply a possibility. Scripture warns us to fear the one who can kill the soul (Mt 10:28). This warning comes, according to Christian faith in the Incarnation, from the human lips of God himself. From the same lips comes, in another theandric speech act, the warning to enter by the narrow gate, the way to life that few will find (Mt 7:13–14; Lk 13:23–27). Yet for the dogmatic universalist we have nothing to fear. Awe and godly fear before the possibility of our own irrevocable fall from grace—take heed, lest you fall—are simply unnecessary. God has certainly decided to save all, and our assurance of this evidently cancels even the warnings of God almighty in the flesh that we should take heed.

Some go further and argue that the salvation of all rational creatures is not simply an actuality, but a necessity. It is simply impossible that God could fail to save every human being. We know this a priori, as it were, apart from any consideration of the words and deeds of God made flesh. Given his own nature, his own infinite goodness and love, it would be impossible for God not bestow eternal blessedness on every rational creature and a fortiori on every human being. On this view God could not justly fail to confer beatitude on any creature capable of it. This is to say that God, in justice, owes beatitude to every creature. It would be unjust for him not to give it, precisely because he would thereby fail to honor the requirements of his own goodness.[8]

Such a view would long have been thought incoherent. Just because God's own will is infinitely good, the sole act his will cannot fail to undertake is to love his own infinite goodness, the goodness that belongs to him by nature. God cannot fail, in other words, to value his own goodness at its intrinsic worth, and to do so in a way that fully matches that infinite worth, since he is alone capable of an infinite act. And because God's justice is precisely coextensive with his goodness, God can no more fail to love his own justice than to love his own goodness. It is one and the same act to love

---

8. For a recent version, at full volume, of dogmatic universalism in this strongest sense, see David Bentley Hart, *That All Shall Be Saved: Heaven, Hell, and Universal Salvation* (New Haven, CT: Yale University Press, 2019). For antidotes, see Christophe J. Kruijen, *Peut-on espérer un salut universel? Étude critique d'une opinion théologique contemporaine concernant la damnation* (Paris: Parole et Silence, 2017), and Michael McClymond, *The Devil's Redemption: A New History and Interpretation of Christian Universalism* (Grand Rapids, MI: Baker Academic, 2018).

either, as what is loved is one and the same. It would seem that any love God has for creatures, even the most abundant, cannot, by contrast, be inevitable for the divine will. It has to be a contingent gift of God's goodness, willed by God as such, a willing beyond what its object, the creature, can possibly elicit. Only God's own goodness cannot fail to elicit an act of love from his will. God's infinite goodness is therefore not an obstacle to the just non-conferral of beatitude on any creature capable of it. On the contrary, God cannot coherently be understood to owe beatitude to any creature. The love of his own goodness cannot require any act on God's part that includes the existence of a creature as its term, still less one that includes the beatifying bestowal of himself on any creature.

The dogmatic universalist will object that God does not, in the typical traditional scenario, simply decline to confer on some the eternal blessedness he decides to confer on others. He damns them eternally. He does not simply punish sin, with the aim of rehabilitating the sinner. He punishes eternally a temporal act of sin, which, while grave, may be over in a moment. In the worst case, he may punish eternally a lifetime of unrepented sin. Still, eternal damnation for even a long life of unbothered sin seems like a punishment infinitely, or immeasurably, out of proportion with the relatively modest temporal magnitude of the crime. As a result, it does not fit even minimally with our standard intuitions about justice; it is unjust, and so cannot be attributed to God.

An argument like this may move even the person who clearly senses the force of the biblical and traditional case against the assertion of universalism as a fact or a necessity. Eternal damnation seems simply unfair, and God is not unfair. Recall, though, that eternal blessedness can also be gained, according to Catholic teaching, by passing human acts, indeed even by a single human act. "Beatitude can be merited by a single act, not only in an angel, but even in a human being, because a human being merits beatitude by any act informed by charity."[9] The reward of eternal blessedness is even more out of proportion with the transitory human acts that merit the reward than is the penalty of eternal loss with the demeritorious acts from which it results. The reward of beatitude is maximally intense in the person

---

9. *ST* I, q. 62, a. 5, c: "Meritum autem beatitudinis, non solum in angelo, sed etiam in homine esse potest per unicum actum, quia quolibet actu caritate informato homo beatitudinem meretur."

who receives it; blessedness cannot be increased in any of the blessed, though there are merited differences of degree between those who are enjoying eternal blessedness. By contrast, the misery of the lost could always be greater, as long as they exist. If it is unjust of God to punish a passing act of sin with the eternal loss of blessedness, it is even more unjust of him to reward a passing act of charity with the gift of eternal blessedness. The dogmatic universalist's appeal to our standard intuitions about justice does not show that God could not justly impose eternal punishment. It shows that these intuitions, if we stick to them and refuse to go beyond them, do not allow us to attribute justice to God at all when it comes to the salvation of finite temporal creatures. Providing any destiny for us beyond the temporal bounds of this finite world would, by these standards, be unjust of God.

The universalist's intuitions place us in a world like that of Aristotle's *Ethics*, which, however noble it may (or may not) have been, was pagan all the way down. In this world there was no inkling that human acts can have eternal consequences, consequences quite beyond the limits of this present world and its history, and thereby inherently out of any measurable proportion to the necessarily finite nature of the acts themselves. This world knew nothing, in other words, of a supernatural destiny held out to human beings by God, a destiny to be reached, or not, by the seemingly insignificant acts of this present life. It belongs to the Christian revelation to teach us that while our acts of course are finite, we do not live in a world where the best outcome of our acts, for good or ill, must likewise be finite. As Pascal memorably depicts it, the Christian revelation confronts us with the claim that our brief life is like a game played just once, but for infinite stakes, where the wager we make with our finite life and its mostly trivial acts can end in infinite happiness, but not without facing the possibility of infinite loss.[10] This is not the justice of the polis, with its calculus of temporal rewards and punishments proportioned to the temporal deed. It is the justice of the cross, where God presents us with his own justice in an unsurpassable way (Rom 3:25–26, again). In the justice of the cross the brief and transitory temporal acts of Jesus, of God almighty in the flesh—offering himself to the Father

---

10. Pascal, *Pensées*, trans. Roger Ariew (Indianapolis: Hackett, 2008), §680, 211–15 (Ariew follows Sellier in his numbering of Pascal's fragments). The "wager," as Pascal makes clear, is not for the Christian, who is certain that we have a supernatural destiny, but for the unbeliever, who is not.

in the upper room, pouring out his blood on the cross, his altar—secure an eternal redemption (cf. Heb 9:11–12). Our own brief and transitory temporal acts are the way we share in the eternal redemption his blood secures, but they are also the way we can profane it (Heb 10:29). An infinite blessing that can be ours by a single act of charity can also be lost by the refusal of that act.

The truly ardent universalist will bite this bullet, and argue that the only act on which the beatitude of the rational creature depends is God's own, the act by which he necessarily loves his own goodness. Just because God inevitably loves his own goodness, from which every creature comes forth, he necessarily bestows blessedness on those among his creatures who are capable of it. Otherwise he would fail to love the goodness from which those creatures come, that is, his own. In this scenario, eternal blessedness cannot, and need not, be won by any act of the creature, any finite act, any more than eternal perdition can be reached by any human act.

In that case, though, it's not clear that we could limit God's bestowal of beatitude only to actually existing creatures. All possible creatures are apprehended by God in his grasp of his own essence, so if his goodness requires the conferral of blessedness on what he thereby apprehends, God would have to bestow blessedness on all possible creatures. Presuming you have to be actual to be blessed, that would mean there could be no merely possible creatures. God would have to actualize (i.e., create) all possible creatures in order to bestow on them the beatitude his goodness requires him to give. The creatures thus actualized would, moreover, be mere spectators of their own beatitude, since they would enjoy it apart from any act of their own—if such a thing were possible.

By now we're rather far removed from the sovereignly free, and freely generous, God of the biblical witness, the God who calls on us to work out our own salvation with fear and trembling, just because he himself is at work in us to this end (Phil 2:12–13). With that we have ruled out the very possibility of fearing God. Eliminated is not only the possibility of servile fear, which flees God's just punishment. Filial fear is also now impossible, since its root is precisely the confident hope of God's goodness and mercy toward us in Christ, which is to say the hope of what we deeply apprehend is not owed to us. If we're owed divine blessedness (because God owes it to himself to give it), then we not only need not, but cannot, fear the God who owes it.

If not even God can keep his own goodness from saving us, there is nothing left to fear—and nothing left to love.

<h2>III. CONSEQUENCES IDEAS
DO NOT HAVE</h2>

I have spoken so far of a crisis of faith. This crisis that lies in the vanishing of our sense that when we have to do with Jesus Christ, we have to do with God almighty in the flesh. The chief symptom of this loss of a proper sense that it is truly God almighty who has become flesh is the decline of the salutary fear of God, visible in a number of different ways.

The topic of this volume is "the crisis of Christology," with which we hope St. Thomas can help us. We might be inclined to suppose that the crisis of faith about which I have spoken is a root a theological crisis, and specifically a crisis in Christology. The crisis of faith concerns, after all, the practical shape of our belief in Jesus Christ, of our faith in him as the Father's only Son become our flesh. We might be inclined to suppose, especially if we are theologians, that bad theology is responsible for deficient faith. In a more or less straightforward way, we might think, bad theology has caused the present crisis of faith, and good theology will overcome the crisis and make it go away.

I am all in favor of good theology, and I have no doubt that there is, unfortunately, a fair amount of bad theology afoot, but I very much doubt that it has any significant causal relation to the crisis of faith that I have described. It is a standard conceit of modern intellectuals, theologians included, that what goes on in our heads changes the course of history, that our books will save the world (assuming we can get people to read them), that the reason for failures of faith is that people have failed to appreciate our theological insights.

This conceit of intellectuals is incredible, in the proper sense of the term: entirely unbelievable. To suppose, as theologians persistently do, that vast social and cultural changes—the rise of secularity, for example—have for good or ill been caused by, and can be explained adequately by, recondite conceptual decisions of theologians requires a wholly implausible idea of how human beings act, of why we do what we do. "To most men," St. John Henry Newman rightly observes, "argument makes the point in hand only more doubtful, and considerably less impressive. After all, man is *not* a reasoning animal; he is a seeing, feeling, contemplating, acting animal. He is influenced by what is direct and precise," and therefore almost never by sentences written in books of theology.[11] There is bad Christology afoot, bad arguments about Jesus, his person and work, perhaps to proportions that constitute a crisis, at least within theology itself. But this is immeasurably more a symptom and reflection of deep changes in modern Christian sensibility—the loss of the fear of God, for example—than it is their cause.

As with intellectuals more generally, theologians are remarkably resistant to the suggestion that their ideas are not as important as they think. Ideas have consequences, we say, and theologians have to take responsibility for those consequences. So to recall a famous—and I think quite incredible—suggestion of Henri de Lubac, the notion of a twofold human finality, natural as well as supernatural, and especially Cajetan's way of articulating that idea, is in some way causally responsible for the rise of modern secularism.[12]

Now, ideas clearly have *logical* consequences, and some of these are necessary. The present question, though, is whether ideas have necessary *causal* consequences. Can ideas, with some kind of inevitability, cause either belief or action? This calls for a bit of reflection.

The case where an "idea"—which is to say, for our purposes, a proposition, like "The final end of the human being is twofold"—is most likely to have a direct effect on belief and action—a causal effect, perhaps—is when

11. I. T. Ker, ed., *An Essay in Aid of a Grammar of Assent* (Oxford: Clarendon Press, 1985), 66–67 (in the original edition of 1870, 91; the passage is drawn from Newman's earlier 1841 essay "The Tamworth Reading Room"). The emphasis is Newman's own. And later: "mere argument is not the measure of assent" (130; 1870 ed., 187).

12. Henri de Lubac, SJ, *The Mystery of the Supernatural*, trans. Rosemary Sheed (New York: Herder & Herder, 1967), xi: "The dualist—or perhaps better, separatist—thesis ... may be only just beginning to bear its bitterest fruit ... While wishing to protect the supernatural from any contamination, people had in fact exiled it altogether—both from intellectual and from social life—leaving the field free for the invasion of secularism." (De Lubac, writing amidst the travails of twentieth-century French Catholicism, says "laïcisme"; I have slightly modified the translation. Cf. *Le mystère du surnaturel* [Paris: Aubier, 1965], 15). That Cajetan and his writings, especially his commentary on the *Summa Theologiae*, were chiefly responsible for the baleful hegemony of what he here calls "the dualist thesis" was a hobby horse of de Lubac's in this work and others over several decades.

the proposition is uttered face-to-face by one person to another.[13] Starting with this case, consider the following.

1. Mary makes a statement to Peter, uttering a proposition p that she evidently believes to be true—say, the proposition "The final end of the human being is twofold." It is quite possible that Peter will not understand correctly what she proposes to him, and if he does in fact understand it, it is quite possible that he will not believe it. There is no guarantee or necessity that Mary's committed utterance of p will result in Peter understanding p, or in Peter believing that p. And this is simply to say that Mary cannot cause Peter either to understand or to believe what she says. Her utterance can certainly be the *occasion* for Peter either to understand p, or to believe that p, but whether he actually does either depends on countless factors over which she has no control, such as how well he grasps the notion of a final end and what he is antecedently inclined to believe about such an end.

2. Even if Peter does come to believe that p when Mary says it, there is no guarantee that he will act in accordance with p, or that p will prove relevant to his overt action at all, even implicitly. People often fail to act in accord with what they believe to be true, even when the belief and the action have the closest possible relation (I believe that it is wrong to lie; I lie). A particular belief and a particular action have no causally reliable connection, even when the content of the belief and the description of the act are intimately linked. "I believe I should always tell the truth, therefore what I just said is the truth" is an inference always open to doubt, even if we accept the speaker's claim about what she believes. I am no doubt more likely, on the whole, to act on a proposition that I believe to be true than on one I believe to be false or have never entertained. But a particular belief cannot necessitate a particular action.

3. A fortiori, if the belief that p has no clear connection, whether by content or inference, to the state of affairs it is supposed to have caused, then the assertion of a causal dependence of that state of affairs on the belief is truly farfetched. A causal relation between belief and action is open to doubt even when the connection between the two is clear, as we have just observed (2).

---

13. I leave aside the effect a proposition might have on the person who entertains it, rather than the person to whom it is uttered. The latter case is the one theologians usually worry about when they say "ideas have consequences."

It is much more obviously open to doubt when the connection between the two is remote, let alone when it is utterly obscure.

Suppose Peter believes, on Mary's authority, that the final end of the human being is twofold. The idea that he will then inevitably set about secularizing the world is not so much wrong as nonsensical. There is no discernible connection between this proposition and any course of action that might be thought of as secularizing, let alone a necessary one. What might holding this belief plausibly motivate (never mind cause) Peter to do? Will he press for the disestablishment of the Church in his country? Embrace atheism, materialism, or naturalism? Lobby to have marriage and education removed from the control of the Church and made subject to the law of the state? For centuries people held this belief and did just the opposite; they still do. Of course, Peter might in fact do any of these secularizing things, though this is probably a case best analyzed along the lines of lying in (2). The point is not that an idea, especially one deeply embedded in a theory (like "The final end of the human being is twofold"), actually has one sort of consequence rather than another. It doesn't have any single sort of consequence at all. Propositions of the form "I believe that p, therefore I necessarily q" are certain to be wrong.

4. When the supposedly causal proposition is not uttered face-to-face but written in a book, the relation between ideas (propositions believed to be true) and their supposed consequences becomes still more tenuous. If the book originated in a place and time well removed from our own, few people will have read the book, and perhaps fewer still understood it, at most only a tiny fraction of those whose way of life (secularity, e.g.) is supposed to be a causal consequence of what stands written in the book. Attributing the grip of secularity on the modern West to something Cajetan, or anybody else, once wrote in a book isn't just implausible. It makes the causal relationships presumed by fortune telling and phrenology seem positively sober by comparison. Secularity isn't the consequence of Cajetan's ideas, and the bad Christology all around us isn't the cause of our current crisis of faith or our reluctance to fear God.

While Christology by itself cannot overcome the crisis of faith, it can help us understand where the problem lies. Christology is not the cause of the crisis, but there can be a Christological diagnosis of it. I will briefly attempt to offer one here. The usefulness of such a theological diagnosis is threefold. It gives us an understanding of the crisis of faith, by locating more precisely where faith in the Incarnation has become deformed, even if unintentionally and by inadvertence. A successful diagnosis helps us, further, to recognize the problem, to spot it even where it might not be obvious. And a good diagnosis enables us, lastly, to offer a reasoned alternative, and so to counteract, to the extent that theology is able, the crisis and faith and its unhappy effects.

IV. SOLIDARITY, GLORY, AND THE SEMANTICS OF THE INCARNATION

At its most basic, St. Thomas proposes the Church's faith in the Incarnation of the Only Begotten Son can be stated as the conjunction of two propositions. (1) *Deus est homo*, God is a human being. (2) *Homo est Deus*, a human being is God.[14] These two propositions do not, of course, say all that the Church believes it necessary to say about Jesus, since to get even the creedal minimum on that score we have to add propositions concerning the *acta et passa Christi in carne*, what Christ did and suffered in the flesh he assumed.[15] Taken together, however, these two propositions, "Deus est homo" and "Homo est Deus," are sufficient to state what is being believed when we say, with John the Evangelist, that the Word became flesh, or with the Nicene Creed, that "true God ... was incarnate by the Holy Spirit of the Virgin Mary, and became man."

These two propositions are jointly sufficient for stating the Church's faith in the Incarnation because, as St. Thomas observes, everything Scripture says about Jesus Christ conforms to, or exhibits, the semantic structure established by one of these two basic propositions. The same goes, all the more, for anything the Church is warranted in saying about Jesus Christ. "Holy scripture," as Thomas puts the point, "attributes without distinction what is true of God to this human being, and what is true of this human be-

---

14. Analysis of these two propositions is the subject of *ST* III, q. 16, aa. 1–2.
15. To recall *ST* III, q. 27, prooemium.

ing to God." Here we have, in reverse order, the two semantic paradigms for Christology just identified. Whatever is true of God (the Son) is attributed to, or predicated of, the human being Jesus—*homo est Deus*. And whatever is true of the human being Jesus is attributed to, or predicated of, God (the Son)—*Deus est homo*.[16]

These semantic paradigms are manifest not only in what we attribute to the human being Jesus and God the Son by nature, but also in what we attribute by action and passion. Thus we rightly say, "The infant in the crib created the stars," *homo est Deus*.[17] And we rightly say, "The Lord of glory was crucified," *Deus est homo*.[18] The complete scriptural and creedal *acta et passa Christi* are thus anticipated by the two basic semantic paradigms for Christology.

For a fuller understanding of these two basic propositions we need to add certain kinds of semantic inflections to each, and consider their truth

---

16. *Summa contra Gentiles* IV, c. 39, no. 3771: "Scriptura sacra indistincte quae sunt Dei homini illi attribuat, et quae sunt illius hominis Deo, ut ex praemissis patet; oportet unum et eundem esse de quo utraque dicantur." From the two basic semantic paradigms required by Scripture it follows, Aquinas here argues that "homo" and "Deus" must be true of the same subject (in Aquinas's terms, the same "supposit" or terminal individual). From this it follows that all the further predicates gathered by the two basic terms "homo" and "Deus" must likewise be true of one and the same subject. Having reached this point, we then try to think out the metaphysics of the Incarnation. The purpose and limit of this metaphysical project is, as Aquinas puts it here, to "save" what Scripture says about the Incarnation, that is, to deploy "person," "nature," and related concepts in a fashion that consistently makes the statements in Scripture come out true. We hold to the basic Chalcedonian picture, complete divine and human natures united in a single person and hypostasis, precisely because it achieves this purpose; it (and in Aquinas's view, it alone) "saves" the semantic paradigms presented to us in the Bible: "Hoc enim solum modo salvari possunt ea quae in Scripturis circa Incarnationem traduntur."

That Aquinas's order of presentation in the *Summa Theologiae* is the reverse should not mislead. He presents in the order of being, moving in general from essence to qualities, causes, and effects of whatever is under discussion. The truth of the basic Christological propositions is an effect, broadly speaking, of the subsistence of a human nature in the person of the Word. But the order of knowing is the reverse, following the axiom that what's known is in the knower according to the mode of the knower. What we first know is the truth of the basic propositions, from which the unity of subject follows (real or ontological subject, since the propositions are true), which is the needed basis for trying to think out the metaphysics of the Incarnation.

17. In Aquinas's formulation, "The Son of man created the stars" (*Filius hominis creavit stellas*). *Super Ioan.* 3, lect. 2, no. 468.

18. *Super Ioan.* 3, lect. 2, no. 468: *Filius Dei cruxifixus est*. See *In 1 Cor.* c. 2, lect. 2 (no. 92), on the verse "If they had known, they would not have crucified the Lord of glory" (1 Cor 2:8). "We can say that a human being created the stars, and that the Lord of glory was crucified ... And by this word [of Scripture: 1 Cor 2:8] the error of Nestorius is destroyed ... since according to this [error] the statement could in no way be verified as true that the Lord of glory was crucified" (*quia secundum hoc nullo modo posset verificari quod Dominus gloriae sit crucifixus*).

value when so qualified or inflected. We need, for example, not only to hold "Homo est Deus" as a basic and irreducible truth about Jesus, but also to ask what becomes of the truth value of the proposition when we add reduplicative qualifications like *secundum quod*, "according as," to generate cases like *Homo, secundum quod homo, est Deus*, "A human being, on account of being human, is God." We cannot, however—and this is the decisive point for present purposes—further reduce these two basic propositions, "Deus est homo" and "homo est Deus." They are both necessary to state what the Church believes about Jesus Christ in an adequate way, which is to say that neither will do by itself.

Equipped with these semantic tools, it is not difficult to locate, or diagnose Christologically, the crisis of faith of which we have been speaking. It consists in a clear, often robust assertion of Christology's first basic proposition, that God is a human being, while the complementary second proposition, that in Jesus Christ we have to do with a human being who is God, is overlooked and ignored, if not denied outright.

To explain briefly. Especially among Catholics, modern piety, catechesis, pastoral practice, and theology warmly embrace the idea that in Jesus Christ, God has truly and fully accepted our human lot, that he has truly made his own all the weakness, frailty, misery, suffering, and death we ourselves experience. From the simplest piety to the most elaborate academic theology, we cling to the conviction of God's complete solidarity with us in Christ. We are, of course, entirely right to do so. Our hope of blessedness and salvation depends on the full solidarity of God the Son with us. As the Letter to the Hebrews teaches, it was fitting that he be like us in all things, that he suffer our infirmities and be tempted as we are, though certainly without sin (Heb 2:17–18, 4:15). Our contemporary piety and theology of solidarity clearly conform to the first of the basic protocol statements for Christology, *Deus est homo*—presuming, to be sure, that the human qualities, actions, and passions we attribute to God the Son actually belong to Jesus, that they are genuine features of his particular human life, or are even capable of belonging to him.[19]

19. To note one example: it is not unusual today for Catholic theologians, following Balthasar, to attribute divine abandonment or God forsakenness to Jesus, and thereby to the person of the eternal Son. Whether this is a feature or characteristic the eternal Son could possibly have, even on account of the flesh (*secundum quod homo*), let alone one he actually has, is less than obvious. On this see Bruce

Not only, however, is "Deus est homo" true, and a Christology of solidarity to that extent warranted. "Homo est Deus," "This human being is God," is also true, and equally basic. In fact the first proposition implies the second, so the first cannot be true unless the second also is. If the statement "Deus est homo" is true, then the person, subject, or terminal individual to which the term "Deus" refers must be one and the same person, subject, or individual as the human being whom he is said to be by this statement, by the predication "est homo."[20] When, therefore, we put "homo" in the subject position, the human being to whom this term refers must be one and the same person, subject, or individual as the God whom he is said to be by the statement "homo est Deus." If the Christologically basic proposition "God is a human being" calls for our recognition of God's solidarity with us in the human being Jesus, the equally basic proposition "A human being is God" calls for our recognition that this same human being unfailingly speaks, acts, and suffers with divine power and authority. With these human lips God speaks in the person of the Son, with these human hands God acts, as this human flesh God suffers. This human being not only lays down his life in divine solidarity with us, he himself takes it up again with his own divine power and authority (Jn 10:18). A legitimate Christology of solidarity, we could say, must be completed by a Christology of glory, a Christology that not only embraces God's compassion for us in becoming flesh but also knows the divine glory that shines forth from his human flesh (Jn 1:14), the glory of God, and not only the mercy of God, in the human face of Jesus Christ (2 Cor 4:6).

If we think, in fact, about how these two basic Christological propositions are connected, not only are both necessary to state the Church's faith in Jesus Christ, and necessary in such a way that the first implies the second. The first is actually for the sake of the second—"Deus est homo" for the sake of "homo est Deus." God is this human being so that this human being can be God.

This naturally recalls the teaching, already emphatic in Athanasius and

---

D. Marshall, "The Dereliction of Christ and the Impassibility of God," in *Divine Impassibility and the Mystery of Human Suffering*, ed. James F. Keating and Thomas Joseph White, OP (Grand Rapids, MI: Eerdmans, 2009), 246–98.

20. As Thomas says in *Summa contra Gentiles* IV, 39, cited in note 16 above; cf. also ST III, q. 59, a. 6, ad 3—the brief conclusion to all the questions on Christ.

Augustine, that the telos or ultimate aim of the Incarnation is the glorification (Rom 8:30) and deification (2 Pt 1:4) of humanity. "The Logos of
God became a human being," in the well-known formulation of Athanasius, "so that we [human beings] might become God."[21] This cannot mean
that God becomes every human being, every *anthropos*, so that in this
quasi-pantheistic way every *anthropos* can be God. Our deification happens
in a different and entirely particular way. God becomes this particular human being so that this human being, Jesus of Nazareth, can be God, and
as a result we can receive a share in the fullness of divine glory that belongs
to him alone: "from his fullness we have all received" (Jn 1:16). Augustine's
formulation brings out this point. "God has become a human being, and in
this way a human being has become God."[22] St. Thomas follows Augustine with precision on this point, taking *Deus est homo* to be for the sake of
homo est Deus, and *homo est Deus* for the sake of our deification (granted
that the passage he quotes from Augustine has turned out to be spurious).
Among the manifold benefits we receive by the Incarnation of the eternal
Son is "full participation in divinity, which is truly the blessedness of the
human being and the end of human life. And this is conferred upon us by
the humanity of Christ. For Augustine says, in a sermon on the Nativity of
the Lord, 'God became man, so that man might become God.'"[23]

A Christology of solidarity, to put the point in a more sweeping way, is
for the sake of a Christology of glory. God's solidarity with us is not an end

21. *On the Incarnation* 54.2–3: ὁ τοῦ Θεοῦ Λόγος...γὰρ ἐνηνθρώπησεν, ἵνα ἡμεῖς θεοποιηθῶμεν. Text
as in Sources Chrétiennes 199 (Paris: Éditions du Cerf, 1973), 458.

22. *Sermo* 186.2 (PL 38, 1000): *sed tamen Deus hominem factum, et ita factum Deus factum*. In
this Christmas sermon Augustine continues, commenting on Jn 1:14, by making it especially clear that
this particular human being, the only son of Mary, is the one of whom it is now true to say that he is
God, *homo est Deus*: "We must confess, therefore, that when he who was the Son of God became the
Son of man, having assumed the form of a servant so that he might be born of the Virgin Mary, he
remained what he was, and assumed what he was not." My translation; for an English version of the
whole, see WSA III/6, *Sermons 184–229Z* (on the Liturgical Seasons), here 25. I am grateful to my
colleague Jim Lee for pointing out this passage to me. Augustine will also say that deification is the
divinely intended aim of the Incarnation; see, e.g., *sermo* 23B.1–3 (Dolbeau 6) (WSA III/11, 37–39),
and David Meconi's analysis of this passage in *The One Christ: St. Augustine's Theology of Deification*
(Washington, DC: Catholic University of America Press, 2013), 90–91.

23. *ST* III, q. 1, a. 2, c: "quantum ad plenam participationem divinitatis, quae vere est hominis
beatitudo, et finis humanae vitae. Et hoc collatum est nobis per Christi humanitatem: dicit enim Augustinus, in quodam Sermone de Nativ. Domini, 'Factus est Deus homo, ut homo fieret Deus.'" For the
text Aquinas here attributes to Augustine, see PL 39, 1997.

in itself. That God fully share our life and our death is not the final purpose of the Word's becoming flesh. He shares our lot so that a human being, the human being Jesus, can act with divine authority and power in our life and in our death. He shares our lot, "Deus est homo," so that human lips can speak divine truth, "homo est Deus." He shares our lot so that human touch can give sight to the blind and life to the dead, and death itself can be destroyed by the human being who can say, "I was dead, and behold, I live forever, and I hold the keys of death and hell" (Rv 1:18).

The Letter to the Hebrews makes with special force this point about how the purposes of the Incarnation are related to one another. In Hebrews we find particularly emphatic statements about God's solidarity with us in the person of the Son. With equal clarity, however, Hebrews insists that God the Son has been made like us in all things not simply so that we can be assured of God's sympathy with us in our weakness, but so that our flesh can offer with divine authority a sacrifice of infinite worth to the Father for the salvation of sinners. The sympathy of the Son of God with us in our weakness is for the sake of the eternal high priesthood of Jesus, and not the other way around. "It was fitting that he become like his brethren in all things so that he might be a merciful and faithful high priest before God, and make propitiation for the crimes of the people" (Heb 2:17).

Unless completed by a Christology of glory, by the certainty that this human being is God almighty in the flesh, our sense of God's solidarity with us becomes deformed. It tempts us, for example, to believe that our salvation consists simply in God's compassion toward us, his sympathy with our lot, and not in the purpose for which he shares our lot—so that he can offer to the Father his own blood for us. It likewise tempts us to believe that we can know the fathomless mercy of God become flesh without heeding the call to repentance that God issues to us with his own human lips.

Among the dispositions called for by the divine acts that Scripture and creed attribute to the human being Jesus—*homo est Deus*—is surely the fear of God, precisely the filial fear rooted in love for the God who has graciously come to share our lot. Not least among these divine acts of the human being Jesus, as I noted at the outset, is to judge the living and the dead. Jesus can judge the world because he is true God in the flesh. If he were not, he simply couldn't, since judgment, as Scripture often teaches, belongs to God alone.

This the Church Fathers rightly emphasized, as St. Thomas points out in the last of the *Summa Theologiae*'s fifty-nine questions on Christ.

Thomas argues, however, that Jesus Christ is not our judge solely in virtue of being true God, our judge only *secundum quod Deus*. In a different way, but no less truly, he is our judge *secundum quod homo*, on account of the knowledge his soul possesses as the human soul of God the Word. The human soul of Jesus, as Aquinas puts it, is more intimately united to God as first truth, and more completely filled with divine truth, than any other creature.[24] To an unsurpassable degree he has, in other words, the immediate vision of God and the knowledge of all things that goes with this vision—including, of course, the full knowledge of each of us, of our actions and our interior life. Jesus Christ is not simply the God who enters into full solidarity with us, *Deus est homo*, though of course he certainly is that. He is also the human being from whom no secret is hid, who knows us better than we know ourselves.[25] God's judgment is agreeable to us, Thomas suggests, because it comes from the God who has consented in love to be our brother, who has shared our lot and sympathizes with our weakness.[26] So we rightly love the human being who is our divine judge, and do not flee him in dread. At the same time, this human being will judge us in the fullest light of divine truth and justice, as he alone knows them, and knows us. So we rightly fear him, and come trembling before him, reverent before both his divine power and his human knowledge. Before him we have the fear that can come only from love, the fear that knows we cannot rightly love him as the God who became our brother unless we also tremble before him as the human being who is God our judge—who is God almighty in the flesh.

24. See *ST* III, q. 59, a. 2, ad 1.
25. *ST* III, q. 59, a. 2, ad 3.
26. *ST* III, q. 59, a. 2, c.

CHAPTER 16

IS JESUS JUDGMENTAL?

Aquinas on Christ as Eschatological Judge

Daria Spezzano

When considering how Thomas Aquinas would respond to the contemporary crisis in Christology, the first question might be, "Which one?" There are many confusions about who Christ is, it seems, in a time when Christ's identity and teachings are often perceived as quite malleable, able to be conformed to our image, rather than the other way around. For instance, in a culture that increasingly accepts the idea of fluidity and self-construction of gender, it is not surprising to see a recent article in the *Journal of Research in Gender Studies* arguing that the Bible, as "a medium of social engineering," presents Jesus as "the supreme androgynous role model meant to inspire social change."[1] One firm tenet of popular Christology, though, is that Jesus does not judge. It is not uncommon to hear those who identify as Catholic claim that Christ's Gospel teachings of inclusivity and tolerance support and promote the freedom to embrace whatever moral decision each individual feels to be good for themselves, no matter how contrary it may be to the Church's teaching—as long as it is approved by our culture, of course. Although the Church is judgmental, the narrative goes, Jesus is not. In fact, like any enlightened postmodern person, the kind of judgmentalism displayed by the Church is exactly what Jesus condemns. I'm happy for Jesus to be my friend, in other words, but not so delighted for him to be my judge.

But according to Thomas Aquinas, I should be. I argue that Thomas of-

---

1. Bobbi Paige Hopkins, "The Bible as a Medium for Social Engineering: Jesus as the Androgynous Role Model," *Journal of Research in Gender Studies* 3 (2013): 78–87, 78.

fers helpful insight to twenty-first-century Christians, allergic as we often are to the doctrine of Christ's eschatological judgment, which can seem to underline God's wrath and justice at the expense of his love and mercy. Thomas's teaching on Christ's power as judge of all the living and the dead, while it certainly encourages holy fear, also shows positively why we need Christ's wise judgment, how it reveals the Father's love, and therefore why it gives the most profound reasons—to those who really will in the end be the friends of Jesus—for gratitude and joyful hope.

THE NATURE OF THE "CRISIS"

First I want to diagnose more clearly the Christological "crisis" or problem that I see at stake in the contemporary Church. On a deeper level, I think, the temptation to reshape Christ to our own image—a perennial one, as Albert Schweitzer famously pointed out[2]— is symptomatic today not only of relativism or individualism but also of a particular underlying discomfort with the fundamental Christian claim: we need a Mediator; we cannot save ourselves. Although every generation of Christians has viewed Jesus Christ through its own lens, we seem now to be at a particularly significant crisis, or turning point, in Western Christianity. Christians today seem increasingly inclined to reject the need for Christ's mediation in favor of a more personalized and self-determined plan of apotheosis, in which Jesus plays a significant but supporting role. New Age spirituality, widely influential on contemporary American religious culture, often promotes the necessity for "unlocking our hidden (divine) potential," proposing a distorted version of *theosis* that is attained by our own effort of "recognizing and accepting that we are divine."[3] Christ, the Church, and its sacraments and tradition of moral teaching may therefore become somewhat optional, even for Catho-

---

2. "Each successive epoch of theology found its own thoughts in Jesus; that was, indeed, the only way in which it could make Him live. But it was not only each epoch that found its reflection in Jesus; each individual created Him in accordance with his own character." Albert Schweitzer, *The Quest for the Historical Jesus: A Critical Study of Its Progress from Reimarus to Wrede*, trans. W. Montgomery (London: A. and C. Black, 1911; repr., Mineola NY: Dover, 2005), 4.

3. Pontifical Council for Culture and Pontifical Council for Interreligious Dialogue, "Jesus Christ, The Bearer of the Water of Life: A Christian Reflection on the 'New Age,'" 2003, 3.5.

lics. Concomitant with the implicit pantheism of this spirituality is often the rejection of divine judgment: "The warmth of Mother Earth, whose divinity pervades the whole of creation, is held to bridge the gap between creation and the transcendent Father-God of Judaism and Christianity, and removes the prospect of being judged by such a Being."[4] The revealed truth about our dependence on the one divine and human Mediator who "will come to judge the living and the dead" can be perilously neglected under the influence of a culture seeking affirmation of more comfortable truth claims that allow the pursuit of autonomous paths to salvation.

Such a trend in popular Christology no doubt reflects a certain Pelagian tendency that is congenial to the self-constructing ideals of postmodernity. But as the Congregation for the Doctrine of the Faith's recent letter *Placuit Deo* points out, this current tendency to neo-Pelagianism goes hand in hand with a neo-Gnostic impulse that seeks a "merely interior" salvation "closed off in its own subjectivism," disregarding the role of the body and the Incarnation itself.[5] Quoting Pope Francis in *Lumen fidei*, the document notes that for this new form of Gnosticism, "salvation consists in elevating oneself with the intellect beyond 'the flesh of Jesus towards the mysteries of the unknown divinity.'"[6] Contemporary reductionist tendencies to think of salvation as self-realization and a disembodied fusion with the divine underlie a rejection of the sacramental economy, the mediation of the Church, and most fundamentally the gift of the Incarnation itself.[7]

The neo-Gnostic trend identified by *Placuit Deo* in particular finds an unfortunate ally, and possibly a source of influence, in some developments in contemporary academic theology. I am reminded of a quote from Joseph Ratzinger's essay "Revelation and Tradition," written in 1966. Ratzinger describes the "urgent task" of the magisterium to defend the "*sarx* of history"—that is, the truth of the revelation of the Incarnation in Scripture—against "the caprice of a *gnosis* which perpetually seeks to establish its own autonomy."[8] A similar concern emerges in *Dominus Iesus*, published in

4. Pontifical Council for Culture and Pontifical Council for Interreligious Dialogue, "Jesus Christ," 2.3.1.

5. Congregation for the Doctrine of the Faith, Letter *Placuit Deo* to the Bishops of the Catholic Church on Certain Aspects of Christian Salvation, February 22, 2018, 3.

6. *Placuit Deo*, 3; see Pope Francis, Encyclical Letter *Lumen fidei*, June 29, 2013, 47.

7. *Placuit Deo*, 12–14.

8. Joseph Ratzinger, "Revelation and Tradition," in Karl Rahner and Joseph Ratzinger, *Revelation*

2000 under Ratzinger as head of the Congregation for the Doctrine of the Faith. The document was written to counter "relativistic theories which seek to justify religious pluralism, not only *de facto* but also *de iure* (or in principle)," based on "presuppositions of both a philosophical and theological nature, which hinder the understanding and acceptance of the revealed truth." The central concern here is with Christological approaches that imply or explicitly posit mediations of salvation alternative to the mystery of the Word made Flesh and his Church, undermining their "absolute truth and salvific universality."[9]

One well-known example is Fr. Jacques Dupuis's later Christology, which led to his notification by the Congregation for the Doctrine of the Faith at the time of *Dominus Iesus*. Dupuis proposed that the divine Logos might bestow truth and grace through other religious traditions in ways unmediated by his humanity, even after the Incarnation.[10] This, as Fr. Thomas Joseph White notes, leaves "room for knowledge of truths about God the Logos that comes not through the humanity of Christ, but by means of other mediators," especially in non-Christian religions.[11] Such a separation between the Word and Jesus, or between the salvific activity of the Word's two natures, reflects a problematic account of the hypostatic union as well as of the revealed truth that the Word Incarnate is the sole and universal mediator of salvation for all humanity.[12]

Like Ratzinger, Fr. Thomas Weinandy, in an essay published a few years before *Dominus Iesus*, characterizes some contemporary Christologies as having Gnostic tendencies. Discussing the work of John Hick, among others, Weinandy notes Hick's rejection of traditional teaching on the uniqueness of

---

and Tradition (New York: Herder and Herder, 1966), 49. Cf. Vatican Council II, *Dei Verbum*, November 18, 1965, 10.

9. Congregation for the Doctrine of the Faith, "Declaration *Dominus Iesus* on the Unicity and Salvific Universality of Jesus Christ and the Church," August 6, 2000, 4.

10. Fr. Jacques Dupuis, *Toward a Christian Theology of Religious Pluralism* (Maryknoll, NY: Orbis Books, 1997), e.g., 298–99, 321. See Congregation for the Doctrine of the Faith, "Notification on the Book *Toward a Christian Theology of Religious Pluralism*, by Father Jacques Dupuis, S.J.," January 24, 2001, I.

11. Fr. Thomas Joseph White, OP, *The Incarnate Lord: A Thomistic Study in Christology* (Washington, DC: Catholic University of America Press, 2013), 105.

12. Fr. Dupuis did, however, genuinely seek to avoid error, and in earlier works criticized pluralistic theologies that undermine the uniqueness of Christ as Savior. For a recent article in defense of Dupuis, see Mark Yenson, "Jacques Dupuis and Chalcedon," *Theological Studies* 80 (2019): 271–92.

the Incarnation in favor of the view that Jesus is one religious teacher among others, albeit one with an "immensely powerful God-consciousness."[13] This, he argues, leads to the idea that "salvation consists in perceiving and living the philosophical truth hidden within ... religious metaphor and myth." Jesus reveals and teaches the truth of this transcendent reality as an exemplar, perhaps in an exceptional manner, but differing from other holy figures like Buddha or Moses only in degree, not in kind.[14] Such a focus on the union of Jesus's human consciousness with God in a manner similar to, though greater than, that of other religious figures, comes at the expense of an ontology of union in the hypostasis of the Word;[15] the Gnostic notion that Christ's salvific work as human is primarily to share this God consciousness with others naturally follows. As a corollary, without a Chalcedonian ontology in which Christ's humanity is the instrument of his divinity, it is also unclear that as human he can exercise divine judgment.

A more recent widespread shift toward contextual theologies in the academy often involves a critical reevaluation of traditional Christology and eschatology, to support "Christologies from below" that locate redemption in the liberating transformation of social structures by a Christ identified with the oppressed. Some influential feminist theologies, for instance, propose a Spirit/Sophia Christology, in which Jesus is again primarily a messenger of divine wisdom, while others reject traditional eschatological teaching, especially about the last judgment, as violent and exclusive.[16] According to a recent *Dictionary of Feminist Theologies*, Christianity's traditional emphasis on the "moral imperatives to be included among the saved," with "clear distinctions between insiders and outsiders," constitutes questionably "exclusiv-

---

13. John Hick, *The Metaphor of God Incarnate* (London: SCM, 1993), 26.

14. Fr. Thomas Weinandy, OFM, "Gnosticism and Contemporary Soteriology," in *Jesus: Essays in Christology* (Ave Maria, FL: Sapientia Press, 2014), 260; this essay was originally published as "Gnosticism and Contemporary Soteriology: Some Reflections," *New Blackfriars* 76 (1995): 546–54.

15. For this reason, White characterizes the Christology of both Dupuis and Hick as tending toward Nestorianism (*Incarnate Lord*, 103–7).

16. For a helpful overview of feminist reconstructions of Christology, see Arnfríður Guðmundsdóttir, *Meeting God on the Cross: Christ, the Cross, and the Feminist Critique* (New York: Oxford University Press, 2010), 27–55. Seminal sources (influenced by liberation theology) include Rosemary Radford Ruether, *Sexism and God-Talk: Toward a Feminist Theology* (Boston: Beacon, 1983), and Elizabeth Schüssler Fiorenza, *Jesus: Miriam's Child, Sophia's Prophet* (London: SCM Press, 1995). For an extended critique of traditional eschatology, see Catherine Keller, *Apocalypse Now and Then: A Feminist Approach to the End of the World* (Boston: Beacon, 1996).

istic, often violent visions of justice." Instead, feminist "visions of judgement are more universalistic and focus on the here and now, on the worth and value of all peoples of the earth. The emphasis is not on a judgment of destruction, but on a new creation."[17] The rejection of traditional teaching on Christ's final judgment as violent is intrinsically related to discomfort with orthodox teaching on the Incarnation because of a perceived connection between patriarchal and abusive treatments of women, and the teaching that Christ was a male human being. Natalie Watson notes that for this reason, "very few feminist theologians stick to traditional orthodox Chalcedonian Christology."[18]

These contemporary theologians share a laudable concern to understand God's plan of justice and salvation for all. Most do not reject the idea that some mediator is necessary, at least as revealer and teacher; yet the thought of all, for the sake of an inclusive pluralism, tends toward the notion that this mediator need not be the Word made Flesh. Once such a soteriology filters out into classrooms, parishes, and popular media, it easily allies with the idea that one may pick and choose among ways of accessing the divine, encouraging, perhaps in the name of tolerance and inclusivity, "the caprice of a *gnosis* which seeks to establish its own autonomy," and a concomitant resistance to the idea of Christ's judgment. Take, for instance, Richard Rohr's popular 2019 *New York Times* best seller *The Universal Christ*, "reclaiming" what Rohr describes as a Christological "panentheism," meaning that everything is an "incarnation of the Divine Presence, the Christ."[19] Jesus (who

---

17. Tina Pippin, "Judgment," in *Dictionary of Feminist Theologies*, ed. Letty M. Russell and J. Shannon Clarkson (Louisville, KY: Westminster John Knox Press, 1996), 158.

18. Natalie K. Watson, *Feminist Theology* (Grand Rapids, MI: Eerdmans, 2003), 36. Watson likewise observes that "feminist theologians have so far not taken much interest in the study of the possibility of a future world, but rather in the healing and transformation/liberation of the present world" (49).

19. Richard Rohr, *The Universal Christ* (New York: Convergent Books, 2019), 43, 53. Rohr distinguishes between the "*first Incarnation* (the general term for any enfleshment of spirit)" in creation, when God the "Infinite Primal Source somehow poured itself into finite visible forms" and "joined in unity with the physical universe," from the "personal, second Incarnation that Christians believe happened with Jesus" (12–13). Rohr explains that the "Christ Mystery"—that Christ is the *Logos* through whom "all things came into being"—means for him that every thing materially incarnates Christ, so that "Long before Jesus' personal incarnation, Christ was deeply embedded in all things—as all things!" (13–14). Writing about the Eucharist, he states that "*The universe is the Body of God, both in its essence and in its suffering*" (134). While Rohr clearly intends to express the beauty of the mystery of God's immanence and transcendence, his language is so imprecise as to blur the distinction between God and creation, seeming to make God, in Thomistic terms, a formal rather than an exemplar cause

is "an inclusive Savior instead of an exclusionary Judge") is "the Christ's historical manifestation in time," but to say "Jesus is God" is "strictly speaking … not theologically correct."[20] Jesus is a model and exemplar for the Christian religion, but the universal Christ can be accessed by getting in touch with one's deepest experience, rather than through specific religious practices.[21] The rejection of the unique mediation of the Word made Flesh might be called a Gnostic move, a search for ways to transcendent truth that bypass the Incarnation. Like the Docetists of St. Irenaeus's time or the Cathars of St. Thomas's, Catholics influenced by this Gnostic tendency today may both disregard such embodied means to salvation as Church, sacraments, and good moral action, and discount Christ's unique role as mediator, savior, and judge in his humanity—perhaps not in principle, but too often de facto.

The credal affirmation that Christ will come to judge the living and the dead is not going to go away, however, and so renewed teaching and preaching on this article of faith seem needed today. I think Thomas offers at least three insights that could be helpful in this effort, all rooted in his thoroughly Chalcedonian Christology and concomitantly hylemorphic anthropology,

---

of creatures. In this way he goes far beyond, e.g., Pope Francis's statements in *Laudato Sí* that all creatures are "imbued with [the] radiant presence" of the risen Lord, who is "mysteriously holding them to himself and directing them towards fullness as their end" (Encyclical Letter *Laudato Sí* of the Holy Father Francis on Care for Our Common Home, May 24, 2015, 100), or that Jesus is now "alive in every creature in … risen glory" (246).

20. Although in some places Rohr makes statements to the effect that Jesus "was always objectively the Universal Christ" (178), in others he separates Jesus and Christ in a way that is confusing, if not misleading: "The full Christian leap of faith is trusting that Jesus together with Christ gave us one human but fully accurate window into the Eternal Now that we call God … This is a leap of faith that many believe they have made when they say 'Jesus is God!' But strictly speaking, those words are not theologically correct. *Christ is God, and Jesus is the Christ's historical manifestation in time. Jesus is a Third Someone, not just God and not just man, but God and human together*" (*Universal Christ*, 19). "We must reclaim Jesus as an inclusive Savior instead of an exclusionary Judge, as a Christ who holds history together as the cosmic Alpha and Omega" (68). Italics original.

21. Rohr, *Universal Christ*: "Every religion, each in its own way, is looking for the gateway, the conduit, the Sacrament, the Avatar, the finger that points to the moon. We need someone to model and exemplify the journey from physical incarnation, through a rather ordinary human existence, through trials and death, and into a Universal Presence unlimited by space and time (which we call *'resurrection'*). Most of us know about Jesus walking this journey, but far fewer know that Christ is the collective and eternal manifestation of the same—and that 'the Christ' image includes all of us and every thing" (47). "Just learn to trust and draw forth your own deepest experience, and you will know the Christ all day every day—before and after you ever go to any kind of religious service. Church, temple, and mosque will start to make sense on whole new levels—and at the same time, church, temple, and mosque will become totally boring and unnecessary" (53).

insights that might perhaps even make the doctrine of Christ as mediator and judge more compelling to contemporary Catholics, and address some of the legitimate concerns of religious pluralists and contextual theologians. The first insight concerns why Christ must be our judge in his humanity, the second has to do with why we need his judgment in the first place, and the third concerns the nature of the judgment, when he will "bring to light what is hidden in darkness" and "each one will receive his praise from God" (1 Cor 4:5). To give a framework for these insights, I first outline Thomas's teaching on Christ as judge.

THOMAS AQUINAS ON
CHRIST AS JUDGE

Thomas discusses Christ's judicial power in numerous texts. I draw from both biblical commentaries and systematic works but begin with *Summa Theologiae* III, q. 59, because the structural placement of this question itself gives insight into the meaning for him of Christ's role as judge.[22] This question is the final one in Thomas's consideration of the mysteries of Christ's life—those things that "were done and suffered" by the Incarnate Word for human salvation.[23] Christ's judgment, then, is the culmination of his salvific activity in his human nature. In the unjust condemnation of his Passion, Christ justly merited exaltation to resurrection and the power of judgment over all.[24] Christ's judicial power in his humanity is due first and foremost, however, to the grace of union with the Word, and consequently his fullness of habitual grace as Head, which gives him "the prerogative to bring souls

22. For a thorough treatment of Thomas on Christ's judicial power in the Scripture commentaries, see Piotr Roszak, "The Judge of the Living and of the Dead: Aquinas on Christ's Power to Judge in his Biblical Commentaries," in *Towards a Biblical Thomism: Thomas Aquinas and the Renewal of Biblical Theology*, ed. Piotr Roszak and Jörgen Vijgen (Pamplona: Ediciones Universidad de Navarra, S.A., 2018), 99–117.

23. *Summa Theologiae* (henceforth *ST*) III, q. 1, prol. All translations of *ST* are based on *S. Thomae Aquinatis Doctoris Angelici Opera Omnia Iussu impensaque Leonis XIII P. M. edita*, vols. 4–12 (Rome: Leonine Commission, 1888–1906). All translations from Latin are my own unless otherwise noted.

24. Question 59 concludes a subsection of questions on Christ's exaltation through his resurrection, ascension, and seating at the Father's right hand in glory, mysteries that are fitting because they increase faith, hope and love. *ST* III, q. 57, a. 1, ad 3; q. 59, a. 3.

to beatitude."[25] Thomas's account of Christ as judge is therefore anchored in the ontological foundation he has constructed earlier in the *Tertia Pars* for the inseparability of Christ's two natures after the union, and the instrumentality of Christ's human nature in his theandric activity.[26] Christ is our judge both as Son of God and Son of Man.

Christ's Judgment as Son of God

In his divine person as "Wisdom Begotten and Truth proceeding from the Father," the Son of God is himself the "law of truth or wisdom," on which "the very rule of judgment is based."[27] Drawing from Augustine (on the Word's role in creation), Thomas explains that the Son is the *ars Patris*, through whom the Father does all things. So judiciary power is properly appropriated to him, because "inasmuch as the Son is his art, so [the Father] judges all things through the Son, as the Son is his wisdom and truth."[28] Thomas's implied parallel between the Son as *ars Patris* in creation and judgment underlines the role of the Word as the alpha and omega, from the beginning through to the end of the divine economy.[29] In his *Commentary on John*, Thomas writes that in the beginning, "all things were made" through the Word (Jn 1:3), the "eternally conceived wisdom" who is "the art full of the living patterns [*rationes*] of all things."[30] Later in the commentary he says that the Son of God, as the *ars Patris* and exemplar of creation, is also the fitting exemplar of perfect virtue for our justification.[31] The principle at work

---

25. *ST* III, q. 59, a. 2, ad 2; a. 3.
26. *ST* III, q. 19, a. 1; q. 50, a. 2, a. 3.
27. *ST* III, q. 59, a. 1.
28. *ST* III q. 59, a. 1, ad 2. Augustine, *De Trin.* 6.2.11.
29. Roszak also alludes to this parallel between creation and judgment, with reference to Thomas's commentary on Colossians, where Thomas explains that Christ is the exemplar of creation, "for in him all things were created" (Col 1:16), and to *ST* III, q. 10, a. 2 ("To Christ and to his dignity all things to some extent belong, inasmuch as all things are subject to him. Moreover, he has been appointed judge of all by God, 'because he is the Son of Man'"). Roszak shows that for Thomas, all things have been subjected to the Son as the principle of creation, and therefore Christ, knowing all things in the Word, is judge of all: "The judge should know the subject of his judgment and Christ has precisely such a competence because the creation of the world happened 'through' Him" (Roszak, "Judge of the Living and of the Dead," 106).
30. *Super Ioan.* 1, lect. 2, no. 77. All citations of the *Commentary on John* are based on R. Cai, ed., *S. Thomae Aquinatis Super Evangelium S. Ioannis lectura*, 6th ed. (Turin: Marietti, 1972).
31. *Super Ioan.* 13, lect. 3, no. 1781.

is that just as the Father works through the Word to bring things into being in creation, so through the Word he brings all things to their end through governance (for rational creatures, this includes their participation in governance through the moral life) and final judgment.[32] The Word fully expresses and manifests the Father's wisdom and truth in creation, in re-creation by grace, and at the end of time, ushers in the new creation, completing the wise ordering of God's plan of salvation in a final rectification of all things.[33]

Thomas again quotes Augustine to explain how the Father's Word will manifest all truth in judging without error: "He who alone is Truth itself pass[es] judgment on us, when we cling to him."[34] Those who "cling to him"—as well as those who don't—can count on his complete knowledge and just judgment of their deepest intentions, thoughts and actions. Thomas writes about the perfection of this future divine judgment in his commentary on 1 Corinthians 4:5:

The Lord coming to judgment "will illumine what is concealed in darkness," i.e., will make clear and manifest those things done secretly in darkness. "And he will make manifest the counsels of hearts," i.e., all the secrets of the heart ... This means both good things, and evil things that have not been covered over by penitence. Third, he mentions the fruit, which the good will carry back from the divine judgment, saying, "and then each one," namely, the good, "shall receive his praise from God." This will be true praise, because God can neither deceive nor be deceived.[35]

For Thomas, like Augustine, judgment by the One who is himself the very *ratio* of Wisdom and Truth ensures that judgment will be without error and

---

32. See *Scriptum super Sententias* IV, d. 47, q. 1, a. 1, qc. 1: "Just as operation pertains to the principle by which things are produced in being, so also judgment pertains to the terminus by which things are brought to their end." In this quaestiuncula, Thomas argues that God's universal and particular judgments correspond to his creation and governance, respectively. Every human being is both a member of the human race and an individual person, and so receives an individual or particular judgment for his own works, corresponding to governance, and also the universal judgment, corresponding to the first production of things in creation, when "a final completion will be given to the world."

33. Jean-Pierre Torrell comments on Thomas's early treatment of the last judgment in the *Scriptum* IV, d. 49, q. 1, a. 1, that "his vision of the last judgment expresses ... the reaffirmation of the lordship of God as creator and savior over the whole universe." Jean-Pierre Torrell, OP, *Le Christ en ses mystères: La vie et l'oeuvre de Jésus selon Saint Thomas d'Aquin*, vol. 2 (Paris: Desclée, 1999), 703. My translation.

34. *ST* III, q. 59, a. 1 corpus and ad 2. Augustine, *De vera religione*, 31.

35. *Super I Cor.* 4, lect. 1, no. 196. All citations from Thomas's commentaries on the Pauline letters are based on R. Cai, ed., *S. Thomae Aquinatis Super Epistolas S. Pauli lectura*, vols. 1–2, 8th ed. (Turin: Marietti, 1953).

absolutely just, because the Lord alone knows the secrets of hearts and the inner truth of each one's conscience.

Christ's Judgment as Son of Man

In the Incarnation, the Word shares his judiciary power with the humanity assumed. Indeed, Thomas emphasizes in q. 59, a. 2, that it is especially through the instrumentality of his humanity that this power of the Word is exercised. Quoting John 5:27 ("He has given him power to do judgment, because he is the Son of Man"), Thomas explains that Christ as human is judge because he is Head of the Church, with jurisdiction over those subject to him.[36] His human soul is eminently capable of judgment, which "belongs to truth as its standard," and therefore to "the man imbued with truth and as it were one with truth," because "beyond all creatures, Christ's soul was more closely united with truth and more full of truth, according to John 1:14: 'We saw him ... full of grace and truth.'"[37] Because of the "overflow of the Godhead in Christ's soul," so that he knows all things possible to a created intellect in the Word in every time and place, "it belongs to him also to know and to judge the secrets of hearts."[38]

In the background here is the work Thomas has done earlier in the *Tertia Pars* on Christ's threefold grace, where John 1:14–16 was a key scriptural authority. Christ's capital grace is the causative overflow to others of his fullness of habitual grace ("of his fullness we have all received"), which is itself the overflow in his soul of the grace of union with the Word, making him "full of grace and truth."[39] Christ's human power to judge flows from his perfection of habitual grace as Head, which gives his humanity the capacity to act as the instrument of his divinity, and makes him the "mediator of God and men" (1 Tim 2:5).[40] In q. 59, a. 3, Thomas explicitly states that Christ's judicial power belongs to Christ as human because of this threefold grace, and also because of the merits he won by suffering unjustly to justify us.[41]

---

36. *ST* III, q. 59, a. 2; a. 3, ad 2.
37. *ST* III, q. 59, a. 2, ad 1; a. 3 ad 3.
38. *ST* III, q. 59, a. 2, ad 3; III, q. 10, a. 2. With reference to 1 Cor 4:5.
39. *ST* III, q. 8, a. 1 and a. 5.
40. *ST* III, q. 7, a. 1.
41. *ST* III, q. 59, a. 3, corpus and replies to the objections.

The one who judges us is the same one who was sent, filled with grace, and suffered for our salvation.

Thomas's further explanations in q. 59, a. 2, for why it is so fitting that Christ as human has judiciary power build on this idea that he is a judge who is also savior of body and soul. God judges us through Christ in his human nature "because of his likeness (*convenientiam*) and kinship" with us, "so that his judgment might be sweeter (*suaviter*)" to us. Here Thomas quotes Hebrews 4:15: "We do not have a high priest who cannot have compassion on our infirmities, but one tempted like us in all things, without sin. Let us go then with confidence to the throne of his grace." The throne of judgment, belonging to Christ by reason of his royal dignity as the Son of God, is the throne of grace administered by Christ as the Son of Man. Hebrews 4:15 appears often where Thomas discusses Christ's judgment.[42] In his *Commentary on Hebrews*, he says this verse shows Christ's "mercy and tenderness … that care for our misery," so no one will believe that "he can do only what is demanded by his justice."[43] Christ as our judge is also our priest, who intercedes for us and offers himself in sacrifice for us, for the remission of our sins and the grace of our salvation.[44] Christ has not just the power, but "also the eagerness and readiness to come to our aid, because he knows, by experience, our misery, which as God, he knew from eternity by simple knowledge."[45] Christ as human has experientially tasted our suffering, and this makes him a compassionate judge. In the *Commentary on John*, Thomas explains that the Father has given the power to judge to the Son of Man because this helps to take away the terror of falling "into the hands of the living God" (Heb 10:31).[46]

Thomas draws on Augustine for two other reasons that Christ is fittingly judge as human; these have to do with his human body and ours. First, because "at the last judgment … 'there will be a resurrection of dead bodies,

---

42. E.g., *Super Matt.* [rep. Leodegarii Bissuntini], ch. 25, lect. 3; *Super Heb.* 4, lect. 2, no. 232; *Super Ioan.* 5, lect. 5, no. 789.

43. *Super Heb.* 4, lect. 3, no. 235.

44. Cf., *ST* III, q. 22, a. 2 and a. 3.

45. *Super Heb.* 4, lect. 3, no. 235. Roszak notes with reference to the Hebrews commentary and to *Super I Cor.* 2, lect. 3, that "The emphasis that the Son of Man will be the one to judge carries a message of hope for man and also the conviction that the judge will be the *optimus iudex*" ("Judge of the Living and of the Dead," 109).

46. *Super Ioan.* 5, lect. 5, no. 789.

which God will raise up through the Son of Man,'" just as souls are raised up through Christ as the Son of God.[47] In q. 56, on Christ's resurrection, Thomas distinguishes between the primary cause of resurrection—the divine justice—and the secondary instrumental cause, Christ's resurrection in his own human body, which communicates the life-giving power of the Word.[48] Christ's resurrection is the efficient cause of the resurrection of both the good and wicked; all will have a resurrected body like him, and even the wicked will receive incorruptibility. But his resurrection is the exemplar cause of the resurrection only of the good, who will also be conformed to his divine Sonship in glory.[49]

It was just for Christ to be exalted in resurrection because he humbled himself in death.[50] But why is Christ's resurrection, as the cause of ours, an instrument of divine justice? The answer seems to be that our resurrection must take place for the effects of judgment to be complete. Although all are individually judged and rewarded or punished in their souls immediately after death, it is only in the final resurrection that all will receive the public and complete fulfillment of reward or punishment owing to their merits and demerits in the body as well as in the soul.[51] Just as the saints will enjoy

47. *ST* III, q. 59, a. 2. Thomas quotes Augustine's *Tractate on John*, 19. For a helpful discussion of Augustine's theology of resurrection, which was influential for the Middle Ages, see Caroline Walker Bynum, *The Resurrection of the Body* (New York: Columbia University Press, 1995), 94–103.

48. *ST* III, q. 56, a. 1.

49. *ST* III, q. 56, a. 1, ad 3. Even the wicked will receive back bodies that are repaired, renewed, and incorruptible; the principle is that what belongs to nature will be restored, but what belongs to grace is given only to the elect; *Super I Cor.* 15, lect. 8, no. 1010. The bodies of the damned will be incorruptible but not impassible, in the sense that although they will not have natural passibility, they will suffer by a kind of spiritual reception of corporeal fire; *ScG* IV, c. 89. The separated souls of the damned before the Resurrection suffer corporeal fire by the dispensation of divine justice in that they suffer "by a certain bondage" to something lower than themselves; *ScG* IV, c. 90; *Questiones disputate de anima*, a. 21; cf. 21; cf. *Scriptum* IV, d. 44, q. 3, a. 1, qa 1. Thomas does not seem to find a fully satisfactory answer to the problem of how spiritual souls can suffer corporeal fire but considers this doctrine to be demanded by Scripture (e.g., Mt 25:41); Thomas often calls on Gregory the Great's *Dialogues* Book 4 as authority here.

50. *ST* III, q. 53, a. 1.

51. *ST* III, q. 59, a. 5; *Comp. Theol.* I, 243–44. With the Tradition, Thomas holds there to be an intermediate state between the particular judgment of the separated soul after death and the last judgment of all after the general resurrection. As the International Theological Commission (ITC) states in its 1992 document "Some Current Questions in Eschatology," there were only a few exceptions to this position in the history of the Christian Tradition (among them the second-century Gnostics), until the twentieth century, when a number of prominent theologians mounted a denial of the intermediate state (4.2–3); among Catholic theologians, the ITC was especially concerned with those who proposed a theory of "resurrection in death," rejecting the idea of a separated soul after death and the deferred

the vision of God more when the delight of beatitude overflows into their resurrected bodies, those in hell will suffer in their bodies what they already suffer in their souls.[52] Thomas argues in his commentary on 1 Corinthians 15 that in addition to the necessity of the reunion of soul and body for the metaphysical completion of human nature, divine justice demands that each will receive back his own identical body, so that he will be rewarded or punished in the same body in which he had carried out good or evil deeds.[53] Thomas explicitly rejects as a "fable" the Gnostic position held by heirs of Platonism from Origen to the Cathars and condemned at Lateran IV (1215), that at the Resurrection the soul would be rid of the material body.[54] The resurrection of bodies is caused by the judge because in the Resurrection the full effects of judgment are fulfilled in one's own body.

Thomas also insists with Augustine that Christ will be judge in his human body at the last judgment because both good and wicked must *see* their

---

final resurrection of that soul's body (2.1). Also see Joseph Ratzinger, *Eschatology: Death and Eternal Life*, 2nd ed., trans. Michael Waldstein (Washington, DC: Catholic University of America Press, 1988) 104–12, 241–60, and White's discussion of Karl Rahner's theory of resurrection in death and rejection of the intermediate state (*Incarnate Lord*, 444–45). See also Andrew Hofer, "Balthasar's Eschatology on the Intermediate State: The Question of Knowability," *Logos* 12, no. 3 (Summer 2009): 148–72. Hofer notes Balthasar's agreement with Rahner on the coincidence of the particular and general judgments and the "super-temporality" of the Resurrection (157–59); he also notes the internal contradictions of Balthasar's own complex thought on the intermediate state (165–66).

52. *ST* I-II, q. 4, a. 5, ad 4 and ad 5; *Comp. theol.* I, ch. 153. Thomas notes in several places that his position differs from that of the Greeks, who "deny purgatory and say that before the resurrection souls neither ascend into heaven nor descend into hell" (*ScG* IV, c. 91; *Super II Cor.* 5, lect. 2, no. 167; *Super Ioan.* 14, lect. 1, no. 1861). The position that the pure separated soul immediately experiences the beatific vision was affirmed in 1336 by Benedict XII in *Benedictus Deus* (on the beatific vision controversy of the 1330s, see Bynum, *Resurrection of the Body*, 279–89).

53. *Super I Cor.* 15, lect. 9, no. 1013. What Thomas means by the "same" body, given his doctrine of the unicity of form, is famously debated. Thomas's position on unicity of substantial form was thought by some to imply that after death, Christ's body, separated from his soul, was no longer identical. Thomas argues that its identity lies in the continuing union of the body with the divine *suppositum* (e.g., *ST* III, q. 50, a. 5). His critics were unconvinced, and in 1286 the theory that the soul is the body's only substantial form was condemned as heretical by John Peckham, the Franciscan Archbishop of Canterbury. The Franciscans had consistently opposed this position; see Antonia Fitzpatrick, *Thomas Aquinas on Bodily Identity* (Oxford: Oxford University Press, 2017), 175–82, for an interesting account of debate over the theory of unicity of substantial form in the centuries following Aquinas. Fitzpatrick concludes that for Aquinas, the body's formal continuity from life across death to the resurrected body lies in its dimensive quantity (159ff.); see *ScG* IV, c. 81, *Comp. theol.* 1, 154. In the *Compendium of Theology*, Thomas argues that divine power alone can bring about the reunion of the soul with the same numerical body. The idea that the accident of dimensive quantity can remain after the substance of the body is corrupted seems parallel to Thomas's understanding of transubstantiation.

54. E.g., *Comp. theol.* 1, 153; *ScG* IV, c. 84. See Fitzpatrick, *Thomas Aquinas on Bodily Identity*, 88.

judge.[55] He explains in his *Commentary on John* that the wicked cannot see Christ in his divinity because this vision is beatitude. Only "the good will see Christ in his divinity and in his humanity."[56] The sight of his glorified human body, displaying the signs of his Passion, will be a reward to his friends, the righteous, but a reproach and torment to those who hate him.[57] The elect will see that they have been saved through his sufferings and rejoice, but "sinners, who have scorned so great a benefit, will be filled with dismay"[58] at the sight. Likewise, Thomas explains, the Gospel of Matthew says that "all the tribes of the earth will mourn" (Mt 24:30) at his coming, "seeing Christ with such power whom they have despised, and such wisdom, whom they did not obey, and the saints with such great brilliance."[59] The wicked are dismayed by being unavoidably confronted with the bodily evidence of the salvation they have rejected, a truth that stares them in the face, as it were, and declares their culpability. For Thomas, there is no bypassing embodied human nature in judgment, whether that of the Incarnate Word or our own. The sight of Christ in his glorified humanity will elicit a final crisis of recognition by those who have been judged as admitted to beatitude or excluded from it with their own cooperation.[60]

INSIGHTS FOR A
RENEWED CATECHESIS

Christ as Judge Is Mediator of Our Salvation

There are at least three ways in which Thomas's account might be helpful for a renewed teaching on Christ's judgment that counters some of the neo-Gnostic and neo-Pelagian tendencies in the contemporary Church out-

---

55. *ST* III, q. 59, a. 2; Thomas draws here from Augustine, *De verbum Domini*, Sermon 127. This teaching is also found in *De Trin.* 1.13. The particular judgment of the separated soul is "invisible"; *ScG* IV, c. 96.

56. *Super Ioan.* 5, lect. 5, no. 789. Parallels are found in *Scriptum* IV, d. 48, q. 1, a. 3 and *Super II Cor.* 5, lect. 2, no. 172. Thomas again quotes here from Augustine, Sermon 127.

57. *Scriptum* IV, d, 48, q. 1, a. 2, ad 2 and ad 4.

58. *Comp. theol.*, 1, ch. 241.

59. *Super Matt.* 24, lect. 3, no. 1963.

60. See *ST* III, q. 59, a. 4.

lined earlier. First, Thomas's explanation of why Christ must be our judge in his humanity is not only thoroughly Chalcedonian but for that very reason, I think, offers a helpful clarification that the primary purpose of this judgment is not merely punitive but primarily salvific, and is in fact a gift of the Father's love. Question 59's placement at the end of the *Summa*'s discussion of the mysteries of Christ's life confirms that for Thomas, Christ's judgment in his human nature brings to completion the saving purpose of the Incarnation, to mediate between, and so unite, fallen humans and God. It is no coincidence that q. 59, on Christ's judicial power, is structurally parallel to the last question on the Incarnation itself—q. 26, on Christ as our Mediator. Question 26 is the last on the consequences of the union and completes a section on Christ's relationship as human with God the Father: his subjection to the Father, his prayer and sacrifice as priest, his sonship and predestination. All these make Christ our principle, exemplar, and mediator, through whom alone we are united to the Father. His judgment completes the work of mediation that he begins in each individual soul in baptism, when he conforms them to his sonship by grace. And, as we have seen, because Christ is judge not only as God but in his humanity, he is a just and compassionate judge who has himself given us everything we need for salvation.[61] In the *Compendium Theologiae*, Thomas notes that in Christ's passion, death, resurrection, and ascension, he acquired for us the goods of salvation, while in his judgment, he distributes those goods to us: "therefore, Christ, in the human nature in which he has accomplished the mysteries of human salvation, is fittingly appointed to be judge over the men he has saved."[62] We can only be judged as righteous at the last because he has given us a share in his own justice at first, and pleads for us to the end. Without Christ's mediation and final judgment, in other words, we would have no access to the Father.

61. Thomas quotes a homily by Gregory the Great on the ascension (*Hom. xxix in Evang.*), to argue that Christ in his humanity, seated at the right hand of the Father, is both our judge and our helper: "it is the judge's place to sit, while to stand is the place of the combatant or helper. Consequently, Stephen in his toil of combat saw Him standing whom He had as his helper. But Mark describes Him as seated after the Ascension, because after the glory of His Ascension He will at the end be seen as judge" (*ST* III, q. 58, a. 1, ad 3). Matthew Levering comments that "Through his paschal mystery, the incarnate Son ascends to the right hand of the Father in order to exercise, in the flesh, the royal and priestly work of ruling and judging all creation, that is, of bringing the Church, as 'the body of Christ' (1 Cor 12:27), to share in the Father's bliss through the Holy Spirit." *Jesus and the Demise of Death: Resurrection, Afterlife, and the Fate of the Christian* (Waco, TX: Baylor University Press, 2012), 51–52.

62. *Comp. theol.* 1, ch. 241.

We Should Approach Divine
Judgment with Holy Fear

But why do we actually need to be judged in the first place? Although the primary purpose of judgment is salvific rather than punitive, secondarily, of course, it *is* punitive for those who will have effectively rejected God's offer of salvation. It goes without saying, perhaps, that Thomas, like all his contemporaries, had a deeper sense than many Catholics today not only of human sinfulness and unworthiness to stand righteously before God, but also of the generosity of divine condescension in making it possible for any human person to do so. In his sermons on the Apostles' Creed given during Lent near the end of his life, Thomas underlines the salutory fear that should prepare us for the coming of Christ to judge the living and the dead: first, because of Christ's wisdom by which he will know every thought, as well as the infallible witnesses of our own consciences which will be revealed; second, because he is all-powerful to carry out his judgments; third, because while this life is the time for mercy, then his justice will be unbending; and finally, because of the "anger of the judge" toward the unjust. The wicked will see him as "wrathful and fearful," while to the just he will appear as "sweet, delightful and kind."[63] Commenting on the final article of the Creed, "I believe in eternal life," Thomas describes the eternal blessings of the just and punishments of the wicked, remarking that this article is placed last because in that way it might always be more firmly impressed in the memory; one should frequently bring it back to mind, in order to be spurred on to good works and draw back from evil ones.[64] Thomas, living in the century that produced the *Dies irae*, is not at all troubled, as some modern theologians might be, that fear of damnation and desire for beatitude are defective or excessively self-serving motives for good behavior; indeed, in his view, servile fear of punishment, while imperfect, can be praiseworthy insofar as it disposes one for penance that turns one back to God.[65]

---

63. *Collationes Credo in Deum* X, Latin text (Leonine ed.), in Nicholas Ayo, *The Sermon-Conferences of St. Thomas Aquinas on the Apostle's Creed* (Notre Dame, IN: University of Notre Dame Press, 1988), 108. My translation.

64. *Coll. Credo in Deum* XV, 156.

65. *ST* III, q. 85, a. 5 and a. 6.

The idea that Christ's mercy is exercised for us in this life and his un-bending justice in the next does not contradict the idea that he is a compas-sionate judge. Thomas says that God's mercy manifests God's goodness in that he bestows perfections to expel the defects that make one miserable.[66] In this life, God shows mercy by offering through Christ the transforming help of grace, with which one must cooperate meritoriously in order to reach the end of beatitude; in the next life, he also mercifully mitigates the pun-ishment justly imposed on sinners and even on the reprobate due to their demerits.[67] But after death, the will in the separated soul is immutable; one can no longer repent or perform acts with moral value because these must be done in the body. Standing before God in individual judgment, the time for conversion and meriting has come to an end.[68] All that is left is the revelation of the truth. Judgment, as an act of justice, denotes "a right decision about what is just," founded on a correct discernment of the truth.[69] Christ judges the dead with a simple unwavering discernment of the truth of how each has

---

66. *ST* I, q. 21, a. 3.

67. *ST* I, q. 21, a. 4, ad 1. Roszak argues that "Thomas' fundamental conviction" is that "the main purpose of judging is the good." With reference to *Super Matt.* 25, lect. 2 ("grace is a weight that in-clines the soul"), he notes that, "theologically, giving an account of one's life on Judgment Day concerns the manner in which man used God's grace" ("Judge of the Living and of the Dead," 113, 114.

68. I.e., after death, saving repentance is no longer possible because for the soul separated from the body, the will is fixed; although it retains the powers of understanding and will, it can receive no new knowledge through the senses that could result in mutability of the will (*ScG* IV, c. 92–95; *De Veritate* q. 24, a. 9, a. 10; *Comp. theol.* 1, ch. 174–75). It is precisely because "judgment cannot be passed perfectly upon any changeable subject before its consummation" that judgment must take place after death, for "many actions appear to be profitable, which in their effects prove to be hurtful. And in the same way perfect judgment cannot be passed upon any man before the close of his life, since he can be changed in many respects from good to evil, or conversely, or from good to better, or from evil to worse. Hence the Apostle says (Heb 9:27): 'It is appointed unto men once to die, and after this the Judgment'" (*ST* III, q. 59, a. 5). The reprobate have in life themselves fixed their end in sin, inclining their will to the evil end in a way that can no longer be changed after death (indeed, the wicked still desire it, while hating the punishments it incurs: *ST* I-II, q. 87, a. 3, ad 1; *ST* II-II, q. 13, a. 4; *Comp. theol.* 1, ch. 175; *ScG* IV, c. 93). See the helpful study by Fr. Lawrence Lew, OP, *Why Can We Not Repent after We Die?* STL Tesina (Washington, DC: Pontifical Faculty of the Immaculate Conception, 2017), esp. 56–77. The idea of saving repentance after death is often part of a theory of universalism; however, this idea proposes a neo-Gnostic account of salvation outside of the body, as Thomas Joseph White, drawing on Aquinas, has argued against Balthasar (*Incarnate Lord*, 426–28). White suggests the possibility rather of a grace offered *in* death to all (*Incarnate Lord*, 413–14). In Purgatory, purification of the will does not change its ultimate orientation to the end; in distinction to the reprobate, the punishments of Purgatory are undergone willingly and so are able to cleanse the soul already fixed in charity (*Comp. theol.* 1, ch. 181–2; *ScG* IV, c. 94).

69. *ST* II-II, q. 60, a. 1; q. 58, a. 4, ad 1.

responded to his mercy and a compassionate remission of some of the punishment due. To our generation sometimes presumptuous about salvation,[70] Thomas's teaching on the humble fear of divine judgment and the necessity of timely cooperation with God's grace is a salutary reminder of God's majesty and merciful condescension in bringing anyone to the gift of eternal life.

Eschatological Judgment Is Adequation to the Truth

Finally, Thomas's teaching gives helpful insight into the nature of Christ's judgment, that is, as final and perfect adequation to the truth. In this life, he says—commenting on 1 Corinthians 4:3, "I do not judge myself"—we should not judge rashly, because we can hide our sins and motives even from ourselves,[71] but in our particular judgment, God will bring to light all that has been mystifying, entangled and obscure.[72] Here there will be no fifty shades of gray. Christ will judge and reward by the rule or ratio of his own perfect truth exactly how much we are conformed to him, that is, how willingly our lives have been ordered by divine wisdom and therefore lived in accord with the objective order of divine justice, in which "it is due to God that that there should be fulfilled in creatures what his will and wisdom require, and what manifests his goodness."[73] The order of justice is founded on God's causal knowledge of things, which establishes the truth of reality; our attempted self-construction of any opposing reality is a futile attempt to live autonomously outside of that order and can only end in self-destruction. In

---

70. The most recent and radical theological proposal for universalism is David Bentley Hart's *That ALL Shall Be Saved: Heaven, Hell and Universal Salvation* (New Haven, CT: Yale University Press, 2019). But universal salvation without strenuous objective moral or religious demands is often popularly assumed in a culture shaped by what sociologists Christian Smith and Melinda Lundquist Denton Christian have termed "Moralistic Therapeutic Deism"; see their *Soul Searching: The Religious and Spiritual Lives of American Teenagers* (New York: Oxford University Press, 2005).

71. *Super I Cor* 4, lect. 1, nos. 192, 195.

72. In the particular judgment, while the separated soul knows only through divinely infused species that give it a confused or indeterminate knowledge of singulars in general, it does know the singulars that pertain to itself, "to which they are determined by former knowledge in this life, or by some affection, or by natural aptitude, or by the disposition of the Divine order" (*ST* I, q. 89, a. 4; cf. *Questiones disputate de anima*, a. 20). The soul can thus retain the memory of the acts on which it is judged.

73. *ST* I, q. 21, a. 1.

the end we will be conformed to truth whether we like it or not. As fearful as this sounds, it should also be deeply consoling for those who will have really sought to love and obey God in spite of every weakness and failure. Christ's judgment is a just reckoning of the whole truth of the moral condition they have forged by their own cooperation with grace—however fumbling—or their persistent rejection of it, to the end.[74] This truth will be made known with perfect clarity; if we have been conformed to justice by being conformed to Christ in faith and charity, we will be judged with "the judgment of reward and approval,"[75] and, passing to beatitude through Christ the Door of Truth, will manifest and rejoice in the truth of God's goodness.[76]

Thomas emphasizes the revelatory nature of the last judgment, when "every eye will see" Christ the Word in his glorified humanity, and the truth of each life with all its circumstances and consequences will be made known to all. In effect, public revelation begun in Scripture will be fulfilled at the last judgment.[77] In his commentary on Matthew 25, Thomas writes that those whose lives are manifestly good or wicked are not judged then because the truth about them is already evident. Only those with a mixture of good and evil—presumably, most of us—will be separated like sheep and goats in a full public accounting, on the basis of our own history of free assent to grace.[78] Thomas underscores too the ecclesial and corporate nature of this judgment; the saints who have been most detached from earthly things will judge alongside Christ by "cooperating in the task of revealing to each individual the cause of the salvation or damnation of himself and others." This

---

74. Ratzinger, *Eschatology*, 209.

75. *Super Ioan.* 3, lect. 3, no. 485. The judgment of each after death will involve "separation and examination." *Super Ioan.* 5, lect. 4, no. 776. Each one of us, as Paul says, will "stand before the tribunal" of Christ (2 Cor 5:10) and "give an account of himself before God" (Rom 14:12).

76. *Super Ioan.* 10, lect. 1, no. 1370: Christ says, "I am the door" (Jn 10:7) because as God, he is the Truth: "no one can enter the door, i.e., to beatitude, except by the truth, because beatitude is nothing else than joy in the truth."

77. *Dei verbum* teaches that "we now await no further new public revelation before the glorious manifestation of our Lord Jesus Christ." Vatican II Constitution on Divine Revelation *Dei Verbum*, 4. At the last judgment, "since there are some other things pertaining to a man which go on through the whole course of time, and which are not foreign to the Divine judgment, all these things must be brought to judgment at the end of time. For although in regard to such things a man neither merits nor demerits, still in a measure they accompany his reward or punishment. Consequently all these things must be weighed in the final judgment" (*ST* III, q. 59 a. 5, ad 1). Then, "each one's salvation or damnation will be made clear to him" by divine power (*Super Rom.* 2, lect. 3, no. 222).

78. *Super Matt.* 25, lect. 3, no. 2096.

dignity will belong especially to the Apostles, "who have left all to follow Christ" (and to those who have preached the divine commandments, so also, perhaps, to Dominicans). Detached from earthly things by voluntary poverty, they are unswayed by them; conformed to truth, they can judge with truth.[79] Perhaps one could say that this full and final revelation, the consummation of *sacra doctrina* giving complete understanding of God's plan of providence for the whole human race, not only completes the revelation of Scripture and magnifies God's goodness but also justly satisfies the natural desire for truth that underlies the Gnostic impulse, even for the wicked who will not have supernatural knowledge of God in the beatific vision.

CONCLUSION: *TE DEUM LAUDAMUS*

Thomas's insights about Christ as mediator and judge offer helpful points for a renewed teaching in response to a postmodern tendency to neo-Gnosticism and the neo-Pelagianism that often accompanies it. Thomas also responds to contemporary concerns by offering a way of arguing, in principle, that to posit the need for mediators of salvation besides the Word made Flesh simply underestimates the universal extent of God's wisdom, justice, and love in Christ. There can be no other mediator and judge but the one who is Truth itself, and who therefore takes into account all the circumstances of each life—religious, personal, and cultural. Christ is the Head of all men and women, in body and soul, and his power to give them eternal life in the Resurrection is in contact with all times and places.[80] Thomas argues that the offer of salvation is extended to all, for "God wills all to be saved" (1 Tim 2:4) antecedently, though consequently he wills that sins be justly punished.[81]

79. *Comp. theol.* I, 245. Cf. *Super Matt.* 19, lect. 1, nos. 1611–19.
80. *ST* III, q. 8, a. 2 and a. 3; q. 56, a. 1, ad 3.
81. *Super I Tim.* 2, lect. 1, no. 62. See also *ScG* III, c.159, no. 2, *ST* I, q. 19, a. 6 and Thomas's commentary on Jn 66:44 ("No one can come to me unless the Father draw him"): "God, in so far as it depends on him, extends his hand to every one, to draw every one; and what is more, he not only draws those who receive him by the hand, but even converts those who are turned away from him … Therefore, since God is ready to give grace to all, and draw them to himself, it is not due to him if someone does not accept; rather, it is due to the person who does not accept." Before the Fall, there was no obstacle to the drawing of God's grace; however, in the state of fallen nature, all are turned away

For Thomas, Christ's judgment in his humanity is a gift of the Father's love; it is his crowning salvific activity as our Mediator, Head, and Priest. The divine Judge was begotten and came into the world not to keep men away from the Father but to give them access to him. Although we should tremble in holy fear, we should hold fast to the Creed and rejoice in hope because it is he, our friend, who is our judge. It seems that Thomas meditated on this often; his biographers record that when he celebrated Mass, at the elevation of the Host, Thomas recited the last part of the *Te Deum*, with its credal formula that praises Christ who freed us by his incarnation and prays that he will come again as judge to bring his own to glory.[82] I finish with his prayer:

> You Christ are the King of Glory
> The eternal Son of the Father
> When You became man to set us free,
> you did not spurn the virgin's womb.
> You overcame the sting of death
> and opened the kingdom of heaven to all believers.
> You are seated at God's right hand in glory;
> We believe that you will come to be our judge.
> Come then Lord and help your people
> Bought with price of your own blood,
> and bring us with your saints
> to glory everlasting.

---

from God, and may resist though God extends his hand. Touching on the mystery of predestination, Thomas goes on to say that "God does not draw all who are turned away from him, but certain ones, even though all are equally turned away. The reason is so that the order of divine justice may appear and shine forth in those who are not drawn, while the immensity of the divine mercy may appear and shine in those who are drawn. But as to why in particular he draws this person and does not draw that person, there is no reason except the pleasure of the divine will." *Super Ioan.* 6, lect. 5, nos. 937–38. Thomas's thirteenth-century perspective on the de facto likelihood of salvation for non-Christians after the Incarnation is arguably more restricted than that of the contemporary Church (cf. *ST* II-II, q. 2, a. 5 on the necessity of explicit faith after Christ). Fr. Thomas Joseph White argues that Thomas does have "a doctrine of the universal offer of salvation by grace to each human being" that could take place in the context of moral decision making (cf. *ST* I-II, q. 89, a. 6) (*Incarnate Lord*, 399).

82. William of Tocco, Ystoria Sancti Thome de Aquino 58, *Ystoria sancti Thome de Aquino de Guillaume de Tocco (1323)*, ed. C. Le Brun-Gouanvic, Studies and Texts 127 (Toronto: Pontifical Institute of Medieval Studies, 1996), 381.

SELECT BIBLIOGRAPHY

Compiled by Braxton Silva

This select bibliography gives only modern works of scholarship. The exact editions and translations of primary sources and magisterial ecclesial documents consulted vary according to the individual contributors of this volume.

Alfaro, Juan. *Fides, Spes, Caritas: Adnotationes in Tractatum de Virtutibus Theologicis.* Rome: Gregorian University Press, 1968.

————. *Esistenza Cristiana.* Rome: Gregorian University Press, 1975.

Anatolios, Khaled. *Athanasius.* New York: Routledge, 2004.

————. "The Ontological Grammar of Salvation and the Salvific Work of Christ in Athanasius and Aquinas." In *Thomas Aquinas and the Greek Fathers,* edited by Michael A. Dauphinais, Andrew Hofer, and Roger Nutt, 89–109. Ave Maria, FL: Sapientia Press, 2019.

Austriaco, Nicanor. "How Did God Create Homo Sapiens through Evolution?" In *Thomistic Evolution: A Catholic Approach to Understanding Evolution in the Light of Faith,* 2nd ed., edited by Nicanor Austriaco et al. Tacoma, WA: Cluny Media, 2019.

Bader, Michael. *Arousal: The Secret Logic of Sexual Fantasies.* New York: Thomas Dunne, 2002.

Balthasar, Hans Urs von. *The Glory of the Lord: A Theological Aesthetics.* Vol. 1. Edited by Joseph Fessio, SJ, and John Riches. San Francisco: Ignatius Press, 1982–89.

————. *Cosmic Liturgy: The Universe According to Maximus the Confessor.* Translated by Brian Daley, SJ. San Francisco: Ignatius Press, 1988.

————. *Theodrama: Theological Dramatic Theory.* 5 vols. Translated by Graham Harrison. San Francisco: Ignatius Press, 1988–98.

————. *Mysterium Paschale: The Mystery of Easter.* Translated by Aidan Nichols. San Francisco: Ignatius Press, 2000.

————. *Love Alone Is Credible.* Translated by D. C. Schindler. San Francisco: Ignatius Press, 2004.

Barnes, Corey L. "Albert the Great and Thomas Aquinas on Person, Hypostasis, and Hypostatic Union." *The Thomist* 72 (2008): 107–46.

————. *Christ's Two Wills: The Christology of Aquinas and Its Historical Contexts.* Toronto: Pontifical Institute of Mediaeval Studies, 2012.

Barnes, Michel René. "Rereading Augustine's Theology of the Trinity." In *The Trinity: An Interdisciplinary Symposium on the Trinity,* edited by Stephen T. David, Daniel Kendell, and Gerard O'Collins. Oxford: Oxford University, 2002.

Barth, Karl. *Church Dogmatics*. Vol. 4.1. Translated by G. W. Bromiley. New York: Charles Scribner's Sons, 1956. [cited by Legge]

———. *Church Dogmatics*. Vol. 4.1. Edited by G. W. Bromiley and T. F. Torrance. Edinburgh: T&T Clark, 1961. [cited by Gondreau]

———. *The Göttingen Dogmatics: Instruction in the Christian Religion*. Vol. 1. Edited by Hannelotte Reifen. Translated by Geoffrey W. Bromiley. Grand Rapids, MI: Eerdmans, 1991.

Bauckham, Richard. *God Crucified: Monotheism and Christology in the New Testament*. Grand Rapids, MI: Eerdmans, 1998.

———. *Jesus and the God of Israel: God Crucified and Other Studies on the New Testament's Christology of Divine Identity*. Grand Rapids, MI: Eerdmans, 2008.

———. *Jesus: A Very Short Introduction*. Oxford: Oxford University Press, 2011.

Baum, William. *The Teaching of Cardinal Cajetan on the Sacrifice of the Mass: A Study in Pre-Tridentine Theology*. Rome: Angelicum, 1958.

Baumeister, R. F., K. R. Catanese, and K. D. Vohs. "Is There a Gender Difference in Sex Drive? Theoretical Views, Conceptual Distinctions, and a Review of Relevant Evidence." *Personality and Social Psychology Review* 5 (2001): 242–73.

Blankenhorn, Bernhard. "The Instrumental Causality of the Sacraments: Thomas Aquinas and Louis-Marie Chauvet." *Nova et Vetera*, English ed. 4 (2006): 255–94.

———. *The Mystery of Union with God: Dionysian Mysticism in Albert the Great and Thomas Aquinas*. Washington, DC: Catholic University of America Press, 2015.

Bobik, Joseph. "Aquinas on *Communicatio*, the Foundation of Friendship and *Caritas*." *Modern Schoolman* 64 (1986): 1–18.

Boersma, Gerald. "The *Rationes Seminales* in Augustine's Theology of Creation." *Nova et Vetera*, English ed. 18, no. 2 (2020): 413–41.

Boland, Vivian. "Truth, Knowledge and Communication: Thomas Aquinas on the Mystery of Teaching." *Studies in Christian Ethics* 19, no. 3 (2006): 287–304.

———. *St Thomas Aquinas*. Bloomsbury Library of Educational Thought. London: Bloomsbury, 2007.

———. "St Thomas's Sermon Puer Iesus: A Neglected Source for His Understanding of Teaching and Learning." *New Blackfriars* 88, no. 4 (2007): 457–70.

———. "The Healing Work of Teaching: Thomas Aquinas and Education." In *Towards the Intelligent Use of Liberty: Dominican Approaches to Education*, 2nd ed., edited by Gabrielle Kelly, OP, and Kevin Saunders, OP, 31–40. Hindmarsh, South Australia: ATF, 2014.

Bonino, Serge-Thomas. "Le sacerdoce comme institution naturelle selon Saint Thomas d'Aquin." *Revue Thomiste* 99, no. 4 (1999): 33–58.

Brown, Raymond E. *An Introduction to New Testament Christology*. New York: Paulist Press, 1994.

Brown, Stephen F. "Thomas Aquinas and His Contemporaries on the Unique Existence in Christ." In *Christ among the Medieval Dominicans: Representations of Christ in the Texts and Images of the Order of Preachers*, edited by Kent Emery and Joseph Wawrykow, 220–37. Notre Dame, IN: University of Notre Dame Press, 1998.

Bultmann, Rudolf. *New Testament Theology*. Translated by K. Grobel. Waco, TX: Baylor University Press, 2007.

Burrell, David. "Creation in St. Thomas's *Super Evangelium S. Joannis Lectura.*" In *Reading John with St. Thomas Aquinas: Theological Exegesis and Speculative Theology*, edited by Michael Dauphinais and Matthew Levering, 115–26. Washington, DC: Catholic University of America Press, 2005.

Bynum, Caroline Walker. *The Resurrection of the Body.* New York: Columbia University Press, 1995.

Cahill, Larry. "An Issue Whose Time Has Come." *Journal of Neuroscience Research* 95 (2017): 12–23.

Cappello, Felix M. *De Sacramentis in Genere, de Baptismo, Confirmatione et Eucharistia.* 7th ed. Tractatus Canonico-Moralis de Sacramentis 1. Turin: Marietti, 1962.

Carnes, Patrick, et al. *In the Shadows of the Net: Breaking Free of Compulsive Online Sexual Behavior.* 2nd ed. Center City, MN: Hazeldon, 2007.

Carr, Anne. "Feminist Views of Christology." *Chicago Studies* 35, no. 2 (1996): 128–40.

Catão, Bernard. *Salut et rédemption chez S. Thomas d'Aquin: L'acte sauveur du Christ.* Paris: Aubier, 1965.

Cessario, Romanus. *The Godly Image: Christ and Salvation in Catholic Thought from Anselm to Aquinas.* Petersham: St. Bede's, 1990.

———. "Is Aquinas's *Summa* Only about Grace?" In *Ordo sapientiae et amoris, Image et message de saint Thomas d'Aquin à travers les récentes études historiques, herméneutiques et doctrinales: Hommage au professeur Jean-Pierre Torrell, OP à l'occasion de son 65e anniversaire*, edited by C.-J. Pinto de Oliveira, OP, 197–209. Fribourg: Éditions Universitaires, 1993.

Cessario, Romanus, and Cajetan Cuddy. *Thomas and the Thomists: The Achievement of Thomas Aquinas and His Interpreters.* Mapping the Tradition. Minneapolis: Fortress Press, 2017.

Chadwick, Henry. *Boethius: The Consolations of Music, Logic, Theology, and Philosophy.* Oxford: Clarendon Press, 1981.

Charlesworth, James H. *Jesus within Judaism.* New York: Doubleday, 1988.

Chenu, Marie-Dominique. *Toward Understanding Saint Thomas.* Edited and translated by A.-M. Landry, OP, and D. Hughes, OP. Chicago: Henry Regnery, 1964. 1st French ed., 1950.

———. "Les passions vertueuses: L'anthropologie de saint Thomas." *Revue philosophique de Louvain* 72 (1974): 11–18.

Clark, Francis. *Anglican Orders and Defect of Intention.* London: Longmans, Green, 1956.

———. *The Catholic Church and Anglican Orders.* London: Catholic Truth Society, 1962.

———. "Les ordinations anglicanes, problème oecuménique." *Gregorianum* 45 (1964): 60–93.

Clark, Russell D., and Elaine Hatfield. "Gender Differences in Receptivity to Sexual Offers." *Journal of Psychology and Human Sexuality* 2, no. 1 (1989): 39–55.

Clarke, W. Norris. *The One and the Many.* Notre Dame, IN: University of Notre Dame Press, 2001.

Coconnier, Marie-Thomas. "La charité d'après saint Thomas d'Aquin: à propos d'une boutade de Bossuet." *Revue Thomiste* 12 (1904): 641–60.

———. "Ce qu'est la charité d'après saint Thomas d'Aquin (2° article)." *Revue Thomiste* 14 (1906): 5–30.

Colish, Marcia L. *Faith, Fiction, and Force in Medieval Baptismal Debates*. Washington, DC: Catholic University of America Press, 2014.

Congar, Yves M.-J. *The Mystery of the Temple: Or The Manner of God's Presence to His Creatures from Genesis to the Apocalypse*. Translated by R. F. Trevett. London: Burns & Oates, 1962. 1st French ed., 1958.

———. "Tradition et *Sacra Doctrina* chez Saint Thomas d'Aquin." In *Église et Tradition*, edited by Johannes Betz and Heinrich Fries, 157–89. Le Puy: Éditions Xavier Mappus, 1963.

Constas, Maximos. "The Reception of St. Paul and Pauline Theology in the Byzantine Period." In *The New Testament in Byzantium*, edited by Derek Krueger and Robert Nelson, 147–76. Washington, DC: Dumbarton Oaks, 2016.

———. "Dionysius the Areopagite and the New Testament." In *The Oxford Handbook to Dionysius the Areopagite*. Oxford: Oxford University, forthcoming.

Coolman, Boyd Taylor. *Knowing God by Experience: The Spiritual Senses in the Theology of William of Auxerre*. Washington, DC: Catholic University of America Press, 2004.

———. "Alexander of Hales." In *The Spiritual Senses: Perceiving God in Western Christianity*, edited by Paul Gavrilyuk and Sarah Coakley, 121–39. Cambridge: Cambridge University Press, 2011.

Corbin, Michel. *Le chemin de la théologie chez Thomas d'Aquin*. Bibliothèque des archives de philosophie, nouvelle série. Paris: Beauchesne, 1972.

Cross, Anthony R. "Baptismal Regeneration: Rehabilitating a Lost Dimension of New Testament Baptism." In *Baptist Sacramentalism 2*, edited by Anthony R. Cross and Philip E. Thompson. Studies in Baptist History and Thought 25. Milton Keynes, UK: Paternoster, 2008.

Cross, Richard. "Aquinas on Nature, Hypostasis, and the Metaphysics of the Incarnation." *The Thomist* 60 (1996): 171–202.

———. *Duns Scotus*. Oxford: Oxford University Press, 1999.

———. *The Metaphysics of the Incarnation*. Oxford: Oxford University Press, 2002.

———. "Thomas Aquinas." In *The Spiritual Senses: Perceiving God in Western Christianity*, edited by Paul Gavrilyuk and Sarah Coakley. Cambridge: Cambridge University Press, 2012.

Cummings, Owen F. "Is Mormon Baptism Valid?" *Worship* 71 (1997): 150–51.

Cunningham, Sean B. "Natural Inclination in Aquinas." PhD diss., Catholic University of America, 2013.

Curiello, Gioacchino. "'Alia translatio melior est': Albert the Great and the Latin Translations of the Corpus Dionysiacum." *Documenti e studi sulla tradizione filosofica medieval* 24 (2013): 121–51.

Daley, Brian E. "Boethius' Theological Tracts and Early Byzantine Scholasticism." *Mediaeval Studies* 46 (1984): 158–91.

———. "A Richer Union: Leontius of Byzantium and the Relationship of Human and Divine in Christ." *Studia Patristica* 24 (1993): 239–65.

Dauphinais, Michael A. "Christ the Teacher: The Pedagogy of the Incarnation According to Saint Thomas Aquinas." PhD diss., University of Notre Dame, 2000.

———. "The Role of Christ and the History of Salvation in Aquinas's Theology of Revelation." *Angelicum* 96, no. 3 (2019): 293–328.

Dauphinais, Michael A., Andrew Hofer, and Roger Nutt, eds. *Thomas Aquinas and the Greek Fathers*. Ave Maria, FL: Sapientia Press, 2019.

Davison, Andrew. *Participation in God: A Study in Christian Doctrine and Metaphysics*. Cambridge: Cambridge University Press, 2019.

Dawson, Samantha J., Brittany A. Bannerman, and Martin Lalumière. "Paraphilic Interests: An Examination of Sex Differences in a Nonclinical Sample." *Sexual Abuse: A Journal of Research and Treatment* 28, no. 1 (2016): 20–45. https://journals.sagepub .com/doi/pdf/10.1177/1079063214525645.

de Couesnongle, Vincent. "La causalité du maximum: L'utilisation par saint Thomas d'un passage d'Aristote." *Revue des sciences philosophiques et théologiques* 38 (1954): 433–44.

———. "La causalité du maximum: Pourquoi saint Thomas a-t-il mal cité Aristote?" *Revue des sciences philosophiques et théologiques* 38 (1954): 658–80.

Dedek, John F. "Quasi experimentalis cognitio: A Historical Approach to the Meaning of St. Thomas." *Theological Studies* 22 (1961): 357–90.

de Gaál, Emery. *The Theology of Pope Benedict XVI: The Christocentric Shift*. New York: Palgrave Macmillan, 2010.

———. "Mariology as Christology and Ecclesiology: Professor Joseph Ratzinger's Only Mariology Course." In *Joseph Ratzinger and the Healing of Reformation-Era Divisions*, edited by Emery de Gaál and Matthew Levering, 93–120. Steubenville, OH: Emmaus Academic, 2019.

de La Soujeole, Benoît-Dominique. *Introduction to the Mystery of the Church*. Translated by M. J. Miller. Washington, DC: Catholic University of America Press, 2014.

Delio, Ilia. *The Emergent Christ: Exploring the Meaning of Catholic in an Evolutionary Universe*. Maryknoll, NY: Orbis Books, 2011.

Deloffre, Marie-Hélène. "Introduction." In Thomas d'Aquin, *Questions Disputées sur la vérité: Question XXIX, La grâce du Christ (De gratia Christi)*, translated by M.-H. Deloffre, 9–148. Paris: Vrin, 2015.

de Lubac, Henri. *The Mystery of the Supernatural*. Translated by Rosemary Sheed. New York: Herder & Herder, 1967.

———. *Corpus mysticum: The Eucharist and the Church in the Middle Ages*. Translated by Gemma Simmonds. Notre Dame, IN: University of Notre Dame Press, 2006.

Denzinger, Heinrich, Peter Hünermann, Robert L. Fastiggi, and Anne Englund Nash, eds. *Compendium of Creeds, Definitions, and Declarations on Matters of Father and Morals*. San Francisco: Ignatius Press, 2012.

De Salvo, Raphael. "The Dogmatic Theology on the Intention of the Minister in the Confection of the Sacraments." STD diss., Catholic University of America, 1949.

Dillon, John. "Monotheism in the Gnostic Tradition." In *Pagan Monotheism in Late Antiquity*, edited by Polymnia Athanassiadi and Michael Frede, 69–79. Oxford: Clarendon, 2008.

Donohoo, Lawrence J. "The Nature and Grace of *Sacra Doctrina* in St. Thomas's *Super Boetium de Trinitate*." *The Thomist* 63, no. 3 (1999): 343–401.

Dorner, Isaak August. *Entwicklungsgeschichte der Lehre von der Person Christi von den ältesten Zeiten bis auf die neueste dargestellt*. 2nd ed. Berlin: Gustav Schlawitz, 1851–56. English translation: *History of the Development of the Doctrine of the Person of Christ*. Edinburgh: T&T Clark, 1863–78.

————. *System der Christlichen Glaubenslehre*. 2nd ed. Berlin: Wilhelm Hertz, 1886–87. English translation: *System of Christian Doctrine*. 2nd ed. Edinburgh: T&T Clark, 1888–91.

Doronzo, Emmanuel. *De Sacramentis in Genere*. Milwaukee: Bruce, 1946.

Dubov, Nissan Dovid. *The Laws of Yichud: Permissibility and Prohibition Regarding the Seclusion of a Man and Woman*. Brooklyn, NY: Sichos In English, 2006.

Dufeil, M.-M. *Guillaume de Saint-Amour et la Polémique Universitaire Parisienne 1250–1259*. Paris: A. et J. Picard, 1972.

Dunkle, Brian. "Thomas Aquinas's Use of John Chrysostom in the Catena Aurea and the Tertia Pars." In *Thomas Aquinas and the Greek Fathers*, edited by Michael Dauphinais, Andrew Hofer, OP, and Roger Nutt, 151–64. Ave Maria, FL: Sapientia Press, 2019.

Dupuis, Jacques. *Toward a Christian Theology of Religious Pluralism*. Maryknoll, NY: Orbis Books, 1997.

Edart, Jean-Baptiste, Innocent Himbaza, and Adrien Schenker. *The Bible on the Question of Homosexuality*. Translated by Benedict Guevin. Washington, DC: Catholic University of America Press, 2012.

Edsall, Benjamin A. *The Reception of Paul and Early Christian Initiation: History and Hermeneutics*. Cambridge: Cambridge University Press, 2019.

Elders, Leo J. *Faith and Science: An Introduction to St. Thomas' Expositio in Boethii de Trinitate*. Rome: Herder, 1974.

————. *Thomas Aquinas and His Predecessors: The Philosophers and the Church Fathers in His Works*. Washington, DC: Catholic University of America Press, 2018.

Elliott, Peter J. *What God Has Joined: The Sacramentality of Marriage*. New York: Alba House, 1990.

Emery, Gilles. "Le sacerdoce spirituel des fidèles chez saint Thomas d'Aquin." *Revue Thomiste* 99 (1999): 211–43.

————. *The Trinitarian Theology of St. Thomas Aquinas*. Translated by Francesca Aran Murphy. Oxford: Oxford University Press, 2007. 1st French ed., 2004.

————. "Biblical Exegesis and the Speculative Doctrine of the Trinity in St. Thomas Aquinas's *Commentary on John*." In *Reading John with St. Thomas Aquinas: Theological Exegesis and Speculative Theology*, edited by Michael Dauphinais and Matthew Levering, 23–61. Washington, DC: Catholic University of America Press, 2005.

————. "Missions invisibles et missions visibles: Le Christ et son Esprit." *Revue Thomiste* 106 (2006): 51–99.

————. *Trinity, Church, and the Human Person: Thomistic Essays*. Naples, FL: Sapientia Press, 2007.

————. *The Trinity: An Introduction to Catholic Doctrine on the Triune God*. Translated by M. Levering. Washington, DC: Catholic University of America Press, 2011. 1st French ed., 2009.

————. "Theologia and Dispensatio: The Centrality of the Divine Missions in St. Thomas's Trinitarian Theology." *The Thomist* 74 (2010): 515–61.

————. "The Dignity of Being a Substance—Person, Subsistence, and Nature." *Nova et Vetera*, English ed. 9, no. 4 (2011): 991–1001.

————. "L'inhabitation de Dieu Trinité dans les justes." *Nova et Vetera* 88 (2013): 155–84.

————. "Kenosis, Christ, and the Trinity in Thomas Aquinas." *Nova et Vetera*, English ed. 17, no. 3 (2019): 839–69.

Emery, John. "A Christology of Communication: Christ's Charity According to Thomas Aquinas." PhD diss., University of Fribourg, 2017.

Evans, C. Stephen. "Introduction: Understanding Jesus the Christ as Human and Divine." In *Exploring Kenotic Christology: The Self-Emptying of God*, edited by C. Stephen Evans. Oxford: Oxford University Press, 2006.

Falsani, Cathleen. "In New Book, Richard Rohr Says the 'Universal Christ' Changes Everything." *National Catholic Reporter*, April 1, 2019. https://www.ncronline.org/news/spirituality/new-book-richard-rohr-says-universal-christ-changes-everything.

Feldmeier, Reinhard. "'Der Höchste': Das Gottesprädikat Hypsistos in der paganen Religiosität, in der Septuaginta und im lukanischen Doppelwerk." In *Die Septuaginta—Text, Wirkung, Rezeption*, edited by Wolfgang Kraus and Siegfried Kreuzer, 544–58. Tübingen: Mohr Siebeck, 2014.

Ferber, Rafael, and Gregor Damschen. "Is the Idea of the Good Beyond Being? Plato's *epekeina tēs ousias* Revisted (Republic 6,509b8–10)." In *Second Sailing: Alternative Perspectives on Plato*, edited by Debra Nails and Harold Tarrant, 197–204. Commentationes Humanarum Litterarum 132. Helsinki: Societas Scientiarum Fennica, 2015.

Ferguson, Everett. *Baptism in the Early Church: History, Theology, and Liturgy in the First Five Centuries*. Grand Rapids, MI: Eerdmans, 2009.

Finley, John. "The Metaphysics of Gender: A Thomistic Approach." *The Thomist* 79 (2015): 585–614.

Fitzpatrick, Antonia. *Thomas Aquinas on Bodily Identity*. Oxford: Oxford University Press, 2017.

Fletcher-Louis, Crispin. *Jesus Monotheism*. Eugene, OR: Cascade Books, 2015.

Fossum, Jarl. *The Name of God and the Angel of the Lord: Samaritan and Jewish Concepts of Intermediation and the Origin of Gnosticism*. Wissenschaftliche Untersuchungen zum Neuen Testament 36. Tübingen: Mohr Siebeck, 1985.

Franklin, R. William, ed. *Anglican Orders: Essays on the Centenary of Apostolicae Curae, 1896–1996*. London: Mowbray, 1996.

Frey, Jörg. "Between Torah and Stoa: How Could Readers Have Understood the Johannine Logos." In *The Prologue of the Gospel of John: Its Literary, Theological and Philosophical Contexts*, edited by Jan G. van der Watt, R. Alan Culpepper, and Udo Schnelle, 189–234. Wissenschaftliche Untersuchungen zum Neuen Testament 359. Tübingen: Mohr Siebeck, 2016.

Froula, John. "*Esse Secundarium*: An Analogical Term Meaning That by Which Christ Is Human." *The Thomist* 78 (2014): 557–80.

Gaffney, Mark. *The Psychology of the Internal Senses*. St. Louis: Herder, 1942.

Gaine, Simon Francis. *Did the Saviour See the Father? Christ, Salvation and the Vision of God*. London: Bloomsbury T&T Clark, 2015.

———. "Is There Still a Place for Christ's Infused Knowledge in Catholic Theology and Exegesis?" *Nova et Vetera*, English ed. 16 (2018): 601–15.

———. "Review of *The Trinitarian Theology of St Thomas Aquinas*, by Dominic Legge, OP." *New Blackfriars* 99 (2018): 108–10.

———. "How Could the Earthly Jesus Have Taught Divine Truth?" In *Christ Unabridged: Knowing and Loving the Son of Man*, edited by George Westhaver and Rebekah Vince, 82–93. London: SCM, 2020.

Gallagher, John F. *Significando Causant: A Study of Sacramental Efficiency*. Studia Friburgensia, New Series 40. Fribourg: University of Fribourg Press, 1965.

Galot, Jean. *Le problème christologique actuel*. Paris: Éditions C.L.D., 1979.

———. *The Person of Christ, Covenant between God and Man: A Theological Insight*.
Translated by M. Angeline Bouchard. Chicago: Franciscan Herald Press, 1984.

———. "Le Christ Terrestre et la vision." *Gregorianum* 67 (1986): 429–50.

Galvin, J. P. "Jesus Christ." In *Systematic Theology: Roman Catholic Perspectives*, edited by
F. Schüssler Fiorenza and J. P. Galvin. Dublin: Gill & Macmillan, 1992.

Gardeil, H. D. *Introduction to the Philosophy of St. Thomas Aquinas*. Vol. 3, *Psychology*. St.
Louis: Herder, 1956.

Garrigou-Lagrange, Reginald. "Le sens du mystère chez Cajétan." *Angelicum* 12 (1935):
3–18.

Gathercole, Simon. *The Pre-Existent Son: Recovering the Christologies of Matthew, Mark
and Luke*. Grand Rapids, MI: Eerdmans, 2006.

Gavrilyuk, Paul, and Sarah Coakley, eds. *The Spiritual Senses: Perceiving God in Western
Christianity*. Cambridge: Cambridge University Press, 2011.

Geenen, C. G. "The Council of Chalcedon in the Theology of St. Thomas." In *From an
Abundant Spring: The Walter Farrell Memorial Volume of The Thomist*, edited by Staff
of *The Thomist*, 172–217. New York: P. J. Kennedy, 1952.

Giambrone, Anthony. "The Prologues to Aquinas' Commentaries on the Letters of St.
Paul." In *Towards a Biblical Thomism: Thomas Aquinas and the Renewal of Biblical
Theology*, edited by Piotr Roszak and Jörgen Vijgen. Pamplona: EUNSA, 2018.

———."*Interpretatio iudaica*: Le monothéisme juif à l'époque du second Temple." *Communio* 45 (2020): 43–60.

Golitzin, Alexander. *Et introibo as altare dei: The Mystagogy of Dionysius Areopagita with
Special Reference to Its Predecessors in the Eastern Christian Tradition*. Thessalonike:
George Dedousis, 1994.

Gondreau, Paul. "Anti-Docetism in Aquinas' *Super Ioannem*: St. Thomas as Defender of
the Full Humanity of Christ." In *Reading John with St. Thomas Aquinas: Theological
Exegesis and Speculative Theology*, edited by M. Dauphinais and M. Levering, 254–76.
Washington, DC: Catholic University of America Press, 2005.

———. "St. Thomas Aquinas, the Communication of Idioms, and the Suffering of Christ
in the Garden of Gethsemane." In *Divine Impassibility and the Mystery of Human Suffering*, edited by James F. Keating and Thomas Joseph White, 214–45. Grand Rapids,
MI: Eerdmans, 2009.

———. *The Passions of Christ's Soul in the Theology of St. Thomas Aquinas*. Münster:
Aschendorff, 2002. Repr., Providence, RI: Cluny Media, 2018.

———. "Jesus and Paul on the Meaning and Purpose of Human Sexuality." *Nova et Vetera*, English ed. 18, no. 2 (2020): 461–503.

González de Cardedal, Olegario. *Cristología*. Sapientia Fidei: Serie de Manuales de Teología. Madrid: Biblioteca de Autores Cristianos, 2001.

Gorman, Michael. *Aquinas on the Metaphysics of the Hypostatic Union*. Cambridge: Cambridge University Press, 2017.

Gray, Sherman W. *The Least of My Brothers: Matthew 25:31–46. A History of Interpretation*.
Society of Biblical Literature Series 114. Atlanta: Scholars Press, 1989.

Griswold, Eliza. "Richard Rohr Reorders the Universe." *New Yorker*, February 2, 2020. https://www.newyorker.com/news/on-religion/richard-rohr-reorders-the-universe.

Grüll, Tibor. "'Monotheism' or 'Megatheism'? Religious Competition in Late Antiquity as Mirrored in the Inscriptions Dedicated to Theos Hypsistos." Academia.edu, accessed April 5, 2021. https://www.academia.edu/5382844/_Monotheism_or_megatheism_Religious_competition_in_late_antiquity_as_mirrored_in_the_inscriptions_dedicated_to_Theos_Hypsistos.

Guardini, Romano. *The Humanity of Christ: Contributions to a Psychology of Jesus*. Translated by R. Walls. New York: Random House, 1964.

Guðmundsdóttir, Arnfríður. *Meeting God on the Cross: Christ, the Cross, and the Feminist Critique*. New York: Oxford University Press, 2010.

Haddad, Jordan. "Modern Biology's Contribution to Our Understanding of Christ's Sufferings." *Church Life Journal*, August 8, 2018.

Hahn, Michael S. "Thomas Aquinas's Presentation of Christ as Teacher." *The Thomist* 83, no. 1 (2019): 57–89.

Hall, Edwin, and Horst Uhr. "*Aureola super Auream*: Crowns and Related Symbols of Special Distinction for Saints in Late Gothic and Renaissance Iconography." *Art Bulletin* 67, no. 4 (1985): 567–603.

Halligan, Nicholas. *The Administration of the Sacraments*. New York: Alba House, 1962.

———. *The Sacraments and Their Celebration*. New York: Alba House, 1986.

Harnack, Adolf von. *What Is Christianity?* Translated by Thomas Bailey Saunders. Minneapolis, MN: Fortress Press, 1986.

Harrison, Verna. "Male and Female in Cappadocian Theology." *Journal of Theological Studies* 41, no. 2 (1990): 441–71.

Hart, David Bentley. *That All Shall Be Saved: Heaven, Hell, and Universal Salvation*. New Haven, CT: Yale University Press, 2019.

Haught, John. *God after Darwin: A Theology of Evolution*. Boulder, CO: Westview Press, 2008.

Hengel, Martin. *The Atonement: The Origins of the Doctrine in the New Testament*. Translated by J. Bowden. Philadelphia: Fortress, 1981.

Hengel, Martin, with A. M. Schwemer. *Jesus und das Judentum, Geschichte des frühen Christentums*. Tübingen: Mohr Siebeck, 2007.

Henry, Michel. *Words of Christ*. Translated by Christina M. Geschwandtner. Grand Rapids, MI: Eerdmans, 2012.

Herrero de Jáuregui, Miguel. "Orphic God(s): Theogonies and Hymns as Vehicles of Monotheism." In *Monotheism between Pagans and Christians in Late Antiquity*, edited by Stephen Mitchell and Peter van Nuffelen, 77–99. Leuven: Peeters, 2010.

Hick, John. *The Myth of God Incarnate*. London: SCM Press, 1977.

———. *The Metaphor of God Incarnate*. London: SCM Press, 1993.

Hofer, Andrew. "Dionysian Elements in Thomas Aquinas's Christology: A Case for the Authority and Ambiguity of Pseudo-Dionysius." *The Thomist* 72, no. 3 (2008): 409–42.

———. "Balthasar's Eschatology on the Intermediate State: The Question of Knowability." *Logos* 12, no. 3 (Summer 2009): 148–72.

———. "The Reordering of Relationships in John Chrysostom's *De sacerdotio*." *Augustinianum* 51, no. 2 (2011): 451–71.

———. "Humbert of Romans on the Papacy before Lyons II (1274): A Study in Comparison with Thomas Aquinas and Pope Gregory X's *Extractiones*." *The Thomist*, no. 1 (2020): 51–102.

Hopkins, Bobbi Paige. "The Bible as a Medium for Social Engineering: Jesus as the Androgynous Role Model." *Journal of Research in Gender Studies* 3 (2013): 78–87.

Huels, John M. *Liturgy and Law: Liturgical Law in the System of Roman Catholic Canon Law*. Montreal: Wilson & Lafleur, 2006.

Hughes, John Jay. *Absolutely Null and Utterly Void: The Papal Condemnation of Anglican Orders, 1896*. Washington, DC: Corpus, 1968.

———. *Stewards of the Lord: A Reappraisal of Anglican Orders*. London: Sheed and Ward, 1970.

Hurtado, Larry W. *One God, One Lord: Early Christian Devotion and Ancient Jewish Monotheism*. Philadelphia: Fortress, 1988.

———. *Lord Jesus Christ: Devotion to Jesus in Earliest Christianity*. Grand Rapids, MI: Eerdmans, 2005.

———. *Ancient Jewish Monotheism and Early Christian Devotion*. Waco, TX: Baylor University Press, 2017.

Iammarrone, Luigi. "La visione beatifica di Cristo Viatore nel pensiero di San Tommaso." *Doctor Communis* 36 (1983): 287–30.

Israel, Jonathan I. *Radical Enlightenment: Philosophy and the Making of Modernity, 1650–1750*. Oxford: Oxford University Press, 2002.

Johnson, Elizabeth A. "The Maleness of Christ." In *The Special Nature of Women?*, edited by Anne Carr and Elisabeth Schüssler Fiorenza, 108–16. Concilium 6. London: SCM Press, 1991.

———. "Redeeming the Names of Christ." In *Freeing Theology: The Essentials of Theology in Feminist Perspective*, edited by Catherine Mowry LaCugna, 115–37. Harper: San Francisco, 1993.

Johnson, Luke Timothy. *The Real Jesus: The Misguided Quest for the Historical Jesus and the Truth of the Traditional Gospels*. San Francisco: Harper, 1996.

Jordan, Mark. "Esotericism and *Accessus* in Thomas Aquinas." *Medieval Philosophy* 20, no. 2 (1992): 35–49.

Joüon, Paul. "Les verbes *BOYΛOMAI* et *ΘEΛΩ* dans le Nouveau Testament." *Revue des sciences religieuses* 30 (1940): 227–38.

Juárez, Guillermo A. *Dios Trinidad en todas las creaturas y en los santos: Estudio histórico-sistemático de la doctrina del Comentario a las Sentencias de Santo Tomás de Aquino sobre la omnipresencia y la inhabitación*. Córdoba, Argentina: Edición del Copista, 2008.

Kähler, Martin. *Church Dogmatics*. 4 vols. Edited and translated by G. W. Bromiley and T. F. Torrance. Edinburgh: T&T Clark, 1936–75.

———. *The So-Called Historical Jesus and the Historical Biblical Christ*. Translated by Carl E. Braaten. Philadelphia: Fortress, 1964.

Käsemann, Ernst. *Essays on New Testament Themes*. Translated by W. J. Montague. London: SCM Press, 1964.

Kasper, Walter. *Jesus the Christ*. Translated by V. Green. 4th repr. London: Burns & Oates, 1985. 1st ed., 1976.

Keating, Daniel. "Trinity and Salvation: Christian Life as an Existence in the Trinity." In *The Oxford Handbook of the Trinity*, edited by Gilles Emery, OP, and Matthew Levering, 442–53. New York: Oxford University Press, 2011.

Keller, Catherine. *Apocalypse Now and Then: A Feminist Approach to the End of the World.* Boston: Beacon, 1996.

Keller, Josephus M. "De virtute caritatis ut amicitia quadam divina. S Thomas, 3. dist. 27, q. 2, a. 1 et 2. 2, q. 23, a. 1." In *Xenia Thomistica*, vol. 2, edited by S. Szabó, OP, 233–76. Rome: Typis Polyglottis Vaticanis, 1925.

Keller, Marie-Joseph, and Marie-Benoît Lavaud. "La charité comme amitié d'après S. Thomas." *Revue Thomiste* 12 (1929): 445–75.

Kereszty, Roch A. *Jesus Christ: Fundamentals of Christology.* 3rd ed. Staten Island, NY: St Pauls, 2015. 1st ed., 2002.

Kister, Menahem. "The Prayers of the Seventh Book of the *Apostolic Constitutions* and Their Implications for the Formulation of Synagogue Prayers." *Tarbiz* 77 (2008): 205–38.

Klimczak, Paweł. *Christus Magister: Le Christ Maître dans les commentaires évangéliques de saint Thomas d'Aquin.* Studia Friburgensia 117. Fribourg: Academic Press Fribourg, 2013.

Klubertanz, George. *Notes on the Philosophy of Human Nature.* St. Louis: St. Louis University Press, 1949.

Koch, Hugo. "Proklos als Quelle des Pseudo-Dionysius Areopagita in der Lehre von Bösen." *Philologus* 54 (1895): 438–54.

Koterski, Joseph W. "The Doctrine of Participation in Aquinas's *Commentary on John*." In *Being and Thought in Aquinas*, edited by Jeremiah M. Hackett, William E. Murnion, and Carl N. Still, 109–21. Albany: State University of New York Press, 2004.

Krämer, Klaus. *Imago Trinitatis: Die Gottebenbildlichkeit des Menschen in der Theologie des Thomas von Aquin.* Freiburger theologische Studien. Freiburg im Breisgau: Herder, 2000.

Kruijen, Christophe J. *Peut-on espérer un salut universel? Étude critique d'une opinion théologique contemporaine concernant la damnation.* Paris: Parole et Silence, 2017.

Ku, John Baptist. *God the Father in the Theology of St. Thomas Aquinas.* New York: Peter Lang, 2013.

Ladaria, Luis. "The Question of the Validity of Baptism Conferred in the Church of Jesus Christ of Latter-Day Saints." *L'Osservatore Romano*, weekly English ed., August 1, 2001.

———. *Teología del pecado original y de la gracia.* 2nd ed. Madrid: Biblioteca de Autores Cristianos, 2001.

Lafont, Ghislain. *Structures et Méthode dans la Somme Théologique de Saint Thomas d'Aquin.* Bruges: Desclée de Brouwer, 1961.

Lagges, Patrick R. "Mormon Baptism Revisited." *Catechumenate* 25, no. 1 (2003): 25–35.

Lanckau, Jörg. "*Hypsistos*: Cultural Translation of Jewish Monotheism in the Hellenistic Period." *Asiastische Studien—Etudes asiatiques* 65, no. 4 (2011): 861–82.

Laumakis, Stephen. "The Sensus Communis Reconsidered." *American Catholic Philosophical Quarterly* 82 (2008): 429–43.

Law, David R. *Kierkegaard's Kenotic Christology.* Oxford: Oxford University Press, 2013.

Lawler, Michael G. "Faith, Contract, and Sacrament in Christian Marriage: A Theological Approach." *Theological Studies* 52 (1991): 712–31.

Le Bachelet, X. "Bonose." In *Dictionnaire de théologie catholique*, 2:1027–31. Paris: Letouzey et Ané, 1903–72.

Le Brun-Gouavnic, Claire. *Ystoria sancti Thome de Aquino de Guillaume de Tocco (1323)*. Studies and Texts 127. Toronto: Pontifical Institute of Mediaeval Studies, 1996.

Leeming, Bernard. *Principles of Sacramental Theology*. London: Longmans, Green, 1957.

Legge, Dominic. *The Trinitarian Christology of St. Thomas Aquinas*. Oxford: Oxford University Press, 2017.

Leroy, Marie-Vincent. "La convenance de l'Incarnation." *Revue Thomiste* 109 (2009): 419–65.

Levering, Matthew. *Christ and the Catholic Priesthood: Ecclesial Hierarchy and the Pattern of the Trinity*. Chicago: Hillenbrand Books, 2010.

———. *Jesus and the Demise of Death: Resurrection, Afterlife, and the Fate of the Christian*. Waco, TX: Baylor University Press, 2012.

Levering, Matthew, and Marcus Plested, eds. *The Oxford Handbook of the Reception of Aquinas*. Oxford: Oxford University Press, 2021.

Lew, Lawrence. "STL Tesina: Why Can We Not Repent after We Die?" Academia.edu, accessed April 5, 2021. https://www.academia.edu/36354794/STL_Tesina_Why_Can_We_Not_Repent_After_We_Die.

Lombardo, Nicholas. "Evil, Suffering, and Original Sin." In *The Oxford Handbook of Catholic Theology*, edited by Lewis Ayres and Medi Ann Volpe. Oxford: Oxford University Press, 2019.

Lonergan, Bernard. *The Ontological and Psychological Constitution of Christ, Collected Works*. Vol. 7. Toronto: University of Toronto Press, 2002.

Lynch, Reginald. *The Cleansing of the Heart: The Sacraments as Instrumental Causes in the Thomistic Tradition*. Washington, DC: Catholic University of America Press, 2017.

Lynn, William D. *Christ's Redemptive Merit: The Nature of Its Causality According to St. Thomas*. Analecta Gregoriana 115. Rome: Gregorian University Press, 1962.

MacIntyre, Alasdair. *After Virtue: A Study in Moral Theory*. 2nd ed. Notre Dame, IN: University of Notre Dame Press, 1984.

———. *Dependent Rational Animals: Why Human Beings Need the Virtues*. Chicago: Open Court, 1999.

Mahoney, Jack. *Christianity in Evolution: An Exploration*. Washington, DC: Georgetown University Press, 2011.

Mainoldi, Ernesto Sergio. "Why Dionysius the Areopagite? The Invention of the First Father." In *Studia Patristica*, vol. 96, edited by Markus Vinzent. Leuven: Peeters, 2017.

Mansini, Guy. "Understanding St. Thomas on Christ's Immediate Knowledge of God." *The Thomist* 59 (1995): 91–124.

———. "'Without Me You Can Do Nothing': St. Thomas with and without St. Augustine on John 15:5." In *Aquinas the Augustinian*, edited by Michael Dauphinais, Barry David, and Matthew Levering, 159–80. Washington, DC: Catholic University of America Press, 2007.

———. "Obedience Religious, Christological and Trinitarian." *Nova et Vetera*, English ed. 12 (2014): 395–413.

Marcus, Joel. *Mark 1–8: A New Translation with Introduction and Commentary*. Anchor Bible. New York: Doubleday, 2000.

Margelidon, Philippe-Marie. Études de Christologie Thomiste: De la grâce à la résurrection du Christ. Perpignan: Artège, 2010.

Marín-Sola, Francisco. *The Homogeneous Evolution of Catholic Dogma*. Translated by Antonio T. Piñon. Manilla: Santo Tomas University Press, 1988.

Marion, Jean-Luc. *Givenness and Revelation*. Translated by Stephen E. Lewis. Oxford: Oxford University Press, 2016.

Marshall, Bruce D. "The Dereliction of Christ and the Impassibility of God." In *Divine Impassibility and the Mystery of Human Suffering*, edited by James F. Keating and Thomas Joseph White, 246–98. Grand Rapids, MI: Eerdmans, 2009.

———. "The Unity of the Triune God: Reviving an Ancient Question." *The Thomist* 74 (2010): 1–32.

McClymond, Michael. *The Devil's Redemption: A New History and Interpretation of Christian Universalism*. Grand Rapids, MI: Baker Academic, 2018.

———. "'Everything Is Christ'—and Other Muddled Messages from Richard Rohr." *Gospel Coalition*, September 16, 2019. https://www.thegospelcoalition.org/reviews/universal-christ-richard-rohr.

McCormack, Bruce. "Karl Barth's Christology as a Resource for a Reformed Version of Kenoticism." *International Journal of Systematic Theology* 8 (2006): 245.

———. "Kenoticism in Modern Christology." In *The Oxford Handbook of Christology*, 444–57. Oxford: Oxford University Press, 2015.

McGinn, Bernard. "'Contemplatio Sapientialis': Thomas Aquinas's Contribution to Mystical Theology." *Ephemerides Theologicae Lovanienses* 95 (2019): 327.

McInerny, Ralph. *Boethius and Aquinas*. Washington, DC: Catholic University of America Press, 1990.

Meconi, David. *The One Christ: St. Augustine's Theology of Deification*. Washington, DC: Catholic University of America Press, 2013.

Meier, John P. *A Marginal Jew: Rethinking the Historical Jesus*. Anchor Bible Reference Library Series 1–5. New York: Yale University Press, 1991–2016.

Merriell, D. Juvenal. *To the Image of the Trinity: A Study in the Development of Aquinas' Teaching*. Studies and Texts 96. Toronto: Pontifical Institute of Mediaeval Studies, 1990.

Meszaros, Andrew. *The Prophetic Church: History and Doctrinal Development in John Henry Newman and Yves Congar*. Oxford: Oxford University Press, 2016.

Migliore, Daniel L. "Karl Barth's First Lecture in Dogmatics: Instruction in the Christian Religion." In *Göttingen Dogmatics*, by Karl Barth, 15–62. Accessed through the Digital Karl Barth Library.

Mitchell, Stephen. "The Cult of Theos Hypsistos between Pagans, Jews, and Christians." *Pagan Monotheism in Late Antiquity*, edited by Polymnia Athanassiadi and Michael Frede, 81–148. Oxford: Clarendon, 2008.

———. "Further Thoughts on the Cult of Theos Hypsistos." In *One God: Pagan Monotheism in the Roman Empire*, edited by Stephen Mitchell and Peter van Nuffelen, 167–208. Cambridge: Cambridge University Press, 2010.

Morard, Martin. "Une source de saint Thomas d'Aquin: Le Deuxième Concile de Constantinople (553)." *Revue des sciences philosophiques et théologiques* 81 (1977): 21–56.

————. "Sacerdoce du Christ et sacerdoce des chrétiens dans le *Commentaire des Psaulms de saint Thomas d'Aquin*." *Revue Thomist* 99 (1999): 119–42.

————. "Thomas d'Aquin lecteur des conciles." *Archivum Franciscanum Historicum* 98 (2005): 211–365.

Morerod, Charles. "Le prêtre chez Cajetan." *Revue Thomiste* 99, no. 4 (1999): 245–80.

Most, William G. *The Consciousness of Christ*. Front Royal, VA: Christendom, 1980.

Murray, Charles. *Human Diversity: The Biology of Gender, Race, and Class*. New York: Twelve, 2020.

Murray, Paul. *Aquinas at Prayer: The Bible, Mysticism, and Poetry*. London: Bloomsbury, 2013.

————. "Beauty in the Prayer of Aquinas." *Ephemerides Theologicae Lovanienses* 95, no. 2 (2019): 235–52.

Navarrete, Urbano. "Response of the Congregation for the Doctrine of the Faith about the Validity of Baptism Conferred in the Church of Jesus Christ of Latter-Day Saints." *L'Osservatore Romano*, weekly English ed., August 1, 2001.

Newman, Carey, ed. *The Jewish Roots of Christological Monotheism*. Journal for the Study of Judaism Supplements 63. Leiden: Brill, 1999.

Newman, John Henry. *An Essay in Aid of a Grammar of Assent*. Edited by I. T. Ker. Oxford: Clarendon Press, 1985.

Nichols, Aidan. *Romance and System: The Theological Synthesis of Matthias Joseph Scheeben*. Denver, CO: Augustine Institute, 2010.

Nicolas, Jean-Hervé. *Synthèse Dogmatique: De la Trinité à la Trinité*. Paris: Beauchesne, 1985. [cited by Mansini]

————. *Synthèse dogmatique: De la Trinité à la Trinité*. Fribourg: Éditions Universitaires Fribourg Suisse, 1985. [cited by Langevin]

Nicolas, Marie-Joseph. "Voir Dieu dans la 'condition charnelle.'" *Doctor Communis* 36 (1983): 384–94.

Nielsen, Lauge Olaf. *Theology and Philosophy in the Twelfth Century: A Study of Gilbert Porreta's Thinking and the Theological Expositions of the Doctrine of the Incarnation during the Period, 1130–1180*. Leiden: Brill, 1982.

Norden, Eduard. *Agnostos Theos: Untersuchung zur Formgeschichte religiöser Rede*. Helsingfors: B. G. Teubner, 1913.

Nutt, Roger W. *General Principles of Sacramental Theology*. Washington, DC: Catholic University of America Press, 2017.

O'Brien, Carl Séan. *The Demiurge in Ancient Thought: Secondary God and Divine Mediators*. Cambridge: Cambridge University Press, 2015.

O'Callaghan, John P. "Imago Dei: A Test Case for St. Thomas's Augustinianism." In *Aquinas the Augustinian*, edited by M. Dauphinais, B. David, and M. Levering, 100–144. Washington, DC: Catholic University of America Press, 2007.

Ocáriz, Fernando, Lucas F. Mateo-Seco, and José Antonio Riestra. *The Mystery of Jesus Christ: A Christology and Soteriology Textbook*. Translated by Michael Adams and James Gavignon. Portland, OR: Four Courts Press, 2011.

O'Collins, Gerald. *Christology: A Biblical, Historical, and Systematic Study of Jesus*. Repr., Oxford: Oxford University Press, 2013; 2nd ed., 2009; 1st ed., 1995.

O'Connor, Edward. "Appendix 4: The Evolution of St. Thomas's Thought on the Gifts." In
    St. Thomas Aquinas, Summa Theologiae, vol. 24 (1a2ae 68–70), *The Gifts of the Spirit*.
    New York: McGraw-Hill, 1964.
O'Connor, Michael. *Cajetan's Biblical Commentaries: Motive and Method*. Leiden: Brill,
    2017.
———. "The Orientation of Human Sexuality: A Thomistic Study of the Inclination to
    Conjugal Union." STD diss., Pontifical University of Saint Thomas Aquinas, 2020.
O'Keefe, John J. "Impassible Suffering? Divine Passion and Fifth-Century Christology."
    Theological Studies 58 (1997): 39–60.
O'Murchu, Diarmuid. *Incarnation: A New Evolutionary Threshold*. Maryknoll, NY: Orbis
    Books, 2017.
Örsy, Ladislas. "Faith, Sacrament, Contract, and Christian Marriage: Disputed Ques-
    tions." *Theological Studies* 43 (1982): 379–98.
Osborne, Thomas M., Jr. "Which Essence Is Brought into Being by the Existential Act?"
    The Thomist 81 (2017): 471–505.
Owens, Joseph. *Human Destiny: Some Problems for Catholic Philosophy*. Washington, DC:
    Catholic University of America Press, 1985.
Pannenberg, Wolfhart. *Jesus—God and Man*. 2nd ed. Translated by Lewis L. Wilkins and
    Duane A. Priebe. Philadelphia: Westminster Press, 1977.
———. *Systematic Theology*. Vol. 2. Translated by G. W. Bromiley. Grand Rapids, MI:
    Eerdmans, 1994.
Parker, Robert. *Greek Gods Abroad: Names, Natures, and Transformations*. Sather Classical
    Lectures. Berkeley: University of California Press, 2017.
Pelster, Franz. "La *quaestio disputata* de saint Thomas *De unione Verbi incarnati*." *Archives
    de philosophie* 3 (1925–26): 198–245.
Peplau, Leitita Anne. "Human Sexuality: How Do Men and Women Differ?" *Current
    Directions in Psychological Science* 12 (2003): 37–44.
Perczel, István. "The Christology of Pseudo-Dionysius the Areopagite: The Fourth Letter
    in Its Indirect and Direct Traditions." *Le Muséon* 117 (2004): 409–46.
Persson, Erik. "Le plan de la Somme théologique et le rapport 'Ratio–Revelatio.'" *Revue
    Philosophique de Louvain* 56 (1958): 545–72.
Pesch, Christian. *De Sacramentis*. 4th ed. 2 vols. Praelectiones Dogmaticae 6–7. Freiburg
    im Breisgau: Herder, 1914–20.
Phelan, Owen W. "'Beautiful Like Helen': A Study in Early Medieval Theological Meth-
    od." *Catholic Historical Review* 106, no. 2 (2020): 202–26.
Pidolle, Laurent. *La christologie historique du pape saint Léon le Grand*. Paris: Les Editions
    du Cerf, 2013.
Pieper, Josef. *The Silence of Saint Aquinas*. South Bend, IN: St. Augustine's Press. Repr.,
    1999.
Pinckaers, Servais. *The Sources of Christian Ethics*. Translated by Mary Thomas Noble.
    Washington, DC: Catholic University of America Press, 1995.
Pine, Gregory. "Magnanimity and Humility According to St. Thomas Aquinas." *The
    Thomist* 82, no. 2 (2018): 263–86.
Pippin, Tina. "Judgment." In *Dictionary of Feminist Theologies*, edited by Letty M. Russell
    and J. Shannon Clarkson, 158. Louisville, KY: Westminster John Knox Press, 1996.

Prudlo, Donald S. *Certain Saints: Canonization and the Origins of Papal Infallibility in the Medieval Church*. Ithaca, NY: Cornell University Press, 2015.

Prümmer, Dominic M. *Manuale Theologiae Moralis secundum Principia S. Thomae Aquinatis*. 8th ed. 3 vols. Edited by Engelbert M. Münch, OP. Freiburg im Breisgau: Herder, 1935–36.

Przanowski, Mateusz. "*Formam servi accipiens* (Phil 2:7) or *Plenus gratiae et Veritatis* (Jn 1:14)? The Apparent Dilemma in Aquinas' Exegesis." In *Towards a Biblical Thomism: Thomas Aquinas and the Renewal of Biblical Theology*, 119–33. Pamplona: Ediciones Universidad de Navarra, S.A., 2018.

Rahner, Karl. *Theological Investigations*. Vol. 5, *Later Writings*. London: Darton, Longman and Todd, 1966.

———. *Foundations of Christian Faith: An Introduction to the Idea of Christianity*. Translated by W. V. Dych. New York: Seabury, 1978.

———. *Theological Investigations*. Vol. 16, *Experience of the Spirit: Source of Theology*. New York: Crossroad, 1983.

Rainbow, Paul. "Jewish Monotheism as the Matrix for New Testament Christology." *Novum Testamentum* 33 (1990): 78–79.

Ramage, Matthew. *The Experiment of Faith*. Washington, DC: Catholic University of America Press, 2020.

Ramelli, Illaria. "Origen, Patristic Philosophy, and Christian Platonism: Re-Thinking the Christianisation of Hellenism." *Vigiliae Christianae* 63 (2009): 217–63.

Raschko, Michael. "Aquinas's Theology of the Incarnation in Light of Lombard's Subsistence Theory." *The Thomist* 65 (2001): 409–39.

Ratzinger, Joseph. "Revelation and Tradition." In *Revelation and Tradition*, by Karl Rahner and Joseph Ratzinger. New York: Herder and Herder, 1966.

———. *Commentary on the Documents of Vatican II*. Vol. 5. Edited by Herbert Vorgrimler. New York: Herder and Herder, 1969.

———. *Behold the Pierced One: An Approach to Spiritual Christology*. Translated by Graham Harrison. San Francisco: Ignatius Press, 1986.

———. *Eschatology: Death and Eternal Life*. 2nd ed. Translated by Michael Waldstein. Washington, DC: Catholic University of America Press, 1988.

———. *God and the World*. San Francisco: Ignatius Press, 2002.

———. *Introduction to Christianity*. Translated by J. R. Foster and Michael J. Miller. San Francisco, CA: Ignatius Press, 2004.

———. *Jesus of Nazareth*. 3 vols. New York: Image, 2007–12.

———. *Gottes Projekt: Nachdenken über Schöpfung und Kirche*. Regensburg: Pustet, 2009.

———. *Dogma and Preaching*. San Francisco: Ignatius Press, 2011.

———. *Theology of the Liturgy: The Sacramental Foundation of Christian Existence*. In *Collected Works*, edited by Michael J. Miller, translated by John Saward et al. San Francisco: Ignatius Press, 2014.

———. "The Church and the Scandal of Sexual Abuse." Catholic News Agency, April 10, 2019. https://www.catholicnewsagency.com/news/full-text-of-benedict-xvi-the-church-and-the-scandal-of-sexual-abuse-59639.

Read, Gordon. "Mormon Baptism Revisited." *Canon Law Society Newsletter* (*London*) 126 (2001): 91–95.

Reale, Giovanni. *Toward a New Interpretation of Plato*. Washington, DC: Catholic University of America Press, 1997.

Reichman, James. "Aquinas, Scotus, and the Christological Mystery: Why Christ Is Not a Human Person." *The Thomist* 71 (2007): 451–74.

Reno, R. R. "A Striking Display of Sophistry." *First Things*, June 16, 2020. https://www.firstthings.com/web-exclusives/2020/06/a-striking-display-of-sophistry?fbclid=IwAR1t11PxQ40PCogxCHFYV6nBRlq9kPTOMNwAQECEk-Yz1BDHtTswOZfrIic.

Revel, Jean-Philippe. *Traité des sacrements: Baptême et sacramentalité*. 2 vols. Paris: Cerf, 2004–5.

Riches, Aaron. "After Chalcedon: The Oneness of Christ and the Dyothelite Mediation of His Theandric Unity." *Modern Theology* 24 (2008): 199–224.

Ridley, Matt. *Genome: The Autobiography of a Species in 23 Chapters*. New York: HarperCollins, 2000.

Rohr, Richard. *Breathing under Water: Spirituality and the Twelve Steps*. Cincinnati, OH: Franciscan Media, 2011.

———. *The Universal Christ: How a Forgotten Reality Can Change Everything We See, Hope For, and Believe*. New York: Convergent Press, 2019.

Rosemann, Philipp W. *Peter Lombard*. New York: Oxford University Press, 2004.

Roszak, Piotr. "The Judge of the Living and of the Dead: Aquinas on Christ's Power to Judge in His Biblical Commentaries." In *Towards a Biblical Thomism: Thomas Aquinas and the Renewal of Biblical Theology*, edited by Piotr Roszak and Jörgen Vijgen, 99–117. Pamplona: Ediciones Universidad de Navarra, S.A., 2018.

Rudy, Gordon. *The Mystical Language of Sensation in the Later Middle Ages*. London: Routledge, 2002.

Ruether, Rosemary Radford. *Sexism and God-Talk: Toward a Feminist Theology*. Boston: Beacon Press, 1983.

Rust, Paul R. "Leo XIII's Decision on Anglican Orders." *Homiletic and Pastoral Review* 61 (1961): 949–51 and 1041–53.

Ryan, Thomas. "Revisiting Affective Knowledge and Connaturality in Aquinas." *Theological Studies* 66 (2005): 49–68.

Salas, Victor. "Thomas Aquinas on Christ's *Esse*: A Metaphysics of the Incarnation." *The Thomist* 70 (2006): 577–603.

Sanders, E. P. *Jesus and Judaism*. London: SCM Press, 1985.

Sanz, Santiago. "Joseph Ratzinger y la doctrina de la creación: Los apuntes de Münster de 1964 (y III). Algunos temas debatidos." *Revista Española de Teología* 74 (2014): 453–96.

Sax, Leonard. *Why Gender Matters: What Parents and Teachers Need to Know about the Emerging Science of Sex Differences*. 2nd ed. New York: Harmony, 2017.

Scheeben, Matthias Joseph. *The Mysteries of Christianity*. St. Louis, MO: Herder, 1947.

———. *Handbook of Catholic Dogmatics. Book One: Theological Epistemology. Part One: The Objective Principles of Theological Knowledge*. Translated by Michael J. Miller. Steubenville, OH: Emmaus Academic, 2019.

Schindler, David L., et al. "Faith and the Sacrament of Marriage: A Response to the Proposal of a New 'Minimum Fidei' Requirement." *Communio* 42 (2015): 309–30.

Schleiermacher, Friedrich. *The Christian Faith*. 3rd English ed. London: Bloomsbury, 1999.

Schmitz, R. M. "Christus Comprehensor: Die 'Visio Beatifica Christi Viatoris' bei M. J. Scheeben." *Doctor Communis* 36 (1983): 347–59.

Schumacher, Michele. "Feminist Christologies." In *The Oxford Handbook of Christology*, edited by Francesca Murphy, 408–24. Oxford: Oxford University Press, 2015.

Schüssler Fiorenza, Elizabeth. *Jesus: Miriam's Child, Sophia's Prophet*. London: SCM Press, 1995.

Schweitzer, Albert. *The Quest for the Historical Jesus: A Critical Study of Its Progress from Reimarus to Wrede*. Translated by W. Montgomery. London: A. and C. Black, 1911. Repr., Mineola NY: Dover, 2005. [cited by Spezzano]

———. *The Quest of the Historical Jesus: A Critical Study of Its Progress from Reimarus to Wrede*. Translated by J. Bowden. Minneapolis: Fortress Press, 2001. [cited by White]

Segal, Alan. *Two Powers in Heaven: Early Rabbinic Reports about Christianity and Gnosticism*. Studies in Judaism in Late Antiquity 25. Leiden: Brill, 1977.

Sesboüé, Bernard. *Jésus-Christ l'unique médiateur: Essai sur la rédemption et le salut*. Vol. 1, *Problématique et relecture doctrinale*. Jésus et Jésus-Christ 33. Paris: Desclée, 1988.

Sherwin, Michael. "Christ the Teacher in St. Thomas's *Commentary on the Gospel of John*." In *Reading John with St. Thomas Aquinas: Theological Exegesis and Speculative Theology*, edited by M. Dauphinais and M. Levering, 173–93. Washington, DC: Catholic University of America Press, 2005.

Smith, Christian, and Melinda Lundquist Denton Christian. *Soul Searching: The Religious and Spiritual Lives of American Teenagers*. New York: Oxford University Press, 2005.

Smith, William B. "Is Mormon Baptism Valid?" *Homiletic and Pastoral Review* 102, no. 8 (2002): 70–72.

Sokolowski, Robert. *The God of Faith and Reason*. Washington, DC: Catholic University of America Press, 1982.

———. *Eucharistic Presence: A Study in the Theology of Disclosure*. Washington, DC: Catholic University of America Press, 1994.

———. *Christian Faith and Human Understanding*. Washington, DC: Catholic University of America Press, 2006.

———. *Phenomenology of the Human Person*. Cambridge: Cambridge University Press, 2008.

Spezzano, Daria. *The Glory of God's Grace: Deification According to St. Thomas Aquinas*. Faith and Reason: Studies in Catholic Theology and Philosophy. Ave Maria, FL: Sapientia Press, 2015.

Spicq, Ceslas. *Agapè dans le Nouveau Testament: Analyse des textes*. Études Bibliques 2. Paris: J. Gabalda et Cie, Éditeurs, 1959.

Spinks, Bryan D. *Reformation and Modern Rituals and Theologies of Baptism: From Luther to Contemporary Practices*. Aldershot, UK: Ashgate, 2006.

Spong, John Shelby. *A New Christianity for a New World: Why Traditional Faith Is Dying and How a New Faith Is Being Born*. New York: HarperCollins, 2002.

Stang, Charles. *Apophasis and Pseudonymity in Dionysius the Areopagite: "No Longer I."* Oxford: Oxford University Press, 2012.

Stein, Edith. *Essays on Women*. Washington, DC: ICS Publications, 1996.

Steinberg, Leo. *The Sexuality of Christ in Renaissance Art and in Modern Oblivion*. 2nd ed. Chicago: University of Chicago Press, 1996.

Stern, Menahem. "Hecataeus of Abdera and Theophrastus on Jews and Egyptians." *Journal of Egyptian Archeology* 59 (1973): 159–68.

Stiglmayr, Joseph. "Der Neuplatoniker Proklos als Vorlage des sog: Dionysius Areopagita in der Lehre vom Übel." *Historisches Jahrbuch* 16 (1895): 253–73, 721–48.

Strauss, David Friedrich. *The Christ of Faith and the Jesus of History: A Critique of Schleiermacher's Life of Jesus*. Translated by L. Keck. Philadelphia: Fortress Press, 1977.

Strousma, Guy. "A Nameless God: Judeo-Christian and Gnostic 'Theologies of the Name.'" In *The Image of Judeo-Christians in Ancient Jewish and Christian Literature*, edited by Peter-Jan Tomson and Doris Lambers-Petry, 230–43. Wissenschaftliche Untersuchungen zum Neuen Testament 158. Tübingen: Mohr Siebeck, 2003.

Szada, Marta. "The Debate over the Repetition of Baptism between Homoians and Nicenes at the End of the Fourth Century." *Journal of Early Christian Studies* 27 (2019): 646.

Tamisiea, David. "St. Thomas on the One *Esse* of Christ." *Angelicum* 88 (2011): 383–402.

Tannen, Deborah. *You Just Don't Understand: Women and Men in Conversation*. New York: HarperCollins, 1990.

Tappé, Mercedes, Lisamarie Bensman, Kentaro Hayashi, and Elaine Hatfield. "Gender Differences in Receptivity to Sexual Offers: A New Research Prototype." *Interpersona: An International Journal on Personal Relationships* 7, no. 2 (2013): https://interpersona.psychopen.eu/article/view/121/html.

Taussig, Eduardo M. "La humanidad de Cristo como instrumento según Santo Tomás de Aquino: Evolución de Sto. Tomás en el recurso a la noción de instrumento para iluminar diversos problemas cristológicos." PhD diss., Pontificia Studiorum Universitas a S. Thoma Aq. in Urbe, Rome, 1990.

Tavard, George H. *A Review of Anglican Orders: The Problem and the Solution*. Collegeville, MN: Liturgical Press, 1990.

Thompson, Thomas R. "Nineteenth-Century Kenotic Christology: The Waxing, Waning, and Weighing of a Quest for a Coherent Orthodoxy." In *Exploring Kenotic Christology: The Self-Emptying of God*, edited by C. Stephen Evans. Oxford: Oxford University Press, 2006.

Torrell, Jean-Pierre. "Imiter Dieu comme des enfants bien-aimés: La conformité à Dieu et au Christ dans l'œuvre de saint Thomas." In *Novitas et veritas vitae: Aux sources du renouveau de la morale chrétienne, Mélanges offerts au Professeur Servais Pinckaers*, edited by C.-J. Pinto de Oliveira, 53–65. Paris: Cerf, 1991.

———. *Christ and Spirituality in St. Thomas Aquinas*. Translated by B. Blankenhorn, OP. Washington, DC: Catholic University of America Press, 2011. 1st French ed., 1996.

———. "La causalité salvifique de la résurrection du Christ selon saint Thomas." *Revue Thomiste* 96 (1996): 179–208.

———. "Le Christ dans la 'spiritualité' de saint Thomas." In *Christ among the Medieval Dominicans: Representations of Christ in the Texts and Images of the Order of Preachers*, edited by K. Emery Jr. and J. Wawrykow, 197–219. Notre Dame, IN: University of Notre Dame Press, 1998.

———. *Le Christ en ses mystères: La vie et l'œuvre de Jésus selon saint Thomas d'Aquin*. 2 vols. Paris: Desclée, 1999.

———. "Le savoir acquis du Christ selon les théologiens médiévaux." *Revue Thomiste* 101 (2001): 355–408.

————. *Thomas Aquinas*. Vol. 2, *Spiritual Master*. Translated by Robert Royal. Washington, DC: Catholic University of America Press, 2003.

————. "Nature and Grace in Thomas Aquinas." In *Surnaturel: A Controversy at the Heart of Twentieth-Century Thomistic Thought*, edited by Serge-Thomas Bonino, OP, 155–87. Ave Maria, FL: Sapientia Press, 2007.

Troeltsch, Ernst. "Über historische und dogmatische Methode in der Theologie, Gesammelte Schriften." In *Gesammelte Schriften*, vol. 2, 728–53. Tubingen: J. C. B. Mohr [Paul Siebeck], 1913.

Tschipke, Theophil. *Die Menschheit Christi als Heilsorgan der Gottheit*. Freiburg im Breisgau: Herder, 1940.

Vacant, A., and E. Mangenot, eds. *Dictionnaire de Théologie Catholique* (DTC). Vol. 2. Paris: Letouzey et Ane, 1905.

van der Horst, Pieter. *Studies in Ancient Judaism and Early Christianity*. Ancient Judaism and Early Christianity 67. Leiden: Brill, 2014.

van Kooten, George H. "Pagan and Jewish Monotheism According to Varro, Plutarch, and St. Paul: The Aniconic, Monotheistic Beginnings of Rome's Pagan Cult—Romans 1:19–25 in a Roman Context." In *Flores Florentino: Dead Sea Scrolls and Other Early Jewish Studies in Honour of Florentino García Martínez*, edited by Anthony Hillhorst, 633–51. JSJSup 122. Leiden: Brill, 2007.

Van Nieuwenhove, Rik. "'Recipientes per contemplationem, tradentes per actionem': The Relation between the Active and Contemplative Lives According to Thomas Aquinas." *The Thomist* 81, no. 1 (2017): 1–30.

Vermes, Geza. *Jesus in His Jewish Context*. Minneapolis: Fortress Press 2003.

Verwilghen, Albert. *Christologie et spritualité selon saint Augustin: L'hymne aux Philippiens*. Paris: Beauchesne, 1985.

Vijgen, Jörgen. "Aquinas's Reception of Origen: A Preliminary Study." In *Thomas Aquinas and the Greek Fathers*, edited by Michael Dauphinais, Andrew Hofer, OP, and Roger Nutt, 30–88. Ave Maria, FL: Sapientia Press, 2019.

Vitz, Paul. "Men and Women: The Psychology of Their Differences and Their Complementarity." Delivered at the annual symposium of the Catholic Women's Forum of the Ethics and Public Policy Center, Washington, DC, June 26, 2019.

Vonier, Anscar. *A Key to the Doctrine of the Eucharist*. Bethesda, MD: Zaccheus, 2003.

Waers, Stephen. "Monarchianism and Two Powers: Jewish and Christian Monotheism at the Beginning of the Third Century." *Vigiliae Christianae* 70 (2016): 401–29.

Waldstein, Michael. "The Analogy of Mission and Obedience: A Central Point in the Relation between *Theologia* and *Oikonomia* in St. Thomas Aquinas's *Commentary on John*." In *Reading John with St. Thomas Aquinas: Theological Exegesis and Speculative Theology*, edited by M. Dauphinais and M. Levering, 92–112. Washington, DC: Catholic University of America Press, 2005.

Wallace, Joel Matthew. "*Inspiravit ei voluntatem patiendi pro nobis, infundendo ei caritatem*": Charity, the Source of Christ's Action According to Thomas Aquinas. Siena: Cantagalli, 2013.

Watson, Natalie K. *Feminist Theology*. Grand Rapids, MI: Eerdmans, 2003.

Wawrykow, Joseph P. "The *Summa contra Gentiles* Reconsidered: On the Contribution of the *De Trinitate* of Hilary of Poitiers." *The Thomist* 58, no. 4 (1994): 617–34.

————. *God's Grace and Human Action: Merit in the Theology of Thomas Aquinas*. Notre Dame, IN: University of Notre Dame Press, 1995.

Weinandy, Thomas G. "Gnosticism and Contemporary Soteriology: Some Reflections." *New Blackfriars* 76 (1995): 546–54.

————. "Aquinas: God *Is* Man. The Marvel of the Incarnation." In *Aquinas on Doctrine: A Critical Introduction*, edited by Thomas Weinandy, Daniel Keating, and John Yocum, 67–89. London: T&T Clark, 2004.

————. *Jesus: Essays in Christology*. Ave Maria, FL: Sapientia Press, 2014.

Weisheipl, James A. "Cajetan (Tommaso de Vio)." In *New Catholic Encyclopedia*, 1st ed. (NCE[1]), vol. 2, 1053–55. Washington, DC: Catholic University of America Press, 1967.

————. *Friar Thomas D'Aquino: His Life, Thought, and Works*. Washington, DC: Catholic University of America Press, 1983.

Welch, Claude. *God and Incarnation in Mid-Nineteenth Century German Theology: Thomasius, Dorner, Biedermann*. New York: Oxford University Press, 1965.

West, Jason L. A. "Aquinas on the Metaphysics of *Esse* in Christ." *The Thomist* 66 (2002): 231–50.

White, Kevin. "The *Quodlibeta* of Thomas Aquinas in the Context of His Work." In *Theological Quodlibeta in the Middle Ages*, vol. 1, *The Thirteenth Century*, edited by Christopher Schabel, 49–133. Leiden: Brill, 2006.

White, Thomas Joseph. "*Dyotheletism* and the *Instrumental* Human *Consciousness* of Jesus." *Pro Ecclesia* 17 (2008): 396–422.

————. "Intra-Trinitarian Obedience and Nicene-Chalcedonian Christology." *Nova et Vetera*, English ed. 6 (2008): 377–402.

————. *The Incarnate Lord: A Thomistic Study in Christology*. Washington, DC: Catholic University of America Press, 2015.

————. "The Infused Science of Christ." *Nova et Vetera*, English ed. 16, no. 2 (2018): 617–41.

Wicks, Jared. "Thomism between Renaissance and Reformation: The Case of Cajetan." *Archiv für Reformationsgeschichte* 68 (1977): 11n7.

Wippel, John F. *The Metaphysical Thought of Thomas Aquinas: From Finite Being to Uncreated Being*. Washington, DC: Catholic University of America Press, 2000.

Wood, Susan K. "The Marriage of Baptized Nonbelievers: Faith, Contract, and Sacrament." *Theological Studies* 48 (1987): 279–301.

Wright, N. T. *Jesus and the Victory of God: Christian Origins and the Question of God*. Minneapolis: Augsburg Fortress, 1996.

————. *The Resurrection of the Son of God: Christian Origins and the Question of God*. Minneapolis: Augsburg Fortress, 2003.

Yenson, Mark. "Jacques Dupuis and Chalcedon." *Theological Studies* 80 (2019): 271–92.

CONTRIBUTORS

GERALD P. BOERSMA is an associate professor of theology at Ave Maria University. He is author of *Augustine's Early Theology of Image* (2016). His research focuses on Latin patristic theology.

MICHAEL A. DAUPHINAIS serves as the Fr. Matthew Lamb Professor of Catholic Theology at Ave Maria University. He has coauthored with Matthew Levering *Knowing the Love of Christ: An Introduction to the Theology of Thomas Aquinas; Holy People, Holy Land: A Theological Introduction to the Bible;* and, most recently, *The Wisdom of the Word: Biblical Answers to Ten Pressing Questions about Catholicism.* He has coedited numerous volumes and has published articles and chapters in books in the areas of Thomistic theology, moral theology, and theological exegesis. He is also a cofounder and codirector of the Aquinas Center for Theological Renewal.

JOHN EMERY, OP, teaches systematic theology at the *Studium* of the Order of Preachers in Buenos Aires, Argentina. His main area of research is the theology of Thomas Aquinas, particularly his Christology. He has a keen interest in the connection between dogmatic and moral theology, as well as between biblical exegesis and systematic theology. He is also a cofounder and codirector of the Aquinas Project, which runs the iaquinas website.

SIMON FRANCIS GAINE, OP, is the first Pinckaers Professor of Theological Anthropology and Ethics in the Thomistic Institute at the Pontifical University of St. Thomas, Rome. He is a fellow of Blackfriars Hall, Oxford, where he was regent from 2012 to 2019. From 2003 to 2020, he was a member of the Faculty of Theology and Religion, University of Oxford. He is the author of *Will There Be Free Will in Heaven? Freedom, Impeccability and Beatitude* (2003) and *Did the Saviour See the Father? Christ, Salvation and the Vision of God* (2015).

ANTHONY GIAMBRONE, OP, is vice director and professor of New Testament at the École biblique et archéologique française de Jérusalem. His research focuses on a range of both historical and theological themes, with a special interest in the Gospels and early Christology. Most recently he is the author of *Rethinking the Jewish War: Archeology, Society, and Traditions* (2021) and *One Sacrifice for Sins: A Biblical Theology of the Priesthood* (forthcoming).

PAUL GONDREAU is a professor of theology at Providence College. Specializing in the thought of Thomas Aquinas, he is the author of *The Passions of Christ's Soul in the Theology of St. Thomas Aquinas* (2002, 2018) as well as numerous essays in Christology, human sexuality, and human anthropology, including "Thomas Aquinas on Sexual Difference" in *Pro Ecclesia* (2021), "Jesus and Paul on the Meaning and Purpose of Human Sexuality" in *Nova et Vetera* (Eng. ed., 2020), and "A Metaphysics of Human Nature in the Christology of Aquinas" in *The Discovery of Being and Thomas Aquinas* (2019). He earned his doctorate in Sacred Theology at the University of Fribourg, writing under the direction of the renowned Thomist scholar Jean-Pierre Torrell.

ANDREW HOFER, OP, is an associate professor and director of the doctoral program at the Pontifical Faculty of the Dominican House of Studies in Washington, DC. Among his works in Christology are 'Dionysian Elements in the Christology of Thomas Aquinas" in *The Thomist* (2008), *Christ in the Life and Teaching of Gregory of Nazianzus* (2013), "Scripture in the Christological Controversies" in *The Oxford Handbook of Early Christian Biblical Interpretation* (2019), and "Augustine's Mixture Christology" in *Studia Patristica* (forthcoming).

DOMINIC M. LANGEVIN, OP, is academic dean and assistant professor of systematic theology at the Dominican House of Studies in Washington, DC, and editor in chief of the journal *The Thomist*. He specializes in sacramental theology. He is the author of *From Passion to Paschal Mystery: A Recent Magisterial Development Concerning the Christological Foundation of the Sacraments* (2015).

DOMINIC LEGGE, OP, is the director of the Thomistic Institute and an assistant professor in systematic theology at the Pontifical Faculty of the Immaculate Conception at the Dominican House of Studies in Washington, DC. He holds a JD from Yale Law School, a PhL from the School of Philosophy of the Catholic University of America, and a doctorate in Sacred Theology from the University of Fribourg. He is the author of *The Trinitarian Christology of St Thomas Aquinas* (2017).

STEVEN A. LONG is a full or ordinary professor of theology at Ave Maria University, and an ordinary member of the Pontifical Academy of St. Thomas Aquinas. He is the author of many scholarly articles and of the books *The Teleological Grammar of the Moral Act* (now in 2nd ed.), *Natura Pura: On the Recovery of Nature in the Doctrine of Grace*, and *Analogia Entis: On the Analogy of Being, Metaphysics, and the Act of Faith*. He coedited, wrote the introduction for, and contributed a further chapter for the book *Thomism and Predestination: Principles and Disputations*.

REGINALD M. LYNCH, OP, is a Dominican priest and a faculty member at the Pontifical Faculty of the Immaculate Conception in Washington, DC, where he teaches historical and systematic theology. He has written on a variety of topics in sacramental, systematic, and historical theology. His current research interests include Aquinas's Eucharistic theology and the reception history of Thomism in the early modern period.

GUY MANSINI, OSB, is a monk of St. Meinrad Abbey and has taught Christology to seminarians for many years. He is now teaching at Ave Maria University.

BRUCE D. MARSHALL is Lehman Professor of Christian Doctrine in the Perkins School of Theology at Southern Methodist University, where he has taught since 2001. He is the author of *Trinity and Truth* (2000) and *Christology in Conflict* (1987), and is presently completing a book manuscript with the working title "Perplexities of Grace: The Church, the Religions, and the Jewish People." For the 2018–19 academic year he served as Rev. Robert J. Randall Distinguished Professor in Christian Culture at Providence College, and he is a past president of the Academy of Catholic Theology.

ROGER W. NUTT serves as provost, associate professor of theology, and codirector of the Aquinas Center for Theological Renewal at Ave Maria University. He is the author of *Thomas Aquinas: De Unione Verbi Incarnati* (2015) and *General Principles of Sacramental Theology* (2017). He has published many scholarly articles on Thomas Aquinas, sacramental theology, and Christology.

MATTHEW J. RAMAGE is professor of theology at Benedictine College in Atchison, Kansas, and an adjunct professor of Sacred Scripture for the online graduate theology program at Holy Apostles College and Seminary in Cromwell, Connecticut. He is author, contributing author, or translator of over fifteen books, including the monographs *Dark Passages of the Bible* (2013), *Jesus, Interpreted* (2017), *The Experiment of Faith* (2020), and *From the Dust of the Earth: Benedict XVI, the Bible, and the Theory of Evolution.* (forthcoming).

DARIA SPEZZANO is an associate professor of theology at Providence College. She holds a PhD in theology from the University of Notre Dame and an MALS from the Liturgical Institute. Her book *The Glory of God's Grace: Deification According to St. Thomas Aquinas* was published in 2015. Recent publications include chapters in *Reading Job with St. Thomas Aquinas* (2020) and *Initiation and Mystagogy in Thomas Aquinas: Scriptural, Systematic, Sacramental and Moral, astoral Perspectives* (2019), as well as articles in *Nova et Vetera, Cistercian Studies,* and *Antiphon.*

THOMAS JOSEPH WHITE, OP, is the director of the Angelicum Thomistic Institute at the Pontifical University of St. Thomas in Rome. He is the author of *Wisdom in the Face of Modernity: A Study in Thomistic Natural Theology* (2011), *The Incarnate Lord: A Thomistic Study in Christology* (2015), *Exodus* (2016), *The Light of Christ: An Introduction to Catholicism* (2017), and *The Trinity: On the Nature and Mystery of the One God* (forthcoming). He is coeditor of the journal *Nova et Vetera,* a scholar of the McDonald Agape Foundation, and a member of the Pontifical Academy of St. Thomas Aquinas.

INDEX

David McEachron